PERSONALITY

McGRAW-HILL SERIES IN PSYCHOLOGY

Harry F. Harlow, *Consulting Editor*

BEACH, HEBB, MORGAN, AND NISSEN · The Neuropsychology of Lashley

BERKOWITZ · Aggression: A Social Psychological Analysis

VON BÉKÉSY · Experiments in Hearing

BERLYNE · Conflict, Arousal, and Curiosity

BLUM · Psychoanalytic Theories of Personality

BROWN · The Motivation of Behavior

BROWN · The Psychodynamics of Abnormal Behavior

BROWN AND GHISELLI · Scientific Method in Psychology

BUCKNER AND McGRATH · Vigilance: A Symposium

CATTELL · Personality

COFER · Verbal Behavior and Learning: Problems and Processes

COFER · Verbal Learning and Verbal Behavior

CRAFTS, SCHNEIRLA, ROBINSON, AND GILBERT · Recent Experiments in Psychology

DEESE · The Psychology of Learning

DOLLARD AND MILLER · Personality and Psychotherapy

DORCUS AND JONES · Handbook of Employee Selection

ELLIS · Handbook of Mental Deficiency

FERGUSON · Personality Measurement

FERGUSON · Statistical Analysis in Psychology and Education

GHISELLI AND BROWN · Personnel and Industrial Psychology

GILMER · Industrial Psychology

GRAY · Psychology Applied to Human Affairs

GUILFORD · Fundamental Statistics in Psychology and Education

GUILFORD · Psychometric Methods

GUILFORD · Personality

HAIRE · Psychology in Management

HIRSH · The Measurement of Hearing

HURLOCK · Adolescent Development

HURLOCK · Child Development

HURLOCK · Developmental Psychology

KARN AND GILMER · Readings in Industrial and Business Psychology

KRECH AND CRUTCHFIELD · Theory and Problems of Social Psychology

LAZARUS · Adjustment and Personality

LEWIN · A Dynamic Theory of Personality

LEWIN · Principles of Topological Psychology

LEWIS · Quantitative Methods in Psychology

MAIER AND SCHNEIRLA · Principles of Animal Psychology

MARX AND HILLIX · Systems and Theories in Psychology

MILLER · Language and Communication

MISIAK AND STAUDT · Catholics in Psychology: A Historical Survey

PERSONALITY

by J. P. Guilford

PROFESSOR OF PSYCHOLOGY

UNIVERSITY OF SOUTHERN CALIFORNIA

1959

New York   Toronto   London

McGRAW-HILL BOOK COMPANY, INC.

To
Jackie, Scotty, and Mike

PREFACE

THIS VOLUME was designed to serve as a textbook for upper-division college students. It was not designed as an exposition of a new system of the psychology of personality, but it has attempted to be systematic and to present the picture of personality from one point of view. It was not designed as a compendium of research on the subject of personality, although it may appear to be that kind of product in places.

No apologies are offered for choosing the comprehensive-appearing title. This *is* personality as viewed by the author. A more restrictive title might have been "Description and Measurement of Personality," but that title has been preempted by Cattell. Another might have been "Personality: A Trait Approach," but this would hardly do justice to the treatment given the subject.

The unifying basis of theory comes from a wedding of the logic of experimental method and factor analysis. The latter, if it is to be used effectively in basic research, should never be separated from the former. In general, much confusion and looseness in treatment of the subject of personality stem from the lack of application of scientific logic and scientific method. In this connection, the experimental approach can, and should, be the cornerstone. Other methods are effective in generating hypotheses, but only experimental procedures can afford us rigorous tests of those hypotheses, leading to dependable conclusions. It must be recognized, of course, that the experimental procedures applied to factor analysis are somewhat different from those applied to the behavior of single individuals.

With the adoption of the experimental approach, variations among persons—individual differences—become the natural and significant variables of investigation. Because there is practically universal agreement that individuals are unique, and uniqueness of individuals inevitably implies individual differences, this concept should prove widely acceptable. Although this brings the study of personality close to differential psychology, it does not make them identical, as will be shown in Chapter 2, where issues are discussed. Neither does it take us too far from the study of the individual, for it offers a needed frame of reference for the description of the individual personality. The nomothetic-idiographic issue also receives attention in Chapter 2. The author believes that it is important to make a stronger distinction than is commonly made between the study of personality and general psychology. The emphasis upon individual differences accomplishes this.

As a single, logical model for unifying the facts of individual differences, there is at present no rival to the model provided by factor theory. The author has attempted to develop conceptions of this model for students in a nontechnical way, realizing that many who legitimately wish to study the subject of personality will have had little or no previous statistical instruction. How successful this attempt has been remains to be seen. The factor model lends itself also to the development of a generalized picture of personality structure for individuals. The picture of personality as a hierarchy of traits is presented in Chapter 5.

The volume is actually in three sections, although not formally so divided. The first five chapters develop the point of view and the logical basis for the measurement of personality and present the factorial and hierarchical models. References to other points of view and approaches are made incidentally, and some general developments of historical importance are mentioned. The middle eight chapters are devoted to the various methods of assessment and to the presentation of good principles of measurement. A strong emphasis is placed upon evaluation of the methods in order to give the student a basis for judging the values and the limitations of procedures that are going to have increasing implications in our society. The last five chapters present the picture of human personality, leaning as heavily as possible upon the results of factorial studies.

In reporting upon the growing picture of personality from this point of view, it has been necessary for the author to inject considerable opinion. This is an author's prerogative, but it is also an author's responsibility to let the reader know where facts end and opinions begin. This should be clear from the manner in which the factors are presented. The factors selected are believed to represent psychologically meaningful concepts. Unfortunately, many analyses fail to yield what the author considers to be psychologically meaningful results, either by reason of the selection of experimental variables or the incidental choice of procedures, as in the rotation of reference axes.

For this reason, criteria of "psychologically meaningful results" are needed. One rather objective criterion is verification of what seems to be the same psychological variable (factor) by independent investigators. Use of comparable procedures is usually important for demonstration of this kind of invariance. Another criterion that may be of logical significance is whether or not the factors fall into a reasonable system, with interrelationships among the factors. The author has attempted to see the forest as well as the trees by putting the factors of each modality, or submodality, into a logical system of some kind. The factors tend to fall into logical categories and in many instances the factors within a category can be arranged in a matrix of two dimensions. The dimensions often have psychological significance as variables of some sort. If a factor fits into such a system it is believed to have superior claim to psychological meaningfulness.

Such systems also give us glimpses of personality structure. Factor analysis has thus far revealed a multitude of basic variables of individual differences, and this multitude of factors is beginning to take shape in terms of logical systems. We have had no very good way of estimating the amount of correlation between factor variables, but this is an important step if we are to develop a picture, based upon empirical evidence, of the general structure of personality in a population. Snatches of such information are given in the last five chapters.

In preparing this volume, I have incurred very great indebtedness to others. There are numerous investigators upon whose work I have drawn and who can be mentioned only in the list of references. There are a few from whom I have made direct quotations or whose material I have used as illustrations, including: Robert G. Bernreuter, Robert I. Blakey, W. Eliasberg, Edwin A. Fleishman, Harry Helson, Walter E. Hempel, Jr., Sibyl Henry, Irving Lorge, Henry A. Murray, Milton E. Rosenbaum, Roy F. Street, and Philip E. Vernon. I am indebted both to them and to their publishers, the American Psychological Association, the Journal of Educational Psychology, the Journal Press, the Sheridan Supply Company, the Stanford University Press, and John Wiley & Sons.

I owe special debts to those who have worked with me during the past ten years on the Aptitudes Project at the University of Southern California and to the Office of Naval Research and the United States Air Force for supporting this and other research. Associated with me on projects have been the following, whose contributions I should like to recognize: Raymond M. Berger, Nicholas A. Bond, Paul R. Christensen, Andrew L. Comrey, James W. Frick, Alfred F. Hertzka, Norman W. Kettner, Donald J. Lewis, Philip R. Merrifield, Marcella A. Sutton McGlothlin, and Robert C. Wilson.

For opportunities in wartime research I wish to acknowledge indebtedness to John C. Flanagan, who invited me into the Army Air Forces Aviation Psychology Research Program and who tolerated much freedom to pursue problems of intellectual abilities, and also to those who contributed most significantly to factor-analytical results: Lloyd G. Humphreys, John I. Lacey, Merrill F. Roff, and Marion A. Wenger. Benjamin

Fruchter, William B. Michael, and Wayne S. Zimmerman have been associated with me in postwar research.

To my wife, Ruth B. Guilford, I am most indebted for relieving me of many duties that would otherwise have detracted seriously from progress in preparation of this volume and for reading the manuscript. Others whom I wish to thank for reading one or more chapters include: Harry Helson, Franklin B. McClung, and Joan S. McClung. They have helped to eliminate errors and have made suggestions but are not responsible for any shortcomings that may remain. In typing the final manuscript, Henry Bedard took more than a typist's interest in producing an accurate product.

J. P. Guilford

CONTENTS

Preface vii

1. Conceptions of personality 1

    Definitions of personality 2
    General aspects of personality 6
    Summary 8

2. Issues and approaches to personality 10

    Reasons for divergent views 10
    Some basic issues 14
    Some secondary issues 25
    Summary 31

3. The prediction of behavior 33

    The main sources of information in prediction . . 33
    Adaptation-level theory 43
    Components of determination 45
    Summary 50

4. Behavior traits 52

    The origins of trait ideas and trait descriptions . . 52
    Some properties of traits 61
    Summary 83

5. The structure of personality 85

    The choice of terms for description of personality . . 85
    Major trends in trait-concept development 89
    A hierarchical conception of personality structure . . 99
    Summary 106

6. Morphological and physiological methods 108

    Some considerations applying to all methods . . . 108
    Morphological methods 113
    Physiological methods 127
    Summary 139

7. Observational methods, ratings, interviews 141

    Rating methods 141
    Direct-observation methods 156
    Interview methods 160
    Summary 168

8. Personality inventories 170

    Development of the inventory 171
    Examples of inventories in current use 172
    Some special forms of inventories 187
    A general evaluation of inventories 191
    Summary 203

9. Interest and attitude measurement 205

    Interest inventories by the empirical approach 206
    General-interest-trait inventories 213
    The nature of attitudes 223
    Thurstone attitude scales 224
    Other methods of attitude measurement 229
    Summary 234

10. Behavior tests 236

    Some general principles of behavior tests 236
    Intelligence tests 240
    Tests of various abilities 246
    Tests of hormetic traits 250
    Tests of temperament 257
    Diagnostic tests of pathology 265
    Summary 268

11. Expressive methods 271

    A general survey of expressive behavior 271
    Assessment of personality from handwriting: graphology . . . 273
    Ratings of observed expressive behavior 280
    Behavior tests of expression 284
    Summary 286

12. Projective techniques 288

    General nature of projective techniques 288
    The Rorschach technique 289
    The Thematic Apperception Test 299
    Other projective methods 303
    General evaluation of projective techniques 309
    Summary 312

13. **Other clinical methods** 315

The integration of information 315
Other methods for gathering information 323
Validation of clinical methods 326
Summary 328

14. **Somatic dimensions** 330

Morphological dimensions 330
Physiological dimensions 336
Summary 341

15. **Dimensions of aptitude** 342

Perceptual dimensions 343
Psychomotor dimensions 348
Dimensions of intellect 359
Some general problems of intellect 395
Summary 405

16. **Dimensions of temperament** 407

A system of temperament factors 408
Factors of general disposition 410
Factors of emotional disposition 414
Factors of social disposition 418
Other potential factors of temperament 423
Summary 430

17. **Hormetic dimensions** 432

Dimensions of need 432
Dimensions of avocational interests 447
Dimensions of vocational interest 458
Dimensions of attitudes 463
Other possible hormetic dimensions 467
Summary 472

18. **Dimensions of pathology** 474

Concerning traditional categories of pathology 474
Dimensions of neurosis 477
Dimensions of psychosis 482
Summary 490

Appendix 493

References 503

Name Index 545

Subject Index 555

Chapter 1

CONCEPTIONS OF PERSONALITY

JUDGING FROM the way in which the term "personality" is used, it is endowed with considerable glamour and prestige. To laymen, generally, and to many professional individuals who deal with people, it is the answer to many problems. It is said to be the reason some persons are liked and others are disliked; it is the secret of popularity and unpopularity. It is said to be something that enables some individuals to "put themselves over" and that fails to make others impressive; it is the secret to success, social or economic, and the reason for lack of success. It is supposed to determine whether we keep our balance and our sanity. It thus keeps most of us out of mental institutions and is responsible for the few less fortunate ones who do not keep out of institutions. Anything so important deserves our most serious attention.

This book attempts to tell the story of what scientists and other professional people have found out about personality. To some extent, and for some people, a scientific approach will necessarily deglamorize any subject. But to those who appreciate the scientific approach, the end result should have a new kind of appeal that is born of deeper understanding and of admiration for the complexity and yet the systematic nature of this phenomenon. From understanding of a phenomenon comes our power to predict and control, in this case to predict and control human behavior and human development.

This chapter and the four immediately following provide an orientation to the subject of personality. They discuss the issues of how personality is defined and, in a very general way, how it shall be approached. In these chapters, a point of view is developed that is consistent with the logic of experimental method and that serves also as a logical basis for measurement of personality. This is done with the conviction that experimental and quantitative methods are eventually essential to the

1

scientific study of any phenomenon and that they should therefore be introduced as soon and as rapidly as is feasible.

The central portion of this volume is devoted to the various methods that have been used in the study of personality, prescientific as well as scientific. Methods are interesting, as such, for they reflect the ingenuity and the efforts of the many people who have attempted to lay hold of aspects of the elusive thing called personality. Many of the methods are in common use for the assessment of individual personalities for various purposes. What we know about personality has come mostly through the use of those methods. It is much easier to evaluate what we know if we also know how the information was derived. Although considerable information regarding the nature of personality can be found throughout the book, this subject is treated most fully in the last section.

DEFINITIONS OF PERSONALITY

The definition of any term is an arbitrary matter. There is no one correct definition, all others being wrong. A certain definition will be adopted for the purposes of this volume, but first let us see what other definitions are more or less current. The understanding of a selected definition is more adequate if we can compare it with other definitions. In England, it is said that an Englishman cannot fully understand his own country until he becomes acquainted with other countries. The same principle applies here.

Origin of the Term

It is natural that such a widely used word as "personality" should have a variety of definitions. After a survey of this matter, Allport (1937) concludes that there are at least fifty different meanings of the term. He reports that "personality" came originally from the Latin word "persona," which was associated with the ancient Greek theater. A Greek player commonly held a mask before his face. The mask was called a "persona" because he talked through it. In time the term "persona" came to apply to the actor and eventually to individuals in general, perhaps with the recognition, with Shakespeare, that "All the world's a stage and all the men and women merely players."

Allport also reports that "personality" is used in at least four distinct senses in the writings of Cicero. It is worth our while to note these meanings, because they embrace most modern conceptions. All of them have their roots in the theater. First, a personality is regarded as an assemblage of personal qualities; in this sense it represents what the person is really like. In this interpretation personality pertains to the actor. Second, a personality is regarded as the way a person appears to others, not as he really is. In this sense, personality pertains to the mask. Third, personality is the role a person plays in life; a professional, social, or political role, for example. A role is a character in a drama. Finally, personality refers to qualities of distinction and dignity. In this sense it pertains to the star performer. Because of the evaluative connotation of this meaning of the term, we do not find such a definition in the scientific setting. In popular usage, a personality in a community is a man of distinction or worth.

Some Classes of Definitions

Instead of quoting the definitions given by particular authors, we shall be content with typical examples that represent classes of meanings. Definitions can be grouped according to various core ideas.

PERSONALITY AS A STIMULUS

A very few who study personality scientifically adopt the idea that personality is one's social-stimulus value. This comes dangerously close to the common, popular idea that personality is something that enables a person to "put himself over." He is impressive or he is not. He has much personality or little. From this point of view, personality then becomes almost identical with reputation. This is clearly a "mask" definition.

Those who take this type of definition seriously argue that it is only through effects upon others that a personality can be known or appreciated at all. Interpreted in the right way, this argument has some merit. But the implication of the definition is that we stop with the "effects" and that we may be interested in only the more immediate effects that most observers appreciate. With the latter interpretation carried to its logical conclusion, this conception would mean that any object—cat, boat, or tree—is to be defined only in terms of the impressions it makes. From this point of view, we might each have as many personalities as there are persons who know us, and an investigation of personality would involve studying, not the individual, but the perceptions, prejudices, and inferences of others who know the individual.

It can hardly be denied that each person has real properties or qualities, independent of anyone's observations. This is not to say that a person is independent of other people, for no one lives in a social vacuum. But neither is it necessary for others to make observations designed to describe a person in order for him to have a personality. The moment we recognize that an observer has gained a wrong impression about the person, we realize that the nature of the person is one thing and the false impression he made is another. It will be admitted later that we do use observations by others and impressions made upon others as material from which to gain information about a personality. But this is not the only source of information and usually such impressions are not regarded as the personality. They are merely signs pointing more or less accurately in the direction of the personality.

OMNIBUS DEFINITIONS

A type of definition that was more popular some years ago than recently usually begins with the words, "Personality is the sum total . . ." and then proceeds to list any of the processes or activities which a human individual is capable of, for example, innate dispositions, impulses, appetites, instincts, tendencies, and habits. The chief source of objection to this type of definition has come from gestalt psychology, which has had a violent antipathy for saying that an individual or anything about him is merely an aggregation of parts. This failure to integrate the parts of the personality is a logical defect that the following definitions correct.

INTEGRATIVE DEFINITIONS

The integrative type of definition emphasizes the organization of a personality; personality is more than the sum of its parts, and that "more than" is its pattern of organization. As an example of this kind of definition, we can do no better than quote from Warren's Dictionary (1934): ". . . the integrated organization of all the cognitive, affective, conative, and physical characteristics of an individual as it manifests itself in focal distinctness from others." An objection to this particular statement might be made with regard to the kinds of characteristics listed, a point we shall discuss later. It should be noted that the end of the statement, "in focal distinctness from others," emphasizes the uniqueness of the individual, a specification that is commonly accepted in other conceptions of personality.

TOTALITY DEFINITIONS

A "totality" definition carries the emphasis upon integration a large step further, almost forgetting the parts entirely. Two statements of this type can be quoted from Warren's Dictionary: ". . . the general characterization, or pattern, of an individual's total behavior," and ". . . the field property or form of the individual's total behavior-pattern." Taken seriously, such definitions would seem to make analysis and, hence a science of personality, logically impossible. If, however, we may interpret them as merely integrative definitions with greater stress on organization, the way is still open for description of personalities and personality in general.

PERSONALITY AS ADJUSTMENT

It is quite common to define behavior as adjustment of an organism to its environment. Individuals tend to develop their own unique procedures of adjustment. Personality, from this line of thinking, is an individual's characteristic pattern of adjustments. If all behavior is adjustment, however, we could just as well say that personality is an individual's characteristic pattern of behavior. Some definitions in this group would limit personality to social adjustments, but to do so would introduce a limitation to the meaning of personality that most of those who deal with personality would reject.

The Definition Adopted

The definition of personality adopted for use in this volume starts logically from an axiom to which everyone seems agreed: each and every personality is unique. This statement includes identical twins, for it is possible to find differences even in pairs of such individuals. A person cannot be unique without differing from others. He is, of course, similar in some respects. But considering his whole pattern of characteristics, he is different from all others. It is in individual differences, then, that we find the logical key to personality, and we shall find later that it is also a most useful, operational key.[1] *An individual's personality,* then, *is his unique pattern of traits.*

TRAITS

This definition of personality is essentially in the integrative class. However, it has the advantage of not attempting to say what kinds of things are integrated. Instead, it uses the general term "trait," which must now be defined. We shall do so by indirect steps.

The definition of personality emphasizes individual differences. This means that we can best know personalities by comparing them with one another. There are no absolute standards for personalities; there are only other personalities from which our frames of reference must be derived. Comparisons of personalities must therefore be made.

It is humanly impossible for us to compare one "person-as-a-whole" with another "person-as-a-whole." The act of comparison is an analytical process. In fact, the act of observation of a single person is an analytical process, as is the act of observing anything. Things, including persons, are known by their properties. An object is round, or sharp, or hard, or all of these things. A person is observed to react promptly, or vigorously, or accurately, or in all of these ways. Properties are abstractions that

---

[1] The emphasis upon individual differences here glosses over an issue that will be discussed at some length in the next chapter.

come by way of analysis from totalities. Our abstraction of a property from a totality does not destroy the totality; it remains the same unitary object it was before. No one can therefore truthfully claim that his abstractions, however numerous, have exhausted the object or will ever completely account for it. But this is not sufficient reason for refusing to analyze. We can extend our observations and thus approach complete coverage of the totality if we have the patience to do so.

Comparisons of individuals are thus commonly made in terms of one aspect at a time, or at least in a limited number of aspects. Persons A and B differ in aspects c, d, e, f, j, and so on; persons X and Y differ in aspects d, f, g, j, m, and t, and so on. More often, our comparisons are between a person Q and the norms (typical qualities) for the population of which Q is a member.

The aspects or properties that we have just been considering are *traits*. *A trait is any distinguishable, relatively enduring way in which one individual differs from others.* "Trait" is thus a very broad, general term. A trait of personality may be as inclusive as a general attitude of self-confidence or as narrow as a specific habit, such as a conditioned muscular contraction in response to a sound. A trait may be a characteristic indicated by behavior, as in the two examples just given, or of physical make-up. The former is a behavior trait, the latter a somatic trait.

GENERAL ASPECTS OF PERSONALITY

Having decided that the abstractions in terms of which personalities are to be described are traits, we shall have to consider what kinds of traits should be included. On this question there is disagreement. Some writers seem to restrict personality to only a part of our behavior traits by occasionally setting personality over against intelligence, probably in accordance with the practice of segregating personality tests from intelligence tests. Probably most writers, however, accept intelligence and all abilities as parts or aspects of personality. But some draw the line when it comes to traits of physique and prefer to exclude physiology as well as morphology from consideration in connection with personality. Since individual differences in body structure and body function come under the definition of trait, however, they can be logically included in personality. A great many psychologists do include them, and many biologists who are interested in personality would most certainly include them.

Modalities of Traits

There will be considerably more discussion on the nature of traits in Chapter 4. Meanwhile, in order to extend a little the conception of the way in which traits account for a personality, let us consider some classes of traits, or *modalities*. For the present, the modalities will be mentioned without much effort to define them. They are illustrated in relation to personality in Figure 1.1.

We could illustrate the modalities as being constituent parts of personality, but this would smack of the omnibus type of conception of personality. We have taken care to refer to traits as being *aspects* of

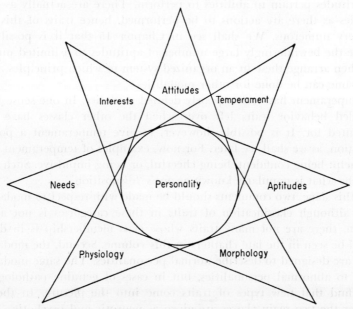

Fig. 1.1 Modalities of traits representing different aspects of personality.

personality and we shall treat the modalities of traits in the same fashion. Figure 1.1 shows personality to be an integrated whole, which can be viewed from different directions. How the viewing is done will be explained in the several chapters on methods. How we arrive at trait ideas through observation in general will be explained in Chapter 4. It is enough for our purposes here to say that as we look at personality from one direction we see one kind of trait and as we look at it from another we see another kind.

There are two kinds of somatic traits—morphological and physiological. Traits of morphology are those relating to structure or feature, such as height, weight, and coloring. Traits of physiology relate to organic functions, such as heart rate, basal metabolic rate, and body temperature.

Three kinds of motivational traits are distinguished, all of which pertain to things we strive to do or to obtain. Needs are perennial desires for certain conditions, such as being noticed, being respected, or being comfortable. Interests are long-standing desires to indulge in certain kinds of activities, such as handwork, thinking, or conversing. Attitudes are distinguished by the fact that some social objects or policies are involved, as seen in attitudes toward the income tax, birth control, the Chinese, and so on.

Aptitudes pertain to abilities to perform. There are actually as many abilities as there are actions to be performed, hence traits of this kind are very numerous. We shall see in Chapter 15 that it is possible to reduce the bewilderingly large number of aptitudes to a limited number and then arrange these in an organized system to which principles apply. The same can be done for other modalities.

Temperament has been a poorly defined modality. In one sense it has included behavior traits left over when the other classes have been accounted for. It is possible, however, to give temperament a positive definition, as we shall see later. For now, examples of temperament traits may help: being confident, being cheerful, or being impulsive. Such traits describe what is popularly known as one's "disposition."

At this stage, two comments should be made with respect to modalities. First, although classification of traits in these categories is not always certain, there are not many traits whose class membership is in doubt, as will be seen in the late chapters in this volume. Second, the modalities given are designed to describe normal personalities. The same modalities apply to abnormal personalities, but in cases of genuine pathology we shall find that new types of traits come into the picture. In the last chapter the two main classes are given as neurotic and psychotic. These two modalities must be added to the picture to account for pathological personalities.

SUMMARY

The importance of personality to laymen and to professional groups of people alike can scarcely be denied. The importance of the subject calls for the best efforts of science to comprehend it. This volume attempts to present a scientific picture of personality.

A very old term, "personality" has many meanings. Even among those who approach it from the point of view of scientific study, we also find varied conceptions. The one idea on which all seem to agree is that each personality is unique. Building upon this idea as a foundation, it is proposed that personality can be defined as a person's unique pattern of traits. A trait is any relatively enduring way in which a person differs from others. This definition places the emphasis upon individual differences.

Traits can be grouped naturally in classes known as modalities. Both traits and modalities are abstractions that arise from viewing personality from different directions. Included are somatic and motivational modalities as well as those of aptitude and temperament. Pathological personalities bring additional modalities into the picture of personality.

Chapter 2

ISSUES AND APPROACHES
TO PERSONALITY

ONE DOES not need to read very far in the voluminous literature on personality to be struck by the fact that there is a somewhat bewildering variation in treatments of the subject. One might even conclude that there is confusion bordering on chaos.[1] Points of view and theories are so numerous that it may be some time before this yeasty state of affairs settles into a more coherent condition, and greater community of viewpoint and language prevails.

It is the purpose of this chapter to help the reader understand the reasons for this diversity of concepts and opinions by highlighting the chief issues involved and by indicating clearly the nature of the issues. The different points of view or theories themselves, will not be treated here.[2] Rather, this volume will emphasize its own point of view and its own theory, which will be developed in subsequent chapters.

REASONS FOR DIVERGENT VIEWS

Although interest in personality is very old, serious, scientific attention to personality as a major objective dates back only about forty years. The somewhat chaotic state of the subject can be attributed, in part, to the many groups who for some reason or other have special interests in the subject and, in part, to the fact that personality study shares the controversial features that have characterized the history of psychology.

Scientific Groups Interested in Personality

The subject of personality comes within the spheres of interest of at least four of the basic sciences—biology, anthropology, psychology, and

---

[1] This impression is given, for example, by the book of readings edited by Brand (1954).

[2] For a recent exposition of different theories, see Hall and Lindzey (1957).

sociology. Biologists such as Roger J. Williams (1953, 1955) have been concerned about individual differences in anatomy and physiology, as well as in biochemistry. Geneticists in general have been concerned with all kinds of human traits in connection with their studies and theories of heredity. Anthropologists such as Margaret Mead (1956) have been concerned with the relation of personality to cultures of different human societies. Sociologists have generally been concerned with many problems of personality, particularly with questions of how the social environment in which individuals live affects personality development and how personality affects social institutions. Of all the basic sciences, psychology is naturally most concerned with problems of personality, since it focuses its interests on individuals and their behavior. We do not have to go into much detail concerning the special interests of these scientific groups to see that each will ask different kinds of questions and will approach its studies with its own theories and methods.

Technological Groups Interested in Personality

Among those interested in personality, the technological groups—those who apply the facts and principles of the sciences to everyday human affairs and to particular problems—outnumber the basic-science groups just mentioned. Each technological group makes its own special demands upon the sciences for the information it needs, for techniques, for facts, and for theory. Each will naturally have some influence upon the directions that are to be taken in scientific investigations of personality. This is especially true where the technologist attempts to find scientific answers to problems for himself. As the issues are discussed later, we shall see how some of them are related to the various interest groups.

PROBLEMS OF PERSONAL ADJUSTMENT

Many technologists are concerned in one way or another with problems of personal adjustment. Psychiatrists, clinical psychologists, and social workers are concerned in a major way with the personal adjustment of their patients or clients, whether the persons involved are maladjusted to the extent of pathology, in the form of neuroses or psychoses, or not. Others in general medical practice often recognize personal adjustment as one of their problems in treating patients, whether such patients fall in the diagnostic category of psychosomatic or not. Physicians may recognize their responsibility to be that of healing the entire person. Psychopathology, especially when it is not attributable to organic causes, is usually described and understood in terms of deviations from normal personality. Maladjustments of lesser seriousness are also regarded as personality manifestations that call for changes.

PROBLEMS OF VOCATIONAL ADJUSTMENT

Another group of technologists is concerned with problems of guidance. Their work is usually not with people suffering from pathology or even from less serious maladjustments. In this case, the guidance sought by the client is concerned with the choice of vocation, courses of study, or both. Vocational guidance involves the assessment of an individual personality to determine its major psychological resources, its significant life goals, and other traits, and to suggest how these indicate the probable wise choice of some vocations and the rejection of others. The choice of a major curriculum of study may depend upon vocational choices, but in many cases it may not. In either case, the selection of courses of study may well be made with reference to the personality of the individual involved.

Still another group is concerned with the matching of persons to job assignments from a different point of view. This group is concerned with personnel selection, classification, and assignment. Having a job to be filled, and knowing what human resources and other qualities are desirable, the personnel technologist must determine which persons qualify. Or having several jobs of different kinds to fill and several applicants, he must decide which ones, by reason of their patterns of personality traits, would be best assigned to each kind of job, and which sorting of the applicants among the jobs would give the greatest over-all satisfaction. Within any one kind of job, some workers will be assigned to work under one set of conditions, including one particular supervisor, and some to work under another set of conditions. Future difficulties might possibly be avoided and more general satisfaction achieved if personal qualities are taken into consideration.

BEHAVIOR PROBLEMS

Those who deal more or less directly with problems of delinquency and crime are continually aware of the personality problems involved. Two trends are largely responsible for this awareness. One arises from the fact that although criminal laws have had to be framed so as to provide similar treatments of classes of criminals, there is a growing recognition that the nature of the individual criminal is an important consideration. Knowing the properties of the individual has therefore become increasingly essential. The second trend concerns the increasing attention being given to the prevention of crime and to continued treatment of the criminal in the form of probation.

The fact that criminal behavior occurs with some individuals and not with others indicates that the cause of such behavior lies to some extent in the area of personality. The prevention of crime and the prediction of its occurrence depend upon knowledge of personality. The apprehension of criminals, their treatment after apprehension, and their disposition by the courts all offer problems of personality. The policeman, the detective, the attorney, and the jurist all realize this. The treatment of the criminal in penal institutions, the determination of his readiness for parole, and the supervision while he is on parole—all involve problems of personality.

PROBLEMS OF PERSONALITY DEVELOPMENT

Larger and more heterogeneous groups than those mentioned above are concerned with personality *development*. The conviction that personality development is somewhat under our control is, in fact, widespread. There can be no doubt, at least, that numerous adults and agencies are acting upon this assumption, among them, parents, teachers, educators of all kinds, religious groups, and other social agencies. Parents, and others, have been guiding developing personalities for many thousands of years, mostly, of course, without any technical knowledge of personality or of the principles of personality development. But the awareness that such information now exists and the apparently increasing difficulty of the problems involved in personality development have prompted parents, with others, to seek new information. The nature of their requests will also have some bearing upon the directions that personality investigation will take.

Points of View within Psychology

The "schools of psychology" have differed considerably in the extent of their interest in personality. For some schools, personality is of no importance as a concept, while for others it is almost a key concept. Among those that are concerned about the nature of personality, there are many differences of opinion, with each school remaining consistent with its own systematic views on psychological goals, methods, and concepts.

Existential, or structural, psychology, with its emphasis upon the nature of conscious experience, naturally has no logical place for personality in its system. Extreme behaviorism, which has attempted to account for behavior in terms of stimulus and response, two external and therefore observable aspects, has had no particular need for the concept of personality. For functional psychologists of all kinds, the language of personality description has been a natural one because of their interest in individual differences. For them, behavior traits and functions are easily related terms. Certain gestalt psychologists, such as Kurt Lewin, have paid considerable attention to personality, while others of that school have not. Because of their central concern with adjustment and maladjustment, all proponents of the psychoanalytical schools of thought have placed personality high on their list of concepts.

Whatever his psychological point of view, the investigator who becomes interested in problems of personality naturally carries his concepts and biases into this field of study. In addition to these major differences among the psychological schools of thought, we must also recognize, as Roback (1955) has pointed out, that differences in conceptions of personality will be injected into the general picture as a result of the personalities of those who write on the subject!

SOME BASIC ISSUES

Some of the issues to be discussed are more basic than others because they help to determine what we are going to make of the subject of personality, what we are going to include in it, and what our main approach and emphasis will be. Among investigators and writers, some emphasize how individuals are alike and others how they are different. Some regard most behavior as involving rather specific responses to specific situations while others regard behavior as more generalized. Some focus their attention on the individual personality while others think of personality in a broad, abstract sense, and if they have a focus of interest it is on traits. These are the issues with which we shall deal first.

The Individual vs. Individual Differences

Should the emphasis be on how individuals are alike or on how they are different? Should the study of personality be directed to finding out the processes and functions by which the typical person operates, or should it be directed to finding the ways in which those processes and functions differ person to person?

FUNCTIONALISTIC VS. DIFFERENTIAL VIEWS

The first of these two objectives is identical with that of psychology in general. In fact, some textbooks on personality read very much like textbooks in general psychology. There is, to be sure, reference to individual differences, but these differences are treated as special cases of common behavior tendencies. To this extent, general psychology also recognizes individual differences. The thing that distinguishes such a treatment of personality sufficiently to give the subject a different title is that there is more emphasis upon the total organization that constitutes an individual personality.[3] This view of personality may be called *functionalistic,* in contrast to that which is called *differential.*

---

[3] There is also, of course, selection of material, with the result that some is emphasized and some neglected; for example, fuller treatment is given to such topics as motivation and emotion and less to such topics as sensation and perception.

While the functionalistic view must be distinguished from general psychology, the differential view must be distinguished from the field of differential psychology. Compared with differential psychology, the latter view is less concerned with the *extent* of differences of various kinds, with the *sources* of those differences, with their relationships to age, sex, and racial origins, and with their *consequences*. In common with differential psychology, the differential view of personality is concerned with discovering all the possible ways in which individuals differ. It is more concerned than differential psychology with the way in which traits go together to make up the total personality; in other words, it is concerned with personality structure.

The functionalistic and differential views differ somewhat as to methodology. The functionalistic approach focuses attention upon relationships between situations and responses and the principles governing them. The differential approach gives more attention to the interrelationships of responses within individuals of a population. It wants to know in what respects behavior is internally consistent or patterned. Consistencies and patterns of behavior lead to descriptions of persons as well as of personality in general. We shall see something of how this is done in Chapter 4.

The differences between the two views are, after all, only relative ones. Actually, the two have much in common. They are like two sides of the same coin. We can learn much about how individuals function by studying how they differ. Similarly, to study the functions of individuals provides knowledge of the traits whereby they differ. Both views can readily accept the idea that each individual is unique.

The study of personality can proceed from both directions, the one source of information supplementing the other. The justification for a separate field known as personality, however, lies in its distinctions from general psychology on the one hand and differential psychology on the other. The key to these distinctions, in turn, seems to lie in the emphasis that is placed upon the individual as a unique organization of traits.

GROUPS FAVORING THE TWO APPROACHES

The last paragraph points out the supplementary nature of the functionalistic and differential views. So far as the basic science of personality is concerned, this reconciliation is sound. But we shall still find biases in one direction or the other among certain interest groups. Some of these preferences are worth noting.

Of all the basic-science groups, perhaps the biologist has the least interest in the individual as such and in his pattern of traits. Next in order are probably the anthropologist and sociologist. Psychologists, who study personality more fully, show relatively more interest in the individual, but they differ considerably in this respect.

Of the technological groups, those concerned with problems of adjustment definitely prefer the functionalistic approach. Those concerned with vocational guidance, selection, and classification of personnel find the differential view and its quantitative descriptions in terms of traits much more useful. The value of information regarding individual differences is also recognized by those concerned with delinquency and crime as well as those concerned with personality development. Although, like the clinical technologists, these groups are concerned with persons, they are more likely to find the trait concepts provided by the differential approach to be useful tools for providing understanding and for indicating treatment. Like the clinicians, however, they find limitations to the value of such information and feel a need for the study of the individual in the light of the common principles of behavior.

Specific vs. Generalized Behavior Traits

The history of psychology has provided another issue that we must face. Going a long way back to the discarded faculty psychology, we find belief in a limited number of very broad powers and other traits. The functional view of modern times has thought along similar lines but has been forced by the experimental evidence to limit severely the scope of functions, powers, or traits. Some forty years ago, behavioristic psychology initiated a program whose objective was to account for all behavior in terms of stimulus-response sequences and patterns. To the extent that this view permits the concept of personality at all, it regards an individual personality as a composite of rather specific habits.

Thus, we have been presented with the question of how specific and how general behavior traits are. On the one hand, we are urged that in order to know a person well we need to obtain information concerning specific biographical facts, what situations he has lived through and what habits he learned in doing so. This point of view is well presented by Guthrie (1944). On the other hand, we have the belief in traits so broad that they affect just about everything we do. The tendencies toward introversion or toward extraversion, proposed by Jung (1923), are examples of such broad trait concepts. The two views illustrated here are as extreme as they could be. As usual, where such divergent views are held, the truth is likely to be somewhere in between. We shall consider the question of where, between the two views, the most reasonable position lies, and of how much of either view we may find it desirable to adopt.

THE SPECIFIC-TRAIT VIEW

First, let us become better acquainted with the general principles of the specific-trait point of view. It is sometimes suggested that the extreme behaviorist views the organism as being "empty." That is, restricting observations to stimuli and responses, he tries to account for everything without resort to any guesses as to what the internal activity is like. We may illustrate this view by reference to Figure 2.1. The large ellipse stands roughly for an organism. This organism is subjected to stimulating forces $S_1, S_2, S_3, \ldots, S_{20}$ in our illustration, to which he may make responses $R_1, R_2, R_3, \ldots, R_{20}$, though not necessarily on a one-to-one basis.

If behavior were actually in the form of isolated *S-R* sequences like $S_1 \rightarrow R_1$ and $S_{20} \rightarrow R_{20}$, we should have the ultimate in specificity. But

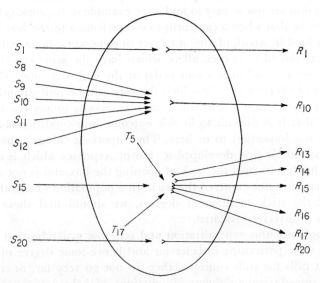

Fig. 2.1 Schematic diagram of an organism, with organized sequences of stimuli (*S*) followed by responses (*R*). Illustrated are the phenomena of stimulus generalization and response generalization as well as traits (*T*).

not even the most rabid specifist would accept this model of the behaving organism. The principle of generalization removes us one important step away from this picture. In the learning of new stimulus-response sequences, we have the processes of stimulus generalization and response generalization.

Stimulus generalization is illustrated schematically by response R_{10} in Figure 2.1. The conditioning has been brought about by application of stimulus S_{10} in close proximity in time to R_{10}, which had previously been dependably elicited by some other stimulus in which we have no particular interest here. We find that in developing the behavior sequence $S_{10} \rightarrow R_{10}$, other stimuli similar to S_{10} also acquire potency to elicit the same response. This is shown in Figure 2.1, the other stimuli being denoted as S_8, S_9, S_{11}, and S_{12}. An example would be Watson's experimental infant, who, being conditioned to fear a rabbit, also responded with fear to other furry stimuli, such as a muff and even Santa Claus's whiskers.

The model for response generalization is also shown in Figure 2.1. In developing the sequence $S_{15} \rightarrow R_{15}$, we find that we have also brought about, to some degree, other sequences in which the stimulus is the same but the responses vary, and yet are similar in some way. Ignore the parts of this model indicated by T_5 and T_{17} for the time being. Examples of response generalization that parallel completely examples of stimulus generalization are not so easy to find. One example of response generalization might be that when a cat learns to escape from a puzzle box in order to obtain food by manipulating a trigger of some kind, he actually seems to learn a *class* of responses, all of which have the same crucial result. Suppose the mechanism is a foot pedal at the end of a rope. There are a number of effective ways in which the rope can be pulled, and the cat uses several of them, without confining his response to any one of them. The fact that it is difficult to fit this outcome into conditioned-response theory is not important to us here. The important thing is that in the same situation we find developed a *class* of responses which is common to a cat that has learned the trick of opening the box and is not common to cats that have not mastered the trick. In a population of cats that have mastered the trick to different degrees, we should find these various responses positively correlated.

Although stimulus generalization and response generalization provide bases for some patterning in behavior and hence some degree of consistency that calls for trait concepts, they do not go very far, as conceived by conditioned-response theory. Predictions of behavior can be made only from very similar situations and with regard to very similar responses. Let us consider next some behavior that should presumably be determined by rather broad traits, such as a trait of honesty. Considering the generally concerted efforts of home, school, and church to make growing children honest in many ways, we should expect a general trait of honesty to be developed. Children on whom the pressures have been greatest (without being resented) should be consistently honest in almost everything they do; others may be consistently dishonest; and still others will range in between, showing more or less consistency.

The extensive research studies of Hartshorne and May (1928) have been commonly interpreted as giving strong support for the specific-trait point of view. These investigators used a variety of tests of deceitful behavior in which children could show more or less tendency to lie, to cheat, or to steal. The intercorrelations of deceitful behavior were generally very low. Statistically, therefore, one cannot tell much regarding the likelihood of a child's cheating or lying in one test from his known behavior in another test. In other words, personal consistency was apparently low.

Whether or not the child lied or cheated seemed to depend upon the specific situation rather than upon a general trait of honesty in the individual child. These results will be referred to again, but first let us see what the general-trait view has to say.

THE GENERAL-TRAIT VIEW

Most psychologists refuse to treat the organism as if it were empty and to attempt to account for behavior exclusively in terms of overtly observable events. It is generally recognized, for example, that an organism brings with itself a rich supply of motives that also determine behavior. Motives help to tie behavior together, to give it threads of consistency, and hence to produce intercorrelations of responses. Other dispositions, such as abilities, interests, and temperament qualities, are also recognized as underlying determiners of behavior. Such dispositions are illustrated in Figure 2.1 by T_5 and T_{17}.

Such inner dispositions have to be inferred from what we can observe in behavior. There is nothing unscientific about this. For years, physicists have been telling us about the nature of the interior of atoms, although no one has ever observed the interior directly. Concepts on the nature of atoms and molecules have been based entirely upon the behavior of things that *can* be observed. The same should be true of the study of human behavior. We should, and do, build up conceptual models of unobserved things from what we can see of observed things. It does not matter if models have to be discarded or changed. This is the way in which a science develops. If we say that we will accept the "true" model or none at all, we have admitted defeat before we start.

There is much more generalization and consistency in behavior than the specifists think, and not all of it need depend upon the principle of conditioning. Many who theorize about the structure of personality conceive of it as being a hierarchy of something like habits, having different levels of generality. This kind of model will be described in some detail in Chapter 5. As has been pointed out, the kinds and amounts of generality are indicated by intercorrelations of behavior. Some degree of generality in behavior was indicated even in the honesty tests of Hartshorne and May. The intercorrelations, although low, were generally positive, and so long as there is positive correlation at all, there is at least some generality. Factor analyses of such intercorrelations have shown the existence of an underlying common trait.[4]

But the specifist can still maintain that doing the honest thing or not doing it is more specific than it is general. In view of the very low intercorrelations, it must be admitted that to this extent the specifist appears

4 Maller (1934); Brogden (1940).

to be correct. Note, however, that this conclusion does admit the existence of a general trait and its involvement in the tests of honesty although the trait's potency for generating consistency of behavior in the children was evidently small.

Before we decide just *how* specific the children's behavior was, there are several things to consider. One is that the subjects were young children, in whom principles of conduct are probably not as operative as they are in older subjects, who have achieved the power to think of moral conduct in abstract terms. This hypothesis should lead us to expect higher correlations for older individuals. Another consideration is that the tests themselves were of low reliability, which made it impossible for them to correlate high with one another. Since the same child was not very consistent in honest behavior from time to time in the *same* test, we should expect him to show similar variability in behavior between different tests. Furthermore, the tests may be regarded as being of low validity. That is, the extent to which they revealed a particular trait was limited by the fact that they also revealed other traits.[5]

Before we conclude, from the study of one particular trait, that traits are more specific than they are general, we must consider whether there might be other traits which would exhibit much greater consistency of behavior, even in young children. Numerous examples of general traits, among children as well as adults, will be given in Chapters 15 to 17. On the other hand, it is possible to find traits that produce less consistency in behavior than honesty seems to, even for adults. For example, Dudycha (1939) found that college students, whose habits should be well formed and whose principles of conduct should be operative, were very low in consistency with regard to punctuality. The behavior observed included returning books to the library on time, turning in assignments on time, meeting appointments on time, and returning change slips to the registrar on time. The intercorrelations of these types of behavior were found to be very low. Yet we should not conclude from this one result that all behavior of college students is specific. Such sweeping generalizations, unfortunately, have been altogether too common.

The truth probably is that the individual personality has traits ranging all the way from very narrow, specific habits, through broadly generalized habits, to dispositions that have even broader scope. The description of the individual in terms of traits at different levels of generality will be relatively more illuminating or useful to some groups of technologists than to others. The view that a personality may be regarded as a hierarchical structure of the kind implied in these statements will be discussed in some detail in Chapter 5.

---

[5] For discussions of reliability and validity, see Chap. 6.

Personal vs. Impersonal Views

In the study of personality, is the interest to be in persons as such or in abstractions about people in general? This question, in turn, presents another issue which, in some respects, is related to the one discussed first but also presents new aspects. Difference of opinion concerning this issue goes somewhat deeper than with the other; furthermore, it involves logical problems of scientific theory and method.

THE PERSONAL VIEW

The personal or personalistic point of view that is often held by clinicians is very well described in the following quotation from Murray (1938): [6]

> Any conceptual formulation of man's experience . . . must necessarily do violence to human feelings. . . . This will be so because it is the substitution of heartless, denotative, referential symbols for the moving immediacy of living. By employing such a scheme, a person's vital movements, once warm and passionately felt, become transformed into a cruelly commonplace formula, which dispossesses them of unique value. . . . The artist's representation of an experience, on the other hand, is a re-invocation of the original . . . equally immediate, exciting, and intense.

Such a view favors the retention of as much of the immediately given, total view of personality in scientific studies as it is possible to achieve.

THE IMPERSONAL VIEW

The basic scientist's reply to the last statement is likely to be that we must lose the individual in order that we may find him. In some respects the difference between the personal and impersonal views is like that between applied and fundamental research. The objective of applied research is to obtain the answer to a problem of immediate concern, pertaining to a particular place, time, and subgroup or population. The information obtained is of limited use, for it usually cannot be generalized. Fundamental research, on the other hand, is designed to obtain information that is more independent of particular circumstances. The results have more general significance and a larger sphere of application.

The difference between the two views can be illustrated by the way each would approach the problem of the effect of cold temperatures on psychological performances. An applied-research approach might consist of comparing the performances of clerks in an unheated room with performances in a normally heated room. A fundamental-research approach

[6] Pp. 17–18.

would involve exploring systematically the performances of individuals of different ages and different sexes in a variety of standard tasks and under systematically varied temperatures. From the latter type of investigation we should expect a set of principles from which we could deduce the answer to the question about clerical performances in a cold room, having at our disposal enough information regarding the kind of individual, the kind of task, and the temperature.

The technologist is naturally concerned about his immediate problem. He is looking for solutions that will help him in his work. He may be impatient with fundamental research that seems slow and that also seems at times to become bogged down in irrelevancies. In his impatience, he may not only attempt to influence the direction that basic research will take but also insist that the investigator of fundamental problems adopt his point of view.

UNIQUE VS. COMMON TRAITS

Technologists who are concerned with problems of personal adjustment must necessarily be interested in persons, one at a time. The impression is often gained, therefore, that each person presents not only a different *pattern* of traits but that he also possesses different traits—traits that are unique to him, traits that no other person possesses. Common traits are qualities that are possessed by many individuals alike. We can compare different individuals with respect to a common trait; we cannot compare them with respect to a unique trait, except to say that person X and no one else has the trait.

G. W. Allport has gone so far as to say that in general each person's traits are his own (1937). This raises the question of whether there are any common traits at all. Allport has insisted that even when it appears that a trait is common, there are individual differences in *quality* as well as in degree. For example, each person's brand of courage is his own, different from that of other people. Allport therefore calls for an approach to personality that can be characterized as a "science of individuals."

The best way to evaluate Allport's suggestion is to take a short excursion into the logic of scientific method, which will be the next major subject of discussion. We might note first some general considerations that should throw light on the matter. It may well appear from observations of the behavior of three persons that the trait of courage is not of the same quality in each of them. We may say that one person shows courage by speaking to a "cold" audience, another by making a daring rescue of a drowning child, while still another shows it by telling his boss what the workers really think of him. First, we could question whether it is proper to speak of all of these instances as revealing a common trait that goes by the name of courage. The three behaviors may indicate primarily three totally different traits, such as social boldness, willingness to take risks of personal injury, and some form of aggressiveness, respectively. It is easy to confuse trait descriptions. But assuming that all three behaviors did show a trait of courage, the trait may merely have appeared different because the behaviors in which it was revealed showed additional common traits that differed from one another. It is essential, for clear thinking, to distinguish between traits, as such, and the behavior in which they are revealed.[7]

IDIOGRAPHIC VS. NOMOTHETIC APPROACHES

In terms of methodology, the personal or personalistic view calls for an approach that has been called *idiographic*. This means the intensive and extensive study of one person at a time. The approach is contrasted with that called *nomothetic*, which calls for the study of many individuals, each probably less extensively. The idiographic approach seeks to understand persons. The nomothetic approach seeks to arrive at general principles that apply to people generally; in this sense it represents the impersonal view.

The differences can be made clearer if we consider some basic differences in the way personality can be investigated. Whatever our views or our methods, when we undertake to study personality, we encounter three main variations. We may study different *persons* and different *traits,* and we may make observations on different *occasions*. In the typical study using the nomothetic approach, interest is likely to be centered upon one trait or a relatively small number of traits with the purpose of finding out how each trait varies in a relatively large number of persons on one occasion or on a small number of occasions. Typically, there are many persons, but few traits and few occasions are involved—perhaps only one trait and one occasion. For any trait, the main reference point will be the average trait position of the population with which the study is concerned. The average measurement is regarded as a group norm for that trait, just as it is for other traits.

In the typical study using the idiographic approach, one person or a very few persons are likely to be studied with reference to many traits. A relatively small number of occasions will probably be involved. The major interest is likely to be in the pattern of traits presented by each person. There may be some interest in *intraindividual* differences, the way in which traits differ within each person. In this connection, the person provides his own reference point, which is his own average, if a

---

[7] This distinction will be discussed in some detail in Chap. 4.

reference point is wanted. By contrast, the nomothetic approach is primarily interested in *interindividual* differences, although it can and does deal as well with the problems of intraindividual differences.

A SUGGESTED RESOLUTION

The heated debate on this issue could have been avoided if a clearer distinction had been recognized between science and technology.[8] The impersonal view and the nomothetic approach belong to basic science; the personal view and the idiographic approach belong to technology. In every science, the individual case is properly regarded as merely an opportunity for making another observation. The single case belongs to history, not to science. Without replications, we have no science. In approaching a final goal, science aims at generalizations that apply to *classes* of phenomena, not at descriptions of particular events.

The idiographic approach is natural in dealing with the practical problems of a particular case. In this connection, however, the technologist can and does use the kind of information, the concepts, and the techniques that have been derived from the nomothetic approach of scientists. Having applied this knowledge, however, the technologist is "on his own" in completing the picture. Because information is always in short supply or its application is not always clear, the technologist may feel that the scientist, in order to be of more help, should take a personalistic approach. What the technologist may actually need, however, is more information of the kind he already has. He is mistaken, therefore, in asking the scientist to take a personal point of view. Nomothetic information contributes much to the understanding of individuals. Idiographic information tells almost nothing about people in general; it belongs to the individual case.

The scientist, left to himself, is likely to go where his own curiosity and personal interests lead him. It is fortunate that he has this freedom, for without it he would fail to turn up those new ideas that eventually prove to be of great importance and usefulness. Probably he could often produce more of the new methods and concepts that the technologist needs if his interests could be channeled in those directions. It is true that the scientific investigator of personality has not given as much attention as he might have to the general problem of the principles governing structures of individual personalities, thereby emphasizing the combinations and interrelationships of traits. This is partly because he needs to know the traits first, and to this problem he has given much more attention. The technologist will have to be reconciled to the fact that

[8] For recent discussions, see Beck (1953), Eysenck (1954), du Mas (1955), and Falk (1956).

he is perpetually working at the points where science ends and art begins. Science can narrow the range within which art is necessary, but it can never eliminate it.

SOME SECONDARY ISSUES

The issues discussed next are called secondary because they have less to do with the main directions that personality study takes. They have some importance, however, since the way in which they are decided will affect what is included and what is emphasized in a treatment of the subject. We shall begin with two issues that bear some relation to the major issues.

The Place of Intuition in the Study of Personality

In connection with the study of personality, we mean by intuition that we reach some conclusion concerning a person after we have acquired a number of bits of information, without the aid of statistical or routine procedures. Intuitive conclusions belong in a class with hunches, guesses (more or less "educated"), and surmises. The use of such terms in the same class with intuition is not designed to disparage the value of intuition but to help in conveying the meaning of the term. Intuitions definitely have their place in the study of personality, and it is our purpose next to see what that place is.

INTUITION IN CLINICAL PRACTICE

The clinician develops a high regard for the process of intuition, for he must use it continually. He can never know everything concerning a given patient. Within the limitations of time and techniques, he obtains what information he can, and from what he thus knows, he arrives at conclusions. He hopes for insights, and if none come he continues to gather further information, hoping eventually to arrive at a conception of what he calls the "total personality." This is a synthetic product, a kind of model that he constructs to represent the individual personality. As such, an intuition may be regarded as a hypothetical construct regarding a single person.

This is entirely proper and necessary. Some trouble arises, however, when the clinician insists, as some do, that scientific studies of personality proceed to utilize such constructs, each unique. The greatest trouble comes when anyone attempts to communicate such ideas to others, for there are no communicative symbols for transferring a complex construct bodily from one person to another. There can be verbal descriptions, but they are analytical and bring us back to trait concepts.

Intuition plays a role in scientific investigation, but not in the same way as it does in clinical practice. The clinician accepts his intuited picture of a personality as being correct and proceeds to make diagnostic decisions and to take action, administrative or therapeutic, on the basis of it. This he must do, if decision and action are to occur. To the scientist, an intuited idea is a hypothesis to be investigated. A good scientist looks at previously known facts, extracts from them, intuitively, a new idea about the probable nature of things, and then proceeds to set up an experimental design to test his hypothesis. After the new facts are in, he again reflects upon all he knows about the subject, arrives at a conclusion regarding his original hypothesis, and perhaps intuitively constructs a new one.

Note that the proper place for intuition in scientific investigations is either before or after the collection of information. *It has no place whatever in the collection of information.* It is at this point where some clinically oriented psychologists go astray. They propose that intuited conclusions be given the status of scientific observations. But there is a vast difference between an observation and an inference drawn from an observation; between fact and hypothesis. Intuition cannot give us facts; it can only give us inferences from the facts. From this it follows that in the scientific study of personality, we cannot observe "total personalities"; observations must necessarily be made in terms of limited aspects, one at a time. More inclusive constructs are built up from information thus obtained.

Concepts for Describing Personality

In what terms shall we describe personality? This question is raised by the fact that in the literature on personality one finds so many examples of terms that are either undefined or very poorly defined, terms, for example, such as "inner core of personality," "deep-seated trends of the personality," "deepest layers of the personality," and "conflict-ridden understructure."

Such expressions have their literary value, but their communication value is very low. It can be questioned whether the writer himself knows exactly what he means by such an expression. If he were forced to put the same idea into simple, straightforward terminology, he might find that the idea he thought he had has vanished. At best, we may regard such expressions as efforts to convey complex, intuitive constructs for which there are no good symbols of expression for communication purposes. At worst, such terms may be symptomatic of an all-too-common fallacy, the assumption that if we can clothe an old idea sufficiently with new terminology, we have a new idea.

EMPIRICAL CONCEPTS

If developments in the study of semantics in recent years have taught us anything, it is that in science, at least, a term should have a *referent* in experience. We should be able to display for observation to others, if necessary, something that the term stands for, and stands for as directly as possible. The thing displayed is known as the referent. This practice is necessary to ensure good communicability. For example, a trait concept should refer to some observable kind of behavior, such as performance on a particular test or kind of test, or the presence of a symptom or group of symptoms that can be specified. Such concepts have been called *empirical,* because they stay close to experience.[9] Some have also been called *operational* concepts, because it is possible to demonstrate to others the operational steps by which the particular experience with which the concept is connected can be brought about. For example, the concept of verbal intelligence or of verbal comprehension in a certain population is indicated by the scores earned by individuals on a vocabulary test.

The basic scientist has no other choice than to favor empirical concepts. To some extent, the technologist will be forced to employ concepts less securely tied to experience, at least to shared experiences, because he always finds it necessary to go beyond established knowledge. For the sake of clear thinking, however, he should favor empirical concepts as far as they are known.

THE CONCEPT OF SELF

The concept of *self* is of special interest in personality study. Some writers refer to the *ego,* some use both terms, but no two authors agree fully on the use of either term.[10] The trouble, of course, is that there are no commonly accepted referents for these terms. In academic psychology, the concept of self has been largely confined to discussions of perception of self and conception of self as special cases of perception and conception. In some nonacademic psychologies, such as that of Freud, the concept of ego is a cornerstone.

It is the author's view that in a well-developed theory of behavior or of personality, the concepts of self and ego will have little place. When they are used in written discussions, they are often superfluous. That is, where the term "self" appears, we could say as much by substituting the word "individual" or "person." The worst thing that can be said about either concept is that it comes dangerously close to animism— the "little-man-within-the-outer-man" idea, which is quite foreign to science.

[9] Hall and Lindzey (1957).
[10] *Ibid.*

Abnormal vs. Normal Personality

The development of personality theory and the directions in which the study of personality have gone have been strongly influenced by those who are concerned with psychopathology. Deviations from the normal, including pathologies, are very frequently regarded as disorders of personality, with the result that normal personalities are often described in terms of categories of pathology, as if everyone had some degree of paranoia, or hysteria, or schizophrenia. We shall consider here the question of whether this belief and practice are justified. There is no doubt that there are continuities between normal and abnormal personality. But several questions should be asked, including how much continuity exists, what kind of continuity it is, and whether there may be any genuine discontinuities.

CATEGORIES OF PATHOLOGY

The general categories of pathology are recognized—neuroses (or psychoneuroses) and psychoses. The former category applies to individuals who are maladjusted to the degree that they need expert attention but usually do not need hospitalization. They suffer from symptoms such as extreme anxiety, compulsions, obsessions, phobias, chronic fatigue, and psychogenic organic disorders such as paralysis, blindness, and asthma. The psychotic group includes patients who are incapacitated and often must have custodial care because they might harm themselves or others. The functional or psychogenic disorders are of more concern to the student of personality than are the organic disorders. Common categories of diagnosis include the several varieties of schizophrenia—such as hebephrenic, paranoid, and catatonic—manics, depressives, and psychopathic deviates, to name the more common ones.

These categories have come down to us from the founder of modern psychiatry, Kraepelin, and have changed very little over the period of more than half a century. Yet, there is considerable dissatisfaction with the categories. This dissatisfaction is supported by studies of the reliability of diagnosis based upon these categories. Agreement between different diagnosticians has been notoriously poor, except for placement within a very few gross categories, such as schizophrenia vs. manic-depressive insanity. Recent research shows that the categories could be somewhat improved.[11] There is, furthermore, much reason to doubt that the present categories of pathology represent unitary traits.[12] In view of all these

---

[11] See, for example, the work of Wittenborn and Lorr, and their associates (Wittenborn and Holzberg, 1951; Lorr and Jenkins, 1953; and Lorr, Jenkins, and O'Connor, 1955). See also Guertin and Schmidt (1955), who found four varieties of paranoids.

[12] See Chap. 18.

circumstances, it is surprising that the categories are sometimes used to describe normal personalities.

NORMAL TRAITS, ABNORMAL SYNDROMES

We obviously need some logical scheme that will take into account the continuity between normal and pathological personality and yet give pathology real meaning. It is entirely possible that categories of pathology can apply to individuals who are recognized as being pathological without also applying to those recognized as being nonpathological. It is not necessary to believe that a particular mental disease is merely an extreme case of what everybody has to less degree. A disease entity is ordinarily known by a combination or syndrome of symptoms, as with the diseases of measles, mumps, or smallpox. It would be ridiculous, for example, to say that each healthy person has a different degree of measles. He has measles or he hasn't.

The analogy between psychological and organic disease may not be complete, but it goes some distance; otherwise we should not talk about psychological "diseases" at all. Measles and smallpox are known for certain kinds of skin eruptions that well persons do not have. Some psychopathological groups likewise have certain symptoms that no well person ordinarily has, for example, hallucinations, delusions of grandeur, and muscular rigidity. To this extent, at least, there is discontinuity between normal and abnormal personalities.

We must still account for the obvious continuities of certain other personality manifestations between the normal and abnormal. We must also consider the common observation that there is some tendency for a pathological syndrome to involve, to accentuated degrees, some of the traits that the person had before he was diagnosed as pathological. For example, the schizophrenic was formerly a shy, withdrawn individual; the melancholic was never much on the happy side and was prone to condemn himself; the manic-depressive was a moody person; and the paranoid was always "touchy." Such continuities in persons are probably the basis of the common practice of describing the normal in terms of pathological concepts.

But these continuities do not provide a necessary or sufficient justification. Continuity in a person and continuity of a personality variable in a population of persons are two different things. It might be pointed out that people who have measles also carry with them the same *behavior* traits through their illness, some of their traits being accentuated along with the experience. To a certain extent, this same principle probably applies in psychopathology. That is, some accentuation of traits may be more incidental than fundamental to the disease in question.

This may not be the whole story, for Moore (1938, 1941) has shown that certain *syndromes* that characterize personalities in some pathological groups existed in prepsychotic persons. For example, the precatatonic is likely to be lacking in gregariousness, to have a preference for indoor activities, to refuse to talk when others disagree, and to give up easily when things become difficult. A prepsychotic manic syndrome includes qualities of marked sociability, irritability, quarrelsomeness, violence of emotional expression, and being a "busy-body." [13] This might be interpreted to mean that the disease was actually developing long before the time of its supposed onset. Before we attribute such a syndrome, present in greater or less degree, to *all* individuals, we shall have to determine whether it is a common syndrome in those who never develop pathologies.

From these considerations, it is not out of order to suggest the hypothesis that the continuity between normal and abnormal personalities is to be found in terms of more limited traits that describe normal and abnormal alike and not in terms of the more inclusive pathological concepts. This hypothesis also implies that pathology in a certain category involves a syndrome or combination of qualities, some of which are accentuations of normal qualities and some of which are not. It can be doubted, in fact, that the pathological syndrome applies at all to large numbers of the normal population, excluding the prepsychotics. Whether or not such syndromes exist generally in the population is a matter for empirical investigation. It cannot merely be assumed. It is perhaps too easy for those who see abnormals every day to also see abnormal syndromes reflected in normal individuals. Seeing such syndromes in only a small proportion of people may lead to the conviction that the same syndromes exist in all people.

Heredity vs. Environment and Personality

The problem of heredity vs. environment is always with us. This problem concerns primarily the development of personalities. Since we have occasion to make only incidental references to development in this volume, the emphasis being on description, we shall be able to sidestep this perennial question. The problem is by no means a simple one, and its satisfactory solution will have to wait until we have adequate descriptive concepts for personality. First things should be put first.

The importance of the problem varies for the different groups interested in personality, as does the tendency toward believing in one determiner of development over the other. At one extreme, the biologists are likely to stress the hereditary determination of traits, with the belief that a personality is primarily a "chip off the old block." At the other extreme,

---

[13] Moore (1938).

cultural anthropologists are likely to stress environmental determination, with the belief that a personality is a "chip off the old culture," as Roback (1955) expresses it. Some even talk as though personality were a feature of the cultural group rather than of individuals, with the implication that the individual owes what personality he has to the cultural group to which he happens to belong.

Biologists must admit that personalities do seem to change, sometimes drastically, under environmental pressures of various kinds. Cultural anthropologists must admit that even within the same culture there are still great individual differences in traits. The most satisfactory view is that heredity sets limits on development but that environment can have effects within those limits. The debate is then concerned with the distance between those limits, the variation in distance from trait to trait, and the extent to which environmental pressures push the individual toward either limit.

SUMMARY

This chapter has attempted to account for the diversity of treatments of personality found in the literature. There are two main sources for this diversity: (1) the many different groups who are interested in personality, both in the basic sciences and in the technologies, and (2) the several theoretical points of view in psychology, where the greatest concern about personality is found. A number of primary and secondary issues arising from these sources affect the approaches to personality, theoretically or operationally.

One view concerning the study of personality is that it should emphasize the ways in which individuals function alike. This view comes close to that of general or basic psychology. Another view favors emphasizing individual differences, which takes personality study in the direction of differential psychology. The thing that most distinguishes the study of personality from both general and differential psychology is the emphasis which is placed upon the way in which things go together to make unique personalities, the emphasis, in other words, upon personality structure. The present volume admits to a bias toward emphasis on individual differences but regards the two views as supplementary.

According to some views, we should describe personalities in terms of relatively specific traits, which are practically identical with habits. According to others, we should describe personalities in terms of relatively broad, generalized traits or dispositions. On this point, it is concluded that personality structure is composed of traits of different degrees of generality and that descriptions at different levels of generality will be found useful to different groups.

Some interest groups want to stress the total individual personality; others insist that we must lose the individual and come out with abstract, descriptive concepts. One view leads to the idiographic approach, which stresses thorough study of one person at a time, and the other leads to the nomothetic approach, which stresses the study of populations, one or more traits at a time. The goal in the first case is to understand individual persons; the goal in the second case is to understand people in general. The personal view and the idiographic approach belong to technology, whereas the impersonal view and the nomothetic approach belong to basic science. This distinction is often not kept in mind, with consequent loss in clear thinking.

Some investigators believe that in order to know an individual personality as a totality, intuition should be included as a means of observation. However, the proper place for intuition comes in the formation of hypotheses, whether by the clinician in attempting to understand a particular person or by the scientist in preparing a research study. Intuitions have no data-gathering function in science.

In the description of personality, empirical concepts, which refer relatively directly to observed experience, should be given preference over vague and ill-defined concepts that have no ready referents. No significant place is seen for the concepts of self and ego in scientific descriptions of personality.

The view that normal personalities can be appropriately described in terms of concepts that apply to pathological categories, such as manic or paranoid, is rejected. Since there are some notable discontinuities between normal and pathological individuals, continuities are more appropriately accepted in terms of less complex traits. Diagnostic pathological groups are best distinguished from normals in terms of syndromes of traits, which may not apply, as syndromes, to genuinely nonpathological individuals.

The problem of heredity vs. environment in the determination of personality has little bearing upon the task of describing personality. The study of this problem is therefore best delayed until appropriate descriptive terms are achieved.

Chapter 3

THE PREDICTION
OF BEHAVIOR

ONE OF the most frequently stated objectives for the science of psychology is to enable us to predict behavior. If we are dealing with people and our aims are practical, knowing what we may expect of them often makes things easier for us and also for them. If our aim is to gain understanding, being able to predict behavior successfully is the best kind of assurance that our understanding is correct. The more complete our understanding of the principles of behavior and the more knowledge we have concerning individuals, the more fully can we predict their behavior.

The purpose of this chapter is to see what kind of information is needed in order to predict behavior and to see where personality traits fit into the picture, for traits contribute significantly to the information on which predictions can be based.

THE MAIN SOURCES OF INFORMATION IN PREDICTION

We cannot predict future events without having information regarding the present or past conditions that have a bearing on those events. Our immediate question is this: "What information do we need for predicting what this particular person will do at this particular time?" It takes special information, of course, in order to predict what a particular person will do at a particular time. Here we shall simply consider the general question, and our answer will be in terms of kinds or classes of information.

In considering all the conditions that may play a role in a person's behavior, we first make a crude distinction between the conditions contributed by the immediate situation in which the person finds himself and those contributed by the person himself. The situation and the organism, then, are the two main sources of information from which prediction of behavior can be made.

The Situation

Let us try to define "situation" without becoming bogged down, as can easily happen, in philosophical debate. For the present let us say that the immediate situation includes all the external energies acting on the organism's receptors at the moment. Usually, except in more exact studies of sensory or perceptual functioning, the psychologist observer specifies a situation in only the crudest terms as he observes it. He notes that the child is sitting on a sand pile, with certain toys at hand, and that three other children are playing close to him when his mother calls, "Willie, come home."

There is usually one element in the situation in which the observer has greatest interest. This aspect of the situation is commonly called the *stimulus*. In the illustration just given, the stimulus was the call "Willie, come home." The remaining elements in the situation are also potential and real determiners of behavior. Let us refer to the remaining elements as *background*. The behavior of the individual will be a function of both stimulus and background. In everyday life, a number of elements in a situation may be about equally potent so far as instigating behavior is concerned, and an observer might consider several elements as stimuli. In a psychological experiment, conditions are usually controlled so that only one element is varied or is of special interest to the investigator, the other (background) elements having been kept constant. But backgrounds, too, can be varied systematically. Hence, the distinction between stimulus and background is often an arbitrary one that is decided by the observer. Usually it is expected that that element which is designated as stimulus is a more powerful determiner of the response to follow than any other element in the situation.

PREDICTION FROM STIMULUS AND BACKGROUND ELEMENTS

A young high school girl is at a party. A boy calls loudly to her using a nickname that she wishes everyone would forget. What does she do? The same boy meets her casually a day or two later at school and calls to her in the same manner. What does she do? In the first instance, she merely blushes and finds no words with which to make a response. In the second instance she stamps her foot, saying, "Don't call me that." The backgrounds made the difference.

A simple experiment reported by Rosenbaum (1956) is a much more systematic illustration of the same multiple determination of response. In this experiment the stimulus and a certain background element were varied and the resulting behavior noted. One of two responses occurred in the subjects, who were university students: they volunteered to be subjects in a psychological experiment or they did not (without realizing that all the time they *were* taking part in a psychological experiment).

In the reading room of the library in the psychological laboratory, the experimenter would approach a student selected at random, inviting him to give a few minutes of his time in an experiment to be performed. Three rough levels of stimulus strength were applied to different subjects: a weak invitation, a moderate invitation, and an invitation with persuasive properties. The total background consisted of the reading room with other students in it. One element of the background was varied in a way that was intended to make the subject's acceptance more or less likely. This was done by letting the subject (*S*) see a neighbor being invited first. The neighbor was a "planted" person who half the time accepted the invitation and half the time turned it down. A third, or neutral condition, omitted this preliminary scene entirely.

In the design of the experiment, each of the three levels of stimulus strength was combined with each of the three background levels of inducement. Fifteen subjects were invited under each of the nine treatments (combination of stimulus and background). In Table 3.1 we see the

Table 3.1

Numbers of students (out of 15) who accepted the invitation to take part in a psychological experiment for three levels of stimulus strength and three levels of favorableness of background condition
(data from Rosenbaum, 1956)

Background condition	Stimulus strength			
	Low	Moderate	High	Average
Positive	6	12	12	10.0
Neutral	0	7	12	6.3
Negative	1	1	11	4.3
Average	2.3	6.7	11.7	6.9

number of subjects accepting the invitation under each of the nine treatments. Especially to be noted is whether the incidence of acceptance increases as a function of stimulus strength and as a function of background favorableness. Both expected relationships occur. If we could vary stimulus strength continuously on a nicely calibrated scale, we might expect the relationship of probability of acceptance to that variable to appear as in Figure 3.1. The relationships shown there are hypothetical but are based upon the known data of Table 3.1.

Let us relate these experimental results to the problem of prediction of behavior. The behavior to be predicted in this case is one of two responses—acceptance or rejection of an invitation. Note that in none of the nine treatments did all 15 subjects accept the invitation, and in only one did all 15 turn it down. Obviously, we would need more information than the two items we know about in order to make perfect

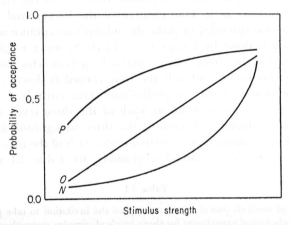

Fig. 3.1 Hypothetical relationship of probability of acceptance of invitation to take part in an experiment to strength of stimulus, for three different levels of favorableness of background (*P* = positive; *O* = neutral; *N* = negative). (*Based upon data from Rosenbaum,* 1956.)

predictions. What that additional information would be like will be mentioned later. With incomplete information we can only say what the most probable response is likely to be. From the information in Table 3.1, we would predict acceptance for the strongest stimulus, regardless of background condition. For a moderate stimulus, we would predict acceptance only when the background condition is positive. In all these cases more than half accepted. For a stimulus of moderate strength and a neutral background we have apparently a fifty-fifty proposition. For all other cases the prediction would be rejection.

The fact that, with one exception, responses were not unanimously in the same direction for any of the nine treatments, that is, some accepted and some did not, indicates that something other than the stimulus and the background element determined the responses. That something else might be in the personality make-up of the individuals. Some may be generous, or interested in science, or suggestible, or they may possess other traits that would favor acceptance of the invitation. Others may be resentful of the disturbance, jealous of their time, or just plain stubborn and hence inclined to decline under the most favorable stimulating conditions. We shall later see an instance of an experiment in which a personality trait is taken into account in prediction.

Temporary Organic and Motivational Conditions

We have just seen that we cannot completely account for behavior in terms of the situation alone. The organism itself brings into the picture some conditions that help to determine responses. Personality traits were mentioned as possible contributors, and we have previously defined a trait as some relatively enduring property of the individual. We must also recognize still another class of determiners of behavior, namely, the individual's temporary organic condition. Because of their temporary character, organic conditions cannot be regarded as personality traits.

One of these important conditions is the individual's state of physical health. Ill health, with its lowering of physical strength, entails a reduction of certain kinds of behavior all along the line. This is noticed most in a disinclination to exert physical effort. Another class of conditions have to do with the individual's state of motivation and his accompanying emotional state. The individual is hungry or he is satiated; he has just been frustrated or frightened; he has just been successful or he has just failed; he is rested or he is fatigued. Any or all of these conditions may have more than appreciable effects upon the behavior of the person over wide varieties of situations.

Personality Traits as Determiners of Behavior

Personality traits are dispositions that tend to persist through the kinds of changes just mentioned. Some of the more enduring "temporary" conditions may appear to bring about changes in personality, as when a person living on a near-starvation diet becomes unsocial, irritable, and depressed.[1] The boundary line between "temporary" and "relatively permanent" is not a very sharp one. Let us say that a change in disposition that lasts over a period of several weeks is a genuine, but temporary, change in personality, but that day-to-day changes associated with organic conditions do not come in the same category. The period between these two lengths of time is logically debatable ground. The fact that when the unusual organic condition has passed the individual returns to his former dispositions indicates that there are stable properties that we may attribute to him. If, however, the previous dispositions do not return, we may conclude that there has been a permanent change of personality.

[1] As reported by Keys, et al. (1950).

Perhaps something needs to be said in defense of our reference to personality traits as determiners of behavior, which implies that they are "causes." It is not uncommon to look upon traits in this manner. G. W. Allport (1937), for example, refers to traits as "determining tendencies," or long-range mental sets, or dispositions of readiness to behave in certain ways. To those who are reluctant to think in terms of "causes," let us say that all we need to mean is that behavior can be partially accounted for, or predicted by, these personal properties called traits. It is not necessary to assume that traits by themselves can bring about behavior or even account for its properties. Behavior does not occur without temporary instigating forces provided by drives or motives on the one hand and by external stimulation on the other. Behavior is a joint product of temporary organic conditions, the situation, and personality traits, all operating together at the moment.

An Experimental Example of Joint Determination of Behavior

The joint determination of behavior by the situation and by a personality trait is nicely demonstrated by an experiment performed by Helson et al. (1956). In this experiment it may be assumed that temporary organic conditions that might possibly have affected the results were constant, or at least were randomly distributed. This is an assumption that we commonly make, implicitly rather than explicitly, when doing an experiment of this kind, unless we are particularly interested in the effects of one or more of these conditions. In this experiment, the stimulus, a background condition, and a personality trait were systematically varied, the investigators noting the effects upon the subjects' responses.

CONDITIONS VARIED IN THE EXPERIMENT

The stimuli were 18 statements of opinion about war as an institution, selected from the Thurstone scale of Attitudes toward War. The statements had been previously calibrated as to degree of favorableness toward pacifism on an 11-point scale on which a statement with a high value indicates a pacifistic attitude. Six statements were selected at each of three different levels on the scale. Two examples of promilitaristic statements and their scale values are:

4.1　It is our duty to serve in a defensive war.

4.4　We should have some military training in our schools.

An example of a neutral statement is:

5.6　War brings out the bad qualities in men as well as the good ones.

Two antimilitaristic statements are:

7.8　The misery and suffering of war are not worth its benefits.

7.8　It is good judgment to sacrifice rights in order to prevent war.

The response that the subject (S) was to make as he heard each statement was to indicate how strongly he agreed or disagreed with the statement. He was to do this by giving a number from 1 to 7 inclusive, where 1 meant "strongly disagree," 4 meant "neither agree nor disagree," and 7 meant "strongly agree." He heard each statement through earphones from a tape recording. Immediately after hearing a statement, the subject would hear voices belonging to persons whom he was led to believe were members of his small group. These "persons" were stating their own numerical judgments of agreement or of disagreement on the same seven-point scale. Their judgments were intentionally grouped near one point on the scale of agreement-disagreement, at one of three levels. After hearing some statements, the subjects would hear judgments of 7, 7, 6, and 7; after others they would hear judgments of 5, 4, 4, 3; and after still others, 1, 1, 1, 2. Thus, there were three levels of background condition. Each was systematically combined with two of the statements at each of the three selected levels on the pacifism-militarism scale. One hypothesis to be tested was that the response of the subject would tend to be biased in the direction of the background level, or level of group opinion.

The third experimental variation was in the trait known as ascendance-submission. The subjects had been given the Allport A-S Reaction Study, which yields scores for individuals on the scale of this trait. For the purposes of the Helson experiment, three levels on this continuum were distinguished—40 per cent of the subjects with highest scores (most ascendant), 20 per cent with near-average scores, and 40 per cent with the lowest scores. With three levels of stimulus quantity, three levels of background condition, and three levels of position on the traits continuum, there were, by all possible combinations, 27 treatments, and since 15 subjects had each treatment, there was a total of 405 subjects.

RESULTS OF THE EXPERIMENT

The reactions of the subjects, in terms of their ratings of agreement vs. disagreement, were expected to show the effects of both situational and personal determiners. Let us first consider the effects of the variations of background condition. If the background had *no* effect, we should expect average ratings of agreement to be approximately equal under the three background conditions. The three means were 5.4, 4.3, and 2.8, corresponding to the background ratings, which average 6.75, 4.00, and 1.25. We see that the subjects did not go all the way with members of their "groups" in making their ratings, but they definitely went in the direction of the background levels.

We can gain information regarding the effect of the trait of ascendance upon the ratings of agreement by looking at the data from a different viewpoint. If we separate all the subjects into three groups on the basis of ascendance-submission scores, and if we also separate each of these three groups in terms of background level—the "agreeing" level, the "neutral" level, and the "disagreeing" level—we find that the three means

Table 3.2

Averages of ratings of agreement vs. disagreement given at three levels of ascendance and for three levels of background agreement
(data from Helson et al., 1956)

Background level	Ascendance level			
	Low	Medium	High	All levels
Agreeing	5.7	5.5	4.8	5.4
Neutral	4.3	4.3	4.4	4.3
Disagreeing	2.5	2.5	3.4	2.8
All levels	4.2	4.1	4.2	4.2

of ratings differ, as shown in Table 3.2. The same data for the most and least ascendant groups are shown graphically in Figure 3.2. The subjects whose scores were moderate for ascendance gave results so close to those

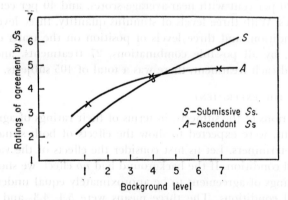

Fig. 3.2 Relationship between the average rating of agreement with statements as given by the subjects and the average level of agreement of background ratings of the same statements, for two extreme groups on the trait of ascendance. (*Data from Helson et al.*, 1956.)

for the submissive group that their two curves would have been almost indistinguishable in Figure 3.2. From the table and the figure we see that the effect of the background ratings was rather small for the ascendant group but rather marked for both the average group and the low group on ascendance.

Figure 3.3 presents the data of Table 3.2 plotted in another way to show the relation of average ratings to ascendance level for the three different background levels. Here we see that when the background level was high, the average ratings of the subjects tended to be high but were least high for the most ascendant group. When the background level was low, the average ratings were generally low but were least low for the most ascendant group. On the average, the most ascendant group was biased relatively little as compared with the other two groups.

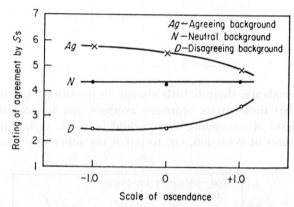

Fig. 3.3 Relationship between the average rating of agreement with statements as given by the subjects and their average level on the trait of ascendance, with three different background levels of agreement. (*Data from Helson et al., 1956.*)

If we think in terms of the degree to which each of the three ascendance groups were *biased* by the background, we get a better picture by examining the deviations of averages from the background averages, the latter being 1.25, 4.00, and 6.75. One implication of the results is that these deviations might be used as objective measures of the trait of ascendance; the greater the deviation, the higher on the scale of ascendance is the individual or the group. The deviations from group opinion at the three trait levels for the three levels of group opinion are shown in Table 3.3. Hypothetical relationships, based upon these data, are shown in Figure 3.4.

From this picture, we see a systematic gain in size of deviation as we go up the scale of ascendance. But before we become convinced that the size of deviation can be used as a measure of ascendance level for individuals, we should note two considerations. From the two curves in Figure 3.4, it is clear that discrimination of levels of ascendance would be good only among the higher levels on the ascendance scale. At lower

Table 3.3

Deviations of the averages of agreement ratings of the subjects from the background agreement ratings (group opinion) at three levels of ascendance and for three background levels (data from Helson et al., 1956)

Background level	Ascendance level		
	Low	Medium	High
Agreeing	1.0	1.2	1.9
Neutral	0.3	0.3	0.4
Disagreeing	1.2	1.3	2.2

levels of ascendance, there is little change in deviation. Another consideration is that these curves represent averages, not individuals. At any particular level of ascendance there would be much variability of individual measures of deviation. Or, to put it the other way around, for a

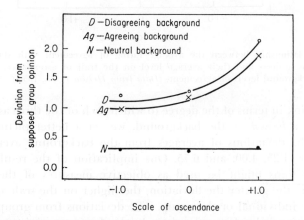

Fig. 3.4 Relationship between *deviations* of ratings of agreement from levels of agreement of group opinion and degree of ascendance of raters, for three different background levels (group-opinion levels). (*Data from Helson et al., 1956.*)

particular size of deviation "score," there would be a considerable range of individual differences in ascendance on the Allport A-S Reaction Study score. We shall have to be satisfied with the fact that the data demonstrate a principle, namely, that human reactions are jointly determined by situational conditions interacting with personality traits. Also to be noted is the fact that only when we keep situational conditions constant do we find that individual differences in behavior indicate individual differences in a trait.

ADAPTATION-LEVEL THEORY

The experiments described above were inspired by a general theory of behavior known as adaptation-level theory. This theory was developed by Helson originally in the context of psychophysics, but it has very general application in psychology. Psychophysics is known as the science that is concerned with the quantitative relationships of reactions to stimulating conditions. Stated in this simple form, the definition seems to apply to the science of behavior in general. However, the emphasis in this definition should be placed on the term "quantitative," for the aim of psychophysics is to state the relation of *measured* changes in a kind of response to *measured* changes in a kind of stimulating condition.

The work of Helson has demonstrated that knowledge of stimulating conditions is not enough; we must also consider conditions within the organism. This is where personality traits come in, as was demonstrated in the second experiment described above. In connection with that experiment, we saw how, by keeping the stimulating conditions constant but allowing individuals to differ in a trait, the resulting differences in response can be used to tell us about individual differences in a trait. This is the theoretical basis for the measurement of traits. We shall see that the picture is somewhat more complicated than this illustration would suggest. But before going into this problem, let us become better acquainted with adaptation-level theory.

Adaptation Level for Lifted Weights

A simple experiment with lifted weights will illustrate the concept of adaptation level (Helson, 1948). Five weights, weighing 200, 250, 300, 350, and 400 grams, were used. As the subject lifted each weight, he gave a judgment on a scale of nine categories, in which 10 points meant "very, very light," 50 points meant "medium," 90 points meant "very, very heavy," and intermediate categories were defined verbally in line with these three. A number of subjects gave judgments of these five stimulus weights, with averages of 34, 50, 63, 74, and 82 points.

Our first interest in these results is to find the quantity of stimulus weight that on the average is called "medium," or that should correspond to an average of 50 points. It happens that one of the weights, namely the 250-gram weight, yielded an average of 50 points. But taking the whole set of data into consideration, it turns out that a weight of 248 is a better estimate of what would correspond, in the long run, to a scale value of 50 points.[2] The weight of 248 grams is therefore said to be at the adaptation level for this experiment. Weights greater than 248 are judged on the heavy side, on the average, and weights lower than 248 are judged on the light side. A weight of 248 grams is at a neutral point for the subjective scale of weight; it would be judged neither heavy nor light, or if so judged, it would yield judgments of heavy and light an equal number of times.

In the context of personality theory, the most interesting aspect of this experiment is that there is evidence that the adaptation level of 248 grams was determined to some extent by predisposition in the subjects who lifted the weights. All of us have had a multitude of experiences in lifting things, and our standards of what we call light or heavy are determined by those experiences. Tresselt (1948), for example, found that professional weight lifters gave her series of laboratory weights a much larger proportion of "light" judgments than did other subjects. In other words, past experiences leave what Helson calls a *residual* level, which enters the picture and helps determine present judgments of a similar nature.

Let us assume that if there were no effects from previous experience, the adaptation level should be equal to the geometric mean of the experimental stimuli.[3] The geometric mean of the five weights used in the Helson experiment is 291 grams. Since the obtained adaptation-level weight is considerably below 291, the inference is that the subjects were predisposed from past experience to regard as neutral (neither heavy nor light) some weight even below 248 grams.[4] Without additional data, we are unable to estimate what that preexperimental adaptation level was.

The estimation of the residual value is not important for our purposes here. What is important is that we have a demonstration of the fact that some condition in the individuals contributed to the resulting behavior (adaptation level) in the experiment. This residual something is analogous to a trait of personality. This is not to say that traits of personality are entirely due to past experiences. To some extent, the residuals called traits may well be determined by heredity.[5]

[2] For procedures by which an adaptation level is estimated from data, see Guilford (1954, p. 332) or Helson (1948).

[3] The geometric mean of the five stimulus weights would be the fifth root of the products of the five stimulus values, that is, $\sqrt[5]{200 \times 250 \times 300 \times 350 \times 400}$, which equals 291. An easier computing procedure would be to find logarithms of the five stimulus values, find their arithmetic mean, and finally the antilogarithm of this mean.

[4] For the purposes of an illustration, we shall assume that no other present conditions have a hand in determining the adaptation level. Helson recognizes the possibility of such other conditions.

[5] It should also be said that the residual affecting judgments of weight in this experiment is an average effect of a number of individuals whose results were averaged. Each person would have his own predisposition, or residual value.

In order to make the analogy between the lifted-weight experiment and the war-opinion experiment more complete, some parallels should be pointed out. In both we have seen that personal qualities—residuals or traits—help to determine the behavior of individuals and of groups. In both, stimulus strength was an effective condition. In both, background conditions were also effective. In two other weight-lifting variations, Helson introduced an extra weight. In one set of judgments of the stimuli, the subject lifted a 900-gram weight just preceding each stimulus weight, and in another set, the subject lifted a 90-gram weight in the same manner. As predicted, the 900-gram background biased the adaptation level upward (to 337 grams) and the 90-gram background biased the adaptation level downward (to 186 grams).

Specification of Stimulus Conditions

The primary concern of this volume is with the description and measurement of personality. We have just seen that the assessment of personality has to be done largely through observations of behavior in one way or another. We can make the most accurate and meaningful assessment of a behavior trait in a person when we have presented a standardized situation or when we can somehow make allowances for effects produced by stimulating conditions. The remaining interpersonal differences can then be attributed to some property or properties belonging to the persons.

In standardized situations, as in good psychological tests, it is important that we be able to specify the stimulating conditions as much as possible. In the experiments cited, the significant aspects of each situation could be made equivalent and we can know when they are equivalent in certain respects and when they are not. It is naturally much easier to control and to specify the conditions of a situation in a psychophysical experiment than in an experiment on social behavior, where situations may be very complex and the operating forces may be subtle. But two experiments involving social situations were described in which relatively accurate controls were exercised and certain calibrations were known. It usually takes considerable ingenuity to accomplish this, but new situations are frequently being brought under control and under operations of measurement, situations that might have been regarded as hopeless candidates before.

COMPONENTS OF DETERMINATION

The statement has been made a number of times that the response made by a person at a particular time is jointly determined by the situation, his temporary personal conditions, and his traits. It has also been said that we infer individual differences in trait positions, or characteristics, from observed responses. We shall consider next the question of the extent to which we may attribute behavior to these three sources, but particularly to traits of personality. This is a very important question for the assessment of trait positions of individuals, for in measurement of individuals on a given trait, we want the individual differences in the observed behavior to reflect individual differences in that trait as much as possible and to reflect differences due to other determiners as little as possible. To the extent that our differences in behavior reflect determiners other than the trait in which we are interested, our measurements are in error.

The Relative Importance of Determiners

Before we can consider more exactly the extent to which a trait contributes to differences in behavior, it is desirable to become acquainted with a concept that may be new to some readers—the concept of *variance*. Let us say that the behavior in which we are interested is of a kind that can be scored on a continuous scale. In the opinion-rating experiment, we found that the average deviation of an individual's ratings from the average rating representing group opinion might be used as a score for the trait of ascendance. If obtained for a large group of individuals, such scores would vary over a range of values. The total amount of variation shown by individuals in the group is known as the variance. If all individuals make the same score, there will be no variance. Similarly, the greater the amount of spread of the scores, the greater the variance.[6]

When behavior scores can be attributed to several independent sources, we can think of the total variance among them as being a sum of components contributed by those sources. By certain statistical methods of analysis,[7] it is possible to estimate what proportion of the total variance should be attributed to different sources. We shall not be concerned with those methods here, but we shall make use of the idea of components of variance. For example, if individual differences in certain scores reflect equally the three main sources of traits, temporary conditions, and situation, we could represent this circumstance by means of diagram A in Figure 3.5, where T, C, and S stand for these three sources, respectively. We shall consider some other hypothetical cases and relate these ideas to concrete procedures for assessing personality traits, for the logic of this approach is important to clear thinking about measurement of personality.

---

[6] Those who are familiar with elementary statistics will recognize that the amount of variance in a set of measurements is measured by the *mean square,* which is the average of the squared deviations of the measurements from their arithmetic mean. The variance is also the square of the *standard deviation.* (See the Appendix for a brief discussion of these terms.)

[7] The methods of factor analysis.

WHEN THERE IS LACK OF CONTROL OF CONDITIONS

Let us consider first the case in which both the situation and temporary personal conditions are allowed to vary somewhat at random among different individuals. Let us say that we want to obtain some idea of the relative amounts of physical courage the individuals of a group possess. There are, to be sure, only certain types of situations in which we should have any opportunity at all to detect differences between individuals in this respect. The situations would have to present some degree of physical

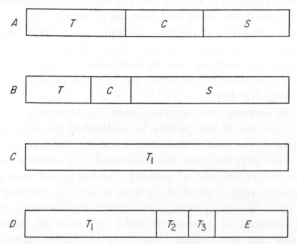

Fig. 3.5 Examples of how the total variance of scores from some methods of trait assessment can be attributed to various sources—traits (T), temporary organic conditions (C), situations (S), and error (E).

danger to the individuals. In everyday life we can wait for such situations to happen and we can note what each person does and whether he shows courage or lack of courage. But some individuals face greater dangers than others, and differences in responses will naturally reflect this circumstance.

This case is of interest to us, because one of the most common methods of evaluating people on traits is to use some kind of rating procedure (see Chapter 7). A rater who has presumably observed each person in day-to-day situations is asked to give each person a value to represent what he considers to be that person's level on a scale of courageousness. We may suppose that such values would be determined to a large extent by differences in situations and to a small extent by personal dispositions, either temporary or permanent. Diagram B in Figure 3.5 might represent such a case. It is true that a rater can, and probably does, make some allowances for the inequality of situations, but how successful he is in this, we do not know. This aspect of the rater's performance adds a second burden to his task: he must evaluate the situation as well as the person.

WHEN THERE IS CONTROL OF CONDITIONS

Ideally, we should like our scores for a trait to be determined 100 per cent by the trait. If we could control all other determiners except the trait, this would be the case, and we could represent it as in diagram C in Figure 3.5.

Note that in diagram C we give the T a subscript to indicate that it is one particular trait. We must now face the possibility that the trait contribution to scores may actually be a multiple one; several different traits may be involved. For example, it was suggested in connection with the experiment on volunteering that an individual's volunteering as a subject for the experiment might reflect his traits of generosity, interest in science, or suggestibility.

In order to measure the particular trait T_1 accurately, we must also rule other traits out of the picture by additional controls. A crude example of how this is done is found in a test for the trait of endurance. The score is the length of time the individual will continue to squeeze a hand dynamometer, in spite of growing discomfort and even pain. Such a score naturally reflects physical strength as well as endurance, particularly if we insist that every examinee hold the dynamometer at the same number of kilograms of pressure. In order to reduce the variance in the scores that is due to strength, two steps are taken. The maximum strength in kilograms is determined for each person. He is then instructed to hold the pressure at half his own maximum squeeze. It is possible, by the statistical procedures of factor analysis, to determine whether or not this condition has eliminated all of the strength component from the total variance of the scores.

THE TEST AS A MEASURE OF TRAITS

By now it should be clear that a good test of a behavior trait is much like a good experiment. It presents to all individuals the same external situation, with the same instructions and the same items or tasks. Apart from the test material itself, the environmental testing conditions—lighting, temperature, freedom from distractions, and other conditions that may be relevant—should also be uniform. All examinees should be in reasonably good health, appropriately motivated as to kind and degree of effort exerted, and free from emotional states that may affect their scores, unless, of course, emotional traits, as such, are to be measured.

Even when the above conditions appear to have been met, we usually find by factor analysis of the scores of tests that we have not approached the ideal expressed by diagram C very closely. In fact, our best tests are more accurately represented in diagram D, where about half the variance can be attributed to trait T_1, a small component to trait T_2, and another small component to trait T_3. We could, and often do, regard as negligible such small contributors as T_2 and T_3.

There are many tests, however, in which the contributions from two or more traits are more nearly equal and in which larger numbers of traits are involved. Such tests are useful for the prediction of behavior that is determined by the same combination of traits. But there are other circumstances in which the meaning of scores from such tests is ambiguous or in which one or more of the trait components is just "dead wood" so far as measurement is concerned. In such cases, the contribution to the scores might just as well be regarded as a kind of error of measurement.

In diagram D, the proportion designated E (for error) indicates determiners other than traits, from whatever sources—sources, in other words, that should have been controlled but were not. Even when we do the best we can, at least a certain proportion of the total variance is from uncontrolled sources. Much of the error comes from situational or personal conditions, both of which vary from person to person.

The last statement seems to contradict the fact that we have applied the same situation to all examinees. It is true that the external situation—the test material—*is* the same for all persons, but each person makes of it something unique to him. Each examinee's attention determines different degrees of exposure to various parts of the test material. Each examinee has his own interpretations of both the instructions and the items of the test. To this extent, the test is a somewhat different one for each individual.

It is true that in some tests we want individual differences in attention and interpretation to be reflected in the differences in scores. This is more true regarding the test items than the instructions. Differences of attention and interpretation may reveal differences in the trait that we want to measure. For example, the test may be designed to measure interest in mechanical things, and the score might be based upon the number of mechanical objects that are noticed on an exposed page where those objects are mixed with several other kinds. For another example, the test may be designed to measure an ability to comprehend correctly, or to measure some other ability that depends upon comprehension. For still another example, misinterpretations might be used to indicate biased attitudes of some kind, such as an attitude toward minority groups. Individual differences of interpretation of stimulus material are of special interest in the projective techniques (see Chapter 12). Differences of interpretation may also contribute, in part, the kind of information we want from personality inventories (see Chapter 8).

But probably in most tests, we should like interpretations of both instructions and items to be uniform for all examinees so that differences in scores will be determined by the trait that we want to measure. Unfortunately, we cannot devise test materials that ensure uniform interpretations. To the extent that interpretation is not controlled in such tests, we have errors of measurement.

The picture of tests that has just been painted may seem discouraging. Actually, it is not discouraging if we do not ask too much of tests. Granted that they do provide us with biased information, from which we may never expect to make perfect predictions, the proper way to evaluate them is to ask whether they give us any useful information that we do not have and could probably not obtain in any other way. If tests give us information concerning properties of individuals, information enabling us to improve predictions of behavior, they make a real contribution.

Other methods of assessing personality traits—ratings, interviews, expressive methods, and so on—could be evaluated on the same basis. The various methods will come under our inspection in many of the chapters to follow. Most of these methods yield numbers to describe trait positions of individuals. The exactness of the number system should not lead us astray when we meet up with a score. As a description of a trait position or characteristic of a person, the score is almost bound to include an error, usually small, but sometimes not so small. This truth should help us to take a more realistic attitude toward obtained measurements of traits. It should prevent our going all the way with test enthusiasts, who accept scores as exact measurements, and it should also prevent our joining the critics of measurement methods, who believe that if there is any error at all, the methods should be done away with. A modulated scale of evaluation of the methods is called for.

SUMMARY

The information needed for the purpose of predicting behavior comes from two main sources. One is the situation, including the focal part (stimulus) and the background, which contains many elements, usually of secondary importance. The other main source is the person, including his temporary organic conditions and his more permanent traits. The organic conditions have to do with present state of health and motivation. All of these sources, including traits, may be regarded as joint determiners of behavior.

Through the experimental control of stimulus, background elements, organic conditions, and traits, the effects of any one of these sources can be determined if it is allowed to vary while the others are held constant. Some experiments were cited in which this type of study of determiners was carried out. The model for such a study is found in Helson's work on the adaptation level.

The adaptation level in a psychophysical experiment is that stimulus value that is most associated with a neutral response when similar but varying stimuli are presented to an individual or a group. Usually some predisposition, or residual level, of the individual being tested helps to determine what the adaptation level will be. A trait is regarded as a kind of predisposition, and in this sense it is in a class with the residual that helps to determine the adaptation level.

In the assessment of a person's trait position, we must apply experimental principles. This means that if we want differences in behavior to indicate differences in a particular trait, we must remove as much as possible the effects of all determiners except the effects of the trait in which we are interested. This involves holding constant the effects of other traits as well as the effects of situational and temporary organic conditions. Behavior tests seem to provide the best example of experimental controls in personality assessment, with certain qualifications that were pointed out.

By use of the procedures of factor analysis, concerning which there will be some additional nontechnical discussion in the following chapters, it is possible to estimate the extent to which a certain trait determines differences in behavior in a certain test, and in this way to evaluate the test as a source of information regarding the trait.

Chapter 4

BEHAVIOR TRAITS

IN THIS chapter we shall attempt to become better acquainted with traits and their properties. The discussion will be restricted to behavior traits because the morphological and physiological traits offer no particular difficulties. We shall first see the logical steps by which ideas of traits come about and the kinds of observations upon which traits are based. We shall see that traits differ from one another in many ways and that some are more adapted to the purposes of description and measurement of personality than others.

THE ORIGINS OF TRAIT IDEAS AND TRAIT DESCRIPTIONS

Trait Names

Carr and Kingsbury (1938) once suggested a logical scheme to describe the way in which we arrive at the idea of a trait and a name for it. The scheme involves three steps, which are followed more implicitly than explicitly. An awareness of the steps should help us to keep better oriented with respect to the nature of traits.

The first step comes immediately from the observation of behavior. We note that people differ in certain ways in the things they do and in the manner of doing them. Some quality is observed to be common to different behaviors and to be exhibited to different degrees. This quality of behavior is described by the use of an adverb because it pertains to actions. We say that a person has acted cautiously, or confidently, or cordially, or rapidly. At this stage, the quality is attributed to behavior and not to the person. There are some students of personality who would leave it this way, but they are probably in the minority.

The second step is to apply the quality to the individual who commits the act. At this stage we apply the adjectival form of description. We say that the person is cautious, confident, cordial, or rapid. The quality has been logically transferred from the action to the actor. Note what this does. The action itself is transitory. When it is finished it is a matter of history. But the person remains, and we generalize the description, applying it on a more permanent basis. The person was here before the action and he is here after the action. If he is the kind of person the adjectives say he is, his behavior was not something just "put on" during the act. It might actually have been confined to the act, of course. But in our ordinary experience we find that people are rather consistent. Having seen this kind of behavior from the person this time, we are inclined to expect similar behavior from him at other times. If we observe behavior of the same kind a second time, and a third, and so on, we have confirmation of our description of the person. Even when there are exceptions, we are inclined to accept the description that applies to the *majority* of his acts.[1]

The third logical step is not a long one. After deciding that we may describe a person, having observed his behavior and having concluded that the quality belongs to him, we refer to the property as a *thing* and give it a noun form. We say that the person has a trait of caution, of confidence, of cordiality, or of rapidity or speed. Nouns are names for abstractions, but so are adjectives and adverbs. Some psychologists strongly object to attaching nouns to abstractions of this sort, as if we were thinking of those abstractions as something objective, perhaps even tangible or palpable. The use of nouns to describe traits should not bother us, however, if we remember what we actually have. Behavior traits are enduring properties of a person, properties that lead us to expect certain kinds of behavior from that person and not other kinds. Whatever it is in the person that ensures persistence of the property is no more mysterious than whatever it is that ensures memory for anything. The endurance of a behavior trait may depend upon the same kind of bodily mechanisms as the endurance of a habit or a conditioned response. There is no more impropriety in using a noun to describe a trait than in using a noun to apply to a particular named habit.

Trait Indicators

The most important idea to extract from the discussion above is that traits are not observed. Behavior is observed, but traits are inferred from the observations. The view adopted in this volume is that traits are properties of persons, not of behavior. The observed behavior that provides the basis for inferring something as to a trait is a *trait indicator*. We see a fighter keep on until he drops exhausted, and we infer that he has a high degree of the trait of endurance. We see someone monopolizing the

---

[1] To the student of learning theory, this might be interesting as a case of "partial reinforcement." Confirmation in some of the incidents is sufficient to determine acceptance of a conclusion.

conversation, talking about himself, and we infer that he has a high degree of the trait of conceit, also of the trait of talkativeness.

GENERAL TYPES OF TRAIT INDICATORS

We shall consider in a general way what it is about behavior that provides the cues from which a *trait position* is inferred, trait position meaning the degree of a trait a person has.

The cue may be *what* the person does or *what he likes* to do. He keeps his belongings in complete order; he seems to enjoy taking risks of personal injury; and he listens to music hour after hour. From these characteristic actions we infer high degrees of meticulousness, adventuresomeness or boldness, and interest in music and perhaps in aesthetic things in general. The traits inferred from this kind of cue are most likely to be motivational; that is, they take the form of needs, interests, and attitudes.

The cue may be in *how well* the person does things. He shows good performance in some things and poor performance in others, as compared with the norms for his group. The trait indicated by goodness of performance is recognized as some kind of ability. The best indicator for an ability level in any respect is, of course, a score derived from a test.

The cue may be the *manner* in which the person does things, not so much his methods as his style of action. He may act tactlessly, thoughtfully, impulsively, or forcefully. From these observations we infer qualities of tactlessness (or low degree of tactfulness), reflectiveness, impulsiveness, and forcefulness. Such traits are likely to be found in the modality of temperament. It is wise to say "likely" here, because under some circumstances forcefulness might mean physical strength, and under other circumstances it might mean enthusiasm (interest) for the particular activity. *What* a person does may also sometimes indicate a temperament trait rather than a motivational trait. For example, the person who criticizes others unduly may show a low degree of tolerance. The cue of *how well* a thing is done usually indicates an ability only, providing we have controlled motivation experimentally in giving the test. In everyday life motivation is also a significant determiner of level of performance.

SPECIAL TYPES OF TRAIT INDICATORS

A number of other possible cues to traits are often considered. Some involve the manner of behaving, or some special way of behaving. One such category is that of expressive movements, those aspects of behavior that have little or no adaptive value and might almost be called mannerisms. The cues, in this case, may come from movements in general, with properties that might be called flourishing, jerky, flowing, or emphatic. Or they may come from emotional expressions that are shown more often than usual in a person, such as sneering, smirking, scowling, or cringing. A later chapter will deal exclusively with the expressive-movement methods, including the use of handwriting samples, as in graphology, and behavior tests in which expressive aspects of behavior are measured and recorded. The most important question to ask is whether expressive aspects of behavior indicate traits of motivation and temperament that we want to know about or whether they indicate only traits of expression as such. It will be found that there is personal consistency with respect to expressive behavior, and the meaning or significance of this consistency presents an important problem.

Another type of cue comes from the kinds of groups in which the person holds membership. The groups may be political, vocational, national, religious, or fraternal. The hypothesis is that the members of a group tend to be of a somewhat stereotyped pattern of personality. Perhaps they select new members of the same kind as themselves and thus perpetuate a stereotype. The "culture" of the group is in turn expected to affect the personality of each member in similar directions, thus making members more alike.

Information about group membership is certainly clear-cut, objective data about a person. Actually, this kind of information will not go very far in leading us to description of personalities. On very few traits would there be strong intergroup differences. In fact, differences between groups on any trait are likely to be small. Although different religious groups have different average positions on the scale of liberalism-conservatism, for example, the amount of overlapping of distributions of individual members is so great that it would be risky to use religious affiliation as the sole cue to this trait.

Some of those who are concerned with the assessment of personalities recommend that the emotional reaction of the *observer* be used as a cue to traits in the person observed. Rather than observe the person to be assessed, the observer examines his own feelings. He may then describe the person as being likable or repulsive, stimulating or soothing, or ingratiating or aloof.

This kind of information, it is claimed, provides impressions that are socially useful, the assumption being that the person who is observed will affect other observers in a similar manner. Such information probably seems important to many interviewers, and to the extent that they can duplicate the emotional reactions of people in general to interviewees, the information would have value. Another value cited for the method is that the impressions gained by the observer can be used as a first step toward better descriptions based on other cues. That is, if we are unfavorably impressed by the person, we can ask what it is that gives this impression. A more analytical examination of the cues that point to traits that impress observers unfavorably may lead to appraisals of significant traits.

However, there are a number of disadvantages to the use of general feelings of the observer as cues. In scientific investigation, of course, such evidence has no status, except as an indication of how one person affects another. There are a number of reasons for concluding that the information is undependable. No two observers are necessarily affected in the same way by the same person. Furthermore, we differ with respect to the behaviors and traits that we like or dislike.[2] Conclusions concerning a person could therefore be wide apart. Only to the extent that the person affects others in the same direction would there be agreement. Even then, the impression indicates some aspect of *popularity* of a person, which does not necessarily tell us what he is like. The reasons for being popular or unpopular may very well depend upon different *patterns* of qualities in different persons. Two popular persons or two unpopular ones might still be very different in personality. Thus, the vague impression given by emotional reactions to others is not sufficiently analytical and may, in fact, reveal more about the observer than about the person observed.

Two Views of Personality: Self and Other

We must make a clear distinction between three quite different things. There is the person as he really is and as we want to know him; there is the person as he sees himself; and there is the person as others see him. Actually, each observer will have his own private view, which will not agree completely with that of any other observer. The views by self and by others have their common elements and hence overlap at many points, but they are not identical. None of these views are completely correct in the sense that they coincide at every point with what the person really is.

In assessing a personality, we are often dependent upon the observations of the person himself and upon observations made by others. The pictures that we can build up from these two sources will differ. We have recourse to another source of information, derived from psychological tests and other techniques, which we hope will be free from the biases that accompany self-observation or observations by others. We may call this source the impersonal or objective view. However, objective methods also fail to give a completely accurate picture of what the person is like. Any picture that we are able to obtain can be only an approximation.

DEGREES OF OVERLAP OF VIEWS—SELF AND OTHER

We can gain some idea of the extent to which the views of self and of others agree by the use of ratings—self-ratings and ratings by others. An

[2] Thomas and Young (1938).

example of this is given by Amatora (1956), who asked 200 boys and 200 girls in grades 4 through 8 to rate themselves and to rate others on 22 different traits, each on a 10-point scale. For each child, the "other" ratings were in the form of averages of the judgments of eight others. The results, which are cited here merely for illustrative purposes, give very little basis for generalizing as to accuracy or agreement between raters in general.

For the boys, the correlations of self and other ratings, trait by trait, ranged from .10 to .67, with a median (average) of .19.[3] Examples of traits on which there was relatively high agreement are:

Courtesy .... .67
Neatness .... .60
Intelligence .... .59
Generosity .... .44

Examples of low correlations are:

Cooperation .... .10
Sense of humor ...... .12
Sportsmanship .... .15
Thoughtfulness ...... .16

For the girls, the correlations of self and other ratings ranged from .11 to .62, with a median of .38. Examples of traits on which there was relatively high agreement are:

Interests .... .62
Dependability .... .58
Intelligence .... .58
Sense of humor ...... .48

Examples of low correlations are:

Sportsmanship .... .11
Courtesy .... .15
Generosity .... .16
Cooperation .... .20

The low average correlations may indicate the generally low amount of overlap of self and other views so far as these 22 traits are concerned for these children. Some of this low agreement may be more apparent than real, reflecting the inability of these young children to comprehend the traits. Because of the unusually large samples, most of the correlations were fairly accurately determined and hence indicate at least *some*

[3] See the Appendix for a brief explanation of the coefficient of correlation.

degree of overlapping. Even if we take into account all extenuating circumstances, the general picture is one of considerable difference between the two views—self and other.

OVERLAPS OF PERSONAL AND IMPERSONAL VIEWS

An example of overlaps of views when we have information from self, others, and impersonal sources is given by Borg and Hamilton (1956). Their subjects were 89 military tactical instructors in the United States Air Force who taught basic military training to new recruits and who were evaluated in five different ways. Teaching performance was rated by the instructors themselves, by their students, by their fellow teachers (peers), and by their supervisors. The fifth evaluation was in the form of a score derived from a situational test.[4] Each instructor was placed, on 12 occasions, in a situation in which the qualities of a teacher should be observable. Observers rated the instructor in each situation on qualities of teaching effectiveness. Since the scores were based upon judgments, there was some subjectivity involved in them, a fact that we shall have to overlook when we regard this variable as impersonal. When the others made general ratings of teaching effectiveness, they based their judgments upon observations of teaching extending over longer periods.

The degree of commonness of the various pairs of evaluations is indicated by the intercorrelations in Table 4.1. In parentheses are given

Table 4.1

Intercorrelations of assessments of teaching effectiveness from different sources
(from Borg and Hamilton, 1956)

Assessments	Variables				
	1	2	3	4	5
1. Student rating	(.90)	.17	.13	.22	.19
2. Peer rating	.17	(.94)	.71	.79	.11
3. Supervisor rating	.13	.71	. . .	.64	.13
4. Self rating	.22	.79	.64	. . .	.01
5. Performance test	.19	.11	.13	.01	(.63)

estimates of reliability for some of the variables. A reliability coefficient is some form of self-correlation, indicating how self-consistent a certain measurement is.[5] The coefficients of .90 and .94 for student ratings and

---

[4] See Chap. 10 for a description of situational tests.
[5] See Chap. 6 for further information on reliability.

peer ratings indicate that there was very high agreement among students and among fellow teachers as to the rank order of the 89 instructors in teaching performance. The reliability of .63 for the performance test indicates that the same teacher showed considerable lack of consistency in teaching effectiveness in the various teaching situations. From a comparison of these three coefficients, we draw the conclusion that impressions of observers of actual teaching in classroom situations are more stable and unvarying than impressions given in simulated teaching situations. These facts should be kept in mind in comparing the intercorrelations of impressions derived from different views, for an unreliable measure cannot correlate as high with other measures as can a reliable one.

In Table 4.1, the highest correlation between impressions derived from different views is that for self-rating with peer rating (.79). Evidently the instructors have considerable common basis for judging themselves and judging others in the same kind of performance—teaching. They evaluate themselves very much in line with the way in which their fellows evaluate them. The next highest correlation (.71) is between supervisor rating and peer rating. Supervisors have probably been instructors of the same subject themselves and would presumably have much the same basis for judgment as the instructors whom they supervise, hence the agreement. The agreement of self-rating with supervisor rating is slightly lower (.64), but still substantial.

Student ratings do not agree at all well with any of the other ratings, demonstrating that students have a very different point of view. What they value in an instructor is evidently very different from what supervisors and teachers themselves value. It would probably be fruitful to attempt to see where the difference of values lies, but that is not of immediate concern to us here. Some of the differences may be attributed to the failure to use common information, in which case, the lack of common value may not be the whole story.

The scores from the performance test correlate even lower with all the other variables. To some extent, the lower reliability of these scores is responsible. But after making allowance for this fact, there is still very low agreement between scored teaching effectiveness in simulated teaching situations and ratings in actual teaching situations.

WAYS OF OBSERVATION BY SELF AND OTHERS

There are several ways in which we use self-observations and observations by others in the assessment of personality traits in persons. We have already seen examples of self-ratings. In making self-ratings, a person is doing more than observing himself. When we ask him to give himself a value on a trait, we are actually asking him to make an inference. It is true that he probably thinks back over his past behavior as a basis for making the rating. He is using remembered past observations, which is not as good procedure as using comparable observations of the present moment, for errors of memory undoubtedly enter the picture to distort it. There is an advantage in one sense, however, and this is that he may utilize a larger number of observations than he could possibly obtain on any one occasion. If he has thought about his own traits from time to time, he may have previously compared himself with others with respect to traits. These are all inferences, and his memory of those inferences may contribute to his present judgment in rating.

Another use of self-reports is less demanding, in that it calls for relatively less inference on the part of the self-observer. This is the personality-inventory approach, which asks the person mostly specific questions regarding his habits, his likes and dislikes, and his attitudes. He may be asked whether he wakes up without difficulty in the mornings, if he would like to engage in knitting, or whether he thinks the practice of tipping should be abolished. Questions can be limited to things on which most persons in a culture have had many opportunities to observe themselves and can probably give ready and truthful answers. The answers are more likely on a simple two-category scale, such as "yes" or "no," than on a scale of five or more points, as in the typical rating scale. Such reports may be regarded as descriptions involving inferences to a small degree, depending upon the nature of the question and what it calls for.

It is true that even the existence of a specific habit has to be inferred. It is a matter of concluding the fact from more than one observation. But the inference involved in the case of such specific traits is relatively direct and therefore more dependable. Obtaining a score by summing thirty such specific and direct inferences in order to measure a more general trait should involve less error than a single rating the person gives for the general trait. There are other issues involved in the use of inventory items, but we shall have to postpone discussion of them until Chapter 8, which is devoted exclusively to the subject of inventories.

In the observations made by others, we have the same kind of situation. The other observer may infer a single trait position for the person being rated or he may give answers to more specific items, as in an inventory or in a check-list type of rating scale (see Chapter 7). Again, it can be expected that the more analytical and specific approach will give a more nearly correct evaluation, as is usually the outcome when the two approaches are compared.

The source of the other person's observations varies. The information may come from knowing the rated person over a period of time and in varied kinds of situations. It may come from an interview that he has with a person who was previously a total stranger. It may come from observations of behavior in a test, such as the situational test of instructor performance referred to above. Or it may come from biographical data given by the subject or by others, as in a written biography, if there is one, or in an application form, or in a case history, or from clinical examinations of various kinds. The information may come from two or more of these sources. From all such information, the other observer can arrive at his inferences as to trait positions of the subject being assessed.

We are not particularly concerned here with the question of which picture of a personality, that developed from self-report or that developed from reports of other observers, is the more correct or useful. Since both are lacking in complete accuracy and since one is likely to provide information and conclusions not given by the other, the two views are to some extent supplementary. Where they conflict, we know that they cannot both be right and we need information from other sources to resolve the differences. The accuracy and completeness of judgments by outside observers can be increased by using composite evaluations that combine judgments from a number of them.

There are certain things that the evaluated person can report about himself that others have little or no opportunity to observe, for example, his thoughts and feelings. Most individuals learn to conceal some expressions of emotion and attitudes and even to deceive others by their actions. Where the person has personal reasons for wanting to give the wrong impression, he can also do this, of course, in his reports about himself. Those who are concerned about obtaining faithful pictures of personalities need to be perpetually on guard against deceptions by word or deed.

SOME PROPERTIES OF TRAITS

In this section, we shall take further steps to build up the meaning of traits in more detail. There are a number of things that we need to know about traits before we can proceed to talk about measuring people. We need to lay a better foundation than we have seen thus far in this volume for the process of measurement. The idea of measuring personality is not very new, but serious attempts at measurement are not so very old.

Behavior traits, not being open to direct inspection, cannot be treated like physical objects, to which measuring rods and other instruments can be applied by manual operations and visual inspection of scales. We need a radically different conception of the meaning of measurement when we apply the operation to behavior traits. As we consider the various properties of traits, we shall note the implications of each property for measurement, and step by step, we shall build up a model that applies to personalities in general, a model that will render measurement a natural and logical process.

Scalability

Many traits are scalable. By this we mean that a trait is a certain quality or attribute, and different individuals have different degrees of it. We have talked about traits thus far as if this were generally true. We shall consider now whether any traits are nonscalable. But first, let us understand more clearly what scalability means.

If individuals differ in a trait by having higher or lower degrees of it, we can represent the trait by means of a single straight line. A straight line is a geometric idea, and here we borrow a geometric idea to stand for a psychological concept. Individual trait positions may be represented by points on the line. One line might stand for a trait of tact-

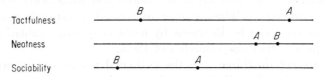

Fig. 4.1 Straight lines representing three assumed traits and selected points representing the characteristic trait positions of two individuals, *A* and *B*, on the three trait scales.

fulness, one for a trait of neatness, and another for sociability. These three traits are represented in Figure 4.1, with the trait positions shown for two persons, *A* and *B*. *A* is very tactful but *B* is rather tactless; both *A* and *B* are quite neat, with *B* slightly neater; and *A* is moderately sociable while *B* is very lacking in that quality. The use of a point to indicate a person's position on a trait continuum is a rather idealized conception. As we shall see later, an individual probably does not stay fixed at one point on a trait. We can therefore only give a *characteristic* or most probable position for him, whereas a point indicates an exact level or degree on a trait scale.

INFERENCE OF TRAIT POSITIONS

How, in general terms, is the degree of a trait indicated for a particular person? How can we decide where he belongs on any trait continuum? There are several kinds of cues, and although we have considered kinds of cues before, we have not gone into the question of what it is about a cue that tells us about trait positions.

One of the signs is the *frequency* of occurrence of a trait indicator. If a person is presented with 50 opportunities to show whether he will be neat rather than slovenly, in how many of them is he actually neat? If another person is presented with 50 equivalent opportunities, in how many will he be neat? A test composed of items is a good operational example, each item being an opportunity for indicating whether the person's reaction points toward the upper end or the lower end of the scale. If it is a test of an ability, passing the item points to a high degree of the trait; failing an item points to a low degree. It does not matter much whether all items offer the same amount of opportunity or inducement. What does matter is that the same or equivalent opportunities be presented to all individuals so that their scores (number or proportion correct, indicating a position) will be comparable.[6]

Another cue to trait position is the *intensity* of occurrence of the trait indicator. In a test of ability, intensity might be regarded as the level of difficulty of items that the person can master. In some kinds of overt, muscular activity, intensity might be reflected in the vigorousness or energy of the response, as judged, perhaps, by amplitude of response or promptness or velocity of response. In other kinds of activity, the amount of emotional component exhibited might serve as an indication of intensity. There are a number of observable emotional components, such as changes in blood pressure, pulse rate, skin conductance, or muscular tension, all of which can be objectively measured. Intensity of response to opinions may also give a cue to the strength of an attitude. One person responds by saying "strongly agree" to most of the favorable statements whereas another person simply responds "agree" to the same statements. The former is probably higher on the scale favoring the idea, whether it be regarding birth control, capital punishment, or the use of chaperones.

Another cue, whose status is not quite so clear as that of intensity, is the *range* of behavior in which a high degree of the trait is indicated. Let us say that our approach to measuring the trait of sociability, or interest in being with people, is in the form of an inventory. We ask each person a list of questions about his liking to be with people in 30 different situations, such as attending a party, a dance, a reception, a bull session, or a church social. Using this cue, we should conclude that the person who responds affirmatively to 25 of these items is more sociable than one who responds that way to only 10. In applying this principle, we might weight all situations equally, or we might weight them differently after finding by experimental procedures that some items are more indicative than others. This illustration should not be taken to mean that range of behavior is the only cue used in inventories. The cues of frequency and intensity are also used in inventories, as we shall see in Chapter 8.

NONSCALABLE TRAITS

A completely nonscalable trait is one that is either present or absent. There is no in-between or gradation of amount of the quality involved.

[6] In this chapter we shall pass over and around many technical problems of psychological measurement. The reader will find such problems discussed in the author's *Psychometric Methods* (1954), and in other writings to which it refers.

When one tries to find examples of completely nonscalable traits, the task is not as easy as it might appear to be. Having a certain phobia or not having it would be an example of a nonscalable trait, as would having a tic [7] vs. not having a tic, or having a certain conditioned response vs. not having it.

At first thought, it might be supposed that color blindness is a nonscalable trait, since individuals are classifiable as color-blind or not color-blind. On second thought, it is recognized that there are degrees of color blindness as well as degrees of color sensitivity. We have here a single color-sensitivity trait with considerable continuity, a trait that

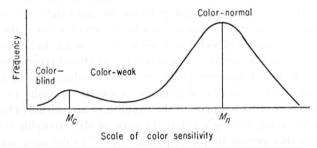

Fig. 4.2 Illustration of a bimodal trait distribution for a trait of color sensitivity (e.g., red sensitivity or green sensitivity).

might be more appropriately regarded as scalable but having a bimodal distribution, that is, having one mode near the average on the scale of color sensitivity for those diagnosed as not color-blind and another mode near the average (low) color sensitivity for those diagnosed as color-blind (see Figure 4.2).[8]

Having a conditioned response was mentioned as an example of a nonscalable trait, but in some respects this trait, too, can be considered scalable. Among the population of those who have the trait at all, there can be variations in the strength of the stimulus-response connection, as indicated by the cues of frequency of occurrence, amplitude of response, and latent time.[9]

From these examples, it will be seen that the class of nonscalable traits is very small after all and that, in fact, most traits are scalable in some way. This indicates that the possibilities for quantitative descriptions

[7] A vigorous, uncontrollable muscular twitch that recurs, such as blinking an eye.

[8] A mode, a statistical value, is that point on the scale at which we find the greatest number of cases in a population or subpopulation. The color-blind group may be regarded as a subpopulation.

[9] Latent time is the amount of time elapsing between the conditioned stimulus and the response. The shorter the time, the stronger the "habit strength" of the connection is inferred to be.

on graded scales are almost unlimited. The problems are to find the appropriate indicators and to develop effective measurement operations.

Unipolar vs. Bipolar Traits

Unipolar traits extend from zero to a great amount (see Figure 4.3). Somatic traits (morphological and physiological) are probably all unipolar. Of the behavior traits, abilities should be regarded as unipolar, the range being from no ability of the kind measured up to the most ability possible.

Bipolar traits extend from one pole to an opposite pole through a zero point (see Figure 4.3). Temperament traits are commonly bipolar. We

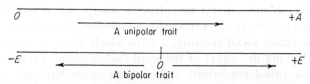

Fig. 4.3 Illustration of a unipolar trait A (an aptitude, such as an ability to remember faces) and a bipolar trait E (an emotional trait, such as cheerfulness vs. depression).

speak, for example, of cheerfulness vs. depression, ascendance vs. submission, or composure vs. nervousness. The zero point comes at a place at which the two named qualities are equally balanced, where a person could be described as having neither the one nor the other quality predominating. Interests should generally be regarded as bipolar, since there are aversions as well as likings for objects of interest. Some persons like mechanical types of activities while others have a distaste for them. It is quite possible that the most extreme aversion is not as intense as the most extreme liking, which would mean that the zero point is not in the middle of the scale but nearer the negative pole. Attitudes are also in the bipolar category. We favor an institution or a practice or we are against it. We are inclined toward favoring peaceful settlement of disputes or toward favoring war or conflict.

LOGICAL AND OPERATIONAL IMPLICATIONS

The distinction between unipolar and bipolar traits is of some logical importance and contributes to clarity of thinking, but it is of little operational or practical importance. Actually, we very seldom have occasion for locating a genuine zero point on a scale, and we lack easy procedures for locating it even if we should want to do so. We also often follow the common statistical practice of using the mean of the values of a population on a trait scale as a reference point and hence as a kind of zero point, around which we have a balancing of positive and negative deviations. This zero point probably rarely coincides with a psychologically meaningful zero point. It certainly would not do so in the case of a unipolar trait and it might be on either the positive or negative side of the meaningful zero in the case of a bipolar trait.

The distinction between unipolar and bipolar traits *is* of some procedural importance in connection with bipolar traits, where we have the problem of determining what qualities are direct opposites and therefore what extremes belong at opposite poles on the same continuum. If we arbitrarily select two qualities as direct opposites, we have some responsibility for showing by empirical methods why they should be so regarded. For example, is the quality of submission the direct opposite of the quality of ascendance? This has generally been assumed. But another hypothesis states that if ascendance is interpreted as social boldness, the opposite quality is not necessarily submission. It might more appropriately be called social timidity, a term which does not necessarily include the "giving in" aspect of the word "submission." Even such qualities as those called conformity and nonconformity have not proved to be direct opposites. In one study,[10] the urge to conform to cultural standards looks more like a unipolar trait, and the indicators designed for nonconformity turn out to represent another unipolar need—a need for freedom or an urge to be independent.[11]

Consistency with Respect to Trait Positions

We have adopted the convention of indicating a person's trait position as a point somewhere on the trait continuum or scale. We must consider now what this actually means and also justify the use of this convention, which was questioned earlier. It seems necessary, for the sake of being realistic, to assume that a person does have minor fluctuations in his trait position from one time or occasion to another. This is known technically as *functional fluctuation* and is observed in fluctuations in behavior, as seen, for example, in variations in scores obtained from the same test on different occasions.

It must not be concluded that variations and scores of the same person in the same test are entirely determined by functional fluctuations in a trait or traits. We have already seen that there are many other possible determiners of differences between scores. All we can say is that even when other determiners are well controlled, as in a carefully administered test of some ability, scores will vary. From what we know about the principles of variability in general, we may venture some hypotheses regarding the variability of a trait position in a person.

[10] Guilford, Christensen, Bond, and Sutton (1954).
[11] See Chap. 17 for further information on this point.

SOME HYPOTHESIZED PRINCIPLES OF TRAIT VARIABILITY

First, we may suggest that the distribution of trait positions for a person in a trait approaches the normal, or Gaussian form, when there is nothing to bias the results. Figure 4.4, diagram A, shows two such distributions for persons J and K on the same trait. J's characteristic position is at point P_j, and K's is at point P_k. Over a large sample of occasions, each person has a considerable range of variation, involving perhaps a quarter of the total scale, but the larger the deviation the less often it occurs, and the

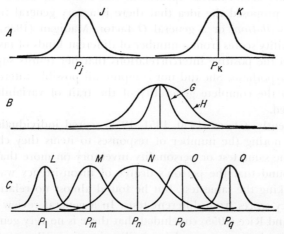

Fig. 4.4 Illustrations of frequency distributions of trait positions of individuals about their respective characteristic (average) trait positions.

smaller the deviation the more often it occurs. In other words, we may expect, from this line of reasoning, that most temporary departures from the characteristic position are small. The distributions for J and K do not overlap; we never find the two persons actually reversed in rank order, K always being higher on the scale. This is not to say that in any kind of *situation* they would never *appear* to be in reverse order. This is a matter of the faithfulness of the trait indicator. We see here another reason for making a distinction between a trait and a trait indicator.

Individuals J and K are shown in diagram A as being equally variable in the trait. This is probably not typical. Persons may differ in degree of instability of trait position as well as in trait position. Diagram B in Figure 4.4 shows hypothetical distributions for persons G and H. These two persons have the same characteristic trait position, $P_g = P_h$, but H has a much greater variability. Consequently, it would be more difficult to measure H accurately in the trait than to measure G, and an obtained score for *G* is probably nearer his characteristic position than is a score for *H*.

CONSISTENCY OF PERSONS

The last-mentioned principle—individual differences in variability—raises some questions. Is a particular person who is relatively more variable in one trait likely also to be more variable in other traits, perhaps even in *all* traits? In other words, is a person consistent in his inconsistencies?

Many years ago, Charles Spearman, the father of factor analysis in psychology, proposed the idea that there is a very general trait of what he called *oscillation,* or a general *O* factor. Madigan (1938) intercorrelated variability scores from a number of different kinds of tasks and concluded from the positive intercorrelations that her results supported the Spearman hypothesis. She did not compute all possible intercorrelations, however, so the complete generality of the trait of variability was not demonstrated.

More recently, Glaser (1950, 1951, 1952) scored individuals for inconsistency by noting the number of responses to items they change when they take the same test or personality inventory on more than one occasion. He found that the person's degree of inconsistency was somewhat stable in taking the same test, but he found almost no relation between inconsistency scores from different tests. In a general review of the subject, Fiske and Rice (1955) concluded that there is no very general trait of variability in similar tests and in similar situations. Personal variability therefore seems to be a relatively specific phenomenon. A person can be relatively variable in one kind of task and relatively stable in other kinds.[12]

There is a peculiar relationship between characteristic scale position and variability that may be responsible in large part for the lack of a general trait of variability. It could be reasonably hypothesized that, on the whole, we shall tend to find the greatest amount of variability among persons of moderate (middle) scale positions and the smallest amount among persons at extreme scale positions. In Figure 4.4, diagram *C* illustrates this principle. With a trait position near the upper extreme, the person has little or no room for variation upward if he is to remain on the scale. He would, of course, have considerable room in the other direction, but he could not have many such variations and maintain an average position close to the end of the scale.

Whether or not this principle holds for the actual relation of variability to scale position, we find that in testing operations the limiting scores of

[12] For other methods proposed for measuring personal variability, see McReynolds (1951), Abelson (1953), and Bouvier (1954).

all items right and of *no* items right do not permit any deviations beyond them, whereas a moderate score permits the greatest amount of room for variability. Glaser (1951) found that in general the principle represented in Figure 4.4, diagram *C*, holds with respect to obtained test results. If we were to make allowance for the trait position of the person when we consider his degree of variability, we might find that there is, after all, much generality in this respect. At any rate, in assessing a person in some trait, it might be worth knowing his degree of stability in the trait as well as his characteristic trait position, if we can obtain this information. As another property of the person, variability, as such, may be worth knowing. The information should also give us a better idea of how accurately we have determined a person's trait position.

CONSISTENCY IN CONNECTION WITH DIFFERENT TRAITS

We can ask the question whether traits themselves differ characteristically in the extent to which there is personal variability. On the scale for trait *X*, for example, we might find a low average variability as compared with trait *Y*, on which we find a high average variability. We should expect that if a trait is strongly determined by heredity, individuals in general would change little on it from time to time. If some other trait is determined mostly by cultural forces that have shifting influences, individuals would change relatively more from time to time. If the trait is itself strongly related to somatic conditions, such as glandular secretions, we might expect variability to accompany the shifting somatic conditions. Not much attention has been given to this particular problem of variability among different traits.

IMPLICATIONS FOR MEASUREMENT

One implication for measurement to be derived from differences in trait stability is that measurements of persons in some traits are more accurate and dependable than they are in others. It would be of some value to know which traits are the more stable and which the less stable, for we should not expect to be able to measure unstable traits with as much accuracy and could compensate for lower stability by testing the person on a larger number of occasions. In other words, to achieve reasonable accuracy, it would be necessary to base our score on a larger sampling of the trait indicators being used. There would still be the difficulty, however, that the person's future behavior would be less predictable where the behavior depended upon that trait than it would be in connection with a more stable trait.

What we are really considering here is the subject of *reliability* of measurements. We have seen that the function fluctuations of a person contribute to deviations from his characteristic or "true" trait position, and these deviations contribute to errors of measurement. We have also seen that in addition to these errors, there are others contributed by behavior fluctuations in the trait indicator. These errors are added to those from function fluctuations. Figure 4.5 is designed to show how the latter kind of error, added to the former, enlarges the total amount of variability, all of which is reflected in scores that would be obtained at different times.

Durability vs. Flexibility of Trait Positions

In addition to the temporary fluctuations in trait positions just discussed we must consider long-term changes or trends. We may consider

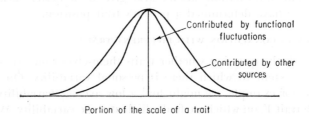

Portion of the scale of a trait

Fig. 4.5 Distributions showing how other sources of error of measurement contribute to increasing the *apparent* dispersion of trait positions of a person on a trait over and above those contributed by functional fluctuations.

such trends during the developmental years of childhood and adolescence, through the years of maturity, or through the years of decline and senescence, or throughout the life span. We may be interested in typical trends for a population or in the changes in an individual. Developmental problems are numerous. Here we shall restrict our attention to some examples in order to gain a general idea of the degrees of durability or of changeability to be expected and to understand the implications of all this for measurement of traits.

As a general introduction to the topic, Figure 4.6 is given to show how trait positions might conceivably change for a single individual over sixty years of life span. The curves for three traits are purely hypothetical. They are drawn on a common scale, with the population-average [13] position the same for all three. We see that from birth this person exhibited an unusually high general-activity level, that is, an inclination to make overt movements. This is shown as remaining at a fairly stable level, with little loss even at sixty years of age, after which it might be expected to drop more rapidly. We see that in some visual-perceptual ability, from the age at which we might be able to test it, there is a fairly steady increase in ability until a maximal level is reached in the early twenties, after which a gradual decline sets in. The curve for the trait of cordiality

[13] Based upon all ages.

is more complex. The trait is at a very low level for the first five years, after which it rises on the scale at an increasing rate but does not reach its first maximum position until the late twenties. The level then recedes during the late thirties and forties, the cause for which would have to be sought in further study of the person. Another high point in cordiality appears just past the age of fifty-five, which would also call for explanation with reasons probably peculiar to this individual.

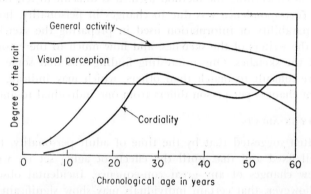

Fig. 4.6 Hypothetical relationships of degree of three traits to chronological age over the first sixty years for a particular individual.

DURABILITY IN CHILDHOOD

A number of studies suggest that there is considerable long-term stability as well as change in certain traits that can be assessed in infants and young children. In a well-known Gesell study,[14] five infants at one year of age were shown in motion pictures to a trained nurse. The pictures were taken both in test situations and in the child's home. The nurse ranked the five infants on each of 15 traits. When the children were five years of age, the assessment was repeated, with the use of new motion pictures. The same nurse again ranked the five children on each of the same 15 traits. The result was that of the 75 ranks assigned the first and second times, 48 were identical; 21 were displaced by 1 rank position, 5 by 2 rank positions, and 1 by 3 rank positions. There was considerable durability of the relative positions of these five children, as one nurse saw them, over a period of four very formative years. Of course, some bias may have entered from the nurse's remembering her first judgments.

A study by Neilon (1948) followed a larger number of children over a much longer time span. In 1932, Mary Shirley wrote personality sketches of 25 babies whom she had studied intensively over a period of two years. Fifteen years later, data were obtainable for 16 of them. The data were

[14] Gesell (1937).

in the form of scores from tests of ability and attitudes, ratings on 23 traits, and interview information derived from the mothers. From these data, Neilon wrote a personality sketch for each adolescent. Ten judges were asked to match the Shirley sketches with the Neilon sketches, with boys' and girls' sketches separated. The accuracy of matching was not impressive. The average number of correct matches for the boys was 2.6 out of 10. The average number for girls was 3.2 out of 5. From lack of information concerning the method used, it is difficult to tell how much the poor correspondence was due to changes in personality, how much to incomparability of information used in preparing the sketches, how much to the writers of the sketches, and how much to the errors of the judges of the sketches. One interesting finding was that some children were more difficult to match than others, which may indicate that the number of changes per person differs from one individual to another.

DURABILITY IN ADULTS

It is often suggested that by the time of adult personality, traits are fairly well fixed and that until the effects of aging set in, we should expect few changes of any great consequence. Incidental observations suggest, however, that certain individuals may show significant changes in some traits, particularly after an experience such as a religious conversion or after psychotherapy, and investigations tend to show that some adult traits are not as fixed as might be expected.

In a survey of studies on this question, Kelly (1955) concludes that there is much evidence of systematic changes in adult personalities, as shown by test scores and ratings. In a particular study,[15] in which some characteristics of 25 women were followed through four years of college, it was found that certain traits persisted through the four years and, on the whole, persistence was greater than change. There were wide individual differences in number of changes recorded. One woman was reported to be 86 per cent persistent, one only 26 per cent persistent, and the average was about 60 per cent. These conclusions pertain only to the traits that were studied, of course, and the percentages pertain to the particular manner in which they were computed.

Striking changes of a more temporary duration are reported in a study of effects of semistarvation on the personalities of 36 young men.[16] These men were kept under observation on a low-calorie diet for a period of six months, followed by a period of rehabilitation. Some of the notable changes attributable to the deficient diet included: increased depression, increased irritability, lowered social initiative and sociability, and loss of sense of humor. There were complaints of loss of intellectual abilities,

---

[15] Roberts and Fleming (1943).
[16] Franklin et al. (1948).

but tests did not show this to be true. There were signs of poor concentration and difficulty in thinking, but under pressure this could be overcome, apparently. It is interesting to note that during the rehabilitation period, improvement was more rapid in behavior traits than in physical well-being, which might indicate that the marked trait changes during semistarvation and after its end should be attributed as much to the subjects' attitudes toward their physical condition as to the amount of nourishment.

IMPLICATIONS FOR MEASUREMENT

In the systematic changes or trends with respect to personality traits, we have two or three indications for practices in assessment. It is clear that we may need to make reassessments from time to time, depending upon the circumstances. Measurements made at one time may not be sufficiently accurate for use at later times. It would be desirable to know in which traits the more significant changes are likely to occur and at what periods during the life span the changes are most rapid. It is also clear that we shall often need norms for different age groups, as well as for sex groups, in order to interpret properly each individual's score within his own subpopulation.

Universality of Traits

By the *universality* of a trait we mean its extensiveness of occurrence in the general population. Some traits apply to every member of the population, for example, the morphological traits of height and weight. Certain abilities may apply quite generally but are not completely universal. Many abilities do not seem to apply to infants and even to young children, because we cannot detect any individual differences at these age levels, at least by any known methods. Achievement variables apply only to those who have had at least a minimum of training of the appropriate kinds. We find interest variables among adults that are not found among children, and there are apparently interest variables among children that do not apply to adults.[17] Many temperament traits seem to have considerable universality, but others have less. The difference is likely to be noticed between temperament traits that are apparent relatively early in childhood as compared with those that become apparent relatively late.

IMPLICATIONS FOR MEASUREMENT

The most obvious implication for measurement of personality from the property of universality is that instruments developed to assess some

[17] Tyler (1955).

traits are not applicable to all segments of the population. It is desirable, therefore, to determine the limits of applicability of each instrument. There are other reasons than lack of universality, of course, for the inapplicability of a certain test. We would not give the same vocabulary test to young children, adolescents, and adults, for example, even though the same basic ability is to be measured. In other words, there are many reasons for unsuitability of a measuring instrument, inapplicability of the trait being only one of them.

Since the restriction in universality in traits is most likely to be related to age, there is reason to investigate the beginnings of appearance of any trait and the manner of its manifestation at the early stages. Much of this kind of research has been done with infants and children.[18] In this connection, a problem of some theoretical importance presents itself, particularly in connection with intellectual abilities. This is the problem of whether the different intellectual abilities that we find in the adult arise by differentiation from the same original ability or whether they have independent beginnings. This problem and the results bearing upon it will be discussed in the chapter on abilities (Chapter 15).

Generality of Traits

By the *generality* of a trait, we mean the extent to which it is exhibited in the behavior of a person. Some traits are evident in almost everything a person does while others are exhibited in only a limited range of his behavior. To state it another way, the generality of a trait is proportional to the number of different trait indicators that apply to it.

Examples of broadly generalized traits would be nervousness, general-activity level, and restraint or self-control. Other traits enter into determination of certain areas of behavior but do not affect all or nearly all behavior. In this connection, we might mention the traits of endurance, interest in art, and affectionateness. There are only certain kinds of situations in which we should be able to detect any evidence as to a person's trait positions for these traits. We should expect to see individual differences with respect to endurance only when there is need for individuals to persevere in an activity in the face of discomfort or pain. Interest in art would be best exhibited in behavior in the presence of art objects or implements or places of exhibit. Affectionateness would show itself in the presence of other persons or in letters or conversations.

Even less-generalized traits would be platform shyness, which is confined to appearing before groups, fear of cats, or fear of some particular cat. With these last examples, we see the continuity between the gen-

[18] For example, see Murphy (1937) and Koch (1942).

erality of traits and the phenomenon of generalization in learning. This does not necessarily mean that transfer of learning is the only basis for generalization of traits. Some of them, particularly the most widely generalized traits, could be determined by broadly effective hereditary dispositions.

Some traits, as we have seen, are restricted in their manifestations by reason of the range of situations in which the trait can operate. Other restrictions occur because the person himself has not generalized the trait. Traits of honesty, loyalty, and cordiality may be given as examples. The person who has not developed clear and strong principles of honesty that make him respond in the honest manner in many types of situations does not have a very generalized trait of honesty. He discriminates more sharply than do most people between different kinds of situations and needs for honesty. Similar statements could be made with regard to loyalty and cordiality. Thus, we can state two general principles with regard to generality of traits: there are some traits that tend to be more or less general among most people; there are also variations in generality of the same trait in different individuals.

IMPLICATIONS FOR MEASUREMENT

There are three implications for measurement of personality in these considerations of trait generality. One is that the more generalized a trait is, the more opportunities we should have for measuring it, since there would be more kinds of behavior from which to select the trait indicators. Our problem would be to determine what kinds of situations would best bring out differences in the trait and be most convenient for assessment purposes. Another implication is that we should be able to predict a wider range of behavior from knowledge of scores on a more generalized trait. A third implication, based upon individual differences in amount of generalization of a trait, is that it would be desirable to find out for each person his degree of generalization of the trait, and more specifically the areas of his behavior to which the trait extends or does not extend.

Organization of Traits

We shall now consider a property of traits that is somewhat related to other properties but which seems worthy of special attention. It pertains to some aspects of traits that have not been fully accounted for by the other properties mentioned. There are actually two aspects to this particular property. One has to do with the *strength* of organization, and the other has to do with *patterns* of organization. The property of organization involves relations of the trait to its indicators.

POORLY ORGANIZED TRAITS

Studies of the degree to which college students are punctual in different ways show considerable lack of consistency.[19] Very low correlations have been found between being punctual in four different ways—returning books to the library, turning in assignments, returning change slips to the registrar's office, and meeting appointments.

A study of students' attitudes toward being punctual is quite enlightening.[20] When questioned about their reasons for wanting to be punctual, students gave seven common, different reasons, such as consideration for others, avoiding unpleasantness, regarding punctuality as important, good quality, and family training. There did not seem to be a single, universally operating core of motivation or drive to be punctual, as such. The correlation between the extent to which the student reported punctuality to be desirable, for whatever reason, and punctual behavior was also very low (about .2).

Although it might still be defensible to speak of a generalized trait of punctuality, the question may well be asked whether punctual behaviors of different kinds are possibly more symptomatic of other traits than they are of a single, common trait. This would have to be determined by correlational studies, relating measures of punctuality in different situations to measures of other traits.

BETTER-ORGANIZED TRAITS

Sociability is an example of a better-organized trait. Let us first consider three scores derived from short inventories and describable as follows:

Liking friends and acquaintances

Being gregarious

Liking social affairs

The intercorrelations of these three scores averaged .44. The three aspects of personality that they indicate would correlate higher than this, after we take into account the fact that none of these scores is perfectly reliable. Adding four other trait indicators, we find that the level of correlation is still nearly the same, the average being .42. The other four are:

Leading on social occasions

Having social poise

Liking to be in the limelight

Not being shy or bashful

The important point demonstrated by this information is that strong correlations among indicators of a trait may be taken as evidence of a

[19] Dudycha (1939).
[20] Dudycha (1938).

well-organized trait. Well-organized traits are unusually strong deter-miners of trait indicators. Since the indicators are determined to a large extent by the same trait, they will correlate strongly with one another. A well-organized trait has more faithful indicators and hence can be assessed more accurately. We can measure more successfully the better-organized traits and we can predict behavior better from the scores for those traits.

PATTERNS OF ORGANIZATION

It was pointed out in Chapter 3 that there are ways of estimating the extent to which the variance (individual differences) in a particular trait indicator (such as a score) is determined by a certain trait. We shall now qualify that statement by saying that such an estimate applies to the population but not necessarily to each individual in that population. The extent to which a trait determines the actions of particular indi-viduals probably differs from person to person. For example, one indi-vidual's sociability is more often or more clearly shown by his liking of friends and acquaintances, whereas another individual's sociability is more often shown by his love of social affairs. If we were to obtain seven scores, one for each of the seven indicators of sociability mentioned above, we should find that not all individuals are shown to be equally sociable in all respects. Two persons with the same total score (where the total is a sum of the seven indicator scores) would not often have identical part scores. This circumstance is consistent with a conclusion reached earlier, namely, that persons can differ in the degree of generalization of a trait. We can now add the qualification that the patterns of generalization can also differ among individuals with respect to the same trait.

By this time the reader may wonder whether, in view of all these exceptions and qualifications, we are justified in talking about the "same" trait at all. Perhaps this question was in the mind of Gordon Allport (1937), when he asserted that no two people have the same trait. The answer is that in spite of all the ways in which the "same" trait can differ in different persons, there is, after all, a common core of similarity if not of identity. Allport's assertion is like that of the ancient Greek philosopher who said that we cannot step into the same river twice. In a sense he was right, but for purposes of communication we still name rivers and there is enough stability to make this practicable over the long period of known history.

Thus we can name traits and expect that something about them is sufficiently stable to justify such a practice. From knowledge of trait scores, we cannot successfully predict indicator behavior in all persons equally well, but there is probably no more economical way of covering predictions of so wide a range of behavior with so little information.

The variation in patterns, however, suggests the possible need for going beyond the information provided by single scores. Whether or not we seek the extra information about patterns will depend upon our purposes and whether or not we find the trait-score information adequate.

Independence vs. Correlation

Considering behavior traits at large, it takes little observation and reflection to lead to the conclusion that some pairs of traits are inter-related in the population. Where this is the case, and the correlation is positive, there is a tendency for a person who is high on the one trait to be high also on the other. For example, among such traits as social aggressiveness, social initiative, and social boldness, we should expect to find considerable agreement of trait positions of persons. The same would be true for such traits as nervousness, sensitiveness, and emotional excitability. Other combinations of traits that we could think of would be apparently unrelated, for example, the traits of friendliness, neatness, and self-control. A person could be friendly without also being either neat or self-controlled, and he could be neat without being either friendly or self-controlled. We might, of course, expect a little relationship between neatness and self-control, but probably not much. Even more independent, perhaps, are the traits of interest in business, self-control, and ability to solve problems.

A GEOMETRIC PICTURE

We previously saw that a trait can ordinarily be represented by a straight line and an individual's characteristic position by a point on that line. Now that we are considering two traits at a time and the question of their degree of intercorrelation or independence, we need to extend that picture. If the two traits are completely independent in the population, that is, if their correlation is zero, we can represent them by two lines crossing at right angles. We arbitrarily put the intersection at the two population means of the two traits (see Figure 4.7, diagram *A*).

Each person in the population to which the traits apply will have a pair of values, one for trait *X* and one for trait *Y*. Figure 4.7, diagram *A* shows three individuals, each with a pair of values that determine his position in this two-dimensional field. Person *J* has a very high position on trait *X* and a more moderate but above-average position on trait *Y*. A perpendicular drawn from the point representing person *J* to each trait line indicates the *projection* of the point on each of those lines. Those projections, or coordinates, represent the two trait positions. Person *K* has a moderately positive position on trait *X* and a moderately negative position on trait *Y*. Person *L* has a moderately negative position on trait X but a high positive position on trait Y.[21] In such a manner, every individual who has characteristic positions on traits X and Y can be represented by a point somewhere in this diagram, his positions being represented by the coordinates on the two *orthogonal* (at right angles) axes, X and Y.

Next, let us consider the nature of independent traits, as represented by orthogonal axes. In diagram B of Figure 4.7, are shown a number of persons' dual trait positions. All of them have an identical, moderate, positive value on Y, but they range over a considerable segment of trait X.

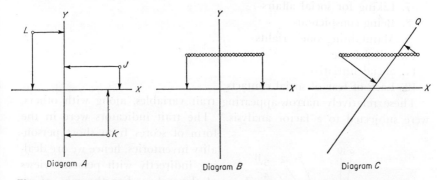

Diagram *A*   Diagram *B*   Diagram *C*

Fig. 4.7 Examples of the representation of two traits at a time in the form of two intersecting lines. In diagrams *A* and *B* the intercorrelations of the traits are zero; in diagram *C* the correlation is +.59.

This is designed to show how there can be variations in one of the traits without also having corresponding variations in the other.

Let us consider next the case in which there is a substantial correlation between the two traits, as in diagram C, Figure 4.7. The correlation between traits X and Q is .59, which is shown geometrically by drawing axis Q at an angle of less than 90 degrees.[22] The same range of positions on X is shown as in diagram B. By drawing perpendiculars to axis Q from the extreme cases, we can obtain an idea of the corresponding range of positions on trait Q. Now it can be seen that we cannot have any variation on the one trait without at the same time having some corresponding variation on the other.

[21] The descriptions "positive" and "negative" here do not necessarily indicate that we are dealing with bipolar traits; they could be unipolar. We are dealing with deviations from means.

[22] For the benefit of the mathematically sophisticated reader, the angle is actually approximately 54 degrees, the cosine of which is .59, which is identical with the correlation. In general, the correlation between two traits represented in this manner is the cosine of the angle of their separation. The cosine of an angle of 90 degrees is .00.

THE PERSONALITY SPHERE

Let us consider next the picture created by a number of similar traits. The traits can be designated by the following descriptive titles:

1. Liking for friends and acquaintances
2. Social leadership
3. Social poise
4. Liking for the limelight
5. Freedom from shyness or bashfulness
6. Gregariousness
7. Liking for social affairs
8. Being conspicuous
9. Maintaining one's rights
10. Self-defense
11. Social initiative
12. Lack of fear of social contacts

These relatively narrow-appearing trait variables, along with others, were subjected to a factor analysis.[23] The trait indicators were in the

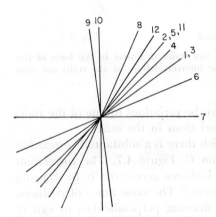

form of scores from short personality inventories, hence we are dealing indirectly with persons' views of themselves. For the sake of an illustration, let us assume that the actual traits approximately coincide with the trait-indicator variables, the scores. This assumption is necessary because we are talking about abstract, but presumably real, traits, whereas it was the score variables that were factor-analyzed. With this assumption accepted, we may represent the twelve trait lines as in Figure 4.8, basing the positions of the lines in this plane upon the results from the factor analysis.

Fig. 4.8 Diagram showing 12 trait lines in relation to one another (determined by their intercorrelations) in a single plane.

The actual procedures need not concern us in this discussion. It is with the end product that we are concerned here.

It will be noted, first, that some of the trait lines are so close together in this plane that they were not drawn separately. Trait 3 (social poise) is practically identical with trait 1 (liking for friends and acquaintances). Traits 5 (freedom from shyness or bashfulness) and 11 (social initiative) are practically identical with trait 2 (social leadership). All of these are

23 Guilford and Zimmerman (1956).

not so very far from trait 4 (liking for the limelight). Standing off by themselves are trait 7 (liking for social affairs), which is closest to trait 6 (gregariousness), and traits 9 (maintaining one's rights) and 10 (self-defense), which are very close neighbors. Remember that so long as two trait lines are separated by no more than 90 degrees, they have some positive correlation with one another. This being the case, only trait 7 is essentially independent of both 9 and 10. Trait 7 bears some relation to all others except 9 and 10, and the last two bear some relation to all except 7.

The important point illustrated by this example is that we have here a two-dimensional system in which these traits and their interrelationships are shown. We would not want to set up different measuring instruments for all of the traits, since many of them would provide closely duplicating information. Actually, two well-chosen trait variables would be enough to provide all the information that we should need regarding a person with respect to any of the qualities represented in Figure 4.8. One of these selected variables could be a measure of trait 7 and another a measure of trait 9 or trait 10, or a combination of 9 and 10. By use of scores for two such trait variables, we could estimate a person's status on any of the other traits lying between them by combining those two scores with appropriate weights.

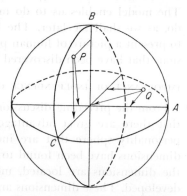

Fig. 4.9 Three independent traits, *A*, *B*, and *C*, shown as dimensions of a sphere. Two individuals, *P* and *Q*, are shown as having positions on the three traits, each person being represented as a single point in three-dimensional space.

There are literally thousands of behavior traits such as those represented in Figure 4.8. Relatively few of them could be represented in the plane shown there, for most of them emphasize other qualities. In other words, we need more than a two-dimensional model to take care of other traits also. It is easy to imagine a third dimension extending through the plane at the origin (intersection of all trait lines) and preferably running orthogonally to the plane, which means that it would also be orthogonal to all the trait lines in Figure 4.8.

Our model then becomes a three-dimensional one, in the form of a sphere (Figure 4.9). However, it has been found that even three dimensions are insufficient to take care of all known traits. By a little stretch of the imagination, we can think of a fourth dimension, orthogonal to the three we already have, and a fifth, and a sixth, and so on. No one ever saw a model of more than three dimensions, but we are talking now about something purely in the realm of ideas, which is where basic mathematics resides. The mathematical model that we can use for description of personality is a hypersphere of n dimensions, where n is an indefinitely large number. Each person can be represented as a point in this n-dimensional scheme, as we saw in relation to two dimensions in Figure 4.7. Such a model is applied solely for the sake of enabling us to think logically and rigorously about traits and measurements of traits. The model enables us to do many things that we could not otherwise do, as we shall see later. The last six chapters of this volume attempt to present a picture of human personality in terms of meaningful dimensions that have been discovered by factor analysis.

IMPORTANCE OF INDEPENDENCE OF TRAITS

From the preceding discussion and from Figure 4.8, it should be clear that there are great advantages to finding dimensions located in the personality sphere that are independent or nearly independent. Such dimensions have been found to be psychologically meaningful, and once the dimensions are located, methods of measuring individuals can be developed. These dimensions are thus of primary significance in terms of meaning and in terms of measuring and describing persons, and are consequently called *primary traits*.[24]

Measurement of independent, or near-independent, traits is highly economical. As we saw above, two measurements can do the work of all 12 traits mentioned in Figure 4.8. The same principle applies throughout the personality sphere. We thus avoid redundancy and duplication of effort, and information is obtained about persons with minimum cost.

Primary traits are less ambiguous in meaning. A little thinking regarding the 12 traits represented in Figure 4.8 will show that 2 fairly unique psychological qualities correspond to the 2 approximately independent traits. In the direction of trait 7, we have variations of interest in people and in being with people. We might call this the dimension of sociability or gregariousness. In the direction of traits 9 and 10, we have a different attribute involved. The traits of "maintaining one's rights" and "defending one's self" indicate a common quality of self-assertion, a trait commonly known as ascendance. The independence of these two dimensions indicates that a person can be very sociable and at the same time be anywhere from extremely self-assertive to extremely lacking in self-assertion. Both self-assertive and nonassertive persons may like social activity with other people or both may dislike it. A self-assertive person

24 Such dimensions need not coincide with any particular experimental trait lines. For example, we could put one primary-trait line between traits 9 and 10 in Fig. 4.8 and another orthogonal to it near trait 7. The primary traits need not be orthogonal, but things are simpler that way.

can take social activity or he can let it alone. So can a nonassertive person. These are conclusions indicated by the independence of the two primary traits of sociability or gregariousness and self-assertion or ascendance. The other traits in Figure 4.8 can be expressed as weighted combinations of these two primary traits. They are not as unusual in meaning, each one representing a confounding of the two primary traits, so far as psychological interpretation goes.

In addition to knowing the positions of individuals on traits, we often want to know about the *differences* among the same person's trait positions on a number of dimensions. These are *intra*individual differences. In more popular terms, we want to know how much stronger a person is in one respect than in another. This information is especially useful in vocational and educational guidance and in classification of personnel.

If a person is considering entering two lines of work, *A* and *B*, and if line *A* demands more of ability *a* than of *b* whereas line *B* demands more of *b* than of *a*, we have in the differences in scores for *a* and *b* some basis for helping him make a choice. If a person is much higher in his interest in one line of activity, such as music, than he is in another, such as painting, we might have some basis for suggesting that he would be happier in music.

The relation of all this to the amount of independence of trait scores is easily explained. Scores for interest in music and scores for interest in painting usually correlate fairly strongly, hence those who like the one are very much inclined to like the other. The difference between the two scores for each person would probably be small and we would have little confidence in it as a basis for making a choice. When two trait scores are uncorrelated, or nearly so, intraindividual differences for the two can be quite large for some individuals. When a difference is large in either direction for a person, we can have some confidence in predicting that he will excel more in one direction than in another or that he will derive more satisfaction from one line of work than another. The search for trait scores that are relatively independent in the population, therefore, bears fruit in guidance and in other places where decisions must be made between alternative kinds of activity.

SUMMARY

The idea of a trait and our naming of it comes about through observations of behavior. We attribute the trait to the person in whom the behavior was observed. Traits are thus inferred rather than observed. General cues to traits are in *what* the person does, *how* he does it, and *how well* he does it. The cues in behavior that lead to inferences concerning traits are called trait indicators.

The observer of behavior may be the person himself or any one of many other persons. The views of a personality given by self-observation and by observation made by others do not coincide with each other or with a view built up from objective-test data, and none of these coincides with the actual personality. Correlation studies give us some information concerning how much the portraits from different views agree.

Most traits prove to be scalable and each one may be represented by a straight line. Each person may be said to have a characteristic trait position on a trait that applies to him. This trait position can be represented by a point on the trait line. Inferences as to trait positions of persons can be drawn from several aspects of trait indicators—the frequency of occurrence of a given indicator, the intensity of its occurrence, and the number of indicators that exhibit the attribute or quality associated with the end or ends of the trait line. Some traits are unipolar (with one extreme attribute) while others are bipolar (two opposite, extreme attributes).

The trait position of a person is not a fixed value, but shows minor fluctuations. This phenomenon is called functional fluctuation and it is one contributor to unreliability of measurements of traits. There is probably more instability in some traits than in others and in one person than in another, but a very general trait of instability is unlikely. Trait positions also undergo long-term changes, particularly those associated with chronological age.

Some traits are more universal than others in the general population, and some traits do not apply to certain segments of the population. Some tend to be more widely generalized than others, in the sense that they have a greater range of trait indicators. Degree of generalization of the same trait also varies from person to person. Some traits are well organized, in the sense that they have strong and dependable indicators. Degree of organization of a trait may differ from person to person, also the pattern of organization.

A general geometric picture or model for representing scalable traits is in the form of a sphere of n dimensions. Trait lines (in the form of diameters) can be drawn anywhere within the sphere, but for economical description and clarity of definition of traits, the primary-trait lines found by factor analysis have distinct advantages. Primary traits are independent, or nearly so, and can be used for describing persons with respect to all attributes represented in the personality sphere.

Chapter 5

THE STRUCTURE
OF PERSONALITY

IN THE chapters just preceding, we saw that one of the most important reasons for studying personality and persons is to obtain information from which we may predict behavior. The information is usually in terms of trait concepts and trait positions. We have seen what kinds of things behavior traits are and, in general terms, how we arrive at the knowledge of positions of persons on trait scales.

In this chapter we shall consider the general question of what kinds of trait concepts will best serve in describing personalities from the standpoint of basic science of personality and how, in general terms, we arrive at those concepts. We shall also develop a model of the total personality that represents all levels of trait generality. The model should help us to see the way in which traits go together in the total personality, as well as provide a general framework for many of the ideas found in earlier and later chapters.

THE CHOICE OF TERMS FOR DESCRIPTION OF PERSONALITY

There are many ways of "slicing" a personality in describing it. But in whatever way this is done, we would come out with a list of descriptive categories. Since analysis of personality in some form is inevitable, how shall we decide on the way to approach it? Let us first set up some requirements for a good list of trait concepts and then find approaches that will satisfy those requirements.

Requirements for Good Descriptive Terms

In this discussion, we shall continue to restrict ourselves to behavior traits, for it is here we find the greatest difficulty in reaching agreement as to trait concepts and trait names. The requirements to be proposed take into account primarily the needs of a basic science of personality. If we can find useful, descriptive language to which those who study personality scientifically can agree, it is probably true that the same language will be found useful by technologists who deal with problems of personality. If technologists find the terminology inadequate, the scientist has probably not completed his job.

First, we shall consider some requirements regarding particular trait concepts, requirements that should determine whether or not the concepts ought to be generally adopted. Then we shall consider requirements regarding the total list of trait concepts, for there are certain desirable features, beyond those applying to particular traits, that apply to a total list.

REQUIREMENTS REGARDING PARTICULAR TRAIT CONCEPTS

The first requirement is that *each term should refer to some demonstrable unity in personality*. By calling for "unities," this statement does not mean that personality should be "broken down" into its simplest "elements" or smallest "particles," by analogy to nuclear physics. It means that however complex or simple the products of analysis of personality may be, there is some degree of coherence or orderliness of the behaviors that indicates a trait. A trait name, to have unique status, should apply to an empirical concept. This test is met if we can point to some clearly observable trait indicators that are associated with it, directly or indirectly. We should find dependable behavior signs for it in performances in the laboratory, in test situations, in clinical operations, or in everyday life.

Some examples of traits that fail to show unitary character will be given here. Many examples of unitary traits are mentioned from time to time in this and in other chapters, particularly in Chapters 15 to 18. Two trait concepts that are purely fictitious entities are "charm" and "impressiveness." This can be seen from a purely logical point of view. Impressions of charm or of impressiveness in a certain person can arise from quite different behaviors and different personal qualities, depending upon the person. These concepts therefore fail to meet the test of consistent signs.

Another example can be given in which empirical investigation has failed to demonstrate a unitary trait. It would seem reasonable to suppose that there is a unitary ability to analyze, in view of the fact that all of us engage in analyzing operations in one way or another in our thinking every day. A factor-analysis investigation of this hypothesis, however, failed to show that analyzing tasks of different kinds show in common a single ability to analyze.[1] Analyzing in one kind of task requires different

[1] Wilson et al. (1954).

abilities than analyzing in another. It is therefore incorrect to speak of an individual's analyzing ability, meaning that he has a characteristic position on a scale of a single trait that goes by that name. This does not mean that we do not analyze or that there is no apparent similarity between analyzing operations of different kinds. It means that a person can do well in some analyzing operations and poorly in others, and this is not a matter of unreliability of measurement or of functional fluctuation. It means that a common underlying ability to analyze is lacking. The same has been found with regard to a supposed common ability to synthesize.[2]

The second requirement for particular trait concepts is a refinement and extension of the first. It is to the effect that *each trait concept should be as exact as possible.* It should pertain to one thing and one only, and it should be capable of clear definition. This does not mean that all traits should be independent or uncorrelated. It does mean that they should be distinct in the sense of having their own consistent patterns of behavior signs. This requirement is desirable for preventing fuzzy and slippery thinking and for promoting mutual understanding among those who deal with personality or with persons.

A third requirement, not as essential, is that *a trait concept should be capable of integration into a general theory of personality.* If we believe that there is general order and system in a human personality, traits must be interrelated in logical ways. A trait concept must fit into a larger conception of personality. The development of a logical framework of theory may have to wait until many of the basic concepts are known, but sooner or later information regarding traits will lead to ideas of a more inclusive picture of some kind. Then the consistency of a trait concept with the general picture and the existence of a reasonable place for it in that picture represent another kind of test of its interpretation and its worth. Later in this chapter, we shall see one kind of theoretical framework that is applied to personality and how trait concepts fit into it. In Chapters 15 and 16, more concrete instances of organizations of traits will be seen.

REQUIREMENTS REGARDING THE LIST OF TRAIT CONCEPTS

The list of trait concepts should be an economical one. We should aim at a minimum number that will serve our purposes. The principle of parsimony that is generally recognized in science urges us to seek a much smaller number of concepts than there are phenomena to be described. There is no hard-and-fast rule regarding the ratio of concepts to phenomena, but the effort is to make that ratio small. This can be

---

[2] *Ibid.*

done by avoiding redundancies. Where trait concepts duplicate one another, it is possible to find more inclusive concepts under which they can be subsumed and by which they can be accounted for.

Running somewhat counter to the preceding requirement is one to the effect that *the list shall provide comprehensive coverage of the phenomena.* No significant aspect of personality should be slighted or omitted in following the urge to be economical. Like the business-minded shopper, we want to "get the most for our money" and yet obtain all the necessities. Each kind of technologist may find a limited number or area of concepts adequate for his purposes, but the basic scientist who adopts personality as his field of study must take a more general and impartial view of traits and give attention to them all. The trait concepts that one technologist does not find useful another one may find very important in his work.

The last requirement in our list is very difficult to satisfy. To be realistic, it can only be stated in relative terms. This requirement is to the effect that *there should be as much general agreement as possible to the list of concepts.* If the first two requirements mentioned were faithfully followed, there would be little question that we should achieve the requirement of agreement, at least among reasonable people. We have long passed the day, as Lorge (1935) has remarked, when acceptable traits can be created "by fiat." Lorge put it very clearly: [3]

> Personality traits cannot be created by the psychologist. If the concept of personality is to have meaning, it must be conceived as an aspect of the individual—an aspect susceptible to quantification. Naming a trait does not make it a trait. . . . Personality traits cannot exist by fiat alone.

Trait concepts "created by fiat" of some authority should be regarded as hypotheses, the same as any other new proposed ideas, subject to verification or rejection on the basis of empirical testing. Unfortunately, the spread of acceptance of such trait concepts has all too often been on the basis of argument and the winning of disciples.

It is easy to find examples of the fate of such concepts. Very early in the efforts to measure personality, there arose the idea of a trait called emotional maturity. Different investigators must have had their own personal conceptions of this trait when they translated it into inventories for measuring it. Four different inventories designed to measure emotional maturity gave scores that were found to intercorrelate over the range from $-.12$ to $+.46$.[4] It is obvious that the concept, as used by these investigators, did not pass the test of empirical examination. We should

[3] P. 278.
[4] Farnsworth (1938).

expect correlations between scores measuring the same trait to be closer to .80.

A similar fate was encountered by the concept of introversion-extraversion. Several inventories developed to measure a trait by this name were obviously based upon different conceptions. Their scores were found to intercorrelate all the way from .19 to .62, none high enough to support the idea that they are alternate measures of the same trait.[5] Intercorrelations of behavior-test scores from tests proposed to measure the same trait have been even lower.[6]

These results should not necessarily be interpreted to mean that there are no such genuine traits as emotional maturity and introversion-extraversion. They mean that no unique set of trait indicators had been found to demonstrate or to represent those concepts. When such demonstrations are provided, and only then, should there be general acceptance of those and other concepts.

MAJOR TRENDS IN TRAIT-CONCEPT DEVELOPMENT

The Trend toward a Very Limited Number of Concepts: Types

In the history of personality theory, we find two distinct, though opposite, trends. One has been the movement toward an enormously large number of trait names; the other toward a minimal number, sometimes the barest minimum of two. The latter is the trend toward *types* of personality. Since it is the older of the two, we shall consider it first.

HOW TYPES ARISE

The classification of persons into type categories is a most natural approach for the beginner in personality studies. It is the method of the "man on the street," who indulges in the popular pastime of pigeon-holing the people whom he knows. It is an effort toward economical evaluation and recognition of persons. The individual finds it expedient to classify people so that he can react one way to persons in one class and a different way to persons in another class. He predicts and controls the behavior of others from what he thinks their classifications or types to be. More serious observers of personality, including literary writers from Theophrastus of ancient Greece on down through the ages, have taken this approach to the description of personalities.

It is significant, as Shuey (1937) has pointed out, that most of the type ideas that have been entertained in psychology have not come from

---

[5] Guthrie (1927); Guilford and Hunt (1931); Guilford (1934).
[6] Schwegler (1929).

academic psychologists but from others. The first types that were given any serious attention by psychologists originated with the medical men— Hippocrates and Galen. The four types of temperament that they suggested are: sanguine, choleric, phlegmatic, and melancholic, terms that have had considerable popular use down the ages.

From the field of psychiatry, we have the famous Kretschmer types.[7] Kretschmer was deeply concerned with the theory that there are behavioral types that correspond to morphological types. He regarded both as constitutional or hereditary. The two main physical types are the *pyknic* (stocky, full-chested) and the *leptosome* (thin, straight, sometimes referred to as asthenic, which means weak). The remaining individuals, more well-proportioned, are called *athletic* (with no necessary implication of interest or ability in athletics). There has been apparently much less interest in the latter group, which is actually sometimes treated as a kind of leftover or miscellaneous group, although obviously a very large one.

The corresponding Kretschmer behavioral types are the *cyclothyme* and the *schizothyme,* corresponding to pyknic and leptosome body types, respectively. The cyclothymic person is distinguished by his tendency to experience cycles of emotional excitement with elation followed by depression of action and feeling. The schizothyme is characterized by his tendency to inconsistencies of action, feeling, and thinking.

These descriptions arose initially from Kretschmer's observations that among the psychotic population with which he was familiar, the manic-depressive cases tended in large numbers toward the pyknic constitutional type while the schizophrenic cases tended toward the leptosome type. The behavioral types were then applied to the general, nonpathological population, with similar terminology. We are not concerned here with the validity of Kretschmer's theories or concepts. More will be said about them in the chapter to follow.

From the psychoanalysts, we have the personality types that are attributed to Freud—his *oral, anal,* and *phallic* types.[8] These are based upon the theory that generalized personality traits develop in the infant and young child and are brought about in connection with the most vivid and pleasurable infantile experiences associated with taking food, elimination processes, and sexual stimulation. From the other great originator in psychoanalysis, Jung, we have had the conception of the contrasting introvert and extravert types.[9]

A few type ideas have originated with academic psychologists. These are of historical interest only, except where they seem to have fore-

---

[7] Kretschmer (1926, 1948).

[8] For a recent discussion of Freud's types, see Bellak (1956).

[9] Jung (1923).

shadowed similar findings in empirical research. William James (1890) suggested that two major categories would be significantly descriptive of individuals with respect to voluntary actions. These he called the explosive vs. obstructed will types. James also distinguished types called tough-minded and tender-minded, concepts that have had some use by psychologists in recent years.[10] Both Binet and Stern distinguished between objective and subjective types on the basis of behavior of two kinds of subjects in psychological experiments. It has been a common recourse of an experimenter who finds some of his subjects behaving in one direction and the others in the opposite direction to invoke the idea of two opposite types as an "explanation." Few, if any, enduring types have arisen in this manner.

SOME DIFFICULTIES WITH TYPES

Those who have seriously proposed types as an approach to scientific description of personalities have had to recognize sooner or later that as few as two categories are simply not enough. They have had to either leave out many individuals who were in neither type category or leave out of account many behavior characteristics not included in the type concepts. For example, Jung later recognized several kinds of introverts and several kinds of extraverts.

In one way or another, the paucity of descriptive concepts is felt, and is either corrected or ignored. It is generally recognized in psychology that two, or even a few more than two, types are wholly inadequate. The main question is whether there should be an attempt to save the type concepts by elaborating them and adding to them or whether they should be discarded in favor of some other descriptive concepts. And there is the further question of whether there will be a need for types of some kind in a scheme of concepts, whatever kind of traits are employed. We shall see answers to these questions later.

KINDS OF TYPES

It will help us to evaluate the type approach and to find answers to these questions if we consider more clearly what types, as such, can mean. Cattell (1946a) has made some useful distinctions among three kinds of types. The popular and semipopular types are what he calls *species* types. Types of this kind are discrete categories or pigeonholes. They are discontinuous and nonscalable. Thinking with regard to them is analogous to the thinking of biologists regarding species of plant and animal life.

When species types are taken over by academic psychologists, they are

[10] Eysenck (1954).

often given scalable properties. They become what Cattell calls *continuous* types. According to this conception, introverts and extraverts occupy the extreme portions of a continuous scale, with a large group of individuals called "ambiverts" in the middle. There are no clear-cut division points, only arbitrary ones, between the middle group and the end groups. With this conception, we no longer have types at all; we have scalable traits. In order to justify the term "type" in connection with any continuous scale, it is necessary to demonstrate multimodal distributions, for example, bimodal or trimodal. Such distributions of actual measurements of a trait in a single population are almost never found. By failure to find the appropriate clustering of persons, the conception of continuous types, then, would seem to have no place in the study of personality.

A third kind of type is called a *syndrome* type. A syndrome in the field of medicine is a combination of symptoms. A syndrome in the study of personality is a combination of qualities or attributes. This is a scientifically acceptable conception of a type since there is the possibility of specifying the combination of attributes involved in the type, and this in turn implies a certain constellation of trait indicators. Whenever a hypothetical type is proposed, with specifications as to its composition, there is a means of testing the hypothesis. Untestable hypotheses are disliked by the scientist. The existence of a syndrome type depends upon the intercorrelations of traits of narrower scope or generality, and such intercorrelations can be demonstrated. In the last part of this chapter it will be seen that the syndrome type is given a place in the structure of a total personality.

The Trend toward a Very Large Number of Concepts

Where type systems have called for an exceedingly small number of trait concepts, there have been other sources that have gone in the opposite direction, calling for an indefinitely large number of concepts and the terms to go with them. The best example is that of Allport and Odbert (1936), who list nearly 18,000 English terms that describe persons; and these were not regarded sufficient! Examples of these terms, sampling by the alphabet, are:

Absentminded	Humble	Negativistic	Temperate
Boastful	Illogical	Obdurate	Unruly
Cheerful	Jealous	Patient	Vain
Diplomatic	Kindly	Quiet	Weak
Effeminate	Loud	Ruthless	Yielding
Fluent	Meek	Secretive	Zealous
Genial			

Fears were expressed by these writers that, without additional terms, it would be impossible to account for all the shades of differences that we find among unique individuals. Carried to the logical extreme, this might mean that we should have a different vocabulary for describing each person. It can be shown that a limited number of descriptive variables will, after all, take care of a very large number of unique individuals. In the field of color perception, for example, three dimensions—white to black, yellow to blue, and green to purple—serve to describe all of the 350,000 colors that are said to be distinguishable. If 10 scalable, common behavior traits, each with only 10 distinct steps, were combined in all possible ways, we could have 10^{10} unique individuals. We have at our disposal many times ten common-trait dimensions if we choose to use all of them.

It must be admitted that even if we place the burden of description of persons on common traits, with any reasonable, finite number that we choose to use, we should find that there will be something in each person left unaccounted for. In this sense, any set of descriptive terms, even 18,000, might fall short. The urge for economy calls for a halt at some reasonable number of concepts for general purposes. It is the author's position that we should give preference to common traits and use them as far as they will serve our purposes. If something of importance is still unaccounted for, additional information of the kind we need can be sought. The study of any particular personality is never complete. What we do not want is to duplicate our efforts unnecessarily by using thousands of overlapping trait concepts where a smaller number will do.

Description in Terms of Primary Traits: Factors

In the preceding chapter the concept of primary trait was introduced. We shall now give this concept additional meaning, without going into the mathematics that underlies factor theory and factor analysis.[11]

To recapitulate previous conclusions somewhat, it was decided that most traits are scalable, which also implies that they are common to members of a population. Some intermediate number of traits will be called for, somewhere between the extremes of two (type theory) and thousands (idiographic approach). The trait concepts must be verifiable unities, as shown ultimately by intercorrelations among the trait indicators. Factor analysis is a procedure for determining from the intercorrelations how many trait variables (common factors) are needed to account for the data and in what directions they lie. Factor theory, as was explained in the preceding chapter, conceives of personality as a

[11] See the Appendix for further information, and for a more complete account, see the author's *Psychometric Methods* (1954) or Fruchter (1954).

sphere of n dimensions. Factor theory and methods seem ideally suited for the purpose of discovering psychologically meaningful and useful dimensions in the personality sphere. The reader can best judge this last statement for himself, when he surveys the results as presented in Chapters 15 through 18.

RELATION OF FACTORS TO TESTS

Let us approach the concept of factors from a different standpoint. We shall use a very simple illustration to demonstrate how the intercorrelation of trait indicators leads to conclusions about the existence of factors and about their properties. We shall also see how the trait indicators can be accounted for, in part, by the factors.

Table 5.1

Intercorrelations of scores from five short personality inventories. The subjects were 213 university students

Trait indicators					Name of indicators
1	2	3	4	5	
.....	.56	.38	.11	−.19	1. Liking for social affairs
.56	.....	.32	−.07	.06	2. Gregariousness
.38	.32	...	.36	.22	3. Lack of fear of social contacts
.11	−.07	.36	.....	.49	4. Self-defense
−.19	.06	.22	.49	.....	5. Maintaining one's rights

The trait indicators of our illustration consist of five scores from short inventories about social habits and preferences. They were among the 12 used in an illustration in the preceding chapter. Here, in addition to the descriptive title for each score, a typical item will be given to help convey the meaning of each trait indicator. The score variables are as follows:

1. Liking for social affairs
   Item: Do you like to have many social engagements?
2. Gregariousness
   Item: Do you prefer to work with others rather than to work alone?
3. Lack of fear of social contacts
   Item: Have you ever hesitated about applying for a job in person?
4. Self-defense
   Item: Are you rather good at bluffing when you find yourself in difficulty?

5. Maintaining one's rights

   Item: Do you ever protest to a waiter or clerk when you think that you have been overcharged?

A factor analysis starts with intercorrelations among all the experimental measurement variables, which, in our illustration, are scores from the five inventories. For the sake of brevity, let us call them tests. Their value as trait indicators will be shown by the results of the analysis. As one result of the analysis, we have the correlations of all the trait indicators with the factors. The five tests of our illustration were analyzed in a large study in which there were altogether 70 similar tests.[12] The results pertaining to the five selected tests will be utilized in what follows.

From the relative sizes of the correlation coefficients in Table 5.1, we see that the pairs of tests that have the most in common, by virtue of their large correlations, are 1 with 2 and 4 with 5. The first two have virtually zero correlations with the last two. We should expect from the correlations alone that we have two factors. Tests 1 and 2 have something in common that is not shared with 4 and 5. Test 3 seems to bear relations with both groups and we should predict that it will be found related to both factors.

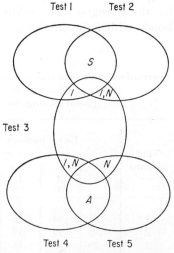

Fig. 5.1 Geometric representation of intercorrelations of five tests and their common components, the factors: *S* (sociability), *A* (ascendance), *I* (confidence vs. inferiority), and *N* (composure vs. nervousness).

We have a graphic illustration of the interrelationships of these five variables in Figure 5.1. Each variable is represented by an ellipse (the shape is not very important). The amount of correlation between two variables is indicated by the overlapping surfaces, to show how much they have in common. The near-zero correlations are ignored in drawing the figure in order to keep it simpler. The significance of the enclosed letters will be explained later.

In Table 5.2, to the left, we have the correlations of the tests with the factors. These are known technically as factor loadings.[13] We see that actually, more than two factors are involved appreciably somewhere among these five variables. The four common factors are designated by

[12] Guilford and Zimmerman (1956).

[13] This is strictly true only when the factors are independent or uncorrelated, as they are in this analysis.

the letters *S, A, I,* and *N.* The strongest relationships are with factors *S* and *A,* with tests 1 and 2 being most strongly related to *S* and tests 4 and 5 most strongly related to *A.* Test 3 is a bit more strongly related to factor *I* than to either *S* or *A.*

We are now ready to interpret the factors psychologically. Factor *S,* being related most strongly to variables 1 and 2, seems to be some psychological quality that 1 and 2 have in common. It is clearly a sociability or gregariousness trait, hence it was called *S,* for sociability. Factor *A* has the strongest relationship to variable 4 (self-defense) but substantial bonds with 5 (maintaining one's rights) and 3 (lack of fear of social

Table 5.2

Correlations of the five trait indicators with the underlying factors or primary traits and proportions of variance of each trait indicator accounted for
(factor loadings from Guilford and Zimmerman, 1956)

Trait indicator	Factor loadings				Proportions of variance accounted for				
	S	*A*	*I*	*N*	*S*	*A*	*I*	*N*	Total
1	.77	.04	.15	−.07	.59	.00	.02	.00	.61
2	.45	.29	.19	−.20	.20	.08	.04	.04	.36
3	.29	.40	.46	.24	.08	.16	.21	.06	.51
4	−.06	.74	.22	.37	.00	.55	.05	.14	.74
5	.02	.46	.09	.25	.00	.21	.01	.06	.28

contacts). From the limited information given here, we should favor an interpretation that stresses standing up for one's self. In the larger analysis other trait indicators were also strongly related that did not necessarily carry the idea of self-defense. Factor *A* (for ascendance) is best defined as self-assertion.

From the larger analysis, factor *N* (for nervousness) was interpreted as composure or freedom from nervousness, and factor *I* (for inferiority) was interpreted as confidence or freedom from inferiority feelings. Referring back to Figure 5.1, we see these four factors represented by their letters in overlapping areas of tests. We see how the different tests share dependence upon them and therefore how they help to account for the correlations seen in Table 5.1.

We obtain a better picture of how much each factor contributes to the total variance of the scores from each test by squaring the factor loadings. These values are seen at the right in Table 5.2, also their sums. These results are shown graphically in Figure 5.2. Showing the total variance for each trait indicator as a long rectangle, the proportions attributed to the four factors are shown, where there is enough to show. The portion at the right in each case with the label U is for unknown components or determiners. This portion would include all kinds of errors in the scores, including functional fluctuation, if any, and specific effects. The total portion not in U, which represents contributions of

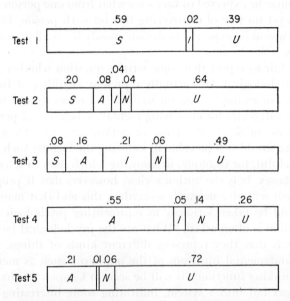

Fig. 5.2 Proportions of total variances of scores from the five tests accounted for by the four factors: S (sociability), A (ascendance), I (confidence vs. inferiority), and N (composure vs. nervousness). U represents unknown sources of variance.

the four common factors that we know about, contributes to the correlations of Table 5.1.

SOME FURTHER ORIENTATION CONCERNING FACTORS

At the risk of being as confusing as it is helpful, this discussion of factor analysis has been necessarily brief and sketchy. A few further general remarks may be of value. The reader who recalls the ideas about traits and their indicators presented in the preceding chapters will recognize that many of those ideas are actually suggested by the factor approach. As early as Chapter 3, it was pointed out that the extent to which a trait determines differences in behavior can be estimated. This was stated as a general principle applying to any trait. Here we see that this may be done when the trait is a factor, and we see something of how an estimation is made.

In connection with the discussion of organization of traits in Chapter 4, it was pointed out that there are patterns of generalization with regard to a trait in relation to its indicators. We see in Figure 5.2 a picture of the extent to which each factor is generalized to each of the indicators. It was also pointed out that individuals differ in their patterns of generalization. It follows from this principle that the proportions of variance represented in a test in Figure 5.2 present an average picture. The picture would of course be expected to vary somewhat from one person to another. We have as yet no way of discovering this for each person, but as usual, individuals would be expected to deviate mostly by small amounts around the average.

It is only fair to report that some writers question whether *any* factors found in psychological data actually represent anything of fundamental significance. For example, Vernon writes: [14] "Factors should be regarded primarily as categories for classifying mental or behavioral performances, rather than as entities in the mind or nervous system." Even if Vernon is right, there would still be value in knowing the factors; such knowledge would be helpful, for example, in knowing which tests to select to represent their classes. It is the author's view, however, that if properly used, factor analysis will give us much more than this and that many obtained factors should be taken seriously as representing psychological reality.[15]

The question is often asked, "What *are* the psychological factors?" The best answer is that they represent different kinds of things. Some may represent fundamental functions of the organism, such as memory functions and thinking functions. It will be seen in Chapter 15 that the intellectual factors fall into a system, indicating some interesting principles of a structure of intellect. It should be fruitful to investigate the properties of such functions by experimental methods and even to attempt to associate them with brain physiology and anatomy. Other psychological factors appear to be broadly generalized habits, for example, the primary attitudes, such as liberalism vs. conservatism or the primary trait of endurance. A few factors are rather obviously somewhat unified areas of knowledge or information. There is a mechanical-knowledge factor, for example, and a factor of social-science information.

From what has been said thus far about factors and primary traits, it can be seen that factor theory provides a general, rational basis for the description of personality. It has its deficiencies for this purpose, but there is no other general theory of such rigorous properties that comes anywhere near as a rival. That there are deficiencies is no reason for discarding a useful theory, particularly when there is nothing comparable

---

[14] 1950, p. 8.

[15] Perhaps the best support to be offered for this statement is to be found in the lists of factor traits in Chaps. 15 through 18.

to take its place. The many practical benefits provide strong justification for the use of factor theory and methods.[16]

A HIERARCHICAL CONCEPTION OF PERSONALITY STRUCTURE

We have seen in preceding discussions something about the model of personality based upon factor theory. This model serves the purpose of thinking about traits in relation to their indicators; furthermore, the methods connected with it provide a way of discovering desirable descriptive concepts and describing tests and other instruments of assessment. We shall now consider another model of personality. This one applies better to the single personality whereas the factor model applies better to populations of persons and populations of measuring instruments. The one model supplements the other and they are consistent with one another.

Traits at Different Levels of Generality

The model to be presented is not essentially new. Similar ideas have been expressed by other writers, particularly Eysenck (1951, 1953a).[17] The model should give additional importance to many of the points covered in the preceding chapter on properties of traits and should also help to apply the factorial model to the individual. The hierarchical picture of personality structure is illustrated in Figure 5.3, where a small segment of a total personality picture is shown.

THE HEXIS LEVEL

Let us say that the lowest level of the structure that shows any significant degree of generalization is the one at which we should find what we call habits of relatively narrow scope. Instead of calling this the habit level, however, the coined term *hexis* is used.[18] From its Greek roots, it means a consistent attitude or disposition of mind. The reason for preferring this new term is that "habit" implies something learned. A more inclusive term is therefore desirable, one that also recognizes hereditary contributions to trait development.

A hexis is a disposition to behave in some consistent manner to a limited range of situations. It is therefore a trait, and like any trait, it must be inferred from observations of behavior. The trait indicators for a hexis

---

[16] See Guilford (1948).

[17] Others include Burt (1949b) and Moursy (1952).

[18] The author is indebted to Professor Robert B. Cross of the Department of Classics at the University of Southern California for this and other suggestions concerning terminology.

are specific actions characteristic of the person. The specific-action level is indicated below the hexis level in Figure 5.3. Some cases of hexitic traits will be mentioned next as illustrations.

In Figure 5.3, we have some arbitrarily chosen traits at different levels to illustrate the nature of personality structure. Much help is available from known factor-analysis results, but in places, we shall go beyond

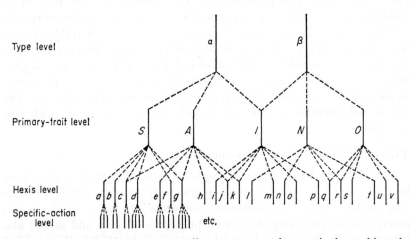

Fig. 5.3 Diagram showing how personality structure can be conceived as a hierarchy of traits at different levels of generality.

known information in order to complete the picture. The hexitic traits used in the discussion are listed together here:

  a. Liking to attend social gatherings
  b. Liking to work with others rather than alone
  c. Liking to start conversations with strangers
  d. Liking to be where there are large crowds
  e. Not letting others impose on one
  f. Liking to speak in public
  g. Liking to hold office in an organization
  h. Being ready to say things in self-defense
  i. Being ready to tackle almost any difficult task
  j. Being able to hold one's own in an argument
  k. When insulted, settling the matter at once

THE PRIMARY-TRAIT LEVEL

By now, the concept of primary traits should no longer be strange to the reader. In previous discussions, we have tended to link primary traits with factors. We must now emphasize certain exceptions, which can be explained in terms of the hierarchical picture of personality structure. We shall note the exceptions after getting better acquainted with all levels. The exceptions provide a reason for not referring to the primary-trait level as the factor level.

In line with previous conclusions, we may say that a primary trait determines to some extent the hexis traits with which it is related, as the latter, in turn, determine to some extent the specific actions. Primary trait S, which is indicated by hexes $a, b, c, d, f,$ and $g,$ is interpreted by the common element that the hexes seem to show—sociability. Primary trait $A,$ indicated by hexes $c, e, g, h, j,$ and $k,$ is interpreted by their common element, which seems to be ascendance or self-assertion. Similar relationships are shown for primary traits I (confidence vs. inferiority feelings), N (composure vs. nervousness), and O (objectivity vs. subjectivity). Objectivity should be interpreted as the disposition to take things impersonally, and subjectivity is hypersensitiveness, a tendency to take things personally.

TYPE LEVELS OF PERSONALITY

In earlier discussions, it was concluded that there is one conception of type that can be adopted for scientific purposes because it fits into the general scheme of other concepts. This is the concept of syndrome types. It seems to fit rather well the conception of more highly generalized traits that bear relations to traits at the primary-trait level.

In Figure 5.3, two such types, alpha and beta, are illustrated. Alpha bears relations to primary traits S (sociability), A (ascendance), and I (confidence). The picture of this combination may well be interpreted as a general, social-adjustment variable. It embraces the positive qualities that a socially well adjusted person would be expected to have. A combination of the negative qualities would be interpreted as social maladjustment.[19]

The existence of type alpha as a unity in personality would rest upon positive correlations among the three primary traits. Although those traits are distinct, they may not be fully independent. The degree of organization of alpha (as a trait) will depend upon the size of the correlations among primary traits $S, A,$ and $I.$ The degree of organization of alpha in any one person will depend upon the similarity of his three trait positions on $S, A,$ and $I.$ There is sufficient independence among those primary traits to provide for individuals who might be very sociable but are lacking in self-assertion and in self-confidence, also for individuals who are not gregarious but who are both socially bold and confident. Other

---

[19] It is probable that a complete syndrome type of social adjustment vs. social maladjustment involves more than these three components.

patterns of differences could be found. Thus, two persons who might have the same trait position on alpha might have different patterns of scores on *S, A,* and *I,* just as two persons of the same trait position on *I* could have different patterns of positions on *j, k, m,* and *o.*

Another example of a type is beta (see Figure 5.3). At the positive pole of beta we should find individuals who tend to be high on primary traits *I* (confidence), *N* (composure), and *O* (objectivity). This combination presents a general picture of emotional adjustment. The high-beta type of person is self-assured, calm, and has a realistic outlook.

RELATION OF FACTORS TO THE TRAIT LEVELS

We now come back to a point mentioned earlier, namely, the reason for not calling the primary-trait level the factor level. While primary traits are best discovered by factor analysis, not all factors discovered are primary traits. Let us assume that the analysis has been well planned and well executed and that the obtained factors do represent psychological unities of some kind.[20] At which level in the hierarchy do the obtained factors belong? This question has not been given sufficient consideration in previous investigations.

Earlier discussions have favored the logical association of factors and primary traits, because in the majority of factor-analytic investigations, the experimental variables have been at the hexis level. This statement implies a general principle. Factors will ordinarily be at the level just above the level of the descriptive variables that are intercorrelated. Traits like alpha and beta would arise from analysis of measurements taken at the primary-trait level. We have in Figure 5.3 only a segment of the total personality structure. There is probably at least one level above what is called the type level here. Some correlation between alpha and beta is suggested by the fact that they share one indicator, primary trait *I.* There might be still other primary traits also shared by alpha and beta, not represented in the picture.

The consequence of all this is that factors reported in the literature may be at different levels in the hierarchy. Eysenck, who has concentrated his analyses on such broad traits as neuroticism, psychoticism, and introversion-extraversion, arrives at factors that are even above the alpha and beta level. Cattell, who has used experimental variables at different levels in his analyses, has arrived at factors at various levels, though they probably tend to be at the level of types alpha and beta. One danger of confusion arises from the use in the same analysis of experimental vari-

---

[20] Like any scientific method, factor analysis must be properly applied in order to obtain meaningful and valid results. There are a number of reasons why an application of the method may go astray, one of the most common being a poor selection of variables to be analyzed. For further discussion see Guilford (1952).

ables from different levels in the hierarchy, which makes the results difficult to interpret.[21]

Some Implications of the Hierarchical Model

Before more is said about what can be done with the model, the reader should be reminded that, like all models, this one can serve only as an approximation of the things for which it pretends to account. It is likely that the levels of generality are not as distinct as the diagram implies. Like other models, the function of this one is to facilitate clear thinking by representing a schematic picture that is simpler than the things it represents.

DETERMINATION BETWEEN LEVELS

We can think of the different levels of the hierarchy as being related in two ways: by way of determination and by way of prediction. The two are not independent, as we shall see. Let us consider relations of determination first. One principle is that specific acts may be determined by certain traits at all levels above them in the hierarchy. In general, therefore, determination is downward.[22] Whether or not the higher-level traits have a very strong determining effect upon specific actions will depend upon how strong or how well organized these traits are.

Let us take an example. A certain person has a very strong general urge toward moral conduct of all kinds. In Freudian terminology, he has a strong superego. We should find that such a person also has moral traits of less general scope. He will be generally honest, generally self-controlled, and willing to take pain or discomfort to reach a worthy goal. Because he is generally honest, we should find that he will usually not deceive, or steal, or cheat. We should also find that the resistance to cheating covers actions in a variety of situations, such as taking examinations, playing games, and making business deals. In this quick survey we have covered the range from a complex syndrome type to specific actions.

PREDICTION BETWEEN LEVELS

With regard to prediction from one level to another, some general principles can also be suggested. Given information regarding a person's

---

[21] Some recent developments of method by Schmid and Leiman (1957) show considerable promise of deriving information about factors at more than one level of generality in the hierarchy from the same analysis. Ahmavaara (1957) has also suggested procedures for determining structure among factors.

[22] Determination may be regarded as being upward when some new action leaves appreciable changes in traits, most clearly felt in narrow habits but possibly effective on up the line. This kind of determination involves us in the whole problem of the role of learning in the development of personality.

status at one level of his personality, how well can we predict his status at another level?

First, there is the general question of whether we can predict more accurately and economically downward or upward in the hierarchy. By predicting economically is meant that we need relatively little information. From the fact that determination of behavior by traits is downward in the hierarchy, as we have just concluded, we should expect that prediction might also be better in that direction. In general, this is true. Knowing that a person stands high on a general need for moral conduct, we automatically have information that he is also probably high on traits of honesty and on habits of *not* cheating, and we would predict that he will avoid cheating in examinations, games, and business deals. Knowing that a person is very low on the same high-level syndrome, we should predict opposite characteristics all along the line. For individuals who are moderate with respect to the high-level syndrome, however, we would be at some loss as to how to make predictions at lower levels.

Let us consider predictions upward. If we find that a person habitually cheats in examinations, this information alone will not tell us whether he has a generalized habit of cheating, although we should expect that more likely than not this would be the case. We would be less certain, however, that it indicates a low position with respect to a primary trait of honesty, which should also mean resistance to stealing and lying. We should be even less certain that cheating in examinations means a generally low character.

These last comments imply another principle to the effect that predictions are better to neighboring levels than to remote levels. This applies in predicting downward as well as upward. If a person is only moderately high for general moral character, there is room for some inconsistency down the line. He can be low in some of the more specific habits, but we do not know from his syndrome score just which ones they are. Added information from the primary-trait level would help us to predict the location of those weaknesses.

Predictions on the same level within the hierarchy should be poorer, in general, than predictions between levels, particularly between neighboring levels. Having sought relatively independent traits at the primary-trait level and at higher levels, we have worked toward low correlations and consequently poor bases for predictions within a level.

SOME APPLICATIONS OF THE HIERARCHICAL MODEL

The traits used in the illustration in Figure 5.3 are mostly from the modality of temperament. We should consider whether the model applies also to other modalities—abilities, interests, and attitudes—and whether the various modalities can be brought into a single hierarchy. With one exception—sociability, which is best classified as a need trait—the traits in Figure 5.3 are in the modality of temperament.

Within the domain of aptitudes, as such, we find a number of signs of logical system. This applies to the psychomotor abilities in one group and to intellectual abilities in another (see Chapter 15). The two systems are somewhat hierarchical. We shall see (Chapter 16) that the primary traits of temperament can be incorporated within a single organized system. The primary traits of needs, interests, and attitudes are so varied that a single, integrated system cannot be offered for them at this time, but certain logical categories are used in Chapter 17.

The manner in which the different modalities can be integrated into a single, comprehensive system is not yet clear. The obvious approach to this is to look for parallels between traits in different modalities. For example, there are a number of interest factors that seem to parallel certain abilities, as we shall see in Chapter 17. In Figure 5.3, we see how at least one trait of need (sociability) works naturally into the structure with traits of temperament.

The applications of the hierarchical model just considered have initially a theoretical importance only, to be followed, if the theory is sound, by practical applications. We can see a rather direct practical application for the model in connection with test practices. The responses to single test items can be regarded as specific acts, at the lowest level in the hierarchy. The total score can be regarded usually as a trait indicator at the hexis level. The score represents an ability (or other trait) involving a generalized habit or hexis. A primary trait is usually indicated by several such total scores, and if we want to measure a person's status with respect to a primary trait, we can often use a composite of scores that indicate the trait in common. At the type level, too, we might measure trait positions by using composites of scores obtained for interrelated primary traits. In this way, the hierarchical model serves as a logical basis for testing practices.

USEFULNESS OF TRAITS AT DIFFERENT LEVELS

The usefulness of traits at different levels differs for the basic scientist and the technologist. To the scientist, usefulness is measured in terms of breadth and depth of understanding and the coherence of things in a general theory. Thus in considering the hierarchical model as a theory, the scientist does not think of one level as being of greater importance than any other.

The question of usefulness has more meaning to the technologist. Since he is primarily interested in persons, he will want to know trait positions of individuals. On which traits will he find the information about trait positions most useful? This will depend upon his particular kind of service and the circumstances pertaining to the individual case, but a few general statements can be suggested.

The clinical psychologist may find information at every trait level useful at some time. General diagnosis is often facilitated most by having scores and other measures of persons on traits at the higher levels. More than other technologists, however, the clinician is likely to want information at the hexis level. This is the kind of trait that gives him an idea about where to go to work on a particular individual. A certain faulty habit may be the key to understanding the patient and his troubles. The patient hates his father; he is in a persistent state of rivalry with a brother; or his wife arouses in him reactions to the same old frustrations as did his mother.

The clinician is perhaps less interested in scores on traits at the primary-trait level. His desire to understand the "total personality" may be one reason for this, and types seem to bring him closer to a picture of a total personality while at the same time requiring less information. The type traits are thus more economical and provide descriptions that are closer to his diagnostic categories. The hexis traits enable him to focus his attention quickly upon a spot that will yield to therapy. On the whole, he has probably not given scores at the primary-trait level adequate trial, and if he did, he might find them more useful than he now seems to believe.

The vocational psychologist should find the primary-trait level most useful. He needs to make many distinctions among traits, distinctions that could not be provided at the type levels. He would not think of going down to the hexis level, ordinarily, for this might call for too much special information and might provide distinctions about individuals that he could not use. He is likely to be interested in traits over a much wider range of the personality than is the clinician, and yet he does not want to lose discriminations such as would be the case if he had information only from the type level. There may be exceptional situations, such as the selection of top executives or police detectives, where it may be known that certain syndromes apply, in which case, information regarding types would be just what the vocational psychologist wants. But for general purposes, the primary-trait level would seem to provide the traits that he needs.

SUMMARY

In considering the list of requirements for the selection of a good set of trait concepts and trait names, we find two somewhat contradictory objectives, one demanding economy of terms and the other demanding comprehensive coverage. Examples of the extreme application of the former objective are found in type systems proposed for description of personalities. One conception of types—the syndrome type—is acceptable for use in a complete, scientific set of concepts. The second objective leads to an unlimited multiplication of terms, which is consistent with the idiographic approach.

A moderate number of trait concepts is needed, in order to steer a course between the two extremes. Factor theory and factor analysis are therefore proposed as providing the answer to the desire to discover trait dimensions in moderate number and the need to satisfy the requirement of empirical verification. Some of the steps in a factor analysis are roughly illustrated and the nature of factors in relation to personality are discussed. It is shown that tests (or other measuring instruments) can be described in terms of factors, as well as persons.

In addition to the model of personality in general as an *n*-dimensional sphere, another model is proposed to represent the individual personality. This is in the form of a hierarchical series of traits at different levels of generality, the most general being syndrome types, the least general being called hexes (which includes habits), and between the two, the primary traits. Factor analysis can be applied to indicators and to measures of traits at any but the top level, culminating in factors interpretable as traits at the level just above.

Traits at different levels are interrelated in terms of determination and in terms of prediction from one level to another. Different technological groups, such as clinical and vocational psychologists, have different degrees of interest in traits at the various levels, depending upon which ones they find useful.

Chapter 6

MORPHOLOGICAL AND
PHYSIOLOGICAL METHODS

In this chapter and in the seven to follow, we shall become acquainted with the great variety of methods that are used in the assessment of personalities for either scientific or technological purposes. We could have gone directly from the general consideration of personality structure in the preceding chapter to the last few chapters on the dimensions of personality. But since those dimensions were discovered through the use of information obtained by the different methods, an adequate understanding of them and an evaluation of them depend upon knowledge of the sources of information from which they came.

The methods of assessment are interesting in their own right. They demonstrate different kinds of trait indicators and how we infer trait positions of persons from them. Some traits are more conveniently evaluated by one approach and some traits by others. Certain principles of personality assessment can be extracted from a systematic survey of the methods such as we shall make.

There is also much that can be learned regarding personality itself from examining the methods. Along with some methods, we shall find that there is considerable theory about traits and about personality in general. Some of these ideas are primarily of historical importance, but some of them are widely accepted ideas today.

SOME CONSIDERATIONS APPLYING TO ALL METHODS

This chapter is devoted to the morphological and physiological methods, but for the sake of orientation toward the survey of methods, it is important for us to be aware first of features that all methods have in common. Certain aspects of each method will be considered as we come to the method. We shall note the purpose of the method, as indicated by its designers and promoters, the essential features of the method, and its important variations.

Features to be Noted

Some of the features to be given special attention are concerned with the following issues: Is the assessment done objectively and impersonally? Does it yield objective measurements or does it yield personal judgments? If there are some elements of subjective judgment involved, to what extent do they determine the measurements? Is the method analytical or global? By "analytical," we mean that the assessments tend to be made in a number of different traits, which gives multiple measurements. By "global," we mean that there is an attempt to encompass a relatively large part of personality in one value or one descriptive sketch.

Finally, we should note the point of view from which the data come, that is, whether the view is in terms of self-description, description by other observers, or neither. In the latter case the view would be an impersonal one, derived from objective data. Results of assessment from some methods do not fit completely in any one of these categories. That is, some data that are primarily from self-reports or reports by other observers can be treated as if they were at least partly objective, such as data from inventories and from check-list ratings.

Evaluation of Methods

Our confidence in a method when used for certain purposes will depend somewhat upon information such as that mentioned in the preceding paragraph. That information, then, contributes to our evaluation of a method. Other information is needed to tell us more specifically how dependable our obtained measurements are as indicators of trait positions. In this connection, we distinguish between the *reliability* of a measure and its *validity*.

RELIABILITY OF MEASUREMENTS

A measurement of a trait is reliable if it is accurate. Every measurement, whether it is a rating, a score, or another kind, is likely to have some degree of error involved in it. The measurement may be a bit too high or too low. It is rarely exactly correct. The important consideration is the size of error, not for any particular person (for this no one can ever know) but for the population in general. This is the general meaning of reliability. When we come to estimating the degree of reliability for methods and for the measurements that they yield, we find that there are actually several types of reliability to be taken into account. Accuracy of measurements means different things when we get into the operation of estimating the degree of reliability.

In Chapter 4, we considered the phenomenon of functional fluctuation, by which we mean the instability of a person's position on a certain trait. From what is known, minor instabilities in trait positions appear to be the rule rather than the exception. We should then expect to find that the measurement of a trait reflects these variations and hence that scores or other measures also fluctuate. We would not expect to obtain the same identical score for a person on a trait on two different occasions.

Tests and other instruments are also imperfect. Even if the person were completely stable with respect to a trait position, he probably would show, from one time to another, variations of scores derived from the instrument. In the usual case, these variations would be added to those due to functional fluctuations, to enlarge the total amount of error in the score. The type of reliability that is affected by these two kinds of fluctuations is known as *stability*.

We can obtain a single number to indicate the amount of stability. This is a coefficient of correlation between two sets of scores obtained from the same instrument given to the same sample of individuals on two different occasions. It is one kind of *reliability coefficient* and it is sometimes known as a *coefficient of stability* but more often as a *retest reliability coefficient*. It tells us the proportion of accuracy we have left after taking into account the amount of instability of persons and the amount of instability of the instrument. If the correlation is very high, we can have much confidence that a score obtained at one time will be close to that obtained at another time.

As might be expected, the size of the coefficient is related to the length of time elapsing between test and retest. The general rule is that the longer the time, the lower the correlation. With longer time intervals, we have more than temporary fluctuations involved. Some of the longer-term trends in traits also contribute something to errors of measurement, for the reason that not all individuals change the same amount or in the same direction during the time interval.

Other estimates of reliability give much more weight to the errors contributed by the measuring instrument and less to functional fluctuation of the individual. If the instrument is a test composed of parts or items, we are often concerned about the *internal consistency* of those parts. Do all parts tell us the same story regarding the trait positions of persons? There are no perfect items. A person fails some and passes others. Where there is less than perfect correlation among items, there will be less than perfect correlation among larger parts of a test. There is positive correlation between two items if persons who "pass" one of them also tend to "pass" the other.

There are many methods of intercorrelating parts of a test. One favorite method is to make two tests out of one by dividing the items into two separately scored groups, with the odd-numbered items in one group and the even-numbered items in another. There are thus two scores for every person in a sample, and these two sets of scores are correlated to obtain a coefficient of reliability for the half-test. By application of the Spearman-Brown formula,[1] we can estimate the degree of reliability of the total test. The longer the test (provided all items are sufficiently similar), the higher the internal-consistency reliability. This coefficient tells how accurate the test is for measuring individuals at the single time the test is given. It tells us nothing about how stable the scores from it are likely to be over time intervals, this being a different kind of information than we obtain from the retest method.

A third general approach to the estimation of reliability is known as the *alternate-forms* method. Sometimes two alternate tests are prepared to measure the same trait. They are composed of the same kind of items, but not the same items. They are like two parts of a longer test. Both are administered to the same sample, with or without an intervening time interval, and the two sets of scores are correlated to estimate the reliability of either form. If there is an appreciable time interval, let us say of a day or more, we would have some functional fluctuation involved, which this kind of estimate of reliability would also reflect. With practically no time interval, the alternate-forms reliability approaches the internal-consistency reliability; with longer time intervals, it gives us information regarding the effects that contribute to errors due both to test content and functional fluctuation. From a practical point of view, it tells us whether two forms of a test are equivalent and could therefore be used interchangeably.

VALIDITY OF MEASUREMENTS

The best synonyms for "validity," when the term is applied to measurements of personality traits, are "relevancy" and "predictive value." Validity is concerned with *what* it is that a test or other instrument measures and *how well* it does so. Are the scores from a particular test relevant for measuring a particular trait? Do they indicate it, and how well do they do so? The measurement of the height of a man in inches tells us how tall he is, but it tells us nothing about how well he can solve mathematical problems. It is not relevant to the measurement of such intellectual abilities. Height measurements are very reliable, but they are invalid for indicating trait positions on intellectual traits. Scores from a kind of behavior test might be relevant for indicating positions on a trait of some intellectual ability, but they would not indicate heights of persons.

[1] See Guilford (1956a).

There are a number of meanings of "validity" in the literature. For our purposes here, two major meanings will be sufficient. One is concerned with relevance. Does the instrument indicate trait positions on a particular trait? We may call this *relevant validity*.[2] If the trait happens to be one found by factor analysis, we speak of *factorial validity*, a special case of relevant validity. The degree of factorial validity of a test is indicated by its factor loading, which, under certain conditions, is the correlation of the test with the factor. There was some discussion of this in Chapter 5, where certain factors were mentioned and their relations to certain trait indicators were given (see Table 5.2). As we saw there, the same test might be valid for measuring more than one common factor. For unambiguous interpretations of scores, we should like to have not only a high factor loading in the test that measures a factor but also near-zero loadings (no validity) for indicating other factors. Short of factor analysis, the usual way of determining that a test is valid for measuring a certain assumed trait is to find out whether it correlates highly with one or more others that were designed to measure the same trait.

The other type of validity stresses predictive value. One could say that in a very general sense a test is valid for measuring anything that it predicts. So long as there is some correlation between this test and any other measure, we can make some prediction (inaccurate though it may be) of that other measure for each person. The most practically useful predictions we should want to make from measures of personality are forecasts of performances in daily life, such as success in school, in jobs, in marriage, or in diplomacy. This we shall call *predictive validity*.

The index of predictive validity in the practical situation is usually a coefficient of correlation between the personality measure and a *criterion* measure of success or of adjustment in everyday life. The higher the correlation between scores and criterion measures, the more accurate the predictions will be. If the correlation with a particular criterion variable is zero, there is no point in using the information provided by the scores in predicting that criterion. This does not mean, of course, that those same scores may not be useful in predicting other criteria. Sometimes the "predictions" pertain to present conditions or statuses of individuals, such as membership in some diagnostic category or in other groups that are defined by such categories as sex, marital status, or delinquency. This special form of predictive validity is commonly called *concurrent* validity.

GENERAL UTILITY OF A METHOD

From the information regarding reliability and validity of trait measurements, as well as from other information, we should be able to gain

[2] Also known as *construct validity* for the reason that the trait adopted is a hypothesized property or a theoretical "construct," a trait idea constructed by the investigator.

ideas of the general value of a method. We should be able to see to what uses the method is well adapted and to what uses it is not adapted, what traits or areas of personality can be best assessed with it, and where better methods are needed. Most methods have their disadvantages as well as their advantages; none are perfect. It should be added that there are other reasons besides reliability and validity that bear upon the advantages and disadvantages of a method. We shall see these as we come to each method.

A general word of caution seems desirable before we examine particular types of methods. There is a common disposition on the part of some people who are not well informed regarding test procedures to ask for nothing short of perfection. If a test is found to have relatively low reliability or validity, the attitude on the part of such people is to say, "Away with it." This is the defeatist attitude, and if it were followed, we would not be using any methods of assessment of personality, except, perhaps, certain morphological measurements for the assessment of morphological traits—height, weight, and the like.

All methods of assessing behavior traits have their limitations. The proper attitude to take is not to keep seeking for the "philosopher's stone," which was said to be able to turn other metals into gold, to keep looking, in other words, for the perfect method of assessment of personality. The proper attitude is to ask whether the method adds anything in the way of information that we could not have without it and whether the amount that it adds is worth the trouble of obtaining the information. If it adds useful information, if we can do appreciably better with it than without, we should not hesitate to use it. In that case, the errors we make in using it are smaller, on the whole, than the errors that would be made without it. In the meantime, we can attempt to improve the method or to develop a better one. We should remember, too, that if a method is at least moderately valid, for every spectacular "miss" there will probably be a greater number of "near hits." [3]

MORPHOLOGICAL METHODS

Reasons for Interest in Morphological Methods

In the study of personality, our interest in morphology and in morphological methods is a double one. The point of view adopted is that morphological traits constitute a part or aspect of personality and hence call for description. We therefore have the problem of what physical traits to measure. Which ones are worth knowing about? Which ones, taken together, give maximum description with minimum effort?

[3] For further discussion of this subject, see Guilford (1946).

In the discussion of types of personality in Chapter 5, the morphological types proposed by Kretschmer were mentioned. Can we say all that is worth saying about a person's physical make-up by assigning him to one of three such classes? Sheldon's three morphological components are alternative descriptive categories for physique. Are these categories better than Kretschmer's and will they provide us with all the information that we need regarding body formation? We shall return to these questions later in the chapter.

The second reason for interest in morphological methods, one that has been more important than the first, is the age-old belief that we can assess behavior traits through information about traits of physique. If this were true, it would solve many of our toughest problems. We should have available some very easy and objective procedures for assessing behavioral aspects of personality. Such an approach would be acceptable only if substantial correlations were demonstrated between certain morphological traits and certain corresponding behavior traits.

The question of correlation between the two kinds of traits is of considerable interest, apart from the possibility of being able to use the one in assessment of the other. Knowledge of such correlations, even when they are found to be small, should help us in gaining understanding of personality structure and in constructing a theory of personality and its development. We shall consider these problems in greater detail later in this chapter.

Discredited Methods of Assessment of Behavior Traits

A few of the methods for assessing behavior traits from physical characteristics may be mentioned. Although long since discredited, they are of historical importance and they also serve as a warning regarding the uncritical acceptance of procedures without appropriate scientific support from empirical facts. Furthermore, the use of these discredited, or pseudo-scientific, methods is not entirely dead, even in these enlightened days of the twentieth century.

PHRENOLOGY

Phrenology is a method that utilizes information concerning the location of elevations and depressions at various positions on the human skull. The basic assumptions are as follows. Human personality can be described in terms of some 30 distinct traits. Each trait has its own "organ" in a given compartment of the brain. A high degree of the trait goes with overdevelopment of its compartment; a low degree goes with underdevelopment. The shape of the skull conforms to these overdevelopments and underdevelopments.

On all these points the phrenologists were mostly wrong. While the existence of a number of basic traits is an acceptable idea, there are undoubtedly many more than 30 (see Chapters 14 through 18), and the ones the phrenologists selected generally lack empirical evidence to support them. Knowledge of anatomy leads to quite different conclusions with regard to localization of function (and therefore of traits) in the brain. It is possible that a very limited number of what today we call factors of personality, such as *visual memory* and *auditory memory*, have somewhat limited localization of functioning, but the great majority of traits probably depend upon very widespread brain activity. Even if certain brain localities were overdeveloped or underdeveloped, it is highly unlikely that the shape of the hard skull would be influenced to any appreciable degree by pressures, or the lack of them, from the underlying brain tissue.

PHYSIOGNOMY

Physiognomy is based upon the use of physical characteristics other than skull conformations—shape of the face, shape of the hand (as in chirognomy), and coloring (blond vs. brunette vs. redhead). The shape of the jaw, for example, is sometimes said to indicate various traits. A broad jaw is said to indicate fidelity and permanency, even firmness and obstinacy. A round, flat chin is said to indicate benevolence and congeniality. A broad, round chin indicates ardent love. An indented chin, with a dimple, indicates a desire to be loved, and a chin with a deep horizontal indentation indicates violent or passionate love, that is, the lower part of the chin juts out while the mouth and upper part recede. Such associations are, of course, purely hypothetical. There is no known support for them. They could possibly serve only for such purposes as the basis for an evening's entertainment!

Where any such hypotheses have been brought under scientific scrutiny, they have fallen seriously short if they have not been entirely discredited. Many traits have been attributed to blonds vs. brunettes, based upon the generalization that the former come largely from human stock that lived for centuries in cold climates while the latter came from stock that lived in warm climates. A study of the incidence of the qualities attributed to the two groups led to the conclusion that there were no significant relationships.[4]

The hypothesis that a long thumb indicates "power of personality" was also examined empirically. "Power of personality" was interpreted as dominance or ascendance. Thumbs of 100 individuals were measured and scores were obtained from the same individuals on the Allport A-S Reaction Study, an inventory for the measurement of ascendance-sub-

---

[4] Paterson and Ludgate (1922).

mission.[5] The correlation proved to be .10, which is not significant (could have happened by chance).

Reasons for Continued Appeal of Discredited Methods

Unsupported and indefensible methods continue to enjoy some degree of popularity. Why? This is an interesting, incidental psychological question, which probably has its answer in what we know about learning and motivation. This is suggested by a number of experimental studies on the problem.

In one experiment, each student in a class of 39 was given a short description of his own personality, a description allegedly derived from inspection of the student's handwriting and from his horoscope.[6] Actually, every student received the same description, a fact that was unknown to any of them. All students accepted the descriptions as being valid! Students thus seem quite ready to accept statements made regarding their personalities by one whom they regard as an "expert" on the subject, particularly when they lack good information to the contrary. Similar results have been reported from two other experiments.[7]

An experiment by Forer (1949) was better designed to find out why descriptions of traits are so acceptable even when they are without foundation. He tested certain hypotheses regarding the types of statements that are most acceptable. He thought that some statements are acceptable because they are almost universally true, that is, they apply to almost everybody. Other statements are accepted because they are ambiguous, thus each person can interpret each statement in the way that applies to him. Other descriptions are stated with much "hedging," and thus avoid extremes. Still other statements are likely to be flattering to the person described. These various properties can be combined in the case of some statements.

In the experiment, Forer administered what was purported to be an interest inventory to 39 students. Later, each student was given a list of statements about himself, presumably derived from his performance on the inventory. Every student, unknown to him, received the same statements as every other student. He was asked to rate the validity of every statement and to say whether it fit his personality.

Out of 13 statements, the average number accepted was 11. Examples of those statements that are almost universally true and the number of students (out of 39) accepting each are:

You have a tendency to be critical of yourself. (38)

At times you have serious doubts as to whether you have made the right decision or done the right thing. (38)

---

[5] Misiak and Franghiadi (1953).   [7] Donceel, Alimena, and Birch (1949).
[6] Krüger and Zeitz (1933).

You prefer a certain amount of change and variety and become dissatisfied when hemmed in by restrictions and limitations. (37)
Examples of statements with hedging are:
While you have some personality weaknesses, you are generally able to compensate for them. (31)
At times you are extraverted, affable, and sociable, while at other times you are introverted, wary, and reserved. (34)
Examples of flattering statements are:
You have a great deal of unusual capacity which you have not turned to your advantage. (23, 15 uncertain)
You pride yourself as an independent thinker and do not accept the statements of others without satisfactory proof. (34)

It appears that all of Forer's hypotheses were supported. Uninformed persons are conditioned to accept statements of "experts" who use methods that are esoteric. They have no reason, of course, to reject statements that are true of everybody. Ambiguous statements, like those of the famed Delphic oracle, can be true or false, depending upon the way one looks at them. Flattering statements carry with them much reinforcing potency. It is no wonder that even a completely invalid method can gain some degree of acceptance.

The Kretschmer Constitutional Types

This is the place to return to the discussion of the Kretschmer types that were mentioned before. We shall consider them in their historical setting and try to assess the validity of Kretschmer's contention that there are strong correlations between physical and behavior types.

SOME HISTORY OF PHYSICAL TYPES

The Greek founder of medicine, Hippocrates, distinguished between two types: the phthistic habitus (long, thin) and the apoplecticus (short, thick). In his medical practice, he noted that the former was relatively more susceptible to tuberculosis while the latter was relatively more susceptible to apoplexy. Rostan (1828) distinguished three types: digestive, muscular, and cerebral, in terms of relative overdevelopment and overfunctioning of those three aspects of physique. The emphasis here is more on functioning than upon anatomy. Viola also distinguished three types, two of them being like those of Hippocrates. The macrosplanchnic exhibits a predominance of trunk development over that of limb development. The microsplanchnic exhibits a predominance of limbs over trunk. The normosplanchnic is better balanced with respect to trunk and limb development.

Naccarati, a pupil of Viola's at Columbia University, correlated the

Viola index of physique with scores from intelligence tests.[8] The Viola index is based upon the ratio of limbs to trunk. A correlation as high as .36 was reported. Later, Sheldon, at the University of Chicago, found distinctly lower correlations in a sample of 450 subjects.[9] The correlation of the Viola index with intelligence scores was .14 and with average grades, .12. The latter results are more in line with the usual correlations found between morphology and measures of behavior traits.

EVALUATION OF KRETSCHMER HYPOTHESES

Kretschmer noticed that schizophrenics as a group tended to be microsplanchnic (which he called asthenic and, later, the leptosome type) and that manic-depressives tended to be macrosplanchnic (which he called pyknic, meaning compact, from the Greek). Further study of these correlations bore out his hypothesis; the correlations seemed to be substantial. He then assumed that the same types apply to the nonpathological population and the same kind of relationships. The two extreme types of temperament he called schizothyme (sensitive, quiet, reserved) and cyclothyme (genial, sociable, emotionally labile).

In countries other than Germany, studies of the Kretschmer hypotheses, with the use of his type concepts, have not given him much support. In the first place, there have been difficulties in typing individuals physically, either for lack of specifications as to how to do it or because his types apply to so few people. Sheldon, for example, found that he could type accurately only 27 per cent of the men he studied. One difficulty was that there were inconsistencies of type indicated in different parts of the body. Because of the faults he found with the Kretschmer typing methods, Sheldon developed his own procedures and theory.

Other investigators who applied the Kretschmer typing procedures to nonpathological subjects have found correlations between physique and temperament to be in the range from .10 to .20, in the right direction but very small.[10] Cabot (1938), studying clearly typed high school boys, concluded that on the whole his results did not support Kretschmer. Eysenck (1950) marshalled evidence from experimental results that can be interpreted as being against the hypothesis that there is a single dimension of cyclothymia vs. schizothymia. Eysenck (1952a) also presented strong evidence that the cyclothymic and schizothymic patterns are not characteristic of normal persons. Using behavior tests, he found that schizophrenics tended to be intermediate to normals and cycloids. He found more differences between the pathological and normal groups than between the two pathological groups. Thus, cycloids and schizophrenics do not differ

[8] Naccarati (1921).
[9] Sheldon (1940).
[10] Mohr and Gundlach (1927, 1929); Burt (1949).

from normals in opposite directions, as the Kretschmer hypothesis calls for, but in the same direction.

Even in pathological groups studied in the United States, the correlations between physique and pathological category are much lower than those Kretschmer reported. Furthermore, in one study it was found that paranoid schizophrenics are physically more like manic-depressives in trunk size than they are like other schizophrenics.[11] There is apparently some common suspicion that Kretschmer neglected the fact that manic-depressives, as contrasted with schizophrenics, develop their psychosis at more advanced ages, when they tend to be more stocky. Ratio of trunk size to limb size cannot, of course, be fully accounted for in terms of age, but to the extent that the ratio is related to age, the Kretschmer correlations would be inflated.

Sheldon's Components of Physique

Sheldon proposed that we think in terms of general *dimensions* of physique rather than types. The three dimensions or *components* are as follows:

Endomorphic: Tendency to roundness, smoothness, softness, large trunk, delicate, tapering limbs

Mesomorphic: Tendency to heavy bones and muscles, squareness, ruggedness

Ectomorphic: Tendency to slenderness, straightness of limb, delicateness

Each person is to be described with respect to his positions on each of three scales, according to Sheldon. A type is thus a particular combination of three trait positions on these dimensions. It takes three scores to express each person's type and to describe him physically.

SHELDON'S TYPING PROCESS

Sheldon adopted a seven-point scale for each physical dimension, with no zero score allowed. Each person's type is expressed by a three-digit number, such as 246, which would mean that the person has a score of 2 for endomorphy, 4 for mesomorphy, and 6 for ectomorphy. A type number of 711 would indicate an extreme endomorph; 171 would indicate an extreme mesomorph, and 117, an extreme ectomorph. A perfectly balanced person with respect to the three dimensions would be a 444, with middle scores in all three components. These four special cases are illustrated in Figure 6.1.

Note that the cases in Figure 6.1 are arranged in the form of an equilateral triangle, with the three extreme cases at the three corners. Every type can be located within the triangle. There is no 777 person nor a

[11] Moore and Hsü (1946).

111 person. Sheldon puts a restriction on the sum of the three component ratings. The sum is not permitted to fall below 9 or to exceed 12. It is this restriction that confines cases almost entirely to a single plane in the form of a triangle.

A plane can be accounted for in terms of only two dimensions; three are unnecessary, as Ekman (1951b) has pointed out. Ekman recommends plac-

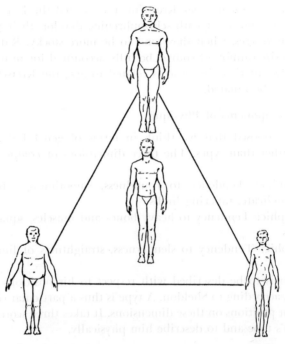

Fig. 6.1 Illustration of Sheldon's three extreme somatotypes at the corners of a triangle and a completely balanced physical type in the center of the triangle.

ing the origin of two dimensions at the ectomorphic corner. This corner would be very close to Kretschmer's conception of a leptomorph (long-thin) type. But the Sheldon system differs from the Kretschmer by the fact that we would go in two directions from the leptomorph rather than one direction (toward pyknic), the two directions being toward the extreme mesomorph in the one case and toward the extreme endomorph in the other.

SHELDON'S TEMPERAMENT COMPONENTS

Sheldon (1942) also proposed three general temperament dimensions of personality corresponding to his three physical components. They are:

Viscerotonia: relaxed, comfort-loving, food-loving, sociable, tolerant, etc.

Somatotonia: energetic, active, dominating, adventure-loving, competitive, etc.

Cerebrotonia: restrained, seclusive, secretive, inhibited, self-conscious, etc.

The typing of individuals in terms of these three components is done by a rating procedure analogous to that for physique. Sheldon obtained the information concerning the temperament components from interviews. There could be other sources of information. Again, persons are given three-digit type numbers, placing most cases within a triangle. Again, two dimensions would be sufficient to take care of all the discriminations implied. If cerebrotonia were placed at the origin, one dimension would extend toward extreme somatotonia and the other toward extreme viscerotonia.[12]

Correlations between Corresponding Components

From the standpoint of theory of personality structure, and because of the possibility of assessing the temperament components indirectly from the more feasible assessment of physical components, we have considerable interest in the correlations between Sheldon's two classes of component scores. Studies by Sheldon (1942) and by others give very conflicting results on this problem. Sheldon had anticipated that, by deriving more sound, basic variables for the description of both physique and temperament, we should find much more substantial correlations between the two aspects of personality, much higher, at least, than the usual correlations in the range from .0 to .2.

SHELDON'S CORRELATION RESULTS

Sheldon (1942) rated a large number of men on both his physical and his temperamental components, with the result that the ratings of corresponding pairs of components correlated .79, .82, and .83, for the pairs endomorphy-viscerotonia, mesomorphy-somatotonia, and ectomorphy-cerebrotonia, respectively. As correlations between morphology and behavior traits, these figures are extraordinarily high. To some extent, we do not know how much, these high coefficients reflect an experimental dependence between the two series of assessments in each case. Sheldon himself typed the men both for physique and for temperament. Even if he did not have the morphological ratings before him when he evaluated the men on behavior traits, he could not help being aware of their ap-

[12] See Ekman (1951*b*).

proximate physical types as he interviewed them for assessment of those traits. Lubin (1950), who doubted the meaningfulness of Sheldon's coefficients, made a statistical study of them. He came to the conclusion that many of the correlations reported by Sheldon are mathematically impossible. This finding suggests biases of some sort in the data or errors of computation.

OTHER TESTS OF THE SHELDON HYPOTHESES

Child (1950) made a direct test of the hypothesis of morphological-temperamental intercorrelations in terms of Sheldon's components by using inventories designed to measure the temperamental components. The inventories were very short, being composed of seven items for each component, but they were developed on a careful, experimental basis. The three intercorrelations, each of physical component with corresponding temperamental component, were .13, .38, and .27, respectively, in the order of the coefficients reported above from Sheldon. An incidental finding was that of the 94 items tried out, all based upon qualities Sheldon believed to be related to his three components, only 20 proved to correlate significantly with the physical components.

Indirect tests have been made by several other investigators.[13] Measurements of the temperament traits were accomplished by various procedures, with traits being selected that would be expected to correlate with the morphological components according to Sheldon's theory of temperament. Very few, and often none at all, of the correlations were significant. One study [14] in which the behavior-trait measures were obtained from the Allport-Vernon Study of Values is an exception to the rule. The investigator reported correlations in the range from .31 to .76 between pairs of measurements (ratings of physical components with selected inventory scores) where they would be reasonably expected. Smith (1949) has pointed out what may be a serious error in the Coffin study, however. Both male and female subjects were included in his sample, and sex differences in both physique and the behavior-trait scores could possibly have accounted for these higher correlations. When Smith repeated Coffin's study, keeping the sexes separate, the correlations were found to be generally less than .10.

Adcock (1950) questioned whether Sheldon's three components of temperament are actual unities, and his intercorrelational study of qualities that Sheldon includes under the components led to the conclusion that at least two of Sheldon's components involve two factors each. It is the author's impression, from comparing Sheldon's descriptions of his

---

[13] Child and Sheldon (1941); Fiske (1944); Smith (1949); Janoff et al. (1950); and Page et al. (1955).

[14] Coffin (1944).

components with the dimensions given in Chapters 15 through 17, that those components involve a number of distinct factors.

Other Relations with Morphological Traits

One class of traits that has received considerable attention in relation to morphology comes under the heading of general intelligence. The index of intelligence has usually been a single score, which has been related to such single variables as height and weight and to indices of body shape.

Katz (1940) tested and measured a group of children, aged three to five, every six months. For boys, correlations of intelligence scores with height and weight were essentially zero at each occasion. With girls, for some reason, the correlations with height ranged from .36 to .40, and with weight, from .27 to .34. These correlations are much higher than those reported by Murdock and Sullivan (1923), which were .14 with height and .16 with weight. They are in line with the finding by Terman (1925) that his superior children tended to be superior in physical traits.

Pillsbury (1936) found that among college students an index of tallness-thinness correlated from .08 to .29 with grade-point averages in four groups. The greatest increase in average grades came between the pyknics and athletics. Pyknics showed the greatest tendency to drop out of school and they came to college in smaller proportions than other men.

Certain physical traits tend to be associated with gravitation to positions of leadership. Gowin (1915) was one of the first to report that executives and leaders in politics and religion tend to be taller and heavier than nonleaders in the same professions. Such conclusions have been supported from different sources.[15]

An Evaluation of Morphological Methods

The measurement of morphological traits, as such, gives the most reliable values that can be obtained in the assessment of personality. Physical weighting and measuring instruments can be used, the only appreciable source of error being that of functional fluctuation, which is not very great for this kind of trait.

The use of the morphological measurements for the assessment of behavior traits, however, is quite another matter. We have already seen much reason to doubt that this age-old objective can ever be satisfied.[16] But we must now consider this problem in larger perspective, apart from the Kretschmer and Sheldon approaches. Let us first consider some logical aspects of the problem and then some additional empirical findings.

[15] Jenkins (1947).
[16] Paterson (1930) summarized much information on this subject.

REASONS FOR EXPECTING MORPHOLOGY-BEHAVIOR RELATIONSHIPS

There are a number of things connected with the development of an organism that should lead us logically to expect relationships between certain physical and psychological traits. We should say "certain" traits, because the demonstration of one or more of such relationships would not be justification for generalizing the same principle to all traits, nor can we see necessary logical connections at every point.

Physical and psychological traits have hereditary causes, at least in part. Therefore, conditions that affect the one group could possibly also affect the other. Both Kretschmer and Sheldon refer to constitutional types and components, as if they were primarily determined by heredity. In their thinking, common heredity is probably regarded as the basis for such physical-psychological relationships as they have expected to find.

The same blood that nourishes the visceral, muscular, and bone tissues in their development also nourishes the nervous system. The hormones in the blood stream may have much to do with the development of both and therefore of both kinds of traits. We are not concerned with personality development as a topic in this volume, yet at this point it is pertinent to consider common effects such as those of hormones. Where glands go seriously wrong, we definitely find parallel changes in physical and psychological traits. Do minor changes or differences in glandular balance also produce similar effects to a smaller extent? This question has not been answered as yet with any degree of certainty.

Another kind of link between morphological and behavior traits might be created by the psychological effects of the former upon the latter. We may develop through the processes of learning some of the behavior qualities we have because of certain physical characteristics that we have. We also cannot get away from the obvious fact that, in general, psychological functioning is dependent upon physical mechanisms.

The effects could be either direct or indirect. Limitation in ability due to the kind of anatomical features a person has would be a direct effect. Psychomotor dexterity might be limited by the way in which bones, muscles, and tendons are organized; so, also, might traits of flexibility, strength, and motor control. If we include physiological characteristics within the physical category also, we can think of other general effects. The chemistry of the blood can probably contribute to a high or a low level of general bodily activity and to the strength of drives, and hence of interests and such motivational traits as endurance.

Indirect effects of physique (and chemique) of the body come primarily through learning. Because of certain limitations in these respects, the individual finds out what he can and what he cannot do. Some individuals accept the limitations and redirect their interests and their efforts whereas others do not accept them. Those who do not accept their limitations may give up in defeat; others show compensatory modes of adjustment.

COMPENSATORY EFFECTS: THE ADLER HYPOTHESIS

Adler's theory of organic inferiority and its psychological consequences is well known. The individual with somatic weaknesses that reduce his ability to compete successfully with his fellows generates feelings of inferiority. There may develop an extraordinary effort to excel in some respect, preferably in the area of the felt source of the inferiority. In view of the plausibility of this hypothesis and its possible bearing upon the generation of correlations between physical and psychological traits, we shall look into a few studies that have been conducted with the aim of testing one or more aspects of the hypothesis.

Faterson (1931) attempted to test the main hypothesis by correlating the extent of individuals' feelings of inferiority and the extent and kind of their physical defects. She examined the medical records of freshmen at the University of Minnesota and recorded each kind of defect reported for every student. She also administered to them Heidbreder's inventory Rating Scale of Personal Traits. In very large samples, the correlation between the number of physical defects (without regard to kind) and the score for inferiority feelings was .16 for the men and .24 for the women. These coefficients indicate a definite relationship in the expected direction, but if the organic defects constitute a determiner of inferiority feelings, they are only one of several determiners and a fairly weak one at that.

Some kinds of defects were found to be more strongly related to inferiority feelings than others. For women, the defects that were particularly related include fallen arches, muscular weakness, heart murmurs, and poor posture. One could question whether the poor posture caused inferiority feelings or whether the latter caused poor posture. We cannot tell from a correlation coefficient alone whether X causes Y or Y causes X or whether neither is true. In the latter case, there may be a common cause of both or there may be some incidental reason for X and Y falling somewhat into line. For men, the most significant defects in relation to inferiority-feeling level were poor posture and curvature of the spine.[17]

One deduction from the Adler hypothesis is that some people turn their attention to music because of auditory defects of which they become more or less aware, directly or indirectly. Farnsworth (1941) tested this deduction in college students. He found that students rating themselves high in musical status had generally better auditory acuity as measured by

[17] It is interesting, from the standpoint of Freudian theory as well, that the defect of undescended testicles was not related to inferiority feelings, as might be expected; in fact, the relationship was in the *opposite direction*.

tests. They also did slightly better on the Seashore tests of musical ability. Results with young children also failed to support the Adler hypothesis.[18]

A similar deduction is that we should find an undue proportion of visual defect among graphic artists. Farnsworth (1941) found no relation whatever. In the Lewerenz test of artistic talents, he found a zero correlation between the score on the color part and the score on the rest of the test. Atwell (1939) found that, in children in grades 3 to 6, art ability, as rated by teachers, correlated with color ability to the extent of .14 to .29 in the different grades. The Adler hypothesis would call for a negative correlation.

We cannot generalize from these special areas of human effort to all others, however. Furthermore, in other areas, some findings do support the Adler hypothesis. Thune (1949) found that weight lifters in a YMCA were more shy, lacking in confidence, and more concerned with body strength and health than other men. Perhaps this could be interpreted as merely a realistic self-appraisal and a rational solution to a problem rather than a case of compensatory behavior. Results that appear to be more pertinent to testing the hypothesis were reported by Harlow (1951). He found that men who were interested in weight lifting in gymnasium work had feelings of masculine inadequacy, also feelings of dependency. However, the interpretation of these results is also in some doubt.

What should be our conclusion concerning the Adler hypothesis? It seems to be true that physical defects and deficiencies can contribute to a detectable extent toward a general feeling of inferiority, but there are other evidently more significant contributors to that trait. There is little evidence that sensory defects dispose individuals toward excelling in the arts. If anything, the opposite seems to be true. There is some evidence that general physical weakness may turn men's attention to exercises that should correct that deficiency. But on the whole, there is little evidence in the population of neurotic or semineurotic efforts that lead to overcompensation on a very large scale. That overcompensation could occur in dramatic form in particular cases that come to the attention of clinicians is quite possible, although it is very difficult to prove such a connection in the isolated case. Certainly, we should not generalize from a few dramatic cases to all humanity.

GENERAL CONCLUSIONS

From the many doubts surrounding the validity and the adequacy of the Kretschmer types and the Sheldon components of morphology, it is clear that we need to restudy the problem of description of physique. Both approaches are inadequate; both cover up too many inconsistencies; both

[18] Farnsworth (1938b)

had to bring in additional concepts, such as "dysplasias." [19] The possible number of simple body measurements is enormous. There must be underlying principles of development that make possible the description of physique in terms of a moderate number of efficient concepts. New concepts of body structure, as a segment or aspect of the total personality structure, might emerge if such principles were known. Factor analysis would seem to be a promising way of going about the solution of this descriptive problem, as it has been elsewhere in the study of personality.[20]

Assuming that we found much more fruitful variables of physique than we now have, it is still unlikely that we should find correlations with behavior traits that would be sizable enough to make practicable the assessment of those traits indirectly through observations of physique. The problem of correlation between the two kinds of traits continues to be important, however, in the effort to obtain a complete picture of personality structure.

PHYSIOLOGICAL METHODS

The Importance of Physiological Functions

Physiological attributes bring us much closer to behavior than do morphological attributes. Among the physiological attributes, we may look for rather direct determiners of behavior traits. We have problems similar to those in connection with morphological traits: Can behavior traits be assessed through physiological evaluations? What kinds of relationships will be found between the two kinds of traits?

BIOCHEMISTRY (APART FROM ENDOCRINOLOGY)

The chemistry of the blood offers a rich potential source of determiners of personal disposition. We have good reason to expect that individual differences in blood composition should have significant effects upon behavior through behavior-trait dispositions. The blood bathes all the body cells and organs. Their efficiency and well-being depend upon what the blood brings to them and what it carries away. We know what a reduction of oxygen supply does to the functioning of the brain. We know what the new tranquilizing drugs and other drugs do to nervous functioning and the consequent effects upon behavior. In spite of the fact that every organism makes an effort to keep the blood in a balanced condition, there may well be room for enough individual differences to bring about corresponding individual differences in behavior traits.

---

[19] Dysplasias are noticeable discrepancies or inconsistencies in body formation of an individual.

[20] Guilford (1957*b*).

Not many studies of chemical assays of the blood and other body fluids, such as saliva and urine, in connection with behavior traits have been reported. One example of such a study is that of Rich (1928), who related the alkaline-acid condition to certain behavior traits. He found that the more excitable subjects tend to have alkaline saliva and urine. The interpretation of this result could be made on the basis of temporary effects as well as on the basis of traits. The excitable person is more physically active and, breathing more rapidly, has less carbon dioxide in his blood, which gives an alkaline reaction. Thus, it would be safer to say that a person tends to be on the alkaline side because he is more excitable rather than to say that he is more excitable because he is on the alkaline side. This seems to be a case of behavior determining a physiological condition rather than the reverse.

ENDOCRINOLOGY

In view of the frequent optimistic assertions regarding the dependence of personality in general upon the endocrine glands, it is surprising that we do not have available more systematic and dependable information concerning correlations of this kind. Dramatic relationships are sometimes observed at the pathological extremes of glandular functioning. Correlations within the nonpathological ranges of functioning are more difficult to demonstrate. The reason probably is that, with the exception of a few traits, such as the maternal attitude in women and male sexuality in men, direct and simple connections are hard to find. The trait of general-activity level, for example, is probably attributable to more than one gland, among other kinds of determiners. In one person, it can be attributed more to one of these sources and in another person, more to some other. Thus, such correlations are probably not usually high or even substantial.

Effects are also indirect as well as direct. For example, connections are sometimes pointed out between glandular disturbances and tendencies to delinquency and crime. The connection may be indirect in that the disturbance makes adjustment difficult for the individual generally and criminal behavior is the by-product. Systematic and comprehensive correlational studies between glandular disposition and behavior traits will require years of patient study before we have the facts.

Functioning of the Central Nervous System

We should expect to find considerable relationship between behavior traits and properties of nervous functioning, involving both the central nervous system and the autonomic nervous system. We shall consider the former system first.

SENSORY FUNCTIONS

Although sensory abilities constitute a kind of personality trait in their own right, sensory functioning is of interest because of its apparent relationship to other aspects of personality. It has been found that neurotics as a group tend to do much more poorly than others in simple tests of sensory acuity.[21] Neurotics are also definitely inferior as a group in tests of vision in the dark.[22] The question is well raised, as it was by the discoverers of these relationships, whether neurotics actually have lower sensory abilities than normals or whether it is some other aspect of the sensory tests in which they fall down. For example, neurotics may do poorly in tests of sensory acuity because of lack of attention to the task, not because of defective sense organs. Eysenck (1947) suggested that the poor showing of neurotics (particularly hystericals) in the dark-vision test is due to fear of the dark. He found that 60 per cent of the men with poor night vision admitted fear of the dark as children or as adults, as compared with 27 per cent of those with good dark vision. These data seem to support his hypothesis.

THE ELECTROENCEPHALOGRAM (EEG)

The electroencephalogram is a continuous recording of electrical activity of the brain. Of greatest interest is the alpha rhythm. In the relaxed person whose eyes are closed, the alpha rhythm is quite clear in the form of a wave of about 10 cycles per second. When the subject is alerted or opens his eyes, the alpha rhythm is likely to be broken up, with rhythms of much higher frequency taking over.

Since individual differences were discovered in the rate or frequency of the alpha rhythm in the EEG, it was inevitable that this variable should be studied in connection with intelligence-test scores. However, most investigators have found no correlation between the two.[23] Exceptions have been noted for feebleminded adults [24] and for eight-year-old boys,[25] where positive correlations were found. Others conclude that there is essentially no correlation between brain waves and intelligence.[26] Walter (1944) has claimed that he was able to distinguish between visual thinkers and verbalizers on the basis of the EEG.

Darrow (1947) concluded that the alpha rhythm has to do with regulative processes, probably of the lower brain centers, and not with integrative activity of the cerebral cortex, which is only in part affected by those processes. The most significant indication found for the EEG

[21] Slater (1944).
[22] Eysenck (1947).
[23] Shagass (1946).

[24] Kreezer (1940).
[25] Knott, Friedman, and Bardsley (1942).
[26] Ellingson (1956).

is the epileptic sign, which is in the form of "spikes" (short waves of unusual amplitude) in the record. Such indicators are found in unusually high proportions of psychopaths (60 per cent) and of delinquents and criminals, but in only 5 to 10 per cent of normals.[27] There is also some indication that brain-wave variations are related to the tendency to anxiety.[28] Except for these few relationships, we have little promise that the EEG will be very significant as a means of assessing behavior traits.

BILATERAL NERVOUS CONTROL

Considerable attention has been given to the fact that we have a two-sided body and a two-sided brain, usually with one side or the other being dominant in each individual. There is the possibility that certain behavior traits might be associated with being right-handed (dextral) or left-handed (sinistral). In the generally right-handed human culture, it is significant that words "dexterity" and "dextrous" are names of good qualities while the word "sinister" is a bad quality. From the fact that a left-handed child and older person does not conform to the cultural pattern, we might expect problems to arise, with consequent effects upon personality. We have also the hypothesis that uncertainty of cortical dominance may lead to speech defects.

There have been some reports of behavior problems arising in connection with the left-handed. There have also been reports of ill effects, in the form of nervousness and speech defects, from attempts to retrain a left-handed child to adopt right-handed habits. The general impression is that it is not so much the dextrality status of the child that causes the difficulty but rather the way in which the child is treated in this connection and the sources of conflict that he encounters.[29]

Two investigators have jointly devoted considerable attention to problems connected with lateral dominance in the act of smiling and its relation to dextrality.[30] Dominance in smiling may be to the right or the left, seen mostly in which corner of the mouth is higher in the act. The underlying theory is that general lateral dominance, as seen in dextrality, is a question of which cerebral hemisphere is dominant or takes the lead. Spontaneous smiling, like the emotional expressions in general, is excited through lower brain centers, perhaps from the region of the hypothalamus. When an expressive movement involves both sides of the face, the question of dominance arises. It was proposed that if the lateral dominance of the lower brain centers is consistent with lateral dominance of the cerebral cortex, there is harmony and the individual's behavior can be better organized. The person who shows this is called a *homolateral*

[27] Walter (1944).
[28] Kennard (1956).
[29] Hildreth (1949a, 1949b, 1949c).
[30] Lynn and Lynn (1938, 1943).

smiler. If there is disagreement of lateral dominance between cerebrum and lower centers, the theory goes, there is a basis for conflicting orders, which shows up in lack of agreement between handedness and dominant side in smiling. A person with this kind of conflict is recognized as a *contralateral smiler.*

In their first study of this hypothesis, involving children and adolescents, Lynn and Lynn found that homolateral smilers tended to have all the "positive" traits, such as aggressiveness, self-confidence, courage, and adventuresomeness, while the contralateral smilers tended to have all the "negative" traits, such as being shy, retiring, timid, dependent, and insecure. Although these findings have not been verified by other investigators, they seem to hold up in a second study by the Lynns (1943) of mental-hospital cases. The correlations reported for two abnormal groups were .60 and .69, and for a group of children, .39. Such promising results call for further investigation.

Another approach having to do with lateral differences emphasizes general facial appearance. Although it might be thought that one side of a person's face is a mirror reflection of the other, this is usually not the case. In fact, in some individuals the difference is striking. Facial asymmetry is best observed by applying a simple photographic trick. The negative of a photograph of a full-face view is cut sharply down the middle, along the ridge of the nose. Two new full-face prints are then

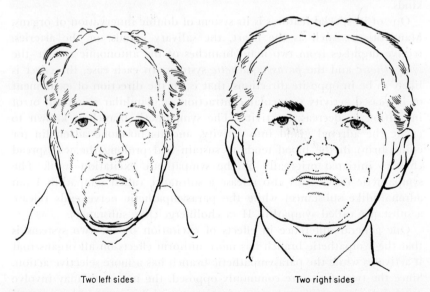

Two left sides   Two right sides

Fig. 6.2 Drawings of two faces of the same man each from a composite photograph, one composed of the right half of his face and the other of the left half.

made, one composed of two right-half views and one composed of two left-half views. Figure 6.2 shows two such composite faces. This technique has been used by Wolf (1943), who reports only a few suggested principles. One principle is that in natural facial expression one side of the face seems to be dominant. Another is that the two sides often suggest different traits or qualities. The implication of the findings to date are not very clear.

A recent study with 18 male undergraduate subjects indicated, in results that were not very decisive, that the rated degrees of asymmetry bear some relation to ratings of neuroticism.[31] Traits attributed to the two faces by observers did not differ significantly, with the one exception of the dimension called vital vs. passive. It was concluded that the apparent relation to neuroticism suggests a constitutional basis for this condition. But it may also be that asymmetry of face, like dysplasias in morphology generally, may be the source of unfavorable comment and hence of social maladjustment and possibly even neuroticism.

Functioning of the Autonomic Nervous System

Our autonomic nervous system consists of connecting links mainly between our central nervous system and our visceral organs. It has to do with regulations of the vital functions of breathing, circulation, digestion, and elimination. It is conspicuous in emotional activities of various kinds.

One of its special features is its system of double innervation of organs. Many organs, such as the heart, the salivary glands, or the arteries, receive impulses from two main branches of the autonomic system—the *sympathetic* and the *parasympathetic* systems. In each case, the effect is likely to be in opposite directions, that is, in the direction of excitement or increased activity (muscular contraction or glandular secretion) or of inhibition or decreased activity. The sympathetic branch is known to excite the adrenal gland into activity, and its hormone adrenalin (or epinephrin) in the blood tends to sustain and prolong the widespread changes initiated originally by the sympathetic excitation itself. The sympathetic nerve ends also release a substance called sympathin I (an adrenalinlike substance) while the parasympathetic nerve ends release a substance called sympathin II (a cholinergeiclike substance).

One general difference in effects of excitation by the two systems is that the sympathetic branch has more uniform effects on all organs that it activates while the parasympathetic branch has a more selective action. Since the two effects are commonly opposed, the net result may involve much interorgan difference in activation vs. inhibition. Another general

[31] Lindzey, Prince, and Wright (1952).

principle is that the parasympathetic system has to do with the domestic functions of nutrition and conservation while the sympathetic system has to do with emergency situations arising in the environment. A stressful situation thus instigates mobilization to meet an emergency through activity of the sympathetic system.

HYPOTHESIS OF CHARACTERISTIC AUTONOMIC BALANCE

With the preceding outline picture before us, we are ready to consider an important hypothesis concerning the relation of the autonomic system to personality. This is the hypothesis that each person has a characteristic status of balance or imbalance between the sympathetic and parasympathetic branches of his autonomic nervous system.[32]

This hypothesis has received considerable attention, particularly from Wenger.[33] Wenger applied a large number of various physiological tests that were believed to offer promise of indicating individual differences along a continuum of autonomic balance. He intercorrelated the tests, using scores from samples of young children and also of young men in aviation-cadet training in the Army Air Forces during World War II, and subjected the intercorrelations to factor analysis in each group. The tests were administered to each person individually while he was in a state of relative rest. Table 6.1 lists many of the tests, with reliability coefficients from retesting after an interval of one day and after an interval of three to four months.[34]

It can be seen from the reliability estimates that, as a class, these tests are far from perfectly accurate as measures of individual differences. There is much functional fluctuation involved, as we should expect. Rate of breathing seems not to be at all constant as a personal characteristic. As we shall see in Chapter 14, a factor of autonomic balance has been found, but only a few of these tests proved to be indicators of it. Some tests proved to be indicators of other factors, such as a thyroid-function factor and a blood-sugar factor.

THE GALVANIC SKIN RESPONSE (GSR) AS A TRAIT INDICATOR

The GSR gives a measure of electrical conductance of the skin (usually of the palm of the hand or fingers) in response to some abrupt stimulus or threat of such a stimulus. It has been a favored technique used in the study of emotional behavior. There seems to be some agreement that it indicates the level of wakefulness or vigilance of the individual at the moment. Those who accept the activation theory of emotion, which regards emotional behavior as primarily behavior at a high level of wakefulness, would recognize the GSR as an indicator of emotion in this

[32] Eppinger (1917).   [34] Wenger (1948).
[33] Wenger (1941, 1942, 1943a, 1948).

sense.[35] It would not tell us what kind of emotional behavior occurs, but how much.

It has been found significant to relate the GSR to emotional development in the child. The GSR has been reported to occur in children as young as three months.[36] In children of nursery school age, there is a negative relationship between the extent of the GSR and the amount of emotional reaction overtly observed. That is, the child who shows more of the one shows less of the other. In each child, there is a common tendency for reduction of overt expression and an increase of the GSR as he matures. This may be interpreted as a shift of emphasis from outward to inward activity under stress. The social environment often frowns upon overt or "childish" expressions and rewards inhibition of them. The organic reactions, such as the GSR, cannot be voluntarily inhibited by direct effort, hence they are not brought under control as the overt expressions are.

There are individual differences in this kind of development. Jones (1950) concludes that there are three types of children in this respect. The types and their characteristic behavior traits are as follows:

Externalizers: Show infantile overt responses and low GSR
  Traits: Excitable, irritable, impulsive, irresponsible, "show-off," bossy, and tense
Internalizers: Show inhibited overt responses and high GSR
  Traits: Deliberate, good-natured, cooperative, responsible, constant in mood, less talkative, less assertive, less animated, less attention-seeking
Generalizers: Show strong positive correlation between the two kinds of responses

It may be that, without systematic training in control of overt expressive behavior, the generalizer type would prevail. The other types may be a joint product of innate emotional disposition toward general emotional responsiveness and the degrees and kinds of training imposed upon them.

As personality dimensions, these types are evidently syndromes high in the hierarchy of traits, provided that empirical research verifies the hypothesis of coherent unities. The Jones type hypotheses have an interesting implication for the use of the GSR as a score variable. If he is correct, a high (or low) score means something quite different in terms of behavior traits when it appears in the internalizer (or externalizer) or in the generalizer types. One would perhaps want to note the combi-

35 Lindsley (1951, pp. 504–508).
36 Jones (1950).

nation of GSR score and the characteristic degree of overt expression shown by the individual.

From the standpoint of methodology, two procedures have been developed for group testing of the amount of palmar sweat. One uses chemically treated paper that is held by the fingertips.[37] The amount of perspiration occurring in a given time can be measured by the darkness of the paper as evaluated by means of a photoelectric cell. The other method uses a bag of crystals held in the hand for a given time interval.[38] The changed color of the crystals indicates the amount of response. This procedure has been used with military troops who were undergoing maneuvers.

MEASURES OF MUSCULAR TENSION

There has been considerable interest in the hypothesis that individuals have characteristic levels of muscular tonus or tension and that this has widespread relations to behavior traits. Many ingenious techniques have been developed for indicating level of muscular tensions, and some of these have been applied to the act of handwriting. The pressure of the writing pencil on the paper has been one common measure. The degree of squeeze exerted on the writing pencil has been another. Some investigators have used the extent of the patellar or knee-jerk reflex as a more general indicator of muscular tension. Still others have sampled muscular tension at various places by taking measures of action currents (electrical activity) of the muscles, such a record being known as an *electromyogram*.[39]

It has been very difficult to establish a trait of general muscular tension, based upon characteristic tensions of the skeletal muscles. Measurements of tension in one muscle group cannot be taken as representative of those in other groups.[40] If the measurements are taken in connection with stimulated action, it is found that the tension depends upon many circumstances in the stimulating situation.[41] Better results have been obtained in connection with autonomic-system responses connected with respiration and circulation, but it is not certain that the trait thus indicated should be known as a "muscular" tension (see Chapter 14).

37 Gladstone (1953).
38 McCleary (1953).
39 Davis (1942).
40 Wenger (1943).
41 Davis et al. (1955).

It has been found that of all muscle-tension measures used, that from the frontalis muscle is most valid for discriminating between psychoneurotic patients and controls.[42] The frontalis-tension score was also found to be correlated with motor irregularities such as fidgeting and tremors. It may be that the brow, because of the frowning reaction, is the focus of tensions going with mental troubles.

PATTERNS OF AUTONOMIC FUNCTIONING

In recent years, some novel views of characteristic autonomic functioning of individuals have arisen from the work of Lacey and his associates.[43] Their work has emphasized reactions of individuals under conditions of stress. Women subjects who were pregnant and hence under some degree of stress were put under a mildly stressful situation by being given a test that emphasized speed of verbal responses. Several autonomic reactions were recorded during this episode.

The significant finding was that each person showed her own characteristic pattern of autonomic reactions in repetitions of the situation. Some reacted relatively more strongly in terms of the GSR, others in terms of systolic blood pressure, and others in some other respects. The rank order of change in each of the functions measured differed from person to person but remained relatively consistent in the same person at different times. This finding helps to account for the relatively low correlations of the various autonomic-function measures commonly found in samples of individuals. In a larger sample of boys and girls aged six to eighteen, results of the same kind were found. The profiles of standard scores for the functions differed from person to person but were rather consistent from time to time in the same person. The retest correlations of individual profiles varied from .43 to .78.[44]

The implication of the work of Lacey and his associates for personality are interesting. The patterns of autonomic responses suggest a type approach to the description of individuals with regard to autonomic functions. It may be more profitable, therefore, to attempt to correlate the type categories, if there are such distinct syndrome types, with behavior traits than to correlate variables (single autonomic tests) with behavior traits. Another aspect would be the amount of variability in a profile. Are individuals who are more uniform in their autonomic reactions of various kinds different from those who show greater variability?

Still another aspect of autonomic responses has been found to be a

[42] Malmo and Smith (1955).
[43] Lacey (1950); Lacey and van Lehn (1952); Lacey et al. (1953).
[44] Lacey and van Lehn (1952).

somewhat stable aspect of individuals. This is a kind of variability score. Continuous recordings of both palmar skin resistance and of heart rate over periods of 15 minutes show arrhythmic fluctuations.[45] Some individuals show very little variability of each kind while others show a great deal, but there is little correlation between the two. The amount of variability of either kind observed during a state of rest has been found to be correlated with behavior in simple reactions. The less-stable individuals tend to have shorter reaction times, to react wrongly to similar stimuli, and to maintain their readiness to react for a slightly longer interval. The general picture is one of greater readiness to make a simple motor reaction. This does not necessarily mean that the less-stable person is generally more impulsive.

General Evaluation of Physiological Methods

The measures of physiological functions are unique among those of human attributes. This is true not only because the techniques themselves differ so much from morphological measures on the one hand and psychological measures on the other but also because of the uncertain status of physiological traits as enduring variables.

RELIABILITY OF PHYSIOLOGICAL MEASURES

From examples of reliability estimates given in Table 6.1, we see that personal consistency in physiological-test scores over a period of time is likely to be relatively low. Even a test such as that for visual acuity does not show as high reliability as might be expected, considering the fact that prescriptions for correction of vision are based upon them, as are decisions concerning medical fitness of applicants. Reliability estimates (retest) for five different methods of testing visual acuity ranged from .80 to .88 for distant viewing (20 feet) and from .71 to .85 for near viewing (12 inches).[46] Medical diagnoses and prescriptions of treatment are based upon measures such as those listed in Table 6.1. It is by no means suggested that these practices be discontinued. The human values that follow from them are definitely sufficient to justify their use. This information concerning reliability of physiological tests, however, should help us to adopt more realistic standards with regard to the use of scores from psychological tests of similar levels of reliability.

The generally low reliabilities and the findings of Lacey and others regarding patterns of physiological measures should lead us to reconsider the conception of physiological traits. Is it meaningful to apply the dimensional model of personality to individual differences in physio-

---

[45] Lacey and Lacey (1957).   [46] Sulzman et al. (1947).

Table 6.1

Physiological tests used experimentally in studies of the hypothesis
of a unitary autonomic-balance trait (Data from Wenger, 1948)

Test	Reliability after 1 day	Reliability after 3–4 months
Salivary output	.88	.85
Salivary pH concentration	.47	.82
Systolic blood pressure	.74	.33
Diastolic blood pressure	.67	.33
Pulse pressure	.64	.44
Heart period	.73	.66
Sinus arrhythmia	.25	.45
Sublingual temperature	.11	.28
Finger temperature	.61	.73
Respiration period	.22	.11
Respiration variability	.64	.28
Oxygen consumption	.57	.10
Lymphocytes in blood	.30	.48
White-cell blood count	.36	.05
Blood sugar	.65	.68
Skin conductance (volar)	.67	.27
Skin conductance (palmar)	.70	.57
Log conductance change	.65	.70
Pupillary diameter	.71	.64

logical functioning? Where such dimensions have been demonstrated by
correlational methods, the inference has to be that any one measure is
usually a somewhat unstable indicator of that variable, or it is an indicator
of a trait that is itself unstable, that is, exhibits a great amount of functional fluctuation. To a large extent, these indicators reflect the determiners that have previously in this volume been called temporary organic
conditions.

VALIDITY OF PHYSIOLOGICAL MEASURES

The validity of physiological tests for measuring individuals on underlying physiological dimensions was touched upon in the preceding paragraph. The degree to which each score indicates trait positions of this
sort is limited by the low reliability of the scores.

As for the validity of physiological tests for indicating behavior traits,
the situation is either relatively hopeful or relatively pessimistic, depending upon one's frame of reference. As compared with morphological tests,
physiological tests stand some chance of making a contribution in this

regard. This is the hopeful aspect. For example, there are the findings of Slater (1944) and Eysenck (1947) that tests of visual acuity and of night vision have substantial correlations (as high as .60) with neuroticism. Although the connection between those physiological measures and neuroticism is somewhat incidental, neither trait involved being a definitive component of the neurotic disposition, the correlations indicate much predictive power and hence validity in this sense.

Wenger (1948) reports correlations in the range of .2 to .3 between scores for the autonomic-dominance factor and scores from inventories for various temperament factors. These are more typical of the correlations reported between physiological measures and behavior-trait measures. They should be compared with typical correlations in the range .0 to .2 between morphological and behavior traits. While this does not offer much promise of general use of physiological measures for the assessment of behavior traits, it does add to the interest in the study of relationships of these two kinds of traits in the total structure of personality.

SUMMARY

Methods of assessment of personality can be roughly classified as objective or subjective. If subjective, they provide information more or less colored by the person's view of himself or by the views of him held by others. Some methods are more analytical than others and provide multiple measures; other methods are global, with an emphasis on personality organization.

In evaluating a method, reliability and validity of the measures are important considerations. Reliability pertains to accuracy of measurements, which depends upon the consistency with which both the method and the individual function. A coefficient of reliability may be obtained by intercorrelating part scores from the same instrument, scores from two alternate forms of the instrument, or scores from retesting. When a time interval is involved, functional fluctuation of traits reduces reliability. Validity pertains to the meaningfulness, relevance, or predictive value of the measures. Validity coefficients indicate how well scores measure a given trait or factor or how well we can predict behavior from them.

Both morphological and physiological measurements are of interest in the assessment of personality. They help to describe the aspects of personality that they were designed to measure. They have been regarded hopefully as possible indirect indicators of behavior traits. The study of their relationships to behavior-trait measures provides some basis for describing personality structure.

Some discredited morphological methods, such as phrenology, physiognomy, and chirognomy, like other invalid methods for assessment of behavior traits, continue to have some appeal among the uninformed, largely because of the plausible, ambiguous, and flattering personality sketches provided as a consequence of their use.

The types of Kretschmer and the components of Sheldon and their corresponding temperamental categories fail to live up to the early promises indicated by the work of these investigators, either as ways of describing morphology or as ways of describing temperament. Better variables for the description of physique are needed.

Morphological measures are generally among the most reliable, but as indicators of behavior traits, their validity is so low as to be expressed usually by correlations in the region of .0 to .2. In spite of these low relationships, there should be interest in the study of their interplay in development of personality, as would be predicted, for example, from the Adler hypothesis regarding physical defects, inferiority feelings, and compensatory behavior.

Physiological variables that have been studied in connection with personality include the chemical properties of the body fluids, including the hormones. Functions of the central nervous system that have been particularly examined in the study of individual differences include sensory powers, the electroencephalogram (EEG), bilateral brain control of handedness and smiling, and asymmetry of the face.

Autonomic–nervous-system functions have been studied a great deal in connection with the hypothesis of a dimension of sympathetic-parasympathetic dominance level, in connection with which a large number of tests have been developed or adopted. Certain tests have received special study in their own right, including the galvanic skin response (GSR) and tests of muscular tension. There is some evidence that attention should be given to the patterning of scores from some of the tests of autonomic functions and to variabilities of scores rather than to single scores or to composite-score variables.

Scores from physiological tests are usually relatively low in reliability, largely owing to the great amount of functional fluctuation that they reflect. To a large extent, they obviously reflect temporary organic conditions. To the extent that they reflect relatively permanent dispositions, we may speak of physiological traits. In spite of their low reliabilities, physiological tests show more promise of correlating with behavior-trait measures than do morphological tests, as we should logically expect.

Chapter 7

OBSERVATIONAL METHODS, RATINGS, INTERVIEWS

SEVERAL METHODS of assessing personality rest in some way upon direct observation of behavior, with consequent judgments given by the observers—self-observers and others. The judgments may be recorded immediately after the observations have been made or some time later. There may have been intention on the part of the observer to look for certain trait indicators or there may not. Whatever the method or approach, the picture of a personality is formed from the observations of the person himself or of one or more other observers. We shall consider rating methods first, since they are also commonly used in conjunction with direct-observation and interview methods.

RATING METHODS

Rating methods come closest to the common everyday practice in which one person, by some acquaintance with another, arrives at conclusions about some of his trait positions. The judgment is likely to be one of two extremes: the person is regarded as either bright or dull, ignorant or informed, exciting or boring, honest or dishonest. Only when the observer begins to compare two or more individuals or when he is forced by circumstances to make finer distinctions on a scale is he likely to do so. Then he recognizes the appropriateness of speaking of more or less of some quality. He is on the way to a judgment that has numerical properties. In employment practices, or other circumstances in which evaluations of persons are common, he may be called upon to rate his fellows. The serious use of ratings for technological and even for scientific purposes has called for considerable investigation into the whole method and for attempts at refinement of procedures.

141

A Bit of History of Rating Methods

Rating scales were used in the evaluation of certain physical variables, such as temperature, wind velocity, and humidity, before appropriate measuring instruments became available. It is commonly believed that Sir Francis Galton, in his studies of imagery and other personal qualities, was the chief initiator of the use of rating scales in evaluating human traits.[1] Galton's interest was in the investigation of heredity. We are reminded, however, that long before Galton's use of ratings a group of people in Indiana who called themselves the New Harmony Colony were using ratings of traits in a surprisingly sophisticated manner.[2] One of the chief interests of the Colony was the improvement of personalities. In this connection, they made ratings of such traits as judgment, imagination, reflection, memory, perception, excitability, courage, and strength.

Some Common Types of Scales

It is not the purpose of this chapter to give a complete account of rating techniques of all kinds. We are concerned more with general principles, with common errors, and with how acceptable ratings may be obtained.[3] The types of scales to be mentioned include: *numerical, graphic, check-list, forced-choice,* and *sociometric* methods. Evaluative statements will be generally withheld until later.

NUMERICAL RATING SCALES

In numerical rating scales the rater is to assign to each person a numerical value for each trait. The numerical values may be defined in verbal terms or they may not. An example of the type with defined numbers is as follows:

How serious-minded is he?

7 Takes everything as if it were a matter of life and death
6 Ordinarily serious and conscientious about things
5 Slightly on the serious, conscientious side
4 Neither serious nor unconcerned
3 Slightly on the relaxed and unconcerned side
2 Ordinarily unconcerned and carefree
1 Seems not to have a care in the world

GRAPHIC RATING SCALES

An example of a graphic scale is given in Figure 7.1. It is to be particularly noted that the judgment is given by making a mark on a

---

[1] Galton (1908).
[2] First reported in 1828; see Ellson and Ellson (1953).
[3] For a more detailed treatment of rating methods see Guilford (1954).

line rather than by stating a number. In this particular form, one trait is given an entire page, which makes possible a ready comparison of the persons rated in a particular trait. By the use of an ordinary linear rule, the numerical value of each rating can be determined to as small a unit as one desires and as one feels justified in using.

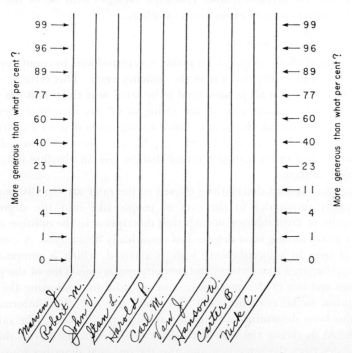

Fig. 7.1 Example of a form of graphic rating scale. The rater puts a mark on a vertical line for each person rated. The percentages are spaced so as to encourage the rater to give a distribution approaching the normal form.

CHECK-LIST RATING SCALES

In one of their studies of character, Hartshorne and May (1929) wanted to obtain ratings of children with respect to generosity vs. selfishness, the judgments being made by the children's classmates and teachers. This was done by using a list of 80 trait names, some favorable and some unfavorable, relating to the aspect of character under investigation. Examples of the terms used are: obliging, thoughtful, unselfish, stingy, cruel, and inconsiderate. The rater was instructed to check every word that he thought applied to each child. The "good," omitted, and "bad" traits checked by the raters were given scoring weights of +1, 0, and −1, respectively. The total score was the algebraic sum of the weights.

This procedure is somewhat reminiscent of the administration of a battery of tests, such as those in the Stanford Revision of the Binet scale, in which each test is scored as passed or failed. A check-list rating form in this sense approaches a form of behavior test. If the items in a check list were in the form of descriptive statements or questions regarding behavior, the form would then resemble a personality inventory. Like the personality inventory, also, check-list ratings could be in the form of self-evaluations or of evaluations of others.

FORCED-CHOICE RATING SCALES

The forced-choice principle in rating was introduced to counteract the general bias in ratings known as the leniency error. This error is sometimes so serious that all persons tend to be rated near the top of the scale, as has been commonly true in the rating of officers in military service. The basic feature of the forced-choice rating method is to require the rater to choose between two favorable qualities or between two unfavorable ones when rating someone rather than to give an absolute judgment on either of them.

The pairs of trait descriptions offered to the rater are equally popular or equally unpopular in the eyes of people like him—the degree of popularity or favorableness of each trait description in the opinion of the rater's group having been determined empirically beforehand. A common type of item in a forced-choice scale is a tetrad, which is composed of two popular trait descriptions and two unpopular ones. One of the popular ones and one of the unpopular ones are valid for indicating the trait dimension to be evaluated, but the others are not. This information has also been determined in advance from empirical data. The rater is instructed to choose the one of the four qualities in the tetrad that he thinks describes the ratee best and also the one that describes him least. The rater may very well know which qualities are popular or unpopular, but he is less likely to know which ones are valid.

In scoring the rater's selections, each valid favorable quality adds one point; each valid unfavorable quality deducts one point; and each invalid quality counts zero. An example of a tetrad, with scoring weights (which, of course, the rater is not given), follows:

-1　Puts on airs
　0　Gabby
$+1$　Punctual
　0　Precise

From the weights, we know that in predicting the criterion or in getting the proper evaluation of a person for some particular purpose, the quality of being "gabby" or "precise" does not matter. We also know that "putting on airs" is an unfavorable attribute and "punctual" a favorable one and that both are valid. We also know that the rater's group regards putting on airs and being gabby as about equally unfavorable and being punctual and being precise as about equally favorable, conclusions that have been predetermined by an experimental trial of the elements in the tetrad. Other tetrads would also appear in the rating form.

In brief evaluation of the forced-choice rating procedure, it might be said that it has not reduced the leniency error to any great extent. This might mean that in general the raters are sufficiently intelligent or informed to sense which qualities are valid as well as which ones are favorable. It has been found that raters can bias the final scores obtained from their judgments, either in the upward or downward direction.[4] Forced-choice ratings tend to be unpopular with raters, who sometimes resent having to make the restricted choices and to say something "bad" about the ratee when they do not believe this is justified.[5]

SOCIOMETRIC RATINGS

Sociometric ratings are used primarily to indicate the popularity of a person among his fellows in a group. With modifications, they may be used to measure other qualities as well. A typical example of sociometric ratings is to ask each child in a classroom to name one, two, or more in his group whom he likes best in some respect, for example, to sit next to, to pal with, or to room with. He may also be asked to rank those whom he names. The procedure naturally works best in groups that have been together for some time.

Common Systematic Errors in Ratings

We cannot evaluate rating methods in general without being aware of the many kinds of error that are involved. We shall now consider some of the main sources of error briefly and note their general effects. We shall also learn something about human nature by seeing how raters go wrong in judging themselves and others.

ERROR OF GENERAL RATER BIAS

Some raters are recognized as lenient raters, rating themselves or others too high on the average, and others are recognized as "hard" raters, rating too low on the average. The extent and direction of a rater's constant error can be determined by comparing the ratings he gives with those given by the average person. It has been found that raters are rather consistent in errors of this kind.[6] "Hard" raters, for example, tend to

---

[4] Highland and Berkshire (1951); Lovell and Haner (1955).

[5] Further discussion of some consequences of the forced-choice technique will be found in Chap. 9.

[6] Dubin et al. (1954).

be hard on themselves also, and to be less confident than others, as well as more conservative generally.[7]

It is generally expected that when raters know that their ratings will affect the status of those whom they rate, they will err on the favorable side. It has been reported that, on the whole, female raters are less lenient than men.[8] Some raters have been found to underrate themselves systematically,[9] but there are more who overrate themselves, as we should expect. So long as we have the same rater or raters judging the same ratees on the same traits, the leniency error need not cause much concern, except for the poor discrimination of ratees at the high ends of the scales. When we want to compare ratings from different sources, however, we encounter the disturbing effects of these general biases.

RATER-RATEE INTERACTION ERROR

The rater-ratee interaction error means that a particular rater tends to rate a particular ratee similarly on all traits. If the rater has a generally favorable impression, he rates the ratee high in most respects; if he has a generally unfavorable impression, he rates him low in most respects. This kind of error has been commonly called the *halo effect* or halo error. Since there are negative halos as well as positive ones, the more general name for the error seems preferable.

Examples of rater-ratee interaction errors are not hard to find. Some instances will be mentioned.[10] In one study, teachers rated different traits of children whom they also selected to represent three defined groups with respect to levels of intelligence and conduct. Seven per cent were selected as being "extremely mentally retarded" (actually their median IQ was about 90, so they may have been underrated for intelligence because of low halos). The teachers attributed very few favorable qualities to this group but many unfavorable ones, such as "lacking in aggressiveness" and "having few interests." The 0.74 per cent of the children who were designated as "geniuses" were rated as outstanding in every way. A group of children selected as "problem cases" were rarely described favorably in any way. Actually their achievement in school was adequate.

Some consequences of rater-ratee interaction errors may be mentioned. Since the rater tends to rate each person similarly in *all* traits rated, overrating some persons and underrating others, positive correlations, even substantial ones, are ensured between different rated traits. In one example of this, college women living together in the same dormitory

7 *Ibid.*
8 Hart and Olander (1924).
9 Shen (1925).
10 Lewis (1947).

rated one another for popularity and also for personal adjustment.[11] The correlation between the two traits, as rated, was .86. It is likely that if personal adjustment had been assessed in some independent manner, perhaps objectively, the correlation would have been much lower. It is likely that if the women had rated other traits, intercorrelations of the rated traits would also have been artificially inflated. Such correlations would be practically worthless for the purpose of studying the interrelationships of different traits.

Another consequence of halo errors is seen in connection with estimates of reliability of ratings. A common procedure for estimating reliability of ratings is to correlate the ratings from two raters (same trait, same sample of individuals) to determine the amount of interrater agreement. If two raters should happen to have the same halo biases with regard to the individuals rated, this circumstance would inflate the intercorrelations of ratings. Unless the raters have previously compared notes or unless they have very similar tastes regarding people whom they like and dislike, however, their biases are likely to be different, and this reduces their agreements. Thus, it is probably true that interrater agreements, and estimates or reliabilities of this kind, are usually reduced. Averaging the ratings from several raters also increases reliability because errors of halo tend to cancel out.

RATER-TRAIT INTERACTION ERROR

Murray (1938) has pointed out a "contrast" error in ratings. This is a tendency for a rater who is toward one extreme of a trait to rate others more toward the other extreme. For example, a person who is himself extremely orderly and meticulous may tend to see and to rate others as lacking in these qualities.

There is just as good reason to expect biases in the other direction, that is, a "similarity" error in rating. Consequently, we may speak of positive as well as negative rater-trait interaction errors. We often expect to find that others are like us in many respects. Landis (1936) found that tall raters tended to overrate the height of others; fat raters tended to overrate the weight of others; and emotionally unstable raters tended to overrate instability in others. The old saying that "misery loves company" perhaps applies in cases such as the latter. The Freudian mechanism of projection also applies here. We attribute to others the faults that we disown in ourselves. To give some further examples, it has been demonstrated that judges sometimes project their own insecurities into their clinical evaluations of others.[12] It has been found that individuals

---

[11] Powell (1948).
[12] Weingarten (1949).

high on the *F* scale, which was designed to measure an attitude known as authoritarian, tend to rate others in the same direction. Those low on the *F* scale, however, do not judge others too low.[13]

LOGICAL ERRORS IN RATINGS

The logical error is the tendency to rate similarly traits that seem to the rater to be logically similar or related. This may be caused by the rater's failure to discriminate the meanings of trait concepts. Or it may be because the rater has some fixed but faulty ideas concerning the structure of personality. In some instances, the effect may be in reverse. That is, the rater may think two traits are independent when actually they are not. The most disturbing result, as in the case of halo errors, is the inflation of intercorrelations of traits that are regarded as more similar or more related than they are. Probably the error in the reverse direction does not occur frequently enough to cause concern. In either case, however, we have another reason for rejecting intercorrelations of ratings as a basis for studying personality structure.

Prevention of Errors in Ratings

Rating errors can be reduced to some extent by the use of superior rating forms and procedures. Numerical rating scales are relatively more subject to biases than other forms. The forced-choice form has shown some promise of reducing the errors of leniency. The graphic form of scale is generally found to be an improvement over numerical forms, particularly in the format shown in Figure 7.1. The chief virtue of this format is that it calls for the rating of all persons in one trait before going to the next trait. This should tend to reduce halo errors, particularly. If a day's time elapses between traits, all halo effects may virtually disappear.[14]

Rating errors can also be reduced by training raters. Raters should be made aware of the different kinds of errors and should be advised as to how to avoid them. They should be given instruction regarding the meaning of trait names and other pertinent terms, and they should be given supervised practice, in connection with which their errors are found and pointed out to them.

An experiment can be cited [15] to show some results from rater training. Two graduate students were asked to rate 38 nursery school children on 15 traits. The raters compared notes after each four to six children had been rated. The amount of agreement for the first four ratees was 25 per cent; for the second four, 80 per cent; and for the next six, 86 per

[13] Crockett and Meidinger (1956).
[14] Johnson and Vidulich (1956).
[15] King et al. (1952).

cent. Agreement means reliability of the interrater type. It does not, of course, ensure validity, but there is the possibility that validity may be increased also.

We might expect that longer acquaintance between rater and ratee would provide a third way of improving ratings, since this would offer more opportunity for making observations. Longer acquaintance may have limited value, as shown by one study.[16] In an officer candidate school, students rated one another at intervals. It was found that the ratings obtained after five days of acquaintance were about as good as any obtained later. This may mean that convictions regarding acquaintances "harden" in a relatively short time, or it may mean that there is little new information to be gained in a somewhat standardized situation after the first few days.

Who Are Good Raters?

Another way to improve ratings, of course, is to select good raters, if there is any basis for such a selection. There is a popular idea that there are good and poor judges of human nature. Expressed in more scientific form, this means that there is a general ability to judge personality. We shall examine this hypothesis and bring together the conclusions from many research studies that bear on this problem.

HOW CAN WE DETERMINE THE GOOD RATER?

The way to find out how good a person is at a task is to try him out on it along with others. Several procedures have been used for determining whether one judge of personality traits is consistently better than another. One procedure is to give a test of ability to read facial expressions. This task is a very limited one, of course, and we could not justifiably generalize very far from the results.

Another procedure that has been more popular is to have the same judges rate the same people in the same traits. How nearly "correct" is each judge? The quotation marks are justified by the fact that we have no good criterion of correct ratings. The average ratings from a number of judges are usually employed as criteria. For all we know, however, the judges might all be wrong in the same direction, reflecting common biases, and any particular judge who differs from the consensus might actually be more nearly right than the pooled judgments. The scores from such a "test" would therefore mean something about the particular ratee's conformity to group opinion rather than his ability to judge personality.

A third method of attempting to measure the good judge of others is to have the examinee answer questions of a personality inventory in a

---

[16] Hollander (1956).

way he thinks others would answer them. The score is based upon the number of agreements with the other person's answers. The "other" might be one person whom the rater knows or whom he has seen in some action, or it might be a specified group of persons. This procedure is regarded as a test of ability to predict behavior of others, or as a test of *empathy*. The task is actually somewhat ambiguous because predicting what a person will do and what he says he does may be two different things. The method is full of pitfalls, as a number of investigators have pointed out.[17] Usually, the person whose behavior is predicted cannot be the same for everybody, hence the test differs from examinee to examinee. The similarity of the examinee's traits with those of the person he predicts is also to be considered. Scores of examinees are thus not comparable for several reasons.

IS THERE A GENERAL TRAIT OF ABILITY TO JUDGE OTHERS?

From the generally positive, but low, intercorrelations among scores of judging ability, there is a little evidence for belief in a general factor, which would be confirmation of the popular notion. In a study with adolescent girls, Wedeck (1947) concluded that there is a common factor or ability of psychological perception. This was more strongly indicated by tests of judging emotional expressions than by rating tests. In general, there is some tendency for similar tests of these kinds to intercorrelate more strongly than others, although the strongest correlations average only about .30.[18]

Vernon (1933) concluded that different abilities seem to apply to accuracy in rating one's self, in rating acquaintances, and in rating strangers, differences that we shall consider later. The most appropriate conclusion to draw at present is that if there is a generalized ability to judge people, it is a poorly organized trait in most individuals. It appears for the most part that abilities of this kind are specific, depending upon many circumstances, such as the combination of rater and ratee, the kind of judgment required, and the information available.

CONDITIONS UPON WHICH GOOD JUDGMENTS DEPEND

Numerous studies have shown under what conditions ratings seem to be more accurate, in the sense of consistency with some criterion. Because the criterion is often to be questioned and because the tests of accuracy have been made on somewhat limited bases, it is uncertain how much we can generalize from the results of those studies. Each conclusion that is drawn has its limitations but should be of some interest.

The age of the rater has received some attention. We should expect

[17] Gage (1952); Hastorf and Bender (1952).
[18] Taft (1955).

that ability to judge, in either a general or a specific sense, would increase with age. This has been found in tests of judging facial expressions [19] and in empathy tests in which each child estimated how well he was liked by others.[20] Children have been known to give ratings that are fairly dependable.[21] How far the development in these respects continues to go is hard to say, but Allport (1937) asserts that adults past the age of 30 are generally superior to those who are younger.

Many studies have been made comparing males and females with respect to abilities to judge others. Quite generally, it is found that female judges are either as good or better than males.[22]

Some investigators find that judges from higher socioeconomic levels are superior.[23] It can be questioned whether this would still be true if intelligence were held constant. Taft (1955) did not find the relationship to hold among graduate students, who were presumably of more nearly equal intelligence but also, perhaps, of narrower range in socioeconomic level. Students from a rural background did have some disadvantages.[24] Older children in a family and children from small families tend to do better than other children.[25] This may be because the former have more contact with adults.

There seems to be no doubt of a positive correlation between ability to judge persons and intelligence of the judge. Correlations typically in the range .3 to .4 have been reported. These findings apply to judgments of an analytical type (trait by trait) and not to global judgments.[26]

The effects of training in psychology upon ability to judge people should be of considerable interest. Early courses in the subject were found to provide no noticeable advantage in judging facial expression.[27] Graduate students in psychology have some advantages [28] in judging people, but graduate students in physical sciences do better,[29] and students in experimental psychology do better than those in clinical psychology.[30] Psychiatrists and social workers share the clinical psychologist's disadvantage.[31] One can question the appropriateness or validity of the tests, of course. It is possible that the clinician's mode of understanding others is something quite different from the kind of performance required by the tests. There is a kind of nonverbal communication between clinician and his client that perhaps does not lend itself to expression in verbal form, which is what ratings require. Other hypotheses

[19] Gates (1923); Walton (1936).
[20] Dymond et al. (1952).
[21] See, for example, Hartshorne and May (1928, 1929) and Amatora (1956).
[22] Taft (1955).
[23] Sweet (1929).
[24] Taft (1950).
[25] Taft (1955).
[26] *Ibid.*

[27] Buzby (1924); Hanks (1936).
[28] Polansky (1941); Luft (1950).
[29] Luft (1950).
[30] *Ibid.*
[31] *Ibid.*

are that the clinical student is himself less well adjusted or that he is too concerned with social relations to be a good observer. The reasons for the clinician's relatively poor showing are not obvious from the information available.

A number of miscellaneous conditions have been suggested as favorable or unfavorable for obtaining good judgments of people. One is that the good judge ranks a little higher in artistic sensitivity; at least he has made higher scores in art-judgment tests.[32] This may be because of his interests in observation and his learned skills in this direction. The emotionally stable are said to be better judges than the emotionally unstable. This should not be surprising, particularly if to be unstable also means to be self-centered.

A few other favorable conditions for good ratings have been mentioned. A good judge is popular with others.[33] A good rater is interested in his task and has a background similar to that of those whom he rates.[34] A good rater, says Allport (1937) is himself hard to judge. Allport attributes this to the "complexity" of the individual's personality. It might mean instead that he is less sociable and hence does not expose himself as much as others do.

There are some qualities that are particularly favorable for accurate rating of one's self. The good judge of self is highly intelligent,[35] emotionally adjusted, and sociable.[36] The good adjustment gives him freedom to become aware of his own weaknesses; and the sociability gives him the views that many others have of him. The good self-judge is also said to have a good sense of humor [37] and not to be conceited.[38]

Some qualities are said to be especially pertinent to good judgments of others. High intelligence is apparently not as important as it is in judging one's self. Probably a minimum level is necessary. It also appears that the intelligence of the rater should not be too far from that of the ratee. The good judge of others is less sociable; he is the detached observer. He has good self-insight, particularly with regard to his own weaknesses.

General Evaluation of Rating Methods

Common errors and biases in ratings, and some of their consequences, have already been discussed, with incidental judgments being passed on some kinds of rating scales as we came to them. We now need to consider the common questions concerning reliability and validity of ratings.

---

[32] Vernon (1933).
[33] Taft (1955).
[34] Conrad (1933).
[35] Adams (1927); Jackson (1929); Vernon (1933).
[36] Adams (1927); Vernon (1933).
[37] Allport (1937).
[38] Jackson (1929).

RELIABILITY OF RATINGS

In view of the great many types of scales, the great variety of persons who rate, the great variety of traits assessed by ratings, and the many other conditions that affect ratings, it is difficult to make universally applicable statements regarding the reliability of ratings. We must also consider two general operations by which reliability of ratings is estimated: the rerate procedure and the interrater-consistency procedure. The former indicates consistency of ratings over periods of time, and the latter indicates consistency over different raters.

The stability of ratings made by the same raters of the same ratees over a lapse of time depends upon a number of things. There is the functional fluctuation of the trait or traits concerned. There are changes in the trait indicators used; that is, the rater remembers and forgets information, and new information comes into the picture. There may be changes in the rater's conception of the trait or traits and changes in the group with whom the ratee is compared, and there is memory of ratings previously given. Some of these influences help to give an impression of stability, others of instability. Everything considered, we may say that the typical rerate correlations (if any can be said to be typical) are in the range .7 to .8, with many lying outside that range.

In an estimation of reliability from the other main approach, many conditions also affect the size of interrater correlations. One of these is the difference in information available to different raters. A study of ratings of nursery school children illustrates this very well.[39] Four children were rated on 15 traits by two raters. One rater had previously interviewed the mothers of two of the children, and the other rater had interviewed the mothers of the other two children. In rating other groups of children without prior contact with mothers, the agreement between the two raters was evaluated at 87 per cent. When only one rater had interviewed mothers, the agreement was only 58 per cent.

There are other differences, even when raters have much the same information available. There are differences in definitions of traits, in the indicators selected and used, and in the weighting of those used. Some of the common systematic errors discussed above contribute to unreliability because the biases are usually not similar for different raters.

Interrater agreement varies all the way from correlations of zero up to something above .9. If there are typical reliability coefficients for this kind of estimate, they are probably in the range of .5 to .6, when one rater's ratings are correlated with one other rater's. When two or more raters' ratings are summed or averaged, the correlations between sums or aver-

[39] King et al. (1952).

ages are higher, owing to some cancellation of errors. One readily controllable condition that can be used to increase the reliability of ratings, therefore, is to utilize more raters. Since there is a law of diminishing returns, however, the use of more than three to five raters in combination ordinarily adds very little to reliability.

VALIDITY OF RATINGS

Reliability estimates of ratings tell us whether we are measuring anything consistently. Validity estimates tell us whether we are measuring what we think we are or whether we can predict anything of importance from the ratings. If we have reliability without validity, we are not assessing what we want to assess. Ratings might be almost perfectly reliable and yet miss the mark. Too often an investigator or other user of ratings is lulled into a feeling of false security. Because he has some ratings of acceptably high reliability, he therefore takes validity for granted. The validity of ratings of behavior traits should rarely be taken for granted. It is never entirely safe to do so.

The process of validation of ratings has never been a very satisfactory operation. A good criterion of what we are trying to assess with the ratings is lacking; otherwise we should probably not be bothering with ratings. In gaining some insight into what it is the ratings of different raters indicate, intercorrelations of rating variables (traits rated) with one another and with other measures and a factor analysis are often very illuminating. It was previously stated that, owing to the many systematic biases involved, ratings are poor material for intercorrelation studies, including factor analysis. This statement is true when the objective is to learn more about traits, but it is not true when we want to learn more about the ratings at hand.

In one study, different teachers rated the same pupils on 12 traits.[40] A factor analysis was done for each teacher, and it was concluded that the teachers were emphasizing the same underlying traits (much less than 12 in number) but that each teacher had her own conceptions of the traits and therefore weighted things differently. In a study of ratings of pictures on the backs of playing cards, certain raters were instructed to evaluate them in terms of color effects, design, and appropriateness of theme.[41] The analysis showed quite different determiners of the judgments. Observers were apparently rating in different terms, including a liking for pictures of romance and adventure, simplicity of design, delicacy or femininity, preference for wealth, luxury, and display, and love for the outdoors.

In an unpublished study, a large group of military officers were

[40] Richards and Ellington (1942).
[41] Guilford and Holley (1949).

rated on several traits, all differently defined and all believed to be important in creative performance. The ratings were made by psychologists after much observation of the officers. The officers had also taken a number of tests of these traits and also other traits. A factor analysis showed that there was a large coloring in most of the ratings, no matter what the defined trait, that could be interpreted as indicating the ability known as expressional fluency, an ability to produce connected verbal discourse. A good hypothesis would be that an overt sign that was both observable and impressive was how well the officer expressed himself. This might account for the apparent coloring of the ratings in several traits with relation to expressional fluency. We might say that this trait was the source of a halo that several raters held in common for each man.

There have been a number of experimental studies on the role of irrelevant cues in ratings. The effect of irrelevant cues, of course, is to reduce validity of ratings. Such cues as the wearing of spectacles or smiling in a photograph were found to make significant differences.[42] Faces with spectacles were rated higher in intelligence, dependability, and industriousness. There may be a positive correlation between wearing spectacles and intelligence score in the general population, but such a relationship was not found among college students. Smiling faces were rated higher in sense of humor, kindliness, and honesty. The same faces had been shown with and without the smile.

Another study demonstrates how irrelevant cues from traits of physiognomy are apparently selected and used by raters.[43] Students rated 24 photographs of saleswomen on behavior traits and also on traits of physiognomy (qualities of eyes, mouth, lips, skin, etc.). The interrater reliability for behavior-trait ratings is indicated by an average coefficient of .52, that for traits of physiognomy, .86. The most revealing correlations are those between the two kinds of traits. Judgments of high moral character tended to go with bright eyes and widened eyes, judgments of low character with bow-shaped lips. Social acceptability was associated with smooth skin, smiling mouth, and being well-groomed. A "gold-digger syndrome" was indicated, for which the cues were a combination of high eyebrows, bowed lips, tilted head, and narrowed eyes. Sexuality was often attributed to the women with relaxed mouth, beauty, thick lips, and much lipstick. The reflection of common stereotypes is obvious.

Lipstick played a special role in another experiment.[44] Six male students interviewed six female students with and without lipstick for 10 minutes each and rated each on 22 traits. There was no indication that the men noticed the difference in presence or absence of lipstick. Girls without lipstick were rated more serious, talkative, and conscientious.

42 Thornton (1943, 1944).   44 McKeachie (1952).
43 Secord and Muthard (1953).

Girls with lipstick were rated more relaxed and more interested in the opposite sex.

These few examples are enough to show that the *meaning* of ratings, i.e., traits that they measure, may be seriously biased away from the trait that we want them to measure. A rater often feels frustrated because he lacks the information he would like to have or he does not know how to use and to weight the information that he has or remembers. It is when decisions come close to guesswork, especially, that irrelevant cues have their greatest influence. In desperation, sometimes, irrelevant information is used, more often unintentionally than intentionally. Whatever the reasons for these biases, they are present, and the result is that ratings are not what they seem. They are affected by errors to an extent not fully indicated by reliability estimates.

The general conclusion to be drawn from the remarks on evaluation of ratings is that we should use ratings only when we do not have and cannot have something better. If we do use them, we should learn all that we can about their accuracy and their meanings.

DIRECT-OBSERVATION METHODS

General Nature of Observational Methods

The direct-observation methods take some steps in the direction of experimental controls. Comparisons with rating methods, as the latter are usually carried out, will show this. Evaluations of traits in persons are usually made on the spot, while observing behavior, or immediately afterwards, whereas ordinary ratings usually depend upon incidental observations and on the memory of the rater. Direct observations are made for definite purposes, whereas ordinary ratings are made on the basis of behavior casually observed, probably with no intention at the time of making systematic evaluations. Direct observations are made in selected situations, because it is believed that the kind of trait indicators one wants to see will thus be forthcoming; ordinary ratings are made on the basis of behavior in incidental situations, which may or may not present observable trait indicators.

Direct observations can be made in situations that are somewhat controlled, as in a school playground, and the general situation can be roughly replicated and the observations repeated. The direct-observation methods therefore have a quasi-experimental nature and yet permit the behavior to take place in a generally natural way. The evaluations with which the investigator emerges are usually in the form of ratings, but the basic information on which those ratings are based would seem to be better than that underlying ordinary ratings.

Types of Direct-Observation Methods

Three general types of direct-observation methods are recognized: *time sampling, incident sampling,* and *controlled diary.*

THE TIME-SAMPLING METHODS

In time-sampling methods, each person is observed at selected time periods. The length of time period may be as short as a few seconds or as long as several hours, depending upon the type of behavior observed, the purpose of the observations, and the number of observations wanted. The distribution of the time periods is also quite varied. They might all occur on the same day or they might extend over periods of months, even years, depending partly on whether there is an emphasis on development.

The things observed and recorded might be merely in terms of the presence or absence of some response or pattern of action, or there may be a quantitative rating of the actions observed, or of some aspects of them. The initial record is expected to stay close to reports of actual behavior. Ratings of traits are properly regarded as inferences, which should be made from inspection of the record.[45]

INCIDENT-SAMPLING METHODS

In incident-sampling methods, certain instances of selected behavior, rather than behavior in selected situations, are observed and recorded. Thus, the report might be a mother's notes on every episode in which her young child cries or pouts, or refuses to eat, and so on. The report includes some statement of the kind of situation and of the probable precipitating stimulus in that situation. The response is described, and its intensity and duration are recorded, as are any notable aftereffects of the response. Another example of this method would be that of the nursery school teacher who jots down incidents noticed for each child during the school day.[46]

THE CONTROLLED-DIARY METHOD

The individual himself, if old enough and intelligent enough, may keep records of his own behavior of selected categories, such as a record of anger responses. This type of daily record may be kept over a period of time, but the self-observer must be exceptionally devoted to science or he will fail conscientiously to keep a complete record. It has been said that in three studies, the frequency of anger responses reported decreased

[45] See Arrington (1943) for a more complete treatment of these procedures.
[46] See Landreth (1940) for further details on this procedure.

progressively over a seven-day period.[47] It did not matter on what day of the week the reporting started. Possibly, the self-reporters changed their standards of what constitutes an anger response, or it may be that the acts of observing and reporting themselves contributed to a reduction of the tendency to anger. Reporting other kinds of behavior would possibly not show the same kind of systematic changes. The observers may also have lost enthusiasm for the study and become less conscientious. Such possibilities must be considered in evaluating the method and in deciding how much confidence to place in it.

Evaluation of Direct-Observation Methods

Although the direct-observation methods have some of the good features of experimental method, they fall short in some respects. They emphasize immediate recording of behavior events whenever possible; furthermore, they provide for somewhat standardized situations that can, in some sense, be repeated, and the observer is set to look for these behavior events. These procedures fall short of experimental methods, of course, because the situation is not fully controlled nor are stimuli systematically varied. Stimuli are not present or absent or varied in some direction at the will of the experimenter. The chief advantage over experimental methods is in the naturalness of the situation in which the behavior occurs. Such situations may be difficult to reproduce in the laboratory.

RELIABILITY OF DIRECT-OBSERVATION RESULTS

The results of direct-observation procedures are in the form of records of behavior (trait indicators) and of interpretations (traits) or evaluations (trait positions). The question of reliability, then, can apply either to reports of behavior or to trait evaluations or ratings.

With respect to reports of behavior, we also have a double question. On the one hand there is the question of agreement among observers who see the same behavior. Will they see the same things? Will their records coincide? In both the time-sampling and incident-sampling methods, typical agreement between observers is usually well above 90 per cent.[48]

On the question of how consistent the child is in his behavior, the picture of reliability is very different. Will the child cry a similar number of times every day? Will he get into fights regularly? Will he play by himself on all occasions? The variability of the typical child in the *frequency* of such behavior is considerable. For crying behavior, correlations of incidence in two halves of the same observation period were .01 to .10.[49]

---

[47] Anastasi (1948).
[48] Landreth (1940).

When the correlation was between lengths of crying spells in two periods, the coefficient was higher, namely, .24.

In a kindergarten group, the same kinds of behavior were recorded as had been recorded a year earlier in nursery school.[50] Some of the actions observed were laughter, talking to self, and use of material. The correlations indicating consistency of different behaviors ranged from −.11 to +.58, with an average of .37. Because the sample was composed of only 11 children, the results are not at all decisive.

These results indicate that children are not very consistent in specific behaviors. A large part of the inconsistency can be attributed to the fact that specific actions are determined largely by situations, and the situations in these studies had not been fully controlled. Trait assessments, had they been obtained, would no doubt show higher levels of consistency.

VALIDITY OF DIRECT-OBSERVATION ASSESSMENTS

From several factor-analytical studies, we have evidence that assessments of traits based upon direct observations of behavior have validity.[51] These studies show that certain behaviors, when observed over a sufficient period of time, are indicators of underlying general traits. For example, a trait of hypersensitiveness was indicated by such behavior as pouting, sulking, poor compliance, and attacking other children not openly but indirectly.

One instance concerning the practical validity of direct-observation methods can be reported in connection with the selection of pilot students.[52] The examinees were observed for about 15 minutes in groups of four while waiting to take a test. The situation was a social one, with the men permitted to talk. The walls of the room were well supplied with pictures pertaining to aviation. The psychologist observer made notes of each person's behavior, from which he predicted likelihood of graduating from pilot training. In two large samples, the correlations with actual passing vs. failing in flying training were .10 and .21. This would hardly be considered a sufficiently accurate prediction for practical purposes of selection.

GENERAL CONCLUSIONS

The direct-observation methods are very time-consuming, usually requiring the time of highly trained, professional personnel, and yield limited information regarding traits for the effort. Experimental methods or behavior tests should be substituted wherever possible. The best

[50] Jersild (1933).
[51] For example, the studies by Koch (1934, 1942).
[52] Guilford and Lacey (1947).

use of the observation methods would be in field studies, for example, in the home of the child. They might well be used as a basis for obtaining ratings, if ratings must be used.

INTERVIEW METHODS

Judging from the frequency with which interviews are used, they represent one of the most popular of all methods of assessment of personality. It seems that rarely is there selection of employees without interviews of some kind at some point in the process. This is true in industry and in civil service jurisdictions. Interviews are repeatedly used in clinical practice as steps in diagnosis and therapy. The clinical use of interviews is too large a subject to be treated here. We shall confine our interests to those interviews whose aim is to arrive at evaluations of persons with respect to traits in vocational or research situations.

Types of Interviews

The kind of interview given will depend upon its purpose and the preferences of the interviewer. Some interviews are *standardized* and some are *unstandardized*. Recently, there have also been some special developments in interviewing called the *stress interview* and the *exhaustive interview*.

THE UNSTANDARDIZED INTERVIEW

The unstandardized interview resembles an ordinary conversation between two people. Often used in the process of selecting employees, the interview is permitted to go in different directions depending to some extent upon the applicant. This is in contrast to the standardized interview in which the same questions are somehow brought into the conversation for every applicant.

Two advantages are often pointed out for the unstandardized interview. Being more casual, it is more natural. Consequently, the interviewee is expected to be more at ease and more like himself; he will resort less to role playing. Furthermore, since there is freedom and time to steer the conversation, the interviewer has a chance to follow up promising leads that arise. Pursuing the conversation in these directions may bring out significant facts.

Disadvantages sometimes mentioned stress the fact that each interviewee faces a different situation, and it is thus more difficult to compare interviewees on an equitable basis. Such a situation also biases the sampling of traits that will be brought out and the ones that will be concealed, for it leaves things somewhat under the control of the interviewee, who, if he so desires, may steer the conversation toward his stronger points and away from his weaker ones.

THE STANDARDIZED INTERVIEW

The amount of standardization of an interview can actually vary a great deal. In the extreme case, the interviewer may ask a fixed list of questions and say little more. In the more liberal case, although he makes sure that certain questions are asked, he may bring in many others. It is possible to use standard forms for recording replies and observations of behavior. Rating forms are sometimes used in conjunction with the interview as a means of summarizing the information obtained. There may also be a standard introductory statement intended to give all interviewees a similar mental set for what follows. In both this and the unstandardized interview, the conversation may be completely recorded for later study or reexamination.

In general, the advantages for the standardized interview are the weaknesses of the unstandardized variety, and vice versa. The standardized form provides all interviewees with a similar situation. We cannot, of course, say that it is identical, but the sampling of behavior will be much the same for all interviewees. Comparisons of individuals are on a fairer basis and information is obtained concerning essentially the same traits in all cases.

The situation faced by the interviewee is somewhat unnatural, but in either form of interview, he cannot escape knowing that he is being interviewed. If just enough time is allowed for asking the set questions, opportunities will be missed for ferreting out some promising bits of information. Except for the need of interviewing on a sort of production-line basis, however, extra time can be allotted for this if it is sufficiently important.

THE STRESS INTERVIEW

The stress interview was introduced to determine how well an individual can keep command of his resources when he is emotionally excited and also to determine how quickly he recovers after the pressure is off.[53] In a somewhat typical application of this procedure, the interviewee appears before a board of three to five interviewers. There may be one or two concealed observers who keep notes and other records.

The interview starts with conversation in a completely friendly manner. The interviewee is instructed to do a performance test in the presence of the board. The test presents a task that becomes rather complicated.

[53] Freeman and Manson (1942).

At the completion of the test, the interviewee is told his score with an expression of surprise that it is so low (regardless of what it is). The whole atmosphere changes to cool disdain for the interviewee, with obvious hints that he will be eliminated if possible.

The interviewee is told to try the test again. This time electric shocks are applied to him, also other distractors. But when finished this time, he is told that he has done much better and the atmosphere becomes friendly again. The interviewee is then told to recall any earlier comments and questions, which is actually a way of giving a memory test. He is then dismissed and ratings are made on various traits. The effectiveness of this kind of interview will be mentioned later in comparison with other kinds, when they are all evaluated.

THE EXHAUSTIVE INTERVIEW

The exhaustive interview is a very long, protracted affair usually given in one continuous sitting. There may be changing interviewers, who keep the interviewee talking without much relief. The purpose is to wear out his defenses, to catch him in inconsistencies, and to see through any façade he may have put on at the beginning. In some respects, this interview resembles the third-degree treatment given to criminal suspects. It has been used in the selection of high-ranking personnel, such as executives.

Evaluation of Interview Methods

Interviews that are intended to provide information regarding trait positions of individuals can, and should, be evaluated on the same basis as any other method that achieves the same kind of end result. As usual, the criteria of effectiveness in this evaluation are reliability and validity of the products of assessment.

RELIABILITY OF INTERVIEW RATINGS

The problems and procedures in estimating reliability of interview results are essentially the same as for ratings of any kind. Intercorrelations of interviewers are used much more commonly than correlations from reinterviewing or rerating by the same interviewer. Rerating can be done best when the interview has been recorded. In the correlation of interviewers' ratings, there is a difference between the case in which the interviews are independent and that in which two or more raters observe the same interview. We should expect higher agreement in the latter case, since the information available is more nearly the same for all observers.

Results show that when the interviews are independent, the correlations between interviewers are likely to be in the range of .4 to .5. An average of .4 has been reported for ratings of different traits.[54] When the interviewers were a vice president, five superintendents, and a director of industrial research, the average intercorrelation was .46.[55] The reliability estimate for a short psychiatric interview was .39.[56] For a civil service interview, intercorrelations ranged from .03 to .41.[57] Larger correlations can be found in the literature on interviewing, but in those cases the ratings were usually based upon additional information from sources such as biographical data, test scores, or both.

When interviewers observe the same interview, the ratings show somewhat more agreement. In a stress interview of police officers under civil service examining, the correlations were .33 to .86.[58] In a nonstress interview of police officers, the range was .53 to .68.[59] In interviews of students who had the prospect of appointments to jobs, the obtained correlations were .40 to .73.[60] These results seem to indicate that under these conditions, the amount of agreement between two members of a pair of interviewers is typically in the range .5 to .6. This is about the same as for ratings in general.

VALIDITY OF INTERVIEW RATINGS

There is much more information on validity of interview assessments than on reliability. This is as it should be, since the meaningfulness and utility of interview evaluations are more important. Two interviewers or raters may disagree very much regarding the worth of an individual, yet each can be right in his own way; the ratings of either can still predict some complex criterion of performance. A combination of two such evaluations can be very worthwhile because there is little redundancy in the information they provide.

In many studies of validity of interview ratings, it is difficult to know how much predictive value to attribute to the interview alone and how much to other sources of information. So often, the rating is made with information of other kinds also available. For example, in one study of the rating of college students for intelligence, the rater had given a 20- to 35-minute interview, preceding which, the student had filled out a detailed information sheet giving facts about himself.[61] The correla-

[54] Odbert (1934).

[55] Uhrbrock (1948).

[56] Bartlett (1950).

[57] Schneidman (1943). In this instance there was a change of interview method as well as interviewer.

[58] Freeman and Manson (1942).

[59] Fearing (1942).

[60] Bass (1951a).

[61] Hanna (1950).

tions of ratings with two college-aptitude tests (Ohio State University Examination and the American Council on Education Examination) were .66 and .71. The intercorrelation of the two tests was not much higher (.77).

The information sheet contained facts concerning membership in honorary societies, leadership activities, choice of hobbies, reading interests, and age of completing different grade levels. It would have been interesting to see how well the test scores could have been predicted from this information alone and also from the interview alone. Of course, since the interview could have elicited the same facts, it would have been possible to do perhaps as well with either source of information in this case. Scores on intelligence tests do correlate substantially with such items as were just cited.

In another study, academic success in college was predicted for 162 freshmen on the basis of tests and an interview.[62] Presumably these were two experimentally independent sources of information. The correlations without the interview information added were .57 and .73, for men and women separately; with the interview added, they were .56 and .73. The conclusion is that the interview information added nothing to that from tests in predicting college achievement.

In a third study of this kind, the entrance examinations were achievement tests.[63] The interview ratings were based also upon biographical information from a personal-data sheet. The criteria of achievement in college were intermediate- and final-examination scores. The interview scores correlated zero with the entrance examinations and essentially the same with the examination criteria.

Validity correlations between interview ratings and criteria of success on different jobs are quite varied, but some of them appear to be higher than those just mentioned for academic success. In a study of police officers,[64] a composite score from an interview correlated .53 with a composite rating for the same traits as shown on the job. Actually, this might be taken as a reliability estimate rather than a validity estimate. A similar correlation, involving a stress interview, gave a correlation of .34. In other words, an ordinary interview appears to be better than a stress interview for this purpose. A correlation of the same composites with ratings of over-all performance as a police officer were .74 (ordinary interview) and .33 (stress interview). Again the stress interview seems inferior to the nonstress form. This might be because some of the traits rated are best assessed when every interviewee is free to do his best. What

[62] Sarbin (1942).
[63] Himmelweit (1950); Himmelweit and Summerfield (1951).
[64] Freeman and Manson (1942).

the stress may do is simply to vary the situation for the interviewees and thus introduce errors of assessment.

Some extraordinary validity coefficients have been reported by Mc-Murray (1947) in employment situations in industry. He reports a correlation of .43 between interview assessments and the criterion of length of time workers remain with the company and correlations of .68 and .61 with rating evaluations of job performance. For truck drivers, he reports a correlation of .61 with a criterion of performance on the road. These figures stand very much by themselves; others are usually far from encouraging when the criteria are performances on jobs.

Interview methods have been tried extensively by those concerned with selection of aircraft pilots. In studies sponsored by the Civil Aeronautics Administration, interviews were commonly held by three-man boards. Typical correlations of ratings from these interviews and ratings of performance in flight school were reported to be in the range .28 to .46.[65] But it was also found that this information added nothing to the predictions that could be obtained from other, less expensive information.[66] After reviewing five years of research on the subject, Viteles (1945) concluded that even a reliable interview made only a slight contribution, considering the time, effort, and cost involved, and added little to information provided by much less expensive paper-and-pencil methods. This was largely because the significant biographical information that was effective could be obtained as readily in group testing as in personal interviews.

The investigations made by Army Air Force psychologists during World War II corroborated Viteles' conclusion. From a 50-minute interview, tried experimentally, two ratings were derived, one for self-confidence and one for general promise of success in flying training.[67] The validity coefficients of correlation with a pass-fail criterion were −.07 for the rating of self-confidence (in a sample of 293) and .06 and .13 for the rating of general promise in two similarly large samples. A Biographical Data Blank derived as a group test, on the other hand, proved to have a validity of .35 to .40.[68]

Interview methods have been used experimentally in an attempt to select successful clinical-psychology students and successful psychiatrists. In the former case, a five-year investigation of rather searching scope utilized many methods of assessment, including interviews.[69] The first interview lasted one hour and the second, two hours. The criterion to be predicted was derived from a week's observations in assessments of various kinds. The ratings made from interviews had some small corre-

[65] Kelly and Ewart (1942).   [68] *Ibid.*
[66] Dunlap and Wantman (1944).   [69] Tupes (1950).
[67] Guilford and Lacey (1947).

lations with the criterion measures but not enough to be of practical value, and they had no more validity than ratings obtained before the interviews. They added nothing to predictions that were possible from test scores for academic aptitudes and vocational interests.[70]

The interview ratings for psychiatrists were made at the time of their application for special advanced training.[71] The criterion was in the form of ratings of performance made by supervisors later. The validity coefficients for average ratings obtained in different years of the study ranged from −.06 to .41. Corresponding validities for scores from experimental tests ranged from .01 to .39. Validities for single interviewers ranged from −.17 to .62, with a median of .05. Assuming that the criterion itself was valid, these results do not appear to be very promising for either the interviews or the aptitude tests that were used.

Since we saw in the discussion of validity of ratings some evidence that the appearance of an individual may serve to provide irrelevant cues to the rating of traits, we may raise the question as to whether the same principle applies to ratings made from interviews. The interviewer sees the physical characteristics of his interviewee. Is he influenced by what he sees?

A study of this question was made in connection with the selection of pilot students in the Army Air Force.[72] Approximately 3,000 students were observed while they took group tests, during a total period lasting about six hours. Each man was rated by three proctors independently on "likelihood to succeed as a pilot," considering whether or not he had a "clean-cut" look. Two hypotheses were being tested. One was that during the medical interview, each man's rating (Adaptability Rating for Military Aeronautics, or ARMA) might be biased by his appearance. The other was that he might be passed or failed later in flying training in part because he "looked like an officer" or did not. The results decisively cleared the interviewers and the instructors and check pilots of suspicions of innocent duplicity of this sort. The correlation of the ratings of physical appearance with the ARMA was only .13, significant but trivial. The correlation with the pass-fail criterion in flying training was almost exactly zero.

GENERAL CONCLUSIONS

In spite of the generally discouraging showing for interviews when their results are placed under the close scrutiny of scientific examination, they will probably still continue to be used.[73] This is partly for lack of

70 Kelly and Fiske (1951).
71 Holt and Luborsky (1952).
72 Guilford and Lacey (1947).
73 As stated early in this section, no attempt will be made to cover clinical uses of

better methods of assessing persons and partly because interviews serve purposes other than that of trait evaluation. In the employment situation, for example, they indicate to the interviewee that there is some personal interest in him. They give the interviewer impressions as to appearance, voice, and social poise of a certain kind. Where such first impressions are important in employees, particularly those who make contacts with the public for the organization, such impressions are presumably worth assessing.

An interviewer can be deceived with regard to impressions gained from an interview, however. The person comes well groomed, but his room at home may be the ultimate in disorder. He is on his guard and puts on his best behavior. He may have considerable acting skill. On the other hand, some persons never appear at their best in an interview; they may actually appear at their worst. This may indicate emotional maladjustment, of course, which the interviewer might want to know about. On the other hand, it may be a purely situational maladjustment. For such a person, the evaluation of his other traits may be biased, as in the stress interview.

It should be quite clear from the studies cited above that where there is an alternative between assessing traits by means of tests and by interviews, the tests should have a decided preference. This is true for the obtaining of biographical data, a thing for which the interview has often been used, as well as for measurement of aptitudes, interests, and temperament traits.

In research, the interview should probably never be used to test a hypothesis. Its most defensible use is for exploratory observations for deriving hypotheses for investigation by better methods. Too often, the investigator himself interviews subjects and makes his own assessments in testing some hypothesis. We saw, for example, what probably happened, no doubt innocently, in the case of Sheldon's correlation of morphological and temperamental components (see Chapter 6). Similar questions of bias have been raised in connection with studies of the authoritarian personality.[74]

There are also dangers connected with the interview in unskilled hands. It has been pointed out that in industry the typical interviewer for employment and other purposes has had two years of high school education, has been previously employed as a clerk, and has had no special instruction or guidance in interview procedures.[75] It is very easy for an interviewer to develop a false feeling of infallibility and an overconfidence

---

interviews. Much of the information sought in clinical interviews pertains to traits at lower levels of generality than those emphasized here.

[74] Luchins (1950).

[75] Uhrbrock (1948).

in his own judgments. The main reason is that he rarely, perhaps never, becomes aware of his errors. We know that learning to do the right thing often depends upon knowing our errors. Without this feed-back, an interviewer receives only reinforcement from what he may regard as his clever intuitions. In this connection, the writer is reminded of an experienced university teacher who declared that he did not need an aptitude test or good examinations, because after looking over his 35 students during his first lecture, he could predict their final grades fairly closely. He may have been more nearly right than he knew!

SUMMARY

Observational methods, often terminating in judgments of fellow men, are very popular and natural. In the scientific and technological settings, they have been developed in various ways to yield estimates of trait positions for individuals. Whether the observations are made casually in the everyday setting, or with intention to observe selected attributes in a semicontrolled situation in which behavior occurs, or in consequence of a face-to-face conversation, the outcome is usually in terms of some kind of numerical description called a rating.

There is much variety in rating-scale forms—numerical, graphic, checklist, forced-choice, and sociometric methods. Most ratings are beset with several kinds of systematic errors—general rater bias (positive or negative), rater-ratee interaction (positive and negative halo), rater-trait interaction (similarity or contrast), and logical errors. Errors can be reduced by using good rating forms and by training raters.

Being a good judge both of self and of others appears to be more specific than it is general. Abilities to judge have been assessed by tests of judging emotional expressions, of accuracy of rating others, and of predicting behavior. A number of personal traits of the rater and conditions of ratings have been investigated in connection with accuracy of ratings.

Rerating consistency and interrater agreement are two forms of reliability of ratings. Neither is very high when only one rater is involved but both are higher when ratings from different observers are combined. Little is known concerning the validity of ordinary ratings, but there is much evidence concerning sources of irrelevant variance in them, suggesting the importance of careful study of the meaning of ratings by intercorrelational methods.

Direct observations are made in time-sampling procedures, incident sampling, and the controlled-diary method. Resulting descriptions of incidence of behavior are very low in reliability because behavior is multiply determined and situations are not sufficiently standardized.

Four kinds of interview are recognized—standardized, unstandardized, stress, and exhaustive. The first two have advantages and disadvantages that can be largely overcome by combining many of the best features of the two. The stress interview appears to be less reliable and valid than comparable nonstress interviews, probably because of its disrupting effects.

An ordinary interview has generally low reliability, with somewhat higher reliability when interviewers observe the same interview. Estimates of predictive validity range from zero to substantial correlation figures, but the usual finding is that ordinary interviews add nothing to prediction of either academic or job performance when there are suitable tests available.

Chapter 8

PERSONALITY INVENTORIES

OF ALL the testlike instruments for assessing nonaptitude traits of persons, the personality inventory has had the most widespread use, at least in the United States. This is so in spite of the severe criticisms, sometimes very bitter, that have been leveled against personality inventories.[1] In order to evaluate these two circumstances, we shall examine the general principles of testing by means of inventories. We shall note some examples of inventories, emphasizing those that offer unique features, and we shall try to arrive at a balanced view.

General Nature of a Personality Inventory

The typical personality inventory asks the examinee to answer direct questions concerning himself and his opinions. The questions may refer to such things as his habits, his feelings, his worries, or his preferences. The opinions may refer to almost anything. The items are often put in the form of affirmative statements rather than questions. If statements, they may be worded in the first-person pronoun, in the second, or even in the third person. There are usually only two or three alternative answers, such as "yes" vs. "no," "true" vs. "false," or "agree" vs. "disagree." A third, or middle, category may be "?," "uncertain," or "cannot say."

Examples of items of the different forms follow:

Do you require less sleep than the average person?

I require less sleep than the average person.

You require less sleep than the average person.

S requires less sleep than the average person.

The use of the third-person pronoun is advantageous when the inventory is to be filled out by one person concerning another person, as in marital counseling where husband and wife do this for one another as well as for themselves.

[1] See particularly Whyte (1954); also Ellis (1946).

Responses are scored on a point basis, with a certain response being given a value of +1 if it is in the direction indicating a high degree of the quality being assessed, and 0 if it is not. Weighted scoring is also sometimes used, with, for example, weights of +1, 0, and −1 in cases where there are three alternative responses, or perhaps with 2, 1, and 0, or 4, 2, and 1. Scoring weights are usually determined by various experimental and statistical methods, to be described briefly later. The weights need not be the same for every item. The larger the range of weights for an item, the better it has been found to be as an indicator and the more it contributes to individual differences in total scores.

DEVELOPMENT OF THE INVENTORY

Origin of the Personality Inventory

The initiation of the inventory method is appropriately attributed to R. S. Woodworth, who developed it during World War I. The story is told that in 1918, General Pershing, Commander-in-Chief of the United States Expeditionary Forces, cabled an urgent request for efforts to screen out the mentally unfit before sending them overseas.[2] Too many new arrivals developed mental disorders that not only disabled them but required the time and attention of other personnel.

Previously, the procedure for such screening had been interviews given by psychiatric interviewers, but there were not enough interviewers. Woodworth, with A. T. Poffenberger, hit upon the idea of giving every man an "interview" by asking him, through printed materials, the kinds of questions that would have been asked by psychiatrists. The list of questions contained the common symptoms associated with mental disorders. The score was the number of symptoms the man reported having. The instrument, known as the Woodworth Personal Data Sheet,[3] was later reported to be very effective in military use.

Thus, in view of its origin, the inventory should be regarded as a form of interview, although less personal than a face-to-face interview. It is a group interview rather than an individual one. In a sense, we could also regard an inventory as a kind of check list. Superficially, we could say that the examinee rates himself on a two- or three-point scale on every item.

In another sense, however, an inventory is like an objective behavior test, and some users so regard it. Each statement or question has been found by experience to discriminate individuals high on the trait continuum from those low on the continuum. As with items in a test of

[2] Zubin (1948).
[3] Woodworth (1920).

ability, an examinee's responses indicate the direction of his position. Although the scoring is completely objective, with predetermined weights, there are certain differences between inventory-type items and aptitude-type items that we shall be concerned about later. These differences preclude the acceptance of an inventory as a completely objective behavior test.

Subsequent Development of Inventories

A few links between the early Woodworth inventory and present-day inventories are of interest. The original emphasis upon general personal adjustment vs. maladjustment has persisted, but there has been a growing tendency toward multiple scoring and the measurement of traits, some of which cannot be said to have much bearing upon decisions regarding personal adjustment.

Donald Laird took the first step in the direction indicated. His Colgate Mental Hygiene Test, part B2, contained items on psychoneurotic tendencies and was designed to detect those persons who needed application of mental-hygiene procedures.[4] Part C2 was designed to measure an assumed trait of introversion-extraversion. Following shortly, there appeared the A-S Reaction Study, by G. W. Allport and F. H. Allport, for the measurement of an assumed trait of ascendance-submission.[5] L. L. Thurstone and Thelma G. Thurstone developed at the University of Chicago the Thurstone Personality Schedule, which was composed of the Woodworth items and many additional ones and was designed to detect those students who needed psychiatric attention.[6]

Hugh Bell developed a more analytical instrument for the assessment of personal adjustment. He found that the Thurstones' items could be grouped logically according to adjustment to home life, to social life, and to personal health, and he developed an inventory that was later scored also for emotional adjustment.[7] Bell recognized that this would give pictures of the person's degree of adjustment in these different directions as the person himself sees things, but it has been found that the scores also agree with impressions of others who are in positions to observe these kinds of adjustment.[8]

EXAMPLES OF INVENTORIES IN CURRENT USE

Of the many inventories that might be mentioned, only a few can be treated here because of lack of space. The selection is based partly on

[4] Laird (1925).
[5] Allport and Allport (1928).
[6] Thurstone and Thurstone (1929).

[7] Bell (1939).
[8] Pederson (1940).

popularity of use and partly on the fact that the inventories illustrate some principles of theory or method.

The Bernreuter Personality Inventory

The Bernreuter *Personality Inventory* (often to be referred to as the BPI) was the first to gain very wide appeal.[9] It was designed to be a general-purpose instrument, indicating degree of maladjustment as well as positions on other trait variables.

Bernreuter began its development with reasoning that went somewhat as follows. Behavior in a certain situation may be symptomatic of several traits. An item in an inventory is a stimulus situation. The same item can therefore be scored for more than one trait. Bernreuter's proposal was thus to let a limited number of items do the work of a much larger number by the economical device of giving each item scoring weights for more than one trait. We shall see later what price has to be paid for this economy.

DEVELOPMENT OF THE BPI

The description of the steps by which the BPI was developed will serve also to tell about some of the operations by which other inventories are produced. Bernreuter wanted an inventory that would measure the introversion-extraversion variable of the Laird C2 inventory, the ascendance-submission variable of the Allport A-S Reaction Study (Bernreuter called his own trait "dominance"), and the neurotic-tendency variable of the Thurstone Personality Schedule. Before beginning his development of the BPI, Bernreuter had hypothesized a trait that he called "self-sufficiency" and had developed an inventory of items for measuring it. This trait was also included in the BPI.

Combining the items from all four inventories, Bernreuter administered an experimental form to a group of students. For this purpose, a very large number of subjects is needed, preferably not less than 400. He scored the items from the four sources to give scores for the four traits that he wanted. His next step is known as an *item analysis*. In terms of operations, this means to correlate every item with each of the total scores. Every item that correlates sufficiently with a total score then becomes a candidate for indicating the trait that this total score represents. Scoring weights for measuring this trait are then determined for each of the alternative responses to this item. The same is done for all other traits. Four scoring keys were thus developed for the BPI. An example follows for one item, with scoring weights to be given the three responses for each scoring key: [10]

[9] Bernreuter (1933).

[10] Quoted through the courtesy of the author and Stanford University Press.

Item: Do you daydream frequently?

Scoring Scale

Response	N (Neurotic tendency)	I (Intro-version)	D (Domi-nance)	S (Self-sufficiency)
Yes	+5	+3	−1	+1
?	−2	0	+2	−2
No	−4	−4	+1	−1

The list of weights informs us that the response "yes" indicates neurotic tendency very strongly; it indicates introversion somewhat strongly; and it indicates lack of dominance and also self-sufficiency rather weakly. The response "no" indicates the opposite trends to about the same degree, as we should expect. The response "?" somewhat surprisingly indicates dominance. It has no bearing on introversion, and indicates some degree of freedom from neurotic tendency. Similar sets of weights would be seen for other items, differing in pattern, of course, from item to item. Some items would possibly not receive any weights for one or more of the scales.

SOME EVALUATION OF THE BPI

Split-half (internal-consistency) reliabilities are reported to be in the range from .77 to .88 and retest reliabilities in the range .65 to .92 with relatively short time intervals.[11] Retest reliabilities after one year were .70 to .77; after two years .56 to .74; and after three years .44 to .72.[12] These reliability figures are somewhat typical for inventory scores in general and they indicate the need for retesting at intervals to bring information regarding these traits up to date for individuals.

Numerous validation studies have been made with the BPI in connection with the prediction of behavior of different kinds, many of the results of which have been summarized by Super (1942). Only a sampling of the results can be mentioned here. It can be said that the BPI has shown some ability to discriminate between pathological and normal groups and to discriminate among different pathological groups, but not to the extent that would make the inventory routinely useful for these purposes. It has shown little or no ability to discriminate between groups with behavior problems and other groups. It is now generally recognized that individuals with behavior problems differ in personality make-up

[11] Super (1942).
[12] Farnsworth (1938c).

from neurotic individuals. The BPI was designed to discriminate the latter.

Students with certain kinds of personal problems have been successfully discriminated. Students who earn at least a part of their living were found to be more self-sufficient and more dominant than others.[13] Student leaders were found to differ from others in the same direction.[14] Individuals with good marital adjustment have been found to score lower on introversion and neurotic tendency than those with poor adjustment. In terms of vocational and personnel selection, reports indicate that the BPI shows some discrimination between successful and unsuccessful YWCA secretaries,[15] teachers,[16] and bank employees.[17]

INTERCORRELATIONS OF THE BPI SCORES

Although the multiple scoring of items is a great step toward economy of effort, it also tends to defeat one of the goals of multiple scoring. The unfortunate effect of multiple scoring of items is to bring about high intercorrelations among some of the scores. The BPI scores N (neurotic tendency) and I (introversion) tend to correlate in the range .90 to .95. This indicates that the two measure essentially the same psychological variable, hence there is almost complete redundancy, and one score would do in place of two. The score for D (dominance) correlates about $-.8$ with the score for N and about $-.7$ with the score for I.

The three traits, as such, are probably not nearly as strongly correlated as these figures indicate. The coefficients of correlation are inflated because of similar scoring weights and the use of the same responses as the basis for two or more scores. Two total scores thus contain many irrelevant components in common. Reference to the weights presented for the single item "Do you daydream frequently?" will show that the weights for N and I are very similar, and those for D lie in the opposite direction. If this situation applies to other items generally, the two keys for N and I would be very similar and they would be generally reversed to the key for D. There is thus not enough freedom for these scores to vary independently. Summing similar weights for two scores would naturally lead to similar totals.

The Humm-Wadsworth Temperament Scale

The Humm-Wadsworth Temperament Scale was developed on the basis of the Rosanoff theory of personality.[18] According to this theory, there are six variables, or *components,* of personality that can be found in

---

[13] Bloom (1936).
[14] Hunter and Jordan (1939).
[15] Anderson (1938).
[16] Super (1942).
[17] McMurray (1932).
[18] Humm and Wadsworth (1935).

normal persons and that stand out more clearly in varieties of abnormals. They are:

Schizoid, autistic: Tendency to inconsistencies, with wishful, daydreamy thinking

Schizoid, paranoic: Tendency to inconsistencies, with ideas of personal persecution and self-importance

Cycloid, manic: Instability of emotions with excited elation

Cycloid, depressed: Instability of emotions with retardation and pessimism

Hysteroid: With character defects bordering on criminal tendencies

Epileptoid: With transitory enthusiasms and inspirations

DEVELOPMENT OF THE H-W TEMPERAMENT SCALE

The H-W Temperament Scale is composed of items, each of which discriminates members of one or more of the pathological groups from a nonpathological population. Many preliminary items were administered in question form to a normal sample and to each of selected pathological samples, with one exception. The criterion group for the hysteroid extreme was composed of prison inmates, on the assumption that individuals suffering from hysteria, in Rosanoff's conception, are criminals at heart.[19] Each item was correlated with the dichotomies of autistic vs. normal, paranoid vs. normal, and so on for all six categories of pathology. Response weights were derived somewhat as Bernreuter did, the main difference being that for the H-W items there was validation of each item against *external* criteria whereas for the Bernreuter items the criteria were provisional scores from some of the same items.

A secondary score developed by Humm and Wadsworth is of special interest. It is known as the "no"-count score and represents the first attempt to derive information as to the probability of an examinee's being influenced by test-taking attitudes, such as trying to look more normal than he is. For most of the items in the H-W Scale, the response "yes" is the pathological one. If an examinee piles up an unusually large number of "no" responses he is suspected of attempting to bias his score in the direction of normality, thus the term "no"-count score. An unusually low "no"-count score would also be suspect, for it might represent a person who for some reason is trying to look worse than he is. There are such individuals. The authors of the H-W Scale recommend that the six scale scores of individuals with the most extreme "no"-count scores not be interpreted at all and that those with less extreme "no"-count scores have their scale scores adjusted. Others have found that this practice does not seem to be very helpful.[20]

[19] Rosanoff (1920).
[20] Arnold (1943); Meehl and Hathaway (1946).

SOME EVALUATION OF THE H-W SCALE

The pathological components that served as the basis for developing scoring keys for the H-W Temperament Scale are best regarded as syndrome types. There is much room for skepticism as to whether such syndromes apply to normal populations in a way that would justify placing normal persons on the same continua with those in the pathological categories.[21]

The authors of the H-W Scale have restricted its general use, having promoted its application in industries. There has consequently been little published research on it. Internal-consistency reliabilities of .67 to .92 have been reported.[22] The lower ones raise some question of the coherence of the items as indicators of unitary variables, e.g., for the epileptic scale.

Reports of studies of validity of the H-W Scale have given quite varied pictures. In one study, the Scale succeeded rather well in discriminating between two small, extreme groups, one of "trouble-makers" in an industry and the other of well-liked employees.[23] In another study, in which 405 white-collar workers were tested and then followed up nine years later, the H-W Scale failed to discriminate among those still employed, those resigning with no adverse record, and those dismissed or resigning while on probation.[24]

One study reported that in a hospital for the insane, the Scale discriminated patients from normal controls only on the normal and the cycloid scores, and only the latter gave scores that agreed with the diagnoses given by psychiatrists.[25] Another study reported that the Scale was almost worthless for diagnosing pathological groups.[26]

There are a few reports of the success of the H-W Scale in predicting performance in employment situations. There is one report of some discrimination between successful and unsuccessful police officers.[27] Unfortunately, the predictions were made on the basis of a combination of the H-W scores and the civil service aptitude-test scores, and it is difficult to say how much of the discrimination should be attributed to each of these two sources.

In the selection of pilot students in the Army Air Force, two scores— hysteroid and paranoid—correlated with passing in flying training to the

[21] See Chaps. 2 and 18 for further discussion of this issue.
[22] Humm and Wadsworth (1935); Dysinger (1939).
[23] Dorcus (1944).
[24] Gilliland and Newman (1953).
[25] Reed and Wittman (1942). The "normal" score is based upon the number of nonpathological responses.
[26] Arnold (1943).
[27] Humm and Humm (1950).

extent of $-.2.$[28] This correlation is in the expected direction and shows about as much validity as any measure of temperament traits showed with the same criterion. A clinical judgment given each student from examination of his profile of H-W scores did not predict success at all.

The Minnesota Multiphasic Personality Inventory (MMPI)

The most widely used inventory in clinical practice is the MMPI, judging from the relative number of reported studies in which it has appeared. Like the Humm-Wadsworth inventory, the MMPI takes its scoring categories from pathological concepts, but it recognizes a larger number.

PURPOSES OF THE MMPI

The main purpose of the MMPI is to help diagnose individuals in the various Kraepelinian categories of pathology.[29] It was not expected that the score categories would represent pure traits or that they would represent discrete causal entities. It was recognized that most patients show mixtures of symptoms from different diagnostic categories. Nor was it expected that the scores would be highly stable over time, since symptoms of pathology come and go as a patient recovers or regresses. There seems to be an assumption that the pathological-category concepts apply also to the normal population. At least this is the implicit assumption of many investigators who use the MMPI for discriminating individuals within the normal population.

DEVELOPMENT OF THE MMPI

The following scoring categories, with brief descriptions, are the ones originally adopted and the ones most frequently used:

Hs. Hypochondriasis: Unwarranted concern with bodily health
D. Depression: Pessimism; low morale
Hy. Hysteria: Dodging duty or problems through physical symptoms
Pd. Psychopathic deviate: Behavior problems; delinquency
Pa. Paranoia: Suspicion and conceit
Pt. Psychasthenia: Beset with doubts, obsessions, and fears
Sc. Schizophrenia: Disorganized thinking and behavior
Ma. Hypomania: Pleasurable excitement
Mf. Masculinity-femininity: Masculinity of interests

As in the case of the H-W inventory, many preliminary items were analyzed by correlation with criteria, each of which was a dichotomy of

[28] Guilford and Lacey (1947).
[29] Hathaway and Meehl (1951a).

a pathological group versus a normal group.[30] The normal group was a large sample of about 500 students and hospital visitors. The pathological criterion groups varied in number from 20 to 50. These are unusually small samples for item-analysis purposes, 100 often being regarded as a safe minimum for such purposes. The results of item analysis were checked to some extent by doing some cross-validation studies, which, in this case, means trying out a scoring key on a new sample of pathological subjects to see whether it discriminates them from normals. The chief danger of error from a small sample in an item analysis is that it could, by chance, be biased in some direction irrelevant to the dimension of personality being selected for study.

THE VALIDATION KEYS

Four special, supplementary scoring keys were developed to give information as to test-taking attitudes and the biases that they may exert upon the basic scores. Three of these keys will be described.[31] An F score was based upon items to which extremely few individuals respond in one direction (true or false). Examples of such items would be:

Everything smells the same. (True)
I believe in obeying the law. (False)

A high F score is taken to mean one of several things: failure to understand instructions; failure to understand items; the examinee is trying to look bad; or carelessness.[32]

The L (lie) score is based upon responses to items that state socially worthy things that are rarely true of anyone. An example would be the response "true" to the item: "I have never taken anything that did not belong to me." A high L score is taken to mean willful falsification, but a low score is not necessarily interpreted as honesty. The L score seems to be a trap for the naïve but not for the sophisticated.

The K scale was designed for two purposes. One was to discriminate between the abnormal person whose scale scores appear to be normal and the genuinely normal. The other was to discriminate between the normal person whose scores appear to be abnormal and the genuinely abnormal. In other words, the K score was intended to detect those who "fake bad" as well as those who "fake good." Low K scores are also taken to mean that the examinee's defenses are down or that he is overly candid, "soul searching," or "self-exposing." It is claimed that this score has

[30] McKinley and Hathaway (1940, 1942, 1944); Hathaway and McKinley (1940, 1942, 1943).
[31] Meehl and Hathaway (1946).
[32] Hathaway and Meehl (1951a).

been useful in improving discrimination of individuals with borderline scale scores.[33] But others report that they find the K score to be of little use.[34]

There is one interesting use of the K score that illustrates a principle that may come to be more generally applied. The K score is sometimes used as a "suppressor" score. This means that the scores for the pathological categories can be modified slightly from knowledge of the K score, thus making some of those scores higher (more abnormal-looking) when K is high and lower (more normal-looking) when K is low.

NATURE AND USE OF THE MMPI

The MMPI is composed of 550 items that are affirmative statements to be answered by the alternatives "true," "false," and "cannot say." It can be administered individually, with each statement on a separate card, the examinee to sort the cards in three piles. This is a unique feature of the MMPI. The items are probably presented more often in the usual booklet form for group administration.

The raw scores are converted to a standard scale that has a mean of 50 and a standard deviation of 10, that is, the common T scale. A T score of 70 or higher in any scale is obtained only by the highest 2 per cent of the general population and hence is taken to indicate a suspicion of pathology. The highest score, even if it is less than 70, is also given attention. In clinical practice, the entire profile is often examined. As a result of experience, it is believed that the shape of the profile provides information that cannot be gained from separate scores. Certain types of profiles are more common among abnormals than among normals. An elaborate coding system has been worked out for the interpretation of profiles.[35]

SOME EVALUATION OF THE MMPI

As for most inventories, the reliabilities of scores from the MMPI are not so very high. Typical coefficients (split-half estimates of reliability) for total scores are in the range .7 to .9. Typical retest reliabilities seem to be in the range .6 to .8. Retesting would seem to be desirable to keep information regarding individuals up to date.

In examining briefly the evidence regarding the validity of the MMPI, we shall give attention first to its use in diagnosing pathology. This has a double meaning: the discrimination of abnormal from normal, and discrimination among categories of pathology for those who are abnormal.

---

[33] Meehl and Hathaway (1946).
[34] Schmidt (1948); Tyler and McMichaelis (1953).
[35] Hathaway and Meehl (1951b).

Meehl (1946) reports that when profiles from the MMPI were interpreted intuitively, about 10 per cent of the normal individuals were wrongly called abnormal whereas about two-thirds of abnormals were correctly so diagnosed in that broad category. Further than that, about two-thirds of the abnormals were correctly classified in the three broad categories of psychosis, psychoneurosis, and conduct disorder. Schmidt (1945) reports that in the study of army personnel, better than chance discriminations were found between normals on the one hand and constitutional psychopaths, neurotics, and psychotics on the other. There was thus some discrimination among major pathological groups.

In differentiating among more limited categories of pathology, the results have not been as satisfactory. In one study, there was significant agreement with the psychiatrist's diagnosis for three categories—psychopathic deviate, paranoia, and schizophrenia—but not for the other scale categories.[36] In another study, the usefulness of two of these same scales—psychopathic deviate and schizophrenic—was found.[37] Other investigators have reported some degree of differentiation.[38]

In evaluating this low degree of accuracy of diagnosis, we need to consider several things. In the first place, psychiatric diagnosis is notoriously uncertain.[39] Agreement among different diagnoses of the same patient is far from perfect. In part, this is because each pathological category itself is not clearly defined. This is particularly true within the broad class of schizophrenics.[40] As stated earlier, each pathological category is complex and irrelevant symptoms are mixed with relevant ones. This circumstance is sufficient to raise the question as to whether such diagnosed groups have been sufficiently valid for use in deriving scoring scales in the Humm-Wadsworth instrument as well as in the MMPI.

The MMPI was not intended for use in discriminating individuals on normal traits in the normal population, yet it has been used a great deal for this purpose. There are a number of studies that should have a serious bearing upon this practice, as well as upon the use of the Humm-Wadsworth inventory for the same purpose. These two inventories were administered to the same college students, and correlations were computed between five pairs of scores that clearly correspond in the two inventories.[41] The correlations ranged from −.05 to +.20 (the latter being between the manic and the hypomanic scores). In this sample, the scales were obviously not measuring the same components or traits. In a larger

[36] Benton and Probst (1946).
[37] Rubin (1948).
[38] Aaronson and Welch (1950); Wauck (1950).
[39] Ash (1949); Doering (1934); Elkin (1946).
[40] King (1954).
[41] Canning et al. (1950).

study with six groups of students, the correlations were much the same.[42] The average coefficients ranged from −.21 (for the paranoid scales in one group of students) to +.30 (for the depression scales in one group). Correlations of scores with student ratings (means of self-ratings and ratings by two others for each student) ranged from .07 to .45 for the H-W inventory and .03 to .33 for the MMPI in the same five score categories.

Both of these inventories were designed to discriminate pathological persons from normals, in various directions of pathology. The studies mentioned above are not crucial tests of validity of this sort for either inventory. Such results as were found in normal populations, however, raise some question as to whether the two inventories would make similar discriminations between normals and abnormals. If it is found that they do not, a somewhat facetious hypothesis would be that paranoids in California, for example, are not the same breed of pathology as paranoids in Minnesota. There is the possibility that in one of the two cases of inventory development, or in both, pathological samples may have been biased in different and perhaps somewhat irrelevant directions.

To return to the subject of using the MMPI in discriminating degrees of normal personality patterns, another study can be cited.[43] Interpretations of the MMPI profiles of individuals were paired with faked personality descriptions provided by the investigator. Students were unable to discriminate between the two descriptions of themselves above the chance level of success. Friends of the students failed to do any better. Quite apart from evidence on validity, the use of the MMPI (or the H-W inventory) for counseling purposes with normal individuals is found to be rather awkward, if not embarrassing, in view of the use of the pathological scoring concepts.

In some of the studies of practical validity for the MMPI scores, a few small relationships have been reported, particularly for predicting grades in college. Correlations near −.3 were reported for the scores of psychopathic deviate and hypomania. There were also indications that a combination of those scores, plus others, would add materially to predictions obtainable from aptitude scores alone.[44] In a medical class, scores for hysteria, psychopathic deviate, and schizophrenia discriminated somewhat between the highest and lowest quarters with respect to grades.[45] In a third study, students with higher L (lie) scores tended to obtain lower grades.[46] It was further reported, however, that experienced psychologists were unable to discriminate the profiles of passing and failing students.

42 Gilliland (1951).
43 Sundberg (1955).
44 Frick (1955, 1956).

45 Schofield (1953).
46 Hewer (1956).

Other studies of predictive validity have found completely negative results. This was true for the prediction of passing in pilot training in the Army Air Force [47] and for the prediction of teaching performance.[48]

The Guilford Factorial Inventories

The main objective of the Guilford inventories is to provide scores for separate factors or primary traits of personality. Several factor analyses served as starting points. In the first analysis, the hypothesis was tested that the symptomatic items designed to indicate the well-known, assumed dimension of introversion-extraversion actually represent more than one primary trait.[49] Later analyses tested similar hypotheses regarding other areas of temperament.[50] Most of the factors have been verified by other investigators.[51]

As information of this sort accumulated, three inventories—An Inventory of Factors STDCR, An Inventory of Factors GAMIN, and Personnel Inventory—were developed.[52] The selection and weighting of items was accomplished by the procedure of internal-consistency item analysis. That is, those items that had been found by factor analysis to indicate a primary trait, and others very similar to them, were first used to provide a preliminary score for the trait. Each of a large number of items was correlated with the preliminary scores to determine its use and its weights.

TRAITS OF THE THREE EARLY INVENTORIES

The traits for which there are scores in An Inventory of Factors STDCR, briefly identified, are:
S   Social introversion; seclusiveness
T   Thinking introversion; reflectiveness
D   Depression; unhappiness; pessimism
C   Cycloid disposition; emotional instability
R   Rhathymia; carefreeness; happy-go-lucky disposition
Traits *S, T,* and *R* may be regarded as three varieties of introversion-extraversion. The opposite pole of *R* may be identified as restraint or self-control. Traits *D* and *C,* taken together, probably account for a large part of the syndrome of neurotic tendency or emotional maladjustment.

The traits scored in the Inventory of Factors GAMIN are:
G   General drive for activity; energy

---

[47] Guilford and Lacey (1947).
[48] Tyler and McMichaelis (1949).
[49] Guilford and Guilford (1934, 1936, 1939a).
[50] Guilford and Guilford (1939b); also an unpublished study with D. W. Dysinger on items, including those in the Humm-Wadsworth inventory that are keyed for measuring the paranoid component.
[51] Mosier (1937); Layman (1940).
[52] Guilford (1940b); Guilford and Martin (1943a, 1943b).

A   Ascendance; social boldness
M   Masculinity (of emotions and interests)
I   Confidence vs. inferiority feelings
N   Composure; calmness vs. nervousness

Traits *I* and *N* are also probably important aspects of the general syndrome of neurotic tendency.

The traits scored in the Personnel Inventory are:

O   Objectivity vs. subjectivity or hypersensitivity
Ag   Agreeableness vs. generalized hostility; belligerence
Co   Cooperativeness (or tolerance) vs. faultfinding disposition

These factors grew out of the analysis of items originally designed to indicate the paranoid disposition. It is questionable whether they have genuine paranoid significance in the normal population, paranoid, that is, in the pathological sense.

THE GUILFORD-ZIMMERMAN TEMPERAMENT SURVEY (GZTS)

The GZTS was designed to cover in a single inventory most of the 13 traits of the three original inventories.[53] Another aim was to reduce or to avoid some of the higher intercorrelations found in the original ones. The highest intercorrelation had been between scores for traits *C* and *D*. Those two traits are therefore represented by a single score in the GZTS. The traits, with some slight changes in symbols and names, are:

G   General activity
R   Restraint vs. rhathymia
A   Ascendance
S   Sociability
E   Emotional stability (combination of *D* and *C*)
O   Objectivity
F   Friendliness (previously called "agreeableness")
T   Thoughtfulness (previously called "thinking introversion")
P   Personal relations (previously called "cooperativeness")
M   Masculinity (of emotions and interests)

Three validation scoring keys have been developed for use with the GZTS inventory.[54] A gross-falsification score is designed to detect the examinee who willfully attempts to make good scores. A subtle-falsification score is designed to detect the examinee who perhaps unwittingly achieves the same kind of result. A careless-deviancy score is designed to detect the examinee who responds in an erratic manner and shows this by giving an unusually large number of extremely rare responses.

[53] Guilford and Zimmerman (1949).
[54] Jacobs and Schlaff (1955).

SOME EVALUATION OF THE GUILFORD INVENTORIES

The split-half estimates of reliability of the scores from the three original inventories range from .80 to .94 and of scores from the GZTS, .75 to .87.

Some information is available to answer the question of whether the scores measure the traits they were designed to measure. The 13 scores from the original inventories correlate moderately with self-ratings and with ratings made by associates.[55] The ratings are of unknown validity and may well be less valid than the scores. A recent factor analysis involving a liberal sampling of all items in the three inventories provides a general verification of earlier conclusions regarding the nature of the factors and the kinds of items needed to measure them.[56]

Some indirect evidence of validity can be cited from a study of effects of a semistarvation diet.[57] After 24 days on a drastically reduced diet, the men made scores showing greater depression and nervousness, and lower sociability, emotional stability, ascendance, confidence, and general activity, in line with rather obvious symptoms. They showed no change in rhathymia and masculinity. The latter result might seem strange in view of the fact that there was marked loss of sex drive. This could mean that the item indicators of masculinity are more attributable to social learning than to biological condition. The score for the trait of rhathymia seemed to be immune to prolonged organic changes such as semistarvation.

Although these inventories were not designed for the purpose of discriminating abnormals from normals or of aiding in the diagnosis of pathological groups, there is some information in this connection, much of it in reasonable directions. Psychotics generally were found to be less sociable and less reflective.[58] Psychoneurotics were characterized by depression, emotional instability, and low rhathymia (overly self-controlled). Delinquents and psychopathic personalities were high on rhathymia, and schizophrenics and organic cases tended to be low on sociability.[59] The suggestion that there is a relation of the scores for *D* (depression) and *C* (cycloid) to neurotic tendency is supported by a correlation of the sum of the two with the Maudsley Medical Questionnaire equal to .88.[60] It is also reported that the *E* (emotionality score) from the GZTS has correlated .80 with the Bernreuter (BPI) score for neurotic tendency.[61]

In spite of these reasonable relationships, it would be premature to propose that patterns of the scores from these inventories might be used as aids in the diagnosis of pathology and of category of pathology. Al-

[55] Guilford and Martin (1944); Carroll (1952).
[56] Guilford and Zimmerman (1956).
[57] Keys et al. (1950).
[58] Steinberg and Wittman (1943).

[59] Wittman and Huffman (1945).
[60] Franks (1956).
[61] Gilbert (1950).

though it may be more reasonable to think that abnormals are more accurately described in terms of concepts that pertain to the normal population than to think that pathological concepts apply to normals, the relationship of normal traits to pathology is not entirely clear. A good hunch is that the essence of pathology involves much more. Pratt (1952) concludes, however, that scores for the factors *S, D, C, R, M,* and *N* have significant discriminating power among ten nosological (diagnostic) categories. From his findings, it would seem that the syndrome types that characterize pathological groups may be describable *in part* in terms of specified patterns of such trait scores.

Another indirect source of validity information comes from the comparisons of vocational groups in terms of the patterns of scores. There is some reasonableness in patterns of scores found for librarians, male and female; [62] for nurses in training; [63] for research-and-development engineers as compared with sales and service engineers; [64] and for teachers as compared with college students.[65] Librarians tend to be low in confidence, ascendance, and general drive. Nurse students tend to be more sociable, emotionally stable, friendly, and masculine than education majors. Research-and-development engineers tend to be lower on scores for ascendance, sociability, and friendliness. Teachers tend to be more restrained, emotionally stable, objective, friendly, and tolerant than students, but lower in general-activity level and ascendance.

There is information concerning predictive validity of some of the scores, some of this from the academic setting. The highest correlations with college grade-point averages were for scores *R* (restraint), *T* (reflectiveness), and *F* (friendliness), the coefficients being .42, .34, and .25, respectively.[66] Similar estimates, but a bit lower, were found for predicting grades in psychology.[67] There is some evidence for similar small predictions of achievement among nurses in training.[68] Also in the academic setting were some promising predictions of teaching performance,[69] and of leadership among freshmen women.[70]

In the industrial setting, a number of the scores were found to correlate with rated success of foremen, scores for traits *O* (objectivity), *Ag* (agreeableness), and *Co* (cooperativeness) being among the most valid.[71] Other scores showing slight relationships were *R* (restraint), *A* (ascendance), and *M* (masculinity). In this study, and in others, we find several curved relationships between the criterion of success and the inventory scores. That is, the trait score that corresponds to the highest average performance

62 Bryan (1952).
63 Beaver (1955).
64 Kirkpatrick (1956).
65 Leeds (1956).
66 Goedinghaus (1954).

67 Bendig and Sprague (1954).
68 Healy and Borg (1951, 1952).
69 Bendig (1955).
70 Bass et al. (1953).
71 Mackie (1948).

is not at the top of the scale but at some position between the middle and the top.

In another organization, executives showed a pattern of scores differing somewhat from that of foremen.[72] In terms of average scores, executives were more sociable, better adjusted emotionally, more confident, and more cooperative or tolerant. Executives who were rated higher for performance in their positions also tended to be slightly higher in the same qualities. These results might be interpreted to mean that the executives, particularly the superior ones, knew better how to earn good scores. It has been found that college students make higher scores in certain traits—A, S, E, O, P, and M from the GZTS—than persons of lower educational status.[73] However, in the case of both executives and college students, we do not know that some of the differences, at least, are not genuine.

An earlier study reported that scores from the Personnel Inventory discriminated significantly between workers clearly recognized as malcontent and as having undesirable temperament and satisfactory workers in regard to personality.[74] In a recent study, correlations of .3 and higher were found between ratings by psychologists of attributes of workers and scores for traits G, A, S, and P of the GZTS.[75]

Cattell's Factorial Inventories

Cattell is another author who has favored the use of factor analysis for deriving the scoring variables in inventories.[76] Since his applications of factor analysis differ from those of most investigators of personality by this approach, however, it is difficult to compare the scored traits directly. Many of his traits seem to be higher in the hierarchy of personality structure than those recognized as being at the primary-trait level in this volume.

SOME SPECIAL FORMS OF INVENTORIES

There are a few special kinds of inventories that deserve mention because of certain unique features that they illustrate. Of most importance here are the forced-choice type of inventory and the biographical-data inventory. Incidental mention will be made of inventories for children and of a special pattern-scoring procedure.

Inventories for Children

Examples of personality inventories for children are found in the California Test of Personality.[77] Different forms of this inventory were

72 J. S. Guilford (1952).
73 Herzberg (1954).
74 Martin (1944).

75 Hilton et al. (1955).
76 Cattell (1957).
77 Thorpe et al. (1939).

designed for four educational groups ranging from the lower grades to the college level. In all of them, a number of part scores are obtained, each for a specified trait. By grouping and summing, two composite scores are obtained, one for personal adjustment and one for social adjustment. Scores from the form at the high school level were found to be better assessments of students than were interview judgments or ratings.[78] A very recently published inventory by Cattell and Beloff (1958) is called the High School Personality Questionnaire.

Forced-Choice Inventories

The first noteworthy inventory with forced-choice items was developed for use in the United States Army during World War II.[79] In the Personal Inventory, each forced-choice item presents a pair of alternative descriptions, one of which is to be chosen by the examinee as fitting him better than the other. Sometimes two favorable attributes are paired, such as:

I've got courage. vs. I am self reliant.

Sometimes two unfavorable attributes are paired, such as:

I wish I weren't so emotional. vs. I wish I were more popular.

The Shipley inventory, as it was sometimes called, showed its usefulness in discriminating from others the men who would later become psychiatric discharges in relatively large numbers. For example, a short, improved form identified 69 per cent of such later discharges while wrongly identifying only 4 per cent of the others.

SOME EVALUATION OF FORCED-CHOICE INVENTORIES

The main objective for this type of instrument seems to have been to avoid the troublesome test-taking biases so often encountered with other inventories. As with the forced-choice rating method, it is believed that the person making a self-judgment is not likely to exercise such a bias if the alternatives are well matched for apparent favorableness. If the forced-choice items accomplish this purpose, they seem to be advantageous; but there are prices to be paid for such an advantage.

One price is the good will of many who take the test. Some persons resent, with reason, being forced to make a choice between two insulting statements such as, in effect: Are you a scoundrel or a dope? Some items are like the question: Have you stopped beating your wife? For example:

I feel nauseated after eating. vs. I feel nauseated after getting excited.

What is the person to say who does not feel nauseated on either occasion?

Another price is in terms of questionable measurement principles. In rejecting one of the alternatives, which may be an indicator of trait *A*,

---

[78] Jackson (1946).

[79] Reported after the war by Shipley et al. (1946).

the examinee is automatically forced to accept the other, which measures trait *B*. If he were truthful, he might justifiably accept both or reject both. This he is not permitted to do. When he indicates strength on one trait, he has to indicate weakness on another. He cannot indicate strength on both or weakness on both. Eventually, ways will perhaps be found to avoid the errors of measurement thus introduced.

There is some evidence that examinees can successfully bias their scores (also bias them unsuccessfully, perhaps in random directions) when instructed to obtain good scores.[80] Success is more likely to be forthcoming if examinees are told in which direction the bias should be, for example, to show high self-confidence.[81] When parallel inventories have been tried, one in the usual form and one in forced-choice form, the results are varied. Sometimes there is a slightly higher validity (with a rating criterion) for the forced-choice form [82] and sometimes there is no differ-ence.[83] We shall have to regard the forced-choice form as being still in the experimental stage. It has not yet lived up to expectations, but per-haps with modifications it will.

Biographical-Data Inventories

The biographical-data inventory generally calls for relatively more factual material, facts concerning the past and present circumstances and activities of the examinee. It stresses particular times, places, and people in the life of the examinee. Some sample items follow:

Between the ages of five and twenty-one you lived away from home a total of:
A. 1 month or less
B. 1 to 6 months
C. 6 months to a year
D. 1 to 4 years
E. More than 4 years
To how many social clubs or organizations do you now belong?
A. None
B. 1
C. 2 or 3
D. 3 to 6
E. 7 or more

DEVELOPMENT OF A BIOGRAPHICAL-DATA INVENTORY

First, all conceivable items of information that might have some indica-tive value for the trait to be measured or the criterion to be predicted are collected or written. These trial items are administered to selected groups.

[80] Gordon and Stapleton (1956); Rusmore (1956).   [82] Gordon (1951).
[81] Longstaff and Jurgensen (1953).   [83] Osburn et al. (1954).

Very large samples, preferably of several hundred individuals, are almost essential. The sample might be composed of people such as students entering pilot training or navigator training, or men just starting out as insurance salesmen. Later, some criterion of success is established, such as passing or failing in training, or the amount of insurance sold during the first six months. Every response to every item is then studied in relation to the criterion. If any or all of the item's responses discriminate between the successful and the unsuccessful, the item is retained, and the scoring weights for its responses are determined.

SOME EVALUATION OF BIOGRAPHICAL-DATA INVENTORIES

Some success has been achieved in the selection of insurance salesmen and service-station managers by this procedure,[84] also in selecting pilots and navigators and other kinds of personnel in the United States Air Force.[85] The validity coefficients for the score for pilots against a pass-fail criterion in new samples were typically in the range .35 to .40.[86] For predicting success of navigator students, the correlations were of the order of .25 to .30. No validity was achieved for selecting school principals by this method.[87]

The biographical-data approach is a kind of "shotgun" affair. It is purely empirical and usually rests on no particular hypotheses about personality traits. The development of a scorable instrument has to be done to meet each and every practical situation. There is little basis for transferring the application of one scoring key to use in a new connection, not, at least, without obtaining new validation data for the score in that situation.

Pattern or Configural Scoring

Configural scoring is based upon combinations of items rather than on single items. That is, in order to earn a weight contributing to a certain score, the examinee has to give a certain combination of responses to two or more items. This procedure has been proposed and tried by several investigators, but its value does not seem to have been demonstrated as yet.[88]

An important difficulty is that any one combination of several responses is likely to occur so rarely that its discriminating value is very low. For

[84] Soar (1956).

[85] Guilford and Lacey (1947); Levine and Zachert (1951). Prior use of the method for selecting pilots had been initiated by E. Lowell Kelly for the Civil Aeronautics Administration.

[86] Guilford and Lacey (1947).

[87] Guilford and Comrey (1948).

[88] Zubin (1937); McQuitty (1941); Fricke (1956).

example, where a pattern of responses is given by only 2 per cent of the cases, we have discriminated only 2 in 100; the remaining 98 all look alike.

To a large extent, significant patterning is already taken into account in scoring single items, for each combination of responses receives a unique, numerical value (combination of response weights). Such implicit patterns give high (or low) weights to consistencies among responses. Any other kind of patterning presumably capitalizes upon certain inconsistencies. Whether the weighting of such patterns very high (or low) would add useful information is still to be determined. It would do so at great cost.[89]

A GENERAL EVALUATION OF INVENTORIES

In this section we shall consider the many criticisms that are commonly brought against personality inventories and also their merits.[90] Inventories do have weaknesses, and we shall attempt to evaluate these and to see what is being done or could be done about them. We shall also consider available information as to the general validity of inventories for different purposes and in different situations.

Some Criticisms of Inventories

Criticisms are usually proposed first on purely logical grounds, and too often they are simply met on the same grounds, with no satisfactory resolution of the argument likely to be reached. Within the context of science and technology, it is incumbent upon both sides of a controversy to present as much supporting evidence as they can. As we take up each major criticism, we shall consider available empirical evidence that bears on the issue.

THE EXAMINEE DOES NOT KNOW HIMSELF WELL ENOUGH

The criticism that the examinee does not know himself well enough to give correct or truthful answers involves essentially two questions. Do the items ask for information regarding things the examinee has never observed or has no chance of observing? Do they ask for judgments and interpretations that are beyond his abilities? The first question concerns observable vs. unobservable facts; the second concerns reporting interpretations or inferences vs. facts.

The degree of insight required is a relative matter. Some items require very little, others a great deal. It should not require much insight to answer the questions:

89 Secord (1955).
90 For some general criticisms, see Cattell (1946a) and Vernon (1938).

Do you prefer to work alone rather than with others?

Have you ever kept a personal diary?

Do you believe that married women should hold jobs outside the home? Few persons who can read the language, excluding the mentally deficient and the psychotic, have failed to achieve the self-knowledge sufficient to prepare them to give meaningful and indicative answers to such questions. Other items require much self-searching that may never have been done before, but some reflection may enable the examinee to reach a representative answer. The writer of items can favor the kind just quoted if he thinks they will serve as indicators and if subsequent item analysis bears out his idea, but for some purposes, it may be necessary to call upon the examinee for some fairly sophisticated decisions regarding himself, decisions that amount to interpretations of his behavior.

Another aspect of the issue is that the examinee should not have too much insight into the psychological import of the items. It is better if he does not have insight into the intentions of the inventory or its items. If he does grasp its intent, he should not have a very fixed impression of his own trait position, particularly if it is in error, lest this knowledge bias his responses. The purpose is to score him on traits that he does not know about by asking him questions that pertain to common things that he does know about.

It could be argued that for items of a less factual nature it does not matter whether he is stating correctly his status with respect to the attribute more obviously stressed by the item. The item, it might be said, has both a manifest and a latent content, and it is not the manifest content but the latent content that is valid for our purposes. To the question "Did you ever hate your father or your mother?" an examinee may respond "no." This is probably not a true statement on his part, but it may reveal something about one or more of his traits, such as an inclination toward repression or lack of self-insight. From this point of view, it is what traits the response to an item indicates that counts, not whether the response represents "correct" reporting. In this case, it is not the person's observation about himself that is of interest to us, it is how he reacts to the item. The same may be true with regard to many items of this sort. To this extent, we need not be concerned about the problem of accurate self-description.

THE EXAMINEE CHANGES HIS RESPONSES FROM TIME TO TIME

The fact that examinees change their responses to items in retesting has been disturbing to some test users. It may suggest that the examinee is very uncertain as to what the correct response for him should be. It suggests a lack of dependability in his answers and hence weakens the dependability of the whole inventory. There has been much research on this point.

The extent to which responses are changed is at first rather disconcerting. An inventory was administered to a group, then immediately readministered to the same group, and readministered again at intervals over a 21-day period. Eight per cent of the responses were changed upon immediate retesting, with an increase to about twenty per cent after 21 days.[91] Most of the changes had occurred by the fourth day. In another study which involved longer time intervals between test and retest, the number of changes was greater: 29 per cent after one year, 35 per cent after two years, and 35 per cent after three years.[92]

Another study compared responses on a printed inventory with responses given by the same persons orally in a psychiatric interview.[93] The incidence of changing of responses amounted to 27 per cent. The investigators looked into the probable causes for the changes, with results that are rather informative. They concluded that most changes were just plain contradictions, no other cause being discernable. Some were the result of actual personality changes that took place in the natural process of recovery from pathological symptoms. Some changes were due to revised interpretations of the items, a cause which others have found to account for about half the changes they have observed.[94] Still other changes were attributed to plain carelessness.

Seen as a statistical problem, these changes in response are a matter of retest reliability for items, and they have a bearing upon retest reliability of total scores. It is the latter that we should be concerned about. It is to be expected that the reliability of a single item would be lower than that for the total score, the reason being that there are compensatory changes, that is, where the response to one item changes to gain a point, another changes in the opposite direction. Lentz (1934) found that although 20 per cent of the responses were changed in retesting, 81 per cent of these changes neutralized one another. Thus, the effect of changes upon total scores was not as great as one would expect from the number of item-response changes.

INTERPRETATION OF ITEMS VARIES FROM PERSON TO PERSON

Misinterpretation of items, some items, at least, cannot be avoided, however well the test is written. The test writer does the best he can. Apparently nonfunctioning items are eliminated consequent to item analysis. There still remain some items that can be misinterpreted by someone. No amount of editing can ensure that an item is functioning

[91] Benton and Stone (1937).   [93] Landis and Katz (1934).
[92] Farnsworth (1938c).   [94] Eisenberg and Wesman (1941).

the same for all examinees.[95] Sometimes a critical reader looks at an item, sees its ambiguity, and pounces upon it. Because of this one bad-looking item, he condemns the entire inventory. He should be reminded that there are numerous other items in the test, and the fact that one item is misinterpreted means little with regard to misinterpretation of others.

As a matter of fact, those who appreciate the value of projective tests, particularly, should welcome the ambiguous items. Actually, it may be the way in which the examinee interprets the item that makes it valid. Because it has passed the hurdle of item validation, something must be giving it predictive value. If an item predicts or indicates trait positions of individuals, it does so in spite of, and perhaps in some cases because of, misinterpretations.

EXAMINEES FALSIFY THEIR ANSWERS

The opportunity for willful biasing of responses and the fact that examinees take advantage of the opportunity has been the most serious criticism of inventories. The problem is not a simple one by any means; there are several facets to it. Investigators have thrown some light on the matter. A number of questions are appropriately asked. Under what conditions will examinees be motivated to give truthful answers and under what conditions will they not? Can examinees make more favorable scores if they try to and can they also make poorer scores? In ordinary uses of inventories, how much biasing of scores does occur? Does such biasing invalidate the scores for measuring the traits? What are the best remedies for the difficulty?

Some critics would reject the use of all inventories because there is an opportunity for willful biasing. Such a decision may be related to a person's general level of belief in the inherent honesty of people in general; some believe, for example, that others are fundamentally honest whereas others suspect everybody of cheating. It is quite possible, however, that many of those who do not believe in the general truthfulness of responses to inventory items would think nothing of accepting responses to application forms or responses to questions during an interview. There are some critics who in one breath may tell you that examinees have insufficient insight to answer the items and in the next will say that examinees can successfully falsify their way to good scores. A very legitimate aspect to the philosophy behind the use of inventories for vocational purposes is the ethical question of whether a person should be given the opportunity to earn an appointment by distorting the truth. Such a question goes beyond the use of inventories, of course.

The motivation behind attempts to bias scores on an inventory are

[95] Willoughby and Morse (1936).

well known or at least reasonably surmised. An examinee may attempt to make good scores in order to look better in the eyes of the examiner and in the eyes of others whose opinions count so far as he is concerned. He may do so to gain a coveted assignment, to prevent hurt pride, or to defeat the purposes of the examiner. The latter may represent the mood of a practical joker or it may express hostility. Some examinees have been known to try to make bad-looking scores; such, for example, has been the case among servicemen, who know that psychoneurotics are exempt from unpleasant and dangerous duties. Some are overconscientious, such as Bible-school students. Others are depressed, and taking a dim view of life, they may modify their responses all along the line. Still others may have an urge for self-punishment. Wherever conditions such as these are known to exist, appropriate caution should be exercised in administering inventories and interpreting the scores.

Quite a number of studies show that individuals, usually college students, can modify their scores, sometimes very considerably, when instructed to do so.[96] Of this there can be no question. Not everybody succeeds, however. Kimber (1947) found that 41 per cent of the men and 26 per cent of the women made the same score or worse. Noll (1951) found that 7 per cent did worse in one inventory and 25 per cent in another. Incidentally, in neither study was there much, if any, correlation between extent of improvement of scores and verbal intelligence. Although many examinees do not succeed when attempting to improve their scores, we should still be concerned about the effects of their efforts. Even when an examinee makes a poorer showing he is giving a biased result that invalidates his score to some extent.

No satisfactory studies have been done to determine how much biasing of scores actually goes on in situations where there should be motivation to do so but in which no instructions are given to try to make good scores. As Bernreuter (1933) has pointed out, the fact that examinees change their average scores so much under instruction to produce biased results indicates that under the normal conditions they have not biased their scores in the favorable direction as much as they could have.

In one study, already-employed police officers were compared with applicants for positions with the police force with respect to scores from two inventories.[97] The applicants made significantly higher mean scores in five of the ten traits involved. We may conclude from this that the hypothesis of willful biasing is tenable but we unfortunately lack information concerning the actual status of the two groups with respect to the traits measured. In another study, two groups of men were compared, one in a research context and the other in an application-for-employment

[96] Heidbreder (1930); Bernreuter (1933); Kelly et al. (1936); Ruch (1942).
[97] Green (1951).

context.[98] The applicants made a better average score in one trait but not in the other. The actual status of the two groups in these two traits was unknown. For this same reason, the results from both these studies are inconclusive.

How much is validity of the scores affected by biasing of responses? Some people are ready to conclude that any faking at all completely invalidates an inventory. Studies seem to show that, when there are instructions to make good scores, some inventories are more subject to successful biasing than others. To the extent that an inventory is resistant to the effects of biasing, we might expect to find some validity left for its scores. There may still be elements of "truth," as Landis (1936) suggests. Although the average score may be changed materially as a result of biasing, there is often considerable dispersion of scores left. Sometimes the dispersion is as great as before.[99] Will the variance of those scores retain any substantial component attributable to the trait we want to measure? This is the crucial question.

One indirect answer to this is to be found in correlations of the same trait scores for the same sample, with the test being taken under the usual testing instruction and then under the instruction to bias scores. Such correlations have been quite varied, from zero [100] through a range of .53 to .54 [101] to a range of .22 to .65.[102] These correlations may be regarded as indicating the relationships between scores with possible set to bias a little and scores with set to bias as much as possible. What should really be known is the correlation between scores obtained under the conditions of zero bias and under normal bias.

The effects of bias upon practical validity were brought out in an experiment with a biographical-data inventory.[103] The AAF Biographical Data Blank was administered to very large samples of aviation students while they were taking classification tests to qualify for assignment to specialized flying training, which they all coveted. One group had the normal instructions. A second group had "relaxed" instructions, in which examinees were given the impression of a more informal, permissive atmosphere. A third group had instructions containing implied threats of punishment if anyone were caught in misrepresentation.

The differences in means were small, in the expected directions, and significant. There was evidently not as much biasing in the favorable direction as there could have been. Previously a high school group of boys had been told to answer in a way that would make them look like good pilot material. They were much more successful.

The correlations of scores of the AAF students with the pass-fail

98 Heron (1956).   101 Kimber (1947).
99 Kimber (1947); Guilford and Lacey (1947).   102 Heidbreder (1930).
100 Bernreuter (1933).   103 Guilford and Lacey (1947).

criterion in pilot training were .40, .28, and .38, for the normal, relaxed, and "threat" instructions, respectively. The results vindicated the use of the inventory under the normal instructions. Even a little encouragement to relax standards of conscientiousness, however, seemed to lead to lowered validity. These results suggest that much can be done to prevent bias and to preserve validity of an inventory by instilling the right test-taking attitude, even under conditions of competition for assignments. Generalization from military to civilian settings, however, would be made with some risk, as would generalizing from more factual-type items to more opinion-type items.

One aspect of the biasing problem seems to be generally overlooked. There seems to be a general assumption that certain extreme trait positions are most desirable and another assumption that all examinees have the same conception of desirable and undesirable attributes. Both of these assumptions are incorrect. For some traits, as we saw before, the optimal trait positions are not at one extreme but at some more moderate places. The optimal point probably depends also upon the criterion to be predicted. An examinee who should decide that being at one extreme is optimal (assuming he had guessed what trait is being measured) and who recognizes which items are valid for this trait and which responses are in the right direction would be likely to overshoot the optimal point.

Actually, there is considerable difference of opinion regarding the most favorable trait positions for different traits. The author has asked students to mark that position on a nine-point scale of a defined trait which they think would be best for a "good" personality. On 3 of the 23 traits so judged, there were choices all the way from 1 to 9. In more than half of the traits, points were selected on both sides of the midpoint (most of the traits were bipolar). In only a third of the traits was one extreme the modal or most popular judgment. Such individual evaluations are another indication of the complexity of the problem.

Edwards (1953) studied popularity judgments of traits in relation to trait scores from another approach. Using averages in judgments of a group of students, he scaled 140 attributes for popularity, the attributes being presented in the form of inventory items. The items were also given as an inventory to the same students, each person responding in self-description in terms of the same attributes. The correlation between the frequencies with which attributes were accepted as self-descriptive and the scale values for popularity was .87.[104] Thus, attributes that are popular on the *average* are also accepted as self-descriptive on the *average*.

There are several possible interpretations of this result. One is that students were biasing responses of self-description in the direction of the

---

[104] Hanley (1956) has found similar correlations.

popular attributes. Another is that the more popular qualities are also the more common in the population, if we accept the word of the students as evidence of actual incidence of the qualities. Another interpretation is that, in rating desirability, students are projecting their own qualities. Still another way of looking at it is that students think that the way they are is desirable; on the whole they are pleased with their own personalities. It must be remembered that these results pertain to averages; *individuals* might not show as much correlation between self-description and judgment of desirability of traits. They would differ in their conceptions of desirability as well as in their attributes.

A number of remedial steps are available to one who would attempt to forestall biasing efforts and prevent their effects. Something can be done in the way of better item writing. Not all items, by any means, need have distinctly favorable or unfavorable answers. For example:

You get more sleep than the average person.

A friend is a person who understands you.

Some items can be so written that the keyed response appears to be unfavorable. For example:

You hate to lose in a contest. (Keyed "no.")

You hesitate to tell a person to mind his own business. (Keyed "yes.")

Some items can be intentionally projective.[105] For example:

A room that is too neat and tidy makes people feel uncomfortable. (Keyed "no" to indicate meticulousness.)

It is hard to see where some people get all their surplus energy. (Keyed "no" for general activity.)

It is likely that the person lacking in the qualities of tidiness and neatness labors under the impression that other individuals, like himself, dislike to see too much of these qualities in others. The person who lacks energy would be the one to respond "yes" to the second of these items. Thus, he does not have to say that he is lacking in energy.

While subtle items, like the projective ones, may be more resistant to biasing,[106] they are sometimes so subtle that they miss the point psychologically; that is, they lack validity.[107] Validity must always be determined empirically.

The other common remedy, an aid in dealing with cases of suspected biasing, is that of validation scores. Examples given above were the "no"-count score of the Humm-Wadsworth inventory; the *F, L,* and *K* scores of the MMPI; and the Jacobs-Schlaff scores for the Guilford-Zimmerman Temperament Survey. Such scores are typically somewhat low in relia-

---

[105] For further examples and discussion, see Guilford, Christensen, Bond, and Sutton (1954); Freeman (1953); Meehl (1945).

[106] Wallon and Webb (1956).

[107] Freeman (1953).

bility and can be used only as suggestive information. Further refinements in measures of test-taking attitudes might be developed.

A SUMMARY ON CRITICISM

In summing up this discussion on the criticism of inventories and their use, it can be suggested that it might help the critic to take a more objective and statistical view. Inventory items are verbal stimuli. Before the items are used for scoring individuals, they have been found empirically and statistically to show some discrimination between groups believed to be high and low on the trait continuum in question. How the examinees will respond to an item depends upon many things, one of which should be the trait. It may be that those high on the trait interpret the item differently from those low on the trait. It may be that the groups differ with respect to some fact of behavior, feeling, or opinion obviously stated by the item. It may be that the item subtly implies something to which the two groups respond differently. In some cases, therefore, it does not matter whether examinees interpret an item as the examiner does or as the critic does.

We usually cannot tell by looking at an item whether it is valid for doing what we want it to do. This is why item analysis of some kind is essential. Scoring weights are based upon the results of analysis. This is not to say that biases in score meanings cannot creep into the scoring keys; they frequently do. The key can be no more valid than the criterion it is aimed to predict. This places considerable responsibility upon the constructor of an inventory to make reasonably sure that his criterion is as unambiguous as possible.

Biases in meanings of scores are by no means confined to inventories. They are also found in completely objective tests of abilities. They are more subtle in the case of such tests and thus are more likely to escape the eye of the critic. Factor analysis often reveals them. Some are due to what Cronbach (1946) has called "response sets" of one kind or another. An example of a response set would be an examinee's bias toward giving the response "true" in a true-false test. If the majority of the items are keyed "true" such an examinee would gain points because of his bias; if the majority happened to be keyed "false," he would lose points, an error in either case.

Other biases arise from the kind of items used. For example, if, in a test intended to measure some particular kind of reasoning ability, the items are put in the form of relatively unfamiliar words, the test becomes instead a measure of verbal comprehension. Another example would be a test of reading comprehension in which the subject matter to be read stresses mechanical information, thus measuring to a marked extent the examinee's mechanical knowledge. Many such tests exist and the irrelevant variances are too often overlooked or are unknown without a factor analysis.

General Validity Information on Inventories

In the early part of this chapter, some information was given concerning validity of particular inventories. We shall now consider this problem in a broader way, stressing practical validity for detecting pathology and for predicting academic and vocational success.

THE DETECTION OF PATHOLOGY

The accuracy and usefulness of personality inventories in general in discriminating pathological from normal individuals in civilian life have been quite varied. Results have ranged all the way from practically no discrimination, as reported by Landis and others,[108] to moderate success, as reported by Benton (1945), Guthrie (1950), and others. If inventory scores do not provide enough information for the diagnosis of the single case, there is nothing against using other sources of information in addition. The reasonable question to ask is whether the information provided by scores adds something useful that cannot be obtained from other available sources.

For use in the military setting, where the inventory originated, the picture has been very different. Eysenck (1952) reported a correlation of .70 in discriminating neurotics from normals. Miles et al. (1946) reported results with a similar correlation. Page (1945) reported discrimination of psychoneurotics from normals with a correlation figure of .75 for the Bernreuter inventory and .80 for another special inventory designed for this purpose.

In a summary of the general usefulness of inventories in the military setting, Zubin (1948) cites an example from the United States Maritime Training Program. Of 1,000 men processed with an inventory, 660 were judged to require no psychiatric interview. Of the 340 who were interviewed but went on into training, 15 had to be discharged for psychiatric reasons, 75 later had mild emotional troubles, and 250 were false positives with no observable difficulties. Of the 660 not interviewed, only three were later rejected for emotional reasons. One of these was reported to be normal at the time he took the inventory and two had falsified their answers. Of the 18 who had to be discharged for psychiatric reasons, 15 had thus been detected by the inventory. In another survey of the subject, Ellis and Conrad (1948) concluded that, in an overwhelming majority of the studies, inventories proved to have value for screening and diagnostic purposes.

[108] Landis et al. (1935).

The same authors speculated as to the contrast of inventory validity in military life with that in civilian life. There were suspicions that in some studies the data were not entirely immaculate. That is, information regarding test scores may have been available to those who later made criterion judgments on the men. In some cases, the criterion interview may have asked some of the same questions as the inventory did. Because of the selective service, the usual sample was, of course, very heterogeneous, with some cases being inducted who were even obviously neurotic or psychotic to an expert observer. Motivational conditions were strongly in favor of validity of the inventories. Men who wanted assignments could "fake good" and men who did not want assignments could "fake bad." There was perhaps more effort to be honest among most men under military discipline than is true in civilian life. Finally, certain symptoms that are not particularly detrimental in adjustment to civilian life cannot be tolerated in military life, for example, dizzy spells, convulsions, and homosexuality.

PREDICTION OF ACADEMIC SUCCESS

Early results on the prediction of grades of college students from scores on inventories were completely discouraging. For six inventories the validity coefficients were essentially zero.[109] Later results have been more encouraging. In one study, the correlations were .08 and .22.[110] Even higher correlations have been reported, some of which were mentioned earlier in this chapter in connection with the MMPI and the GZTS inventories. Differences have been found between high achievers (more introverted and self-sufficient on the BPI) and low achievers.[111]

Gough (1953*a*) has developed a scale empirically for predicting achievement in high school by correlating preliminary items with grades. The scale proved to have a validity coefficient of .44 in new samples of high school students but a validity of .18 for achievement in college, indicating that somewhat different qualities may be important at the two levels of education. Gough has also developed an empirical scale for predicting achievement in college, which proved to have a validity of .38 for predicting college achievement and .36 for predicting high school achievement.[112] The latter result indicates that there is much in common, after all, between the qualities other than aptitude that are involved in achievement at the two levels. The college scale is one of several in Gough's California Personality Inventory.

[109] Stagner (1933).
[110] Jackson (1946).
[111] Neel and Mathews (1935); Greene and Staton (1939); Super (1942).
[112] Gough (1953*b*).

PREDICTION OF VOCATIONAL SUCCESS

An over-all picture of the validities of inventories for prediction of success in different job assignments is provided by Ghiselli and Bartol (1953). Averaging available validity coefficients from many sources for different inventories, different organizations, and different criteria, the authors presented results for a number of occupations. Some of their data are given in Table 8.1. From this information, we may conclude

Table 8.1

Typical validity coefficients for predicting success of different kinds of workers from knowledge of scores on personality inventories

Worker group	Validity coefficient	Number of samples
Salesmen	.36	12
Sales clerks	.36	8
Trades and crafts	.29	8
Clerks	.25	22
Protective workers	.24	5
Foremen	.18	44
Supervisors	.14	8

that the greatest chance of predicting success occurs in connection with sales personnel. Other groups, except for those in skilled trades and crafts, also have to deal with people in one way or another. Although the degree of prediction is limited in any case, inventory scores probably provide information that cannot be obtained in other known ways. They usually correlate approximately zero with aptitude scores, and hence contribute something that does not duplicate that kind of information.

Such validation results are about the same in the military setting, where the criterion is one of job performance. In the experimental studies of pilot selection in the Army Air Force, inventory scores did about as well as any other assessments of nonaptitude traits. Correlations in the neighborhood of .2 were generally about the best that could be obtained,[113] except for biographical-data inventories, for which correlations as high as .4 were found.

In contrast to the success in detecting cases of pathology, these results show strikingly inferior validity. There may be several reasons. One may

[113] Guilford and Lacey (1947).

be that the abnormals were mostly eliminated before they reached the point of assignment to training. It is possible that, if pathology is sufficient to contribute to failing performance, it is fairly obvious and requires no test to eliminate the person before entrance to training. Possibly a person who is highly motivated tries hard and succeeds in spite of his emotional handicaps. Possibly emotional maladjustments have very little to do with success or failure in training. Possibly teachers and supervisors overlook peculiarities of temperament and make allowances for them in evaluation of students and workers. Criteria of success are often very unreliable. However this may be, aptitude tests are distinctly superior to temperament inventories in predicting performances in training and in job assignments.

In the study of effects of adjustment and maladjustment upon work performance, perhaps criteria other than work performance should be used. There are the possible effects of maladjusted people upon fellow workers and supervisors, effects which, by reason of compensatory efforts, may not be reflected in reduced production but are tallied rather by the wear and tear on human beings, by mistakes and roughness of operation, and by general unhappiness of associates. These are all human values that are difficult to measure in terms of dollars and cents, but they are values nevertheless. Perhaps they deserve more weight in the processes of evaluation of personnel.

SUMMARY

The first inventory of importance originated as a substitute for a psychiatric interview. The inventory is still a kind of standardized group interview that can be scored by the use of a predetermined point system. Some inventories continue to emphasize the detection of the pathological and the maladjusted and some, in addition, aim to aid in the diagnosis of abnormals. Other inventories are designed to measure traits of normal people, with the possibility that abnormal people can also be described in part by the same trait concepts.

A typical inventory is developed by the originator's first adopting certain trait concepts. He then selects and writes the items that he thinks have a chance to be indicators of one or more of these traits. He segregates two groups, one high on the trait scale and one low. Correlating each item with this criterion of the trait, he selects those items that are valid and adopts scoring weights in accordance with the statistical results.

The first general-purpose inventory, with multiple scoring, was the Bernreuter Personality Inventory. Inventories based upon scoring categories drawn from pathological syndromes are the Humm-Wadsworth Temperament Scale and the Minnesota Multiphasic Personality Inventory. The use of both has been extended to differentiation among normal individuals on the same traits. The Guilford inventories—Inventory of Factors STDCR, Inventory of Factors GAMIN, Personnel Inventory, and the Guilford-Zimmerman Temperament Survey—were based upon traits discovered by factor analysis. Special forms of inventories include a forced-choice type and the biographical-data inventory.

Personality inventories have been the subject of considerable criticism, some of it justified, some not. On the one hand, it is feared that the typical examinee does not know himself well enough to state the facts called for. On the other hand, it is feared that he knows too much, that he can, and does, bias his responses to items in ways that give him better-looking scores (or worse-looking scores, depending upon his motivation). There is concern about the unreliability of responses to items and about misinterpretations of items. Much of the criticism can be attributed to lack of understanding of techniques of test development. Steps have been taken to remove some of the weaknesses of inventories, but there is still much room for improvement.

Inventories show their best validity and usefulness in connection with the first purpose for which they were developed—to screen out the potentially emotionally unfit from entering military service—for a number of reasons. Their use in detecting and diagnosing maladjusted and pathological persons in civilian life leaves much to be desired, but they contribute new information that can be helpful. Validity correlations indicating the degree of predictive value in academic and vocational areas are generally very low when performance criteria are used. In spite of this poor showing against such criteria, where it is important to understand individuals better in terms of trait concepts, personality inventories have much to offer.

Chapter 9

INTEREST AND
ATTITUDE MEASUREMENT

AN INTEREST may be defined as an individual's generalized behavior tendency to be attracted to a certain class of activities. The expression "generalized behavior tendency" implies nothing more than that an interest is a general trait. The term "attracted" signifies that the individual gives attention to, seeks out, goes toward, or strives to obtain something that has potential value for him. Being attracted to certain activities implies that interests are most likely to determine *what* a person does rather than how he does it or how well.

INTERESTS AND OTHER MOTIVATIONAL TRAITS

Our definition of interest places it in the general area of motivation. Along with *needs* and *attitudes,* interests form a class of traits that might be called dynamic. But to avoid some other connotations of that word, the new term *hormetic* will be applied, a term whose root, like that of "hormone," means an "instigator."

Having classified interests in this way, we need first to distinguish them from motives. There are several differences. Motives pertain to more particularized goals, whereas interests pertain to *classes* of goals, as indicated in the definition. Motives are also temporary conditions, fluctuating in strength according to the state of deficiency or satiation, whereas interests, like all traits, are of relatively long duration at relatively more stable strength.

Attitudes will be defined later in this chapter, but the class of traits called *needs* should be distinguished from interests here, for this will help us better to understand interests. Like interests, needs develop as more or less permanent motivating conditions. Unlike an interest, however, a need pertains to the individual's attraction toward a certain condition or status rather than toward certain activities. A desired condition might be that of being loved or admired or of having fame or fortune. Examples of particular traits of interest and need will be seen later in this chapter and in Chapter 17.

Vocational and Avocational Interests

Vocational psychology has naturally favored the use of vocational categories in the descriptions of interests of people. Knowledge of a person's interests in things mechanical, artistic, or scientific seems immediately useful and applicable. But we may question whether vocational interests represent unitary traits and whether they are appropriate for a basic psychology of interests. When we define interests as broadly as the term is defined above, linking them with the field of motivation, we see that they go well beyond the vocational sphere. There are avocational interests as well as vocational interests, and we shall see in Chapter 17 that the former outnumber the latter. The most popular inventories for measuring interests, those of Strong and Kuder, stress vocational variables. We shall consider these two inventories at some length because most is known about them and because they represent some interesting principles and techniques of test development that also apply more generally.

INTEREST INVENTORIES BY THE EMPIRICAL APPROACH

In this section we shall consider three interest inventories that were developed by an approach that is known as empirical. In part, the empirical approach means that there is little or no consideration of psychological theory regarding the fundamental nature of interests or regarding basic interest traits. In part, it means that such inventories are developed to meet some immediate technological needs and that considerable arbitrariness is involved in the choice of traits included in the inventories.

The Strong Vocational Interest Blank for Men

The Strong Vocational Interest Blank for Men is composed of 400 items and is scored for more than 40 interest variables [1] or categories of interest. The first 280 items are names of objects or activities, to each of which the examinee is to respond by one of three letters: *L* for liking the idea, *I* for being indifferent to it, and *D* for disliking it. Among these items are the following kinds:

100 occupations, given by name
36 school subjects
49 amusements, including sports, games, and magazines

[1] Strong (1943, 1945).

48 common activities, such as making a speech

47 kinds of people, such as energetic people, pessimists, foreigners, etc.

There follow four sets of ten things each, the examinee being told to rank each set of ten as he prefers them:

10 activities

10 general features of jobs

10 well-known men in various occupations

10 positions of leadership in an organization

Next follow 40 paired activities, the examinee being told to choose one, and finally a list of inventory items and traits on which the examinee is to rate himself.

PURPOSE OF THE INTEREST BLANK

The purpose of the Vocational Interest Blank (which will be referred to sometimes hereafter as simply VIB) is to determine whether the examinee has interests similar to those of successful people in each of several occupations. The occupations for which the VIB is scored are mostly at higher occupational levels. Actually, it is not accurate to say that the VIB is limited to the assessment of interests. Many of the items included are very similar to those found in inventories used to measure traits of temperament. As to general use, the VIB was designed for application to vocational and educational guidance and not for vocational selection or classification purposes. It was not intended to measure vocational aptitudes, and so far as is known, it does not do so.

DEVELOPMENT OF THE STRONG VIB

The major assumption on which the Strong VIB was based is that individuals who are reasonably satisfied with an occupation are distinguished from other individuals in general by the fact that they tend to possess a unique pattern of interests. Another assumption is that the extent to which any person's interest pattern approaches that of a given occupation is proportional to the number of specific interests he has in common with the occupational pattern. This is determined by the number of responses he gives that are in agreement with the typical individual in that occupation. The first empirical step, then, in developing a collection of items to be scored for an occupation is to determine how persons in the occupation respond to the items in contrast to the way in which persons outside that occupation respond.

The technique involves administering a large number of trial items to hundreds of men in many occupations. In order to develop a scoring key for a particular occupation, Strong selected a "criterion" group for that occupation. It was composed of men who had been employed in it for several years with more than a minimum salary. The assumption was that they were reasonably well satisfied with their occupation. The number in a criterion group was usually about 300, the actual numbers ranging from 100 to 1,000, approximately. The group of "men-in-general" excluded those in the criterion occupation when the scoring key for that occupation was being derived. They represented a variety of occupations at the business and professional levels. This group numbered nearly 5,000, representing 106 different occupations.

For every item, Strong determined the percentage responding each way to an item, both in the criterion group and in the men-in-general group. The scoring weight to be used in connection with each response was determined by the difference between its pair of percentages. For example, the engineers said that they liked the idea of being an advertiser by a much smaller percentage than did men in general, hence response *L* receives a weight of −2 for the engineer score. Engineers disliked the idea of being an advertiser by a larger percentage than did men in general, hence the response *D* receives a weight of +2 for the engineer score. The larger the difference in percentages, the greater the scoring weight attached to a particular response to a particular item. This process was repeated for all items under each occupation for which a scoring key was developed.

In taking the test, an examinee is instructed that he must respond to every item. Each occupational key is then applied to his responses, and the weights attached to his responses are summed algebraically to give a "raw" score. These raw scores are not comparable from one occupational-interest scale to another. To make measurements comparable, Strong converts the obtained raw scores to standard scores. The standard score is in turn given a letter designation, according to the following principles:

A means any standard score that is made by the highest-scoring 70 per cent in the occupation in question.

B+, *B*, and *B−* include those in the next 26 per cent.

C+ and *C* include those in the lowest 3.5 per cent, *C* indicating the lowest 1 per cent.

THE NONOCCUPATIONAL SCALES

In the course of time, Strong developed some additional scoring scales that do not pertain to specific occupations but were designed to supply some additional information that would provide useful supplements to the occupational scores.

The Interest Maturity (IM) scale was designed to determine whether the examinee's interests are mature, like those of an older man, or immature, like those of a younger man. Studies of the changes of interests of men over the range of ages from fifteen to fifty-five showed that many changes occur between fifteen and twenty-five as compared with changes after twenty-five.[2] The maturity key was empirically developed by comparing responses to the items by a group of men at fifteen and a group at twenty-five. When an examinee is scored with the Interest Maturity key, a low score is taken to mean that his interests are relatively unstable and may change considerably as he grows older. A high score is taken to mean that little further change is to be expected. The maturity score is accordingly used to tell the counselor about how much confidence he should have in the *occupational* scores of an examinee.

The key for the Masculinity-Femininity (MF) score was based upon differences in responses of men and women to the items of the VIB. The obtained score for an examinee is taken to indicate whether his interests tend to resemble those of men or those of women relatively more. This score is also used as supplementary information in connection with the occupational scores. Some of the occupations for which there are scores may be roughly classified as being more masculine or more feminine. If the examinee's occupational scores are high for masculine occupations and if the MF key indicates generally masculine interests, there is more assurance that the occupational scores are correct. If there should happen to be a discrepancy, that is, a low MF score combined with a high masculine occupational score, the latter would be discounted somewhat. Some examples of masculine occupations are: engineer, farmer, purchasing agent, and chemist. Some examples of feminine occupations are: musician, artist, journalist, and minister. Some occupations are regarded as neutral, for example: physician, psychologist, mathematician, realtor, and architect.

The Occupational Level (OL) key was developed from the contrasting ways in which business and professional men responded as compared with unskilled workers. There has been considerable debate as to just what the OL score means. There is some support for the belief that the score indicates the level of occupation at which the examinee will be most likely to derive satisfaction.[3] There seems to be some agreement that the OL score does not indicate level of general drive or motivation to progress within an occupation.

THE GROUP SCALES

It has been found that some of the occupational scales have very high intercorrelations, either positive or negative. For example, the scale for physicist correlates .91 with that for mathematician, .93 with that for chemist, −.83 with that for life insurance salesman, and −.76 with that for sales manager. Many such correlations indicate much redundancy, which means wasted effort in testing. It also means that some scales could

---

[2] Strong (1931).

[3] Barnett et al. (1953).

well be combined, giving a single score to represent a group. By study of the intercorrelations, Strong found it reasonable to form eleven groups, for each of which there could be a single more comprehensive, yet meaningful, score. A few examples, with illustrative component occupations, follow:

   I. Artist-physician-psychologist
   II. Scientist-engineer-mathematician
   V. Teacher-minister-personnel manager
  VIII. Accountant-banker-office worker
   X. Advertiser-lawyer-journalist

Group scales are useful in two ways: in guidance of younger men who need not make specialized decisions until later and in confirmation of decisions based upon some of the occupational scores.

RELIABILITY OF THE STRONG VIB SCORES

The reliabilities estimated for the Strong VIB occupational scores are rather typical of those found for inventories in general.[4] From correlations of odd and even scores, the estimates range from .74 to .94, with a mean of .88. For correlations from retesting after one week, the average estimate is .87. From retesting after five years, the average is .75. From retesting after ten years, it was found that most of the estimates ranged from .6 to .8.[5]

VALIDITY OF THE STRONG VIB SCORES

Investigators have attempted to examine the validity of the Strong VIB in a variety of ways. Perhaps the fairest question we can ask regarding the occupational scores is whether individuals who go into occupations that are consistent with their high scores are more satisfied than those who do not. The satisfaction might come either from the kind of work or from congeniality with other workers in the same occupation who presumably have similar likes and dislikes, tastes, values, and other dispositions such as are assessed by the VIB.

Redlener (1949) located people for whom he had scores on the VIB and who were in occupations for which there are VIB scores. He asked each person to state how well he liked his job and also how well he liked his occupation. The reason for asking about both occupation and job was that he expected to find some individuals who might like one and not the other. It turned out that the correlations between corresponding Strong VIB scores and ratings of satisfaction were the same in the two cases, namely, .46. This is a fairly respectable level of validity, comparing

---

[4] Unless otherwise noted, the reliability estimates reported here are from the VIB manual (Strong, 1945).

[5] Powers (1956).

favorably with the validity often found for academic-aptitude tests in predicting average grades in college.

Some of Strong's own validation studies have been less direct. Such, for example, is the case with the study to be described next, in which the purpose is to predict which men will change occupations and which will not, the hypothesis being that those in occupations consistent with high scores on the VIB would be less likely to change. There are, of course, many reasons for changing occupations, lack of satisfaction being only one of them.

Strong (1951) followed up 400 men 20 years after they had taken the VIB in college. For 240 men who had not changed their occupations, the agreement between high scores and choice of occupation was reported to be 91 per cent of what it could possibly be under the circumstances. For 160 men who had changed their occupations, the corresponding level of agreement was 77 per cent. Men who continued in their occupation had a higher average score for it than those who changed. In another study,[6] it was found that men changing occupations had a higher average score for the occupation changed to than for the occupation changed from. The VIB thus predicts to some extent the likelihood of a man's staying or not staying in his selected occupation.

A number of investigators have correlated the Strong VIB scores with grades in college courses. Significant correlations should be most promising where the grades are in subjects like engineering, mathematics, and sciences, for which there are rather directly corresponding interest scores. In general, all such correlations have been quite low, even where substantial ones might be expected. While a number of correlations between .2 and .3 have been reported, most of the correlations are lower.[7] The conclusion is that we cannot predict much about grades from knowledge about scores from the VIB. One possible reason for this is that a group of students who are in courses of their chosen specialty tend to have a narrow range of interest scores. A more probable reason is that, of the multitude of determiners of grades, interests play a minor role.

Another approach to the validation of the Strong VIB is the attempt to predict success in an occupation. There is very little information of this kind. Ferguson (1952) reports that in one study the correlation between the amount of life insurance sold annually and the corresponding VIB score was .37. The correlation with the selling of casualty insurance was .25 in another study. These correlations, though quite small, indicate some promise of adding to predictions of success in selling insurance. There is no basis for generalizing to predictions to be expected in

---

[6] Strong (1945).

[7] Segel and Brintle (1934); Melville and Frederiksen (1952).

other fields, and it should be remembered that the VIB was not intended for use in selection of personnel.

GENERAL EVALUATION OF THE VIB FOR MEN

The VIB for men has proven itself to be of value in providing information regarding vocational interests (and other predispositions), which seem to be related to satisfaction in occupations and possibly in some small degree to success also. Compared with other inventories, some of which will be described later, the VIB is very inefficient, by reason of its cumbersome weighted scoring and its overlapping measures. It also falls far short of a comprehensive coverage of all occupations, of which there are several thousand. It is rather limited in use, providing guidance into only the higher occupational categories. Studies [8] have shown that examinees can readily bias scores, particularly in the upward direction, when they are motivated to do so. This strongly suggests that the VIB be used only as the author of it intended, in the guidance situation.

The Strong Vocational Interest Blank for Women

The Strong VIB for women is similar to that for men. It contains 410 items and is scored for 18 occupations. In addition to some of the occupations also scored for men on the men's VIB, there are keys for occupations of librarian, social worker, nurse, stenographer-secretary, and housewife. There is a secondary score for masculinity-femininity. As compared to the VIB for men, on which there has been rather steady research over a period of about thirty years, there is as yet comparatively little information published regarding the usefulness of the VIB for women.

The Gregory Academic Interest Inventory

The Gregory Academic Interest Inventory [9] is another example of an inventory developed on an empirical basis. It is mentioned because of its one unique feature—the fact that it was designed to help college students make a choice of major subject, vocational or otherwise, in which they will find satisfaction. It is composed of 150 items and is scored for 28 major fields. Each scoring key was developed after the Strong model, contrasting responses of a group of students in the particular major with other students in general. The following four specializations within the field of engineering represent the kind of differentiations the Gregory inventory was designed to make:

Public service engineering
Mechanical engineering

8 Steinmetz (1932); Longstaff (1948).
9 Gregory (1946).

Electrical engineering
Civil engineering
Other examples within the field of education are:
Elementary education
Secondary education
Physical education
Nonvocational majors within the usual liberal arts college are also covered
with scoring categories.

GENERAL-INTEREST-TRAIT INVENTORIES

There has been a recognition on the part of other test makers that
the number of vocational categories is very large and that developing
scoring scales for each one would be both cumbersome and uneconomical.
The intercorrelations of such scales indicate that there are common, underlying interest variables. There is the further implication that a relatively small number of more basic interest variables might be sufficient
to cover a very large range of vocations. The Kuder Preference Record
(Vocational) is a good example of an interest inventory based upon this
principle.

The Kuder Preference Record (Vocational)

The Kuder Preference Record (Vocational), which will often be
abbreviated hereafter as the Kuder PRV, or as simply PRV, rests upon
the major assumption that there are relatively unique patterns of interests
for somewhat coherent *areas* of vocation.[10] It has a single scale for each
of ten such areas. A further assumption is that the pattern of interests
for a particular vocation can be indicated by combinations of these scales.
The number of combinations of scores from only ten scales can be enormous, certainly enough to cover a multitude of particular occupations.
One of the major objectives in the development of the PRV was to arrive
at score variables whose intercorrelations would be as near zero as possible, thus avoiding the redundancy that is so common in some other
inventories. Each score should then provide little or no information that
any other score duplicates.

The purposes often stated for the Kuder PRV include calling the
attention of students to areas of vocation in which perhaps they do not
know that they have interests and in guiding them away from unwise
choices that may have been made more or less by accident. Another
purpose is in connection with the counseling of employees, aimed toward
finding assignments in work that will give them satisfaction. This does

10 Kuder (1946).

not mean that the PRV is intended for use in personnel selection or classification.

GENERAL NATURE OF THE KUDER PRV

Kuder's inventory is composed of 160 forced-choice items. Instead of being asked to say whether he likes or dislikes an activity as in the Strong and the Gregory inventories, the examinee is asked to state his *relative* likes and dislikes among three given activities by ranking them. For example, the examinee is given the following list of three activities:

Build a bird house

Write an article about birds

Draw sketches of birds

He then indicates the one he likes best and the one he likes least. The third is, of course, automatically ranked between the other two. In scoring, the activity liked most is given a weight of 2, that liked next a weight of 1, and that liked least a weight of 0.

Notice that the three activities pertain to three different areas, implying three vocational areas that might be described as mechanical, literary, and artistic. These are three of the scoring categories. In the latest edition of the PRV there are ten scoring categories. In the items, the ten areas are combined systematically so that the examinee is by implication making choices between all possible pairs of categories, each a number of times.

The total score for each category is the sum of the weights that the category receives in all its comparisons. Each raw score is transformed into a standard score on a scale that applies to all scoring categories and is expressed in terms of norms from a general population. A profile of the scores is then prepared, showing the high and low areas of interest. The ten scoring categories are:

Mechanical	Scientific	Literary	Clerical
Computational	Persuasive	Musical	Outdoor
	Artistic	Social Service	

SOME CONSEQUENCES OF THE FORCED-CHOICE ITEMS

The use of the forced-choice type of item entails some consequences that we need to know about if we are to interpret intelligently some of the results from the PRV and other inventories of its type. Because the examinee ranks his preferences for activities belonging to different scoring categories, his scores indicate primarily his *relative* positions on the different interest traits. Such scores are called *ipsative*.[11] Each person's scores are distributed around his own average. Scores of the more usual type, when forced-choice items are not used, give trait positions for individuals that are distributed about the general population average for each trait.

[11] Cattell (1944).

These are called *normative* scores. Scores from the Kuder inventory should not be treated as if they were ordinary normative scores.

Another consequence is that the averages of scores, person to person, tend to be about the same, which does not represent the true state of affairs. This feature, and others just mentioned, may be made clearer by study of Figure 9.1. Three hypothetical persons, *J*, *K*, and *L*, are represented there. For each person, ten "true" (normative) scores for different interest variables are assumed, all on the same common measurement

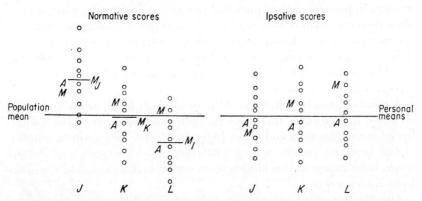

Fig. 9.1 Hypothetical distributions of Kuder *PRV* scores of three individuals, *J*, *K*, and *L*, as they would be obtained in ipsative form, at the right, and their corresponding normative scores at the left. Mechanical and Artistic scores are indicated by *M* and *A*. The normative means for the three persons are indicated by M_j, M_k, and M_l, respectively.

scale. Person *J*'s scores tend to be high, with a mean M_j that is well above the general population mean for all such interest variables. Person *K*'s personal mean is close to the population mean and person *L*'s personal mean is somewhat below the population mean. If these three individuals were to take an inventory like the Kuder PRV, each person's scores in different traits would maintain the same rank order, but the three means would all approach the population mean.

Consider the scores for mechanical interest (*M*), which are arbitrarily chosen among the normative scores for illustrative purposes. The three individuals come in the rank order of *J* highest and *L* lowest, with very little difference. On the ipsative scales at the right, they come in reverse order and the differences are greater. Consider, also, the scores for artistic interest (*A*). In the population, the differences are relatively large, with *J* highest and *L* lowest. The ipsative scores for the same interest variable become almost identical. These two examples of trait scores show what can happen when means of all individuals are arbitrarily equated. One could undoubtedly find examples of a trait score that would remain in the same rank order in spite of the transformation from one system of scores to the other. But it is obvious that there is likely to be much scrambling of rank orders in the process.

There are both advantages and disadvantages in the use of ipsative scores in the Kuder procedure. One advantage is that, since the examinee is forced to make choices, even where there may be little difference among his ten trait positions, there are bound to be some marked differences among his Kuder scores. Ties in scores are highly unlikely. This ensures a profile with both high and low scores and exaggerates whatever differences in preference the individual has. Decisions between interest variables therefore seem definite and certain and based upon good evidence. An interpreter of a Kuder profile should remember, however, that the sizes of many differences are more apparent than real. Accepting the profile at its face value may result in unwarranted confidence in making a preferential decision between fields of interest.

A disadvantage is that no profile can be high in all traits or low in all traits. It is probable that there are individuals who have quite a number of strong interests and other individuals who have quite a number of low interests. On the Strong VIB profile such instances can and do occur. Information of this kind is often useful, and it cannot be obtained from Kuder scores.

Another important consequence of the forced-choice items is that the intercorrelations tend to be negative. Actually, about two-thirds of the intercorrelations are negative, although most of them hover around zero, as Kuder wanted them to do.[12] It is the forced-choice aspect of his items that brings about such correlations. Other investigators have found rather high positive correlations among items on literary, artistic, and musical activities when no forced-choice items were used.[13] The reason for the biased correlations from the Kuder scales is that in each item one interest is pitted against another. The examinee cannot express strong interest for both or low interest for both. If he chooses one in preference to the other, he is, in a sense, rejecting the other. Giving one a higher value (scoring weight), he gives the other a lower value. This is the basis for negative correlations.

Investigators often correlate the Kuder scores with other variables as if they were normative measurements. Such correlations are also biased, and the general tendency should be in the downward direction, in line with biases in their intercorrelations. Such correlations make *some* sense, because there is, after all, some positive correlation between ipsative and normative scores for the same variable. If an individual's mechanical score is low among his own scores, it will tend to be low among the

[12] See Guilford and Lacey (1947).

[13] Average intercorrelations greater than .6 were reported by Guilford et al. (1953).

mechanical scores for the population. For the correlation of two trait scales in the population, it is normative scores that we should use. The use of ipsative scores as if they were normative scores is, in this instance, very likely to give a biased result and hence a certain amount of misinformation. The biasing effect of forced-choice scores probably affects other statistical operations as well as correlation.

USE OF THE KUDER PRV SCORES

In his Manual,[14] Kuder has provided suggested lists of occupations to be considered by those with a high score in each of the ten scales and lists of occupations to be considered in connection with combinations of high scores. These lists were first based upon logical considerations, but as empirical information has accumulated, many of the recommendations have been supported by data. Among groups of individuals in different occupations who have been given the PRV, typical profiles are provided in the Manual for 53 of them.

RELIABILITY OF THE KUDER PRV SCORES

In the Manual, Kuder gives estimates of internal-consistency reliability for his ten scores. They range from .80 to .98, with an average of .91. Quite a number of other investigators have presented estimates of retest reliability, with time intervals from one to four years.[15]

There seems to be little difference in stability of scores between high school and college students, contrary to what we should expect from Strong's findings. For men, the typical coefficients in different scales range from .50 to .80, with an average of .65. For women, the corresponding figures give a range from .59 to .78, with an average of .68. On the whole, there is so much change in scores that retesting would often be desirable to bring the information regarding counselees up to date.

VALIDITY OF THE KUDER PRV SCORES

Validity of the Kuder inventory has been examined in a number of ways. One of the approaches to this problem has been to correlate scores of a scale with self-ratings of interest in the same category. In one study, the correlations for the different scales ranged from .39 to .66, with an average of .54.[16] In another study, the ipsative nature of the scores was recognized.[17] For each person, the ranking of Kuder scores was correlated with the ranking of his expressed interest in corresponding school subjects. The average correlation was .48.

[14] Kuder (1946).
[15] Rosenberg (1953); Herzberg and Bouton (1954); Herzberg et al. (1954).
[16] Crosby and Winsor (1941).
[17] Frandsen and Sessions (1953).

The interpretation of the outcome of such studies is somewhat uncertain. If the correlations were very high, we might conclude that students knew their own interests well enough without having interest scores to inform them. If the correlations were very low, we should conclude that either the ratings or the scores or both are of low validity. Since the correlations turned out to be of moderate size, we may conclude that the scores are aimed in the direction of what the students think their interests are, but there is plenty of room to supplement the student's general impressions with more exact information that is possible from inventory scores.

Another approach to the validation of the Kuder scores has been to correlate them with the corresponding Strong scores. The parallels are only approximate, of course, since Strong has a finer breakdown of occupational categories. In four groups of subjects, the coefficients between logically corresponding scales ranged from .30 to .48.[18] Recalling the remark earlier to the effect that the ipsative nature of the Kuder scores would tend to reduce their correlations with normative scores of other variables, we may interpret these results as representing substantial agreement of the kind of traits measured by both the Strong and Kuder scales involved.

Still another approach to validation is to predict the general nature of a Kuder profile to be expected for some special interest group, then compare the obtained average profile with that predicted. This was done with student interest groups, including such areas of activity as publications, band, religion, and athletics. The profiles were reported to be significantly different for these groups.[19] The same approach to validation, of course, applies to the various occupational profiles reported by Kuder in his Manual, where they approach reasonable expectations.

The method of validation that is of most practical value for an interest inventory is to see how it predicts satisfaction with chosen occupation. Two studies bear directly on this type of validity. One group of students was tested and a year later the students gave ratings of satisfaction with their kind of work. The rating was correlated with whether or not they chose a line of work in accordance with one of their two highest Kuder scores.[20] From these data the author has estimated a correlation of .39.[21] In another study, ratings of both job satisfaction and occupation satisfaction were correlated with whether or not the worker was engaged in work consistent with his high Kuder scores. The two coefficients were .24 and .58, respectively.[22] Satisfaction with the kind of work thus seems to be more predictable than satisfaction with a particular job in the occu-

18 Stanley and Waldrop (1952).
19 Magill (1955).
20 Lipsett and Wilson (1954).

21 A coefficient of contingency.
22 Redlener (1949).

pation, as one might expect. Another study provides indirect evidence of a similar nature. It was found that men who were tested in high school and who, seven to nine years later, were in occupations consistent with their Kuder scores had higher average scores in the scales corresponding to their categories than did men who were in occupations not consistent with their Kuder scores.[23] This was true for all but three of the scoring categories, and for these three there were inadequate samples to make a test.

In the prediction of school grades from Kuder scores, the picture is about the same as we saw for the Strong inventory. In quite a number of studies the correlations were either close to zero or were usually not above .30.[24] In two investigations, the Kuder scores did not predict which students would complete their courses of study.[25]

Frandsen (1947) tested a hypothesis of Strong that interest scores will predict achievement only over a long period of time and should not be expected to predict achievement in single courses or for a period of one semester. Frandsen used as his criteria of achievement the scores in comprehensive examinations in different fields. From this approach, it was found that the scientific score correlated .50 with the achievement score in natural science and .34 with the score in social studies. The scientific score also correlated .54 with number of courses taken in the natural sciences and .32 with number of courses taken in the social studies. The correlations between achievement scores and number of courses taken in corresponding fields were low. In support of the Strong hypothesis, it can also be reported that Kelly and Fiske (1951) found a correlation of .47 between the Strong score for psychologist and achievement in psychology during the next four years.

Mindful of the ipsative nature of the Kuder scores, investigators have correlated *relative* interest scores with *relative* achievement in corresponding subjects. That is, for each student the rank order of his scores was correlated with the rank order of his grades; then all correlations were averaged.[26] The student also ranked his own interests in the same subjects. The average correlation of Kuder scores with grades was .27 and with ratings of interest .48. The average correlation between ratings of interests and grades was .51. It is quite possible that the last correlation was biased by the fact that the students knew their grades and perhaps rated interests somewhat in line with that knowledge.

For the prediction of vocational success, the Kuder inventory has

23 Levine and Wallen (1954).

24 Frandsen (1945); Phillips and Osborne (1949); Hake and Ruedisili (1949); Borg (1950); Long and Perry (1953).

25 Bolanovich and Goodman (1944); Samuelson and Pearson (1956).

26 Frandsen and Sessions (1953).

shown no promise. It failed to predict which students would pass or fail in pilot training.[27] It also failed to predict the rated success of supervisors in an aircraft industry.[28] There may be other areas in which significant predictions of success can be made, but the accuracy of prediction is likely to be small.

BIASING OF KUDER PRV SCORES

The Kuder scores have been found to be quite susceptible to willful biasing. It appears to be easier to bias particular scores downward than upward.[29] Even high school students have succeeded in biasing scores either favorably or unfavorably.[30] In an employment situation, men applying for appointments as police officers made higher average scores in certain scales, such as social service and mechanical, than did police already employed.[31] While we do not know that these differences do not represent genuine differences between two populations, one hypothesis is that the applicants were trying to make a good impression.

The Guilford-Shneidman-Zimmerman Interest Survey

The Guilford-Shneidman-Zimmerman inventory (to be referred to as the GSZ inventory) is mentioned because it offers two or three novel features. Like the Kuder inventory, it aims to cover a wide range of interest areas with a few trait scores. It differs from the Kuder PRV in that the choice of scoring categories was based upon the best information available at the time as to the interest factors or primary-interest traits.[32] There was recognition that this information was incomplete, but it went a long way in suggesting what the basic variables of interest are. The GSZ inventory also differs from the Kuder inventory by asking for absolute judgments of liking of activities rather than forced-choice judgments.

THE SCORE VARIABLES OF THE GSZ INVENTORY

There are nine main scoring categories with two sub-categories under each. The variables are as follows:
Artistic: Appreciative and Expressive
Linguistic: Appreciative and Expressive
Scientific: Investigatory and Theoretical
Mechanical: Manipulative and Designing
Outdoor: Natural and Athletic
Business-Political: Mercantile and Leadership
Social Activity: Persuasive and Gregarious

27 Guilford and Lacey (1947).
28 Comrey and High (1955).
29 Longstaff (1948).
30 Cross (1950).
31 Green (1951).
32 Guilford et al. (1948).

Personal Assistance: Personal Service and Social Welfare

Office Work: Clerical and Numerical

The distinction between appreciative and expressive was found in an earlier factor analysis [33] and it has been verified by a more recent analysis.[34] Some of the other distinctions are in terms of professional or intellectual level, for example, the categories of Investigatory and Theoretical under Scientific, and the categories of Manipulative and Designing under Mechanical. Recent factor-analytical studies have supported all the major categories except that those of Artistic and Linguistic were found to belong together under two aesthetic interest traits, which should be distinguished as Appreciative and Expressive.[35] Very high correlations, however, between Investigatory and Theoretical (.87 and .96), between Clerical and Numerical (.85 and .80), and between some of the other pairs under the same major categories indicate that in some cases one score would do the work of two.

VOCATIONAL AND AVOCATIONAL INTEREST SCORES

Another novel feature of the GSZ inventory is its distinction between liking activities used as a means of earning a living and the same activities used as a hobby, to be enjoyed for their own sakes. For each of the 18 score categories, 2 scores can be obtained, one a vocational score and one an avocational or hobby score. One reason for this distinction and for the inclusion of a hobby score was the belief that, in a society where leisure time is on the increase, individuals need guidance in the selection of hobbies as well as vocations. Another reason was that a hobby score might reflect more genuine interest in an area by ruling out of the picture the prospects of various financial returns. A hobby score might then be a kind of confirmation of fundamental interest in the direction of some vocation as well.

Some findings of Super (1941) support this reasoning. He was able to conclude that men whose avocations resemble their vocations are more satisfied with their work and show less desire for a change of occupation. Changes of occupation that are in the direction of avocations tend to increase job satisfaction. There was also the finding that some men who do not find satisfaction from their kind of work can compensate for this and find their choice of occupation more acceptable if they have found satisfying avocations. This would be another reason for guiding men into satisfying avocations.

Results show that there is considerable independence between voca-

33 Lurie (1937).

34 Guilford, Christensen, Bond, and Sutton (1954).

35 *Ibid.*

tional and hobby scores in the same area. Actually zero correlations (.04) were found in two instances, in the mercantile and gregarious categories. The highest correlations were found for the two clerical scores (.63) and two numerical scores (.59).

Some Special Forms of Interest Inventories

A number of efforts to extend or to modify the procedures for measurement of interests are worth noting in passing, primarily because of their novel features.

PICTORIAL INTEREST INVENTORIES

Two serious attempts have been made to produce interest inventories using pictorial items in place of verbal items, with the hypothesis that the material is more realistic and hence might elicit more faithful responses regarding genuine interests. The pictures are of people at work in various occupations, with several pictures for each occupation. In one of these inventories,[36] greater objectivity was introduced by making it a memory test. All pictures are shown to a group of examinees, then a memory test is given to see how many pictures of each occupational category are remembered. The hypothesis is that the pictures of an occupational group will be remembered in proportion to the interest in them and in that occupation. In the other pictorial inventory,[37] pictures were presented in pairs for forced-choice responses. The scores from these two inventories were neither sufficiently reliable nor valid for use in measuring interests.

AN INTEREST INVENTORY FOR CHILDREN

More than one attempt has been made to develop an interest inventory for children. One of these is an inventory for children in grades 4 to 6.[38] In such an inventory, interest categories suitable for children have to be used, since most adult categories do not apply. As yet, the score reliabilities are not high enough to meet customary standards.

INVENTORIES OF NEEDS AND NONVOCATIONAL INTERESTS

At the beginning of this chapter an interest was defined in a broad sense, including nonvocational as well as vocational areas of motivation. Two or three inventories stress nonvocational interests and need traits. The most popular of these has been A Study of Values, by G. W. Allport and P. E. Vernon, published in 1931. These writers adopted as their scoring categories the six hypothetical major areas of human values as proposed by the philosopher Eduard Spranger. These values (which are

[36] Older (1944).
[37] Pierce-Jones and Carter (1954).
[38] Hawkes (1952).

actually very broad interest categories) are: theoretical, economic, aesthetic, social, political, and religious.

The Edwards Personal Preference Schedule, a recently published inventory that emphasizes traits of need, is based upon the hypothetical traits of need proposed by Murray.[39] Examples of the traits are: deference, exhibition, autonomy, affiliation, succorance, abasement, change, nurturance, and aggression. Another inventory of traits of needs and interest that were found from factor analyses is the DF Opinion Survey.[40] Examples of its traits are: need for attention, need for freedom, need for diversion, liking for thinking, liking for adventure vs. security, and cultural conformity.

THE NATURE OF ATTITUDES

Definitions

An attitude is a disposition a person has to favor or not to favor a type of social object or social action. Social objects include such things as institutions—the church, the public school, marriage, or government—and they include social groups—a race, a nationality, or some other class of individuals. Customs such as gambling, bull fighting, or auctions are considered a kind of social action. Another kind of social action would be some practice such as censorship, capital punishment, or taxation. Still another would be some form of political life such as democracy, communism, or fascism. Psychologically, an attitude involves beliefs as well as feelings, a characteristic that distinguishes attitudes from interests.

Opinions

An opinion is a statement of belief or feeling regarding something, hence opinions are often used as trait indicators regarding attitudes. They are obviously not always accurate indicators, but when expressed under appropriate circumstances, opinions can be expected to correlate highly with attitudes. A person may hold one opinion in public and a conflicting one in private. For instance, Schanck (1932) cites the example of a loyal churchman in the community that he studied who took a public stand against card playing but admitted privately that he enjoyed the practice. It is well known that there are home owners who profess tolerance toward certain minority groups and who yet sign agreements with their neighbors not to sell property to members of those groups.

Some years ago, La Piere (1934) reported an experiment on attitude toward the Chinese. The experimenter traveled about the country with

---

[39] Edwards (1953*b*).
[40] Guilford et al. (1954).

a Chinese couple, stopping at 66 sleeping places to spend the night and at 184 eating places to eat. The group was refused service in only one place. The proprietors of all these places later received a questionnaire asking if they would serve Chinese. Ninety-three per cent of the restaurant proprietors and ninety-two per cent of the sleeping-place proprietors said they would not. A control group gave similar figures. The results show very contradictory reactions on the part of these proprietors.

Many of these apparent contradictions can be attributed to the fact that the overt behavior is multiply determined, as was stressed in Chapter 3, and that the attitude, which may be in agreement with the opinion, has only a small part in determining the behavior. Or it may mean that cases are involved in which attitudes depart only a little in either direction from complete indifference. It may be expected that a man with very deep convictions on some matters will show more agreement between opinion and overt behavior.

THURSTONE ATTITUDE SCALES

Efforts to measure attitudes of individuals and groups began in earnest when Thurstone proposed a method some 30 years ago.[41] His method of attitude-scale development is so unusual among measurement procedures that it will be described in some detail.

Thurstone Technique of Scale Development

Thurstone's method of scale development rests upon certain propositions, which may be stated briefly:

1. For any attitude there is an attitude continuum of favorableness.
2. An expressed opinion is an indicator of a person's attitude position.
3. Each opinion indicates a certain position of attitude on the continuum, and hence has a scale value.
4. A person's position on the attitude continuum is the average position of the opinions that he endorses. It should be expected that each person will endorse only statements of similar value on the scale.

STEPS IN SCALE CONSTRUCTION

First, some opinions are needed. Instead of attempting to write the opinions himself, Thurstone collected them from people like those on whom the scale was later to be used. For example, if the scale were to be about attitude toward labor unions, each person would be asked to write down how he felt about the subject. In this way, statements that

[41] Thurstone (1928).

seem natural to most people are likely to be written and a wider coverage of different shades of opinion is likely to be achieved. It may be that some very extreme statements will be lacking and will have to be written by the scale maker. It may also be that very few indifferent statements, neither favorable nor unfavorable, will be written and will thus have to be added.

The next step is to edit the statements. Double-barreled statements are to be eliminated. For example, the sentence, "Labor unions raise wages for members but raise the cost of living for everybody," contains two ideas, one favorable and one unfavorable. Ambiguous statements, such as "Union members refuse to be bossed," should also be eliminated, for it is not clear in this sentence by whom the members refuse to be bossed. Every statement must be pertinent to the particular continuum; in other words, it must be valid or indicate position on the attitude. It should express belief regarding the issue. Some statements seem so factual that almost everyone would agree to their truth. Such is the case, for example, in the statement, "Labor unions have grown during the past 20 years." The statements should reveal personal biases and feelings.

The next step is to scale the statements. Each statement is written or typed on a separate card, and each of a number of judges is asked to sort the statements, usually in eleven categories along the attitude continuum, attempting to keep the differences in favorableness equal between all pairs of neighboring steps. This procedure is known as the *method of equal-appearing intervals,* a psychophysical method. It has been found that a group of 25 intelligent judges is sufficient to do the item scaling. It has also been demonstrated a number of times that the judge's own position on the attitude scale has practically no bearing upon how he evaluates the opinions. For example, anti-Semitic Arabs in Beirut judged opinions of Jews very much like American students did.[42] The correlation between the two sets of scale values was .93. Displacements of opinions were very small and not generally in the predicted direction.

After the judges have finished, the average scale position is computed for each statement. Statements that spread too widely over the continuum are discarded. They may be ambiguous and invalid. The next objective is to select a small number of statements, usually 20 to 25, to constitute a scale. If there are enough good items about equally spaced, two alternative forms are made up. The items in each form are best arranged in random order, not in order of scale value.

The following items selected for a scale of attitude toward college football are given in descending order to illustrate what kind of values opinions receive by these methods. They had been evaluated on a nine-point scale.

[42] Prothero (1955).

8.1 Football is the leading activity of a university.
7.1 The successful football team puts a college on the map nationally.
6.0 College football unifies the student body.
5.0 Football provides a means of letting off steam.
3.5 College football should be subordinated to studies.
2.0 The player gets so little from the game that it isn't worth his while.
1.2 College football is a racket for pecuniary purposes only.
0.5 I firmly believe that it should be abolished.

A completed scale of 20 to 25 calibrated items is ready for use in measuring the attitude position of an individual or the average position for a group. The attitude position of a person is the average scale value of the opinions that he endorses as expressing his own beliefs. Thurstone and his associates developed and published a number of scales, including the following:

Attitude toward War
Attitude toward the Church
Attitude toward God
Attitude toward Treatment of Criminals
Attitude toward Capital Punishment
Attitude toward the Law
Attitude toward Birth Control
Attitude toward Communism
Attitude toward the Negro
Attitude toward Censorship

Evaluation of the Thurstone Attitude-Scale Methods

Many questions have been raised concerning several aspects of the Thurstone methods of attitude-scale construction and there have been a number of investigations to test the soundness of his assumptions and procedures. There have been questions as to how stable the scale values of opinions are over a period of time; as to whether the scale values will be biased depending upon the attitude positions of the judges; and as to the equality of units on an attitude scale. Finally, there is the general question applied to all measuring instruments—are the scales reliable and valid?

STABILITY OF OPINION VALUES

In order to examine the stability of scale values of opinions after considerable lapse of time, Farnsworth [43] rescaled the opinions from the Thurstone attitude scales on war and on religion. Both scales had originally been constructed about 1930 at the University of Chicago. Farns-

[43] Farnsworth (1943); Ayad and Farnsworth (1953).

worth rescaled the opinions on war ten years later and the opinions on religion 20 years later, both at Stanford University.

In 1940 the country was living under the shadows of war in Europe. Would this perhaps make a difference in the values of opinions about war? There was a systematic shift of opinions toward the pacifist end of the scale, with an average change of 0.7 of a unit. Thus, on the background of war atmosphere, the same statements tended to seem less militaristic. We do not know how much of this may have arisen from the Stanford setting as compared with the Chicago setting. In spite of the shifts in value, the correlation of scale values from the two sources was .97, which indicates a very high degree of stability as to rank order or relative placement. Thus, the opinions would give scores that tend to rank-order individuals properly, but comparisons of score levels from the two scales would be inaccurate.

In the rescaling of the opinions on religion, 39 per cent of them showed significant shifts, 35 per cent of them in the more religious direction. The average changes were from 0.5 to 1.2 units on the 11-point scale. The correlation between the two sets of scale values was .99. From the two studies, we can conclude that although there may be slight differences of *level* of items on a scale from one population of judges to another, or from one time to another, the relative values of opinions will remain remarkably constant.

ATTITUDE LEVELS OF JUDGES OF OPINIONS

It was stated above that studies have well supported Thurstone's contention that the attitude positions of the judges have no bearing upon their scaling of opinions. There has been one proposed exception to this rule. Hovland and Sherif (1952) asked Negro judges to rate opinions expressing attitudes toward the Negro and found that the results were very different from those from non-Negro judges. This would seem to be a questionable procedure for scaling opinions and actually has little bearing on the Thurstone assumption.

EQUALITY OF SCALE UNITS

Studies show that there is some inequality of units on attitude scales.[44] This probably has little effect upon the scores of individuals or the averages for groups, but it makes questionable the comparability of numerical values assigned to different attitude scales. There are other possible reasons why values on different scales are not comparable. This is not serious, except when one wishes to compare directly an individual's scores from different scales.

[44] Webb (1955).

RELIABILITY OF ATTITUDE-SCALE SCORES

The usual type of reliability investigated for attitude scales is the correlation of scores made by the same group of individuals on two forms of scale of the same attitude. From a large number of such results, it can be said that the correlations range from .40 to .95, with an average of about .77.[45] The lower correlations indicate that either something is wrong with the scales constructed (they may contain irrelevant opinions) or the attitudes in question are not well organized in individuals of the population. The average of .77 indicates that as a class of instruments, attitude scales show much inaccuracy of measurement of individuals. The figures just given apply to a single form of an attitude scale. A combination of the two scores from two forms for the same attitude would give appreciably higher reliability of measurement.

VALIDITY OF ATTITUDE-SCALE SCORES

One of the approaches taken to validation of attitude scales is to compare average scores of two or more groups who would be expected to differ significantly on particular scales. For example, on the scale of attitude toward the church, active church members show a higher average score than inactive members. The three major religious groups in the United States—Protestants, Catholics, and Jews—have been compared on a number of scales and their average differences are generally in predicted directions.[46] More will be said concerning the validity of attitude scales in general later in this chapter.

Some Modifications of Thurstone-type Scales

Two significant variations of the Thurstone type of attitude scales are worth noting. One is a generalized form of scale and the other is the combination of scales to measure primary attitudes found by factor analysis.

THE REMMERS GENERALIZED SCALES

At Purdue University, Remmers and his associates hit upon the economical procedure of developing scaled opinions that would apply to several social issues or practices of similar kinds.[47] For example, opinions regarding different racial groups, pro and con, are likely to read about the same. To the extent that there are identical opinions, one group name can be substituted for another. Single sets of opinions tend to apply to similar social practices, social activities, and to courses of instruction. There is some danger, of course, that some opinions worded to

45 Ferguson (1952).   47 Remmers and Silance (1934).
46 Ferguson (1952).

apply to one object or issue might be inappropriate, even absurd, when applied to another, but such opinions can probably be avoided. The principle of the generalized scale can possibly be applied to advantage, within certain limits.

FERGUSON'S PRIMARY-ATTITUDE SCALES

From factor analyses of ten of the Thurstone attitude scales, Ferguson (1944*a*) became convinced that three primary attitude variables account for individual differences in scores from all ten. He named these primary attitudes *religionism,* which accounted for the attitudes toward evolution, God, and birth control; *humanitarianism,* which accounted for the attitudes toward capital punishment, treatment of criminals, and war; and *nationalism,* which accounted for the attitudes toward communism, censorship, law, and patriotism. He developed three new scales to measure these three factors, with generally higher reliabilities than for the typical Thurstone scale.[48]

OTHER METHODS OF ATTITUDE MEASUREMENT

The Attitude Inventory

Attitude inventories resemble other personality inventories in many ways.[49] They resemble the Thurstone scales in that they are composed of opinions as items. They differ from the Thurstone scales in that the opinions are not scaled and that when an examinee takes an attitude inventory he must respond to every item by choosing one of several alternative responses, usually one of two to five levels of agreement vs. disagreement. The opinions are either favorable or unfavorable to the issue in question, neutral items being of no use in discriminating among individuals. Very extreme opinions are usually avoided because they are accepted by so very few and would therefore make few discriminations. The most discriminating items are moderately favorable or moderately unfavorable. They are selected by the process of internal-consistency item analysis, which has been described in the preceding chapter.

It has often been found that scores from attitude inventories are more reliable than those from corresponding Thurstone-type attitude scales. There may be several reasons for this, one of which is that in taking the inventory the examinee must make some kind of a reaction to every opinion, whereas in taking the scale he has the option to mark or not to mark. Individuals differ in their marking habits so that some

---

[48] Ferguson (1944*a*).

[49] Concerning procedures for attitude-inventory development, see Likert (1932) or Edwards (1957).

mark very few and some mark several opinions. This tends to bias individual scores on a Thurstone-type scale. The more opinions an examinee marks, the more the average of his opinions endorsed tends to go toward the center of the scale.

General Evaluations of Verbal Attitude Scales and Inventories

In either case, inventory or scale, the scores represent an approach to the measurement of individuals' attitude levels through self-description. While we do not expect that the self-view will give a completely accurate picture of the actual disposition of the person, we expect the two to be strongly correlated. As usual, we stand the chance of some risk of incorrectness in such information. One test of the usefulness of such information is in the accuracy of the predictions we are able to make from it.

PREDICTION OF BEHAVIOR FROM ATTITUDE SCORES

Experiences involving attempts to predict overt behavior from knowledge of attitude scores have not been very reassuring. Pace (1950) made one rather ambitious study intended to determine the answer to this question. On the one hand, he asked over 1,000 alumni of Syracuse University to indicate their degree of appreciation of each of several areas of activity, such as music, literature, religion, politics, and civic affairs, in response to inventory items. The list of activities suggests that the study pertains more to interests than to attitudes, but the results may have some bearing upon prediction from attitude scores. At another time, Pace questioned each person on the extent to which he engaged in activities in these various fields. The correlations between favorable attitude toward (appreciation of) fields and corresponding amount of activity in the same fields were near zero for politics, science, and civic affairs but were .40 for music, .37 for art, and .33 for literature. When taking into account the undoubted inequality of opportunity for activity in some of these fields, perhaps the low correlations are not too surprising. It should be noted that both assessments, for interest and activity, were derived from self-reports or self-observations, a condition ordinarily favorable for positive correlation.

Other predictions of behavior from attitude measurements are even less impressive. A near-zero correlation was found between favorable attitude toward punctuality and actual punctual behavior of students.[50] Punctual behavior was in the form of returning books to the library on time, returning registration slips to the registrar's office, and keeping appointments. A zero correlation was also found between scores for attitude toward cheating and actual cheating behavior in an examination.[51]

[50] Dudycha (1938).
[51] Corey (1937).

Morale studies have been very common in various industrial organizations, undoubtedly based on the hypothesis that favorable attitudes toward management, superiors, and practices and policies of the organization must necessarily have some bearing upon performance of workers. From a review of such studies,[52] we are led to the conclusion that the correlations between attitude scores and performance of workers are usually below .20. This is true whether the criterion of performance is quantity of production or ratings, or whether it is incidence of such behavior as absenteeism, turnover, or accidents. Exceptions have involved rather specific attitude variables correlated with selected criteria.

How are we to account for the apparently very low value of attitude scores for predicting overt behavior? Do we have the wrong measures of attitude? Do we have the wrong criteria of performance? Is the overt behavior determined by such a multitude of things other than attitude that correlations cannot be far from zero? Are the criterion measures themselves unreliable or irrelevant?

Some or all of the above questions should be answered in the affirmative. In practical validation of attitude scores in this manner, we should ask first what kind of behavior should be predictable from them. We should not overgeneralize to the effect that, since the few studies reported find almost no correlation, there is probably no kind of overt behavior that attitude scores will predict.

If we consider where in everyday life attitudes are likely to play more important roles, we think of such things as voting behavior. We may think also of attitudes having much bearing upon what a teacher teaches, what a preacher preaches, and upon what an editorial writer will say in his column. If the assessment of people's attitudes from what they will say under standardized conditions is of no value in predicting behavior, the public-opinion polls would have to close up shop.

Predictions from attitude scores may more often than not have a low degree of accuracy. But, as usual, it is a question of whether the increased margin of accuracy that they may provide is worth the gathering of the information. There is also the possibility that measurements of attitudes by other than the opinion approach will be more successful in this respect. We shall now examine some of those alternative methods.

Some Indirect Methods of Assessing Attitudes

Some methods of attitude assessment are called "indirect" because they do not involve asking the subject to make or endorse statements of opinion. The purpose of the method may be well concealed from the subject. By inference, his behavior is expected to reveal his position on an attitude.

[52] Brayfield and Crockett (1955).

The methods vary all the way from objective behavior tests to disguised inventories and projective techniques.

OBJECTIVE TESTS OF ATTITUDES

One of the more promising objective tests is disguised to look like an ordinary information test.[53] In a test of attitude toward labor, that is, being prolabor vs. antilabor, Weschler (1950) used an "error-choice" method. Planted among multiple-choice information items, for which there are correct, factual answers, are a number of items for which no correct answer is provided. An example of such an item is:

During the strike wave of April 1948, the per cent of estimated working time lost was (*a*) 1.1%, (*b*) 2.2%.

The correct per cent was 1.6. It is assumed that the prolabor examinee will choose answer (*a*), since it defends labor, while the antilabor examinee will choose (*b*), since it puts more of an onus on labor. The score is the number of responses biased in favor of labor. The validity of the score is indicated by the fact that a known prolabor group made an average score of 17, whereas a known promanagement group made an average score of 12.4. An estimated correlation between scores and known membership in these two groups is .64. Although this correlation does not indicate the degree of prediction of overt behavior to be expected, it does indicate that groups of known biased attitudes can be strongly differentiated by the scores.

Other objective tests have capitalized on the expectation that an individual's "logical" reasoning will be biased by his attitudes. A test of syllogisms contains items pertaining to social issues, where an unwary examinee can be led to wrong conclusions by virtue of his beliefs.[54] Other objective tests depend upon the principle that attitudes may bias perceptions and memories.[55] An example is a memory test for a list of faces, half of them white, half Negro. The relative number of Negroes recognized later is taken to be a score for attitude toward the Negro. Still another test is composed of jokes about minority groups.[56]

A test of the attitude called liberalism-conservatism approaches inventory form in some respects.[57] Each item describes a social situation, asking the examinee "What would you do?" Five alternative answers are available, of which the examinee chooses one. The scores were reported to discriminate 25 known liberals completely from 25 known conservatives and to correlate .72 with scores from an inventory.

[53] Hammond (1948).
[54] Morgan (1943, 1945); Morgan and Morton (1944).
[55] Seeleman (1940, 1941).
[56] Gordon (1947).
[57] Pace (1939*a*).

A number of studies have been reported in which a sociometric technique was used.[58] Most of these studies have been done with children as subjects and concern attitudes toward the Negro. Each of the children in a mixed classroom may be asked to name those with whom he would prefer to eat, to play, or to pal around. In nonmixed groups, pictures of dark Negroes, light Negroes, and white children may be shown to the class, each child being asked to state the same kind of preferences. The attitude "score" for a white child would be the relative number of Negroes selected. There are a number of difficulties encountered with such procedures. Current customs, degree of acquaintance, and parental teachings were found to be among the determiners of the children's responses.

PROJECTIVE TECHNIQUES IN ATTITUDE MEASUREMENT

A number of attempts have been made to assess attitudes indirectly by different projective techniques (see Chapter 12). Some investigators [59] have asked subjects to make predictions about the future, expecting that in what they say they will reveal their attitudes. In another approach with children, a doll-play technique was used.[60] Each child was told to construct a dramatic scene, using dolls. From the results, inference was made concerning attitudes. In what may be called an "empathy" test, the examinee is asked to state what he thinks the prevailing opinions are in his population.[61] The assumption is that in saying what people in general believe he projects his own beliefs. In an adaptation of the Thematic Apperception Test, a subject is shown pictures of people interacting in some way and is told to make up a short story about the scene.[62] From the story material, inferences are drawn regarding the attitude shown by the subject toward, for example, labor. Still others have used a sentence-completion test, in which very short beginnings of sentences are given, and the examinee is expected to reveal his attitude in what he says in completing the sentences.[63]

EVALUATION OF THE INDIRECT METHODS

All these indirect methods must be regarded as still in the experimental stage. None of them have been given a very thorough tryout, with several different attitude variables involved. They leave a general impression

[58] Horowitz (1936); Helgerson (1943); and Deri et al. (1948).
[59] Carmichael (1938); Bartlett (1938, 1939).
[60] Dubin (1940).
[61] Travers (1941); Wallen (1943).
[62] Proshansky (1943).
[63] Rotter and Willerman (1947). Other indirect methods are discussed by Campbell (1950).

of quite varied reliability, with estimates all the way from .0 to .9. A characteristic reliability level seems to be about .6. Validities are generally unknown. Very often the criterion for validation of the indirect methods has been corresponding attitude scores from a verbal inventory. Where this type of validation has been attempted, correlations with these direct measures have been typically near .5. Intercorrelations of the indirect-method scores for the same attitude variables have been generally low. Most of these methods obviously need much more experimental development, with intercorrelational studies to help determine what they measure. Of the various indirect methods that have been tried, the disguised-information test seems to be the most promising.

SUMMARY

Interests and attitudes have been defined as traits belonging, along with needs, in the general category of motivational traits. They determine what we are for or against, what objects, conditions, activities, and practices we favor or seek after, and what ones we reject or avoid.

Inventories designed to measure interest traits have, in general, avoided psychological theory of fundamental human interests and have emphasized vocational categories for the purposes of measurement. Inventories such as the Strong Vocational Interest Blank for Men (and a corresponding one for women) and the Gregory Academic Interest Inventory have been developed on an empirical basis. They score the strength of an interest in terms of how well the examinee's responses to items agree with those of a vocational or educational group.

The Kuder Preference Record (Vocational) aims to measure strength of interest in a limited number of *areas* of vocational activity. It employs a forced-choice type of item in which the examinee ranks his preferences for liking different activities. The Guilford-Shneidman-Zimmerman Interest Survey adopts scoring categories along the lines of basic or primary-interest traits, in so far as they are known from factor analysis. It provides scores for avocational interests as well as vocational interests.

Interest inventories give scores that have a reasonable degree of accuracy, but scores are not highly stable over periods longer than about two years for examinees below the age of 25. Validity of the scores for predicting satisfaction with kinds of work in terms of stated satisfaction and tendency to change or not to change occupations has been fairly well demonstrated. They have very little value for predicting course grades but some small value for predicting vocational success in selling insurance. Their defensible use is restricted to that of vocational and educational guidance.

The Thurstone attitude scales are unique among assessment methods.

They are composed of statements of opinions, pro and con, regarding social issues such as censorship, communism, and capital punishment. The numerical value of each opinion has been determined by a method of calibration. An examinee's score on any scale is the average of the values of the opinions he endorses as expressing his own views. Inventories provide another procedure for the assessment of attitudes through verbal reactions.

As compared with scores from interest inventories, scores from attitude scales and inventories tend to be a bit lower in internal consistency and stability. Their validity for predicting overt behavior has been disappointing, but it is possible that the kinds of behavior that investigators have attempted to predict are inappropriate. It is probable that the determination of much overt behavior is so complex that attitudes make a relatively small contribution.

Efforts have been made to develop measures of attitudes by means of objective (behavior) tests and also by means of projective and sociometric procedures. Some of these methods have promise but need further development.

Chapter 10

BEHAVIOR TESTS

THE UNIQUE feature of behavior tests is that they evaluate persons from systematic and relatively controlled observations of samples of behavior. There is probably a popular notion that tests are confined to the measurement of intelligence, or at least to the measurement of abilities. Such is not the case. In this chapter, we shall see that there have been many attempts, some of them moderately successful, to measure traits of interests and other motivational traits, traits of temperament, and even pathological dispositions. Many of these efforts will be described, including situational tests and some approaches to measurement of non-aptitude traits through perceptual responses.

SOME GENERAL PRINCIPLES OF BEHAVIOR TESTS

The Sampling of Behavior

There are several guiding principles that determine the selection of the behavior that is to be sampled in a test. There are apparently some testers who believe that the entire personality of an individual enters into and helps to determine everything that he does. If this were true, it should not matter very much what behavior we sample for the measurement of any trait. A little thought, however, will lead us to doubt the practicality of such an idea. As a general principle, the idea may be logically correct. But it does not take much experience in testing to realize that certain samples of behavior are relatively better for revealing individual differences in one trait and other samples are better for revealing differences in other traits. In fact, we find by analysis that most behavior traits are of negligible significance in each kind of test behavior, if they play any role at all in determining individual differences.

BEHAVIOR AS A TRAIT INDICATOR

Our first principle, then, is that for the assessment of a particular trait we select the kind of behavior in which we believe the trait to be an important determiner, preferably the most important determiner. If possible, we want the scores from the test to indicate positions of individuals on the trait in which we are particularly interested and in no other. The trait must be sufficiently general to extend its influence to the behavior we select to indicate it, and furthermore, the trait must be a strong determiner of the scores.

It is true that more than one trait can be assessed from information derived from the same sample of behavior. Scoring different aspects of the performance—its speed, its accuracy, its stability, or its unusualness— might indicate such qualities as rate of movement, precision of muscular control, uniformity of motivation, or originality, respectively. There would be some economy of effort if we could often proceed on this basis, that is, by multiple scoring of the same behavior.

Multiple scoring presents its problems, however, as we saw in connection with responses to inventory items. When different scores come from the same behavior, they are likely to show relationships that are not necessarily true of the traits involved. Too often, even a single score is at once an indicator of two or more traits, which means that we have ambiguous information about a person. This difficulty would probably be increased by multiple scoring. Because of such considerations, the usual practice has been to employ one test to measure one trait.

CRITERIA FOR SELECTION OF BEHAVIOR SAMPLES

Since we must select functional behavior samples of many kinds to use in tests, we need some criteria for making appropriate choices. Certain requirements are observed by test makers, consciously or unconsciously.

One requirement is that the test must be economical, both for the examiner and the examinee. It should not take from either any more time or effort than is necessary. In this connection, we have to consider both the administration and the scoring that requires the judgment of the examiner. A clerk can do the scoring of an objectively scored test.

Objective scoring is a desired goal for another reason: behavior of all persons will be evaluated the same regardless of the scorer. We cannot say that objective scoring removes *all* human judgment from the picture, for judgment certainly enters the picture at places in the process of developing a test. But after the test is constructed and the scoring key is decided upon, all examinees are treated exactly alike in the evaluation of their responses. There are some kinds of tests of certain traits, such as creative-thinking abilities, in which at least some subjectivity of scoring has seemed necessary. There have to be decisions of "pass" or "fail" for responses to items in such well-known intelligence tests as the Stanford Binet. On the whole, however, the goal of objective scoring has been quite broadly achieved.

A test should present an acceptable situation. It should appear reasonable to those who take it and to those affected by decisions based upon the results. This is a problem of public relations, more specifically, the problem of *face validity*. The public that supports testing programs and that is affected by the results will find tests more palatable if they appear to be pertinent. Face validity is required in addition to genuine validity, of course, and is not a substitute for it. Another aspect of reasonableness is that tests should not be harmful or insulting to examinees. If it is necessary to upset the equilibrium of examinees as a part of the conditions of testing, there should be some general warning in advance and some opportunity for declining to be tested.

TYPES OF TEST MATERIAL

Some test forms are preferred to others because they satisfy many of the criteria mentioned above. Printed tests have many advantages, particularly in the economy provided by group testing. They also provide a permanent record of the behavior of the examinee. They are by no means confined to verbal material.[1] Even some of the manual psychomotor abilities have been tested by means of printed tests. Performance tests usually require equipment or apparatus, which is relatively expensive, and they are usually administered individually or to very small groups.[2] Motion-picture tests have been so expensive that only a few attempts have been made to develop them.[3] For testing perception of movement, for instance, they are the most natural form. There are other uses to which they can be adapted to advantage and they offer unusual possibilities for control of presentation of material. Furthermore, they can be administered to large groups if it is so desired.

Aptitude vs. Nonaptitude Tests

The general use of behavior tests for measuring traits other than abilities is a relatively recent development. Such tests present problems not encountered in tests of abilities. Some contrasts are of considerable interest, particularly with respect to problems of motivation.

THE PROBLEM OF MOTIVATION IN TESTS OF ABILITY

One of the temporary personal conditions to be controlled in testing is the motivation of examinees, its level and its kind. In giving tests of abilities, examinees should have uniformly high motivation, if possible. This does not mean maximum motivation, for we know that in general

---

[1] For descriptions of great varieties of printed tests, see Guilford and Lacey (1947); see also Chap. 15 for illustrations.

[2] See Melton (1947).

[3] See Gibson (1947).

the level of motivation that is optimal for performance is something short of maximum. In terms of best performance, a person can try too hard for his own good. It is usually assumed that if every examinee is trying reasonably hard to do his best without becoming disorganized to any appreciable extent, we have controlled level of motivation about as well as we can.

In a test of ability, examiners frequently tell the examinee something about the nature of the ability being measured. This should be another effective means of control, for it should direct the attention of the examinee to the significant things he is to attempt to do. It should emphasize the nature of the task in a way that makes more uniform the manner in which different examinees go about the items. The test should then measure more nearly the same trait or traits for all examinees.

A lack of explicit instructions leaves the task somewhat ambiguous to the examinee. An example of this is the digit-symbol test, a part of the Wechsler-Bellevue Intelligence Scale. It is usually assumed that the test measures ability to form new associations. The instructions commonly used make no mention of this. By determining how many associative connections examinees remembered after they had taken the digit-symbol test it was found that some of them learned and remembered the associations between digits and symbols and others did not.[4] Some thus seem to take it as a learning-and-memory test while others do not. When the test was given with instructions changed to inform the examinees that they were to learn associations, much more memory for the associations was found in memory tests following the digit-symbol test.

In general, if instructions are left ambiguous as to objectives, a test may easily measure some trait other than the one intended. If the examinees should generally agree upon an objective other than that intended, the test measures some ability not intended. If there is considerable difference of opinion among examinees, the test measures one ability more for one person and another ability more for another. If examinees waver in their interpretation of the objective, a large proportion of random error is introduced into the scores. The implication of these considerations is very clear. A test of ability should usually be clearly structured for examinees. Even then, the examinee will not always do the items in the way intended.

MOTIVATION IN OTHER TESTS

In contrast to tests of ability, tests of motivation and temperament traits call for concealed objectives. It is important that the examinee not know what trait is being measured. If all examinees know what trait

---

[4] Luchins and Luchins (1953).

is being measured and how the test measures it, they might make perfect, or nearly perfect, scores. The variance among scores will at least be severely reduced, and what variance remains might represent ability to achieve the objective, which is to obtain a good score.

The examinee likes to be told that the test has some objective, some purpose. In a nonaptitude test, he is consequently often given some irrelevant objective, either by direct statement or by implication, to satisfy this need. Here some questions of professional ethics arise that are difficult to answer. Sometimes the pretext for the test is obviously so lame that the examinee distrusts it. He may even "see through" the subterfuge. But in leaving instructions without something about aims, we lose much control that is needed to standardize conditions for different examinees.

We are thus forced to steer between the horns of a dilemma. The test maker should attempt to give enough information to guide examinees in the same direction but not enough to give a clue as to how to make a score that is better than is deserved. One general principle that helps in this connection is to make the test look like a measure of some kind of ability. There seems to be no way around this much of a step in the direction of deception as to purposes.

INTELLIGENCE TESTS

Whole books have been written about tests of intelligence and other abilities without exhausting the subject. We can do very little in the way of a review of these topics in the part of one chapter. Only the highlights can be noted. We shall try to see intelligence tests in their proper general perspective, to note their present status, and to estimate their over-all value. We shall do the same for other tests of ability in the section to follow.

A Historical Perspective

The intelligence test and the IQ are an established part of our present-day culture. Probably no other concepts offered by psychology and its technologies are so well known. How did this come about? From the beginning, intelligence tests were developed without much attention to empirically tested basic theory and almost always with an eye on the need for practical applications. This circumstance has had much to do with the direction their development has taken.

TESTS BEFORE BINET

The first efforts to measure intelligence by means of tests, efforts which later proved to be abortive, were those of Sir Francis Galton, in England.

From the biological tradition, before Darwin and after, psychology had inherited the two important concepts of instinct and intelligence. These were regarded as two different modes of determination of behavior, the one unlearned and the other learned. Learning was regarded as the key to intelligence, and to this day we frequently see intelligence defined as learning ability. From the British tradition in philosophy came the idea that association of ideas is the key to learning. This might have suggested that tests of intelligence should emphasize learning or the formation of associations, but it apparently did not. Ideas are traceable ultimately to sense impressions, and this became the basis for Galton's selection of tests. They emphasized measures of sensory acuity and sensory discrimination. Galton gave some simple motor tests, also, but these were more incidental to his general aim to study the hereditary basis of human qualities, mental and physical.

James McKeen Cattell, who assisted Galton in his testing investigations, brought the tests to the United States and later administered them to freshmen students at Columbia University, with the idea of determining whether they would predict academic achievement, which was presumably regarded as another indicator of intelligence. The validity correlations turned out to be very low, which proved to be a severe blow to the young test movement.

THE BINET INTELLIGENCE TEST

The fact that Alfred Binet and Theodore Simon were commissioned to find a means of discriminating the educational laggards is well-known history, as is the fact that this led to the first successful intelligence test. It is usually overlooked that prior to this historical event, Binet had spent many years as an experimental psychologist studying the nature of thought processes. It is fairly clear from his early conclusions and even from his discussions of intelligence, that he regarded human intellect not as a single function but as a collection of "higher" mental processes, such as judgment, common sense, memory, imagination, and critical resistance to suggestion. Had he set about the task of developing methods to measure intellect apart from an immediately practical use, he might well have come out with a multiple-score instrument. The immediate use for the instrument that he developed for the Paris schools was to arrive at a single administrative decision for each child. The child was or he was not to be segregated for special instruction. For this purpose, a single score sufficed. In constructing his intelligence scale, however, Binet introduced considerable variety into his battery of tests. The different mental functions as he knew them were to be represented.

INTELLIGENCE TESTS AFTER BINET

The first Binet-Simon scale was published in 1905, a first revision followed in 1908 and a second revision in 1911. Several American revisions soon followed, the most popular of which was the Terman scale produced at Stanford University and published in 1916. The second Stanford revision appeared in two forms, L and M, in 1937.[5]

By 1917, Otis had developed a form of intelligence test that was in printed form and could be administered in groups. Various revised forms of this test are still popular today. The Army Alpha Examination was developed by a group of psychologists under the direction of Robert M. Yerkes during World War I. A nonverbal test known as the Army Beta Examination for use with illiterate soldiers was also developed. Following the war, tests similar to the Otis test and Army Alpha were developed to measure aptitude for academic learning at various educational levels from the elementary grades through college entrance.

Nonverbal tests were also developed for individual administration. These were designed for individuals with language handicaps produced by one reason or another, for immigrants or children of immigrants, or for the deaf or otherwise handicapped. These tests, which stress such things as form boards, picture puzzles, and block or paper designs, are called intelligence tests although they do not correlate very high with verbal tests of intelligence.

Two kinds of measurement scales have become popular in connection with intelligence tests: mental-age scales and point scales. The latter have been more popular for group tests, in which the immediate score is usually the number of correct responses to items. The former have been more popular for individual tests like the Binet, in connection with which the concept of mental age was originated. A particular mental age describes a test performance that is typical of the performance of a child with that chronological age. For example, if a child passes tests or items such as a typical ten-year-old child would pass, his mental age is ten, regardless of what his chronological age might be. It is possible to find mental-age equivalents for point scores and this is often done in tests for children.

As is well known, the IQ is the ratio of the mental age to the chronological age. A child who develops at the average rate has an IQ of 100. For individuals over fifteen, adjustments are made in the chronological-age figure that is used to compute the IQ. Other adjustments are made in the Stanford revision of the Binet scale to ensure that the average IQ for the general population will be close to 100.

[5] Terman and Merrill (1937).

The Wechsler Intelligence Scales

Partly because of the inadequacy felt in using the Binet-type scales with adult examinees, the Wechsler-Bellevue Intelligence Scale (WBIS) was constructed.[6] Later, a Wechsler Intelligence Scale for Children (WISC) was developed. These scales have shared popularity with the Stanford revision in recent years.

The content of the WBIS is worth noting. First of all, there is a general verbal part and a general nonverbal or performance part. The verbal part is composed of the following subtests:

General Information

General Comprehension (intended to measure judgment or common sense)

Arithmetical Reasoning

Digits Forwards and Backwards (lists of 3 to 9 digits to be repeated exactly either in forward or backward direction, as told)

Similarities (determine how two given things are alike)

Vocabulary

The performance tests include:

Picture Completion (determine what is missing in each picture)

Picture Arrangement (put four pictures from a comic strip in correct temporal order)

Object Assembly (jigsaw puzzles)

Block Design (construct color-pattern designs in duplication of given patterns)

Digit Symbol (a code-substitution test, each digit to be substituted for one of nine symbols, which are given in random sequence)

The subtests are short, some with only ten items each. Usually, two composite point scores are obtained as well as a total point score, which can be transformed into an equivalent value on the IQ scale. The WISC is similarly constituted.

A Brief Evaluation of Intelligence Tests

This highly condensed evaluation of intelligence tests will follow the usual pattern, with remarks on their reliability and validity, and some comment regarding their social usefulness and their psychological significance. It can be safely said that of all the kinds of tests that psychologists have created, those known as intelligence tests have been most eminently successful and have had the greatest social consequences. In some respects, they have been too successful, for they have led to feelings of complacency that have reduced motivation to make improvements in measurement of

6 Wechsler (1944).

abilities and in understanding them more fully. The particulars in support of this statement will be seen in subsequent discussions and in Chapter 15.

RELIABILITY OF INTELLIGENCE TESTS

Total scores from intelligence tests have internal-consistency reliabilities that are usually above .90. Retest reliabilities depend upon the time interval. An immediate retest usually gives a reliability coefficient near .90. The figure may drop to .8 after about five years and continue to fall with time at a decreasing rate. In retesting adults who had taken the Army Alpha in college 30 years earlier, Owens (1954) found a correlation of .77 for the total score. We can say that whatever intelligence tests measure, they do so with considerable consistency and stability and that there is relatively little functional fluctuation in the *average* person over periods of years. As some studies have shown, this does not mean that particular individuals may not change considerably, usually owing to such circumstances as experience, education, or health.

VALIDITY OF INTELLIGENCE TESTS

Intelligence tests beginning with Binet were generally designed to assess the kind of abilities needed to succeed in schoolwork. The key subjects for the elementary grades are reading and arithmetic, with much greater emphasis upon the verbal ability needed in reading since so much of what is learned comes in verbal form. The first question that we can raise regarding validity of intelligence tests is whether they measure the qualities generally agreed to belong to the concept of intelligence. There has never been agreement on a definition of intelligence. The tests have been aimed at discriminating between the bright and the dull and between the mentally more mature and the less mature. Intelligence-test scores have correlated with ratings of brightness in the vicinity of .7. Typically, the raters have been teachers and they have undoubtedly had in mind the qualities that it takes to do well in school.

Tests that justify the same label should show very high intercorrelations. Total scores from different verbal-intelligence tests have intercorrelated in the range .7 to .9. Correlations between verbal and nonverbal total scores have been lower, as have the intercorrelations among different nonverbal test scores. Correlations between some subtests may be as low as zero, indicating that the total score is sometimes made up of components that may have much independence.

Designed originally for predicting academic success, intelligence tests have shown their greatest practical validity in that area. In the elementary grades and in high school, correlations between verbal-intelligence scores and achievement in terms of school marks have been typically in the range .5 to .7. In college, the results vary considerably from one kind of school subject to another, but for predicting grade-point averages the validity is often in the range .4 to .5. One reason for the lower validity at the college level is that the range of ability is narrower, hence correlations tend to be lower. Another reason is the greater diversification of subject matter, which calls for assessment of abilities outside the limited area that predicts success in reading and arithmetic.

In vocational affairs, we should expect that verbal-intelligence tests would predict success wherever the work involves or resembles academic activities. In summarizing numerous validation studies from vocational situations, Ghiselli and Brown (1948) present some "average" validity coefficients in different general fields. The data came from the use of different tests, in different work situations, and with different criteria of success; thus they can give us only rough ideas. Some of the average validity coefficients for different vocational groups were: skilled workers, .55; supervisors, .40; clerical workers, .35; salesmen, .33; protective workers, .25. There was no validity for groups of sales clerks (average of −.09) or of unskilled workers (average of .08). In some groups, therefore, the results indicate definite usefulness for selection purposes, in other groups, little or none. In all cases, there is much room for improvement of prediction by the use of additional methods of assessment if we can find the right ones.

INTELLIGENCE AS A UNITARY TRAIT

It was suggested above that Binet apparently regarded intelligence as a collection of different abilities. About the time Binet was presenting the first edition of his scale, Spearman, in England, was first proposing the idea of factor analysis. He proposed the hypothesis that there is a single, general ability, g, that plays a role in everything we do that involves cognition. Applying his early procedures of analysis to a few tests of intellectual qualities, Spearman thought that he demonstrated the truth of his hypothesis. He also thought that this justified Binet's practice of throwing a large variety of tests together into a single battery that gives a single score. Each component test, said Spearman, measures g and its own specific contribution. By summing the scores from many such tests, the amount of g for an individual comes through strongly and the specific components cancel one another out.

Thus, Spearman lent statistical support for the practice of a single score for intelligence. To this day, British psychologists quite generally adhere to the belief in a unitary general factor but recognize the importance also of additional *group factors*. Group factors are of limited generality but are not specific. They correspond generally to what have been called primary traits in previous discussions. In the United States,

Thurstone has been the leader in promoting the hypothesis of multiple factors of the primary-trait type and in providing a generalized type of factor-analysis procedure that is quite commonly used. By this procedure, we find little or no evidence for a unitary intellectual ability, such as Spearman's *g*, but much evidence for a large number of primary intellectual abilities, probably more than 50 (see Chapter 15).

TESTS OF VARIOUS ABILITIES

In the course of time it was realized that intelligence tests would not predict successful behavior in all vocations and that they left untouched certain significant abilities. There are also needs, increasingly felt, to seek more analytical information concerning the talents of individuals. These circumstances have called for the production of tests for abilities outside of the intellectual area and of tests of relatively independent attributes within that area.

Vocational-Aptitude Tests

One important area of vocational endeavor in which success has not been predicted very well by intelligence tests is that involving mechanical things—the construction, operation, and maintenance of machines of different kinds. Another area is that of clerical work. Special tests have been developed for both areas.

MECHANICAL APTITUDES

Thorndike once proposed that we should make an important distinction between abstract intelligence, which is of academic significance, and mechanical intelligence.[7] It was learned that the prediction of performance in mechanical types of work must be done with tests that are different from the kind employed in the usual intelligence tests.

Subsequent studies of tests designed to measure mechanical aptitude by means of factor analysis have fairly well described the primary abilities in the general mechanical area.[8] Some of these tests stress certain psychomotor abilities, such as general bodily *psychomotor coordination* (for those who operate large machines such as aircraft) and *hand dexterity* and *finger dexterity* (for those who do manual work requiring craftsmanship). Others involve abilities to deal with spatial problems, such as *spatial orientation* (keeping one's bearings in one's immediate surroundings) and *spatial visualization* (thinking of transformations of what one sees). The last two are classified as intellectual abilities (see Chapter 15). In

[7] Thorndike et al. (1926).
[8] Guilford and Lacey (1947).

addition, an important factor is identified as *mechanical knowledge*. This is the fund of basic and common information that the growing person acquires formally or informally with regard to tools and their use and commonly known principles of engines and other devices.

Thus, the concept of mechanical aptitude is somewhat variable in its reference; it is one thing for the operator of machines and something else for the builder and the repairman. Aptitude in these different directions can now be specified in terms of primary abilities, as we have just seen.

CLERICAL APTITUDES

Special tests of clerical aptitude have been in common use. They usually include measures of the primary ability of *verbal comprehension*, the weightiest component of most verbal-intelligence tests, and possibly one or two other components of verbal intelligence. Unique components have to do with rapid and accurate identification of letters and numbers and ability to alphabetize.

Differential Aptitude Batteries

Most test publishers now present among their offerings a battery of aptitude tests each of which is to be scored separately. The intercorrelations among them are sufficiently low to ensure that each provides information not covered by others. A profile of scores is more likely to be used than a single composite score. These batteries differ in their compositions, but the multiple-scoring principle is used with each of them.

An example of a differential-aptitude battery is the aircrew-aptitude battery developed in the Army Air Force during World War II. This battery is composed of about 20 different tests, some psychomotor, some printed. The wartime objective was to classify students for training as fighter pilots, bomber pilots, navigators, bombardiers, flight engineers, or as none of these. By experience, it was found that a different combination of scores from selected tests, differently weighted, would best predict success in these different specialties. In so far as it was possible, each man was assigned to the specialty in which he had the highest score provided he was sufficiently interested in it.

Tests of Primary Mental Abilities

A few published aptitude-test batteries have been based upon the rational basis of factor theory and the empirical basis of factor-analytic results. The aim is to obtain scores each of which is relatively "pure" for measurement of a certain aptitude factor.

One published battery of this type is composed of the Thurstone

Primary Mental Abilities tests, also known as the Thurstone PMA tests.[9] In two batteries prepared for two age levels—seven to eleven and eleven to seventeen—tests called Verbal Meaning, Space, Reasoning, and Number are included. At the older age level, Word Fluency is included, and at the younger level, this is replaced by Perceptual Speed.

Another published battery primarily for senior high school level and for older individuals is the Guilford-Zimmerman Aptitude Survey.[10] The seven parts included are:

Verbal Comprehension
General Reasoning
Numerical Operations
Perceptual Speed
Spatial Orientation
Spatial Visualization
Mechanical Knowledge

The factors involved are described in Chapter 15, and some of the tests are illustrated there.

THE USE OF PRIMARY—MENTAL-ABILITY TESTS

In addition to the fact that the particular factor-test scores are less ambiguous in psychological meaning than those from the usual test, there are other advantages for factor scores. There is greater flexibility in their applications and greater potential validity for various practical purposes. Some investigators who have correlated factor-test scores from a *single* test with practical criteria are disappointed not to find validity coefficients higher than for the usual type of aptitude test. In fact, in predicting a criterion that is itself factorially complex, involving a number of the primary mental abilities, a single factor-test score often has a lower validity coefficient than do scores for certain other tests. Such an investigator is ready to give up factor tests completely. He apparently does not understand that to predict a complex criterion well we need to combine tests of all the relevant and significant primary abilities. It may happen that some other test does combine two or more of the factors involved in the criterion and hence predicts more than any one factor test can do alone.

A number of extensive investigations tend to show that, with the right combinations of factor-test scores in composites, we can achieve appreciably greater practical validity than any single test can show.[11] Each criterion, such as grades in a particular course or kind of training, in-

[9] Thurstone and Thurstone (1947).

[10] Guilford and Zimmerman (1947, 1956b).

[11] Harrell and Faubian (1941); Ellison and Edgerton (1941); Goodman (1944); Guilford and Lacey (1947); Shaw (1949); Guilford and Zimmerman (1956b).

volves its own pattern of primary abilities. It takes somewhat different combinations of factors, each with different weights in different composites, to yield optimal validities. Usually no one complex test, such as an intelligence test, combines the right components that, taken together, can do as well as a composite made up of weighted factor-test scores.[12]

Tests of Empathy

Some relatively new developments in the way of testing abilities are concerned with social behavior. The abilities assumed to be involved come under the general heading of *empathy*. It is assumed that there are abilities to perceive something regarding the thinking, feelings, and intentions of other individuals. This subject was touched upon in Chapter 7, where the ability to judge others in connection with rating traits was considered. We shall give some further attention to the various types of tests of empathy here. They are still very much in the experimental stage.

One of the simpler and more fully developed tests is the Kerr Empathy Test. The task presented to examinees is to give judgments as to the likes and dislikes of people in general for common experiences. In one part, they are to rank types of music for general popularity; in a second part, they rank magazines, also for popularity; and in a third part, they rank annoying things for general unpopularity. The score is based upon the closeness of the individual's ranks to those known to hold in the kind of population for which judgments are to be made. This three-part test shows substantial internal consistency, with average intercorrelations of about .65.[13] It also shows some promise of predicting the personal popularity of examinees (where degree of popularity is based upon sociometric ratings) [14] and with job satisfaction.[15] It is not known as yet just what the test measures. A reasonable hypothesis would be that it measures inclination toward conformity with group values.

Another principle that has been applied experimentally in empathy tests is to ask the examinee (*E*) to predict the behavior of others. The behavior predicted is often in the form of responses to inventory items.[16] The score is based upon the number of agreements with responses actually given by the person whose behavior is being predicted. A variation of this approach is to ask *E* to respond to items as he believes some specified group would be likely to answer, for example, teachers or administrators [17] or a typical member of the examinee's own group. Still another variation is to have *E* observe the behavior of a stranger, or

---

[12] For other advantages of primary traits, see Chap. 5.
[13] Van Zelst (1953).
[14] Van Zelst (1953); Kerr and Speroff (1954).
[15] Van Zelst (1953).
[16] Steinmetz (1945).
[17] *Ibid.*

strangers, in a motion picture and then answer questions about them. In one study, four selected children were shown in 10 minutes of interview and 10 minutes of group discussion.[18] The use of common subjects to be predicted standardizes the test to some extent for all examinees.

The prediction-of-behavior approach offers many pitfalls and many chances of errors.[19] This is particularly true when observers predict behavior of different individuals on different occasions. There are several possible sources of bias, depending upon the extent to which an examinee's responses agree with those he is attempting to predict. If his own personality is similar to that of the individual predicted (whom we shall call simply "*O*," for "other"), and if he recognizes this fact, his task is much easier. He may put *O* in some stereotyped category and predict responses accordingly. If he is lucky enough to hit upon a good pattern of traits in the assumed stereotype, he may do exceptionally well; if he misses, he misses badly. If both the examinee and *O* respond as they think a good personality should, and if they agree on what a good personality is like, a good score is made.

There are still other types of judgments examinees are called upon to make in other experimental tests, such as the degree of popularity of others or of self [20] or of opinions that would be accepted by others in a discussion group.[21] There is still much experimental work to be done in this general area. Intercorrelations of different tests are generally very low. Scoring problems still must be ironed out. There is no good information as to what traits the empathy scores actually indicate. In Chapter 7 some evidence was cited that suggests there may be a unitary empathic ability, but the chances seem more favorable for quite a number of abilities in this area. We may find eventually that the field is best described in terms of primary social-intelligence abilities or in terms of numerous rather specific abilities, or both.

TESTS OF HORMETIC TRAITS

The hormetic category includes all motivational types of traits—needs, interests, and attitudes. Behavior tests have been proposed or developed for certain of these traits, with more or less success. We shall consider some of the more interesting examples.

Behavior Tests of Interests

Many kinds of tests have been proposed for the measurement of interests.[22] One type bases the score on the length of time certain classes of

18 Stone et al. (1954).
19 Gage et al. (1954*b*); Gage and Cronbach (1954).
20 Gage et al. (1954*b*).

21 Gage and Exline (1953).
22 Cattell et al. (1950).

objects will hold the gaze of the examinee when a number of different classes of objects are exposed for inspection. Another type of test determines how much the examinee remembers of each class of object shown. Another type is based upon speed of reading material regarding different areas of interest. Another uses a measure of the galvanic skin response (GSR) in reaction to different statements.[23] All these tests have in common the assumption that the degree of performance or reaction is proportional to the level of interest for the stimulus involved.

An approach that deserves special mention uses information tests, the assumption being that an individual will acquire during his everyday experiences more knowledge about those areas of activity concerning which he has more interest. The person interested in mechanical things will have picked up more of this kind of information than the person without such an interest. Similarly, a person interested in becoming an aircraft pilot will have absorbed more information in the field of aviation than the person with little or no interest. This approach was given a limited trial in the Army Air Force during World War II.[24] A test called General Information included items on information regarding airplanes and aviation. Another test called Technical Vocabulary included terms pertaining to piloting an airplane and also terms pertaining to navigation. Factor analysis did, indeed, show that both measured to a small extent a trait that could be called *aviation interest*.

Except for the information-test approach, none of the methods described above for measuring interests seem promising. Reliabilities are quite varied and intercorrelations of scores are low where we should expect them to be quite high. Even the information approach can be readily questioned on both logical and empirical grounds. It is obvious that interest is not the only basis for having or not having information in a field. Opportunities to acquire information in the field differ considerably. A person with low interest chances upon situations that force information upon him. A person with strong interest lives where he lacks the opportunity to acquire knowledge of the field or he is kept too busy with other things. If we could equate opportunities for acquiring information, the principle would stand a much better chance of working for us. Analysis of the Technical Vocabulary test (pilot score) mentioned above showed that it measures the factor of *verbal comprehension* (which any nontechnical vocabulary test also measures) and the factor of *mechanical knowledge* both slightly more strongly than it measures *aviation interest*.[25] These extra traits could probably have been minimized by im-

---

[23] For an explanation of the GSR test, see Chap. 6.
[24] Guilford and Lacey (1947).
[25] *Ibid.*

proved test construction, but probably not much could be done about the weak measurement of the interest factor.

Tests of Persistence

Efforts to measure qualities of persistence have been more successful. For the purposes of discussion, we may say that persistence is a tendency to pursue goals without being deterred by obstacles. Some of the tests involve merely keeping on voluntarily at a task whereas others involve increasing discomfort and even pain. Both performance tests and printed tests have been found to measure the same qualities. Some examples of performance tests, with brief descriptions, are: [26]

Holding the breath (score is total time in four trials)

Maintained handgrip (time examinee holds handgrip at half his maximum strength)

Shock test (time examinee will continue to take an increasing electric shock)

Aiming test (time examinee will continue to practice voluntarily before he says he is ready to take the test)

Some examples of printed tests are:

Reading test (time examinee will continue to attempt to read where print becomes worse and eventually unreadable)

Word-building test (time examinee will keep trying to build words out of six given letters)

Analysis of all such tests has shown that two distinct traits are measured.[27] One seems to be sheer willingness to keep on at a task, with no implication of taking punishment in the process. The other is willingness to withstand discomfort or pain in order to show a good performance. The latter trait is better named endurance.

Persistence tests of the type described have been found to correlate significantly with teachers' ratings of children.[28] They have also been found to correlate with grades in college to an extent that would add something to the predictive information derived from aptitude-test scores.[29]

Level of Aspiration

Of all the motivational qualities that may contribute to successful achievement in life, that of ambition or aspiration to achieve seems most important. Roe (1953) found such an attribute to be one of the most significant traits in common to high-ranking scientists in different fields. Over the past 30 years, we have seen considerable investigation of aspira-

---

[26] Thornton (1939); Hartshorne and May (1929).   [28] Hartshorne and May (1929).
[27] Thornton (1939).   [29] Howells (1933); Ryans (1938).

tion to succeed or to improve, particularly in laboratory studies. Aspiration of the laboratory variety has been in the form of desire or expectation in connection with improvement in testlike tasks. Although it is not known whether this particular motivation is in common with the more general will to succeed, the studies have represented an effort toward development of tests that will possibly indicate that quality.

NATURE OF LEVEL-OF-ASPIRATION TESTS

The typical level-of-aspiration test is conducted somewhat as follows. A task is selected that should seem intrinsically interesting and challenging. It is a task of moderate difficulty and one in which most examinees can show improvement during a few trials. Certain performance tasks have been popular for this purpose, such as pursuit activity, maze tracing, or key-punch operation. Some typical printed test materials have involved reading (speed score), cancellation of letters or digits, or digit-symbol substitution.

Several steps are applied to bring out supposed differences in aspiration level. After the first trial, the examinee (E) is informed of his score. He may also be told the average score made by his group. In some variations of the test, E may be given fallacious scores after certain trials in order to ensure that he can experience some degree of failure or success. His reaction to this information can then be observed. After being informed about his score, E is asked to state what score he will make on the next trial. Sometimes the instruction places the emphasis upon prediction, sometimes upon his intention or upon his desire. Some 10 to 12 trials may be given, repeating the step of informing E each time and asking for his prediction or goal score on the next trial.

Several different scores may be derived, the most common one being the goal-discrepancy (GD) score. This is the sum of the differences, each between the last performance score earned and the prediction of the next. A flexibility score is based upon the sum total of all *shifts* in predicted scores, positive or negative, or the number of shifts made. A responsiveness score may be the percentage of *typical* changes in predicted score, where "typical" means raising a prediction after a gain in performance and lowering it after a loss.

THE MEANING AND VALUE OF ASPIRATION SCORES

The goal-discrepancy score has achieved a fair level of internal-consistency reliability, with estimates from .65 to .97 being given.[30] Intercorrelations of GD scores from different tasks vary considerably, with estimates of .25 to .70 being given.[31] These correlations depend upon

[30] Gardner (1940); Ausubel and Schiff (1954).
[31] Gardner (1939); Gould (1938); Eysenck (1947); Ausubel and Schiff (1955).

several circumstances that have been demonstrated by experiments: similarity of the two tasks, or their apparent similarity; similarity of scoring methods and whether the scores are obtained from the same or different testing situations; levels of performance in the two tasks; success or failure in this task or in some preceding task; [32] and having or not having knowledge of group performance.[33]

Does the GD score measure level of aspiration? There is much question as to whether it measures aspiration even in the laboratory or testing situations. There are several hypotheses as to what trait or traits the score measures. A high GD score has been thought to measure the traits of confidence, ambition, subjectivity, and wishfulness; and a low score to measure realism, cautiousness, self-protection, and fear of failure. Still other hypothesized traits involved include dissatisfaction with status, feeling of security, and respect for intellectual achievement.[34] Actually, it has been difficult to demonstrate correlation with any of these variables when ratings were used as criteria.[35] The GD score has shown only near-zero correlations with academic achievement.[36]

This type of test is open to many criticisms on logical grounds. The test is based upon several hidden, questionable assumptions. One is that all examinees start with the same status on the performance of the task, and others, that they have the same rates of improvement and the same upper limits. For good experimental controls, these conditions should be satisfied. There should also be equivalent levels of interest in the kind of task presented to examinees. As Rotter (1942) has pointed out, there is ambiguity in the question "What score will you get next time?" It might mean "What do you hope to get?"; "What do you plan to get?"; or "In view of what you know, what score would be a reasonable expectation?" With so many sources of determination of the GD scores, it is probable that many different traits are measured and that these differ from one task to another and from one condition of administration to another.

There is some evidence that level of aspiration is not a unitary trait but depends upon the area of endeavor. Hills (1955) hypothesized that for college students there would be varying degrees of ambition to achieve in social, academic, professional, and economic directions. He used an inventory approach. The lowest intercorrelation of scores was between social and academic (.21) and the highest was between academic and professional (.59). There were reasonable relationships between means of

[32] Frank (1935); Jucknat (1937); Escalona (1940); Heathers (1942).
[33] Gould and Lewis (1940); Gilinsky (1949).
[34] Gardner (1940).
[35] Frank (1941).
[36] Himmelweit and Summerfield (1951); Schultz and Ricciuti (1954).

scores and the specialization of groups of students in college work. The correlations with a GD score were essentially zero.

Tests of Character Traits

Certain traits come under the popular category of character because of their ethical implications. Psychologically, they can be placed in the category of motivational traits. They represent urges toward certain kinds of conduct that are socially approved. The classical studies of Hartshorne and May (1928, 1929) brought into the picture a large variety of tests of honesty vs. deception, selfishness vs. unselfishness, and of self-control.

TESTS OF HONESTY AND DECEPTION

Tests of honesty have pertained to three forms of deception—cheating, lying, and stealing. The kind of test will depend upon which of these aspects is being assessed. Some forms of tests of cheating are in a category known as "peeping" tests. The examinee is to do a puzzle or other task that cannot be done correctly without the aid of vision. He is told to close his eyes and is given the impression that he is not being watched. The extent to which he succeeds is a measure of the amount of cheating. One difficulty with this type of test is that it is not certain that E opens his eyes, if he does, with an intention to cheat. Another is that some Es may get more done per "peep" than others.

Another type of test of cheating behavior is known as the self-scoring method. Having taken a test, such as one on spelling, errors are determined by the examiner. Papers are then returned to the examinees who are told that, after all, they are to be permitted to score their own papers. The amount of discrepancy in number of errors made and reported is the score. In other tests in this category, examinees take part in athletic events, keeping their own scores and not knowing that examiners are checking up on them.

A test designed to indicate the strength of tendency to lie may be in the class known as overstatement tests. Given some questions of information, E is told to check those to which he knows the answers the first time through. He is then told to give answers to the items in a second time through. The number of items checked in excess of actual knowledge is the score. In another test from the same category, E is presented with a list of book titles, some of which are fictitious. He is to check the titles of the books he has read. The number of fictitious titles checked is the score. Another variation is to give E all genuine titles. After he has checked those he has read, he is quizzed to see whether he probably has done so.

Tests of honesty with property may come in a category of planted-money tests. Each child is given a kit of material to use, with coins included. His score is the amount of money that does not come back when the material is later collected.

It is easy to think of flaws that may exist in these tests, and many hypothetical defects may well be effective. The proof of the worth of a test, however, is in terms of what it does. Hartshorne and May have reported reliabilities from .62 to .87 for various forms of tests that they used (from correlations of alternate forms). They have also reported correlations with teachers' ratings of honesty in the range .10 to .40 for single tests and .40 for a composite score. The tests therefore detect something in the children that is related to teachers' impressions of their habits of honesty.

TESTS OF UNSELFISHNESS

Tests of unselfishness and inclination to serve others emphasize the tendency to contribute work for the benefit of others, to give money for charitable purposes, and to give money for things from which all the child's group would benefit.[37]

In the first of these three categories, children were given the opportunity to come to school a half-hour early in order to make pictures for hospitalized children. The scores were the number of mornings the child came and the number of pictures he made. There were differences in parental attitude and control involved, of course, and other circumstances helped to determine behavior in this test.

In the second category, in one example, each child was given a certain sum of money. He was allowed to decide how much he would give to a charity and how much he would use in buying ice cream for himself. In the third category, the schoolroom was given a sum of money. Each child was asked his opinions as to how the money should be spent—dividing it all among the children, buying things for the school, buying things for their own room, or giving it to some outside charity. The ranking of these and other alternatives by each child was compared with a considered best ranking from a "service" point of view. His score was based upon his agreement with the ideal ranking.

The tests of service or unselfishness each correlated with ratings given by teachers and classmates in the range .13 to .32. Combinations of them correlated .24 to .51. Intercorrelations ranged .12 to .40. There seems to be some thread of consistency running through the different scores and the ratings. Considering the looseness of control involved in the test situations, it is perhaps not surprising that the correlations were low.

TESTS OF SELF-CONTROL

Three types of tests of self-control are worth mentioning here. One type has to do with resisting temptations of various kinds, another with

[37] Hartshorne et al. (1929).

inhibitions of emotional expression, and the third with endurance of pain.

In the Hartshorne-May studies, tests with temptation were in the form of tasks lasting as much as 40 minutes, with some tempting distractor available to each child—a toy safe with a penny in it, an interesting-looking puzzle, or a box of candy sitting on his desk. The extent to which the child did something with the distractors furnished the self-control score. In the emotional-expression test, E would be told to "keep a straight face" while efforts were taken to make him do otherwise, such as tickling him with a feather, putting a foul-smelling substance (asafoetida) under his nose, or bringing a noisy object close to his face. A pain-enduring test measured the length of time a child would continue to accept increasing pressure on a fingernail.

As in the case of other groups of tests, we do not know whether a unitary trait is operating or whether there are possibly two or more distinct traits involved. We shall attempt to see what primary "character" traits there are in Chapter 17. It should be added that the kinds of tests mentioned here are still regarded as experimental and have not been used in general testing practice.

TESTS OF TEMPERAMENT

In the survey of behavior tests whose primary purpose is to measure traits of temperament, we encounter a situation that makes classification of them difficult. On the one hand, certain classes of tests have been developed to measure hypothesized traits. On the other hand, other tests have been developed with less definite ideas as to what they should be used to measure. The former approach to test development is, of course, more acceptable.

We find tests that were designed to measure such adopted traits as suggestibility, introversion-extraversion, and masculinity-femininity. We also find tests that are better classified in terms of their content or approach, such as word-association tests, situational tests, and perceptual tests. Actually, the last-mentioned groups have been used in the attempt to assess quite a variety of traits, nontemperamental as well as temperamental.

Tests of Suggestibility

Behavior tests designed to measure what was believed to be a trait of suggestibility were among the earliest nonaptitude tests to be developed. Binet experimented with them, believing that resistance to suggestion is an important aspect of intelligence. The behavior of dull and feeble-minded children brought this to his attention. Four kinds of suggestibility tests are commonly distinguished. Two of them depend upon the production of sensory and perceptual effects; one depends upon the production of muscular activity; and one comes under the heading of prestige suggestion.

One of the sensory tests has to do with the sense of smell. In one version of such a test, six small bottles containing liquids are presented to the examinee to sniff and to match each substance with its appropriate name.[38] Only two of the bottles actually have odoriferous substances in them. The number of matchings made to the four odorless samples is the score. Another popular sensory test is based upon illusory warmth. Subjects are in a group and each subject holds a coil of wire in his fingertips. The experimenter can be seen to manipulate a rheostat, which is supposed to increase the physical heat in the coils. Sometimes it does and sometimes it does not. The readiness of the examinee to report warmth when it is illusory is the measure of suggestibility.

One of Binet's tests is known as line progression. The examinee is to estimate the length of line shown by drawing a reproduction of it. The first dozen lines systematically keep increasing in length, after which there are no more increases. Suggestibility is shown by E's increases after the lines become equal. A weight-progression test of similar nature is also used.[39]

Tests involving muscular activity in response to suggestions are sometimes called ideomotor-action tests. An old form of this is the Chevreul pendulum. E holds in his fingertips a string, at the end of which is a small weight. He is told repeatedly to imagine that his hand is moving forward and backward, or from right to left. The amount of swinging of the pendulum is the indicator of the trait. Other muscular effects suggested are hand rigidity (E cannot lift his hand from the table) and hand levitation (E's hand is rising from the table).[40] The body-sway test is more commonly used.[41] E is told as he stands erect with eyes closed that he is swaying forward (or backward). A string attached to him runs to an apparatus that registers his movements.

In a prestige-suggestibility test, the emphasis is on the examinee's readiness to accept group opinion or the opinion of those whom he admires or of those in high status. A test of this kind assesses E's readiness to accept or reject opinions in accordance with the way that he believes the prestige source believes. We saw in Chapter 3 an example of an experiment in which it was shown that such a test indicates differences in the trait of ascendance. It may be that what has been regarded as

[38] Lindberg (1940).

[39] Most of these tests are described by Hull (1933) and experiments based upon them are also reported.

[40] Remmers et al. (1940).

[41] Hull (1933).

prestige suggestibility is the same as low ascendance or it may be that falling in line with prestige sources indicates two separate traits, as can and does often happen.

Curious as it may seem, some of the tests designed to measure suggestibility are among the most reliable (internally consistent) that we have. This is because the suggestibility reaction tends to be a kind of all-or-none affair. If a person responds in the suggestible direction, he is likely to do so to a considerable extent.[42] Scores tend to be very high or very low with relatively few in the middle, in contrast to most other score distributions, which are unimodal rather than bimodal. Retest reliability after some time is comparatively low. Most of the tests are apparently unusually sensitive to conditions under which they are given. There are often low correlations between different tests of suggestibility, values from zero to approximately .60 being reported.[43] This indicates more than one primary trait in the area, as we shall see in Chapter 16.

Tests of Masculinity-Femininity

Other good examples of behavior tests of a hypothesized trait are found in the area of sex differences. There have been a number of tests in which it is found that males tend to give different responses from females. One of the earliest of these utilized proverbs.[44] It was found empirically that when examinees are instructed to respond to each proverb by judging it true or false, males tend to accept certain proverbs more often and females to accept others.

Some parts of the Terman-Miles measure of masculinity-femininity are behavior tests.[45] One is based upon reactions to ink blots, which are ambiguous and hence open to differing interpretations. Male and female interpretations were found to differ in response to certain blots, which were then retained in the test for scoring purposes. An information test can also be discriminating, since there are some facts that males are more likely to know and other facts that females are more likely to know.

Goodenough (1942) has developed a word-association test for discriminating the sexes. She chose ambiguous words, such as "ring." Males are more likely to associate "ring" with bells or sports whereas females are more likely to think of something worn on the finger. From the experimental use of a large number of potential stimulus words, a test composed of discriminating words was developed.

Situational Tests

A situational test presents to the examinee a lifelike but contrived situation involving social interaction. The situations are selected be-

---

[42] Hull (1933).
[43] Littell (1946).

[44] Weinland (1930).
[45] Terman and Miles (1936).

cause it is believed that they will bring out differences in personalities. The examinee knows that it is a test but he does not know what traits are being assessed. He may have some ideas of his own on this point. The scoring is done by observers who take notes, as in the time-sampling method (see Chapter 7).

BRIEF HISTORY OF THE SITUATIONAL TEST

The situational test has had an interesting history. It originated in Germany during the 1920s in the setting of military psychology.[46] By 1935, it was reported to be in general use in all military branches and also in use for selection of teacher trainees. It was adopted in England for military testing and in civil service testing. It was introduced into the United States by the assessment staff in the Office of Strategic Services during World War II, in an experimental program for the selection of OSS personnel.[47] It is reported that by 1951 the situational test had become somewhat common in civil service and in industry.[48]

GENERAL ASSUMPTIONS OF THE SITUATIONAL TEST

From the beginning, the emphasis in situational tests was upon the selection of potential leaders of some kind. The basic assumption has been that we need to see a person performing in a complex, lifelike situation in order to obtain a proper view of his personality. A global view of personality is preferred, and a descriptive picture that is built up piecemeal is mistrusted.

THE LEADERLESS-GROUP-DISCUSSION TEST

A special kind of situational test is known as the leaderless-group-discussion (LGD) test. The test is usually conducted somewhat as follows. A small group of four to eight similar persons (similar as to age, sex, status, socioeconomic level), who know one another no more than casually, are seated in a circle.[49] A topic is assigned to the group for discussion. Two observers are present to take notes and to score the individuals. Each member of the group is rated for degree of leadership shown or for suitability for some assignment. A check-list procedure has been found definitely best for this purpose.[50]

There is a possibility of having a fairly good objective score in the proportion of the time each person talks. A talking-time score has correlated .65 with ratings for supervisory ability and .65 with how much the observer thought the person talked.[51] Another possibility is that the amount

[46] Ansbacher (1951).
[47] OSS Assessment Staff (1948).
[48] Bass (1954).
[49] Bass and Klubeck (1952).
[50] Bass and Norton (1951).
[51] Bass (1951).

of time the person talks is an important cue for the observer's rating of leadership ability. If so, it might replace the rating.

RELIABILITY OF SITUATIONAL TESTS

Most of the satisfactory information we have concerning reliability of situational tests comes from the use of the LGD test. This information is of two kinds: interrater agreement and retest correlation.

Correlations between observers' ratings of the same performances have averaged .67 and .75 in two reports.[52] Several circumstances seem to affect the amount of interobserver agreement. There is better agreement when the average ratings of groups are moderate and when the size of groups is moderate (about six).[53] Interobserver agreement is not assurance of validity, of course, since observers may be agreeing upon irrelevant aspects of personality. We shall consider validity of the ratings shortly.

Retest reliability of the ratings from the LGD method have ranged generally from .75 to .90.[54] This kind of reliability is lower if the two assessments of a person are made in different groups, which indicates that to some extent the evaluation of a person is partly a function of the group in which he is tested, as we should logically expect. A more accurate evaluation would be obtained, then, if he were assessed several times in different groups. A retest correlation for an objective score (time talking plus talked to) was found to be usually below .4.[55] The OSS group reported retest reliabilities for other types of situational tests to be scattered, generally below .50.[56]

VALIDITY OF SITUATIONAL TESTS

In the impression of those who do not appreciate the many possible sources of error from lack of experimental control, the face validity of the situational tests, including the LGD test, is very high. There should be considerable acceptability for such tests from laymen. In spite of the realistic feature of the complexity of the situation, it can be questioned whether, after all, the situation is representative of those in which the examinee will later perform. Performance in a leaderless-group discussion may well assess the person's behavior in a face-to-face discussion. To the extent that leadership in daily life depends upon performance in such circumstances, the predictions should have some validity. There is much evidence to support this expectation. There was little evidence to support the validity of the OSS assessments, perhaps because the military work of the men involved had to be done under such diverse circumstances.

[52] Bell and French (1950); Bass (1951a). Bass (1954) later drew the general conclusion that interrater correlations are usually in the low .80s.

[53] Bass and Norton (1951); Bass (1954).   [55] Semeonoff (1952).

[54] Bass and Norton (1951).   [56] OSS Assessment Staff (1948).

Some rather significant correlations have been reported between scores from the LGD test and supervisory performance, validity coefficients of .29 and .43 being mentioned for civil service settings.[57] An average correlation of .39 was reported with merit ratings of ROTC students who had taken the LGD test.[58] Correlations from .25 to .60 were reported with "buddy" ratings made by fraternity brothers for general esteem.[59] Correlations of LGD scores with objective criteria of leadership for sorority girls were smaller, being .36 for number of positions held in the university and .10 with number of positions held in the sorority.[60] Correlations with rating of leadership potential given by fellow students have varied considerably, coefficients from .17 to .42 being mentioned.[61]

A number of conditions seem to influence the size of the LGD scores and hence should contribute to the lowering of validity estimates. The larger the discussion group, from two to twelve, the lower the average score. This should call for a standardized size of group. There has been some study of the possible intentional biasing of scores by examinees. Experiments have been done on effects of coaching selected students on how to make good scores. Students who were given a few minutes of coaching showed a small average gain in scores.[62] High scorers gained more, low scorers less. With long-term training, however, there were considerable gains in scores.[63] When a whole group was coached, there was less over-all initiative and less consideration shown for others.[64]

Giving the examinee extra inducement to make a good score, such as promising him that his score will have some bearing upon his grade in a course, had little effect.[65] This may mean that the person who wants to make a good score accepts the test as one of ability in the ordinary case and does his best. There is some question of motivation in those who know their abilities in group discussion are poor and who have little aspiration to do well in it. Scores for this type of performance might therefore reflect aspirations as well as abilities.

Some light on what LGD scores measure has been provided by correlations of those scores with known measures of other traits. Correlations with verbal-intelligence-test scores are usually in the range .25 to .35.[66] Some correlations with scores from the Guilford-Zimmerman Temperament Survey add information on this point. Correlations with A (ascendance) range from .25 to .44; with S (sociability), from .27 to .31; and with T (reflectiveness), .19 to .26. The high-scoring person in the LGD test is

[57] Vernon (1950*b*); Mandell (1950).
[58] Bass (1954).
[59] Bass and White (1951).
[60] Bass (1954).
[61] Bass, Klubeck, and Wurster (1953).

[62] Klubeck and Bass (1954).
[63] Pepinsky et al. (1952).
[64] Klubeck and Bass (1954).
[65] Bass (1954).
[66] Vernon (1950); Bass (1954).

therefore likely to be more verbally intelligent, more ascendant, sociable, and reflective, all of which conclusions seem reasonable.

Apart from the LGD test, situational tests have not been conspicuously valid for predicting practical criteria. No validity was found for the selection of pilot students.[67] The basis for the ratings of predicted success in pilot training was observation of each man in a group of four who worked together assembling a puzzle of the Wiggly Blocks type. In a large study on the selection of clinical-psychology trainees, three situational tests were employed.[68] Correlations with the criterion of success were in the proximity of .20. More recently, military instructors (of basic training) were assessed in 12 problem situations and rated for probable teaching ability. The correlations of these ratings with ratings made by students, peers, and supervisors who were acquainted with the instructors' performances in the classroom were below .20.[69]

From all this one gains the impression that the performance of a situational test is quite variable, sometimes valid and sometimes not. Since the evaluations of persons rest ultimately upon ratings, situational tests probably suffer from many of the weaknesses of rating methods. It would seem that they have the advantage over ordinary ratings in that samples of actual behavior are observed. But this immediately raises questions concerning the samples of behavior selected. Other considerations raise the question of how well situations are controlled and thus equated for all examinees, as a good test should do. In the instances in which some validity, practical or otherwise, has been shown, it would be of interest to see whether weighted combinations of scores from tests of abilities and other traits would not do as well or better in prediction of the same behavior.

Perceptual Tests of Personality Traits

In recent years we have seen develop a rather enthusiastic vogue for the assessment of traits, other than perceptual, from the use of perceptual tests. This may have been instigated to some extent by experience with projective tests, to some extent by the knowledge that examinees misinterpret inventory items, and to some extent by the knowledge of habitual errors of perception in experimental psychology. In the field of psychophysics, for example, we have known for many years that when subjects are told to judge differences between stimuli in three categories, "greater," "less," or "doubtful," some will give a large number of "doubtful" judgments and others will give very few. The differences in this respect are suspected to be not a matter of sensory sensitivity but a mat-

[67] Guilford and Lacey (1947).
[68] Kelly and Fiske (1951).
[69] Borg and Hamilton (1956).

ter of traits such as caution, lack of interest, or inattention. Such individual differences in behavior might therefore be put to work assessing nonperceptual traits in an objective test that can be well disguised.

Some general principles or assumptions are explicitly recognized as a logical basis for this approach. The first is that a person's perceptions are determined by his own nature as well as by the stimulating conditions. It follows that the person reveals his behavior traits in the way in which he perceives things. The extent to which the latter is true depends upon the degree to which perceptions are determined by stimulating conditions versus personal traits. The proponents of this approach assume a considerable degree of determination of perceptions by traits.

THE WITKIN TESTS

Witkin et al. (1954) provide an example of the investigation of the use of perceptual tests to measure traits. These tests have to do with the individual's perception of the vertical dimension within the space in which his body is oriented. In the Rod and Frame test, in a dark field, the examinee adjusts a rod to make it "straight" (vertical). Each trial starts with either *E* being tilted or the square frame within which the rod appears being tilted. In the Tilting Room test, *E* looks into a small room that can be tilted. *E*'s task is to make the room "straight," either by telling the examiner what to do or by manipulating controls himself. In the Rotating Room test, there is the added feature of having the room and *E*'s chair rotated on a circular track, giving *E* a feeling of centrifugal force.

The scoring principle for all three tests is that a score indicates the degree to which *E*'s response is in line with visual appearances. A low score is obtained when *E* tends to approach the correct vertical. High scores are believed to stress *E*'s dependence upon the visual sense and low scores to stress his use of kinesthetic and tactual cues.

It is very difficult to evaluate the Witkin tests. Many substantial correlations are reported with varieties of assessments of hypothesized traits. There is little guiding theory to help and little is known regarding just what either the criteria or the perceptual tests measure. It will take further intercorrelational studies, using measures of better-known components to clear up the meaning of the Witkin-test scores.

GENERAL EVALUATION OF PERCEPTUAL TESTS

A consideration of the literature on perceptual tests leaves one with the distinct impression that the enthusiasm for them has been very much overdone and is largely unjustified.[70] It appears, thus far, that the total

[70] See, for example, Klein's discussion (1956). See Helson (1953) for a review of this subject.

variances in scores from perceptual tests under a wide range of conditions have only small contributions from nonperceptual traits. There are numerous difficulties. The stimulus situation, after all, is usually the chief determiner of what we perceive, except for schizophrenics and others who are beset with illusions. In normal individuals, it would take a very ambiguous stimulus to leave much room for individual differences. With many stimuli such as have been used, the trait variance is usually to be found in *errors* of perception. Errors are usually very small. Even when errors are large, there are potentially many possible trait determiners of what is perceived. Before any one kind of error can be depended upon to indicate clearly one particular trait, much better experimental controls will have to be introduced.

DIAGNOSTIC TESTS OF PATHOLOGY

Testing that is aimed at diagnostic examination of pathological individuals falls naturally into two classes: that designed to distinguish pathological individuals from normal ones, and that designed to distinguish among categories of pathology. Interest in finding or developing behavior tests that can aid in these directions has been fairly well divided between the development of tests to discriminate neurotics and those to discriminate psychotics. We shall consider efforts in these two directions.

Diagnosis of Neuroticism

Tests with considerable variety have been applied in the attempt to find some that will discriminate between neurotics and normals. There has been considerable success in this. Three classes of tests, both verbal and nonverbal, have been found valid for discriminating between neurotics and normals.

Among the nonverbal tests, we find a few fairly successful tests of sensory, psychomotor, and emotional functions. Neurotics as a group have been found inferior in tests of visual acuity and in tests of seeing in the dark, with correlations as high as .60.[71] Neurotics were also found to be inferior in tests requiring dexterity, such as hand dexterity and rail walking.[72] They show more body sway while standing, without suggestion,[73] and also in the body-sway test of suggestibility.[74] In the handgrip test of persistence, neurotics for some reason show a better performance than normals.[75]

---

[71] Eysenck (1945, 1952). See Chap. 6 for further discussion.
[72] Eysenck (1952); O'Connor (1952). [74] Eysenck (1945, 1952).
[73] Eysenck (1952). [75] O'Connor (1952).

Luria's [76] test of emotional disturbances has probably not been ex-ploited as much as it might have been. Essentially, the test goes as fol-lows. The examinee does two things. He responds to a stimulus word with an associated word and presses a rubber bulb with his right (preferred) hand simultaneously. His left hand rests on a device that registers invol-untary muscular contractions. Disturbances are shown by the usual signs connected with word-association responses and also by disruptions of any kind for reactions with the hands. Eysenck (1952) has reported that a score for right-hand reactions correlated .47 with the neurotic-normal dichotomy.

Using the galvanic skin response, two investigators found that the conditioning of this response takes place more rapidly for anxiety cases than for normals (8 trials vs. 22) and reconditioning also occurs more rapidly (5 trials vs. 11).[77]

Among the verbal tests used with the hope of discriminating neurotics, two are worth noting here. One is a word-association test with two alter-native word responses given along with each stimulus word, the examinee to choose one. The test has been keyed for scoring on the basis of previ-ously determined diagnostic value for each response.[78]

Another verbal test is based upon food preferences.[79] Twenty names of foods are presented to the examinees with the instruction to say whether or not they like or dislike each food. In two large groups, neu-rotics disliked four foods on the average while normals disliked only about one on the average. This kind of discrimination has been verified in an independent study, with even stronger differences.[80] While there is great similarity as to which foods are most disliked for both neurotics and normals, 70 per cent of the neurotics disliked more than three foods while only 5 per cent of the normals did so.

Diagnosis of Psychotics

Tests used in the attempt to discriminate psychotics of one kind or another have been largely in the nature of aptitude tests of the kinds composing the Stanford-Binet or the Wechsler-Bellevue scales.

MEASURES OF DETERIORATION

There has been some interest in assessing the amount of intellectual deterioration that has occurred incident to psychosis. For this purpose a comparison of scores in tests that emphasize previous learning, such as vocabulary tests or information tests, has been made with scores in tests involving new learning or reasoning. The main hypothesis is that, in

[76] Luria (1932).
[77] Welch and Kubis (1947).
[78] Eysenck (1952).

[79] First reported by Wallen (1945).
[80] Gough (1946).

deterioration, learning and reasoning abilities are lost more rapidly than previously learned information. The Shipley (1940) test was designed for this purpose and contains a vocabulary test that represents a measure of information and a test involving seeing relationships that represents a measure of abstract thinking. The difference in mental-age equivalents from the two tests shows some discrimination between psychotics and normals.

APPLICATION OF THE SCATTER PRINCIPLE

The use of differences between scores from different kinds of aptitude tests has been generalized considerably in recent years with the hope of obtaining differential diagnosis among psychotic types. The basic assumptions are somewhat as follows. It is supposed that normal development results in rather uniform status of an individual in all intellectual abilities.[81] This assumption may have arisen from a deep-seated belief in a unitary trait of intelligence. When it is found that individuals do not perform equally well in all aptitude tests, the inference is that something has happened to disturb an even development, something from outside intelligence itself. The second major assumption is that uneven intellectual development is due to emotional disorders. Emotional disorders do this by first affecting the individual's interests and through this his abilities. Consequently, unevenness in scores should indicate different kinds of emotional disorders and hence different psychotic conditions. The *amount* of intraindividual variability in a person should indicate the likelihood of psychosis of some kind.

There are several things wrong with these assumptions. First, it is well established by now that intelligence, apart from pathology, is not a unity. There are major variations among a normal person's positions on different primary abilities. If a psychotic person is uneven in his abilities, he could well have been uneven before his pathology developed or would have been uneven had he been normal emotionally. In fact, it has been demonstrated that normal and pathological groups exhibit about equal degrees of personal scatter in aptitude scores.[82]

Second, there is nothing known to support the idea that interests determine development of abilities to any significant degree. In fact, where correlations have been estimated between corresponding interests and abilities, they have been found to be generally low.[83] Third, the psychotic categories are not so well discriminated in terms of kinds of emotional disturbances. Even granting the assumptions, diagnoses are sufficiently

[81] Mayman et al. (1951).
[82] Gilliland et al. (1943).
[83] Results of Adkins and Kuder (1940) on this problem seem to be rather typical.

uncertain that we should not expect very clear-cut diagnostic differentiations of pathological groups on the basis of aptitude scores.

VALIDITY OF SCORE SCATTER

What are the facts regarding the many efforts to validate scatter scores and difference scores? In general, the findings have been negative; that is, they indicate a failure to support the hypothesis on both counts. Where positive findings have been reported, it is not uncommon for some other investigator to find serious flaws with the research.[84]

In the first place, the subtests of either the Wechsler-Bellevue or the Stanford-Binet scales are inadequate for determining personal differences between scores. Some subtests are very short and their scores are unreliable. Differences between the subtests are even less reliable.[85] To obtain reliable difference scores, we need basic scores of very high reliability and low intercorrelation. Otherwise, the differences are largely composed of chance errors.[86]

In the second place, there is indirect evidence that essentially the same scatter of scores exists before as during a period of pathology. Onset of pathology and recovery from it seem to make little difference.[87] Rigorous studies of patterns of scores in relation to categories of pathology do not support the hypothesis when age and sex differences are taken into account.[88] A factor analysis resulted in grouping patients according to their abilities, not according to their pathological categories.[89]

All in all, one is inclined to agree with Wittenborn and Holzberg (1951) that, until more is known about the matter, tests of intellectual abilities be confined to the measurement of intellectual qualities. Progress on this general problem will depend upon several essential conditions: more clear-cut pathological categories; better experimental controls of samples selected for study; and use of more reliable and more independent (uncorrelated) tests.

SUMMARY

Behavior tests take samplings of behavior of individuals, with sample behavior determined by the test instructions and the test content. The behavior sampled depends upon what trait we wish to measure; it is

[84] Magaret and Wright (1943); Jastak (1949); Rabin and Guertin (1951).

[85] McNemar (1957) has found the average reliability of all difference scores from the Wechsler tests to be .60, with one as low as .25.

[86] Lorr and Meister (1941). For proof of this, see Guilford (1954, p. 394).

[87] Jastak (1949).

[88] Gilliland et al. (1943); Jastak (1953).

[89] Frank (1956).

selected because we believe that it maximizes individual differences in the trait and minimizes differences in other respects.

The kind of material used in tests, such as printed matter, apparatus, or motion pictures, is partly determined by the trait we propose to measure and partly by considerations of economy. Printed tests are generally favored where they will serve the purpose. Aptitude tests vs. non-aptitude tests present different problems, particularly with regard to motivation of the examinee, which we should like to control as to degree and direction.

Intelligence tests represent psychology's first major conquest in the goal of personality measurement. From the first tests of Binet to the current ones, intelligence tests have stressed the prediction of academic success. They have thus emphasized aptitudes for development in reading and in content subjects that depend upon reading and for development in arithmetic as a secondary objective.

Nonverbal intelligence tests have been found to measure somewhat different abilities, different from those in tests of verbal intelligence and different from those in one another. The general success of intelligence tests in predicting success to some degree in various vocational areas has been at once an achievement and a source of complacency regarding the measurement of aptitudes.

There are trends at the present time toward multiple scoring of aptitudes in collections of tests known as differential-aptitude batteries. Some of these batteries emphasize the selection of scoring variables in terms of the primary mental abilities. Special aptitude tests have been developed or are being developed in the general areas of mechanical aptitude, clerical aptitude, and more recently, social aptitudes, which come under the heading of empathy.

Behavior tests of interests, attitudes, and other motivational or "hormetic" traits are still generally in the experimental stage. There is some indication that interests and attitudes can be measured to some extent by means of information tests. Experimental tests of persistence (and endurance) have been quite successful but have not seen much practical application as yet. Considerable research on the measurement of level of aspiration has brought forth nothing that can be considered ready for practical validation. Experimental tests of honesty vs. deception, of service or unselfishness, and of self-control have been demonstrated to be useful for research purposes but have seen almost no practical application.

Some of the behavior tests of temperament traits are very old, particularly those in the area known as suggestibility. Several objective tests have been developed for measurement of masculinity vs. femininity. A relatively new test designed to assess qualities of leadership is known as the situational test. A special, popular form of the situational test is the leaderless-group-discussion (LGD) test, in which a small group is given a topic to discuss. The LGD test shows some promise in the assessment of individuals for some particular purposes, such as supervisory assignments, where face-to-face handling of people is important, but it is not promising for the measurement of particular traits. The use of perceptual tests for the measurement of nonperceptual traits has had considerable promotion in very recent years, but outcomes of research on this approach have been disappointing.

Diagnostic tests of pathology have been urgently sought for some time. The objective has been to distinguish between pathological persons and normal ones and also to help discriminate among varieties of pathology. Quite a number of different tests have shown discriminating power in distinguishing neurotics from normals. Discriminations of psychotics from normals have not been so successful.

Some principles pertaining to special aptitude tests, such as parts of intelligence scales, have been exploited in connection with diagnosis of pathology. It has been supposed that psychotics, because of their emotional disorders, show more variability among different test scores and that certain patterns of high and low scores should be diagnostic of patients with respect to pathological categories. Rigorously designed and controlled experiments generally do not support these ideas and procedures. Under improved testing circumstances and with improved conceptual categories of both abilities and pathology, this general approach might show some promise.

Chapter 11

EXPRESSIVE METHODS

WE SHALL now consider a class of possible trait indicators that has been fascinating to many psychologists and to laymen alike, particularly to descriptive writers. These indicators are in the form of behavior, but unlike the behavior sampled in ordinary behavior tests, the aspect stressed here is secondary or incidental to the business of living. Expressive behavior, or, more accurately stated, expressive aspects of behavior, may be regarded as mostly nonadaptive. It is what gives the overt behavior of an individual its obviously distinctive flavor or style.

There is much popular conviction that an individual's personality is more or less on display in the manner in which his behavior is embellished. Perhaps it is the uniqueness of such mannerisms and the awareness of the fact that personalities are unique that leads to the expectation that the two things—expressive behavior and personality—are strongly connected. From this point of view, a person wears his personality for all observers to see.

It is not unfamiliar language that speaks of an "arrogant walk," a "self-righteous stance," a "conceited toss of the head," a "self-confident flourish," a "sincere handclasp," "miserly steps," or "dishonest, shifty eyes." Literature abounds with such expressions, which are accepted by readers as being meaningful. We shall examine some of the steps that have been taken by psychologists and others in attempts to capitalize on such potential trait indicators, and we shall try to come to some conclusion as to their validity and value.

A GENERAL SURVEY OF EXPRESSIVE BEHAVIOR

The most systematic consideration of this subject was presented some years ago by Allport and Vernon (1933). As an orientation to the subject, we shall note briefly something of the "repertoire" of expressive movements that might be considered in a thorough study of this field. In addition to observable movements, as such, there are postures and there are products of movement in the form of handiwork or of literary or artistic production of some kind.

Postures

How does the person stand, sit, or lie? What are the characteristic positions or dispositions of his musculature in different body regions when he is in a state of rest or relative inactivity?

While standing or sitting, the body generally may be erect, stiff, and generally immobile, or it may be comfortable, relaxed, or even slouched. When lying down, the body may be supple, curled, or contorted. In general, the chest and shoulders may present a "chesty" appearance or a droopy sag. The head may be tilted, arched, bent, or bowed. The face may be drawn and haggard or twisted and contorted. The eyes may be downcast or staring, the mouth set in a pouting, sneering, or smirking position.

Movements

There are certain qualities of movement that may be noted in many body regions. We might note that different persons' movements are vigorous, expansive, dainty, crude, clumsy, heavy, sluggish, or vivacious. Different persons' performance of tasks might be described as rapid, precise, orderly, or hurried. Some of these qualities, of course, can be objectively scored. Some are best rated for lack of obviously measurable variables. The face is especially expressive, of course, in connection with emotional reactions. Many faces carry rather habitual expressions that could be described as sad, suspicious, kindly, stuporous, vacuous, and the like.

Various mannerisms or incidental movements of different kinds may occur. The hands may be continuously fussing with objects; fists may be clenching and unclenching; fingers may be kept drumming on the table, or pulling the hair, or rubbing the chin. The head and face may be involved, the head making short, quick nods or tossing movements, and the face grimacing or twitching.

Special activities such as walking, running, dancing, or talking also have potentialities for unique features. One person's walking may be described as bobbing, others' as plodding, skipping, or rolling. Other aspects of walking gait are speed, length of stride, balance, and rhythm. Personal styles of dancing might be described as stiff, supple, gliding, choppy, or heavy. Handshakes are strong, lingering, listless, or pumping. Laughs are of explosive, chuckling, giggling, or wheezing types. In talking, several aspects have their qualitative flavors. The voice itself is soft, dull, nasal, shrill, or gruff. In manner of speaking, the person is loquacious, taciturn, stammering, or slurring. His conversation is punctuated with gestures, is halting, or is intimate and confidential.

Products of Behavior

The expressive aspects of behavior show up in terms of more permanent records in things that the person produces. Whether he is an expressive artist or not, there are some aftereffects that can be found in consequence of his behavior. Something of the person's personality may possibly show up in the kinds of things he prefers in the way of products made by others, such as his dress, his home furnishings, or his motor car.

If the person is a creative artist, performing artist, writer, composer, or scientist, we can see the results of his thinking and his aspirations and judgments. His personality may show up in his style or in the contents or subject matter of his productions. He may write an autobiography, which may be revealing from what one can read between the lines as well as from what the person says about himself. Literate persons are likely to leave samples of their handwriting, all of which have unique features.

Possible Roles of Expressive Indicators

We shall give attention to the methods of attempting to assess personality from samples of handwriting in the next section. Before leaving our general survey of potential expressive cues to personality, however, a general statement should be made. We have been considering the existence of a multitude of personal peculiarities in the form of postures, movements, and products. The implication has been, and usually is, that these are signs or indicators of the kinds of traits we have been considering heretofore and for which we have seen that there are quite a number of more direct methods of assessment. Whether expressions are or are not useful indicators of traits of aptitude, temperament, and motivation, they certainly present aspects of appearance and of superficial peculiarities of behavior. They thus form a class of traits that might be worth study in their own right, particularly since they can have so much to do with impressions made on other people. We shall see, later, examples of how observations of expressive qualities lead to stereotyped conceptions of more fundamental traits.

ASSESSMENT OF PERSONALITY FROM HANDWRITING: GRAPHOLOGY

According to Wolfson (1951), the Chinese were noting what they thought were relationships between handwriting and personal qualities as early as the eleventh century. By 1622, Carmille Baldi published the first known treatise on graphology. Graphology has apparently had its advocates at all times, at least since that date, and has held the attention of some persons with scientific interests as well as of laymen. As recently as 1943, Eliasberg, referring to the historical Munich meeting between Britain's prime minister and Hitler, wrote in these enthusiastic terms:

> Let us assume that Chamberlain would have neglected the type-text of the document of 1938 and have looked instead at the signature above his own. That signature would have revealed to him more of the true meaning than the wording. He might have seen the vulture swooping down for prey, or, more soberly expressed, he would not have overlooked the overstrain of that person who, in his hands, wielded the balled-together might of 80 million people, with no control.

It is probably safe to say that the attitude of psychologists in general has been that of skepticism. Yet, articles on the relations of handwriting to personality have appeared by the hundreds since 1928. A number of psychologists have done serious research studies on the subject. We shall note a sampling of these studies, placing greatest emphasis upon the more recent and better-controlled studies.

Scientific Studies of Graphology

One of the earliest serious investigators of graphology was Binet, whose studies were somewhat limited. He found that three graphologists could judge correctly from handwriting samples, in excess of chance, such qualities as sex, intelligence, and being criminal vs. noncriminal.[1] An enthusiast for graphology, Saudek (1928) devoted some years to the study of the subject. He reported results along with claims for remarkable successes, as compared with those found by more recent investigators generally. His findings are difficult to evaluate because of the nature of his studies and his reports.

PROBLEMS AND METHODS

The studies of graphology differ in some respects from one another in the kinds of questions asked, the kinds of interpreters or observers used, and the criteria of personality assessment used for validating the graphological approach. On the one hand, there are two schools of thought as to how personality traits are to be inferred from the handwriting sample. There are those who prefer the "gestalt" approach, insisting that the general impression gained by the observer shall be the information used. Others prefer to be analytical and to take their cues from different aspects of the sample, such as type of loops, angle of slant, degree of spacing,

---

[1] Binet (1906).

width of lines, and so on.[2] From this point of view it is believed that each aspect has its own story to tell regarding different traits.

Studies differ, too, on whether the observers or interpreters are to be experienced graphologists or naïve individuals, such as college students. On the one hand, it is maintained that the method should be given full opportunity to work, in the hands of those who know how to use it. On the other hand, it is thought that, if handwriting is revealing of personality, a minimum of experience should be sufficient to show some validity if there is any. If the description of handwriting samples is to be analytical and objective, of course, this is no issue. Where general impressions are used as information, studies generally show that professional graphologists do better, but only slightly better, than students, as we shall see in the discussion that follows.

DISCRIMINATION OF ABNORMALS FROM NORMALS

It was inevitable that, like most methods, graphology should be tried in an effort to discriminate abnormal individuals from normal ones. In one study, ten abnormals were matched with ten normals.[3] The abnormals wrote what they remembered of a story. The normals copied in their own handwriting the stories of their mates. Pairs of these samples were presented to 25 nongraphologists and to a graphologist who claimed ability to detect abnormals. The mean scores were 5.1 and 6.0, respectively, both very close to the chance level of 5 correct. A sample of one graphologist is not adequate, of course, to test the differences between the two kinds of observers. The results show, however, that if there were observable differences in the handwriting peculiarities of the two groups, the observers were mostly unable to use them in discriminating normals from abnormals.

Eysenck reports three studies involving judgment by graphologists.[4] In one, 50 patients copied items of an inventory and also answered the items regarding themselves. The copies, without the answers, were given to a graphologist with the instruction to answer the questions as she thought the patient should. There was agreement between the graphologist's answers in 62 per cent of the cases, whereas 50 per cent would have been expected by chance. It was not known, of course, how correct the patients were.

In another study, a psychiatrist wrote a personality sketch of each patient. The graphologist was asked to match handwriting sample with sketch in groups of five patients. The average number of correct matchings

[2] Lewinson and Zubin (1942) have made a serious attempt to arrive at objectively measured variables in handwriting.

[3] Pascal and Suttell (1947).

[4] Eysenck (1947).

was 2.4, where 1 would be expected by chance. A nongraphologist made an average score of 0.7. It appeared from the results that some patients were easier to judge from their handwriting or from the personality sketch than others. This possibly means that some persons express their traits better in their handwriting than others do. To the extent that there is expression at all, this would be a reasonable hypothesis.

In Eysenck's third study, a graphologist rated samples of handwriting for degree of neuroticism on a five-point scale.[5] The criteria of neuroticism were in the form of behavior tests and also psychiatric diagnoses. The correlations were .21 and .02, respectively. This might mean that the behavior-test scores were more valid than the psychiatrist's ratings. But since the tests involved motor activity, it may merely mean that there were *psychomotor* traits in common to the scores and the graphologist's ratings of handwriting, also a psychomotor task.

ASSESSMENT OF TRAITS FROM HANDWRITING

A more exacting demand to make of graphology is that it serve as a basis for assessing traits of persons. Studies of this kind have been done using both graphologists and nongraphologists as observers and using both ratings and test or inventory scores and the like as criteria.

In an unpublished study, the author obtained samples from 20 individuals who did not know that their handwriting would be used for graphological purposes. Ten of these samples are shown in Figure 11.1. These individuals also rated themselves toward one or the other extreme on 13 different traits. Their ratings were agreed to by persons who knew them well. The 20 samples were presented to four practicing graphologists and to 33 students, all of whom were also asked to rate each person in one direction on each of the 13 traits.

The graphologists agreed in advance that the most difficult trait to judge from handwriting is the sex of the writer. They were correct in judging sex in 72 per cent of the cases, their best success. They did almost as well in judging some other traits: firm vs. yielding, 66 per cent; slow vs. quick, 65 per cent; and accurate vs. inaccurate, 62 per cent. They judged the samples in the wrong direction almost as decisively in several traits: plastic vs. set in his way, 38 per cent; self-restraint, 37 per cent; and selfish vs. unselfish, 43 per cent. Their over-all percentage of accuracy was 54.2, not far above chance.

The students also did best in judging sex of the writer, with an accuracy of 63 per cent. Other traits with higher accuracies were: firm vs. yielding, 58 per cent; and slow vs. quick, 56 per cent. Their poorest record

5 Eysenck (1948).

was made with: self-restraint, 43 per cent; and plastic vs. set in his ways, 45 per cent. Their over-all accuracy was 52.7 per cent, not far behind that of the "experts."

Two things are noteworthy in comparing the two groups of observers. Traits on which there is highest accuracy of judgment for graphologists are also highest for students, and traits with greatest disagreement from

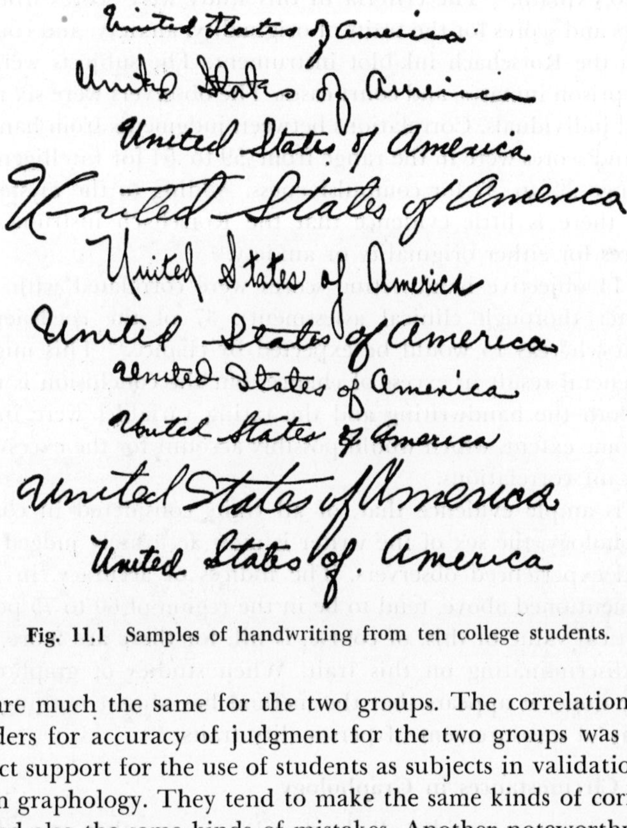

Fig. 11.1 Samples of handwriting from ten college students.

ratings are much the same for the two groups. The correlation between rank orders for accuracy of judgment for the two groups was .92. This is indirect support for the use of students as subjects in validation experiments on graphology. They tend to make the same kinds of correct judgments and also the same kinds of mistakes. Another noteworthy result is that, while the graphologists had higher percentages of accuracy in some traits, this was somewhat balanced by greater inaccuracy in others so that over-all means of accuracy were not far apart. The results indicate biases on the part of judges; biases that are accentuated in the graphologists. They evidently develop stereotyped ideas as they gain experience, accentuating biases with which they may have started.

In many other relatively recent studies, the validity of either naïve or experienced observers' judgments from handwriting samples are zero or

only slightly on the positive side. This has been true when the criteria
were in the form of ratings,[6] scores from the Bernreuter Personality Inventory,[7] or stories from the Thematic Apperception Test [8] (see Chapter 12).
Similar lack of validity was found when samples of writing were scored
for 16 aspects and the 16 scores were factor-analyzed.[9] None of the 5 handwriting factors were found related to any of 13 inventory factor scores.

There is one notable exception to the usual finding, which is very
difficult to explain.[10] The criteria in this study were scores from intelligence tests and scores for the traits of originality, anxiety, and compulsiveness from the Rorschach ink-blot instrument. The subjects were college
students, prison inmates, and court cases. The observers were six relatively
untrained individuals. Correlations between judgments from handwriting
samples and scores were in the range from .59 to .64 for intelligence down
to the range .32 to .37 for compulsiveness. Adding to the mystery is the
fact that there is little evidence that the Rorschach instrument yields
valid scores for either originality or anxiety.[11]

When 14 objective handwriting scores were correlated with 21 rated
traits (after thorough clinical assessment), 37 of the coefficients were
significant whereas 15 would be expected by chance.[12] This might seem
to be a general result in excess of chance, but the conclusion is not clear
because both the handwriting and the rating variables were intercorrelated to some extent, which would possibly account for the excess number
of significant correlations.

There is ample evidence that, of all traits considered in connection
with graphology, the sex of the writer is most accurately judged by both
naïve and experienced observers. The indices of accuracy, in addition
to those mentioned above, tend to be in the region of 60 to 75 per cent.[13]
The practical value of this, of course, is nil, for there are more accurate
ways of discriminating on this trait. When studies of graphology are
rigorously done, it appears that the method has almost nothing to offer
in the way of measurement of personality traits.

Limiting Circumstances in Graphology

When we stop to consider all the possible sources that may play parts
in determining a person's style of handwriting, its limited meaning and

6 Birge (1949).

7 Middleton (1941).

8 Secord (1949).

9 Lorr et al. (1954).

10 Castelnuovo-Tedesco (1948).

11 As to validity for assessing originality, see Roe (1946); for assessing anxiety, see
Bijou (1947) and Stewart (1950).

12 Pascal (1943a).

13 Eisenberg (1938); Goodenough (1945).

usefulness for assessment of personality are not so surprising. There are anatomical features of the hand and arm to be considered. According to Williams (1955), it takes 11 drawings to show the individual differences in the way in which the extensor muscle of the index finger is attached. Differences in tendon patterns on the back of the hand require eight different pictures. Much of the individual differences in style of hand-writing, then, might be attributable to these anatomical differences. These implied relationships have not been established, but they serve as the basis for a good hypothesis to be investigated.

Individuals also learn handwriting from different sources. There are different systems emphasized by different schools and different teachers and parents at different times. Children who follow a particular system of writing tend to show many similarities in their hand scripts, depending upon the extent to which they conform to common teaching and strive to reach the same goal. If personal styles deviate from the general pattern taught, it may be that individual styles are intentionally cultivated and adopted. It might be said that herein lies the opportunity to reveal personality. This is also merely a hypothesis that still seems to lack general support. Some styles are undoubtedly rather accidentally or incidentally acquired. A child admires some older person and imitates him in many ways, including the way he writes. Another child wants to be different from all others in the style he adopts and finds a very unusual model to imitate. Still another is just accidentally rewarded for some particular effort to change his style. He might just as well have been rewarded for another. It might be worthwhile to make a survey as to probable beginnings or moments of decision regarding adoption of handwriting styles by a large number of people.

Reasons for the Acceptability of Graphology

Some rather incidental studies in psychology suggest a possible reason for the conviction that handwriting indicates personality traits. From a few studies, we have the uniform result that people agree remarkably well as to the most appropriate association between lines and adjectives.[14] Consider the seven adjectives and seven lines in Figure 11.2. Try to match each adjective with its most appropriate line before reading footnote 15.[15] There is considerable agreement of individuals on such matchings, indicating some stereotyped associations that have plausibility but no necessary connections. A person's writing may look as if he is a placid, relaxed individual because his writing has a quality like line *A*. Another person's writing seems to have a high position on a trait of firmness

[14] Lundholm (1921); Poffenberger and Barrows (1924); Guilford and Guilford (1931).

[15] The most popular associations are: playful *C*, furious *F*, sorrowful *E*, tranquil *A*, hopeful *G*, firm *D*, and dead *B*.

because his writing emphasizes heavy strokes on the order of line *D*, and so on.

The reasons for the continued appeal of graphologists to many laymen and for the confidence shown in their judgments of personality are very similar to those given in Chapter 6 in connection with the invalid morphological methods. The interpreter of handwriting samples makes statements about each individual that are true of almost everybody; he makes flattering statements; he makes ambiguous statements; and when he says something unfavorable, he immediately balances it by adding some-

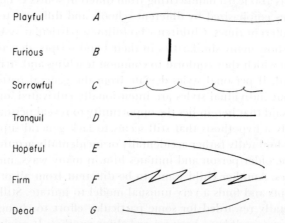

Fig. 11.2 Illustration of popular associations between adjectives and lines. Which line seems to go naturally with each adjective?

thing favorable. These reasons, coupled with the plausibility of stereotyped associations of lines and behavior qualities, tend to maintain what appears to be a virtually useless method.

RATINGS OF OBSERVED EXPRESSIVE BEHAVIOR

It would seem that observing expressive behavior on the spot would offer more cues than observing the products of such behavior. Much expressive behavior leaves no products, hence must be observed when it happens. There are two approaches to the assessment of such behavior, one a subjective approach depending upon the perceptions of an observer, and the other an objective one that measures and thus obtains scores for certain aspects of the behavior. We shall consider the subjective approach first. Most of the research by this approach has emphasized observations of the speaking voice. A few studies have focused attention upon walking, dancing, and performance on individual behavior tests.

Observations of the Speaking Voice

Can we tell anything about an individual's personality by listening to his voice as it might come to us over a radio or a public-address system? A number of experiments by Fay and Middleton were devoted to this question. The speakers were high school or college students of both sexes. The observers who listened to the speakers were usually college students. Among the traits that the listeners were to rate were the Spranger value types [16] (aesthetic, economic, political, religious, social, and theoretical), intelligence, the Kretschmer types (pyknic, athletic, leptosome), personal adjustment, and three traits scored for the Bernreuter Personality Inventory—self sufficiency, introversion, and confidence.[17] In other experiments, there were to be judgments as to whether each speaker was telling the truth or was lying in making factual statements, whether the speaker's statements of opinion sounded persuasive, and whether the speaker had leadership qualities.[18] The numbers of speakers were usually small, often in the range from 9 to 15. The numbers of raters were much larger, ranging from about 30 to more than 100.

Usually the interrater correlations were positive, showing general agreement of impressions gained by different listeners. For a total group (average ratings of speakers), a typical reliability was something like .55. This means that there was consistency in kind of impressions made by different speakers upon the raters. Are the impressions in the directions of the traits to be assessed?

The general picture with regard to validity is one of no validity at all to some small positive correlations in a few experiments. For the ratings of intelligence, the correlation was .33 for the 12 cases. It is possible that two lucky accurate judgments accounted for most of this correlation, for the four boys of average IQ were actually rated lower on the average than the four dull-borderline boys.

Twelve speakers were put in their six Spranger-types criterion groups with an over-all accuracy of about 24 per cent, where an accuracy of 17 per cent would be expected by chance. The placement of nine speakers in the Kretschmer categories was done with a contingency correlation of .37. The judgments of adjustment of 15 freshman girls correlated .11 with ratings of adjustment given by their sorority sisters and .40 with scores from an adjustment inventory. Correlations between average ratings of speakers and scores for self-sufficiency were .07 and .10; with scores for introversion, −.05; and with scores for confidence, .09 and .14.

Listeners were able to judge the difference between truth telling and

---

[16] Spranger (1928).
[17] Fay and Middleton (1939, 1940a, 1940b, 1941a, 1941c, 1942a, 1944).
[18] Fay and Middleton (1941b, 1942b, 1943).

lying with an accuracy of about 56 per cent, where 50 per cent would be the level of chance success. Listeners saw very little difference among speakers for degree of convincingness of their statements, the indices ranging from .85 to 1.04. Ratings for leadership of 15 freshman male speakers correlated .08 with ratings of 10 seniors who knew them.

A study by other investigators was done for the purpose of determining whether persons show their degrees of dominance feeling (probably a combination of ascendance and confidence) in their speaking voices.[19] Extreme cases on this trait, as determined by an inventory score, had their voices recorded. Students who listened to the 16 voices judged each speaker as either dominant or nondominant. They were correct 64 per cent of the time in the first playing of the voices and 61 per cent in the second. When asked to say what cues they observed in making their judgments, they frequently mentioned that a dominant voice is dramatic, well modulated, nonhesitant, and mature. It was found that these cues sometimes led listeners astray so that some speakers were judged incorrectly more often than the chance level of 50 per cent. Here we see what some particular stereotypes may be like.

The most striking aspect of all these results is the substantial amount of interrater agreement upon how the voices impress them coupled with the very low and nonexistent agreement of ratings with criteria. The best hypothesis is that raters are agreeing upon errors of judgment. Certain voices are commonly believed to sound this way or that with respect to traits. Again and again, the writers mention the apparent use of stereotypes by the listeners. There were very strong agreements with respect to certain speakers. If these stereotypes happened to agree with the criteria, correlations were increased. This kind of situation calls for the use of much larger samples of speakers in such experiments in order to minimize the effects of biases.

Observations of the Act of Walking

Can we tell how dominant a person feels by the way he walks? From a total of 238 women who took an inventory on dominance feeling, the eight highest and eight lowest-scoring women were selected.[20] A 30-second motion picture was taken of each woman, showing a sample of her manner of walking. The pictures were shown to a hundred students who were simply to judge in which direction each sample appeared to be. The percentage of correct discriminations was 63.5. This is above the chance level, but we have to remember that only the very extreme cases were involved. Two of the pictures were judged *incorrectly* to an extent

[19] Eisenberg and Zalowitz (1938).
[20] Eisenberg and Reichline (1939).

that was in excess of chance, indicating that stereotypes of dominance were probably operating and these two women did not fit the stereotype.

Observations of the Act of Dancing

Eighteen high school girls danced to four musical selections in their stocking feet and were under observation, each for 30 minutes.[21] Twenty-two movement variables were noted and recorded. The girls had also taken An Inventory of Factors STDCR (see Chapter 8). From correlations between some of these scores and some of the expressive-behavior variables, the authors could conclude that the shy, inhibited girls tend to keep the trunk straight, arms down, shoulders high or medium, and fail to rise on their toes. They also tend to maintain a generally rigid posture and to be slow moving. A deviation score was derived, based upon the number of scores in which a girl deviated from the modal (most popular) response. The deviation score correlated .48 with trait D (depression) and .46 with trait C (cycloid disposition). The two scores indicate aspects of neuroticism and the correlation may mean that deviating or nonconforming movements while dancing might help to discriminate neurotics.

Observations of Behavior in Performance Tests

In one study, many different activities were required of the subjects, for they were observed while taking different performance tests.[22] It would be more accurate to say that their expressive behavior was scored rather than rated, but the study is mentioned here because the chief interest was in relating expressive aspects to a particular temperament trait that was assessed by means of an inventory.

The subjects were the 9 most and 8 least dominant men among 216 and the 21 most and 21 least dominant women among 238, where dominance was based upon a score for dominance feeling. Certain trends were indicated by the results. For both men and women, it was observed that the dominant persons tended to perform many movements rapidly. Dominant men tended to cover more than the normal amount of area in writing and to apply more pressure. They tended to be less persistent in endurance tests (possibly because of impatience?), to walk more slowly while under observation, and to show less tension when writing under the instruction for maximum speed. Dominant women, unlike the men, tended to show more persistence in endurance tests. These relationships would very likely be much less clear in the total population, with the middle of the range for dominance left in.

21 Franklin et al. (1948).
22 Eisenberg (1937).

Observations of Written Speech

Written speech is a product, of course, but aside from certain editings and corrections, it is, in terms of its content, exactly what the person put on paper. Only a few studies can be mentioned for there have been very few.[23] One method of using compositions is to ask observers to match them with personality sketches. This has been done with an accuracy reported to be better than chance.[24] Another method has been to ask for matchings of themes from the same writer. These have also been matched with accuracy better than chance.[25]

Some objective signs have been tried out in connection with written compositions. It was suggested that the frequency of the use of the first-person pronoun should indicate egocentrism. Anderson (1939) found that writers are not very consistent in this respect. The ratio of number of verbs to number of adjectives has been proposed as an indicator of emotional stability [26] and as an indicator of different types of neuroticism.[27] On the whole, written speech has been disappointing, though little explored, as a source of personality indicators. It is probably less promising than oral speech because it is more deliberate and more under the inspection of self-criticism and under self-control.

BEHAVIOR TESTS OF EXPRESSION

Tests of expressive behavior have been in the stage of experimental development. One test, the Downey Will-Temperament Test, was published in 1922. Experimental tests that are worthy of note include Mira's myokinetic tests and some of the examples of tests used by Allport and Vernon (1933) in their extensive studies from this point of view.

The Downey Will-Temperament Test

After study of graphological methods, Downey came to the conclusion that if handwriting is to be used seriously for the assessment of personality, it should be done by observing the act of handwriting itself under different conditions. A number of the parts of her test require the examinee to write the expression "United States of America" under different instructions. A few examples will show how she used handwriting behavior to indicate supposed traits.

Examinees are told to write the expression first in their normal style and normal rate of speed then later to write it as rapidly as possible. Downey assumed that the difference in time indicates a trait of "free-

---

[23] See Sanford (1942) for a review on this subject.
[24] Vernon (1936).
[25] Allport et al. (1934).
[26] Buseman (1925, 1926).
[27] Balken and Masserman (1940).

dom from load." The more nearly the normal rate approaches the maximum rate, the less "load" normally applies to the individual and the more free he is to "let himself go." Instructed to write the expression in a disguised style (after some practice), the examinee is supposed to show his degree of flexibility. Told to copy a given model, the closeness of imitation is taken to indicate interest in detail.

It has never been demonstrated that the scores from the Downey test measure traits that have any great degree of generality or usefulness. At this time, the test is mainly of historical importance. However, it would seem that if handwriting behavior is ever to furnish the indicators of significant traits, her approach would be a promising one to cultivate. Other promising aspects, which she did not attempt to use in a group test, include degree of grip pressure and of writing-point pressure. For example, Pascal (1943*b*) found in a small sample of examinees correlations above .5 between handwriting pressure and pressure range, on the one hand, and ratings of energy and expressiveness on the other.

The Mira Myokinetic Tests

The basic assumption of the Mira tests is that every mental attitude is accompanied by a muscular attitude.[28] The equipment needed is a drawing board with sheets of paper. The board is set in three different positions for the examinee to use in different trials—horizontal, vertical in front of *E,* and vertical edgewise toward *E.* The examinee is blindfolded and instructed to draw 10 lines of different general form—straight, zig-zag, chains, etc.—in each position of the board, with each hand. The products are scored for directions, trends, and variability. The interpretations seem thus far to be based upon hypotheses rather than on established facts. Directions up vs. down in general trend are taken to indicate optimism vs. pessimism. Directions outward vs. inward are taken to indicate extraversion vs. introversion. Outward directions also indicate aggression toward others or liberalism. Which interpretation to place upon outward movements must presumably rest upon other signs. Inward movements are also taken to indicate autosuggestion and selfishness.

The Allport-Vernon Tests of Expressive Movement

Some of the common kinds of activities involved in the Allport and Vernon (1933) tests were walking, strolling, reading aloud, and counting. There were also tests involving estimating distances and the sizes of objects, sizes of angles, and weights. Arm movements were involved in making these estimates. There were measures of hand grip and of tapping rate, also tests involving handwriting and the drawing of figures, with the feet as well as with the hands.

[28] Morris (1951).

Types of scores included rate of movement, distances or areas covered in making specified movements, vigor of movement, and pressure involved. Reliabilities (retest) usually ranged between .5 and .9, indicating reasonable degrees of personal consistency over relatively short time intervals. Intercorrelations of scores were generally small, with the general principle that the more similar the tests, the higher the correlations. Without a factor analysis, certain clusters of tests were noticed, in terms of higher intercorrelations. Four clusters were among speed scores, area covered by movements, scores involving emphasis, and scores involving outward (centrifugal) movements. The last finding would lend some support to the use of outward movements in the Mira tests.

A General Evaluation of Expressive-Movement Tests

The picture of test development in the area of expressive movement is one of experimentation. There has been very little demonstration of connections between expressive-movement scores and nonexpressive behavior traits. A possible exception is in the case of pressure scores. It appears at this stage that such correlations are likely to be so small that other approaches to the assessment of the same behavior traits are likely to be more valid. There is a distinct possibility that we shall find primary traits of expression as such, and for a complete picture of personality, they deserve attention in their own right. Knowledge of their interrelationships with other behavior traits, even though small, will help to complete our conception of personality structure.

Enough has been found in studies of ratings of nonexpressive behavior traits to indicate that there are many popular stereotyped ideas concerning things indicated by expressive behavior. A study of these popular associations might be profitable for use in training raters to avoid the use of misleading cues when they assess others by direct observation.

SUMMARY

Expressive aspects of behavior are primarily in terms of muscular movements that are rather incidental to the business of living; they are largely nonadaptive. The uniqueness of each person in this respect and the uniqueness of each personality has suggested that expressive behavior can be a rich source of indicators of nonexpressive traits. The body's repertoire of expressive movements is very large, involving many body parts and many occasions for body movement. Postures, movements, and products of movements have been utilized for observation.

Graphology, or the assessment of behavior traits from samples of handwriting, has been an age-old dream. In spite of claims often made for this method, even quite enthusiastic ones, acceptable, rigorous studies indicate little or no validity for the method. This is true when general impressions of specimens are the basis and also when analytical approaches are the basis. It is true for both experienced and inexperienced observers. Limiting circumstances for such a use probably lie in the anatomy of the hand and in formal and informal learning of handwriting styles. The persistence of belief in graphology may rest, in part, upon stereotyped associations between impressions that lines make and human qualities.

Observations of expressive aspects of behavior, either in the form of ratings or the form of test scores, usually fail to show much correlation with assessments of nonexpressive traits by other methods. Ratings of traits from the speaking voice and from walking, for example, indicate very strongly that observers are biased by stereotyped ideas that they have in mind. Both ratings and behavior-test scores of expressive aspects of behavior show considerable interrater agreement and retest reliability. On the one hand, this seems to indicate agreement of observers upon errors of interpretation. On the other hand, it indicates somewhat generalized traits of expression, which may be largely confined to expressive behavior but which may bear some small degree of relationship with nonexpressive traits.

Chapter 12

PROJECTIVE TECHNIQUES

DURING THE past 30 years, projective techniques have gained enormous popularity among clinical psychologists. Oldest and best known of these is the Rorschach ink-blot instrument. Probably next in popularity is the Thematic Apperception Test. Beyond these two methods, we have a proliferation of other techniques that make special use of projective principles. We shall examine the two best-known procedures in some detail and give some attention to a few others that present unique features. First, let us consider some properties that projective techniques have in common.

GENERAL NATURE OF PROJECTIVE TECHNIQUES

Unstructured "Tests" [1]

In contrasting projective techniques with behavior tests and personality inventories, it is often emphasized that the former are "unstructured" whereas the latter are "structured." By this is meant that tests and inventories, by reason of their detailed instructions and their contents of stated items, provide the examinee with a quite definite task to perform. He is expected to do what he is told to do. He is not supposed to decide for himself what he will do or how he will go about the task.

In an unstructured instrument there is a minimum of instruction. In administering the Rorschach ink blots, for example, the examiner hands E a card and asks him simply "What might this be?" in accordance with Rorschach's original practice. In another projective technique, the draw-a-person method, the instruction is simply "Draw a picture of a person." The intention is to leave the way as wide open as possible for the examinee to do what he will. He is not completely free, of course, for he knows

---

[1] In the opinion of the author, the expression "unstructured tests" is a contradiction of terms. A test by definition, if not by usage, presents a structured situation, hence the author's general avoidance of the expression "Rorschach test."

that he is in a kind of test situation. He is likely to comply with the limited instructions, which, after all, give some direction to his behavior.

SUPPOSED ADVANTAGES OF LACK OF STRUCTURE

The ambiguity of the task and of the materials given in a projective instrument is believed to be most desirable. It is claimed that this imposes minimal restraints upon the examinee. As a consequence of the ambiguity and the freedom from restraints, it is believed that the examinee will reveal his "total personality."

The exercise is highly disguised as to its purpose and as to the traits E will show. He does not realize, therefore, what and how much he is revealing about himself. Material that would otherwise be inhibited, as in responding to an inventory, comes out. It is often said that these conditions induce E to exhibit the "deeper layers" of his personality. By "deeper layers" is apparently meant the things of which he is unaware in his own personality. E is free to follow his own lines of interest, thereby revealing what his stronger motives are. The informality and the freedom are said to promote a favorable attitude and to ensure E's cooperation in taking the examination.

These asserted assumptions call for critical examination on logical grounds. Before we take any evaluative steps, let us bring into the picture more concrete information of the methods, how they operate, and what kinds of results are obtained with them.

The Nature of Projection

The term "projection" is used in this connection in a very general sense. The concept is by no means limited, as Freud used the term. The Freudian concept involves a person attributing to others the thoughts, feelings, and attitudes that he has himself but disavows. The "projection" in projective techniques simply means that the examinee puts himself and his traits into his reactions, so to speak, in response to the material given him. In a very broad interpretation, we might include projective techniques among the expressive methods. Some do so regard them. The expressive methods have been very much limited to motor activity, however, whereas projective-technique reactions are more likely to emphasize some other kind of activity.

THE RORSCHACH TECHNIQUE

Origin and Development

The originator of the technique that bears his name was Herman Rorschach, a Swiss psychiatrist.[2] The unusual originality exhibited in

[2] Rorschach (1942).

Rorschach's use of ink blots was probably due in part to his freedom from the restrictions of current psychological theory of his time. He had some half-formulated theories of his own that furnished some guide to his research with ink blots. He was not the first to use ink blots, but he was the first to use them in the way that he did and probably the first to introduce colors other than black into them. He tried out a large number of ink blots before selecting the 10 that became the material for his instrument. His lack of sophistication in test theory and in the accepted practices in test development was both a help and a hindrance. It permitted him to adopt many novel features in his technique, but it also left a number of serious weaknesses.

Fig. 12.1 An ink blot of the type appearing in the Rorschach series.

The Rorschach ink blots were perhaps most enthusiastically received in the United States, where several individuals have been instrumental in promoting their use, among them Samuel J. Beck, Marguerite Hertz, and Bruno Klopfer. Current scoring systems can be largely attributed to their efforts. Before long, a Rorschach Institute was formed and a journal was started to be devoted to the Rorschach instrument.

General Nature of the Rorschach Technique

The material is composed of 10 heavy cards, each with a complex ink blot. An example of such an ink blot may be seen in Figure 12.1. The blot is always bilaterally symmetrical because it was found that examinees prefer them this way, other experimental blots being too frequently "rejected" (no responses given). Some blots are in black, white, and grey, and others are in two or more chromatic colors, mostly in pastel shades.

Administration

In its usual form, the Rorschach instrument is given individually. The examinee holds the card in his hands. He is permitted to turn it as he pleases and to take his own time. *E* states orally what he sees and the examiner records *E*'s responses. After the last blot has been given, an inquiry follows in which *E* tells where he saw each object that he reported and explains what he thought made him see the object. The responses and *E*'s additional information constitute a *protocol*.

Very elaborate scoring systems have been developed. In general, the most common source of information the scorer uses is the determiner of *E*'s response, that is, whether the response is determined by form, color, or shading, and so on. Scoring categories and interpretations of Beck (1944, 1951) will be discussed briefly here.[3] Some of the scores recommended by Beck are:

Scores for intellectual qualities

R Response productivity (total number of responses; said to indicate intellectual productivity or "responsivity")

F+ Number of accurate forms (indicates clarity of perception and discrimination, also motivation to be clear and accurate)

W Number of objects based on whole blot (indicates abstracting ability or theorizing behavior)

D Perception of details (indicates a concrete or practical approach)

Z Relationships between blots (indicates organizing ability)

A Animal content (indicates sterility of thought, since animal responses are among the most common)

P Number of popular responses (high *P* meaning passive submissiveness to one's group; low *P* meaning rebellion against conventionality)

Scores for temperament and motivational qualities

C Number of color-determined responses (e.g., ocean, sky, blood; indicates general emotionality)

CF Primarily color determined, but some form determination (indicates immature emotionality; self-gratification)

FC Reverse of *CF* (indicates more mature emotional disposition)

Y Shading-determined responses (indicates painful emotions; anxiety)

V Vista associations (third-dimensional effects; similar meaning to *Y*)

T Texture responses (e.g., fur; means vague anxiety, affect, or love hunger)

S Responses determined by white spaces (indicates resistiveness; negativism; stubbornness)

M Movement responses, especially human movement (indicates artistic talent and imagination)

It will be noted that there is a kind of common-sense reasonableness to the connection between the personal emphasis upon response determiners and the psychological interpretations attributed to them. Such interpretations have been offered generally without proof of the actual connections and have been used without much questioning. Some infor-

[3] See, also, Klopfer and Kelley (1946) and Bell (1948).

mation as to validity of one or two of these scores will be mentioned later.

It should also be said that other interpretations of responses emphasize their content. The objects seen and mentioned by the examinee might be commonly frightening, such as snakes or lightning; others might indicate an unusual interest in sex; and still others an attitude of masculinity or of femininity. Such use of responses to the ink blots is much less common, however, than the scores based upon determiners of responses, such as were indicated above.

A Multiple-choice Form of the Rorschach

It was to be expected that to meet the demands for large-scale testing, as in the military situation, some form of group testing should be considered for the Rorschach. Presentation of the blots to groups can be accomplished by projecting them on a screen, which is the usual method in group testing. In order to circumvent the need for asking the examinee to write down all his responses, which might well arouse much resistance from him, a list of alternative responses has been selected for each blot. *E* is instructed to select the most appropriate response out of a number or to select more than one and to state the rank order of appropriateness. It has been determined by empirical studies which responses are given more often by abnormals than by normal individuals. One score that has been used is the number of abnormal responses that *E* selects. The multiple-choice Rorschach is usually associated with Harrower-Erikson.[4] It is readily seen that the uses of the group form are very limited and that in many ways it departs from the lack of structuring that has been regarded as one of the Rorschach instrument's important virtues.

Evaluation of the Rorschach Technique

Since the Rorschach technique has been proposed as a means of assessing certain traits of individuals and does so in terms of scores, it is justifiably subject to the same approaches to evaluation as we have utilized in connection with other methods. There are some investigators who maintain that it is the clinician's final decision regarding a person that should be examined for reliability and validity. On these grounds, we could never attribute obtained indices of reliability and validity to the instrument alone but to the instrument coupled with particular interpreters. How much of the result should be attributed to the interpreter and how much to the instrument would be hard to say. With such in-

4 Harrower-Erikson and Steiner (1945).

formation from a population of interpreters, however, some kind of average figure would be a reasonable indicator of the value of the instrument. No study of this kind has involved more than a very few interpreters. We shall devote most of our attention to the value of the Rorschach scores since they are presumably the information from which the interpreter reaches his decisions. If the information has no predictive power, it is difficult to see how the interpreter is able to extract valid predictions from it.

RELIABILITY OF THE RORSCHACH SCORES

Retest reliabilities seem to be the most acceptable type for the Rorschach scores. Some coefficients of this type may be cited from Eysenck (1952). From samples of both normal and abnormal individuals, the coefficients ranged from −.10 to .86. Most values were in the range .5 to .6, with several below .4. The retest reliability for the score from the Harrower-Erikson form of the instrument has been reported to be .62.[5] So far as single scores from the Rorschach are concerned, then, the degree of stability is not very high over time. There is considerable fluctuation of personal trait positions, or of the functioning of the instrument as such, or of both.

VALIDITY OF RORSCHACH PRACTICES IN GENERAL

The question of validity of the Rorschach instrument is a complex one. The technique has been used for many purposes and in many ways. We shall consider the different uses in turn and take note of any unusual variations in methodology as we come to them. Efforts have of course been made to use the technique for discriminating between normals and abnormals, and in some instances, for discriminating among pathological groups.

Apart from pathological populations, it has been used in attempts to predict academic success and vocational success of different kinds, in spite of the fact that it was not intended originally for such purposes. The fact that its promoters have claimed that it measures personality traits, including some intellectual abilities, has opened it to the challenge to predict behavior where such traits may be regarded as significant. In our survey of validity information, we shall also be concerned with how well it measures traits as such.

VALIDITY FOR DETECTING PATHOLOGY

For the Rorschach technique as usually administered, the success in distinguishing neurotics from normals and for detecting different degrees

[5] Wittson et al. (1944).

of neuroticism has been almost negligible. Two experienced Rorschach interpreters rated 120 subjects in four categories for degree of neuroticism, using only their Rorschach protocols as their information. The categories ranged from normal to extremely neurotic. The correlations with the criterion of neuroticism were .17 and .16 for the two raters.[6] In the Army Air Force during World War II, 180 diagnosed anxiety cases were compared on Rorschach scores with 290 aviation cadets. There were no apparent differences.[7] The failure of the Rorschach technique to discriminate between patients with and without anxiety diagnosis was duplicated in another study.[8] Several experienced interpreters failed to discriminate ten anxiety cases from ten nonanxiety cases significantly better than chance. Wittenborn and Sarason (1949) reported that there are so many cases of discrepancy between responses of pathological vs. normal and mentally deficient vs. normal that they recommend against using the Rorschach method for making individual diagnoses of this kind.

The Harrower-Erikson multiple-choice form apparently does better in discriminating normals from abnormals. This should not be surprising, since the keying of diagnostic responses had been determined empirically. In one study, 100 patients were compared with 100 applicants for employment. The scores detected 69 per cent of the pathological persons while wrongly identifying 23 per cent of the normals.[9] In a military setting, scores from 208 normals were compared with those from 416 psychiatric cases. The results were regarded as too unfavorable to justify recommending the method for screening purposes.[10] There were too many false positives (40 per cent) for the number of abnormals detected (59 per cent). From another source, we are told that the validity for discriminating neurotics from normals can be indicated by a correlation of .18.[11] Thus, the Harrower-Erikson form of the technique presents a picture of only limited validity for the normal-abnormal discrimination.

VALIDITY FOR DIAGNOSIS OF PATHOLOGY

How much useful information can be obtained from the Rorschach method for putting pathological patients in their proper diagnostic categories? This picture, too, is disappointing. In one study, Rorschach examiners were asked to sort 199 patients in five diagnostic categories. The results were reported to be not significantly different from chance success.[12] In another study, Rorschach scores failed to discriminate satisfactorily among patients in three groups: psychopathic personality, psychoneurotics, and schizophrenics.[13] Other investigators conclude their

6 Eysenck (1952).
7 Bijou (1947).
8 Stewart (1950).
9 Challman (1945).

10 Wittson et al. (1944).
11 Eysenck (1952).
12 Wittenborn and Holzberg (1951*b*).
13 Knopf (1956).

studies with warnings against making diagnosis on the basis of Rorschach information alone.[14]

VALIDITY FOR INDICATING MALADJUSTMENTS

Information from the Rorschach ink blots has usually failed to discriminate between those who are regarded as maladjusted and those who are not. One instance in which there was some validity will be mentioned first.[15] The Rorschach score was a special one, obtained by what is known as the Munroe check-list method.[16] The criterion was in the form of "buddy" ratings in small groups of 24 and 22 male students. The average correlation of .41 was obtained.

In a very extensive genetic study, 145 adolescents were given the Rorschach every two years from age eleven to age eighteen.[17] They were also interviewed in order to provide a criterion of level of adjustment. Several purported signs of adjustment and of maladjustment in Rorschach results were compared with the adjustment criterion. The indicators, if followed, would have meant that there were at least some neurotic signs in as many as 90 per cent of the cases. Signs of adjustment appeared in from 15 to 95 per cent of the cases. On specific symptoms, 69 per cent were identified as unproductive, 52 per cent as rigid and constricted, and 69 per cent as emotionally unresponsive (46 per cent as being completely unresponsive), and 63 per cent as being disturbed by strong emotional stimuli. The life histories of these adolescents belied these diagnoses. The ratings of adjustment (criterion) correlated just about zero with the signs of adjustment (Rorschach).

In a study of 151 normal persons who were divided by psychiatrists into two groups, adjusted and maladjusted, most of the Rorschach signs failed to discriminate and some of them discriminated in reverse.[18] Some fourteen-year-old boys were assessed for degree of adjustment by a number of methods. The Munroe score from the Rorschach failed to correlate with any other signs of adjustment.[19] When the criterion of adjustment was based upon the MMPI scores, the Rorschach signs of maladjustment of women in military service did not agree.[20] Thus, for the few studies mentioned, with one exception, the various Rorschach indices of adjustment have failed to discriminate different criterion levels on this very general trait.[21]

[14] Sacks and Lewin (1950).
[15] Holtzman (1952).
[16] See Munroe (1942).
[17] Ives et al. (1953).
[18] Brockway et al. (1954).
[19] Tindall (1955).
[20] Winfield (1946).
[21] Hundreds of studies have been made concerning the Rorschach instrument. Reviews

PREDICTION OF ACADEMIC SUCCESS

In an exceptional study of 101 freshmen women, it was concluded that the Munroe score was superior to either the Bernreuter Personality Inventory or the American Council on Education Examination (a college-aptitude test) for predicting grades.[22] Using the same Rorschach score, no validity was found for predicting achievement in an officers candidate school.[23] Other investigators have found little in the Rorschach results to account for overachievers or underachievers.[24] The Harrower-Erikson score was found to discriminate students on probation from other students in one study [25] but correlated zero with grades in another.[26] It is impossible to say why there should be prediction in one academic setting and not in another without knowing more about the circumstances, and this would usually mean knowing more than the investigators have reported or could report.

VALIDITY IN VOCATIONAL PREDICTIONS

We have a few results regarding the performance of Rorschach information in predicting general employability of applicants, in predicting success in pilot training, and in discriminating superior military officers and creative artists.

A hundred unemployed persons were interviewed, after which they were placed in three levels of employability.[27] The Harrower-Erikson scores correlated .24 with this criterion, which shows some relationship but not enough to justify much confidence in the Rorschach score. This conclusion assumes, of course, that the judgments based upon interviews were valid.

During World War II, the Army Air Force examined two large groups in the regular Rorschach manner.[28] Single scores from the Rorschach and also predictions of passing in pilot training (using a nine-point scale based upon examination of the Rorschach information) were correlated with the training criterion of pass vs. fail. The correlations could well have arisen by chance. In another large sample, the Harrower-Erikson form of the Rorschach was found to be not valid. After the war, 20 expert Rorschach interpreters were asked to predict pass or fail for 20 pilot students.[29] Only three of the experts had as many as 14 correct predictions, where 10 predictions would have been right by chance.

---

such as those of Kelly (1954) and of Butler and Fiske (1955) present a general picture of some studies indicating positive results, offset by as many others indicating negative results.

22 Munroe (1942).
23 McCandless (1949).
24 Rust and Ryan (1953).
25 Osborne and Sanders (1949).

26 Montalto (1946).
27 Balinsky (1945).
28 Guilford and Lacey (1947).
29 Holtzman and Sells (1954).

Further bits of information pertain to military officers and artists. A multiple-choice form of the Rorschach made very poor discriminations between officers rated excellent and a group of officer candidates.[30] A group of 20 of the leading painters in the United States were given the Rorschach, which failed to indicate that they were an exceptionally creative group.[31]

In general, the Rorschach techniques have almost completely failed to predict vocational success in the few instances where validation studies have been done. Perhaps it is too much to ask this kind of validity for the Rorschach methods. The founder probably never intended his instrument for this purpose. Yet, the followers who claim that it measures a large number of traits that should be pertinent to vocational success virtually challenge the interested and the skeptical alike to make such studies.

It would be more expeditious to attempt to find out what primary traits are assessed by the Rorschach scores, then to validate the scores for vocational areas where those primary traits should be involved. A number of factor analyses of the Rorschach scores have been attempted, none being satisfactory, since they are not good material for analytic purposes.[32] When *specific responses*, each "scored" separately, were factor-analyzed, it was found that the factors do not support the Rorschach scoring categories very well.[33]

SOURCES OF ERROR IN RORSCHACH SCORES

It helps some in accounting for low reliability and validity, and in improving them, to locate sources of error. Some experiments have demonstrated what some kinds of errors can be. In the Army Air Force setting, the Rorschach results from nine different examiners were compared.[34] The hypothesis was that the individual examiner has something to do with eliciting large or small numbers of responses from the ink blots. The average total scores (R) for the nine examiners varied from 15 to 25. This is somewhat serious in view of the fact that, if the R score is changed, other scores are changed, for many of them are strongly correlated with R since they are parts of R.

The attitude of the examiner, known as his "permissiveness," may have much to do with the number of responses. Three examiners each administered the ink blots under three intentionally selected attitudes—normal, rejecting, and accepting.[35] It was found that 20 of the 23 Ror-

[30] Jensen and Rotter (1945).
[31] Roe (1946).
[32] Wittenborn (1950a, 1950b); Williams and Lawrence (1953).
[33] Wittenborn (1949a).
[34] Guilford and Lacey (1947).
[35] Lord (1950).

schach scores obtained were related to these conditions, but differences between examiners were more important than differences between attitudes.

It is often said of projective tests that the examinee knows so little about the method that he cannot willfully modify his scores. This assertion overlooks the fact that, for one thing, an examinee may not express orally all the responses he thinks of. Censorship can operate consciously; probably it can also operate unconsciously. In one study, students were given the blots twice, once with the instruction to "fake good" and once with the instruction to "fake bad." [36] The meanings of the same scores under these conditions must have changed considerably, since they correlated as low as .16. Patterns of scores for individuals were also significantly changed. It is not known how well the students achieved the goals of the two instructions, but the instructions did something to them, something that may have invalidated the scores.

Another study demonstrated that *E*'s belief as to the purpose of the examination influences his responses.[37] A group was told, for example, that the Rorschach technique aims to "discover serious emotional disturbances." Examinees tended to give lower total scores, more good forms, more popular responses, and fewer aggressive responses.

Some Analogs of the Rorschach

There are, in addition to the multiple-choice form, a number of variations of the Rorschach, using the same ink blots but administering them and scoring the responses differently. We shall not take space to consider them here. It is of interest, however, to mention two methods using material other than visual as a basis for projective responses, one employing auditory stimuli and the other tactual.

In one form of the auditory test, known as Skinner's *verbal summator* or more recently as the *tautophone,* vowel sounds are presented in succession and are repeated until the examinee reports that he hears something meaningful.[38] This method gave some small discriminations among abnormal groups but was not considered very powerful for this purpose.[39] In another form, the sounds are of voices, natural sounds, conversations, etc.[40] Such stimuli would not be as ambiguous as the vowel sounds. The tactual method presents to blind or blindfolded examinees a bas-relief of some sort to see what the examinee makes of it.[41]

[36] Carp and Shavzin (1950).
[37] Henry and Rotter (1956).
[38] Shakow and Rosenzweig (1940).
[39] Grings (1942).
[40] Wilmer and Husni (1953).
[41] Morris (1951). See also, Harris (1948) and Smith and Madan (1953).

THE THEMATIC APPERCEPTION TEST

The Thematic Apperception Test (TAT) grew out of work at the Harvard Psychological Clinic, under the leadership of Henry A. Murray.[42] The theoretical background was mainly Freudian or psychoanalytical. The purpose of the TAT was to reveal the patient's needs, motives, values, and basic attitudes, if some degree of redundancy will be permitted in stating this list. It was believed that the method would uncover trends in the examinee's mental make-up of which he is unaware or which he would not otherwise expose to an observer. The main Freudian "mechanism" upon which the technique is supposed to rest is that of *identification,* as we shall see.

General Nature of the TAT

The TAT material consists of pictures, mostly involving people in various combinations and situations. There is much ambiguity as to what is going on in the picture, as to the interrelationships of the people, and as to identity of the people. In one picture, even the sex of the person is not clear. Emotional expressions of the people can be interpreted in various ways. Objects are so blurred and indistinct in some pictures that there is much room for individual interpretation. One "picture" is just a blank card.

In the administration of the TAT, the examinee is instructed to tell a story about each picture. The task is presented to *E* with the implication that it is a test of his "powers of imagination." In this way he may take the task as a challenge to do his best as he would in taking an intelligence test. This instruction is said to frighten some examinees because they realize their own weaknesses in imagination or in the invention of stories. The story is to cover several points: What led up to the scene? What is going on? What are the thoughts and feelings of the people? What will be the outcome of the story? The examiner records the essential elements of the story. There is a review of the stories during which the examiner can probe for associations, memories, and further details.

There is no standard scoring procedure, yet there is some agreement as to which indicators reveal what traits. The clinical psychologist's goal in its use is to arrive at a personality sketch. This is composed of statements about traits without much effort to report finely graded quantitative descriptions.

Some Evaluation of the TAT

Because the results from the TAT are given so much in qualitative rather than quantitative terms, it is difficult to apply to them the usual

[42] Murray (1943, 1951).

criteria of reliability and validity. Attempts in this direction have been made, however, and some information of this kind can be reported.

RELIABILITY OF TAT ASSESSMENTS

One concern with the TAT assessments of individuals has been the amount of agreement among different interpreters of the same stories. Correlations between interpreters have varied over such wide ranges that it is impossible to state a typical figure for agreement of this kind.[43] A general principle is that agreement increases when interpreters have shared similar experiences and when they agree in advance upon concepts and signs. As in rating methods, however, agreement may mean that such interpreters tend to confirm one another's errors.

Retest reliabilities have been generally moderate to low, as retest reliabilities go. Estimates have been .80 after two months, .60 after six months, .50 after ten months, and .46 after one year.[44] Some very low reliabilities have been reported.[45]

VALIDITY OF THE TAT

In considering validity for the method, in principle, including assumptions upon which it was based, we have information that should be of some help. A few experiments have been done to determine whether induced motivation of specific kinds will have some bearing upon the kinds of stories produced. Stories have been found to reflect the effects of deprivation of food [46] and the effects of failure in a test of ability.[47] After the subject is rebuked for the poor quality of his stories, later stories tend to include more aggressive words, as one should expect in response to frustration.[48] Pastore (1949) has found considerable fault with such experiments. At best, they provide only *indirect* evidence of validity for the TAT. In another experiment in which sex motivation was aroused, examinees made *fewer* references to sex in their stories.[49]

The assumption that the examinee identifies himself with some person in a picture has been tested in one study.[50] Interpreters were asked to judge with whom the examinee had identified himself, from an inspection of his story. They agreed to the extent of 89 per cent. We have no indication, however, that the interpreters were correct in their decisions.

Some apparent support for validity of the TAT for personality description comes from a comprehensive study involving one examinee who was

[43] Tomkins (1947).
[44] *Ibid.;* Sanford et al. (1943).
[45] Child et al. (1956).
[46] Sanford (1936, 1937); Atkinson and McClelland (1948).
[47] McClelland et al. (1949).   [49] Clark (1952).
[48] Bellak (1944).   [50] Mayman and Kutner (1947).

described by a number of experienced interpreters.[51] Each of 17 interpreters was given 150 statements that might be applied to the examinee
and was asked to sort them for the degree to which they applied to the
examinee, as judged from his TAT stories. The same 150 statements were
ranked by 29 clinicians who used all *other* clinical information available
regarding the patient. The consensus of the latter judgments constituted
the criterion. The correlations of the rankings of the items by the 17
experts with this criterion ranged from .22 to .76, with an average of .60.

Two things about this study leave us in some doubt. One patient is
hardly enough for a very comprehensive validation study, to say the
least. By chance, he might have been a case that was especially revealing
or unusually unrevealing in terms of TAT stories. There is also the
possibility that both the experts and the criterion clinicians rated highest
(most descriptive) the statements that apply more universally or that
clinicians are more accustomed to use and rated low those that rarely
apply or are rarely used. This kind of bias in common to the two groups
might account for much of the positive correlation obtained. In another
large study, TAT scores for 10 traits showed no validity in terms of
correlation with evaluations from several other methods of assessment
of the same traits.[52]

There has been some interest in validity of the TAT for prediction of
overt behavior. This would seem to be a natural interest in connection
with any method of assessment. A special problem arises in this regard for
projective tests because of a particular issue that does not apply to other
methods. It is well agreed that the TAT, especially, obtains indications
of the "fantasy life" of the person. Is there sufficient relationship between
one's fantasies and one's overt behavior, so that knowing the one we can
predict the other?

Where correlation studies have been made, the validity of this kind for
the TAT appears to be very questionable. Among adolescent boys, the
correlation found between TAT assessments and teachers' ratings of behavior averaged .11.[53] In another study with children, negative correlations were actually found.[54] Obviously, such results require some speculation. Several hypotheses have been suggested concerning the relation
between fantasy and overt behavior.[55] One hypothesis is that behavior
that is prohibited will be expressed in fantasy but will tend to be avoided
overtly. Behavior that can be and is freely expressed overtly will not
appear in fantasy. These hypotheses would account for negative correlations.

According to additional hypotheses, approved behavior that is desired

[51] Little and Shneidman (1955).
[52] Child et al. (1956).
[53] Sanford et al. (1943).
[54] Symonds (1949).
[55] Bellak (1950).

but not achieved is likely to appear both in fantasy and overtly. It might be suggested that this would be an optimal condition for applying the TAT to elicit indicative information. There may be other occasions in which the person suppresses expressions, in both fantasy and overt forms. The last two conditions mentioned would provide sources of positive correlations between fantasies and overt behavior. It should be an implication of these various hypotheses that, with so many sources of both positive and negative relationships, it would appear not to be safe to attempt to predict the one kind of behavior from the other without having additional information as to the person's state of success or failure and his tendency to suppress or not to suppress either or both at the time of examination.

The suggestion of self-censorship in connection with the TAT raises the question of how much of this may be effective in the normal use of the instrument. One study of administration of the TAT with instructions to the examinees to bias their scores can be cited.[56] In two administrations, 24 veteran patients were instructed to "fake good" and to "fake bad." The resulting stories showed some changes in both directions, but there was more change in the bad direction than in the good direction. The latter finding could be interpreted to mean that there was some "faking good" in the normal administration of the TAT.

Validity of the TAT in prediction of vocational success has been studied very little. Because of the important roles that motivation is believed to play in vocational performance, it is a legitimate question to ask regarding practical validity of this sort. There are two sources of information. In a study of 20 leading American artists, the TAT failed to detect the fact that they were an exceptionally creative group.[57] In the experimental selection of pilot students, the TAT failed completely to predict the distinction between passing and failing students, either from single or collective scores or from a single intuitive prediction of success.[58] From this limited information, we find no promise as yet for vocational-selection uses of the TAT.

Adaptations of the TAT

There have been a number of variations and applications of the TAT to meet special problems, and the story-writing type of response from examinees has been adapted to other stimuli, such as sounds (emotional vocalizations, dialog, animal sounds, etc.)[59] and described situations (Sargent Paper-and-Pencil Test).[60]

---

[56] Weisskopf and Dieppa (1951).
[57] Roe (1946).
[58] Guilford and Lacey (1947).

[59] Stone (1950).
[60] Morris (1951).

The best-known adaptation is that of McClelland and his associates for measuring need for achievement (abbreviated as n Ach.).[61] From the use of eight specially selected pictures, they report that the scores have low reliability (split-half .65 and retest .22). Correlations with college and high school grades have varied from −.14 to .51, from results of their own studies and those of other investigators.[62] From reports of experimental work with the test, one gains the impression that responses are oversensitive to temporary conditions and hence may not indicate clearly the more permanent traits we should like to know about.[63] We lack information as to just what the scores do represent psychologically.

OTHER PROJECTIVE METHODS

The number of different projective techniques is growing, new ones being suggested from time to time. It appears that almost anything a person can do in an incompletely structured situation, where there is much freedom for individuals to behave differently, can be utilized as the basis for a projective method. We shall first give more than passing attention to three of the better-known techniques—sentence completion, Rosenzweig Picture-Frustration Test, and the Szondi test—then mention a number of others more briefly, emphasizing unique features.

Sentence Completion

The development and promotion of sentence completion as a projective technique can be credited largely to Rotter (1951) and Rohde (1946, 1957). A more recent newcomer, when compared to the Rorschach and the TAT, sentence completion lacks the extensive experience that has accumulated with the "big two." In some ways it seems more promising than either.

GENERAL NATURE OF SENTENCE-COMPLETION TESTS

It is best to speak in the plural number, for there are several variations of this technique. The material consists of short beginnings of sentences. Examples might be:

1. I like _____
2. The happiest time _____
3. I regret _____
4. A mother _____
5. I failed _____

6. Sometimes _____
7. I hate _____
8. My stomach _____
9. The future _____
10. Most girls _____

[61] McClelland et al. (1953).
[62] Parrish and Rethlingshafer (1954); Ricciuti (1955); Krumboltz and Farquar (1957).
[63] McClelland et al. (1953).

The instructions are simple, often suggesting that the examinee write rapidly, giving his first thoughts. Complete sentences are called for and E is encouraged to express his feelings.

It will be noted from the sample items that the sentences begin with things that may well lead to common trouble spots for individuals who are in difficulties. They pertain to potentially embarrassing thoughts, to hostilities, inferiority feelings, or anxieties. They remind one of the word-association method used by some of the early psychoanalysts. The sentence form is more structured than a single stimulus word and might therefore bring the examinee more pointedly to areas that should be explored.

The method of scoring, or of utilizing the responses otherwise, depends upon the purposes for which the test is used. Those with a more psycho-analytical bent may prefer an intuitive approach, which involves a general inspection of the answers and a decision as to what they signify.[64] Others, more inclined toward a trait approach and toward quantification, may develop a scoring key for each trait that they want to assess from the responses. In the latter case, there can be some selection of sentence beginnings that are promising in desired directions, as in assessing level of hostility feelings. There is considerable subjectivity in scoring sentence completions, but check-list methods can be applied to the responses after some experience with the items.

EVALUATION OF THE SENTENCE-COMPLETION TECHNIQUE

Scoring can be fairly reliable. In one study, scoring by a check-list method for the general trait of pathological vs. normal, the agreement between two scorers was indicated by a correlation of .89 and the odd-even reliability was .85.[65] Agreement between two scorers who used the intuitive method was indicated by a correlation of .68. How typical these figures may be is not known.

In the same study, psychiatrists had separated a large sample of military personnel into three groups—those fit to return to duty, those needing convalescence, and those to be discharged. The check-list score correlated with this criterion to the extent of .61; the intuitive score (for two scorers separately) correlated .41 and .39. Clearly, in terms of both reliability and validity, the check-list scoring was superior to the intuitive scoring.

When the test was used for screening purposes in a college group, validity coefficients for predictions of maladjustment were .77 for males and .64 for females.[66] This was after development of an empirical key in other groups. In a high school group, however, no validity was found

---

[64] Holsopple and Miale (1954).   [66] Rotter et al. (1949).
[65] Bijou (1947).

for differentiating maladjusted students, but leads were found that could be profitably followed up in individual cases.[67]

Advantages claimed for the sentence-completion test are that it is easily administered, to individuals or to groups, and comparatively easily scored and interpreted. There are certain disadvantages, including the fact that its purpose is less well concealed than in the case of other projective techniques. The material is much less attractive than that of the Rorschach or the TAT. The fact that sentence completion requires some effort on the part of the examinee is sometimes unattractive to him. Some examinees fail to give enough in the way of completions to reveal much about themselves, and there is the obvious opportunity for E to give intentionally misleading answers.[68]

The Rosenzweig Picture-Frustration Test (P-F)

The P-F test was designed to measure primarily three different kinds of reactions to frustration:

Extrapunitive. (E attacks his environment, overtly or covertly.)
Intropunitive. (E turns his aggression on himself; blames self; denies frustration; expresses mollification.)
Impunitive. (E glosses over the problem; is conciliatory; minimizes importance of the frustration.)

NATURE OF THE TEST

In each item a cartoonlike line drawing is shown with two people in conversation. A mishap has occurred or an injury is inflicted and one person speaks; he may say, for example, "It's a shame I spilled the coffee on you," or, in a theater, "That girl in front of us talks so much we can't hear the show." A blank "balloon" is left in which E is to write what the other person says. E speaks for an injured person, a step designed to encourage him to identify himself with that person and to react as if he were in the scene.

EVALUATION OF THE P-F TEST

Studies tend to show that retest reliabilities of the scores from the P-F test are generally moderate (.4 to .8).[69] Validity information generally does not support the test. In a study of semistarvation, the male subjects showed a marked, observed drop in frustration-tolerance level or an increased level of irritability, which would lead one to expect increases in the extrapunitive scores and decreases in the others. The men were tested on the twenty-fourth day after the beginning of the starvation diet

[67] Wilson (1949).
[68] Rotter (1951).
[69] Bernard (1949a, 1949b).

and also on the twelfth day after the end. No differences in average scores were found.[70]

Other studies fail to provide evidence of validity for the P-F scores.[71] One of the investigators found that aggressive persons could make low extrapunitive scores and also high intropunitive scores.[72] Further probing revealed that some examinees were responding the way they would *like* to be rather than the way they should if they were consistent with their usual behavior.

The Szondi Test

The Szondi test is unique among projective instruments, unique in its material and its task as well as in the theory underlying it. According to the theory, there are eight basic biological motives in man. We recognize these unconsciously in others and we like the people whose strongest drives are like our own.

The test material is composed of 48 reproductions of photographs of male and female individuals arranged in six sets, eight in each set. The eight components are: homosexual, sadist, epileptic, hysterical, catatonic, paranoid, depressed, and manic. Given a set of eight pictures, the examinee is to select the two he likes best and the two he likes least. The scoring is based upon the number of pictures of each type that are liked.

Many investigators have devoted much time to the study of the Szondi instrument, with generally negative results. Reliability is near zero.[73] A factor analysis of judgments of simply liking or disliking each picture resulted in groupings of the pictures, not in line with Szondi's theory but in terms of such superficial characteristics as bearded vs. clean-shaven faces; smilers vs. nonsmilers; or male vs. female.[74] It appears that if there is any validity at all in the theory or in the test, the very subtle motivational features involved are greatly overshadowed by the superficial features of appearance.

Techniques Based upon Motor Activity

A number of projective techniques call for the examinee to produce something in the way of drawings or paintings. In the techniques examined thus far in this chapter, either perceptual or intellectual behavior is the basis of information used by the examiner. The techniques utilizing motor activity and its products could well be classified with expressive-movement methods in which traits are inferred by inspection of the product.

---

[70] Franklin and Brozek (1949).
[71] French (1950); Lindzey and Goldwyn (1954).
[72] Bernard (1949a).

[73] Cole (1951); Guertin (1951).
[74] Gordon (1953).

THE BENDER-GESTALT TEST

In the Bender-Gestalt test, nine simple figures in line drawings are to be reproduced by the examinee. E's behavior is observed while he draws and his drawings are scrutinized for clues to his personality. Examples of some of the clues and their supposed meanings are as follows. Broken lines indicate personality disturbances. Oversimplification indicates immaturity or regression to a less mature stage. Leaving openings in what should be closed figures indicates a general habit of leaving things undone.[75] As a rule, little empirical evidence is offered to support such interpretations. To the uninitiated they smack somewhat of the kinds of associations represented in Figure 11.2, associations that seem plausible on the surface but that may be entirely without substance. Use of the test in the diagnosis of pathology has not been very successful, except possibly for certain cases of brain damage.

THE DRAW-A-HUMAN-FIGURE TEST

In this test, the examinee, while under observation, draws a picture of a human person.[76] Having drawn one figure, he is asked to draw another of the other sex. An inquiry is then held, with E telling what he can about his reasons for drawing what he did and about his reactions to the figures. Some examples of the kinds of interpretations given are interesting. If E draws a figure of the opposite sex first, this is taken to mean that he has some uncertainty regarding his own sex membership. Popeyes are taken to indicate sexual excitement. Long, outstretched arms are interpreted as ambition.

When one investigator studied the Machover hypothesis regarding uncertainty of sex he found that 90 per cent of the male subjects and 68 per cent of the female subjects draw a figure of their own sex first.[77] If the Machover hypothesis is correct, this would mean that about a third of the females were uncertain regarding their sex! In another study, no significant difference was found in averages for the masculinity-femininity score from the MMPI for those drawing their own sex first vs. those drawing the opposite sex first.[78]

OTHER MOTOR PROJECTIVE TESTS

A test similar to the one just described calls for drawing a house, a tree, and a person. It is called the House-Tree-Person (HTP) test.[79] Another test asks E to draw a "doodle" in response to each of 40 stimulus words.[80] Finger painting has been adapted to projective methods.[81] The

[75] Halpern (1951).
[76] Machover (1951).
[77] Frank (1955).
[78] Granick and Smith (1953).

[79] Morris (1951).
[80] Rapkin (1953).
[81] Napoli (1951).

examinee's paintings are observed for selection of colors, kind of motions made, and choice of subject matter.

There would seem to be no end to the variety of behavior that can be adapted to projective use. One is reminded sometimes of Freud's use of dream interpretation as a source of information regarding the individual's personal problems. In that connection, we are reminded that the meaning of a particular dream symbol is by no means dependable for all cases. It often has unique significance for the particular individual. The same limitation may apply to the results of many of the projective techniques. Presumably the more clinically oriented psychologist takes this into account. The more psychometrically inclined, who wants to treat responses from projective techniques as if they have fixed meaning, would do well to remember this possible limitation.

Projective Techniques Involving Construction

In some projective methods, the examinee is given some elements from which he is to build up a structure of some kind. In the World test, he is given 252 pieces, each piece an object, from 15 different categories and is told to make something from them.[82] In Shneidman's Make-a-Picture Story (MAPS) technique, background pictures are given as miniature stage settings.[83] Figures of human individuals of different ages, sex, and races are given. *E* is told to set the stage and then to explain the situation. In Lowenfeld's Mosaic test, *E* is given many colored shapes and told to make something of them.

Some Miscellaneous Projective Techniques

Several other projective procedures do not fall into any defined category. The Blacky pictures were developed on the basis of Freud's theory of personality development.[84] The characters are: Blacky (a dog), Mama, Papa, and Tippy (a sibling), all being drawn in silhouette. Blacky is a male or female, depending upon the sex of *E*. Different groupings of the characters are shown, to which *E* is to react by telling stories, answering questions, and stating preferences.

A newly developed procedure is based upon judgments of facial expressions.[85] In another procedure, *E* is told to name three things that he regards as being impossible and to explain his responses.[86] In still another, *E* is told to name the most unpleasant thing he can think of and to draw a picture of it.[87] There is one technique that calls for the completion

[82] Morris (1951).
[83] Shneidman (1948).
[84] Blum and Hunt (1952).

[85] Glad and Shearn (1956).
[86] Diamond (1947).
[87] Harrower (1950).

of drawings; [88] another shows short motion-picture scenes, *E* telling what the action represents to him.[89]

GENERAL EVALUATION OF PROJECTIVE TECHNIQUES

Some Logical Criticisms

While there has been widespread enthusiasm for projective techniques, they have not been without critics. Cattell (1946a), for example, puts the Rorschach technique in a class with patent medicines. He particularly takes exception to two unjustified claims.[90] One claim is that more information is derived from application of the Rorschach ink blots than is provided by the scores. The same might actually be said for any test. In fact, those who are partial to projective methods have sometimes looked for such information.[91] The "more information" is in the form of an intuitive judgment, the validity and value of which is difficult to demonstrate. As we saw earlier in connection with the sentence-completion test, and as we shall see in the next chapter, wherever intuitive conclusions are pitted against objective summarizations of information, intuition is likely to come out second best. As Cattell (1944a) points out, if there is anything in the way of subjective information that is useful, we should find out what it is and have it put into the form of objective scores.

It is often said that a projective instrument is designed to assess the "total personality," not separate aspects of it. In Cattell's terminology, this is a "charming misconception." No matter how the results of a projective technique are presented, descriptions are in terms of trait concepts. An interpreter or anyone who communicates the results to others has no other choice. Since trait concepts are used, therefore, much care should be taken to ensure that they have as much unique and unambiguous communication value as possible. On this matter, the users of projective techniques have been negligent.

Goodenough (1949) brings out another warning that should be taken seriously. It is sometimes apparent that a particular examiner or interpreter tends to project his own personality into reports of his examinations. Each examiner tends to stress certain trait concepts and to find certain qualities relatively frequently as compared with other examiners. Stereotypes of interpretation develop, reflecting the examiner's own personality. Projective techniques thus may have a double meaning.

That the unstructured nature of projective methods is a unique virtue

88 Franck and Rosen (1949).
89 Lundin (1949).
90 Cattell (1944b). See also, Steinmetz (1948).
91 For example, see Mayman et al. (1951).

can well be questioned. As Secord (1953) points out, the distinction between structured and unstructured instruments has been overemphasized. There is some structure in projective techniques and there is some lack of structure in inventories and even in aptitude tests. An ideal test is highly structured. This is in line with the frequent assertion in earlier chapters that a good test is like an experiment. If we cannot achieve uniform structuring in a test for all examinees, the next best thing is to obtain information as to what structuring we do achieve for each person. This information might make some difference in the interpretation of his scores.

The Validity Problem for Projective Techniques

Although many attempts have been made to validate the various projective methods, in general they have been put to practical use in advance of validation and in spite of meager support from the studies that have been completed. We have seen from discussions of validity of some of the more common projective instruments in preceding sections that, except for rather isolated reports, the validity picture is dark. A recent conclusion is in line with this picture. After studying ten men intensively by various procedures, Smith, Bruner, and White (1956) concluded that projective techniques underrate capacities, strengths, and stability of their subjects. They fail to reveal creative ways in which the individuals learn to cope with their problems and they fail to show ways in which attitudes affect conduct.

It is possible to overlook the failure of projective techniques to predict vocational success, since they were not developed for that purpose. As mentioned previously, our information on this point is limited to performances of creative artists, military officers, and aircraft pilots. To this information, we may add the conclusion of Viteles (1945) that projective methods failed in pilot selection in the Civil Aeronautics Administration research. While we can overlook such failures, we should expect some success in connection with the diagnosis of psychopathology. But here, again, there is not enough success to justify the apparent faith in the methods.

It would appear, then, that projective techniques in their present forms, and without more supporting evidence than we now have, should be confined to use as aids in psychoanalytic approaches to the understanding of persons. As in the analysis of dreams, they provide snatches of information here and there, which, fitted together with other information, help to build up a picture of an individual and his problems. They are not well designed to measure general traits, but they may give suggestions of general traits that may be profitably investigated further in the individual by better methods.

The clinician's convictions regarding validity may well be based upon actual validities that are statistically very small in the population. If this is true, it does not take much correlation between two things in a population to give the impression of a genuine relationship.

The Outlook for Projective Techniques

It would seem necessary for future developments in projective techniques to go in one of two directions. Either more substantial evidence should be found for validity of the techniques in their present form, or present forms should be superseded by much better ones. The projective principle, which capitalizes on revelation of personal idiosyncracies in what we do, seems to be sufficiently promising. If a principle is useful, we should put it to work in some way. We saw in Chapter 8 that projective types of inventory items can be made to contribute to differentiation among trait positions of individuals. The fact that each item is diagnostic with respect to a trait is determined by empirical procedures. The important implication is that *the projective principle works in spite of the restrictions of some structuring.*

This fact should provide the key as to how the projective principle may be put to work in using other material. Other examples may be found in assessment of the syndrome type of masculinity-femininity in parts of the Terman-Miles inventory.[92] In that inventory, psychological sex differences are determined experimentally for responses to ink blots, to stimulus words, and to other stimulus material. The secret of success in these instances is that some experimental control is introduced. The controls are not completely rigorous, but *they narrow the alternatives while leaving enough leeway for the projective principle to work.* When there are adequate controls, with two alternative responses, one indicating the direction of masculinity and the other the direction of femininity, we obtain an automatic interpretation of the outcome for the item. In the usual projective-technique item, the lack of control leaves the meaning of the result so wide open that it is surprising that there can be much consistency at all in the psychological meaning of the response that emerges.

It is possible to combine controls and the projective principle in the same test in a way that should measure traits now poorly measured by the Rorschach ink blots, for example. If seeing clear form in the Rorschach ink blots indicates an intellectual trait (and the author is quite willing to admit that it probably does), let us obtain a good score that is especially designed to indicate that trait. Let us use more than 10 items and let us be sure that the response to each one of them gives us information upon this particular trait. A test like the Street Gestalt Completion

[92] Terman and Miles (1936).

test,[93] which presents incomplete silhouettes of familiar objects, or the Mooney closure test,[94] of similar nature, would probably do very well for this purpose. Whether or not they do so would be determined first by a factor analysis of these two tests along with the Rorschach $F+$ score. If the analysis were to indicate a common factor, it would then be apparent that there were two behavior tests to replace the less dependable $F+$ score from the Rorschach instrument.

If the tendency to see form rather than color in the same object, or to have the form rather than the color determine one's perception, measures an important trait, a color-form test especially designed for the purpose should be set up. The same proposal can also be made for the tendency to see human movement in the ink blots. The Rorschach ink blots seem to have low potentialities for eliciting movement responses. If it is important to have a dependable score for tendency to see movement in blots, a longer series of blots with higher potentialities could be developed. In how many of them does E see movement? [95]

The courses of action just recommended are those of the psychometrician, whose goal is to measure people on traits. If an important goal of a technique is to derive scores for individuals, the psychometric route to that goal should be taken. It might be objected that even if there were 30 or 40, or even more, dependable scores, something would still be missed. If something more remains to be known, it should be discovered. If the present projective techniques can give any clue as to what it is, and if it can be identified, better tests can probably be developed for it also.

The multiple-test approach, which this line of thinking involves, would, of course, entail considerably more work than does a single projective instrument. But if the patient or client is to be known thoroughly, time must be devoted to the task. A thorough medical examination may take several days. Should a thorough personality examination take less? As in medical testing, a preliminary, rough examination and a general picture of symptoms may be a good start. It would suggest which traits need to be studied more intensively and which traits are probably of little importance for understanding the particular case. This would be one way of economizing on testing effort in the multiple-test approach.

Some of the appeal of a projective technique probably comes from the fact that here and there, apart from scores, something about a particular person's performance gives an important clue that is well worth following up. There is also the clinician's interest in more specific habits and atti-

[93] Street (1931). See Fig. 15.3.
[94] Mooney and Ferguson (1951).
[95] Barron (1955) has developed such a test.

tudes, which are not clearly revealed by trait scores. There is also the partiality to an intuitive type of inference, which seems to emerge in one summative operation, starting with available information.

The preliminary examination of a patient could be done either with some present form of projective technique or with a comprehensive battery of very short tests of traits, or both. The exploration of specific habits and attitudes will probably always require methods additional to either projective techniques or trait tests. Intuitions are not precluded when there are more dependable scores from trait tests, and their desirability should not be offered as an argument for less accurate information.

SUMMARY

Projective techniques are distinguished from other methods of assessment by the use of unstructured tasks and ambiguous materials. The examinee is given a minimum of instruction, and within the limits of the testing situation and the kind of material, he is free to go in his own directions and to give his own unique responses. It is hoped thus to obtain information concerning his personality by the fact that he projects himself into his responses.

The two best-known procedures in this general class are the Rorschach ink-blot technique and the Thematic Apperception Test (TAT). The former is used primarily to derive some 30 different (but experimentally interdependent) scores, each of which is interpreted as a measure of some trait, intellectual, temperamental, or motivational. In spite of the widespread popularity and use of the Rorschach ink blots, the reliabilities of scores tend to be relatively low, and validities, although quite varied, are generally near zero. This statement regarding validity applies to use of the instrument in discriminating pathological from normal individuals, for diagnosis of more particular pathologies such as anxiety, for indicating degree of maladjustment in the general population, and for predicting academic and vocational success. Studies show that responses from the method are not as exempt from test-taking attitudes as has often been claimed for projective techniques in general.

The TAT utilizes pictures of people in ambiguous situations and relationships, to which the examinee responds by composing stories. The basic assumption is that he identifies himself with one of the characters, and in reporting upon this character, he is revealing his own trends in motivation as they affect his fantasy life. Interpretations of TAT results may be in terms of scores, but they are usually in terms of intuitive impressions. Owing to rather complex relationships between fantasy and overt behavior, predictions of the latter from TAT results proves to be somewhat precarious. Results are also rather sensitive to temporary conditions, including test-taking attitudes, and have shown little or no validity for predicting academic or vocational success.

There are many other projective techniques of different forms. The sentence-completion type of technique is an important step beyond the word-association procedure of the psychoanalysts and seems to have some promise. The Rosenzweig Picture-Frustration Test aims to measure traits involved in ways of meeting frustrations by the use of cartoonlike pictures. The Szondi test presents pictures of adult persons for statements of preferences, on the assumption that each examinee will tend to prefer those persons who have high degrees of traits in line with his own high trait positions.

A number of techniques involve motor responses, which might actually put them in the class of expressive-behavior methods. One of the best known of these is the Bender-Gestalt Test, which asks the examinee to reproduce with pencil and paper some simple designs that he is shown. Other techniques involve the free drawing of a person or of a combination of house, tree, and person. Others involve the use of "doodles" and of finger painting.

Another class of techniques involves construction of some kind—in the form of stage settings with figures of people or in the form of mosaic patterns. Still other techniques call for interpretations of emotional expressions, family scenes composed of dogs, or motion-picture snatches.

Criticisms of projective techniques in general have been aimed at what appear to be unjustified claims, for example, that the interpreter can extract intuitively something from the results that objective scoring could not supply and the claim that, unlike other methods, projective techniques give at once a picture of the "total personality." Dependence upon the techniques has gone well beyond what has been justified by rigorous validation studies.

The greatest supposed strength of projective techniques has also been their greatest weakness. This is the lack of control, which violates experimental principles of obtaining univocally interpretable information. The experimental principle can, however, be applied along with the projective principle to take appropriate advantage of both. So long as an outcome of any projective technique is to be in the form of trait scores, a psychometric approach is involved. This means that the best psychometric procedures should be applied, including observance of analytical and experimental principles.

The continued use of projective techniques in their present form can be justified only in terms of rough surveys or explorations, which yield hypotheses only, to be followed by the acquisition of more dependable information bearing upon those hypotheses.

Chapter 13

OTHER CLINICAL METHODS

THERE REMAIN a few miscellaneous procedures that can be grouped under "clinical methods" for want of a better class name. They are not the only methods used by clinicians, as we have seen before. Commonly used in clinical practice also are interviews, inventories, projective techniques, and behavior tests. The relative emphasis placed upon different methods will depend upon the individual clinician and his problems.

Also to be considered in this chapter is the problem of integration of information regarding personalities. We have encountered this problem incidentally from time to time. We must now take a closer look at it, and we shall begin with that subject.

THE INTEGRATION OF INFORMATION

Two General Approaches to Integration

After a number of trait scores and other bits of information concerning a person have been obtained, how is this material to be integrated to obtain a more unified picture? There have been two general answers to this question and there has been considerable difference of opinion concerning these two answers. Some of the issues mentioned in Chapter 2 come to the fore as well as some of the considerations mentioned in connection with projective techniques in the preceding chapter. One of these approaches is known as *statistical* or *actuarial* and the other is known as *intuitive,* involving professional judgment.

SUMMATION EQUATIONS

Some kind of additive equation is commonly used as a statistical procedure for combining information. The information is in quantitative form, including scores, ratings, or other measurements such as age, years of education, or years of married life. Even membership in categories, such as being married or single, criminal or noncriminal, can be treated as quantitative by giving to the classes certain values such as 0 and 1. In summing values of the various kinds, we may weight them differently or we may not. The weights can be based upon professional judgment or upon empirical results, as in a *multiple-regression equation*.[1]

A common criticism of the use of additive equations for combining information is that the individual does not act that way. He faces a complex situation, which he interprets (integrates) as best he can; then he organizes a response that he hopes will be successful. Although a number of his traits may bear upon the end result, they do not operate separately and by piling one upon the other. The analysis of the determiners of actions into components, the subsequent measurement of those components, and the prediction of behavior from a sum of the components is said to be an unrealistic procedure.

Such a criticism indicates a misunderstanding of the role and use of mathematics in science. We do not need to say that nature necessarily operates in the way that equations say that it does. Nature only needs to act *as if* the equations apply. Equations are humanly constructed models, designed to achieve a better understanding of how things occur and a better control over them. The proof of the value of equations is in terms of how well they work, in terms of prediction and control. To find that we can predict behavior by summing bits of information in the way some equation prescribes does not commit us to a belief that a person "acts that way."

If the chief objection is to the idea of summation, it can be quickly pointed out that this is not the only objective manner of combining information. Other kinds of equations involving products or other operations are quite possible. Profile methods provide still other possibilities of mathematical, yet nonadditive, procedures.

PROFILES

Profile methods and profile charts have been mentioned earlier in connection with a few of the standard inventories and tests. An example may be seen in Figure 13.1. In using this kind of device, we must transform the obtained scores for all the different traits involved into standard scores on a common scale. The usual practice is to equate frequency distributions of scores for different traits so that there will be identical means and dispersions for all traits in the population from which the norm data were derived. This is an arbitrary procedure applied for

---

[1] The multiple-regression method yields weights that give maximum accuracy of prediction for the combination of measures used and the sample of individuals to which they were applied. For further information on multiple regressions and multiple correlation, see textbooks on statistics.

C SCORE	G General activity Energy	R Restraint Seriousness	A Ascendance Social boldness	S Social interest Sociability	E Emotional stability	O Objectivity	F Friendliness Agreeableness	T Thoughtfulness Reflectiveness	P Personal relations Cooperativeness	M Masculinity (of emotions and interests)	Centile rank	Nearest T score
10	30 29	30 29 28 27	30 29	30	30 29	30 29	29 28 27 26	30 29 28	30 29 28	30 29 28	99	75
9	28 27	28 27 26 25	28 27 26	29 28	28 27	29 27	25 24 23	27 26	27 26	27		70
8	26 25	24 23	25 24 23	27 26	26 25	26 25	22 21	25 24	25 24 23	26 25	95 90	65
7	24 23 22	22 21	22 21	25 24	24 23 22	24 23	20 19 18	23 22	22 21	24	80	60
6	21 20 19	20 19 18	20 19 18	23 22 21	21 20 19	22 21 20	17 16	21 20	20 19 18	23 22	70 60	55
5	18 17 16	17 16	17 16 15	20 19 18	18 17 16	19 18 17	15 14 13	19 18	17 16	21 20	50 40	50
4	15 14 13	15 14	14 13	16 15 14	15 14 13 12	16 15 14	12 11 10	17 16 15	16 15 14	19 18	30	45
3	12 11 10	13 12 11	12 11 10	13 12 11 10	10 9 8	12 11 10 9	9 8	14 13	13 12 11	17 16 15	20	40
2	9 8	10 9 8	9 8 7	9 8 7 6	7 6	8 7 6	7 6 5	12 11 10	10 9 8	14 13 12	10 5	35
1	7 6 5	7 6 5	6 5 4	5 4 3	5 4 3	5 4 3	4 3 2	9 8 7	7 6 5	11 10 9		30
0	4 3	4 3 2	3 2	2 1 0	2 1 0	2 1 0	1 0	6 5	4 3 2	8 7	1	25

Inactivity Slowness	Impulsiveness Rhathymia	Submissiveness	Shyness Seclusiveness	Emotional instability Depression	Subjectivity Hypersensitiveness	Hostility Belligerence	Unreflectiveness	Criticalness Intolerance	Femininity (of emotions and interests)	

Copyright 1949, SHERIDAN SUPPLY COMPANY, Beverly Hills, California

Fig. 13.1 A profile chart showing the variations in score levels of one individual in ten traits measured by the *Guilford-Zimmerman Temperament Survey*. Score positions left clear have been found most favorable for successful performance of foremen; positions with single crosshatching are fair; and those with double crosshatching are least favorable. Validity coefficients tend to be small. For other types of work assignments the favorable and unfavorable regions might well be somewhat different. (*Profile chart shown through the courtesy of the Sheridan Supply Company.*)

convenience. The use of the profile for a particular individual is open to two different approaches. The information can be summarized and reported in terms of a single, integrative value or it can be interpreted intuitively.

The Need for Intuition

The statistical or actuarial approach adopts the rules of combination of data in advance and applies those rules uniformly to all individuals of a class or population. The intuitive approach, on the other hand, while applying some principles based upon experiences, is free to apply new rules to each case if this seems necessary or desirable. Each case does offer some problems of its own and the same items of information may not be known regarding every person. There is usually more information than can be shown in a profile or included in a multiple regression equation. A particular case calls for seeking information that is not included in profile or equation. All these reasons indicate the need for professional judgment, much of which must involve intuition at many points.

General Evaluation of Clinical vs. Actuarial Approaches

The real issue between the two approaches is whether, given the same information, it will be better to combine the data according to pre-established rules or to make an educated guess as a way of extracting conclusions. Is the clinician justified in rejecting the more objective and rigorous procedures for combining information in making predictions, as he often does? A number of studies give results bearing upon this question, more often indirectly than directly, but nevertheless with some degree of relevance.

OVERCONFIDENCE IN INTUITIONS

There is good reason to believe that a preference for the intuitive approach is fostered by an overconfidence in its results. Meehl (1954), who made an extensive survey of publications bearing upon the actuarial vs. intuitive issue, cites an example of overconfidence in clinical judgment. An experienced clinician was reported to have given a certain test to many patients who had also taken the Wechsler-Bellevue scale. He "noticed" that the correlation between the two was "pretty good." The actual correlation turned out to be only .04. How could he have reached such an erroneous conclusion?

Speaking in more general terms, one trouble is that the clinician or counselor is likely to remember his hits and to forget his misses. The law of effect, so prominent in learning theory, must surely apply here. Too often he does not know *when* he misses. He does not have the necessary feedback of information that would tell him when he is right and when he is wrong. Without information to the contrary, it is natural for us to believe that we are right. Thinking we are right is reenforcing. Furthermore, when we think of "clever" hypotheses, the reward we feel for being so clever also helps to build up the conviction that we are right. In these ways does a belief in the infallibility of our judgments develop.

RESULTS FROM INTUITIVE VS. ACTUARIAL PROCEDURES

It must be admitted that good studies comparing intuitive and actuarial procedures are hard to find. The ideal study would provide clinician and statistician with the same information. Each would combine the data in his own way and would emerge with a prediction concerning the outcome in behavior. In some studies that have been done, each operator usually started from his own favorite procedures, which provided different information. In other studies, the clinician had an advantage in that he had available not only the statistician's information but also some of his own, for example, test scores, which both had in common, plus results from an interview. Recognizing the weaknesses of studies comparing the two approaches, let us see as best we can what the results tend to indicate.

A frequently quoted study in this connection is that of Sarbin (1942) on predictions of grades of college freshmen. Clinical predictions correlated .35 and .69 for males and females, respectively. Statistical predictions based upon high school ranks and aptitude scores only correlated .45 and .70, respectively. The clinical information included results from an interest inventory, a temperament inventory, a personal-data form, and an interview. Adding the clinical procedure to the statistical procedure did not improve predictions materially.

Wittman (1941) studied by two procedures the predictions of whether or not patients would benefit from shock treatment. One procedure used a check list of 30 weighted items of information. The weights had been selected by psychiatrists and hence were probably not the same as the optimal ones that would have been found by ordinary multiple-regression procedures. The intuitive predictions were made by three psychiatrists. The percentage of correct predictions from the check list was 81. The average percentage from the psychiatrists' predictions was 44. In a similar study, the check-list procedure gave 68 per cent correct predictions and the psychiatrists gave 41 per cent. [2] The correlation coefficients corresponding to these percentages were .61 and .21, respectively.

An earlier study involved prediction of success of a thousand parolees from a state prison. [3] The bases for prediction were, on the one hand,

[2] Wittman and Steinberg (1944).
[3] Burgess (1928).

21 objective facts, combined without weighting, and on the other, the judgments of two prison psychiatrists. The psychiatrists proved to be better in predicting successes, with 80 and 85 per cent correct judgments, compared to 76 per cent for the objective score. They were worse in predicting failures, with percentages of 30 and 51 as against 69 for the objective procedure. The difference in the two cases probably arose from the fact that the psychiatrists predicted more successes in general. If we combine cases of success and failure predicted we find an over-all advantage for the objective method.

In the prediction of success of therapy for 33 psychoneurotic patients, each of three "mechanical" methods was found to be superior to judgments of all clinicians.[4] The mechanical methods for sorting profiles were adopted in advance. Eight clinicians made intuitive predictions based upon the profiles. The average accuracy for the clinicians is indicated by a result of 62 per cent correct. The corresponding percentages for the three mechanical methods were 73 to 80.

In the study of selection of graduate students in clinical psychology, a great many methods of assessment were tried out.[5] One general conclusion was that scores from the Strong VIB alone were as effective as all the clinical information combined. Another was that clinical judgments added nothing to objective information in predicting criteria of success.

After surveying 20 such studies, Meehl (1954) came to the conclusion that statistical methods have proved to be better than or equal to clinical methods, with one exception. This is probably a conservative statement. Although, as pointed out above, really crucial experiments on this subject are rare, the cumulative effect of results from experiments that bear on the question seem to support Meehl's general conclusion. The implication is not that we do away entirely with clinical intuitions, for they will always be needed where objective methods leave off, but that we use the objective methods of integrating information and reaching decisions just as far as they have proved to be valid and that we seek to extend the areas in which such methods are used.

In addition to the greater over-all validity of statistical summaries of information, there is considerable saving of costs in terms of professional time. Kelly and Fiske (1951) estimated that it required seven man-days of clinical-expert time to duplicate the performance (in terms of prediction) of the Strong VIB. A lower-paid clerk can handle the statistical operations called for in the objective methods of integrating data. Those methods, to be sure, involve considerable time and effort in preliminary research, when the procedures of combining data are derived. In the

4 Barron (1953b).
5 Kelly and Fiske (1951).

practical situation, too, there is always the necessity of rechecking validity of the same procedure to determine whether it is still working in spite of possible changes in conditions. In the long run, however, such effort seems to pay.

Methods of Interpreting Profile Data

Several different procedures other than intuitive have been proposed recently for integrating information found in profiles of scores. Some of these consider certain properties of a profile—its level, its degree of scatter, and its form or shape. Another kind of approach is to determine whether an obtained profile approaches some ideal profile that is thought to be representative of a defined group of individuals. Still another looks for particular patterns of scores that possibly have unique meaning.

PROBLEMS IN CONNECTION WITH IDEAL PROFILES

In one use of profiles, decisions are made as to probable future success in an occupation, or satisfaction in it, or as to probable diagnosis in some pathological category by noting how closely the person's profile of scores approaches the typical one for that occupation or category. This presents a double problem: the nature of the ideal profile, and how we can indicate the closeness of approach to it for a particular case. The first of these two problems will be discussed here and the second later.

The derivation of an ideal profile for any defined group is no simple task, for there is much variation among members within the defined group. Some groups conform more closely to their average patterns than do others. The more closely individuals of a group all approach the same profile, the more sense it makes to attempt to match individual profiles with the ideal group profile.

An example of this difficulty was found in the attempt to derive an ideal profile for home economics women on the Kuder Preference Record.[6] At first, when profiles from women trained in home economics and later employed in appropriate positions were compared, no typical pattern could be found. A species of home economics women with similar patterns of interests did not seem to exist. The total sample was then broken down into two subgroups according to kind of employment—teachers and business women. Each group then tended to show more coherence in terms of profile pattern. Teachers were higher in scores called artistic and social service and lower in the score called persuasive. Business women were higher in the persuasive score and lower in the social service score. A further breakdown for business women gave even more distinct patterns. Clearly, the choice of populations for the purpose of deriving ideal profiles must be made with considerable care.

[6] Lehman (1944).

QUANTITATIVE DESCRIPTIONS OF PROFILES

There are several objective features of a profile of scores that can be described in terms of single numbers. Such numbers may provide information that is predictive or otherwise useful. The general elevation of a profile can be indicated by a sum or average of its scores. What we have by way of information, however, is an unweighted sum of scores, which is nothing more nor less than a regression equation without weights.

Another objective feature of a profile is its degree of *scatter* of scores. This can be expressed in a single number by computing an average deviation or a standard deviation of the profile scores. The possible usefulness of such an index in connection with aptitude scores was discussed in Chapter 10. The possible significance of scatter, as such, for nonaptitude scores has not been investigated to any extent. Unevenness of scores for interests is expected and is regarded as favorable for finding the points of strongest interest for an individual. Unevenness of temperament scores might suggest the hypothesis of lack of balance and hence maladjustment. On this point, we have no information and apparently little speculation.[7]

The third main feature of profiles—shape (apart from variability)—is not easily expressed by any numerical value. It is possible, however, to indicate how similar the shape of an obtained profile is to an ideal profile in ways that yield quantitative values.

PROFILE SIMILARITY

The similarity of an obtained profile to an ideal one can be indicated in a number of ways. There may be interest in general level, in which case this can be expressed in terms of a simple difference in averages of the two sets of profile scores—obtained and ideal. A comparison of scatters of the two may be indicated in a similar manner, the difference between two average deviations or two standard deviations. For the comparison of shapes, du Mas (1949) has suggested a simple index of profile similarity and Cronbach and Gleser (1953) have suggested another. A correlation coefficient for the relation between the two sets of scores would provide some information but probably not enough. Two profiles could correlate very strongly and yet be very far apart.

CLASSES FROM COMBINATIONS OF SCORES

Lykken (1956) objects that most indices of profile similarity do not tell us enough, and he is probably right. He proposes a rather complicated validation approach that should take care of all cases if it could be

_____
[7] Apart from the kind mentioned in Chap. 4 in the discussion of intraindividual variability.

followed out. In principle, his procedure calls for grouping individuals in classes, each class representing a different combination of scores from a profile. The average criterion score would be determined for each class. This average could then be used as the prediction of a person's criterion performance. The difficulty with this procedure would be the very large number of classes and the very small numbers of cases in most of the classes. Even if a very coarse scale of two scores for each of ten traits were adopted, there would be 1,024 possible classes. If scales of more than four steps were adopted, the numbers of cases with combinations of extreme scores would be very small.

FAVORABLE AND UNFAVORABLE REGIONS

A simple and practical procedure of interpreting profiles is to mark off the score region for each trait within which the highest criterion scores are obtained. We see an example of this in Figure 13.1. There we have for each trait the range of score values for men who are likely to be most successful as supervisors, also the ranges of probable moderate and poor success. The profile of one individual is also shown. Six of his ten scores fall in the most favorable region and none in the least favorable region. Experience with predictions from such information could be further validated. This method takes into account the fact that optimal score regions are not always at the very top of the scale but even extend down to the middle score category in some instances. The Lykken method would not be able to take this fact into account without having at least three score intervals for almost every trait.

Most methods fail to provide the possibility for using information regarding special combinations of two or more scores, an exception being the Lykken procedure. Such special combinations are likely to be discovered by clinical observations. For example, it is likely that if a person has a low score on G (general activity) in the GZTS (see Figure 13.1), his low scores on such traits as O, F, and P may indicate little future trouble in getting along with people. A high G score combined with low F and P scores, particularly, is likely to mean trouble. For another example, a high M (masculinity) score combined with high O (objectivity) and high A (ascendance) scores may indicate a callous, overbearing person who lacks finer sensibilities. In general, such combinations, which may indicate syndrome types, would be missed by most current methods.

OTHER METHODS FOR GATHERING INFORMATION

Case-History Material

Certain demographic information—age, sex, socioeconomic level, etc.—concerning a client or patient is regarded as obviously needed for general background information, if for no more direct purpose. Such information is ordinarily used informally with little effort to combine it with other information in order to make predictions in a rigorous manner. As in the case of biographical data in general, each item of information can be validated for different purposes and total scores can be derived for making predictions of outcomes.[8]

Personal Documents

Personal documents include such things as autobiographies, letters, diaries, recordings, and artistic products, such as writings and paintings. At many points the use of such material coincides with certain expressive methods described in Chapter 11. A product is something tangible for all to see. While such information is of limited value for scientific purposes, it can be a rich source of hypotheses to be investigated. It can also be useful for understanding the individual, and hence can be of value in clinical practice.

There are a number of disadvantages in the use of such material, as Allport (1942) has pointed out. Samples of such material are not representative, for some individuals leave such products, others do not. The material requires interpretation; its meaning with regard to personality is not self-evident. It is desirable to check up on the facts, if factual material is involved, and checking up is not always easy. Some individuals may actually write so as to deceive. Biographies are touched up to make certain persons look better and perhaps to make others look worse. Crucial facts may be omitted or distorted. There is self-deception to be considered. Errors of memory occur to modify the facts. There is a liberal mixture of fact with interpretation, and always the writer is selective in what he includes and what he leaves out. The study of a product is about as complex a task as the study of the person himself, and being once removed from the person, the product is likely to be of considerably less value than the person himself as an object of study.

THE DISCOMFORT-RELIEF RATIO (DRQ)

One step is taken toward a more objective indicator that can be applied to personal documents by the *discomfort-relief-quotient* (DRQ) index.[9] This index is in the form of a ratio of the number of words indicating discomfort (suffering, tension, unhappiness, or pain) to the number of words indicating relief (comfort, satisfaction, or enjoyment). It can also be scored in terms of numbers of sentences or of thought units. When applied to statements made during interviews, the index has not

---

[8] See Chap. 8 for a discussion of the biographical inventory.
[9] Dollard and Mowrer (1947).

worked very well,[10] but it is at least one attempt to put evaluation of personal verbal expressions into more objective form. It also suggests that other indices might be developed.

Personal Constructs

Clinicians sometimes bemoan the fact that there is a dearth of methods especially designed to study the individual as such. This means essentially a study from the idiographic point of view. It is true that in the development of method the normative view has generally prevailed and that normative information is used in describing the individual. Considerable success for achieving different purposes has followed this general practice. Recently, G. A. Kelly (1956) has come forth, after years of investigation, with a unique procedure for study of the individual.

Kelly's main thesis is that the important source of determination of a person's behavior is in his own conception of the world in which he lives. Most important in that world as he sees it are the individuals who are or have been most closely associated with him, such as mother, father, brothers, sisters, teachers, preachers, husband or wife, employer or supervisor, and so on. The way in which the person interprets these people and their relations to him and what he expects from them have much to do with his behavior, for good or for ill. If he is in trouble, some of his constructs or interpretations may need to be modified.

THE REP TEST

In connection with his practice Kelly uses a test designed especially for the purpose of understanding the particular individual, known as the Role Construct Repertory Test, or Rep test. The test is administered somewhat as follows. The examinee names a number of people whom he knows, usually about 20. He is then offered the names of three of these people at a time in different combinations. He is instructed to say which two are most alike and how the third differs from the other two. The aim is to see how E classifies these individuals and how he differentiates them.

From the judgments given by E, a matrix of similarities between these persons is made up. A factor analysis is performed to give a picture of the structure of E's conceptions of the people who presumably have meant the most to him. From this picture it is ascertained, with E's help, whether desirable changes may be called for. The results are thus not in terms of trait scores or even in terms of profiles, but rather in terms of a structure of ideas and attitudes. There may be similarity of structures among different individuals, which may provide the basis for extracting general principles that will apply beyond particular individuals. Whether or not

[10] Auld and Mahl (1956).

the Rep test is the answer clinicians have been looking for, it does provide an example of how the individual may be studied systematically. It probably will not provide all the information that the clinician needs to know.[11]

VALIDATION OF CLINICAL METHODS

Problems in Clinical Validation

The validation of the clinician's judgments presents some unsolved problems. Wherever he claims to assess particular traits for which there are well-accepted criterion measurements, in the form of behavior-test scores, for example, we can readily apply the usual validation procedures. When he claims to predict academic or vocational success for which there are the customary criteria, there are also no problems. Even when he makes one of his "global" or integrative judgments based upon an intuitive grasp of heterogeneous information, we can still arrive at a conclusion as to how well he has done if the terminal use of a judgment is some predicted outcome that can be assessed as present or absent or as present to different degrees.

But when his judgment is in the form of an impression of his patient that cannot be adequately communicated verbally, we encounter trouble. To a large extent, in dealing with a patient he must more or less "play by ear." He is engaged in a running sequence of reassessments as new bits of information come to light or new facets of personality seem to be shown. There are no criteria for such impressions, and yet it is on the basis of such impressions that action must often be taken.

This problem actually involves us in the whole question of psychological or social perception, of how one person who is in interaction with another keeps reacting in accordance with his interpretations of that other person, revising them as he goes along. It is safe to say of such impressions that much is erroneous. If one were to venture a wild guess as to an over-all correlation between impression and fact, including all significant facets, it might be a rather low value. But in human interaction, there is no escape from dependence upon such perceptual information. Actually, the impression that one person has of another at the moment involves the temporary thoughts, attitudes, and emotions perhaps more than it does the more permanent dispositions we have called traits. Appropriate reaction to the other person is guided by feedback information arising from the give and take of interaction. Perhaps it is the rapid corrective action that gives the clinician the impression that

---

[11] Other approaches to the statistical study of individuals by using factor analysis have been tried by Cattell, Cattell, and Rhymer (1947) and by Baldwin (1946).

he is doing better in his current evaluations than he really is. It is only fair to say that the feedback information also corrects his perceptions. On the other hand, his own actions may often succeed better than he knows.

Validity Against Global Criteria

It seems logical that if clinical judgments are global in character they might well be validated against criteria of like complexity. Some years ago Vernon (1936*b*) suggested and investigated a matching procedure that was designed for this purpose. The assumption was that composite assessment and composite criterion both involve things that trait descriptions cannot duplicate. It was expected that such pairs of assessments could be more accurately matched than anything that fell short of such completeness.

The things often matched, however, have been personality sketches, or verbal descriptions, which involve a step, or more, in the direction of trait concepts. Sketches have been matched with samples of handwriting, with themes, and with personal documents of other kinds, and with one another. The matching has been done in small groups of five to six individuals, which allows a strong chance element to enter the picture. Numerous difficulties have beset the method, as Secord (1952) has pointed out, which is probably one reason this procedure has not been frequently used.

A notable example of validation of clinical assessment against a clinical type of criterion is found in the OSS assessment studies.[12] Assessment ratings, which tended, after all, to conform to trait descriptions, were obtained for men just entering training and were later correlated with ratings similarly obtained in combat areas. Correlations of .3 to .5 were reported. Since the final assessments were similar in character to those prior to training, however, these figures may be more properly regarded as retest reliabilities with much intervening time and many intervening experiences.

Prediction of Particular Behavior Outcomes

The prediction of particular behavior outcomes from clinical judgments has not had an outstanding record, as should have been clear by this time. Some examples were given of this kind of prediction in the discussion of clinical vs. statistical methods of combining data. Predictions of several kinds of behavior were mentioned—academic achievement, response to shock therapy, success of parolees, and success of therapy among psychoneurotics. Some degree of validity was demonstrated for such predictions, but the accuracy was usually lower than that for predictions

[12] OSS Assessment Staff (1948).

from composite information statistically derived. It would not be important to add other examples here except for the fact that claims have been made or expectations have been expressed of such predictions from clinical judgments.

A number of attempts were made to predict success vs. failure of pilot students during World War II in the Army Air Force.[13] Predictions of probable success were made on a nine-point scale from each of several sources of information, including the Rorschach technique, the Thematic Apperception Test, an hour-long interview, two personality inventories, and observations of students while they were taking an Interaction test, a psychomotor test, and a stress test. In so far as these different predictions could be intercorrelated, we have essentially validation of the kind mentioned in the preceding section, one global impression being validated against another. The highest intercorrelation of this kind was .19, most of the correlations being near zero. The correlations of these predictions with the pass-fail criterion in pilot training were also generally near zero.

A postwar study of the same kind of validation was made under more favorable conditions.[14] Of 100 selected students, 50 had passed their training successfully and 50 had failed for reasons of personality defects. In sets of 20, representing 10 passing and 10 failing students in each set, detailed protocols were presented to well-experienced clinical psychologists, three to seven of whom made predictions for each set. The protocols included results from six instruments, four of them being common projective techniques, one involving biographical information, and one being a score from a psychosomatic-symptom inventory. The predictions from the 20 psychologists were correct in 4 to 14 cases out of 20, with an over-all average of 10.2 correct; almost exactly chance accuracy. The results were no better when majority opinion was used for predicting success.

From all such results as we have seen in this chapter, it can be concluded that there are definite limitations in the prediction of behavior from clinical procedures of the intuitive type. As to the ability of clinicians to understand others, from factual information and from direct observation and interaction, we have almost no information. Validation studies of this type of assessment will have to wait until better experimental procedures have been developed.

SUMMARY

Although the average clinician appreciates the collection of information regarding a person in terms of trait scores and other bits of information, he often prefers to integrate that information and to extract

---

[13] Guilford and Lacey (1947).
[14] Holtzman and Sells (1954).

from it an impression of the total personality by an intuitive approach rather than by means of a prearranged, objective method. His experience tends to give him confidence in his power to extract intuitively from scattered information more than is possible by additive or other mechanical methods of combination.

Although few crucial studies designed to test the relative validities of these two approaches have been done, numerous comparisons of results from the two have led to the conclusion that, in the predictions of behavior outcomes, the intuitive approach is probably never better and usually comes off second best. This does not mean that there is no validity in clinical judgment based upon intuitive evaluation of data, for validity for some kinds of predictions has been demonstrated. No adequate validity studies have been made and no procedures for validation have been devised for assessing the accuracy of the clinician's moment-to-moment understanding of a patient.

Profiles of trait scores provide a special method of combining material for possible interpretation by the clinician or counselor either intuitively or in some quantitative manner. Several numerical methods have been suggested for describing properties of profile—level, scatter, and shape—and for indicating how similar a given profile is to some ideal type of profile. Other procedures have been suggested for understanding persons from combinations of profile scores.

Methods of gathering trait-indicating information that are favored relatively by clinicians include case-history methods and the use of personal documents. A unique Rep test has been designed for the purpose of describing an individual's personal constructs, a personal construct being a person's way of conceiving his more intimate world, including the people whom he knows best and who have the most effect upon him. This seems to be the first rigorous method designed for the systematic study of the individual from the idiographic point of view. It suggests that other such methods are possible.

Chapter 14

SOMATIC DIMENSIONS

In this and the remaining chapters, we shall attempt to obtain as clear a picture as is possible at this time of the structure of the entire personality as described in terms of dimensions. In doing so, we shall stress the findings of factor analysis in the form of primary traits and syndromes. We shall have to go beyond the known primary traits in many places in order to round out the picture. We shall not be on very sure ground in the consideration of syndrome types, for the reason that information regarding the organization of traits is generally lacking. For this purpose, we need to know from empirical sources about the intercorrelations of primary traits. Attempts will be made to inject as much logical organization into the picture as seems permissible at this time. We shall begin with the somatic aspect of personality, which includes the dimensions of morphology and physiology.

MORPHOLOGICAL DIMENSIONS

Factor-Analytical Studies of Morphology

Some ten reports have come to the attention of the author in which a total of 32 factor analyses have been done with measures of morphology. Fortunately, each analysis was based upon a population that was homogeneous with respect to sex and relatively homogeneous with respect to age. Such experimental controls are very important. If we allowed age to range considerably in our sample, intercorrelations among all physical measurements would be much higher and it might appear that we have only one factor—general size. If there are any significant differences in the morphological factor structures of males and females, these differences would be obscured when the measurements of both sexes were included in the same analysis. Of the 32 analyses, 16 were done with male groups and 16 with female groups. Two were done with samples of infants nine days old; [1] fifteen were done with children; [2] six with adolescents; [3] and nine with young adults.[4]

Conclusions Regarding Known Morphological Factors [5]

As each factor is discussed, the measures or experimental variables that are sufficiently related to it to be worth mentioning will be given. They are listed in order of their apparent strength of relationship to the factor, from the most to the least related.

General head size [6]

The related variables are: breadth of head, height of head, length of head, interpupillary distance, and breadth of face. The finding of a factor of *general head size* [7] means that there is freedom for the general size of head to vary somewhat independently from sizes of other body parts. There are limitations to this, of course.

Since heads also vary in *shape,* some, for example, being long and narrow, others short and thick, it is likely that there are also three more narrow factors, including head length, head width, and head depth. To test for the relative independence of such factors we should have to include in the same analysis at least two, and preferably three, measures in each of these directions. The intercorrelations of the three basic head dimensions—length, breadth, and depth—are all positive, indicating a factor of *general head size.*[8]

Trunk length [9]

In the trunk area, we find considerable evidence that there are three size factors, one of which is *trunk length.* The measures found related to this factor in one or both of two analyses are: sitting height, sternal length, and trunk length.

---

[1] McCloy (1940*a*).

[2] McCloy (1940*a*); Burt (1949*a*); Mullen (1940).

[3] McCloy (1940*a*); Mullen (1940).

[4] McCloy (1940*a*); Hammond (1942); Rees and Eysenck (1945); Thurstone (1946*a*, 1946*b*); Moore and Hsü (1946); Heath (1952).

[5] Some of the factor analyses left much to be desired in the way in which they were conducted. It is nevertheless possible to ascertain which of the factors appear to have been verified in more than one analysis.

[6] Thurstone (1946); Moore and Hsü (1946).

[7] It will be the general policy to italicize names of factors on their first appearances, and sometimes elsewhere, to distinguish them from names of experimental variables.

[8] Howells (1951) found a factor that may be interpreted as head width. He also found evidence for factors of *face* length and *face* width as well as ear size. We should therefore probably make a distinction between factors of cranial size and face size.

[9] Thurstone (1947); Burt (1949*a*).

Trunk depth [10]

Measures of size of trunk from front to back have been taken at a number of places. Circumference measures also indicate this factor to some degree. The measures are: chest thickness, abdominal depth, chest circumference, and hip circumference. The abdominal measure and hip measure show relationship to a chest-size factor because of some consistency between depth of bodies in these neighboring regions. This does not preclude possible later finding of a separate abdominal-depth factor.

Trunk width [11]

The related measures are: chest breadth, shoulder breadth, hip breadth, and chest circumference. Again, measures of neighboring structures, this time shoulders and hips, show some relation to a trunk factor.

There is some uncertainty as to whether there is enough independence between chest measurements vs. abdominal measurements vs. hip measurements to provide the basis for size factors in those three regions separately. If so, the three factors just mentioned might be more properly called chest factors. At any rate, the intercorrelations among the three trunk factors just listed are probably such that there is a higher-order *general* trunk (or chest) factor in addition to the three more limited ones. This would be analogous to the *general-head-size* factor mentioned above. Studies have been more analytical and liberal in selecting trunk measures than they have in selecting head measures.

General body length [12]

Length measures taken at widespread places in the body generally intercorrelate positively. There is a tendency toward consistency in length in all body regions from which measurements have been taken. This is over and above local length factors, of which we have just seen an example in the trunk region. Since the growth of length of bones is known to depend upon instigation from the pituitary gland, we should expect most bones to be affected similarly. This does not mean that we need expect perfect correlations of length of all bones and hence of length in all body regions. Lack of perfect correlation leaves room for localized length factors.

Measures that appear to be related to the *general-body-length* factor are: total height, sitting height, sternal length, arm span, arm length, upper-arm length, lower-arm length, hand length, leg length, upper-leg length, lower-leg length, nose length, and ear length. Again, it should be pointed out that not every measure was used in every analysis.

[10] Thurstone (1947); Moore and Hsü (1946); Burt (1949a).
[11] Thurstone (1946, 1947); Moore and Hsü (1946); Burt (1949a).
[12] Thurstone (1946a, 1946b); Moore and Hsü (1946); Burt (1949a); Howells (1951); Heath (1952).

Muscular thickness

The morphological factors considered thus far pertain mainly to skeletal features. Two studies indicate that there is a factor of *muscular thickness*.[13] The measures involved are: forearm girth, circumference of neck, maximum leg girth, calf girth, ankle girth, breadth of hand, height, knee girth, and wrist girth. The presence of height among these otherwise muscular measures probably indicates that measures of muscular thickness or bulk are related to an over-all body-size factor in which height has considerable importance.

Other Possible Morphological Factors

Other morphological factors have been found, each in a single investigation. They may hold up in subsequent analyses and are hence well worth considering here. We may regard them as hypotheses of dimensions having some empirical support. McCloy (1940*a*) reported a factor that he interpreted as growth of fat. It was determined by measures of thickness of subcutaneous fat deposits in the chest, back, and arm regions by means of a "pinching" test. Thurstone (1947) reported a factor that might be interpreted as hip width, indicated by measurements of hip width, hip circumference, and chest width. Thurstone (1946) also found a factor interpreted as hand size, related to variables of hand length, hand breadth, and arm span.

Heath (1952) reported two other factors pertaining to her female population, one called girth above the waist and the other called girth below the waist. Heath's experimental variables had been selected for use in providing information for garment makers, not for the purposes of factor analysis. They therefore included a number of girth measurements, which are not as good as linear measurements for factor-analysis purposes. The two girth factors that she reports reflect this bias in selection of measures. They may represent two second-order factors of trunk size and hip size, factors that could be reasonably expected.

Some General Implications of Factor Studies

It is apparent that much remains to be done in completion of the picture of human morphology from the factorial approach. From what we have seen, however, and from other information that we have, certain predictions can be made concerning the future of studies by this approach.

AGE AND SEX DIFFERENCES

One general finding of some interest is the relative consistency of factor structure as seen in results from both sexes and from different age groups,

[13] Moore and Hsü (1946); Heath (1952).

in so far as that structure can be seen. Blumenfeld (1946) has reported intercorrelations for different groups ranging in age from seven to fifteen years. Although he did not perform factor analyses, his coefficients are sufficiently similar from one group to another to indicate that factor structures are much alike. Other studies indicate much similarity of factor structure between children and adults.[14] There may be some unique morphological factors found for infants and for postpubertal females as compared with males, but all such possibilities are still to be generally explored. Racial differences pose another special problem.

THE KIND OF STUDY NEEDED

An ideal study of morphology by the factor-analytical approach should observe certain conditions. Samples of individuals should continue to be homogeneous as to sex, age, and racial origin. The selection of experimental variables should be systematic, comprehensive, and searching. Measurements should be made of bones, muscles, and fat in different body regions. If there is to be thorough coverage of aspects in a way that would investigate the Sheldon hypotheses regarding his components, measures of viscera, hair, and skin should also be made. Some of these measures cannot be obtained from the living organism, of course. Only by such thoroughness can we expect to answer all significant questions regarding the morphological aspects of personality and arrive at an adequate set of descriptive concepts.

A HYPOTHESIS CONCERNING MORPHOLOGICAL STRUCTURES

From what is known already concerning morphological factors, we can make some guesses as to what the total factor structure will be like. The picture is of a hierarchical character, similar in type to that proposed for personality in Chapter 5. We may expect that there will be a general body-size variable, as a third-order factor. We may expect several second-order factors, such as head size, trunk size, and limb size. There is possibly enough independence between arm size and leg size and between these and hand size and foot size to justify further discriminations of this kind. There may be a factor of pelvis size, separate to some degree from trunk size or chest size. None of these possibilities should be overlooked.

At the first-order level, we should expect a number of linear-measurement factors such as we already have for dimensions of the trunk. Such variables are limited in scope or generality. They should not be regarded as specifics, since there are several alternative ways in which each can be assessed. The problem connected with these factors is to determine what particular measures are most representative of each one at this level.

[14] McCloy (1940*a*).

In the operations of assessment, also, there is a need for taking into account the contributions of the second- and third-order factors when we take linear measurements of parts for the assessment of first-order factors. There is a similar need for taking into account the contributions of any third-order factor when making assessments of second-order factors.

CORRELATIONS WITH BEHAVIOR TRAITS

It should not be expected that measures of the morphological factors will necessarily correlate much higher with behavior traits than the physical variables heretofore utilized for this purpose. In fact, some of the basic measures, which would be utilized in assessment of the factors, have already been studied in relation to behavior traits, with correlations usually in the range from .0 to .2. Not all morphological dimensions have been studied in relation to all behavior traits, hence there is still some chance of finding higher correlations here and there. When the various factors are assessed so that other factors of higher order are taken into account or their influence is eliminated from the measurements, there may be slightly higher correlations.

The goal of assessing behavior traits indirectly through morphological measurements is likely to continue to be a "will-o'-the-wisp." This rather pessimistic appraisal of the situation almost removes one reason for enthusiasm for the study of morphology, but it still leaves the other objective of seeking a rational and systematic, yet comprehensive, way of describing this aspect of personality, and it leaves morphology in the picture to be considered in a general theory of personality development and organization.

RELATIONS OF FACTORS TO MORPHOLOGICAL TYPES

What of the relations of morphological factors to the Kretschmer types and the Sheldon components? If the factor picture of morphology that seems to be projected is correct, many more distinguishable dimensions are involved than would be called for by the Kretschmer types or the Sheldon components. Do we find anything among the known factors of morphology that would support either general theory of physique?

In terms of general personality theory, both Kretschmer's types and Sheldon's components may be regarded as possible syndrome types, a concept that was defined in Chapter 5 as a relatively consistent combination of primary traits. A syndrome type, conceived as a linear dimension, stands for a weighted combination of simpler or more basic dimensions, such as factors at the lower levels in the general hierarchy of personality structure. The combination of factors would be selected to compose the syndrome in accordance with their intercorrelations in the population.

We may well ask whether it will be possible to specify the Kretschmer

types and the Sheldon components in terms of combinations of morphological factors and their weights in the combinations. A combination,
for example, might be: relatively greater general body length combined
with relatively smaller thickness factors in the ectomorph and relatively
greater breadth and muscular thickness for the mesomorph. We should
anticipate difficulty in specifying the composition of Kretschmer's types
in terms of factors because they are not sufficiently well defined. For
example, the pyknic individual is known to a large extent by his having
a bulky chest. But how should the three factors—trunk length, trunk
width, and trunk depth—be weighted in the specifications? This same
question was raised by Burt (1949a) after finding two factors in the trunk
region.

Similar difficulties may pertain to the Sheldon components. Lorr and
Fields (1954) were led to question the validity of the Sheldon system
after performing a factor analysis by what is known as the Q technique. In
this technique, persons are correlated rather than measurement variables.
Lorr and Fields selected five extreme individuals to represent each of the
three components. Each person was assessed in 36 of Sheldon's experimental variables and then each person was correlated with every other
person. Two factors were sufficient to account for all the intercorrelations,
one extending from ectomorph to endomorph (that is, with two contrasting groups of ectomorphs and endomorphs at opposite extremes of a
bipolar factor) and one unipolar factor representing the mesomorph
group. These results agree in part with Ekman's (1951) logical analysis
of the Sheldon system of components.[15]

The consequence of these considerations is that we should determine
the best descriptive syndrome types in physique by correlational procedures. Whatever the traditional types of Kretschmer and Sheldon have
enabled us to do, we should be able to do as well or better with factorially
discovered syndrome types.

PHYSIOLOGICAL DIMENSIONS

The Factor Approach to Physiological Dimensions

The physiological aspects of personality have been less extensively
explored by factorial methods than the morphological aspects. The analyses that have been made have been directed toward two areas, the area
of autonomic function and the area of muscular tensions.

Most studies have been focused on the general hypothesis that there
is a major dimension of autonomic-nervous-system balance, that is, a

---

[15] In a similar study, Howells (1952) found three factors, none of which agreed in a
simple way with the Sheldon components.

dimension of sympathetic vs. parasympathetic dominance. The functions that have been measured in this connection have to do with circulation, respiration, salivation, body temperature, conductivity of the skin to electric current, metabolism, and so on.

Analyses based upon physiological functions have presented some unique difficulties. Among several measures of the same function, some are experimentally interdependent. For example, as the quantity of salivary output decreases, acidity increases because the acid component is less diluted. Pulse pressure is measured by the systolic pressure minus the diastolic pressure, hence it is positively related to the former and negatively related to the latter. Another difficulty is that retest reliabilities of physiological measures are generally low, as pointed out in Chapter 6, owing to functional fluctuations and to the fact that the scores are largely affected by temporary conditions, environmental as well as systemic. In consequence of these conditions, intercorrelations of physiological measures of individual differences are generally low and are sometimes also distorted. It is possible to see in the factor-analysis results, however, that certain systematic variations in intercorrelations do exist, that they can be verified, and that they can be attributed to meaningful underlying variables or factors.

Some Physiological Factors

To date, only four physiological dimensions in the form of factors have been reported and only one of these has had much verification in repeated studies.

Sympathetic vs. parasympathetic dominance

The hypothesized autonomic-balance factor has been found five times by the same investigator.[16] It has been found in the use of samples of young children and samples of Army Air Force personnel. The measures, which were used in from two to five studies in which the factor has appeared, are: heart period, palmar conductance, sublingual temperature, salivary output, sinus arrhythmia, and pulse pressure. The measures were taken while the examinee was in a state of relative rest. The sympathetic-dominant person tends to show a higher palmar conductance, sublingual temperature, sinus arrhythmia, and pulse pressure, also lower heart period and salivary output.

Wenger studied the relationship of autonomic-dominance-factor scores to certain scores from personality inventories and to psychosomatic disorders and psychoneuroses. The inventories were An Inventory of Factors STDCR, An Inventory of Factors GAMIN, and the Guilford-Martin Personnel Inventory. Significant correlations were found with five of the

[16] Wenger (1940, 1941, 1942, 1948).

inventory scores: depression (r = .31), cycloid disposition (.27), composure vs. nervousness (−.13), objectivity (−.23), and cooperativeness (−.26). From these results, we may conclude that those with sympathetic dominance are inclined to be depressed in mood, emotionally unstable, nervous, hypersensitive, and intolerant and faultfinding—a generally neurotic picture. The general interpretation of this might be that the sympathetic-dominant person is perpetually reacting to an emergency of greater or less seriousness.

Army Air Force personnel returning from combat areas with diagnosis of operational fatigue deviated from normal personnel in the direction of sympathetic dominance, and psychoneurotic personnel deviated further in the same direction.[17] This result might be taken to mean that those with combat fatigue were suffering from a mild psychoneurosis and both groups were reacting with residual fear to the combat situation. A small group of 21 ulcer patients had essentially normal scores. A small group of 16 asthma patients showed an average tendency toward sympathetic dominance. The cause-and-effect relationships here are not very clear. Patients of these different types who show sympathetic dominance may be in mental trouble because of their autonomic condition, or they may be reacting in a somewhat panicky manner to their mental troubles.

There is some evidence of the hereditary basis for individual differences on the dimension of autonomic balance.[18] Studies of similarity of pairs of twins, ordinary siblings, and randomly chosen children seem to support this idea. The correlations were .45, .30, and .05, for the three kinds of pairs, respectively.

Tension

It is apparently a quite common belief that individuals differ in their levels of general muscular tension. We know persons who give the impression of being tense and others who appear to be relaxed. Studies of intercorrelations of actual measurements of habitual muscular tension in different muscle groups, however, do not show a great deal of personal consistency.[19]

The best evidence for a tension factor has come from variables that are not measures of muscular tension. They have to do, instead, with respiratory and circulatory variables.[20] The measures and their loadings are: respiratory period, rating of tension, variability in respiratory period, diastolic blood pressure, and pulse pressure. If it were not for the rating of tension as observed by others in this list of variables, we should have difficulty in identifying this dimension as a tension factor.

Because actually measured muscular tensions are so uncorrelated with

17 Wenger (1948).
18 Jost and Sontag (1944).
19 Malmo and Smith (1955).
20 Wenger (1943); Duffy (1946).

one another and with this factor, it is best to call the obtained factor simply *tension*. It must be characterized by some property other than general, chronic muscular contractions. It is best interpreted in terms of things to which it is related. In addition to the circulatory and respiratory functions, as indicated above, certain other rated qualities have been found related to it, such as restlessness, energy, emotionality, impulsiveness, lack of fatigability, and lack of emotional control.[21] Assuming the ratings to be valid, they suggest that the tension involved, if it is tension, is more nervous than muscular. Its relations to what is called "anxiety" and to the factor of nervousness are unknown.

Plutchik (1954) interprets the tension factor as being a state of chronic mental conflict. There is a constant state of readiness to respond, which seems to have nervous rather than muscular involvements. Consequences may be seen in the form of blocked or impeded motor responses and in psychosomatic disorders. Freeman (1948) agrees, essentially, in describing such a trait as a disposition to inhibit overt behavior.

Thyroid function

Wenger (1948) reports evidence of a factor of *thyroid function* from three different analyses, one based upon children and two upon Air Force personnel. Two variables carry the load of demonstrating an underlying common variable. They are: volar conductance and oxygen consumption. The oxygen-consumption variable identifies the factor because of its long-recognized use as an index of thyroid function. Volar conductance is a score for conductivity of the skin of the forearm to electric current. The greater the degree of perspiration under resting conditions, the higher the score. Greater perspiration in regions of the body other than the palms of the hands and soles of the feet indicates rate of production of body heat.

Blood sugar

The measure of sugar content of the blood of individuals identifies this factor.[22] The related variables are: blood sugar, sublingual temperature, variability of respiration, and diastolic blood pressure. Relations of variables other than blood sugar to this factor are relatively weak.

FUTURE STUDY OF PHYSIOLOGICAL DIMENSIONS

There are a number of scattered investigations that suggest the directions that future study of physiological dimensions may take. The field is by no means well explored. There are glandular, hormonal, and biochemical aspects that have not as yet been touched by correlational

---

21 Wenger (1943).
22 Wenger (1948).

methods. Some of the studies that may suggest dimensions to be investigated are concerned in one way or another with fluctuations or variability of physiological functioning.

There is the Hersey hypothesis that men undergo rhythmic cycles.[23] In industry, Hersey found by intensive and frequent interviews and other observations, that male workers undergo cycles of productivity and morale. Cycles for some individuals are as short as 14 days while for others they are as long as 52 days, with an average of about 35 days. At the high points of the curve, a man shows increased productivity and zest for work. Somewhere between these periods, he shows a disinclination for mental effort, planning, and concentration. But it is said that the low periods for some men seem to be the "breeding ground" for later exhibitions of creative production. Only one other investigator, to the knowledge of the writer, has found supporting evidence. A rhythmic cycle of about 48 days was found in handgrip measures in one subject.[24] A fluctuation pattern that is as dramatic as this one is reported to be would seem to merit serious attention.

Other studies have emphasized the *extent* of variability of physiological functioning as possible indices of traits. It has been found that such variability measures tend to discriminate pathological groups from normal ones, the psychotic persons tending to be *more* stable than normal and the neurotic persons tending to be *less* stable.[25]

Most of the measures of physiological functioning that have been factor-analyzed have been obtained while the examinee is in a state of relative rest. There is much interest in recent work on individual differences in reactions under stress. It has been demonstrated that individuals have their own characteristic habits of responding with different parts of their autonomic equipment. In one person's response, circulatory changes may be emphasized most; in another, it may be respiratory changes; in still another, it may be gastric or intestinal changes.[26] Each person is found to be rather consistent from time to time in his own pattern of responses to stressful situations.

These personal patterns direct attention to individual differences in *differences* between scores, or in profile types, and raise some problems as to the adequacy of a dimensional approach to this area of personality. In view of individual patterns of organic responses, it is interesting that two factors of pathology—a gastrointestinal reaction and a cardiorespiratory reaction—have been reported.[27] The former is featured by severe

[23] Hersey (1955).
[24] Weinland (1947).
[25] Sherman and Jost (1945); Freeman (1948).
[26] Lacey (1950); Lacey and Van Lehn (1952); Malmo et al. (1950); Lacey et al. (1953).
[27] Lorr and Rubenstein (1955, 1956).

gastric, intestinal, and bowel symptoms and frequent headaches, whereas the latter is featured by severe respiratory symptoms and being consistently tired and worn out. The relations of these two factors to the normal stressful responses are not known.

SUMMARY

A large number of factor-analysis studies of morphological measures, based upon samples of both sexes and of ages from infancy to young-adult levels, indicate the promise of this approach for revealing the trait structure for body build. A hierarchical system of dimensions seems indicated, with first-order factors pertaining to linear measures of parts such as head, chest, pelvis, arms, hands, legs, and feet; with second-order factors pertaining to general sizes of the same regions; and with a higher-order factor pertaining to total body size. Of these possible factors, a half dozen have been found and verified. Other possible factors involve muscular development and fat deposit. Thorough and comprehensive analyses remain to be done. Such analyses should include measures of tissues other than bones, muscles, and fat.

It is proposed that syndrome types of physique be developed on the basis of empirical studies involving intercorrelations of the factors at the lower-order levels. Whether or not this approach would verify either the Kretschmer types or the Sheldon components remains to be seen.

Physiological aspects of personality have been explored very little by factor-analysis methods. Among the factors that have been found are: *sympathetic vs. parasympathetic dominance, tension, thyroid function,* and *blood sugar*. Significant but low correlations have been found between the first two of these and ratings and inventory scores for behavior traits, and between the first and incidence of operational fatigue, psychoneurosis, and asthma. Aside from the last two of these factors, dimensions associated with glandular functions and with biochemistry offer an unexplored field.

Chapter 15

DIMENSIONS OF APTITUDE

THIS CHAPTER might have been entitled "dimensions of ability." The term "aptitude" is preferred because it is less inclusive. The term "ability" applies to the goodness of performance in any particular task as well as to a trait of a person. Goodness of performance is measured directly by means of a score, which is an observable variable. Dimensions of personality are underlying or inferred variables. The term "ability" is also used in reference to dimensions of personality when we employ the expression "primary ability." Thurstone introduced this term to apply to dimensions discovered by factor analysis. We shall therefore use the term "ability" in its very general sense, but restrict the term "aptitude" to underlying dimensions of ability.

Another general statement should be made regarding the concept of aptitude. It has a forward-looking implication, suggesting that the individual is prepared to perform with some level of excellence (or lack of it) or to learn (change in a performance). The idea of preparation is in line with the general definition of "trait" as that term has been used throughout this volume. A trait is a preexisting and predetermining condition of the individual.

A distinction is sometimes made between aptitude and achievement, the latter meaning how well an activity is performed *after* practice. We shall see that some of the dimensions of ability turn out to be areas of knowledge, such as mechanical, mathematical, or social science. The justification for calling these variables dimensions of *aptitude* is that they, too, prepare a person for a certain level of performance in given activities and for learning new things.

Looking backward, we can see that probably any aptitude, even though it is not recognized as obviously representing a particular area of training or education, owes its status in part to previous learning and hence to that extent is a variable of achievement. In connection with the nature-nurture issue as it applies to aptitudes, the most realistic view at present is to regard learning as continuous with heredity. By this is meant that heredity provides the mechanisms with their potentialities; stimulation and organic reaction (which implies learning) provide further development. This does not mean that heredity carries each aptitude up to a point and then learning takes over. Interaction of the two determiners probably continues as long as the organism continues to develop.

In surveying the dimensions of aptitude we shall note the primary abilities as indicated by factor analysis in three general areas—*perceptual, psychomotor,* and *intellectual.* If significant facts happen to be known in connection with a factor, these will be mentioned. As much system as possible will be injected into the factors of an area, and their logical interrelationships will be pointed out. Some attention will be given to the concept of intelligence and to the relations of the intellectual factors to learning and development in general.

PERCEPTUAL DIMENSIONS

Some of the perceptual primary abilities have to do with sensitivity of different kinds within each sense modality. The sensitivity may be in the absolute sense, that is, a lower or higher threshold (the lower the physical energy to which the organism responds, the lower his threshold), or in the relative sense, that is, ability to make fine discriminations of certain kinds. Primary abilities having to do with attention can be placed in the perceptual category on the ground that attention is preparation to observe. Most of the more complex functions in perception, such as perception of forms, patterns, and relations between forms, are classified with the intellectual aptitudes, for reasons that will be clearer when we come to them.

Dimensions of Sensitivity

The senses of vision, audition, and kinesthesis and the sense associated with the semicircular canals have been partially studied by factor analysis, with some rewarding results.

VISUAL-SENSITIVITY FACTORS

Using sensitivity measurements obtained at different wavelengths in the visible spectrum, Jones (1948, 1950) has twice found three distinct factors, which can be interpreted as *red sensitivity, green sensitivity,* and *blue sensitivity.* Red sensitivity has its highest loadings for tests at wavelengths in the region of 600 to 660 mμ (millimicrons). Green sensitivity has its highest loadings in the range 540 to 580 mμ. Blue sensitivity has its highest loadings in the range 450 to 470 mμ.

The three-factor picture of color sensitivity agrees very well with the traditional hypothesis that there are three color-receiving mechanisms of some sort. It has been known for a long time that there are three general types of color blindness. The *protonope* individual is insensitive to the longest visible wavelengths and sees orange and yellow as one color.[1] The *deuteranope* sees a complete spectrum but confuses reds and greens. The *tritanope* is insensitive to the shortest wavelengths and is extremely rare in the population. Color-weak persons of two types are known as *protanomalous* and *deuteranomalous,* corresponding to the red-

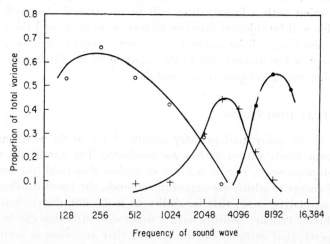

Fig. 15.1 Systematic relations of contributions of three auditory-sensitivity factors to total-score variances for tests at different sound-frequency levels. (*Data from Henry,* 1948.)

and green-blind, which are more numerous than the blue-blind. The three factors found by Jones in normal individuals indicate continuity of the three abilities in the general population.

AUDITORY-SENSITIVITY FACTORS

One study by Henry (1947) has found three primary abilities for hearing tones at different pitch levels in the audible range. A *low-frequency auditory sensitivity* has loadings for quite a range of frequencies, we may say to about 2,048 cps (cycles per second), as shown in Figure 15.1, where factor loadings have been plotted as a function of sound-wave frequency. An *intermediate-frequency auditory sensitivity* seems to cover a range from approximately 2,048 to approximately 6,000 cps. A *high-frequency auditory sensitivity* covers a range beyond 11,000 cps, which is about as high as the experiment went. From the curve for this factor, shown in

[1] Pickford (1956).

Figure 15.1, we might predict that it would cover all audible frequencies at the upper end of the scale.

The finding of these three distinct primary abilities suggests that the physiologist might do well to look for three separate mechanisms for responding to tones of the three categories of frequency. It has been known for a long time that males and older people are relatively defective in hearing tones of the highest frequencies, presumably a relative weakness in factor C. When scores were obtained for the three factors A, B, and C of Figure 15.1, it was found that the greatest losses occurred for factor C and the least for A.[2] The correlations between the three scores and measures of reading attainment varied from one factor to another. There was no correlation for factor A, some for B, and more for C. This is consistent with the fact that accurate hearing of speech is dependent upon the higher frequencies. Learning to read may be dependent upon the accurate hearing of words.

AUDITORY-DISCRIMINATION FACTORS

Three auditory-discrimination factors have been reported. In descriptions of the factors here, some of the kinds of tests that have been found related to each factor will be mentioned. They are listed in order of decreasing degree of relationship to the factor.

Pitch discrimination [3]

Pitch–Vocal (E compares spoken monosyllables having small differences in pitch.)

Pitch–Pure (E compares single-frequency tones.)

Pitch–Short (E compares tones of very short duration.)

Memory (Seashore Tonal Memory test, in which melodies of two to six tones are repeated with one tone changed, E to say which one.)

Loudness discrimination [4]

Loudness (E compares tones for loudness when pitches also differ.)

Loudness–Complex (E compares tones for loudness when not limited to one frequency.)

Loudness–Pure (E compares tones of single frequency.)

Male Voices (E recognizes voices heard earlier.)

Auditory integral [5]

Silence (E compares time intervals marked off by clicks.)

Loudness–Pure

Loudness–Complex

Time–Sound (E compares durations of tones.)

[2] Henry (1947).
[3] Karlin (1942).
[4] *Ibid.*
[5] *Ibid.*

There can be little or no doubt concerning the kinds of aptitudes involved in the first two of these factors. The abilities to discriminate either pitch or loudness can be indicated either by using pure tones or by using tones of varying degrees of complexity, even as complex as spoken voices. Karlin called the third factor "auditory integral" because judging either loudness or time intervals indicates the factor. His reason was that the total quantity of tone heard depends upon a product of loudness and time. But the fact that a test for judging *empty* intervals leads the list is against this hypothesis. It is likely that in this factor-analytical solution there was a partial confounding of two factors, one of which is ability to discriminate time intervals and the other to discriminate loudness differences.

KINESTHETIC SENSITIVITY

Two investigators have found a factor of *kinesthetic sensitivity*,[6] which is defined as an ability to sense positions of parts of the body nonvisually, at rest or in motion.[7] Some related tests are:

Bending test (*E* stands on ball of one foot, eyes closed.)

Standing test (*E* stands on ball of one foot, eyes closed.)

Postural Discrimination—Angular (*E* adjusts his tilted chair to match position in which he was previously put.)

Postural Discrimination—Vertical (*E* brings tilted chair to upright position.)

Kinesthetic sensitivity should be important in psychomotor performances of many kinds, such as athletic, acrobatic, or musical performance. It probably makes some small contribution to the variances of scores from tests of psychomotor abilities that we shall see later.[8]

FACTORS ASSOCIATED WITH THE SEMICIRCULAR CANALS

The receptive organs for the static sense are attached to each inner ear. The most significant parts of these organs are the semicircular canals. In each organ the three canals are so located that they respond differently to movements of the head, forward vs. backward, from side to side, and in rotary motion.

The number of separate abilities of sensitivity involved is not clear from present results. Bass (1939) found what appeared to be a single general static-sense factor. Scores for sensitivity to rotation with the head

---

[6] Bass (1939); Fleishman (1954).

[7] McCloy and Young (1954).

[8] Actually, we may have two kinesthetic factors here rather than one. The first two tests listed are of one kind and the last two of another, the two kinds having been used in different analyses.

in three positions—erect, on one side, and bent forward—intercorrelated sufficiently to indicate such a factor.

McCloy and Young (1954), however, suggest that there may be two distinct factors, one based upon the functioning of the two vertical canals (sensitivity to forward-backward and sideways movements) and the other based upon the horizontal canal. The sensitivity of the latter should be important in whirling activities such as those encountered in figure skating and ballet dancing. It is probably safe to say that there is a *static-sensitivity* factor. Whether this should be regarded as a second-order factor, and whether there are also two related first-order factors in addition, is still to be determined.

An Attention Factor

At least three independent investigators have found a factor that can be called *attention*.[9] The kinds of tests that indicate it are:

Digit Series (Sets of three digits are spoken at rapid rate by the examiner. *E* responds with + or −, according to rules.)

Letter Lists (A list of 14 letters is read, each to be responded to with + or −, according to rules.)

Letters *ABCDE* (Every time *E* writes these five letters he receives a new instruction, e.g., to interchange *D* and *E*.)

In all the tests that indicate this attention factor, routine, but sometimes intricate, directions must be followed in dealing with simple material such as letters or numbers. The examinee must be very alert or he will fall behind or make errors. Alertness in making quick, adaptive responses to changing stimuli in accordance with rules seems to be characteristic of good performance on tests of this factor. We should not generalize our conception of the ability so far as to say that it is a general "power of concentration" or a general "power of voluntary attention." So far as we know, it may be restricted to a narrow class of tasks like those mentioned above.

Other Perceptual Factors

Length (size) estimation

We saw earlier factors involving discrimination of differences in pitch and in loudness. There are probably many other such perceptual factors of narrow scope. One of these is known as length estimation.[10] The factor probably also applies to judgments of size. Two tests illustrate the kind of tests related to the factor:

---

[9] Woodrow (1939b); Gibb (1942); Wittenborn (1943).
[10] Woodrow (1938); Guilford and Lacey (1947); Roff (1952); Hertzka et al. (1954).

Ratio Estimation (*E* estimates the percentage a line of one length is of another.)

Figure Estimation (*E* compares two figures for size.)

Sensitivity to visual movement

An ability to detect minimal movements was investigated in connection with aviation psychology. The bombardier formerly had to be sensitive to small drift motions in viewing events in his bombsight. Pilots should be aware of changes in the indicators on their display panel and should judge seen movements as their airplanes approach a runway for a landing. Such tasks served as the basis for development of certain motion-picture tests.[11] The tests were analyzed and together defined a factor that could be interpreted as sensitivity to visual movement.[12] The tests were:

Drift Direction (A spot shown in one quarter of a complete circle moves in some direction that *E* is to report.)

Integration of Attention (Pointers or other indicators are moving in five dials. *E* is to report every time each indicator goes into a danger zone.)

Landing Judgment (*E* sees view taken from a cockpit of a plane during landing. He is to tell at which point the wheels will touch the runway.)

Unexplored Perceptual Areas

The general perceptual domain has been only partially explored by factorial methods. Nothing decisive seems to have been reported on primary abilities in the tactual, olfactory, gustatory, or organic senses. There are probably other factors to be discovered in the areas of visual and auditory perception, as well as in connection with attention. Since attention is very much determined by motivation, however, individual differences in attentive behavior may largely be accounted for in terms of motivational factors, discussed in Chapter 17.

PSYCHOMOTOR DIMENSIONS

The psychomotor abilities have been of great interest to teachers of physical education as well as to vocational psychologists. Interest in them among basic psychologists has been slight, for some reason, as compared with interest in intellectual abilities and other traits. A relatively new group of technologists, the human engineers, are keenly interested in psychomotor abilities, since the limits of man's psychomotor reactions

[11] Gibson (1947).
[12] Roff (1952).

have considerable bearing upon the kinds of machines and equipment he is expected to use. Like the physical educator, the teachers of dancing and of acrobatics should find a knowledge of psychomotor abilities most useful.

The Analysis of Psychomotor Abilities

Factor analyses of psychomotor abilities have employed three general kinds of tests—tests of physical fitness, apparatus tests, and printed tests. Physical-fitness tests have been the favored approach of those concerned with physical education, health, and athletics in general. Vocational psychologists and others have generally favored apparatus tests to printed tests, owing to the obvious involvement in muscular movements, but have attempted to convert to paper-and-pencil form, for the purpose of group testing, as many of the psychomotor tests as could be so adapted.

Analyses of psychomotor tests have presented some difficulties. All except the printed test forms have had to be administered individually, or at best, in very small groups. This involves considerable research effort. Another handicap is that it is sometimes difficult to provide tests that involve rather isolated groups of muscles, for example, hand movements only, with minimal wrist and finger involvement. As we shall see later, such isolation and control by body parts seem to be very desirable if we are to obtain clear-cut results and explore the functional unities systematically and exhaustively.

To make things more difficult, some investigators have not used sufficient care in the choice of tests to be analyzed together. For example, left-hand and right-hand scores are sometimes included from the same test, and minor variations of the same test are also included. Both conditions tend to favor a kind of test that is represented more than once and to give an exaggerated impression of its importance for indicating the factor, if indeed they do not also bias the impression as to the nature of the factor.

Another practice, not so serious, is that most analyses tend to be confined to one of the three kinds of tests—physical fitness, apparatus, or printed. If this were completely true, we could not be sure whether a factor found in one kind of test is or is not the same as one found in another. It turns out that correlations across the categories of tests tend to be low, indicating that in general they do measure different abilities. Since printed tests can effectively sample only finger and hand movements, abilities pertaining only to those units may be thus indicated. Since physical-fitness tests very often involve the whole body, they tend to indicate gross body-movement abilities. Apparatus tests can be adapted to finger and hand movements or to movements of larger parts of the body. They might be expected to indicate some factors in common with printed tests and perhaps some in common with physical-fitness tests. Results tend to show that this is the case.

Recognized Psychomotor Aptitudes

The psychomotor factors fall into classes according to the kind of ability involved—*strength, impulsion, speed, precision, coordination,* and *flexibility.* Impulsion means the rate of initiation of a movement. Precision actually applies in two ways—precision in holding positions and precision of movements. The former may be called *static precision* and the latter *dynamic precision.* Flexibility is a matter of looseness of joints, which permits greater extent of movements. The other categories should be recognized from their names.

The psychomotor factors are also classifiable according to another principle, namely, the part or parts of the body involved. Some of the psychomotor abilities seem to involve the entire body, or large parts of it; others involve restricted body regions, such as the trunk, limbs, hand, fingers, or vocal organs. We shall take note of both kinds of classification in noting the different factors. With each factor will be given a few representative tests that have indicated it.

STRENGTH FACTORS

General strength [13]

Leg strength
Shoulder strength
Back strength
Handgrip strength
Shot-put (various weights from 3 to 24 pounds)

Trunk strength [14]

Abdominal pivot (*E* pushes body around with hands, with back arched.)
Push-ups (Lying prone, *E* pushes body off floor with arms.)
Leg raising (*E* raises leg to height of head, in sitting position.)

Limb strength [15]

Dips (In standing position, *E* alternately squats and rises.)
Chinning (*E* pulls own weight up with arms to put chin over horizontal bar at arms' length over his head.)
Rope climbing (*E* uses arms only.)
Push-ups (see description above)

[13] McCloy (1940a); Carpenter (1941); Wittenborn (1945b).
[14] Hempel and Fleishman (1955).
[15] Hall and Wittenborn (1942); Shapiro (1947); Hempel and Fleishman (1955).

There is some possibility that arm strength and leg strength will also appear as somewhat separate, but correlated, factors when enough arm-strength tests and leg-strength tests are analyzed together.

IMPULSION FACTORS

It is not yet clear which factors should be included under this heading. The clearest case of such an ability is the factor of *limb thrust*. *General reaction time* and *tapping* may not belong in the same category, since tests of the two kinds involving the hand are not correlated.[16] As defined above, impulsion means the rate of initiation of an act. Other interpretations of such factors have stressed the concepts of "energy mobilization," "speed of ballistic (explosive) movements," and "dynamic energy." [17]

General reaction time [18]

Reaction time to light
Discrimination reaction time (*E* notes which stimulus came before reacting.)
Choice reaction time (*E* reacts differently to each of two or more stimuli.)
Reaction time to sound

The usual simple-reaction-time test involves a finger or hand movement in response to a simple stimulus signal. There is much evidence that it should be regarded as a general factor, applying to many parts of the body.[19] The ability seems not to depend upon what sense modality is involved, but there are enough differences in reaction-time ability for different muscle groups to suggest that there may be, after all, some more limited, regional reaction-time factors.[20]

Limb thrust [21]

Vertical jump
Standing broad jump
Shot-put (various weights)
Short dash
Bar vault

It may be that more searching analysis would show that there is some degree of independence between separate arm- and leg-thrust abilities.

[16] Seashore et al. (1941).
[17] McCloy and Young (1954).
[18] Thurstone (1944); Rimoldi (1951); Fleishman (1954).
[19] Seashore and Seashore (1941); Seashore et al. (1940).
[20] Seashore et al. (1941).
[21] Wendler (1938); McCloy (1940b); Carpenter (1941); Shapiro (1947); Hempel and Fleishman (1955).

Tapping [22]

Tapping, index finger

Tapping, turnbuckle (*E* turns turnbuckle with fingers.)

Tapping, four fingers (in turn)

Pegs, handicap (*E* removes and replaces pegs in holes, holding all in the hand.)

Since finger work seems to be the motor component emphasized in these tests, this factor may be confined to the finger units.

Articulation speed [23]

Maximum rate of oral reading

Normal rate of oral reading

Speed of articulation (repeating a consonant)

Spelling (in a dictation test)

It would seem that rate of initiation of oral speech movements is the common element in these tests. The factor might be called "vocal impulsion," if this interpretation is correct. This is the only psychomotor factor of speech reported. There are probably others yet to be found.

MOTOR-SPEED FACTORS

Motor-speed factors are distinguished from impulsion factors by the fact that they emphasize rate of a movement after it has been initiated. Some investigators have sought evidence for a general motor-speed factor, but without much success.[24] Intercorrelations of speed-of-movement tests have generally been rather low. But there have been higher intercorrelations among scores from similar tests, providing the basis for speed factors of limited scope. Factor analyses have shown where the common speed abilities apply, and three localized speed variables have been found.[25]

Arm speed [26]

Ten-Target Aiming (*E* aims at ten targets in succession. Score is number of correct responses per unit of time.)

Two-Plate Tapping (*E* taps alternately on two plates some little distance apart.)

Rotary Aiming (*E* touches succession of buttons with finger tip.)

[22] Wittenborn (1945*b*).

[23] Carroll (1941).

[24] For example, see Harrison (1941).

[25] Rimoldi reports evidence that might be interpreted as supporting the hypothesis of a general motor-speed factor, but his tests were designed to measure a trait that he called "tempo" instead of speed. Instructions were for *E* to perform at his natural rate, but he evidently knew his reactions were timed. Harrison (1941) found an average correlation of .44 between natural and maximum rates in various tests, hence Rimoldi's factors might be speed factors.

[26] Fleishman (1954).

Hand speed [27]

Pin Stick (*E* loops string around each of series of pegs.)

Tapping, Large (*E* writes dots in scattered circles, each $7/16$ inch in diameter.)

Tapping, Small (same, with $1/8$-inch circles.)

Santa Ana Finger Dexterity test (*E* removes each square peg from hole, turns it 180 degrees, and resets it.)

Finger speed [28]

Log Book Accuracy (*E* marks spaces in an answer sheet; a speed test of finger movements.)

Tapping, Small (*E* puts dots in circles $1/8$ inch in diameter.)

Square Marking (*E* makes a cross in each square, squares being closely spaced.)

Marking Accuracy (another answer-sheet marking test)

STATIC-PRECISION FACTORS

Static balance [29]

Bending (*E* stands on ball of foot, eyes open, bends over.)

Foot Balance II (*E* balances on one foot, with right foot held behind left knee.)

Standing (*E* stands flat on one foot, eyes open.)

Two-foot Rail Balance (*E* walks, heel-to-toe, on 1-inch board.)

Arm steadiness [30]

Track Tracing (*E* moves stylus in slot at arm's length.)

Steadiness Aiming (*E* keeps delicately balanced stylus in hole at arm's length.)

Cox Eye Board (*E* threads cord through eyes in pegs in a row.)

Hex Nut Steadiness (*E* stacks series of small, hexagonal nuts.)

While some of the tests in the lists for these two factors involve a certain amount of movement, the movement is usually slow and deliberate. In tests characteristic of the next factors the movement is usually rapid, if not of the thrust type.

DYNAMIC-PRECISION FACTORS

Three factors are known in the category of dynamic precision, involving body balance in motion, arm aiming, and hand aiming.

---

[27] Rimoldi (1951); Fleishman and Hempel (1954a).

[28] Guilford and Lacey (1947); Fleishman (1954); Fleishman and Hempel (1954a); Guilford and Christensen (1956).

[29] Bass (1939); Hempel and Fleishman (1955).

[30] Fleishman (1954); Hempel and Fleishman (1955).

Dynamic balance [31]

Jump and click heels together (as many times as possible while in the air)

Jump and balance (*E* jumps upon edge of box and maintains his balance.)

Rate of jump (*E* jumps upstairs one step at a time, feet together, then backwards downstairs.)

Arm aiming [32]

Pursuit Aiming II (*E* traces through series of small openings $\frac{1}{16}$ inch in diameter, in a maze pattern.)

Pursuit Aiming I (*E* traces circles $\frac{3}{16}$ inch in diameter, putting a dot in each.)

Punch Board (*E* puts pin through tiny holes rapidly.)

Hand aiming [33]

Irregular Dotting Pursuit (*E* places dots in small circles on paper.)

Circle Dotting (*E* puts three dots in each small circle.)

Rotary Aiming (*E* touches each button in a series rapidly.)

COORDINATION FACTORS

Tests of coordination factors involve the use of patterns of muscles in combination and in sequence. Three such factors have been found, one involving gross body parts, one for the hand, and one for the fingers.

Gross body coordination [34]

Cable Jump (*E* jumps through a cable that he holds.)

Rotary Pursuit (*E* keeps stylus on a button on a revolving disk.)

Hurdle Jump

Rudder Control (*E* corrects loss of balance in his seat by manipulating rudder controls with his feet.)

Complex Coordination (*E* operates stick and rudder controls to effect certain light patterns to match others.)

From the list of tests under this factor title we conclude that muscles of arms and legs, and sometimes also of the trunk, are involved. It remains to be seen whether an arms-only and a legs-only factor of coordination will be found.

From one study it has been suggested that there are two gross-body-coordination factors, one for rough adjustments and one for fine adjust-

---

[31] Hempel and Fleishman (1955).

[32] Fleishman (1954); Hempel and Fleishman (1955).

[33] Hempel and Fleishman (1955).

[34] Guilford and Lacey (1947); Shapiro (1947); Fleishman (1954); Hempel and Fleishman (1955).

ments.[35] The one mentioned above and found most often is the "rough-adjustment" ability in gross coordinations. It is the one that predicts to some extent whether pilot students will pass or fail. The "fine-adjustment" factor needs further study. It might possibly be the same as the factor called dynamic balance above. In other words, it may be a general move-ment-precision factor.

Hand dexterity [36]

Marble Board (*E* places marbles in a groove.)
Santa Ana Finger Dexterity test (described above)
VDL Rings (*E* removes small rings from small pole.)
Dowel Manipulation [*E* arranges suspended pieces to make a continuous dowel (cylindrical stick).]

Finger dexterity [37]

Purdue Pegboard, both hands
Purdue Pegboard, Assembly
O'Connor Finger Dexterity test
Speed of Manipulation "A" (*E* removes washers from pegs.)
Nut and Bolt (*E* completes nut-and-bolt assemblies.)

The manipulation of small objects by means of hand and finger move-ments has been recognized as being very important in many tasks in in-dustry; hence dexterity tests have been in use for many years. It has also been recognized that there is a difference between hand dexterity and finger dexterity, a fact that factor analysis has substantiated. Many dex-terity tests measure both abilities—more than the data presented here indicate—but it is possible to devise tests of the one that do not also measure the other appreciably.

There is much information concerning the validity of dexterity tests for predicting work success in industry. From the nature of the tests that are often used, it is difficult to say how much of this validity to attribute to hand dexterity and how much to finger dexterity. Correlations of test scores with criteria that measure *quantity* of output tend to be near zero.[38] Correlations with rated *quality* of work, however, have been as high as .63 or even .70.[39] Multiple correlations (between a combination of scores and a criterion) are as high as .65 to .74.[40] There can be little question that where fine hand-manipulation work is involved, selection of workers who have high dexterity scores would be desirable. The failure to predict

[35] Fleishman and Hempel (1956).
[36] Wittenborn (1945*b*); Goodman (1947); Fleishman (1954); Fleishman and Hempel (1954*a*); Hempel and Fleishman (1955).
[37] Fleishman (1954); Fleishman and Hempel (1954*a*); Hempel and Fleishman (1955).
[38] Long and Lawshe (1947).
[39] Tiffin and Greenly (1939).
[40] Henshaw (1937).

quantity of handwork is an interesting finding. It probably means that amount of work output is much more a matter of motivation or temperament than it is of aptitude. At least we can conclude that for predicting output, measures of some traits other than dexterity are called for.

Dexterity is also probably important for the painting artist. After considerable research, Meier (1939) came to the conclusion that good dexterity is a family characteristic of artistically gifted children. Their families tend to have more than the usual share of skilled craftsmen of one kind or another.

FLEXIBILITY FACTORS

Flexibility of movement has been recognized as a trait for a long time by those concerned with athletic training. It depends upon the looseness of the joints and determines the range of movement of parts associated with those joints. Only those individuals with a high degree of flexibility can indulge in the stunts of the acrobat and particularly of the contortionist. The question faced by the analyzer of personal traits is whether flexibility is a general trait, characteristic equally at all joints, or whether there are certain classes of joints that have the property to different degrees in the same person. Psychologists find two flexibility factors, one for the trunk and one for the legs.

Trunk flexibility [41]

Back Down Wall test (*E* bends over backwards, hands on a wall, as far as possible.)

Table Vault test (Placing hands on table, *E* vaults over it, landing on his feet.)

In both tests, it would seem that the freedom of the spinal column to bend and twist is the significant aspect for good performance.

Leg flexibility [42]

Toe Touching (*E* touches toes with fingers without bending knees.)

Kicking Height

Leg Bend (*E* squats slowly on right leg.)

The fact that only two flexibility factors have been found should not be taken to indicate that there are no others. Flexibility tests have been neglected in practically all studies of psychomotor dimensions.

A Matrix of the Psychomotor Factors

The last statements apply also in other areas of psychomotor performance. It is likely that factors are still to be discovered in other categories. In this connection let us consider Table 15.1, in which the known psycho-

[41] Hempel and Fleishman (1955).
[42] *Ibid.*

Table 15.1

Matrix of the psychomotor factors, with columns for kinds of abilities and with rows for parts of the body involved

Part of body involved	Type of ability						
	Strength	Impulsion	Speed	Static precision	Dynamic precision	Coordi-nation	Fexibility
Gross	General strength	General reaction time		Static balance	Dynamic balance	Gross body coordina-tion	
Trunk	Trunk strength						Trunk flexibility
Limbs	Limb strength	Limb thrust	Arm speed	Arm stead-iness	Arm aiming		Leg flexibility
Hand		Tapping			Hand aiming	Hand dexterity	
Finger			Finger speed			Finger dexterity	

motor factors are systematically arranged. Each column is devoted to a particular kind of ability, such as strength, speed, or coordination. Each row is devoted to the part of the body involved, with a row at the top to take care of those abilities that seem to involve the whole body in one way or another. A possible row for speech organs has not been included, since there is only one such factor known.

POSSIBLE ROLES OF WHOLE-BODY FACTORS

Some of the factors in the top row of Table 15.1 seem to play the role of general factors—general strength and general reaction time. They represent consistencies across body regions, and they are indicated by the fact that regional tests intercorrelate positively across regions. Other factors in the first row seem rather to indicate a total-body characteristic—static balance, dynamic balance, and gross body coordination, for example. These abilities pertain to total-body performances of some kind. They do not particularly suggest that they owe their existence to intercorrelated regional factors in their category, though we may find that such a structure exists in those columns of factors also.

When the question is raised as to why there should be regional psychomotor factors rather than just general ones, we can only speculate. One reasonable hypothesis would be that heredity has more to do with *general* psychomotor factors, such as strength, speed, coordination, and flexibility, whereas exercise and training have more to do with *regional* factors. For example, the pianist develops relatively strong fingers; the cyclist, strong legs; and the coal fireman, strong arms, shoulders, and trunk. Not to be overlooked, however, is the fact that anatomical peculiarities have very much to do with localized psychomotor abilities, and these could possibly have relatively independent hereditary determination.

OTHER POSSIBLE PSYCHOMOTOR FACTORS

Perhaps the chief value of the matrix of psychomotor factors is that it suggests where we should look for undiscovered factors. It suggests that there is a hand-strength factor and a finger-strength factor, separate to some extent from general strength. In every column there are vacant cells where new factors may be found. The main reason they have not been found, if they exist, is probably that the kinds of tests needed to indicate them have not been developed, or if developed, they have not been subjected to factor analysis. We can see from the position of a cell in the table the kinds of tests that would be needed to indicate the unknown factor.

What about possible factors that could not necessarily find a place in the matrix as now constituted? There are a number of such possibilities. McCloy and Young (1954) suggest that there is a factor of "muscular endurance," an ability to repeat a performance a number of times in succession before giving up. They propose the hypothesis of another factor having to do with "circulatory-respiratory endurance." This involves keeping on with vigorous activity until one is "winded." This seems to be more appropriately affiliated with the list of physiological traits rather than psychomotor traits. Both abilities to perform in the ways specified may involve the motivational factor of *endurance* (see Chapter 17), which is a willingness to accept pain or discomfort in achieving a goal.

McCloy and Young also cite evidence for a factor having to do with ability to change direction, as in running, thus revealing an efficiency of footwork. They also name another factor, "agility," which is defined as an ability to change body positions rapidly. It might be remarked that there is something suggesting an element of impulsion combined with coordination and possibly speed in the nature of such activities. If this logical analysis is correct, what is called agility of feet or of other body parts may turn out to be a syndrome type. The concept of "power" used in physical education may also be a syndrome involving speed or impulsion and strength. One might entertain the hypothesis that a combination of speed and strength describes impulsion, and that the impulsion factors are really syndrome types. But it would hardly be appropriate to regard simple-reaction-time tests or tapping tests as measures of power. The concept of impulsion factors seems to remain a basic one, and power is best accounted for in terms of a syndrome.

Somatic Implications of Psychomotor Factors

The various kinds of psychomotor abilities surely depend upon both anatomical and physiological properties of the individual. The relations of coordination and flexibility to anatomical traits are perhaps easiest to understand. Correlation studies between morphological traits and psychomotor abilities should offer a promising field for study. This should be true also in connection with the factors of strength and speed. For the corresponding physiological properties we shall have to consider nervous as well as muscular functions. What brain parts and functions account for individual differences in impulsion, for example? What are the relative roles of visual and static-sense sensitivity in the factors of static and dynamic precision? These are but a few of the unanswered questions regarding this general part of the structure of personality.

DIMENSIONS OF INTELLECT

We have just seen that it is possible to organize the psychomotor factors that we know into a kind of system. It has become increasingly clear that the dimensions of intellect can also be organized into a meaningful structure.[43] We shall make use of that structure as a basis for considering the intellectual abilities.

General Plan of the Structure of Intellect

The general plan of the structure of intellect may be seen in Figure 15.2. The first major division of intellectual factors is into a small group of memory abilities and a much larger group of thinking abilities. The thinking abilities subdivide into three categories—*cognitive* abilities, *productive* abilities, and *evaluative* abilities.

The factors of cognition have to do with the discovery of information and the rediscovery or recognition of information. Productive abilities have to do with the use of known information, whenever and however it is called for, sometimes in order to generate new information. Evaluative abilities come into play when it is necessary to determine whether things cognized or things produced are suitable, correct, or adequate, or whether they otherwise meet requirements. The factors of productive thinking subdivide further into two groups—convergent-thinking abilities and divergent-thinking abilities. *Convergent* thinking proceeds toward one right answer, that is to say, a determined or a conventional answer. *Divergent* thinking goes off in different directions, as in searching, varying the course of thinking behavior.

[43] Guilford (1956*b*, 1957*a*).

PRINCIPLES OF CLASSIFICATION OF FACTORS

Within each of the five main categories of factors we have two principles for classifying the factors. One principle subdivides them according
to the kind of product involved—the kind of thing remembered, the kind
of thing known, the kind of thing produced, and the kind of decision
reached. We shall see more precisely what these subcategories mean as
we come to them. They are used in Tables 15.2 through 15.6.

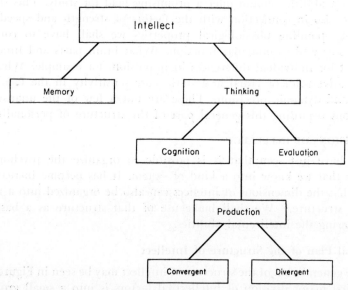

Fig. 15.2 General plan of the relationships among the various main categories of
intellectual abilities. Corresponding to each of the five terminal rectangles is a matrix
of factors, these matrices being represented in Tables 15.2 through 15.6.

A second principle of classification of the intellectual factors cuts across
the first. It has to do with the kinds of material or content upon which
the functions of memory and thinking operate. There are three classes
of content known to apply in this way—*figural, symbolic,* and *semantic.*

Figural content may be in visual form, the units of which have shape,
size, color, and so on as properties. We also have figures in auditory form,
such as melody, rhythm, and speech sounds. Tactual objects have some
of the same figural properties that are better known in vision. There
are also probably kinesthetic figures, in the form of patterns of felt movement that can be experienced or thought of.

Symbolic content is best represented by such elements as letters or
digits and such units as syllables, words, and sentences, where meaning
does not matter. Semantic content is in the form of meanings or abstract

ideas. Abilities in the semantic category are tested by means of meaningful verbal material. If the distinctions between figural, symbolic, and semantic content are not clear from these definitions and brief comments, they should come out more clearly as we encounter examples of abilities related to them.[44]

The known intellectual primary abilities that contribute to the total structure of intellect will be mentioned in the major groups indicated in Figure 15.2. Each factor will be defined and its known properties taken into account. Usually, two or three illustrative tests will be listed for each factor, some of which will also be accompanied by sample items.

Memory Factors

The tests from which memory factors have been discovered usually involve giving the examinee some material that he is to inspect or some material composed of paired units that he is to learn to associate. All the examinees are given the same amount of time for learning. There is almost always a fairly prompt testing of how much was retained, which usually involves reproduction or recognition of the material by E or E's giving one member of a pair of units in response to the other member presented.

Because of the experimental confounding of learning efficiency and goodness of retention, recall, and recognition in the scores thus obtained, it is not certain where to place the emphasis in interpreting this class of factors. They may thus represent ability to memorize, ability to retain, or ability to use learned material in recall and recognition, or any combination of these abilities. The shortness of the time interval over which retention is tested should probably not mean that we are excluding ability to retain learned material, since we know from experience in the laboratory that there is generally strong correlation between goodness of early recall and goodness of later recall.

The known memory factors are presented in a matrix in Table 15.2. It will be seen that the classification under the three kinds of content apply and that there are general kinds of things remembered—substance, associations (or relations), and systems (in the form of order).

SUBSTANCE-MEMORY FACTORS

Examining the first row of Table 15.2 we encounter an unusual cell in the first column, unusual for having more than one factor listed in it. We may find that the abilities dealing with figural content can be quite generally distinguished along the lines of sense modalities when more

---

[44] An earlier category term for "symbolic" was "structural," and an alternative for "semantic" was "conceptual." The terms used in this chapter are less ambiguous.

Table 15.2

Matrix of the memory factors

Kind of thing remembered	Kind of content		
	Figural	Symbolic	Semantic
Substance	Visual memory Auditory memory	Memory span	Memory for ideas
Associations		Rote memory	Meaningful memory
Systems	Spatial order		Temporal order

is known about them. We have two known figural-substance-memory abilities—visual and auditory—as shown. There is some indication of a kinesthetic-memory ability,[45] and there could well be such separate abilities in connection with other sense modalities, at least those in which figural properties apply.[46]

Incidentally, in this group of figural-substance-memory abilities, we have evidence from objective methods (factor analysis of behavior-test scores) of the "imagery types" that Galton proposed many years ago. Instead of types of imagery, however, we now speak of dimensions of memory for sensory material, each individual having trait positions on all of them. Pure imagery "types," in the sense of exceptional strength in one of the abilities combined with weaknesses in all others, would be very rare, as most investigators have long since concluded regarding Galton's types.

The figural-substance-memory abilities and their representative tests are:

> *Visual memory:* The ability to recall, recognize, or reproduce material presented visually [47]
> Reproduction of Designs (*E* reproduces, by drawing, an outline geometric figure.)
> Map Memory (*E* selects map sections identical with parts of a larger map previously inspected.)

[45] Burt (1949).

[46] Christal (1958) has found a separate ability for remembering color, which opens up the possibility of other, more specialized abilities in this particular area.

[47] Carlson (1937); Guilford and Lacey (1947); Kelley (1954).

Auditory memory: The ability to recall or recognize patterns in perceived sequences of auditory stimuli [48]

Musical Memory (memory for musical compositions heard)

Rhythm (*E* judges whether patterns of taps are same or different from those previously heard.)

Other substance-memory factors are:

Memory span: The ability to recall immediately a series of symbolic elements in correct order after a single exposure [49]

Memory Span—Digits

Memory Span—Letters

Memory for ideas: The ability to reproduce previously presented ideas, not verbatim [50]

Picture Recall (*E* reports facts from previously inspected pictures.)

Memory for Ideas (*E* reports facts from a prose passage heard previously.)

There is little scientific knowledge concerning the usefulness of the substance-memory abilities. In a general survey of research on artistic talent, Meier (1939) concluded that visual memory is of considerable importance. Individuals with artistic talent seem to observe better and to remember more of what they observe in a literal sense, which probably means the factor of visual memory, since Meier was dealing with the graphic arts.

In education that stresses content courses, the remembering of ideas would seem to be one of the most important objectives. This suggests that it is time we learned more about the principles of memory for ideas. We might also find that measures of the factor of memory for ideas in individuals would make a unique and worthwhile addition to tests of academic aptitude.

ASSOCIATIVE-MEMORY FACTORS

There are but two known associative-memory factors, those for symbolic and semantic content. None has been found for the learning and memory of associative connections between units of figural content, for the probable good reason that this kind of test has not been analyzed.

Rote memory: The ability to remember units of material in naturally meaningless connections [51]

Word-Number (*E* memorizes numbers associated with words.)

Color-Word (*E* memorizes words associated with colors.)

[48] Karlin (1941).

[49] Kelley (1954).

[50] *Ibid.;* Zimmerman (1953).

[51] Carlson (1937); Wittenborn and Larsen (1944); Guilford and Lacey (1947); Kelley (1954).

Meaningful memory: The ability to remember meaningful connections between units of material [52]

Sentence Completion (*E* supplies missing words in sentences previously exposed.)

Related Words (*E* memorizes related words in pairs.)

FACTORS OF MEMORY FOR SYSTEMS

Christal (1958) has recently reported the discovery of two new memory factors which also have logical support because they are parallel to other factors that we shall see later in other areas of intellect.

Memory for spatial position: The ability to remember locations of objects

Space Memory (*E* identifies the locations on the page of some symbols that he has studied earlier.)

Position Memory (*E* recalls positions on the page of some number-word combinations that he has studied for another test four hours earlier.)

Memory for temporal order: The ability to remember the order in which events occurred

Position Recall II (*E* recalls on which of four pages, which he has studied successively, each of a number of figures had appeared.)

Sequence Memory (*E* recalls the order in which tests had been administered to him three days previously.)

These two factors call for a third row to the matrix of memory factors, where until recently there were only two. This fact suggests that still other rows may have to be added as we learn more about memory abilities. Another fact that suggests the same conclusion is that in other areas, as we shall see, more than three rows are needed to take care of all the factors. The three rows now in the memory matrix seem parallel to rows of similar factors in other areas.

Considering together the three main classes of memory abilities, in the three rows of the matrix, we may note some implications that are worth mentioning. In the past, experimental psychologists have devoted almost all their attention to memory for associations. This may be attributed to the fact that investigation of learning has been dominated by the stimulus-response model in psychology. From the investigation of individual differences, we find that memory for substance and memory for systems are also to be considered. It is quite possible that in accounting for the phenomena connected with these two types of memory, additional principles of learning will be needed. It is also possible that some of the results obtained in the study of associative memory can be better under-

[52] Kelley (1954).

stood if we remember that substance memory or systemic memory may have been involved.

Experimental studies have generally failed to find any localization of "traces" in the brain resulting from learning. These studies have also emphasized the learning of associative connections, and the prevailing conception of physiological processes has been some form of pathway hypothesis. It seems plausible that there should be a much better chance of finding localized brain mechanisms or properties for such functions as visual memory and auditory memory. In recent years Penfield (1958) has been accumulating evidence that electrical stimulation of certain points on the human cerebral cortex serves to revive in rather full detail memory for things experienced. Such events would seem to represent instances of substance memory.

Cognitive Factors

The primary cognitive abilities have to do with the possession of information—its discovery and its rediscovery or recognition. They fall into a matrix of three columns and five rows, as shown in Table 15.3. The

Table 15.3

Matrix of the cognitive factors

Kind of thing known	Kind of content		
	Figural	Symbolic	Semantic
Units	Visual cognition Auditory cognition	Symbolic cognition	Verbal comprehension
Classes	Figural classification		Semantic classification
Relations	Eduction of figural relations	Eduction of symbolic relations	Eduction of semantic relations
Systems	Spatial orientation	Eduction of symbolic patterns	General reasoning
Implications	Perceptual foresight		Conceptual foresight

rows are identified in terms of the kinds of things known—*units* (of information), *classes, relations, systems,* and *implications.*

Judging from the column headings in Table 15.3, we should expect the units of thought to be in the form of figures, symbols, and meanings. This is borne out by the factors in row one.

> *Visual cognition:* The ability to cognize visual units [53]
> Peripheral Span—Single (*E* names single letters flashed in peripheral vision.)
> Dark Adaptation (*E* recognizes letters in dim illumination.)
> Street Gestalt Completion (*E* identifies objects in incomplete silhouettes. See Figure 15.3.)
> Mutilated Words (*E* identifies words with partly erased letters.)

Fig. 15.3 Sample item from the Street Gestalt Completion test. What is the object?

The preponderance of letter-material tests in this list calls for comment, since letters have been mentioned as examples of symbolic content. It is probably the figural properties of the letters that give these tests so much in common with the Street Gestalt Completion test. Cognition of single letters is probably more dependent upon their figural properties, whereas the cognition of syllables and words is more dependent upon symbolic properties. We shall see that the best tests of a parallel ability of *symbolic cognition* are composed of words.

In all the tests listed above, seeing under difficult circumstances is a common element. This condition is needed in order to make the tests sufficiently difficult for the examinees. Otherwise they would all make perfect scores and we should have no variance and no tests at all.

There is a little validity information concerning tests of this factor, some of it indirect. It is quite possible that the $F+$ score from the Rorschach technique is a measure of this factor, although evidence on this point is lacking. It has been found that ability to see good whole form in the Rorschach ink blots is highly correlated with rated creativity

[53] Thurstone (1944); Pemberton (1952); Wilson et al. (1954); Mooney (1954).

in chemists.[54] If the validity is due to the involvement of the factor of visual cognition in the $F+$ score, we could substitute for the Rorschach some completely objective tests for this factor in predicting creativity in chemists. In another connection it was found that scores from the Street Gestalt Completion test tended to be lower for delinquents than for non-delinquents.[55] The reasons for this are not obvious, but the matter may be worth following up.

Auditory cognition: The ability to cognize sound patterns, as in oral speech [56]

Haphazard Speech (E hears phrases spoken with unusual inflections and pitch changes.)

Illogical Groupings (E hears phrases spoken with unusual groupings.)

Singing (E cognizes words in voice singing with piano.)

The kind of tests in this list seems clearly analogous to that under the factor of visual cognition. The hearing or seeing of an organized form of some kind is required in both cases.

It is reasonable to expect to find other factors of this kind in the tactual and kinesthetic modalities, where perceived forms occur. The factors in this cell of the cognition matrix are also clearly analogous to those in the first cell of the memory-factor matrix. In both cases new tests of tactual and kinesthetic material will have to be designed to investigate the possibilities of such additional factors.

Symbolic cognition: The ability to cognize symbolic units [57]

Anagrams (E rearranges four-letter words to make other words.)

Scrambled Words (E rearranges letters given in nonsense order to make familiar words.)

Incomplete Words (E supplies missing letter in each word.)

All of the tests known to be related to this factor involve cognition of very familiar words under difficult circumstances. It is not known whether the ability is sufficiently general to apply to other types of symbolic material (numbers and other simple symbols). At any rate, it is the word structure that must be recognized; meaning is apparently of no importance in the individual differences in such tasks, at least for educated individuals.

Word recognition, as such, is an important aspect of ability to read. In many cases of reading retardation there may be deficiency in this one respect. The entire task of obtaining information from printed material, of course, goes well beyond word recognition, involving reasoning abilities as well as cognition of meanings.

[54] Stein and Meer (1954).
[55] Jones et al. (1955).
[56] Karlin (1942).
[57] Pemberton (1952a).

Verbal comprehension: Knowledge of meanings of words

Most ordinary vocabulary tests

Reading Comprehension (*E* answers questions concerning a paragraph he has just read and can refer back to.)

General Information (Part of the Army Alpha Examination; in fact, most content or factual examinations in school are strongly related to this factor.)

The factor of verbal comprehension has been found numerous times. A simple vocabulary test is almost always the strongest and purest measure of it. This factor has generally dominated verbal-intelligence tests, predicting academic achievement from the lower grades through the graduate school. The fact that it would do so has fostered the practice of weighting it heavily in intelligence tests.

Verbal comprehension is undoubtedly a very important trait in a verbal civilization, but its relatively strong predictive power and its obvious role in education has often obscured the importance of other intellectual factors. The overemphasis upon it in testing and in education may have led to serious neglect of other desirable qualities in the general population. A clearer knowledge of the other intellectual abilities should enable us to reappraise the current approaches to encouraging intellectual development through education.

FACTORS FOR KNOWING CLASSES

The matrix in Table 15.3 calls for three abilities to know *classes* of units, two of which are known—those for figural and semantic classes. In the one case the groupings are in terms of figural properties, such as size, shape, and color, and in the other they are in terms of abstract meanings.

Figural classification: The ability to classify units according to their figural properties [58]

Figural Classification (*E* assigns a figure to a class that is defined by three similar figures. See Figure 15.4.)

Picture Classification (*E* assigns a pictured common object to a class defined by three members.)

The objects involved in tests of this factor have been visually presented. Is there perhaps another parallel ability to classify in terms of auditory-figural properties, and also abilities to classify according to tactual and kinesthetic properties?

Semantic classification: The ability to classify verbal concepts [59]

Word Classification (*E* states which of four words does not belong to the group, e.g., horse, man, canary, flower.)

[58] Guilford et al. (1956*b*).
[59] *Ibid.*

Verbal Classification (*E* states in which of two groups a word belongs,
or neither.)

The phenomenon of concept formation has been of considerable interest in psychology. Whether a large part of the process of concept
formation can be accounted for in terms of these classification abilities
is yet to be determined. On one point the factor-analysis results have some

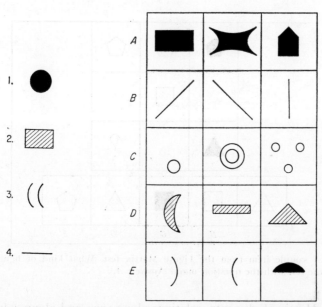

Fig. 15.4 Sample items from a test of *figural classification*. To which group at the right
does Figure 1 belong? Figure 2, and so on? Answers: 1, *A;* 2, *D;* 3, *C;* and 4, *B.*

information to offer. The classifying abilities represent something beyond
seeing similarities. Two tests that involve seeing similarities were analyzed,
along with the tests that defined these two factors. They showed no relationship to the classification factors.[60]

FACTORS FOR KNOWING RELATIONS

Many years ago Spearman (1927) proposed the idea that one of the most
significant aspects of his *g* factor (general intellectual ability) is the ability
to educe relationships. Given two "fundaments," we ordinarily see some
kind of relationship between them. Recent analyses show that an aspect
of intellect is, indeed, eduction of relations, but there are three such
abilities, and they are only three of many other components of intellect.

60 *Ibid.*

To educe a relation is to extract it from the information given, in other words, to discover it, or rediscover it.

> *Eduction of figural relations:* The ability to discover relations between objects by reason of their figural properties [61]

Figure Analogies (Given: Figure *A* is to figure *B* as figure *C* is to what? *E* selects one of five possible figures as his answer.)

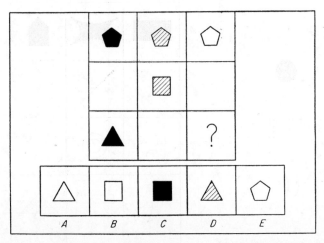

Fig. 15.5 A sample item from the Figure Matrix test. What kind of figure should appear in the cell with the question mark? Answer: *A*.

> Figure Matrix (*E* discovers relations along rows and along columns of a three-by-three matrix of figures and finds a figure to fill a vacant cell. See Figure 15.5.)

> *Eduction of symbolic relations:* The ability to discover relations between objects by reason of their symbolic properties [62]

Seeing Trends II (*E* discovers the letter relationship that appears in a sequence of words.)

> Example: ANGER   BACTERIA   CAMEL   DEAD   EXCITE
> (Answer: Initial letters are in alphabetical order.)

Correlate Completion II (*E* discovers similarities in spelling changes in pairs of words.)

> Example: AM   MA   NOT   TON   TOOL   _____
> (Answer: loot)

[61] Green et al. (1953); Guilford, Green, Christensen, Hertzka, and Kettner (1954); Guilford et al. (1956*b*).

[62] Guilford et al. (1956*b*).

Eduction of semantic relations: The ability to discover relations in conceptual material [63]

Verbal Analogies (similar to Figure Analogies)

Example: CLOTH : DYE :: HOUSE : _____

(Alternative answers: shade   paint   brush   door   wood)

Word Matrix (similar to the Figure Matrix test)

Example: GROUND   STREET   AUTOMOBILE

AIR   ROUTE   _____

(Alternative answers: airplane   bird   kite   balloon   cloud)

Although the abilities to see relationships have been regarded as being very important by Spearman and others who have been concerned with individual differences, relatively little has been done with them or about them. Figure-analogies and verbal-analogies tests have sometimes appeared as parts of intelligence tests, but their contributions to total scores have usually been rather slight, as indicated by factor analysis of total scores. The experimental psychologist might have given more attention to relations, as such, in studies of learning and reasoning. The role of relations in transfer of training may prove to be of considerable importance. Reasoning as a concept might well be defined more empirically as relational thinking, that is, thinking that makes extensive use of relations. We shall encounter other abilities having to do with relations in other areas of intellect.

FACTORS FOR KNOWING PATTERNS OR SYSTEMS

It might be thought at first that a pattern or a system among units of information is merely a complex set of relationships. While this idea may be logically sound, the abilities involved in cognizing systems seem to be not only distinct from those involved in seeing relationships, but also quite different from one another, as we shall see. In each case we have to deal with some kind of organized total structure.

Spatial orientation: The ability to structure the perceived arrangements of objects in space, with reference to the observer

Guilford-Zimmerman Spatial Orientation (See Figure 15.6.)

Thurstone's Flags, Figures, Cards (*E* states whether two views of the same object in rotated positions are mirror images.)

Instrument Comprehension (AAF) (*E* states which of five pictured airplanes is flying in the direction indicated by readings in two dials.)

Spatial orientation is the best known of several abilities having to do with visual space. When first reported, it was commonly confounded with

---

[63] Green et al. (1953); Guilford, Green, Christensen, Hertzka, and Kettner (1954); Berger et al. (1957); Guilford et al. (1956*b*).

another important factor known as *visualization*,[64] which we shall encounter later. In the Air Force research the two factors were effectively separated, and this separation has been verified many times.[65]

There is evidence for a spatial-orientation factor in young children,[66] in fact, as early as the age of seven.[67] There is possible evidence for such a factor in lower animals. A factor called "visual insight" has been reported in connection with maze-learning tests applied to rats.[68] It is possible that a factor known as "goal gradient" is a spatial-orientation

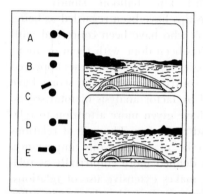 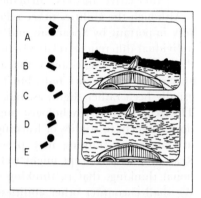

Fig. 15.6 Two sample items from a spatial-orientation test. If the position of the boat changes with respect to the background as we go from the upper picture to the lower, which symbol shows what the change is like? The dot in each alternative answer indicates the position of the tip of the boat's prow in the upper picture and the rectangle represents your view of the boat in the lower picture. The correct answer is *D* for the first item and *B* for the second. (*From Part V of the Guilford-Zimmerman Aptitude Survey, courtesy of the Sheridan Supply Company.*)

factor.[69] It should not be surprising to find that an ability so elemental and so essential is shared by lower animals, especially since learning of locations seems to be one of their most common achievements. Interpreted in line with cognition theory, the mastery of a maze by a rat may be regarded as the learning of a "cognitive map." [70]

Certain studies with adult human subjects seem to show other possible factors of spatial orientation. The Army Air Force results [71] suggest a factor called "space II," which seems to involve only the ability to distinguish right from left. They also suggest a factor called "space III," which seems to be an ability to maintain orientation with respect to the vertical. It might be suggested that the factor spatial orientation is a visual

---

[64] Kelley (1935); Thurstone (1938).
[65] Guilford and Lacey (1947); Michael et al. (1950, 1951).
[66] El Koussy (1935).
[67] Emmett (1949).
[68] Vaughn (1937); Van Steenberg (1939).

[69] Wherry (1939, 1940, 1941).
[70] Tolman (1948).
[71] Guilford and Lacey (1947).

structure, that space II is somehow related to dextrality, and that space III is dependent upon the force of gravity and our learned reaction to it. In either case, the last two factors could both be regarded as kinds of kinesthetic structures. There may be also an ability to cognize auditory-space structure and an ability to cognize tactual-space structure. These hypotheses are still to be explored.

There is yet a fourth possible space-orientation factor. This one has to do with maintaining personal orientation with respect to the compass points, as indicated in two factor analyses.[72] This may be a limited, learned structure among those individuals who have come to rely on the compass points as a frame of reference.

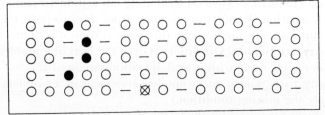

Fig. 15.7 A sample item for the factor of *eduction of structural patterns*. What is the rule by which the circle in each of the first four rows has been blackened? It is the first circle after the first dash. The last row has been marked accordingly with an X. (*From the test Circle Reasoning by Robert I. Blakey.*)

There is much information regarding the practical validity of measures of spatial orientation. It was found to be one of the most important mental resources in connection with learning to pilot or to navigate aircraft.[73] It may be important wherever machines are to be operated in such a way that spatial features are important. From 18 samples of auto mechanics, it was found that tests of spatial orientation correlated with a criterion of success to the average extent of .32.[74] Small validities of .2 to .3 have been reported for predicting leadership criteria.[75]

> *Eduction of symbolic patterns:* The ability to discover patterns or systems among symbolic elements [76]

Circle Reasoning (*E* discovers a system by which series of small circles are marked. See Figure 15.7.)

[72] Guilford et al. (1952); Roff (1952). For further interpretations of spatial and visualization factors, see Michael et al. (1957).

[73] Guilford and Lacey (1947).

[74] Ghiselli and Brown (1951). In many instances, some of the validity might have been attributable to the factor of *visualization*.

[75] Carter and Nixon (1949*b*).

[76] Green et al. (1953); Guilford et al. (1956*b*). Also possibly a "structural" factor found by Chein (1939).

Letter Triangle (*E* discovers the system by which the alphabet is arranged among letters in a triangular pattern, then fills a blank.)

Sample item:

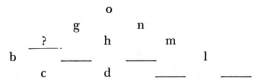

(Answer: f)

General reasoning: The ability to comprehend or structure a problem in preparation for solving it

Guilford-Zimmerman General Reasoning (an arithmetic-reasoning test)

Ship Destination (*E* computes distances from ships to ports taking into account actual distances, wind direction, current direction, etc.)

Necessary Arithmetical Operations (Given the facts of a problem, *E* has to say merely what arithmetical operations are needed.)

Necessary Facts (Given an incomplete statement of a problem, *E* is to supply the missing condition.)

From the last two tests for the factor of general reasoning we see that *E* need not actually solve problems, as he does in the first two tests. He need only show in some way that he understands the set of interrelationships of facts.[77] This is a conceptual structure or organization, seemingly analogous to those in connection with spatial orientation and eduction of symbolic patterns.

General reasoning is probably the second most important factor in most verbal-intelligence tests. It is needed to account for achievement in arithmetic (in large part) and related subjects. The factor is related to grades in a large number of college subjects,[78] but not to achievement in advanced mathematics, which indicates one psychological difference between advanced mathematics and arithmetic.[79] Abilities in mathematical thinking are more likely to be found in the symbolic columns than in the semantic ones, since it deals so much with relating symbols according to rules.

FACTORS FOR KNOWING IMPLICATIONS

Organisms learn what to expect of things, and expectation has a future reference. The higher the type of organism and the more experienced, the farther ahead it can extend its expectations and project present information into future events. While foresight has long been regarded an

[77] Guilford et al. (1956a); Kettner et al. (1957).
[78] Guilford and Zimmerman (1956b).
[79] Hills (1955b).

important aspect of intelligence, it was not brought into focus as a particular aspect of intellect until fairly recently. It turns out to involve two known factors and perhaps an additional unknown third (see Table 15.3).

Perceptual foresight: The ability to explore visually courses of action in order to select the most apparently effective ones [80]

Competitive Planning (*E* completes as many squares as possible in a game in which he plays for the two opponents. See Figure 15.8.)

Route Planning (*E* locates the point, of several offered, through which one must pass in tracing a printed maze from start to goal. He does not actually trace the path in writing.)

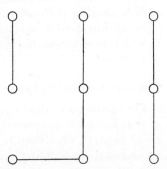

Conceptual foresight: Ability to anticipate the consequences of a given situation in terms of events [81]

Pertinent Questions (Presented with a described situation calling for a decision, *E* is to ask four questions regarding things he should know.)

Fig. 15.8 An item to illustrate the test of Competitive Planning. The examinee is to play the game for both opponents. Each opponent, by drawing one line at a time according to rules, attempts to complete as many squares as possible. The examinee is given credit according to the efficiency with which he plays the game. (*From a test developed by the United States Army Air Force. See Guilford and Lacey, 1947.*)

Example: You have two locations available for opening a hamburger stand. If you intend to open a stand at one of these locations, what four questions have to be considered in making a choice between them?

Alternate Methods (*E* lists as many as six different ways for accomplishing a given task.)

Example: You have a large number of books covering a great variety of subjects. Give six ways in which you could organize the books in shelves so as to find readily the material you want.

In other analyses, with entirely different tests, a factor called "penetration" was found.[82] It appears to be logically the same as conceptual foresight. For example, a test called Social Institutions asks *E* to list, in turn, things that are wrong with institutions such as tipping, divorce, and elections. Only "penetrating" or "farsighted" responses are accepted and scored.

No foresight factor has been found for the symbolic column, but it is

[80] Berger et al. (1957).
[81] *Ibid.*
[82] Wilson et al. (1954); Guilford et al. (1956*b*).

reasonable that there should be one and that we should find such an ability important for the mathematician, who does well to see several steps ahead. Perceptual foresight may be suggested as being significant for players of chess and checkers, for electricians who do wiring or plan circuits, and for architects and other layout planners. Conceptual foresight would seem to be more important for planners such as executives, who deal with ideas. In a survey of variables that predict leadership criteria, Stogdill (1948) concluded that "farsightedness" has correlated .25 to .55 with leadership performance. It is not known whether conceptual foresight was involved as a factor in any of the assessments of farsightedness to which he referred, but his conclusion lends support to the suggestion just offered.

Convergent-thinking Factors

The convergent-thinking class of abilities takes its name from the kinds of tests involved. In general, they call for one right answer (at least one *keyed* answer), which can be determined closely, if not exactly, from the information given. This class of factors is displayed in the matrix of Table 15.4. The familiar column headings appear, and row headings that bear some resemblances to those for the cognitive abilities are given.

Table 15.4

Matrix of convergent-thinking factors

Kind of thing produced	Kind of content		
	Figural	Symbolic	Semantic
Names	Object naming		Concept naming
Correlates		Eduction of symbolic correlates	Eduction of semantic correlates
Systems			Ordering
Transformations	Visualization	Symbolic redefinition	Semantic redefinition
Unique implications	Symbol substitution	Numerical facility	

FACTORS FOR PRODUCING NAMES

Names are units, and they stand for other units of material or of thought. The first row in this matrix thus bears some resemblance to the first row in Table 15.3.

> *Object naming:* Facility in thinking of names for familiar perceived objects or properties of objects [83]

Form Naming (*E* names common forms presented in random order.)

Color Naming (*E* names familiar colors given in random order.)

> *Concept naming:* The ability to name relations and class concepts [84]

Picture-Group Naming (*E* gives a class name for a group of five pictured objects.)

Word-Group Naming (*E* gives a class name for a group of five words, e.g., movie, game, carnival, bowling, circus.)

Verbal-Relations Naming (*E* states the relation that one word of a pair bears to another, for two pairs at a time, e.g., silence—sound; darkness—light.)

FACTORS FOR PRODUCING CORRELATES

> *Eduction of symbolic correlates:* The ability to produce a response to fulfill a relationship given with a symbolic unit [85]

Correlate Completion II (See description and item under the factor *eduction of symbolic relations.*)

Letter Series (*E* extends a letter series by giving two more letters.)

Example: A R B R C R D __ __

(Answer: R E)

It was noted that Correlate Completion II served to illustrate the factor *eduction of symbolic relations* as well as this one. The examinee has two operations, one of which is to see what relation is involved in the given pairs (such as AM MA   NOT TON) and the other of which is to complete another pair of words by giving a correlate (for example, in this case, TOOL _____). Incidentally, this test is an example of how two factors can be measured about equally well by the same test, thus making its scores ambiguous as to meaning. Letter Series, the other example of a test for eduction of symbolic correlates, also measures the factor of *eduction of symbolic patterns.* It resembles the test Letter Triangles, which measures the same two factors. Knowing that a test measures two factors and knowing what aspects of the test are responsible, we are in a better position to develop tests that are more nearly univocal for both factors.

[83] Found in only one analysis thus far, that of Carroll (1941).
[84] Guilford et al. (1956*b*).
[85] *Ibid.*

Eduction of semantic correlates: The ability to produce a response to fit a given or implied conceptual relation [86]

Vocabulary Completion (*E* gives a word to satisfy a definition and a given first letter.)

Example: The wife of a king   (q) _____

Inventive Opposites (*E* gives two antonyms for a given word, first letters being provided.)

Example: STRONG   f _____   w _____

A FACTOR FOR THE PRODUCTION OF SYSTEM

Ordering: The ability to arrange steps or events in a reasonable sequence [87]

Picture Arrangement (*E* rearranges four pictures from a comic strip in the appropriate sequence.)

Sentence Order (*E* rearranges three sentences in the most appropriate order.)

Example:

_____ Many roads were blocked and houses flooded.

_____ The river overflowed because of the heavy rains.

_____ Traffic was held up all over the area.

FACTORS FOR PRODUCTION OF TRANSFORMATIONS

Visualization: The ability to manipulate or to transform an object into another visual arrangement

Guilford-Zimmerman Spatial Visualization (*E* states which of five alarm clocks is in correct position after specified changes have been made in an initial clock. See Figure 15.9.)

Punched Holes (*E* shows by pencilled drawing where holes will be in paper after it is folded, holes cut out, and unfolded.)

Since its separation from the factor spatial orientation, visualization has been verified as a separate factor a number of times. We have considerable information concerning the validity of measurements of the factor. A validity of .41 has been reported for predicting grades in engineering drawing and descriptive geometry.[88] Validities averaging about .3 have been reported in connection with a number of mathematics courses, and with astronomy and physics.[89] In an industrial setting scores for visualization predicted rate-of-pay increase for engineers in an aircraft factory with a correlation of .31, and also predicted rank-order ratings of performance of operations analysts with a correlation of .46.

[86] *Ibid.*
[87] Berger et al. (1957).

[88] Guilford et al. (1955).
[89] *Ibid.;* Hills (1955).

Symbolic redefinition: The ability to reorganize units in terms of their symbolic properties, assigning new use to elements [90]

Camouflaged Words (*E* finds the name of a sport or a game by combining the end of one word with the beginning of the next in a sentence.)

Example: To beat the Hun, tin goes a long way.

(Answer: hunting)

Hidden Figures (*E* indicates which of five figures is concealed in a more complex figure.)

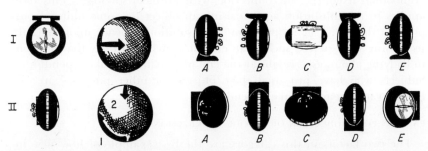

Fig. 15.9 Two items from a test of visualization. In each item, imagine the clock turned as the arrow or arrows on the sphere indicate. Which clock at the right shows how the clock will look after the turn or turns? The first and second turns in item II must be made in correct order. The correct answers are *B* and *C*, respectively. (*From Part VI, Form B, of the Guilford-Zimmerman Aptitude Survey, courtesy of the Sheridan Supply Company.*)

In the last test it would seem that figural properties are the significant ones involved in the reorganization. One suggestion is that we should regard arrangements of lines as being systems of symbolic elements. Perhaps a better suggestion is that a related figural-redefinition factor is confounded with the symbolic-redefinition factor, which has been found in only one analysis thus far. If the latter hypothesis is correct, we shall have to remove visualization from its present place in the convergent-thinking productive factors. There are actually strong arguments for placing visualization in a new transformation row in the matrix of cognitive factors.

Semantic redefinition: The ability to shift the function of an object, or part of an object, and to use it in a new way [91]

Gestalt Transformation (*E* indicates which of five objects has a part that can be adapted to some new purpose.)

Example: Which object could best be used to start a fire?

A. Fountain pen

B. Onion

[90] Guilford, Frick, Christensen, and Merrifield (1957).
[91] Wilson et al. (1954); Hertzka et al. (1954).

C. Pocket watch

D. Peanut

E. Bowling ball

(Answer: C, by using the face cover as a condensing lens)

Object Synthesis (E is given two familiar objects from which to make a new one.)

It is quite reasonable to suggest that the redefinition abilities described here are actually polar opposites of what has gone under the name of "functional fixedness" in connection with problem solving.[92] This term applies to the inhibition against using an object for some unusual purpose. In the Maier string problem [93] the solution depends upon the subjects using some object, such as an electric switch or a relay that happens to be lying about, as a weight at the end of a string to make a pendulum. Subjects who have just used these objects for other purposes are less likely to use them to make a pendulum.[94]

FACTORS FOR PRODUCTION OF UNIQUE IMPLICATIONS

The two factors in this category are the best example of how new information can be extracted from combinations of other information according to rules of procedure. It happens that in both cases the inference or conclusion follows rigorously from the given data, hence the class name "unique implications."

Symbol substitution: The ability to manipulate figural symbols according to rules in order to reach conclusions [95]

Sign Changes (E substitutes one algebraic sign for another and solves simple equations.)

Form Reasoning (E solves equations presented in the form of simple figures according to rules. See Figure 15.10.)

Numerical facility: The ability to manipulate numbers rapidly and accurately

Guilford-Zimmerman Numerical Operations (composed of simple addition, subtraction, and multiplication problems)

Number Series (Army Alpha) (E gives two numbers to continue a series of numbers with relationships.)

The factor of numerical facility has usefulness in helping to predict achievement in some college courses and in technical training such as navigation. For some unknown reason, scores for this factor have corre-

[92] Duncker (1945).

[93] Maier (1931).

[94] Birch and Rabinowitz (1951). See also Adamson (1952).

[95] Green et al. (1952); Guilford et al. (1956b).

lated in the range .3 to .4 with leadership criteria.[96] In a test of very simple operations such as this one, where speed of work is of considerable importance, it may be that the score has in it a component of general motivation to do well. Such a component could be reasonably related to leadership behavior.

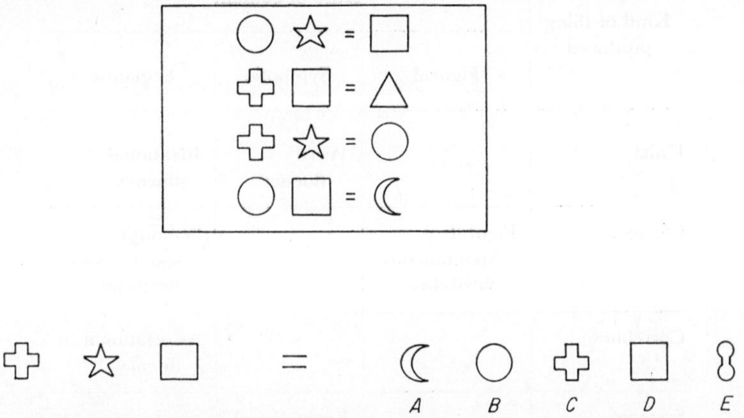

Fig. 15.10 Sample material from the test Form Reasoning. Given the equations for the combinations at the top, what is the figure equalled by the combination of three figures, taking the combinations of two at a time in turn? Answer: *A*. (*From a test prepared by Robert I. Blakey.*)

Divergent-thinking Factors

Divergent thinking is defined as the kind that goes off in different directions. It makes possible changes of direction in problem solving and also leads to a diversity of answers, where more than one answer may be acceptable.

FACTORS INVOLVING PRODUCTION OF UNITS

Word fluency: The ability to produce rapidly words fulfilling specified symbolic requirements [97]

Prefixes (*E* writes list of words, each beginning with a specified prefix, such as "con-" or "pre-.")

Word Listing I (*E* writes words, each containing a specified letter.)

Rhyming (*E* lists words rhyming with a word such as "moon.")

Two items of information can be mentioned concerning predictions from scores for word fluency. They have been found related to creative performance of students of sciences and of arts in college.[98] They have

[96] Carter and Nixon (1949*b*).
[97] First found by Thurstone (1938), this factor has been verified by many others.
[98] Drevdahl (1956).

Table 15.5

Matrix of divergent-thinking factors

Kind of thing produced	Kind of content		
	Figural	Symbolic	Semantic
Units		Word fluency	Ideational fluency
Classes	Figural spontaneous flexibility		Semantic spontaneous flexibility
Correlates			Associational fluency
Systems		Expressional fluency	
Transformations	Figural adaptive flexibility	Symbolic adaptive flexibility	Originality
Implications	Elaboration *		Elaboration *

* Now appears to be one factor but it may be a confounding of two, a figural and a semantic factor.

also shown small correlations (.2 to .3) with leadership criteria.[99] The reasons for these findings are not very obvious and call for speculation. In a highly speeded test of word fluency, possibly a motivational component, rather than the more obvious aptitude factor, is responsible for the relationships.

> *Ideational fluency:* The ability to call up many ideas in a situation relatively free from restrictions, where quality of response is unimportant [100]
>
> Thing Listing (*E* names things having one or two specifications, e.g., things both solid and edible.)
>
> Brick Uses (fluency) (*E* lists uses for a common brick, the score being the total number of responses.)

[99] Carter and Nixon (1949*b*).
[100] Taylor (1947); Wilson et al. (1954); Guilford and Christensen (1956).

FACTORS INVOLVING SPONTANEOUS SHIFTS OF CLASSES

The next two factors involve spontaneous shifting, and from this fact they might be expected in a row of the matrix devoted to transformations. But there are other divergent-thinking factors that qualify better for such a row. The production of varied classes of units is a clear characteristic of one of the factors to be mentioned next but not of the other.

> *Semantic spontaneous flexibility:* The ability or disposition to produce a diversity of ideas when free to do so [101]
> Brick Uses (flexibility) (*E* names uses for a common brick. His flexibility score is the number of *classes* of uses.)
> Unusual Uses (*E* names several different, unconventional uses for common objects, such as a newspaper.)

Recent studies indicate that semantic spontaneous flexibility is the psychological opposite of *perseveration* (a kind of rigidity) in thinking.[102] Perseveration is a tendency to continue doing what one is doing until fatigue or some intrusion puts a stop to it. So far as we know, the perseveration involved here is an inertia with limited influence, possibly confined to the clinging to a class idea.

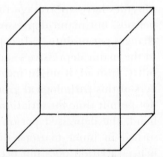

> *Figural spontaneous flexibility:* Tendency to see rapid alternations in perceived visual figures

When we gaze at certain ambiguous figures, such as an outline cube, a line drawing of a staircase, or a rotating lawn sprinkler, we see it first in one perspective then suddenly in another. Our perception reverses itself repeatedly so long as our gaze is held on the object. There are individual differences in the rates with which these changes occur. When the outline cube (see Figure 15.11) is observed under a passive attitude to let the cube change as it will, the slowest rate has been found to be about 2 shifts per minute and the most rapid rate about 150 per minute, with an average of about 20. This is after the person sees the first change, which often takes longer.

Fig. 15.11 An example of the outline cube; an ambiguous figure. As you stare at it, first one square comes to the front then the other.

It has been known for a long time that each person tends to have a similar position in his group with respect to rates of fluctuation for different figures.[103] A factor analysis has shown that this is true for three

---

[101] Wilson et al. (1954); Guilford, Frick, Christensen, and Merrifield (1957).
[102] *Ibid.*
[103] Porter (1938).

quite different perceived objects.[104] Some other tests of the factor are:

Retinal-rivalry reversals (A different view is presented to E in each side of a stereoscope. E sees first the one then the other.)

Windmill alternations (E views a slowly rotating windmill wheel at an angle.)

There is some question regarding the suitability of listing this factor in a group having to do with producing a diversity of classes. We can think of the alternative perceptual organizations as being in different classes, but by the nature of the tests there are usually only two classes thus involved. A possible exception is in the retinal-rivalry test, in which more than two alternatives are possible. Figural tests involving classes in ways similar to that in Brick Uses should be studied in relation to fluctuation tests. Certainly, inertia and spontaneity are important properties of both the figural and semantic tests for these two factors.

One interesting fact is known concerning the characteristic rates of fluctuation of ambiguous figures for certain pathological groups. Schizophrenics have an average rate that is about the same as that for normal persons, but manic-depressives have an average rate of only two or three changes per minute.[105] It is possible that this difference is not attributable to the manic-depressive's status on the factor of figural spontaneous flexibility. Instead, it might mean something regarding the attention of members of this pathological group. The manic may be so flighty that he does not permit time for satiation of one phase of the perception. On the other hand, the depressed person may be so phlegmatic in general, or so absorbed in inner matters, that stimuli make insufficient impression and hence satiation does not occur. These are guesses, of course, and call for experimental study. A more general point would be that the same behavior test may measure a certain trait in a normal population but different traits in pathological populations.

A FACTOR OF FLUENCY FOR PRODUCING CORRELATES

Associational fluency: The ability to produce words from a restricted area of meaning [106]

Controlled Associations (E writes a number of synonyms in response to each word given, e.g., "soft.")

Simile Insertions (E writes adjective completing a simile.)

Example: As _____ as a fish

---

[104] Thurstone (1944).

[105] Hunt and Guilford (1933); Cameron (1936).

[106] Among the earliest to identify and report this factor were Taylor (1947) and Fruchter (1948). Reports of fluency factors go back to Hargreaves (1927), but they were not differentiated along the lines described here until much later.

Associational fluency is very much like the factor eduction of semantic correlates, to which it is parallel. It might even be regarded as an ability to produce a variety of correlates to the same stated relation and a given unit. The one is a convergent-thinking ability, the other a divergent-thinking ability. In the former case, one rather clearly determined response is called for; in the latter case there must be searching, either to give a number of different responses, as in the Controlled Associations test, or to give one of a number of acceptable responses, as in the similes test.

A FACTOR INVOLVING PRODUCTION OF SYSTEMS

Expressional fluency: The ability to produce organized discourse [107]
Four-Word Combinations (*E* writes four connected words, the first letters of which are given.)
Example: Y_____ c_____ t_____ d_____ (Possible answer: You can throw dice.)
Simile Interpretation (*E* completes a sentence that states an analogous idea.)
Example: A woman's beauty is like the autumn, for it

_____

(Possible answer: shows many changes of color.)
The trait of expressional fluency has probably deserved more attention than it has had, at least from a professional point of view. It can be a very impressive human quality. The person who can put his ideas into apt and colorful speech with considerable ease is likely to win followers and to persuade others to his views.[108] It is possible that this trait is the source of halo when raters attempt to evaluate other traits. In an unpublished study 100 military officers were rated by several psychologists on several traits that were believed to contribute to creative performances. Ratings of other traits were found correlated with the factor of expressional fluency much more than one should have expected. However this may be, in his review of traits related to leadership performance Stogdill (1948) found "fluency of speech" correlated .15 to .61 with criteria in different studies.

The fluency factors taken together must surely have much to do with ability to write successfully. Ideational fluency should give the writer something to write about. Expressional fluency should help him to put

---

[107] Carroll (1941); Taylor (1947); Guilford and Christensen (1956).

[108] Assuming that the same factor is shown in oral speech as well as in written speech. Actually, it has not been demonstrated that any of the verbal-fluency factors that have been found pertain also to oral responses. Rogers (1953) concluded in favor of separate written and oral fluency factors, but his evidence can be interpreted in other ways.

his ideas into organized discourse. Associational fluency should give him the word-finding ability that he needs.

None of the four fluency factors that are known is in the figural column. The system of the factors suggests that there are corresponding fluency abilities in the figural category. Such factors may provide some of the basis for creative art—fluency with visual-figural content in the case of the graphic arts, fluency with auditory-figural content in the case of the composer and arranger, and fluency with kinesthetic-figural content in the case of the choreographer and interpretive dancer. Fluency factors in the symbolic column might be important for the mathematician.

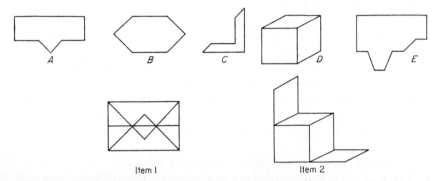

Fig. 15.12 Sample items from the Hidden Figures test. Which of the five simpler figures at the top is concealed in each of the item figures? Answers: 1, *A*; 2, *D*. (*The test Hidden Figures is based upon figures originally designed by Gottschaldt, 1926.*)

Fluency factors in the semantic column have already been mentioned as being important for the writer.

FACTORS INVOLVING DIVERGENT TRANSFORMATIONS

> *Figural adaptive flexibility:* The ability to give up one perceived organization of lines in order to see another [109]

Hidden Pictures (*E* finds faces whose lines are concealed as parts of larger objects.)

Gottschaldt Figures A (*E* perceives a simpler figure that is a component of a more complex figure. See Figure 15.12.)

> *Symbolic adaptive flexibility:* The ability when dealing with symbolic material to restructure a problem or a situation when necessary [110]

Match Problems (*E* is told to remove a certain number of matchsticks—sides of squares or triangles—to leave a certain number of complete squares or triangles. See Figure 15.13.)

[109] Thurstone (1944); Botzum (1951); Roff (1952); Pemberton (1952).
[110] Wilson et al. (1954); Berger et al. (1957); Guilford, Frick, Christensen, and Merrifield (1957).

Planning Air Maneuvers (*E* selects most economical path a given airplane should take in skywriting two capital letters in succession.)

Factors of adaptive flexibility are of special interest in connection with
the concept of rigidity, which has received so much attention in recent
years. Rigidity is an ill-defined concept; it has been used broadly to
describe stereotyped or persistent behavior in many areas, including perception, thinking, motor activity, and even attitudes. Scattered studies
have tended to show, however, that rigid behavior in one of these areas
is not necessarily correlated with rigid behavior in others.[111] It is very
unlikely, therefore, that there is a single common factor of rigidity. If we

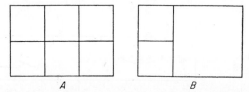

Fig. 15.13 Illustration of an item from the Match Problems test. If each line is a
match, can you take away four matches in *A*, leaving three squares and nothing more?
If you work under the assumption that the squares must be of the same size you would
not reach the solution in *B*.

may accept the idea that rigidity is the psychological opposite of flexibility, the finding of more than one flexibility factor in the area of
thinking alone supports the last conclusion.

Some studies have tended to show what flexibility is *not*. One hypothesis
was that flexibility is an ability to shift mental set quickly, as in performing simple, routine tasks. The factor-analysis results did not support this
hypothesis.[112] Ferguson has suggested the hypothesis that rigidity is a
personal disposition in which negative transfer of training predominates
over positive transfer.[113] This would mean that the rigid person tends
to persist in using a response or meaning or an association in the wrong
place. A recent analysis did not show that tests involving such misuse of
learned behavior are related to adaptive flexibility.[114]

We are left, then, with the definitions of adaptive flexibility given
above, which stress freedom from persistence of approaches, permitting
restructuring. There is some evidence that flexibility can be promoted
by rewarding a person when he tries out different approaches and rigidity

[111] Fisher (1950); Oliver and Ferguson (1951); Scheier and Ferguson (1952); Schaie
(1955); Wolpert (1955).

[112] Kleemeier and Dudek (1950).

[113] Oliver and Ferguson (1951).

[114] Guilford, Frick, Christensen, and Merrifield (1957).

of thinking can be promoted by leading a person to expect that there is one right answer or that there is one right method.[115]

Originality: The ability or disposition to produce uncommon, remotely associated, or clever responses [116]

Plot Titles (clever) (*E* writes a number of titles for each of several short stories. The score is the number of titles rated clever.)

Consequences (remote) (*E* lists consequences of some hypothetical events, e.g., repeal of all laws. The score is the number of distantly connected consequences given.)

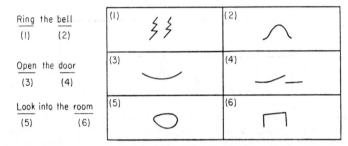

Fig. 15.14 Sample items from the test Symbol Production. The examinee is to produce symbols (as at the right) to stand for corresponding words (at the left). (*From a test designed by Raymond M. Berger.*)

Symbol Production (*E* is given short sentences and is to draw one simple symbol to stand for the noun and one for the verb. See Figure 15.14).

Quick Responses (*E* responds within five seconds to each of 50 stimulus words, giving the first word he thinks of. The score is based upon weights, where each response is weighted in indirect proportion to its commonness in the population.)

Four tests are mentioned to represent originality in order to show that quite different measures all indicate the same trait, each stressing one of the aspects of the definition of the factor—remote associations, cleverness, and uncommon responses.[117] Repeated analyses have failed to find more than one factor of originality.

Other studies show that measures of originality based upon these principles all correlate with criteria that may be accepted as indicating originality outside test situations. For example, Licht (1947) used a score based upon the number of common responses given in word associations.

[115] Schroder and Rotter (1952).

[116] An originality factor was first reported by Hargreaves (1927) and again much later by Wilson et al. (1954).

[117] Wilson et al. (1953).

Higher average scores (indicating lack of originality) were made by people such as executives, salesmen, teachers, and politicians. Lower average scores were made by scientists, artists, musicians, engineers, and writers.

Drevdahl (1956) reported that scores for originality correlated .33 with teachers' ratings of creativity of students in science and art. Barron (1955) reported that several tests, including some of those mentioned above, correlated with ratings of originality in military officers to the extent of .30 to .45. A composite score from the tests correlated .55 with the same rating criterion. The same composite score correlated positively with ratings of traits that the investigators called "independence of judgment" and "preference for complexity." It would seem, then, that scores from originality tests agree with something that is judged to be originality by observers.

Some defense is necessary for placing originality in the same row of the matrix with flexibility factors. This implies that it can be regarded as a semantic adaptive flexibility. There is little doubt regarding its placement in the semantic column, for it is measured by verbal tests. The main question is whether giving clever, uncommon, and remotely associated responses indicates flexibility. It is not unreasonable to think so, for it is the nonflexible person who gives the trite, the conventional, and the obvious responses.

FACTORS INVOLVING VARIED IMPLICATIONS

Elaboration: The ability to supply details to complete a given outline or skeleton form

A factor found in a study of abilities that were believed to be involved in planning was called elaboration.[118] It pertains to the specification of details that contribute to the development of an idea or the variations of an idea. Two tests represent it, one figural and one semantic, which may indicate that the factor is a confounding of two separate factors, one figural and one semantic. The two tests are:

Planning Elaboration (*E* fills in many details to make a briefly outlined plan work.)

Figure Production (*E* adds to simple given lines as many other lines as he likes in order to make meaningful figures. The score is based upon the number of additions made.)

RELATION OF CREATIVITY TO INTELLECT

The mention of factors of fluency, flexibility, and originality in this section suggests that in the category of divergent thinking we should find the human resources most directly concerned with creative thinking and

118 Berger et al. (1957).

creative production. To a large extent this must be true. Some of the validity information mentioned tends to support this conclusion. The relations of fluency factors to creative writing were suggested above. The factors of semantic spontaneous flexibility and originality must also be credited with potential usefulness in writing.

The general absence of corresponding fluency factors in the figural column and to some extent in the symbolic column is probably due to the fact that tests that would appropriately demonstrate such factors have not been analyzed. Possibly they have never been developed. It is to the figural factors in the divergent-thinking matrix that we should look for certain creative abilities in the arts.[119] It is in the symbolic column that we should look for abilities of special value in the creative mathematician and others whose stock in trade is in the form of letters, numbers, and other symbolic elements. We should not forget, however, that other abilities outside the divergent-thinking category play significant roles in creative, productive work in everyday life.

Evaluative Factors

Evaluative abilities have to do with testing information and conclusions as to their suitability, acceptability, goodness, or correctness. This involves the question of standards or criteria. The evaluative factors differ in terms

Table 15.6

Matrix of the evaluative factors

Type of decision	Kind of content		
	Figural	Symbolic	Semantic
Identity of units	Figural identification	Symbolic identification	
Logical relations		Symbol manipulation	Logical evaluation
Systemic consistency			Experiential evaluation Judgment
Goal satisfaction			Sensitivity to problems

[119] The author has elaborated upon this idea elsewhere (Guilford, 1957c).

of criteria of judgment as well as in terms of the usual three content categories that we have encountered in all other areas of intellect.

FACTORS INVOLVING JUDGMENTS OF IDENTITY

We frequently encounter the need to determine whether or not two units of information are identical. Two out of three potential abilities of this kind are known.

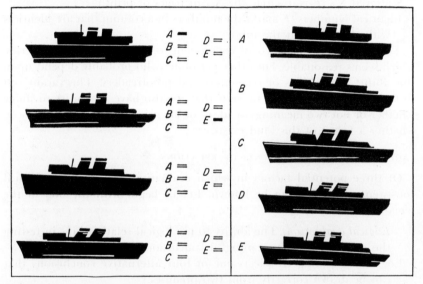

Fig. 15.15 Sample items from a test of figural identification. Which steamboat at the left is exactly like which steamboat at the right? The answers to the first two items are already marked as they should be. (*From Part IV of the Guilford-Zimmerman Aptitude Survey, courtesy of the Sheridan Supply Company.*)

> *Figural identification:* The ability to identify a given figure among similar figures
>
> Guilford-Zimmerman Perceptual Speed (*E* matches each pictured object with one among five similar ones. See Figure 15.15.)
>
> Identical Forms (*E* matches a given figure with one among several similar ones.)

Figural identification was first found by Thurstone (1938) and has been verified numerous times under the name he gave it—"perceptual speed." The change in name here is in line with the place it is given among the evaluative factors.

There is some experimental evidence of the usefulness of this factor in predicting practical criteria. It has had some small, consistent predictive value in the selection of aviation personnel in the Air Force.[120]

[120] Guilford and Lacey (1947).

In industry, it is reported that Thurstone's Identical Forms test correlated .64, .66, and .65 with ratings of job success of welders, assemblymen, and inspectors.[121] As in the case of certain tests mentioned earlier, the speed aspect of this test may introduce a motivational component in connection with leadership behavior.[122]

> *Symbolic identification:* The ability to identify groups of letters, digits, etc., among similar units [123]

Scattered X's (*E* is to circle the X's in pages of print.)

Identical Numbers (*E* marks the numbers in a column that are identical with that given at the top.)

Tests of this type are favorite components of clerical-aptitude batteries, which seems reasonable. For other personnel who probably depend upon this ability, one thinks of typesetters and proofreaders. The vacant cell in the row with this factor suggests that we also have an ability to judge whether or not two meanings or ideas are identical. It remains to be seen whether a factor of this kind exists.

FACTORS INVOLVING JUDGMENTS OF RELATIONS

Of three potential factors in which evaluation is in terms of logical consistency, two seem to be known. Let us begin with the one in the semantic column.

> *Logical evaluation:* The ability to use logical relationships in testing the correctness of a meaningful conclusion

Logical Reasoning (*E* selects one of four alternative conclusions that can be drawn correctly from two premises.)

Example: No birds are insects. All swallows are birds. Therefore:

A. No swallows are insects.

B. Some birds are not swallows.

C. All birds are swallows.

D. No insects are birds.

(Answer: *A*)

Inferences (*E* selects one statement among five that can follow logically from a single given statement.)

Originally reported by Thurstone (1938), who called it "deduction," this factor has been verified a number of times. It is believed that the emphasis in interpreting it should be on the act of testing the soundness of a conclusion rather than on the act of drawing a conclusion. Ability

[121] McMurray and Johnson (1945).

[122] Carter and Nixon (1949*b*).

[123] Coombs (1941); Wittenborn (1943, 1945*a*); U.S. War Manpower Commission (1945); Dysinger (1950).

to draw conclusions would fit logically into the convergent-thinking category, probably in the last row of the matrix.

> *Symbol manipulation:* The ability to use logical relationships to test the correctness of a conclusion from symbolic statements [124]

Symbol Manipulation (*E* is given a statement in terms of defined symbols and relations. He judges whether a given conclusion is true or false.)

Sign Changes II (*E* indicates which interchange of algebraic signs will make a given equation correct.)

In the case of the two factors just described we have essentially the task of judging the soundness of a conclusion in terms of its logical consistency with given information. The information is in verbal form in the one instance and in symbolic form in the other. At first thought, it does not seem possible to have a task involving logical consistency of figures or of figural properties—not, that is, until we think of geometry. Ability to handle the logical aspects of geometry may depend upon the factor occupying the first cell in the second row of Table 15.6.

FACTORS FOR JUDGING IN TERMS OF SYSTEMIC CONSISTENCY

> *Experiential evaluation:* The ability to appraise aspects of a situation in terms of internal consistency [125]

Unusual Details (*E* detects two incongruities in each picture; e.g., a flag and smoke flying in opposite directions; door with no doorsteps.)

Social Situations (*E* tells which of several courses of action would be wiser in a social-problem situation, such as being late for an appointment.)

> *Judgment:* The ability to make wise choices of action in a somewhat ambiguous situation [126]

Practical Judgment (*E* selects the best course of action out of five given in solution of a predicament.)

Practical Estimations (*E* makes rough quantitative estimates based upon common experience, e.g., estimating which of four named objects is most nearly square.)

There is some doubt concerning where to place the factor of judgment in the category of evaluative factors. From the fact that in analyses it has sometimes been confounded with the factor of semantic redefinition, it is probably strongly correlated with that trait. This would be statistical evidence for placing judgment in a row for judging transformations.

---

[124] Guilford, Green, Christensen, and Kettner (1954); Guilford et al. (1956*b*).
[125] Hertzka et al. (1954).
[126] First found in AAF wartime research (Guilford and Lacey, 1947).

Because the ability involves the weighing of circumstances, taking into account different aspects of situations, it is logically similar to experiential evaluation, and hence has been temporarily listed with that factor.

Judgment seems to come closest to the popular conception of "common sense." It is evidently not a very strong unity, judging by the fact that it never has a very substantial loading in any test and sometimes fails to appear at all when it is expected. This may mean that judgments in the tests as well as in everyday life depend very much upon specific personal experiences. If there is any truth in the popular notion of the importance of common sense, and if judgment tests indicate it to any useful degree, the factor should be of considerable interest. Stogdill (1948) concluded that "commonsense judgment" correlates .28 to .69 with leadership criteria. Since the predictors and the criteria in many of these studies probably depended heavily upon ratings, it is difficult to evaluate his conclusion.

A FACTOR INVOLVING JUDGMENT OF GOAL SATISFACTION

In two investigations of abilities involved in creativity, it was found that individuals differ systematically with respect to their readiness to recognize that a problem exists.[127] This ability is grouped with the evaluative factors for the reason that a kind of judgment is involved. When we appreciate the fact that we are short of a goal, we still have a problem; when we think we have reached our goal, a problem no longer exists for us. As long as we are satisfied with things as they are, we make no effort to improve matters, thereby losing opportunities to be creative. This was the logic relating such an ability to creativity.

Sensitivity to problems: The ability to recognize that a problem does exist

Seeing Problems (*E* lists problems that might arise in the use of common objects such as a candle.)

Seeing Deficiencies (*E* points out ways in which a proposed plan or activity is faulty.)

The kinds of items used in this connection have presented objects, procedures, or plans of a rather practical type. It is not known whether the factor also applies to theoretical problems in such areas as science. Presumably, the vacant cells in the same row of the matrix would call for sensitivity to problems in such areas as mathematics (symbolic) and the arts (figural). The heading of the row is Goal satisfaction, since in a very general sense, being aware of problems is a matter of judging whether motives are or are not satisfied. The last row of other matrices pertain to implications, and the last row here can also be so regarded. The impli-

---

[127] Wilson et al. (1954); Guilford et al. (1956*b*).

cation in the product evaluated is that we do or do not need to do something more about it.

SOME GENERAL PROBLEMS OF INTELLECT

Implications of the Structure of Intellect

The systematic organization of the intellectual factors, as shown in the general plan in Figure 15.2 and as filled in with the known factors in Tables 15.2 through 15.6, has many implications for psychological theory, for education, and for testing practices.[128] Briefly, the most important implication for us to note here is the great richness of human resources that exists in the general domain of intellect.[129] Those who search for simple answers and for a single key to unlock the door to the understanding of intellect will be disappointed. At first, the number and variety of intellectual abilities seems overwhelming. This apparent complexity, however, is considerably mitigated by the principles of classification of the factors, which simplify things for us a great deal. As for testing practices, no longer should we favor one or two of the abilities, letting them determine our impression of the total intellectual stature of an individual. No longer should we fail to respect talents other than those emphasized in verbal-intelligence tests.

A POSSIBLE BEHAVIORAL COLUMN

In Chapter 10 we saw that efforts are being made to bring within the sphere of psychological measurement what is often called "empathic ability." This is an assumed ability to know psychological dispositions of other persons—their perceptions, thoughts, feelings, and attitudes, as well as their traits. In solving these problems, it is possible that we should envisage the matter in a way that is analogous to what we have already seen regarding the structure of intellect. The understanding of such abilities would be of utmost importance to all those who deal directly with people in any professional way—politicians and teachers as well as psychiatrists, psychologists, and social workers.

Thorndike (1926) and his associates once proposed the idea that there are three kinds of intelligence—abstract, mechanical, and social. It is now clear that these distinctions were made on the basis of content. In the light of the organization of the primary intellectual abilities as described above, we can see that Thorndike's abstract intelligence subdivides into two areas—symbolic and semantic. His concept of mechanical intelligence

---

[128] Guilford (1956*b*, 1957*a*).

[129] For an earlier survey of aptitude factors, see French (1951), and for a very recent one, see Oléron (1957).

was much too narrow, for there is the general area including the figural factors, which might be called "concrete intelligence." It includes abilities significant for mechanical types of activity, but it also includes many other abilities of little or no importance to mechanical operations. The Thorndike hypothesis of a social intelligence is a challenge to see whether such a concept can be fitted into the structure of intellect as currently conceived.

Perhaps the best way to fit social intelligence (or empathy) into the present scheme would be to assume a fourth kind of content and a fourth column of factors in each category. It is reasonable that there should be abilities involved in the cognition of the behavior of others (and of ourselves). As in the other content areas, cognition of behavior could be in terms of units. The units could be in the form of reactions, attitudes, or traits; this point is not yet clear. Whatever the units, we can think in terms of classes of behavioral units, of relations between them, and of constellations or patterns composed of them. We can also reasonably think in terms of shifts or changes in behavior and in terms of implications, for we often attempt to foresee where perceived behavior is leading, and to predict what will happen next.

It would also be reasonable to think of abilities pertaining to productive thinking about behavior. Let us consider the area of divergent-thinking abilities, for example. An extension of the divergent-thinking matrix into a fourth column would involve fluency in responding to the behavior of others or to their known dispositions, temporary and enduring; originality in dealing with other individuals; and flexibility in the ways of thinking about human problems.

A fourth kind of content calls for a fourth kind of test material. One error possibly made thus far in conventional research on empathy is too much dependence upon verbal material. It may be true that there is much translating back and forth from one kind of material to another on the part of individuals in everyday life, and this would probably extend to testing operations. But there must be limitations to this. At any rate, it would be well to seek types of test material that emphasize behavioral content, and this may often require motion-picture presentations.

A GENERAL THEORY OF INTELLECT

Having considered the possible extension of the structure of intellect to include social intelligence or empathy, we are ready to ask whether it might be possible to bring about a more unified conception of intellect. In considering the known intellectual factors, we noted that the same categories of content apply throughout and also the same categories of operations. Although the kinds of products are not identical in all matrices of factors, there is enough commonality to suggest that when enough of the intellectual primary abilities are known we shall find that the same product categories do apply throughout—units, classes, relations, systems, transformations, and implications.

If we assume that this is true, we can then combine all the matrices of factors into a solid figure of three dimensions, as shown in Figure 15.16.

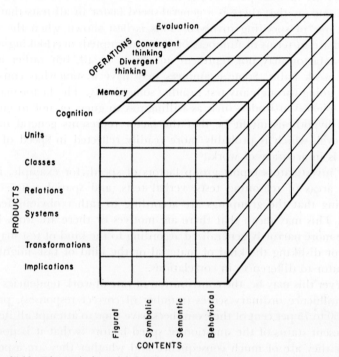

Fig. 15.16 Theoretical model for the complete structure of human intellect.

In this diagram each cell is also three dimensional. It represents the intersection of three dimensions or variations—a certain operation combined with a certain kind of content and a certain kind of product. With five kinds of operations, four kinds of material, and six kinds of products, we have $5 \times 4 \times 6$, which equals 120 cells. Nearly 50 of the factors thus hypothesized are known, representing almost as many cells (since at least two cells are now known to include more than one factor). The vacant cells are a challenge to those who would like to know more about the range and variety of components of intellect.

It should be emphasized that the model is purely theoretical and is subject to change as we acquire additional information. For example, there is some doubt concerning the placement of certain factors within the system. The chief value of the model for the scientist is its suggestions for future research. The principles involved should be of value to scientists and professional people who are concerned with problems of ability.

Possible Speed Factors in Intellect

From a number of sources we have had suggestions from time to time that there are mental-speed factors involved in tests of intellectual qualities.[130] Some say that there is a general-speed factor in all tests that have some degree of speeding involved. This is best shown when the scores analyzed are in terms of numbers of items attempted, overlooking errors.

Such a factor may not represent an ability at all, but rather a generalized work habit. Some examinees may have a somewhat consistent habit of going through any test rapidly, some slowly. The factor may also involve general attitudes, such as willingness to guess or not to guess.[131] A third hypothesis might be that the factor represents general motivational level, which is probably more readily reflected in speed of work than it is in accuracy of work.[132]

Some investigators report group factors of speed; for example, in the general areas of reasoning tests, verbal tests, and spatial tests.[133] It is interesting that the groupings are according to rather obvious features of tests. This may mean that there are motives or there are work habits that are more narrowly generalized according to the kind of test material. Liking or disliking the kind of material or the kind of task might be a contributor to differences in correlations.

However this may be, the contribution of rate-of-work tendencies seems not to influence ordinary scores (number of correct responses), particularly if 50 to 75 per cent of the examinees have time to attempt all items.[134] The present status of the question of speed factors is that it is doubtful whether they are of much consequence and whether they are aspects of intellect. We saw earlier that certain speed tests have correlated with leadership behavior, a result that is consistent with the hypothesis that speed tests measure to some extent a motivational component.

Achievement Factors

Factor analysis has demonstrated that there are somewhat coherent dimensions of fields of knowledge that apply to certain populations, educated and partly educated. These are much more clearly shown if we analyze achievement tests than if we analyze grades. The analysis of grades

---

130 Woodrow (1938); Davidson and Carroll (1945); Tate (1948).
131 Myers (1952).
132 Thurstone (1937).
133 Davidson and Carroll (1945); Lord (1956).
134 Lord (1956).

from different courses usually gives a strong general "grade-getting" factor, which represents all the personal qualities that contribute toward garnering similar grades from different instructors in different courses.[135]

Among the more clearly defined achievement factors are *mechanical knowledge, general culture, social studies,* and *mathematics.* The mechanical-knowledge factor is shown by tests of information about tools and their functions, common equipment, like the automobile, and machine parts.[136] General culture is indicated by scores from information tests about amusements, fine arts, and literature.[137] Social studies knowledge is indicated by information possessed regarding political, social, and economic events, geography, and history.[138]

Intelligence and Learning Ability

We still frequently hear and read the glib statement that "intelligence is the ability to learn." We shall now consider briefly a number of questions that this statement raises. We have convincing evidence that intelligence is not a unity; is there, then, a unitary trait of learning ability? If so, is it related to any or all of the dimensions of intellect? The evidence bearing on these two questions comes from intercorrelations among rate-of-learning scores and from correlations between such scores and measures of intellectual abilities.

INTERCORRELATIONS OF RATES OF LEARNING

"Ability to learn" could mean one of two things—rapidity of learning or the level of achievement attained after practice. Investigators of this problem have usually interpreted ability to learn in the former sense. First, it should be said that the measurement of rate of learning has not been on a very satisfactory basis. The usual research practice has been to find the difference between initial scores and final scores from a task on which individuals engage in a period of practice. One difficulty is that individuals do not all begin at comparable positions on their learning curves for the task. Some may start where a spurt of progress is common, while others may start nearer their top-performance level where little further gain can be made.

Another difficulty is that such difference scores are often very unreliable. To take the extreme case, if there were a perfect correlation between initial and final scores (they would ordinarily be highly correlated, since such correlations are essentially retest-reliability coefficients), every gain would be the same. With no variability among the gain scores, there

---

[135] Carroll (1943); Comrey (1949).
[136] Guilford and Lacey (1947); Comrey (1949).
[137] Carroll (1943).
[138] Carroll (1943); Guilford and Lacey (1947).

would be no correlation among gain scores from different tasks or with any other scores.

Woodrow (1939*d*) has demonstrated mathematically that there should be the same factors in gain scores as in initial and final scores, since the gain scores are derived from them. If the terminal scores do not represent a single unity, the difference scores also probably do not.

Briefly, the studies of intercorrelations of gain scores show that the coefficients are generally low, as one should expect from the low score reliabilities.[139] This holds true for animal learning as well as human learning.[140] There is some indication of group factors, but not of a single general factor;[141] however, analyses have not been carried far enough to determine whether these factors are the same as those found in initial and final scores. According to Woodrow, they should be. Until the difficulty of obtaining comparable gain scores from different individuals is surmounted, we shall not be able to interpret gain factors satisfactorily. We have an answer to our first question, however. Learning ability, as indicated by rate of learning, is not a unity, but there may be a number of somewhat generalized learning abilities.

CORRELATION OF LEARNING RATES WITH INTELLECTUAL MEASURES

Many of the studies have correlated learning-rate (gain) scores with scores from intelligence tests. Most of the results show zero correlations. This was true for maze learning [142] and for learning in a perceptual task and a space-problem task,[143] as well as for gain in knowledge in beginning psychology during a semester.[144] One study is an outstanding exception.[145] Gains in school knowledge over periods of 11 weeks and 1 year in the seventh and twelfth grades, respectively, correlated .49 with IQ. This is more in line with common observation, so far as school learning is concerned. But it is probable that both the IQ test and the measures of achievement stressed the factor of verbal comprehension, only one of many components of intelligence.

Other examples in which gain scores were related to particular factors of intellect involved gains in a space-problem task and factors of rote memory and verbal comprehension, in which the correlations were .42 and .20, respectively.[146] The thing to be concluded from all these studies is that we should seek to answer the question of what kinds of gains are related to what intellectual factors.

[139] Husband (1939); Heese (1942).
[140] Campbell (1932); Dunlap (1933); McCulloch (1935).
[141] Husband (1939); Heese (1942).
[142] Thompson and Witryol (1946).
[143] Simrall (1947).
[144] Carlson et al. (1945).
[145] Tilton (1949).
[146] Simrall (1947).

Effects of Learning upon Aptitude Factors

We have just considered the possible role of the intellectual factors in learning. We now turn the relationship the other way around and ask what may happen to factors as a result of learning. This involves us eventually in the problem of how factors develop and the possible roles of heredity vs. environment in this connection. We shall not venture very far into this important problem.

THE FERGUSON THEORY

According to a theory proposed by Ferguson (1954), the primary abilities, particularly those of intellect, are produced mainly through the processes of transfer of training. The ancient hypothesis of formal discipline held that exercising the mind in any way strengthens the mind generally, or it strengthens certain powers called "faculties." Logically, intellectual factors are somewhat like faculties. They differ in that factors are much more limited in scope and are discovered by empirical research, not by armchair speculation alone.

According to Ferguson's theory, we have families of habits, and positive transfers are more likely to occur within these families than between them. Similarities of operations within families would be one basis for such transfers. We can also see from the system of factors in the structure of intellect that similarities of content—figural, symbolic, and semantic—might also serve as a basis.

The Ferguson theory receives some very general support from two studies in the academic setting. One study was designed to show, in three different high school curricula, the possible effects of instruction upon gains in intelligence-test scores.[147] The significant finding in view of Ferguson's theory is that the academic, commercial, and shop curricula seemed to promote development relatively more in verbal, numerical, and spatial-visualization components of the intelligence test, respectively. In another study it was found that different college courses were associated with different rates of development in verbal vs. numerical abilities.[148]

Studies aimed at testing effects of certain kinds of training upon particular factors have not been very conclusive. Woodrow (1939a) found no gains in verbal-comprehension scores that could be attributed to practice on seven verbal tasks. One reason might have been that the college students, whom he used as subjects, were too near their peak of develop-

---

[147] Brolyer et al. (1936).

[148] Hartson (1936). Some very indirect evidence on the Ferguson theory is that populations differing as to race or sex yield some differences in factors and factor loadings from the same tests. See Dudek (1948–1949) and Michael (1949).

ment in this ability. Another reason might have been that he used the wrong kind of practice. The practice tasks were like the game of anagrams, for example, hence they were in the symbolic category, not semantic.

Three studies pertain to effects of engineering courses upon the factor of visualization. One study found apparently no change after a six-week course.[149] A second found a slight gain after a nine-week course in drafting.[150] A third reported marked gains.[151] The general impression left by such studies is that the gains in status on a factor are likely to be very small, if measurable, after limited amounts of training.

Positive results from such experiments tend to give the Ferguson theory added plausibility, but negative results do not disprove it. The kind of learning that ordinarily promotes development of a factor may be informal and may occur over a period of years. Effort should be made, however, to determine whether the thinking abilities, particularly, can be developed by formal training of appropriate kinds. Knowing what the abilities are like should suggest the kinds of training that may be needed to promote their development.

Changes in Factor Composition of Tests with Practice

There is another question concerning the effects of practice on factors. This has to do with the relative importance of a factor at different stages in the learning process. Does late performance in practice draw upon the same human resources as early performances do? Are there any progressive changes in factor loadings as learning progresses?

In a pioneer study on this problem, Woodrow (1938) had subjects practice over a period of 39 days on seven verbal tasks. The factor loadings changed considerably, those for verbal comprehension decreasing in importance. His conclusion was that subjects change in their methods of performing a task as learning occurs. In six psychomotor tasks and six nonmotor tasks, Greene (1943) also found marked changes in factor loadings. As a rule, one factor involved in a test gained in importance while others lost.

The most systematic studies of this problem have been made by Fleishman and Hempel (1954*b*, 1955). In one typical study eight scores were selected at different points during the total learning period. The task being performed was work on the Complex Coordination test. In each item of this test the examinee has to make a pattern of movements with hand and foot controls in accordance with a pattern of three exposed lights. The score is the number of items completed correctly in a given time interval. A number of common factors, both psychomotor and intel-

---

[149] Faubian et al. (1942).
[150] Churchill et al. (1942).

[151] Blade and Watson (1955).

lectual, are involved in the performance on this task. Figure 15.17 indicates graphically the relative contributions of five of the common factors and the specific component to the total variances of scores at the eight stages of practice.[152]

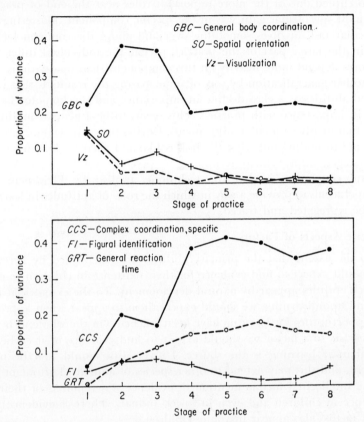

Fig. 15.17 Changes in contribution of factors to total variance of scores in the Complex Coordination test as practice continued. (*From data of Fleishman and Hempel, 1954b.*)

From Figure 15.17 it can be seen that at the beginning of practice the more important factors were gross body coordination, spatial orientation, and visualization. Early in practice the relative importance of gross body coordination first rises then falls again, to remain at a fairly high level. Both spatial orientation and visualization decline progressively, the latter more rapidly at first, both occupying a near-zero level of importance during the last half of the practice period. Another intellectual factor,

[152] A specific component of a test contributes to reliability but not to the correlation of the test with anything else, so far as is known. Psychologically, it is an ability unique to the particular test.

figural identification, never of very great importance, seems to hold a more or less consistent place.

The factor of general reaction time was of relatively low importance at the beginning but gained steadily during most of the practice period and occupied one of the more important roles near the end of practice. The most spectacular gain was in the specific component. Mastering this particular task involves something over and above the common factors, and in the latter part of the practice period the individual differences in scores depend more heavily on this component than on anything else.

Another generalization by way of summarizing the results is that intellectual abilities as a class decline in importance and psychomotor factors gain in importance with practice. This seems to be a general finding in tasks that involve muscular adjustments. During the early stages, cognition is an aid in finding out what the task is like and what to do. During the later stages, improvement is limited by psychomotor abilities. A more general conclusion is that the technique applied by Fleishman and Hempel seems to provide a way in which the roles of aptitudes in learning can be segregated and traced.

Genetic Aspects of Factors

To the extent that the primary abilities are determined by heredity, we should expect to find evidence for their existence in children as early as such abilities appear by natural development. To the extent that they depend upon learning, we should expect them to appear when appropriate opportunities for learning have been reached. On the whole, if heredity is basic to a factor we should expect to find evidence of it earlier in life than if learning is the source. Universality should also be more evident, and this may extend to other species of animals. For one or two of the intellectual factors mentioned, evidence was reported of their occurrence in children and even in lower animals. There is evidence that other factors also appear in young children.[153]

THE GARRETT THEORY

Garrett (1938) proposed the general theory that children begin life with one undifferentiated intellectual ability, and that differentiation of the primary abilities occurs with development. The strongest early experimental evidence cited in support of this theory was the observation that intercorrelations of different kinds of tests tend to be large for young children but become lower and more uneven for older children and adults. One incidental reason for this experimental result might be that when children are young they are developing in all abilities more rapidly than

[153] Thurstone and Thurstone (1942); Richards (1941). Richards and Nelson (1939) have analyzed scores for children as young as 18 months.

when they are older. Even in a group with relatively narrow age range, every ability is related to age and hence abilities seem to be related to one another. This might be in part responsible for the higher intercorrelations of tests for younger children.

The obvious experimental test of the Garrett theory is to analyze the same tests at different age levels, each group being very homogeneous as to age. Such analyses have been done, but they have not been sufficiently systematic or comprehensive to yield a dependable answer to the question. Some of them give the theory support by showing a slight increase in the number of factors [154] and a decrease in correlations between factors.[155] The number of factors in any study has been small, ranging from two to six as compared with the very large number we have seen in this chapter. One more recent study shows practically no change [156] and another even shows a decrease in number of factors with age.[157] We are therefore left very much in the dark as to the merits of the Garrett theory. The problem still remains, and with larger and better-designed experiments we should be able to find the answer.

SUMMARY

The three major groups of dimensions of aptitude include the perceptual, psychomotor, and intellectual abilities. The perceptual dimensions include abilities pertaining to sensory functions. Interpretable factors have been found for the visual, auditory, kinesthetic, and static senses. A factor of attention has been found, also a very small number of factors for more complex perceptual function, out of what must be a potentially much larger number.

The primary psychomotor abilities fall into a logical system that distinguishes body regions—gross body movements and movements involving the trunk, limbs, hands, fingers, and possibly the vocal organs. For each part, similar kinds of ability are often found—strength, impulsion, speed, precision (static and dynamic), coordination or dexterity, and flexibility. Psychomotor abilities are of most concern in athletics, physical education, and in certain vocational areas.

Factors of intellectual abilities are numerous and they have been organized into a system called the "structure of intellect." This is a logical

[154] Balinski (1941); Garrett (1946).

[155] Richards (1941).

[156] Jones (1949). Jones interprets his results as supporting the theory, but the evidence is weak, for at ages 7, 9, 11, and 13 he found 4, 5, 4, and 6 factors, respectively. A disturbing aspect of his results was that a factor might go out at one age and come back at another. See also Curtis (1949).

[157] Chen and Chow (1948).

structure in which two major categories are composed of memory factors and thinking factors. The thinking factors are subdivided into three areas—cognition, production, and evaluation. The production group is further subdivided into convergent-thinking abilities and divergent-thinking abilities. The result is five groups of intellectual factors, distinguished by the kind of operation performed.

Each of the five groups is organized according to two principles. One principle is classification according to the kind of product involved; for example, in the cognitive group there are abilities for knowing units of thought, for knowing classes of units, for knowing relations between units, for knowing patterns or systems, and for knowing implications. The second principle has to do with the kind of content with which thinking deals—figural, symbolic, or semantic. Each group of factors, for cognition, memory, or thinking abilities of a kind, can be represented in the form of a matrix, with three columns for the kinds of content and with as many rows as there are kinds of products. Because similar products are involved in all areas, the entire collection of intellectual factors can be included within a three-dimensional theoretical model. The model adds a place for abilities in the general area of social intelligence or empathy, by analogy to abilities involving the three kinds of content already included. Many vacant cells in the model suggest undiscovered primary intellectual abilities. The everyday activities of problem solving and creative thinking may eventually be at least partially accounted for in terms of certain combinations of the intellectual factors.

The definition of intelligence as learning ability is not defensible, for intellect is not a unity, nor is learning ability. The relations of primary abilities to learning have been studied from a number of points of view. Some studies have investigated the role of primary abilities in learning of different kinds. Others have investigated the possible role of learning in the development of primary abilities. Both kinds of studies should now proceed on an enlightened basis. The genetic relations of aptitudes to heredity should also be more fruitfully investigated.

Chapter 16

DIMENSIONS OF
TEMPERAMENT

APTITUDES PERTAIN to *how well* the person performs. Temperament traits have to do with the *manner* in which his actions occur. Neither aptitudes nor temperament traits have much to do directly with *what* a person does; this is primarily a matter of motivational traits, which we shall find featured in the chapter to follow. In the operating organism, of course, we cannot divorce either aptitudes or temperament completely from motivation. In motives, we find reasons for performing at all, or for performing with different degrees of effort and hence of attainment, and to some extent, motives provide reasons for performing in one manner rather than in another.

Problems in the Analysis of Temperament

Many of the analyses of temperament traits by factorial methods have been based upon responses to inventory items. Sometimes the variables correlated have been the single items and sometimes they have been scores from homogeneous lists of items. The basic information, then, comes from the person's reports about himself. These variables—item scores and inventory scores—are not in the same category as self-ratings of traits, for the items usually deal with more specific habits, opinions, likes and dislikes. We should remember, however, that there is a possibility that some of the factors found from such data may not coincide with factors found from analysis of performance-test scores. It is difficult to check on this point, because the traits with which we are dealing when we use inventory items are not, as a rule, readily assessed by means of behavior tests. If there were behavior tests for them, we should probably not be analyzing inventory items and scores.

Another source of data analyzed in the study of temperament factors is provided by observations of behavior by outsiders. The subjects in this case have usually been children or adult patients, and the observers have been teachers or psychologists. The observations have been recorded in various forms. Sometimes they are like ratings of traits, with some degree of generality; at other times, they are ratings of more specific qualities. They may be symptoms that are reported as being present or absent, or they may be overt behaviors that are rated or reported as present or absent. Thus, as a rule, the ratings have been of the check-list variety.

Ordinary ratings of abstract traits are full of the effects of rater biases of different kinds and hence are poor material for factor-analysis purposes. Although responses to inventory items and check-list reports are not in the same class as ordinary ratings, they are not free from some of the dangers of bias. (The subject of biases from test-taking attitudes was discussed in connection with inventories in Chapter 8.)

The subjects who participate in factor-analytical studies are not applying for jobs or other coveted assignments, and their cooperation is usually solicited. Some biases and their effects are still quite possible. If examinees differ in their general tendency to try to make good-looking scores, and if they agree on what are the "good" responses, factor analysis should show the effects of this in the form of a general "halo factor." A general halo factor of this kind has never been reported.

What probably happens is that there are limited areas in which such biases operate with some consistency. In one study it was found that biases seemed to operate around two focal points.[1] One bias was around a factor of self-confidence and showed up in terms of significant correlations of the self-confidence scores with a number of other scores. The fact that a feeling of adequacy should spread its effect to scores in other areas, while troublesome, probably did not do a great deal of damage to the picture of the factors. Another focus of such spread of effect was in connection with the quality of hypersensitivity. It appeared that there were many items that were designed for other factors but about which some examinees tended to feel sensitive. Their responses accordingly tended to increase correlations between the hypersensitivity scores and the scores of other factors thus affected.

A SYSTEM OF TEMPERAMENT FACTORS

In the survey of temperament factors that follows, an attempt has been made to organize the primary traits of temperament in a systematic manner, somewhat like that applied to the aptitude factors. The results are not as satisfactory as in the preceding chapter, but some semblance of order is helpful in viewing the dimensions as a group.

[1] Guilford and Zimmerman (1956a).

We find, first, that the temperament factors fall into three major groups of dispositions, depending upon the spheres of behavior in which they apply. Some of them seem to apply to many kinds of behavior, or to behavior in general, while others are more restricted to emotional aspects of behavior and still others to social behavior. The temperament factors can therefore be listed in three columns of a matrix, with headings of General, Emotional, and Social (see Table 16.1).

Table 16.1

A matrix of temperament factors

Kind of dimension	Areas of behavior involved		
	General	Emotional	Social
Positive vs. negative	Confidence vs. inferiority	Cheerfulness vs. depression	Ascendance vs. timidity
Responsive vs. unresponsive	Alertness vs. inattentiveness	Immaturity vs. maturity	Socialization vs. self-sufficiency
Active vs. passive	Impulsiveness vs. deliberateness	Nervousness vs. composure	Social initiative vs. passivity
Controlled vs. uncontrolled	Restraint vs. rhathymia	Stability vs. cycloid disposition	Friendliness vs. hostility
Objective vs. egocentric	Objectivity vs. hypersensitivity	Poise vs. self-consciousness	Tolerance vs. criticalness

Within each major group it is possible to apply, at least roughly, the same subcategories. There is general bipolarity of the factors, hence there is also bipolarity of the headings. As may be seen from the first-row category of Table 16.1, some factors seem to represent positive vs. negative attitudes of persons toward things in general, toward themselves, and toward their social environment. From the second-row category we see that some factors pertain to being responsive vs. unresponsive. The remaining rows distinguish their triads of factors as showing contrasts of active vs. passive, controlled vs. uncontrolled, and objective vs. egocentric. Further explanation of the meaning and significance of those distinctions will be given as we come to the factors in those categories.

FACTORS OF GENERAL DISPOSITION

This section and the next two will be devoted to a survey of the known temperament dimensions as shown by factor analysis, following which there will be a treatment of other proposed dimensions. In treating each factor we shall note the qualities associated with it, the kinds of populations in which it has been found and from what kinds of information, its place in the general scheme of temperament factors, and finally, some of the facts that have been shown in scientific studies bearing upon the factor.

Confidence vs. inferiority feelings

Positive vs. negative attitudes, such as this one, are shown most clearly in whether or not the individual tends to advance to meet his environment or to retreat from it. A dimension of confidence vs. inferiority feelings hardly needed factor analysis to discover it. Factor analysis, however, has done much to sharpen our concept of the dimension. The factor has been found from the analysis of inventory items as answered by adults [2] and by children,[3] and from the analysis of inventory scores.[4] It has been found from the analysis of symptoms of adults [5] and of ratings based upon the observations of children.[6]

We may summarize the qualities belonging to either pole of this dimension as follows. (Whatever property is mentioned for the one pole, its opposite may be inferred for the other.)

Confidence:

Feels adequate (e.g., feels he can accomplish the things he wants to do)

Feels accepted (e.g., believes that others like him)

Believes in himself

Has social poise (e.g., not embarrassed in doing or saying the wrong thing)

Inferiority:

Is egocentric (e.g., feels that a lecturer is talking about him)

Feels discontented with status (e.g., wishes he were either taller or shorter than he is)

[2] Mosier (1937).
[3] Cattell and Gruen (1954).
[4] Guilford and Zimmerman (1956a).
[5] O'Connor (1953); Lorr and Rubenstein (1955).
[6] Lorr and Jenkins (1953).

Feels need for improvement

Has feeling of guilt

Has crying spells

It is particularly interesting to note in passing some of the possible determiners of confidence vs. inferiority feelings, since so much attention has been given to this subject. A study of hundreds of behavior-problem children tends to show that adverse home conditions, as such, have little relation to the trait, whether those conditions be physical, mental, moral, or social.[7] The attitude of the child toward those conditions, however, does make a difference. Thus it is the discrepancy between those conditions and the child's aspirations that matters.

Another interesting finding is that the more intelligent the child, the greater his proneness to inferiority feelings. Feebleminded children rarely exhibit feelings of inferiority. Either they are unable to appreciate the discrepancy between their own accomplishments and those of others, or they have become reconciled to their condition. It was similarly found among male college students that those who are low in both aptitude and achievement are likely to be more confident than better students.[8] Some of this might be a matter of façade, but in part it probably means that they have lived up to their expectations, which were not very high.

We saw in Chapter 6 that physical and health defects of students were not very generally associated with feelings of inferiority. In men, only one defect—curved spine or poor posture—was significantly correlated. In women a number of defects were related. Correlations of *number* of defects the individual had with inferiority score were .16 for the men and .24 for the women.

Some possible consequences of confidence or inferiority feelings in behavior are of interest. A very general conclusion seems to be that inferiority feelings have little or no consequences in the form of behavior problems. Compensatory effects seem significantly rare in behavior. Ackerson (1943) found little evidence of any in behavior-problem cases. Farnsworth (1938) found that children with auditory defects do not tend to excel in music or children with visual defects in artistic performance.[9]

In terms of validity in vocational predictions, Stogdill (1948) has reported correlations of .12 to .59 between assessments of degree of confidence and leadership criteria. The meaning of this relationship is not completely clear. Some persons may become confident because they find that they can lead successfully. Others who are confident may seek to lead or may have leadership responsibilities thrust upon them.

[7] Ackerson (1943).

[8] Wrenn et al. (1936).

[9] Farnsworth (1941).

Alertness vs. inattentiveness

The factor of alertness vs. inattentiveness was found in a factor-analytical study of Jung's well-known hypothesis concerning a major dimension of personality—*introversion vs. extraversion*.[10] Following his own interpretation of extraversion, one might well place the emphasis on general alertness to or interest in the environment. The factor of alertness vs. inattentiveness is a matter of keeping in rapport with the environment versus being inattentive or absentminded. A person high on this dimension says that he keeps in close touch with things going on around him, that he is not less attentive than the average person, and that he is alert to things in his immediate surroundings. Since these qualities are stated in such similar manner, there can be some suspicion that the trait that they indicate in common is a specific one. The factor does need further verification, but since it fits into the general framework in Table 16.1, it can at least be tolerated as a promising hypothesis.

As a trait it is not logically identical with the aptitude factor of attention, mentioned in the preceding chapter, for the latter is indicated in performing tasks under the instruction to work accurately. A general attitude of alertness would be a matter of spontaneous attention to things in general, as its place in the responsive vs. unresponsive row of Table 16.1 indicates.

Impulsiveness vs. deliberateness

As the factor name implies, this is a tendency to react promptly without thinking. Formerly regarded as an aspect of rhathymia (to be discussed next), it is now fairly clear that it stands as a separate dimension. It has been found in adults, by the use of inventory items and scores only.[11] From the impulsive person himself we learn that he:

Acts on the spur of the moment without thinking things over

Often says things and later regrets them

Does not plan his work beforehand

Works "by fits and starts"

Certain small relationships between impulsiveness and some aptitude factors are of interest. Measures of this temperament trait have correlated .25 with measures of expressional fluency and .22 with measures of ideational fluency.[12] Correlations with other fluency factors seem to be zero. The impulsive person thus seems to have an advantage in certain speed tests of thinking. Another significant correlation of .17 was found with measures of the factor of hand speed. Correlations with other psychomotor speed factors are unknown.

[10] Guilford and Guilford (1939*a*).
[11] Guilford and Guilford (1939*a*); Layman (1940); Guilford and Zimmerman (1956*a*).
[12] Guilford, Christensen, Frick, and Merrifield (1957).

Restraint vs. rhathymia (rath-uh-me-uh)

This dimension is best defined as a self-controlled, serious, conscientious disposition versus a happy-go-lucky, carefree, and unconcerned disposition. In the analysis of inventory items the factor had the following distinguishing qualities: [13]

Is not happy-go-lucky

Is not carefree

Stops to think things over before acting

Does not crave excitement

In a later analysis of inventory scores it had the following qualities: [14]

Is restrained rather than carefree

Does not crave action or excitement

Is serious rather than unconcerned

In this analysis the factor lost its impulsiveness aspect, which went with other variables to indicate the impulsiveness factor discussed above. The two dimensions may be correlated somewhat.

Eysenck (1955a) has proposed the hypothesis that restraint vs. rhathymia is equivalent to introversion-extraversion. In connection with this idea, he developed the hypothesis that conditioned responses are formed more quickly in introverts and extinguished more slowly. Franks (1956) found support for the Eysenck hypothesis from two directions. He found that neurotics classified as dysthymics (extreme introverts) tend to learn conditioned responses (eyeblink or galvanic skin response) more quickly and their responses are extinguished more slowly than those of normal subjects. Hysterics (extreme extraverts) differ from normals in the opposite direction. Franks found the correlation between a score for the factor restraint vs. rhathymia and rate of conditioning to be .48 for the eyeblink and .25 for the GSR. The correlation with rate of extinction in the eyeblink response was −.37. Individuals with higher restraint scores condition more quickly and extinguish more slowly, in line with predictions.

There is some practical-validity information concerning the factor. A correlation between a score for restraint and average grade in college was found to be .42.[15] Scores for this trait would have added appreciably to predictions that were possible with aptitude scores alone. The validity for predicting grades for women students in another university was found to be .33.[16] The same kind of score has been found related in a small way to rated success of supervisory and administrative personnel, the optimal average performance being found for men whose scores for restraint fall between the average and the highest scores.

[13] Guilford and Guilford (1939a); see also Morris and Jones (1955).
[14] Guilford and Zimmerman (1956a).
[15] Goedinghaus (1954).
[16] Bass, McGehee, Hawkins, Young, and Gebel (1953).

Objectivity vs. hypersensitivity

A number of investigators have found a factor that can be interpreted as hypersensitivity. Although the negative qualities are most striking and seemingly the most numerous, the existence of a positive pole has been indicated. Over the years a number of writers have suggested or tolerated the idea that there is an objective-subjective dimension of personality. Sometimes it has been linked logically with introversion-extraversion and sometimes not. Objectivity vs. hypersensitivity probably comes as close to the hypothesized objective-subjective trait as any factor that is known. The strong egocentric coloring of the negative pole is probably something more than has usually been meant by "subjective," however.

The factor has been found by analysis of inventory items,[17] inventory scores,[18] and observed behaviors of children.[19] The qualities extracted from these results (describing the negative pole) are:

Feelings are easily hurt

Is hypersensitive (e.g., disturbed badly by criticism)

Worries over humiliating experiences

Has ideas of reference (e.g., believes others are reading his thoughts)

Is prone to unwarranted sympathy (e.g., feels sorry for all the people in the world)

Is bothered by feelings of guilt (e.g., feels unworthy)

In young children the behavior going with hypersensitivity includes pouting, sulking, and poor compliance. When hypersensitive children attack others, it is likely to be an indirect attack.

FACTORS OF EMOTIONAL DISPOSITION

Four of the five emotionality factors seem to be intercorrelated so strongly that sometimes it is difficult to separate them in factor analysis. There is also a kind of halo effect operating in examinees as they respond to inventory items, which contributes to the apparent correlations among these factors. Scores indicating emotional immaturity, cycloid disposition, depression, and nervousness thus appear to represent a common syndrome that would account for a large part of neuroticism. The person who feels he is not mentally well is likely to answer inventory items in a way that earns scores in all these directions. The person who feels mentally well is likely to earn scores in the opposite directions. Along with the neurotic syndrome as indicated by these emotionality factors, we are also likely to find scores indicating inferiority feelings and hypersensitivity.

[17] Mosier (1937); Gordon (1951); also an unpublished study by the author.
[18] Guilford and Zimmerman (1956a).
[19] Koch (1942).

Cheerfulness vs. depression

As with other factors of emotionality, we have more descriptive terminology for the negative or unfavorable pole of this factor. Depression catches more attention because it is troublesome, whereas cheerfulness is not. From analysis of inventory scores and items we gain the following picture of persons habitually on the depressed side: [20]

Is emotionally depressed (e.g., often has the "blues"; the future does not seem very optimistic)

Feels physically depleted (e.g., has often felt listless and tired for no good reason)

Is worried and anxious (e.g., has often lost sleep over his worries and over possible misfortunes)

Is not cheerful (e.g., not usually in good spirits)

Has periods of loneliness

From this picture we see that there are physical as well as mental aspects of depression and that the opposite of depression is cheerfulness. Although depression may indicate that everything is not well with the individual, a distinction should probably be made between normal and pathological depressions. In the latter case we have something else added; it is not simply an extreme extension of this dimension of temperament (see Chapter 18). Neither is the opposite of the depression represented here the state or trait of hypomania. The latter includes something besides cheerfulness.

Emotional immaturity vs. maturity

The two poles of this factor are mentioned, with the socially less desirable one first in order to fit the general Responsive vs. unresponsive heading in Table 16.1. The emotionally immature individual is more easily described, the over-all picture being that of a person who in general reacts emotionally like a child. The picture is similar to the one that Jones (1950) has called the "externalizer" type. A person of this type has not learned to control the overt components of his emotional responses. Emotional immaturity seems to have additional qualities, however, such as we see in the following lists.

From the analysis of ratings we find that the emotionally immature person is [21] looking for sympathy, conceited, quarrelsome, infantile, self-centered, and demanding.

From the analysis of inventory scores we find these descriptions: [22]

---

[20] Mosier (1937); Guilford and Guilford (1939a); Guilford and Zimmerman (1956a).
[21] Gibb (1942); Brogden (1944); Cattell (1945a).
[22] Guilford and Zimmerman (1956a).

Has perseverative emotions (e.g., finds it difficult to go to sleep at night because experiences of the day "keep running through his head")

Is emotionally excitable (e.g., is often in a state of excitement)

Is emotionally immature (e.g., is upset very much to lose in a competitive game)

Daydreams

From the observations of behavior of young children we find that when emotional development is retarded they cry, whine, manipulate their hair and scalp, and refuse to cooperate.[23]

Nervousness vs. composure

The opposed pictures of this bipolar dimension are of the jittery, jumpy, and tense person at one extreme and the calm, relaxed person at the other. The less happy disposition is mentioned first in agreement with the active vs. passive class name, since nervousness is activity in a disorganized, emotional way, whereas composure is inactivity.

What is probably one and the same factor has been indicated from several kinds of information. As indicated by analysis of inventory items, the nervous person: [24]

Is easily disturbed by distracting stimuli

Is unable to relax easily

Is easily startled by unexpected stimuli

Is rattled easily in exciting situations

Frequently suffers from insomnia

Has nervous habits, such as chewing a pencil, biting nails, etc.

Perspires easily

As indicated by inventory scores, the nervous person: [25]

Is nervous and jumpy (e.g., long-continued noises "get on his nerves")

Is perpetually fatigued (e.g., wakes up in the morning feeling tired)

Is restless (e.g., cannot sit without fidgeting)

Is tense-excited vs. calm-relaxed

Symptoms noted in nervous patients are consistent tenseness, sleep is difficult and interrupted, consistent irritability, loss of control under stress, and possible agitation or panic with anxiety.[26] This list seems to link the factor with the common symptom of anxiety, though things going under the name of anxiety probably differ from one another a great deal.[27]

---

[23] Koch (1942).

[24] Guilford and Guilford (1939b); Layman (1940).

[25] Guilford and Zimmerman (1956a).

[26] Lorr, Rubenstein, and Jenkins (1953); Lorr and Rubenstein (1955).

[27] Goodstein (1954), for example, found poor agreement among different measures of anxiety.

The factor seems to have been found in young children who responded to inventory items [28] and in others who were observed, with the following indicators: [29]

Is inclined to constipation

Has nervous habits pertaining to the mouth

Handles other parts of body manually

Shows expressive movements such as squirming

Has nervous habits connected with the feet

It was found in other young children by means of observations of motor activity, that the nervous child shows excess movements while sitting at a table or while sitting on the floor.[30]

A factor that may be interpreted as nervousness vs. composure has been found in the analysis of behavior-test scores derived from human subjects.[31] Other behavior tests applied to rats have also indicated a factor that can be similarly interpreted.[32] The tests were:

Amount of defecation and urination in an open field

Wire T test (time *E* hesitates in a starting cage)

Activity test (as in an activity wheel)

Wire Tunnel test (time spent hiding in a tunnel)

There is an element of fearfulness or timidity shown by some of these tests, which makes complete identification with nervousness uncertain.

Stability vs. cycloid disposition

This factor has been characterized as an evenness of mood vs. a tendency to fluctuating moods. Whatever the control that is implied by the classification of this factor in Table 16.1, it operates somewhat like the governor on an engine, which prevents the engine from running away. When some people start to change in either the elated or the depressed direction, they tend to go all the way; others seem to have some moderating influence to dampen the changes. As indicated from analysis of inventory items, the cycloid disposition is described as follows: [33]

Has ups and downs in mood (either with or without apparent cause)

Goes easily from happiness to sadness

Is moody

Often feels miserable

Poise vs. self-consciousness

As a dimension of personality, poise vs. self-consciousness involves having an objective view of one's self and feeling at ease in situations vs. an egocentric view in which there is an emotional oversensitivity to being observed by others. From common experience one could almost fill out

---

[28] Cattell and Gruen (1954).

[29] Koch (1942).

[30] Koch (1934).

[31] Cattell (1955).

[32] Billingslea (1942).

[33] Mosier (1937); Layman (1940).

the picture for self-consciousness which has been given by two analyses of inventory items: [34]

Is embarrassed when entering a room after all are seated

Finds it difficult to speak in public

Suffers from stage fright

Hesitates to volunteer remarks in class

Is bothered by people watching him while at work

Feels uncomfortable to be different from others

It might be thought that self-consciousness is a direct opposite to sociability, but the results do not show this. Sociability is classified with the interest dimensions [35] in the next chapter. A person can evidently be sociable, in the sense of liking people and social affairs, yet be self-conscious. A person who is not self-conscious is not necessarily sociable. There is probably some correlation between poise vs. self-consciousness and both *gregariousness* and *ascendance vs. timidity*, but the extent of either relationship has not been determined.

FACTORS OF SOCIAL DISPOSITION

The social dispositions fall roughly into the same categories used for the general and emotional ones, with five factors having been found in the area. This does not exhaust all the factors having to do with social behavior. We shall find others pertaining to social needs, interests, and attitudes in the next chapter. Here we shall consider the social-behavior traits that more clearly belong under the general heading of temperament.

Ascendance vs. timidity

This trait has often been called "ascendance-submission," but accumulating evidence seems to show that the person of low ascendance does not necessarily submit to others. Submission has a quality of dependence about it, also a low status with regard to need for freedom. The opposite quality selected is accordingly timidity, which, in this context, does not mean a general timidity or fearfulness. Ascendance should also be interpreted as "social boldness" or "self-assertion" rather than as "dominance." There is no necessary implication of a desire to dominate others.[36] Such a slant would bring into the picture a motivational quality, probably the factor called *aggressiveness*, discussed in the next chapter.

We obtain the most complete picture of the indicators of this factor from analyses of inventory scores and items.[37] The qualities commonly found for the ascendant person, in terms of what he says, are:

[34] Mosier (1937), who called the factor "platform shyness"; Layman (1940).

[35] Under the name of *gregariousness*.

[36] This implication has also been questioned on clinical grounds by Anderson (1940).

[37] Layman (1940); Guilford and Zimmerman (1956a).

Maintains his rights (e.g., protests to a waiter or clerk if this is called for)

Takes social initiative (e.g., would enliven a dull party)

Does not mind being conspicuous (e.g., does not dislike being watched at his work)

Is a social leader (e.g., in conversation is a talker rather than a listener)

Is not reticent (e.g., does not dislike to talk about himself)

A similar factor was found in the analysis of ratings of young children, as shown particularly in the form of independence of adult affection, respect for property rights, and ascendance.[38] This factor might have gone somewhat beyond ascendance. A similar factor has been found in the analysis of behavior tests.[39] One is also tempted to say that a similar factor was found in the observation of young puppies. In one study the following syndrome of reactions, observed at feeding time, seemed to be consistent in some puppies: barking, threatening, taking fighting posture, and pushing.[40] In another study of groups of four puppies each, a dominance hierarchy developed by the eighty-fifth day.[41] In both instances the characteristic behavior probably indicated something in addition to ascendance, and, of course, it lacked most of the indicators that we find for the trait in humans.

It has been natural to expect that the trait of ascendance would be among the most important for leadership performance, and there has been much study of ascendance in this connection. The evidence is by no means unanimous to the effect that ascendance is favorable for leading. Among young children a correlation of .20 was found between ratings of "bossiness" and of leadership.[42] In adolescents the correlations were a bit higher for the same two variables, being .28 and .29 for boys and girls, respectively.[43] In older groups there is still some correlation, but bossiness and aggressiveness are resented.[44] Others find that the importance of ascendance depends upon the kind of situation in which leadership is needed. For example, when the situation involved two high school students doing an intellectual problem together, leadership performance correlated −.27 with scores for ascendance derived from an inventory.[45] Much also depends upon the criterion of leadership. Thus in the same study a positive correlation of .30 was found with the objective criterion of leadership in student activities.

The same variation of results was found in college groups. In a group of sorority women an inventory score for ascendance correlated .27 with a leadership criterion in student activities but −.29 with leadership within sororities.[46] The same score for ascendance correlated .37 and .42 with

[38] Richards (1940).
[39] Cattell (1955).
[40] James (1955).
[41] James (1949).
[42] Ackerson (1942).

[43] Tryon (1939).
[44] Stogdill (1948).
[45] Carter and Nixon (1949*b*).
[46] Bass et al. (1953).

scores from a leaderless-group-discussion test on two occasions, and .35 with scores for attempted leadership (participation score).[47] It would seem, then, that a score for ascendance predicts best the type of leadership behavior that involves face-to-face interaction in group activities, where not too much intimacy is involved.

Negative correlations have been found between scores for ascendance and average grades, but the correlations have been small.[48] It was also found that men who were low in both scholastic aptitude and achievement averaged higher than other men in scores for ascendance.[49]

Socialization vs. self-sufficiency

Bernreuter first proposed a trait of self-sufficiency and included items for it in his Personality Inventory. It has been fairly well verified as a separate dimension of personality, although under somewhat different names, by two investigators.[50] It can be characterized as a matter of independence in personal matters, an inclination to work alone and to depend upon one's self. To elaborate upon this, let us note some of the most strongly related inventory items:

Never feels lost when there is nothing to do
Prefers to do his own planning alone
Enjoys evenings he must spend alone
Prefers to work things out in his own way
Finds things to do in his spare time

There is some evidence of a relationship between the trait of self-sufficiency and creative work. Among students of science and arts who were rated for creative performance, there was a correlation of .33 between ratings and scores for self-sufficiency.[51] Creative art students had a higher average score than creative science students. It may be the individualistic attitude involved in self-sufficiency that accounts for its small relationship to creative performance, especially in art as compared with science. Others have found a positive correlation between scores for self-sufficiency and scores from an intelligence test.[52]

Social initiative vs. passivity

At least two investigations indicated a factor called social initiative [53] and others have found what appears to be about the same, reporting

[47] *Ibid.*
[48] Goedinghaus (1954).
[49] Wren et al. (1936).
[50] Stott (1938); Layman (1940). Morris and Jones (1955) also report a factor characterized by qualities such as "going it alone" and "knowing himself."
[51] Drevdahl (1956).
[52] Wren et al. (1936).
[53] Layman (1940); Guilford, Christensen, Bond, and Sutton (1954).

the factor under the name of "social resourcefulness" or some similar term.[54] From these sources the qualities of social initiative are:

Makes friends easily

Organizes clubs

Does not stay in the background

Easy to converse with

Is asked to plan parties

Makes suggestions used in meetings

Does extra work he was not told to do

This trait is sufficiently different from ascendance to merit more attention, particularly in relation to leadership behavior. Little or nothing seems to have been done in study of the implications of this dimension.

Friendliness vs. hostility

It is difficult to find a single opposite quality for friendliness. In fact, it is not easy to find a single term for the positive pole. This factor implies agreeableness and compliance at the positive pole and hostility and belligerence at the negative pole. The only justification for placing it in the controlled vs. uncontrolled category is that hostile or belligerent attitudes are either brought under control or they are not.

Analysis of inventory scores shows a number of qualities descriptive of belligerence or hostility: [55]

Resists controls (e.g., has very much resented being given orders)

Has contempt for others (e.g., sometimes thinks most people are stupid)

Is hostile (e.g., bears a grudge against someone who has injured him)

Is irritable (e.g., has become so angry at work that he threw tools about or broke them)

Descriptive of the positive pole is the quality:

Enjoys friends and acquaintances (e.g., enjoys getting acquainted with most people)

Probably the same factor has been found in the analysis of symptoms of patients.[56] The related symptoms are:

Has some degree of hostility

Perceives the world as hostile

Is hostile toward authority

Is suspicious

There may be a counterpart of this factor in lower animals. A factor found in rats was called "tameness," [57] and a factor found in dogs was called "docility or responsiveness." [58]

---

[54] Stott (1938); Gernes (1940).

[55] Guilford and Zimmerman (1956a); also verified by Holley (1951) and by an unpublished study by the author.

[56] Lorr et al. (1953).   [58] Anastasi et al. (1955).

[57] Vaughn (1937); Van Steenberg (1939).

In human subjects scores for friendliness have correlated .25 with average grades in college. This could mean that the agreeable, compliant student has a slightly better chance for good grades than the student who is possibly rebellious. There are sometimes relations between scores for the same factor and rated success of supervisory personnel, with the optimal scores between the average and the top.[59] This is one of the traits for which a very low score can indicate trouble in getting along with others and possible violence if the low score is combined with high scores on ascendance and masculinity.

Tolerance vs. criticalness

This means a tendency to accept others and to overlook their weaknesses vs. being hypercritical. It has been found from inventory items and scores a number of times.[60] The analyzed variables make it easier to describe the negative end of the dimension:

Finds fault with human nature (e.g., believes that many men will shirk their duties whenever they can do so)

Finds fault with industry (e.g., believes that many men deserve higher pay than their bosses)

Is suspicious of hypocrisy in others (e.g., believes that most people who help others really dislike to do so)

Distrusts honesty of others (e.g., does not believe that others can be trusted completely)

Finds fault with society (e.g., believes it takes money to get a square deal in court)

The factor of tolerance vs. criticalness [61] has been one of the traits most often found related to criteria in industry. In this case, the higher the score the better the personnel, in a linear relationship between criterion and scores. This trait seems to be one of the most important for good personal relations and for popularity with others. A low score in it combined with a low score in friendliness vs. hostility is likely to mean trouble. There is a small predictive validity for happiness in marriage [62] and for success in discussion groups.[63] Stogdill (1948) reports correlations of .44 to .69 between assessments of a logically similar trait (cooperativeness) and performance in the way of leadership.

[59] Mackie (1948).

[60] Harding (1941); Holley (1951); Guilford and Zimmerman (1956a); and an unpublished study by the author.

[61] In two of the author's published inventories, this trait has been named "cooperativeness" and "personal relations."

[62] Adams (1946).

[63] Bass et al. (1953).

OTHER POTENTIAL FACTORS OF TEMPERAMENT

The factors of temperament that have been surveyed do not exhaust the description of temperament. Many other temperament traits have been proposed from time to time, some rather persistently. Some of the traits that have been put forth as important dimensions of temperament have been investigated to some extent by factorial methods but the results are not yet sufficiently clearly verified to justify listing them as established factors. Some of them turn out to be syndromes of primary traits. Such is the case, for example, with the dimension of *masculinity vs. femininity,* which will be discussed first.

Masculinity vs. Femininity

In more than one analysis a factor has been found that is most appropriately identified as masculinity vs. femininity for the reason that the indicators of it have in common the fact that they describe sex differences. Wherever a number of the experimental variables in an analysis are of the kind that indicate consistent sex differences, such a factor may be an outcome. The indicators of masculinity-femininity are as a rule also indicators of various other factors. For example, women admit more freely than men to the statement that they are emotionally excitable and that they are more fearful of certain objects or situations. Being emotionally excitable also indicates emotional immaturity, and being fearful indicates low adventuresomeness or a desire for security.

Thus, masculinity vs. femininity should be regarded as a higher-order factor or as a syndrome type. It is not a very stable variable as measured by common tests and inventories. Scores from instruments like the MMPI, the Terman-Miles test, the Strong Vocational Interest Blank, and so on, have correlated in the range .41 to .73 when both males and females are included in the sample,[64] and .21 to .40 when only one sex is included.[65] Each score, therefore, indicates a somewhat different area of sex differences, for these intercorrelations are definitely lower than the internal-consistency reliabilities of the various scores. It is interesting to note in passing that a factor analysis of the 12 subtest scores from the Terman-Miles test indicates two or more factors. These factors may actually be contributors to the total score in addition to the factor of masculinity vs. femininity.[66]

Some of the more common indicators as shown by factor analysis of inventory scores are: [67]

---

[64] Heston (1948); Shepler (1951).
[65] Nance (1949); de Cillis and Orbison (1950).
[66] Ford and Tyler (1952).
[67] Guilford and Zimmerman (1956a).

For masculinity:

Has masculine vocational interests (e.g., being a truck driver rather than a florist)

Has masculine avocational interests (e.g., going to a baseball game rather than to a dance)

Inhibits emotional expressions (e.g., does not cry easily)

For femininity:

Is sympathetic (e.g., being sorry for a helpless bird)

Is easily disgusted (e.g., by odors of perspiration)

Likes social limelight (e.g., does not mind being the center of attention)

The only moderate correlations among scores of masculinity-femininity from different tests and inventories have some implications that should not be overlooked. First, the dimension of masculinity vs. femininity, at least as operationally defined by these scores, is a shifting concept. In interpreting any one of the scores it is well to consider the areas of sex difference that are emphasized by that score. Certainly, one should be slow in drawing any inferences regarding homosexuality from the fact that a man makes a low score or the fact that a woman makes a high score on an MF scale. Other information is needed before such an interpretation would be justified.

Some validation information is available concerning scores for masculinity-femininity. In predicting average grades for college men no significant relationship was found, but for women the correlation was .47 when aptitude is held constant.[68] The correlation between the masculinity score and aptitude was −.33. Thus, the more feminine college women tended to have higher aptitude, but the more masculine ones made higher grades. The more feminine ones probably had other interests and distractions.

In predicting leadership a masculinity-femininity score correlated negative with several criteria.[69] The hypothesis was proposed that the democratic leaders who tend to be preferred are less masculine than others. In a leaderless-group-discussion test applied to college women a masculinity-femininity score correlated .56 with the average efficiency of discussion in a group. That is, a group of women tended to discuss a subject more efficiently if they were on the masculine side for women in general.

Personal Tempo

There seems to be a popular idea that there are fast people and there are slow people. This implies a very general trait of personal tempo, which means that in their natural everyday activities persons have characteristic rank positions in terms of the natural speed with which they

---

[68] Goedinghaus (1949).

[69] Bass, Wurster, Doll, and Clair (1953).

do things. Intercorrelations of natural speeds of different activities, however, do not uniformly support the hypothesis of general personal tempo.

There is some evidence of such a factor in the rate-of-movement aspect of behavior of rats in two investigations.[70] Intercorrelations of rate-of-movement scores for human subjects of about the same age do not indicate a general factor.[71] They do tend to suggest group factors, that is, consistency of speed in limited areas of similar movements. Rimoldi (1951), who factor-analyzed a large number of such scores, found a number of factors, each rather restricted in scope and limited according to parts of the body involved and types of movement. There is some suspicion that these factors might have been speed factors in whole or in part, since the subjects knew that they were being timed. The same might be said regarding other correlations among presumed tempo scores. One may ask an examinee to perform at his natural rate, but he knows he is taking a test, and if he has reason to suspect that he is being timed he may perform at something greater than his natural rate. There is a substantial correlation between speed and tempo scores obtained from the same tasks.[72]

Perseveration

The idea that there is an important dimension of perseveration has been a persistent one for many years. Spearman (1927) thought that a very general factor of this kind had been demonstrated. He defined it as a mental inertia or lag, and thought that the opposite qualities are quickness and originality. It has often been suggested that the factor is indicated in many ways and in many aspects of behavior—sensory, perceptual, emotional, motor, and in thinking.

An example of sensory perseveration is seen in the critical fusion rate for visual flicker. Looking at a slowly revolving disk composed of two segments of different color, we see an alternation of the two. As the rate of rotation increases, we see a flickering light, and at some critical rate flickering gives way to fusion into a smooth, "mixed" color. There are individual differences in the critical rate for fusion. Those persons who have a low rate for fusion are greater perseverators; the lag in their nervous systems is greater, hence the brain responses overlap and the two colors appear mixed. Those who see the flicker at higher rates of rotation are low on the scale of perseveration; there is not enough lag to overlap the excitations.

An example of a perceptual perseveration is found in the rate of fluctuation of ambiguous figures. The perseverator has a longer period without

---

[70] Vaughn (1937); Van Steenberg (1939).
[71] Harrison and Dorcus (1938)· Harrison (1941).
[72] Harrison (1941).

change; the low perseverator has more rapid fluctuations. Perseveration in motor tasks is expected to show up in the inability to reverse one's movements, as in writing the letter *S* forward then backward, and so on. Thinking perseveration is thought to be illustrated by the use of persisting images, ideas, or methods. Emotional perseverations might be in the form of reverberating anger, fear, or grief.

DISPOSITION RIGIDITY

In more recent years we have heard relatively less of perseveration and more of "dispositional rigidity." The term has been used to cover approximately the same range of phenomena. Many intercorrelational studies and some factor analyses have been made to test the hypothesis of a single general trait of rigidity. Cattell (1946*a*), who is partial to the idea of very broad factors, concludes that of the many studies, the majority find a rigidity factor. This is in spite of the fact that zero correlations, also many very small ones, commonly appear among different tests designed to measure rigidity. Rim (1955) has reported four group factors among perseveration tests, and Weisgerber (1955) has also reported four factors. Oliver and Ferguson (1951) found a rigidity factor confined to motor tests, and even Cattell's (1946*bc*) rigidity factor was almost confined to motor tests. Shevach (1938) found some evidence of a factor among children but not among adults.

GROUP FACTORS OF PERSEVERATION

The best conclusion seems to be that there is no very general factor of perseveration or rigidity, but that there are a number of group factors of this kind, at least in the normal population. A motor-rigidity factor has been mentioned. Its scope is unknown. In connection with thinking abilities, it was pointed out that perseveration or inertia of thinking appears to be opposite to the quality known as semantic spontaneous flexibility and that persistence in direction of thinking appears to be opposite to the quality known as figural adaptive flexibility.[73] It is reasonable to suppose that there are two additional forms of perseveration or rigidity opposite to the thinking abilities of figural spontaneous flexibility and semantic adaptive flexibility. It is not likely that the five factors mentioned here exhaust all kinds of rigidity that exist.

There may be a general trait of rigidity in the sphere of pathology. Such a condition is reported to appear among the feebleminded [74] and among brain-injured psychotic cases.[75] Even if it is proven by statistical analysis that the trait is general in pathological populations, however,

[73] Guilford, Frick, Christensen, and Merrifield (1957).
[74] Kounin (1943).
[75] Gelb and Goldstein (1920).

this should not mean that we can extend the concept of a general-rigidity trait to the normal population.

Oscillation

Another very general trait proposed by Spearman (1927) has been called "oscillation." This concept means a consistent tendency for a person to be variable in his behavior vs. being stable or uniform. The term "oscillation" implies rhythmic fluctuations in the form of waves, with peak performance interspersed between lower levels. Whether the changes are regular or not, the results should show up in the form of personal positions with regard to variability vs. uniformity of performance in particular tasks.

A typical test of this hypothesized dimension consists of 60 trials of five seconds each in some rather routine and perhaps repetitive task. The oscillation score is some measure of variability of the 60 scores. Such variability scores can attain a fair level of reliability (approximately .65), which lends some confidence to the idea that they measure a personal property of some kind. Whether or not they measure a single unitary trait or any common factor at all depends upon the intercorrelations of such scores obtained from different tests. The general picture is one of somewhat low intercorrelations, with higher correlations among scores derived from similar kinds of tests.[76] This looks as if there are group factors among them, not a single unity. Whether the group factors, when and if they are found, are actually oscillation factors remains to be seen.[77]

There is evidence that such scores may indicate something quite different from oscillation or variability, as such. In rats, certain variability scores were found related to other measures that indicate emotionality.[78] Other variability scores for humans were reported to be related to a trait called "steadiness of character," a person who is more variable in performance having less of this trait.[79] Some support for the relation to character qualities comes from the fact that variability scores were found related to a factor called "character integration"[80] in one study and to a factor that might be called "persistence" in another.[81]

Possible Factors of Suggestibility

Suggestibility has been one of the most fascinating subjects in psychology, fascinating in large part because it has been surrounded with much mystery. It is commonly believed that one person is more suggestible than another, but little unique meaning is conveyed by stating that a

[76] Madigan (1938); Glaser (1952).
[77] For a review of this subject, see Fiske and Rice (1955).
[78] Hall (1937).   [80] Cattell (1943).
[79] Walton (1936, 1939); Cummings (1939).   [81] Brogden (1940).

person is suggestible or not suggestible. The reason is that this trait concept has often been more or less equated with a number of other different concepts, such as obedience, impulsiveness, compliance, submissiveness, or gullibility.

Suggestibility has also been traditionally connected with the phenomenon of hypnosis. It is commonly thought that a person goes into a state of hypnosis as a result of suggestion, and that this state itself is one of heightened suggestibility. Those who have studied hypnosis intensively sometimes reach a conclusion that the hypnotic state and hypnotic phenomena are quite varied, depending upon the person and the method of inducing hypnosis.[82] About the last thing that we should expect, then, is to find a unitary dimension of suggestibility. If our expectation is correct, are there varieties of suggestibility or are the phenomena of suggestion to be accounted for in terms of other known traits?

Suggestibility has also been traditionally tied up with the psychoneurotic disorder known as hysteria, whose symptoms, such as blindness, deafness, or paralysis, are said to be adopted in response to suggestions. An example is the patient who feels numb in an arm and is unable to move it during an accident and therefore suffers from continued paralysis that has no organic basis such as severed or blocked nerves.

ANALYSIS OF TESTS OF SUGGESTIBILITY

The dimensions of suggestibility, whether there be one or more than one, is a matter of intercorrelation of the supposed indicators, as usual. In Chapter 10 some of the typical tests of suggestibility were briefly described. Investigators who have obtained intercorrelations of such tests report values that seem to fluctuate to an unusual degree from one study to another where the same tests have been used. This peculiarity of tests of suggestibility indicates that there is something unstable as to what a particular test measures. Those who have administered tests of suggestibility know very well that a minor slip or change of conditions may make a considerable difference in the reactions of examinees. The resulting scores thus seem to be unusually sensitive to temporary testing conditions. This might well have been expected in view of the subtle stimulation to which we hope some examinees will respond in suggested directions.

Apparently no one has found a single dimension that accounts for all kinds of tests of suggestibility.[83] Eysenck (1947) proposes three factors. One he calls "primary suggestibility," which he found related to the body-sway test, the Chevreul-pendulum test, and the arm-levitation test. All of these involve motor responses consequent to verbal suggestion that the body or the arm is moving in certain directions. Another factor he

[82] Young (1941).
[83] Littell (1946).

called "secondary suggestibility," related to the tests of progressive lines, odor suggestion, and warmth suggestion. All of these involve unwarranted or illusory sensory or perceptual outcomes apparently consequent to suggestions that the examinee is smelling odors, feeling warmth, or seeing increases in lengths of lines where there are no increases. A third factor is called "prestige suggestibility." This is related to tests that indicate how strongly E accepts the opinions of authorities or of his peers.

It would be nice to be able to say that these three reasonable suggestibility factors have been established. However, there are some discordant results that give us cause for hesitation to do so. Under the most indicative conditions the average intercorrelation among tests of primary suggestibility was .50.[84] In another study intercorrelations of four tests of primary suggestibility averaged $-.07$.[85] In the former case it was known that the test scores were highly reliable (approximately .90); in the latter case reliabilities were not reported. In the former study the average intercorrelation of scores from tests of secondary suggestibility was .15, where reliabilities were of the order of .30 to .50. In the second study the average intercorrelation of five tests was .06.

Among six scores designed to measure tendency to conform to group opinion, intercorrelations averaged .30, and it was concluded that one common factor would account for them.[86] The six scores came from reactions of acceptance of opinion on similar sets of attitude-scale items, however. The strong similarity among the tests would seem to make them alternate forms of virtually the same test, hence we do not know how general the common factor is. It might be specific to this kind of test. This study thus adds little support for belief in the hypothesis of a factor of prestige suggestibility.

There are indications that factors other than those of suggestibility are involved in suggestibility tests. In one study it was found that tests involving suggestions for active muscular responses do not correlate very well with tests involving suggestions for passive muscular responses, for example, tests calling for raising the arm vs. tests calling for lowering the arm.[87] The better tests of the factor of primary suggestibility and those more strongly related to hypnotizability are of the passive type. Sometimes a surprisingly high correlation (e.g., .56) appears between a perceptual test (autokinetic phenomenon [88]) and a motor test (Chevreul pendulum), which are not expected to indicate the same factor.[89]

---

[84] Eysenck and Furneaux (1945).
[85] Benton and Bandura (1953).
[86] Ferguson (1944c).
[87] Eysenck and Furneaux (1945).
[88] Seeing movement in a small stationary spot of light in the dark.
[89] Littell (1946).

SUGGESTIBILITY, HYPNOTIZABILITY, AND NEUROTICISM

The relations of suggestibility tests to hypnotizability and to neurosis are somewhat revealing but also somewhat puzzling. While some investigators conclude that no behavior tests correlate consistently with a rating of hypnotizability,[90] others report consistently substantial correlations for certain tests. In three samples hypnotizability was reported to correlate with the body-sway test to the extent of .64 to .73, and to correlate with the warmth-illusion test to the extent of .51 to .68.[91] Since the correlation between these two tests was near zero, combined they predicted hypnotizability with an accuracy indicated by correlations of .92 and .96. One inference from these findings is that the scale for assessing hypnotizability emphasizes both primary and secondary suggestibility. This is not surprising, in that both perceptual and motor "tests" are applied in rating depth of hypnosis achieved.

One puzzling feature is the fact that the body-sway test has correlated substantially with degree of neuroticism and also with hypnotizability, whereas neuroticism in general is essentially unrelated to hypnotizability. Eysenck (1947) has offered the plausible hypothesis that the body-sway test is actually a double one, indicating two different basic traits. One is an *ability,* the ability to exhibit ideomotor activity. Ideomotor activity is the tendency for an idea of a body movement to be translated into the movement. The other component of the sway test is an *attitude* toward the instructions, which also determines the extent of the body sway. Eysenck supposes that hypnotizability is related to the ideomotor-ability component, whereas neuroticism is related to the attitude.

IMPROVEMENTS IN TESTS OF SUGGESTIBILITY

What seems to be needed in studies of the area of suggestibility is further intensive experimental work on the tests so that we can know under what conditions we obtain the kind of intercorrelations that we do. If they vary as much as they seem to, the samples of examinees being of adequate size, there must be good and sufficient reasons. Having established standard forms of tests, considerable further intercorrelation study and analysis are definitely needed, which would include measures of traits other than those of suggestibility in order to gain as much information as possible regarding components of the tests.

SUMMARY

The dimensions of temperament pertain primarily to the *manner* in which a person's behavior occurs, as distinguished from what he does

90 Friedlander and Sarbin (1938).
91 Furneaux (1946); Eysenck (1947).

or how well he does it. They account for what is popularly known as an individual's "disposition." Most factors of temperament can be grouped into three broad classes, depending upon whether they refer to a person's attitudes toward his general environment, his emotional characteristics, or his inclinations in dealing with his social environment.

Within each of these three categories we find more or less common distinctions between factors, that is, whether the person is inclined toward a positive or a negative disposition, whether he is responsive or unresponsive, active or passive, controlled or uncontrolled, and objective or egocentric. The naming of opposite directions in each case is a function of the general bipolarity of the dimensions in the domain of temperament.

Among the better-known dimensions of temperament are the factors of confidence vs. inferiority feelings, restraint vs. rhathymia, objectivity vs. hypersensitivity, cheerfulness vs. depression, emotional immaturity vs. maturity, nervousness vs. composure, stability vs. cycloid disposition, ascendance vs. timidity, socialization vs. self-sufficiency, friendliness vs. hostility, and tolerance vs. criticalness.

The commonly found factor of masculinity vs. femininity is regarded as a syndrome type, with somewhat fluctuating properties, depending upon the aspects of sex differences emphasized. A consequence is that scores for the dimension obtained from different standard tests and inventories do not intercorrelate as well as one should expect of measures of the same trait.

A proposed general trait of personal tempo does not seem to hold up in correlational studies. There seem to be group factors of this type, but they may not be clearly distinct from psychomotor-speed factors. A proposed general trait of perseveration is not well supported. There are several factors, each of which seems to indicate one kind of inertia or rigidity, depending upon the area of behavior involved—psychomotor, perceptual, or intellectual. A proposed general factor of oscillation (or of variability of behavior) also lacks support. Personal consistency in variability of performance seems to be more specific than general. Where there appear to be group factors, the traits thus indicated may be better interpreted as something other than dimensions of variability.

There is much evidence supporting belief in three factors of suggestibility—primary, secondary, and prestige suggestibility. There are many puzzling exceptions, owing to widely fluctuating intercorrelations of tests of suggestibility. Further study of the tests and factors of suggestibility is needed, and more must be learned about the relationships of these factors to hypnotizability and to neurotic disposition.

Chapter 17

HORMETIC DIMENSIONS

THE HORMETIC dimensions of personality include all those dimensions that have to do more or less directly with motivation. Included under motivation are the biological drives, which are dependent upon organic needs. Because other needs develop through experience, we have many kinds of valued conditions, such as order, comfort, achievement, and freedom. We also have classes of valued activities, which means interests, avocational as well as vocational. More complex motivating conditions come under the heading of attitudes. Needs, interests, and attitudes constitute the major categories of hormetic dimensions.

DIMENSIONS OF NEED

A survey of the traits that can be called needs shows that they can be grouped roughly under five categories—*organic, environmental, achievement, self-determination,* and *social* needs.

Organic-need Dimensions

Most organic needs, such as those of hunger, thirst, and sex, fluctuate with time, depending upon the length of time since the most recent gratification or satiation. In this sense they belong in the class of determiners of behavior recognized in this volume as temporary organic conditions. In spite of these temporary fluctuations, it is possible to recognize that each person has a characteristic average level in each of these drives that is true of him over long periods of time, and hence the idea of organic-need traits can be accepted. A person could possibly be assessed as being relatively high or relatively low in his characteristic strength of drive in each of these directions.

HUNGERS FOR SUBSTANCES

There is popular recognition of the glutton, who seems to overvalue food in general and to demand unusual quantities of it. We are told that this may often be attributed to frustrations and lack of fulfillment of other motives rather than to the organic demand for nourishment. Whatever the source, a trait position seems to be roughly determined.

There is some question regarding the unitary nature of each of the recognized organic needs, hunger in particular. Young (1948) has shown that rats exhibit at least 11 different hungers for different substances (some of which are not food materials), including carbohydrates, fats, proteins, thiamin, riboflavin, salt, phosphorus, sodium, calcium, water, and oxygen. A rat that has been deprived of any of the food components for a time shows the effects of this by a decided preference for a food that contains it. Preferred foods are more "palatable" to such an organism; they are especially valued. A good hypothesis seems to be that when he is deficient in any component the rat learns which foods are most satisfying because those foods have the effect of reducing his particular needs. The important point for us here is that each specific need seems to operate relatively independently and hence is a basic unit of drive function.

It would probably be difficult to demonstrate corresponding unitariness of such very specific drives in humans. Even if we could do so, such specific drives could hardly become the basis for separate traits, and they therefore more properly remain among the temporary organic conditions. One implication, however, is that the so-called sex drive might also have a number of components, some of which are more highly valued or featured by different individuals. The fact that the drive comes under the single label of "sex" should not prevent us from looking for more basic components, with patterns of strengths and weaknesses.

FACTORS RELATED TO ORGANIC NEEDS

No serious attempts have been made to determine whether there are systematic individual differences with respect to characteristic levels of organic drives in general, either in terms of the major categories or in terms of more specific needs.[1] Incidental factor-analytical studies have revealed two or three that seem to depend upon organic needs.

Male sex drive

In naming this factor, it is qualified as "male" sex drive because it has been found only in analyses of behavior of males. It is to be expected that somewhat different indicators would be involved in the assessment of female sex drive. Three analyses of inventory scores and items have shown the kinds of self-reported behavior and feelings that characterize this factor: [2]

[1] The famous Kinsey reports (Kinsey et al. 1948, 1953), of course, have presented dramatic data indicating wide individual differences in strength of sex drive.
[2] Cattell (1950a); Barnes (1952); Cattell and Miller (1952).

Has sex drive (e.g., not troubled with doubt about sexual adequacy)
Favors sex predation (e.g., believes men are superior to women)
Has antifeminine feelings (e.g., believes woman's place is in the home)
Wants to make love to a beautiful woman
Likes sex appeal in a woman
Likes a novel with love interest

There is also some indication that the factor is inversely related to a desire for cleanliness.

There is some suspicion that the factor found by Barnes and that found by Cattell are somewhat distinct. The former, characterized by the first three indicators, plus the reference to cleanliness, may reflect what Freud has called the "phallic" level of development. The latter seems to reflect the romantic aspects that Freud regarded as the more mature male-sex manifestation. Thus, we may have two male-sex factors, but probably with considerable correlation between them.

General activity: A general tendency to be physically active and energetic

In human subjects the indicators have been in the form of responses to inventory items: [3]

Exhibits a rapid pace (e.g., eats and walks rapidly)

Exhibits energy (e.g., feels bubbling over with excess energy)

Has a drive for activity (e.g., keeps "on the go"; can turn out a lot of work)

Likes action (e.g., happiest when involved in rapid action)

What seems to be a similar factor is found in ratings of behavior of young children.[4] A similar factor has been found from behavior tests given to dogs [5] and to rats.[6] Large individual differences have been found in rats in running tests, such as amount of running in a squirrel cage. The least active rat in one study ran only 60 feet in 15 days, whereas the most active rat ran about 20 miles.[7]

Experiments with lower animals tend to throw light on the nature of the factor of general activity. It appears that any one of a number of organic drives can be contributory to the production of the general level of physical activity. The level of activity at the moment may be a joint resultant from several motives. Correlations of about .4 have been found

---

[3] Guilford and Guilford (1939*b*); Adcock (1952); Guilford, Christensen, Bond, and Sutton (1954); Morris and Jones (1955); Guilford and Zimmerman (1956).

[4] Koch (1934); Richards and Ellington (1942).

[5] Royce (1955); Anastasi et al. (1955).

[6] Rundquist (1933); Anderson (1937); Hall and Lindsley (1938); Hall (1941).

[7] Rundquist (1933).

between a general-activity score and measures of strengths of drives.[8] A correlation of .72 was found with metabolic rate.[9] Correlations of activity scores with blood-sugar level and with body weight were zero.[10] A characteristically "tuned-up" physiological state seems related to high position on the dimension of general activity.[11]

There is some evidence of the hereditary basis for the trait of general activity. Two selected strains of rats were bred over several generations, the most active and the least active being selected to become parents of the next generation.[12] The two strains progressively separated in activity level, the difference becoming more marked for females than for males, until the inactive group ceased to reproduce and the experiment was over.

Validity information for measures of the factor of general activity comes from two sources. Scores for it correlated .27 with a criterion of leadership behavior in the form of student activities and .23 with assessments in a leaderless-group-discussion test.[13] Stogdill (1948) reported "physical activeness" to be correlated with criteria of leadership behavior in the range .20 to .47. From scattered unpublished sources we gain the impression that a person with a very high score in this factor will not adapt so well to sedentary work, and that a person with a very low score will have difficulty in getting his work completed under pressure of time. Some of those with very low scores have been found to suffer from a hypothyroid condition, hence any person with a very low score should probably have a medical examination.

There is some evidence for a more narrow physical-activity factor that might be called an interest in physical fitness or an interest in athletics. The person high on this dimension says, in effect, that he likes to take part in (noncompetitive) sports (in order to promote health and healing) and to command others.[14] Women also indicate such a factor by expressing interest in tennis, swimming, and horseback riding.[15] If this factor indicates need for physical exercise as such, it belongs here among the organic needs. If it turns out that the emphasis should be on liking for athletics, however, it is more properly classified among the interests.

[8] Anderson (1937).
[9] Hall and Lindsley (1938).
[10] *Ibid.*
[11] A factor that Cattell (1946*a*) has called "surgency" probably comes close to general activity, but as nearly as one can tell from logical considerations, his surgency is a syndrome type, for it seems to involve the qualities of rhathymia, impulsiveness, and cheerfulness.
[12] Rundquist (1933).
[13] Bass, Wurster, Doll, and Clair (1953).
[14] Guilford, Christensen, Bond, and Sutton (1954).
[15] Gernes (1940).

Environmental-need Factors

This group of factors contains those that put the emphasis upon environmental conditions desired by the individual. There are three such factors.

> *Need for a soft environment:* Desire for a comfortable, orderly, warm, approving, and supporting environment

One analysis of inventory scores indicates liking for quite a number of favorable environmental conditions, including: [16] continual feedback from others, approval of others, comfort, others persuaded to his point of view, affection from others, orderly surroundings, system and planned activities, having friends, and cleanliness.

The picture given by this list of qualities is one of general infantilism. While dependence is suggested, this does not seem to be the most distinguishing feature. Besides, there is another factor, which we shall see later, that better qualifies for the name "dependence." Individuals who have this need for a soft environment very strongly are unable to face the rough places in life and would have difficulty in adjusting to camp life, to some aspects of military life, or to an unfriendly group.

> *Meticulousness:* Need for order, system, neatness, and cleanliness

Three analyses of inventory scores show the following list of indicators: [17]

Likes things kept in order

Is meticulous (e.g., believes it is important to have things done "just so")

Likes planning (e.g., prefers to follow a set plan in his work)

Likes cleanliness (e.g., likes to wash his hands before every meal)

Has an attitude of "no nonsense" (e.g., believes workers waste too much time joking as they work)

A cluster of symptoms of patients seems to indicate the same dimensions.[18] Such a person is careful and painstaking, concerned about order and system, sets high standards for himself, and highly motivated for achievement. The factor was called "conscientiousness," but it appears to be meticulousness confounded with the factor of general activity. The two factors may be correlated in the general population.

The factor meticulousness might have been called "need for order," but it seems clearly to be more than that. It also seems to share with the previous factor, need for a soft environment, a liking for order and

[16] Guilford, Christensen, Bond, and Sutton (1954). Gernes (1940) reported a factor that may be the same, with indicators in general that call for being aided.

[17] Holley (1951); Barnes (1952); Guilford, Christensen, Bond, and Sutton (1954). See also, Adcock (1952), who found a factor called "obsessional tendency."

[18] Lorr and Rubenstein (1955).

cleanliness. The reasons for valuing those conditions are probably different in the two cases. Order and cleanliness may be valued in the latter case because they make things easy and uncontaminated for the individual. They may be valued by the meticulous person more because they repre sent high standards of personal rectitude. There is some uncertainty about whether meticulousness should be classified among the needs or among the interests, since valued kinds of activities are also involved. The emphasis is upon the end products of the activities, which justifies the grouping of the factor here among the environmental needs, the end products being in the form of environmental conditions.

Meticulousness has shown significant relationships with measures of three intellectual factors—with correlations of $-.33$ with verbal comprehension, $-.22$ with logical evaluation, and $-.14$ with originality—when measures for all factors were composite scores.[19]

Need for attention: Desire to be noticed by others

In one analysis of inventory scores the following qualities characterize this need: [20]

Likes to receive recognition (e.g., to be in the news)

Likes to achieve status (e.g., to have prestige)

Likes to show off (e.g., doing queer things to attract attention)

Indulges in autistic thinking (e.g., dreams of doing heroic deeds)

Similar factors called "exhibitionism" [21] and "flashy exhibitionism" [22] have been reported, with similar indicators. From observations of behavior problems among boys, analysis indicated a similar factor with the qualities of attention-getting behavior, overaggressiveness, and bravado.[23]

From these pictures we gain the impression that the need is to be noticed for acceptable behavior if possible and for unacceptable behavior if necessary. The relation to behavior problems, and perhaps to crime, is fairly apparent. From the basic principles of learning we obtain the suggestion for the prevention of unwanted attention-demanding behavior —make sure that it is not rewarded.

Achievement-need Factors

During the past decade we have seen considerable interest and effort devoted to attempts to measure an assumed unitary trait of "need achievement." In the two decades preceding that we saw considerable research on attempts to measure "level of aspiration." In the former case, "achieve-

---

[19] Guilford, Christensen, Frick, and Merrifield (1957).

[20] Guilford, Christensen, Bond, and Sutton (1954).

[21] Gernes (1940).

[22] Barnes (1952).

[23] Hart et al. (1943).

ment" has not been very precisely defined, and in the latter case, the same is true of "aspiration." We may well ask, in the two cases, achievement of *what* and aspiration for *what?* Operationally, "what," in connection with aspiration level, has been excellent performance in this or that laboratory task of some kind. It has been found that aspiration to improve in such tasks depends upon the kind of task. The same may be true for need for achievement. The question of the generality of desire for achievement is one calling for correlational analysis. In what spheres of activity are there common or consistent individual differences in desire to excel or to succeed? The results thus far indicate three general variables. There are probably more.

General ambition: Desire to "succeed," to achieve fame and fortune

It may seem like the crudest common sense to propose that there is a variable of this kind to represent needs for achievement. But the empirical data lead to this conclusion. Two analyses of inventory scores show the following indicators: [24]

Has high general aspiration level (e.g., anticipates superior wealth and fame)

Has initiative (e.g., is resourceful leader in group activities)

Likes recognition and prestige (e.g., likes to be looked up to)

Is impatient (e.g., wishes time would go more rapidly)

Believes money is important (e.g., few things in life more important than money)

Does not believe in miracles

A similar factor, reported under the title of "self-assertion," appears to be much the same as the one labeled ambition here.[25]

If the list of qualities above included only the first, third, and fifth, one would be inclined to put this factor down as merely a general expression of a stereotype to which it is popular in our culture to subscribe. It may be that the factor represents little more than that, an expression of a personal ideal that has been adopted from the culture. Yet, it could hardly be denied that such ideals are effective; they bring out efforts where there might otherwise be little motivation. The other qualities tend to broaden the meaning of this variable somewhat. The people who have these ideals of personal success also show that they have drive, for they are impatient; they do something about it, for they take the initiative; and they do not look to outside help, for they do not believe in miracles.

Another kind of achievement is represented by the next factor, a more specialized kind, and yet one with considerable generality.

[24] Holley (1951); Guilford, Christensen, Bond, and Sutton (1954).
[25] Cattell and Miller (1952).

Persistent effort: Self-imposed urge to keep working at a task

This factor is found in behavior tests and has been noted by three investigators.[26] The factor has been found in populations of children as well as of adults.[27] The kinds of behavior tests and kinds of scores that indicate it are:

Time spent voluntarily in word building (given six letters)

Time spent in reading (where difficulty increases to the extent of the reading becoming impossible)

Picture Inhibition test (adding numbers in the presence of distracting pictures)

Persistence Adding (speed score taken late in a period of adding)

Nonvariability in Adding (standard deviation of 30 part scores)

There is some fairly recent information upon the validity of a test of persistent effort for predicting college grades.[28] The task was the solution of number-series problems. One score was the length of time the examinee kept on working voluntarily and another was the number of times he went back to try problems skipped earlier. The correlations of these two scores with average grades were .30 and .25. Using these scores in combination with aptitude scores would have increased accuracy of prediction of grades appreciably.

Endurance: Willingness to withstand discomfort or pain in order to achieve a goal

In tests of endurance increasing discomfort or pain is applied to the examinee, who is permitted to give up at any time. The score is the length of time he will continue to take the punishment. Two analyses have brought out the factor, both of which were designed as studies of persistence.[29] In both, the tests divided, some going with the preceding factor and some with this one. The tests that best define this factor are:

Withstanding pain from pressure of blunt point on the back of the hand

Withstanding pain from an electric shock

Maintaining handgrip pressure (at half of *E*'s maximum grip)

Holding the breath

Factors of Self-determination Needs

The next four factors owe their membership in the same category to the fact that in some way they are concerned with self-directed behavior. We can understand better what this means by seeing what the factors are.

26 Thornton (1939); Brogden (1940); Rethlingshafer (1942).
27 Rethlingshafer (1942).
28 French (1948).
29 Thornton (1939); Rethlingshafer (1942).

Need for Freedom: Desire to be free from restrictions, regulations, and restraints; to be a free agent

Found most commonly by analysis of inventory scores and items, this factor is characterized by the following attributes: [30]

Is a nonconformist (e.g., dislikes restraints and restrictions)

Dislikes organization and system (e.g., dislikes following a rigid schedule)

Dislikes order (e.g., believes a man should be allowed to leave his clothes scattered about the room)

Shows personal independence (e.g., likes to make his own decisions)

Other factors, probably the same as this one, are Whisler's (1934) "independence," Barnes' (1952) "flexible ascendance," and Lorr's (1951) "freedom from social regulation vs. favoring social codes and governmental organization," although the latter may be somewhat confounded with attitude toward religion. Two of Lorr's indicators were "nonmoralistic" and "pagan."

Self-reliance vs. dependence: Desire to depend upon one's self; to be a responsible agent

Another time-honored virtue receives scientific support in the factor of self-reliance vs. dependence. The bipolarity for this dimension is indicated by empirical data. A number of analyses of inventory-derived information indicate the scope of manifestations of this trait.[31] From adult populations we find the following associated attributes:

Is dependable (e.g., scrupulous in discharging his obligations)

Is self-reliant (e.g., depends upon his own judgment)

Does not crave attention or approval

Is not dependent upon others (e.g., does not go to others for aid or advice)

Is not subservient (e.g., not willingly submissive)

Does not expect to be waited on

At the high school level similar qualities pertain to the factor: [32] seldom late when he must get up without being called, dislikes being late for appointments, and conscientious in his work. And from analyses of observed symptoms we have this picture: [33] shows sense of responsibility, rarely blames others for his difficulties, has consideration for tomorrow, makes no use of complaints, shows concern for others, able to delay his impulses, and sees a task through. Cattell and Miller (1952) found a

---

[30] Guilford, Christensen, Bond, and Sutton (1954).

[31] Gernes (1940); Barnes (1952); Guilford, Christensen, Bond, and Sutton (1954).

[32] Stott (1938).

[33] Lorr and Rubenstein (1955).

factor that appears to be similar, which they called "appeal." Gordon (1951) reported a similar factor of "responsibility."

There is one reservation that may be expressed regarding this factor as well as others in this group that were found from responses to inventory items. From this source, the unity shown might be attributed to some extent to an *ideal* of behavior. The person admires and would like to attain the qualities that hang together to represent the factor. We have some evidence that the factor is something more than an ideal, however, in the fact that similar qualities hang together when observed and reported by outside observers, as in the study by Lorr and Rubenstein (1955). While it might be said that these observers, too, were responding in line with a stereotype of an ideal, it could also be said that they were merely recognizing an implicit unity in behavior.

> *Cultural conformity:* Acceptance of conventional ethical codes and
> a desire to see them observed

This factor represents a willing renunciation of self-direction in favor of direction by the code of the group, or an adoption of group precepts as principles of self-direction. From different kinds of assessments and from different age groups, we have abundant evidence of the existence of this factor. Let us begin with the attributes of cultural conformity as shown by analysis of information from inventories. The conforming person: [34]

Has urge to satisfy his conscience

Likes to conform to social policies and standards

Likes to see discipline maintained

Favors competition

Believes in honesty (e.g., in examinations)

Admires thoroughness and carefulness

Similar inventory-based factors have been called "acceptance of conventional ethical principles" [35] and "self-sentiment." [36] A similar factor was found by analysis of behavior tests: [37]

Success (*E* marks traits that he thinks are more promising of success.)

Stories Test (Each story has an ethical point, *E* to make ethical choices.)

Two analyses of observations of children indicate a similar factor. One was called "docility, conformity, conscientiousness," and had the following indicators: [38] accepting requests for help or participation, showing persistent effort, and participating in group work. The other had the

---

[34] Brogden (1940); Holley (1951); Barnes (1952); Guilford, Christensen, Bond, and Sutton (1954).

[35] Whisler (1934).

[36] Cattell and Miller (1952).

[37] Brogden (1940).

[38] Koch (1942).

following related, observed behaviors: [39] complying with routine, responding well to authority, respecting property rights, and facing reality.

It might have been natural to expect that the need for conformity to the group mores would be at the opposite pole from the need for freedom, since the latter implies a lack of conformity. This was the expectation in one study,[40] but the results turned out otherwise, with these two traits represented by different dimensions. One thing that separates the two traits is that cultural conformity has a strong ethical aspect, whereas need for freedom appears to have no such implication. The logical consequence is that a person may have an urge to conform to social and cultural mores and yet be a lover of freedom. In this sense, he is a nonconforming conformist. We may also have a person who is unready to accept the social and cultural mores and yet cares little for freedom. This kind of result should be a warning against accepting preconceived ideas regarding what attributes are direct opposites.

It might be supposed that cultural conformity has a negative relationship to creativity, particularly to the factor of originality. Such did not prove to be the case.[41] There was, however, a correlation of $-.21$ with a measure of verbal comprehension.

Honesty: Avoidance of lying and cheating

Although generally positive, but low, correlations have commonly been found among various tests designed to measure honesty, only one analysis has clearly brought out a factor of honesty.[42] The indicating tests were:

Peeping test (E cannot succeed without opening his eyes.)

Lie score (E scores his own paper in an information test in which some items have no answers.)

False Book List (E checks titles of books he has read.)

Overstatement (E states what he knows, then is tested on his knowledge.)

Honesty (an inventory on cheating in different situations)

As indicated in the definition, this factor, so far as we know, is confined to lying and cheating. We do not know whether it is sufficiently general to extend to stealing as well, since no tests offering opportunity to appropriate property belonging to others were analyzed with those in the list.

OTHER POSSIBLE CHARACTER FACTORS

It should have been clear before we progressed very far in this group of self-determination factors that most of them fall in the popular category of character traits. So far as the psychological point of view is concerned,

---

[39] Richards (1940).

[40] Guilford, Christensen, Bond, and Sutton (1954).

[41] Guilford, Christensen, Frick, and Merrifield (1957).

[42] Brogden (1940).

we cannot be directly concerned with character as a concept. A trait is an aspect of character when it pertains to ethical aspects of conduct. Science does not deal directly with ethical values; it does not undertake to say what behavior is right and what is wrong. This is an ethical decision. Since conduct is behavior, however, problems of character come under the examination of psychology along with other behavior. Those persons who are particularly concerned with conduct, good or bad, should find the factors of this group of particular interest.

Before we leave this group of self-determination factors, we need to consider the possibility that there are others. For example, Brogden (1940) reported a factor that he interpreted as "self-control." In the Character Inquiry studies of Hartshorne and May, tests of self-control played a prominent role. Brogden's self-control factor was defined by the following tests:

Slang C (a test of knowledge of slang terms)

Duty (*E* chooses between duty and pleasure or between negligence of duty and some punishment.)

Reading Preference (*E* ranked "wholesome" and "unwholesome" books for order of preference.)

Self-sufficiency (an inventory)

The factor is not listed here as an established primary trait because we are not certain that it is not actually some other factor already listed. In some respects it appears similar to the factor of restraint vs. rhathymia, mentioned in the preceding chapter. The latter represents a kind of generalized self-control or seriousness of purpose vs. letting one's self go.

Is there a *general* factor of character? Many years ago a general factor of character was reported by Webb (1915) and was called factor *w* for "will character," defined as persistence of motives. Spearman adopted it as a general factor of will power alongside his general intellectual factor *g*. Years later, Maller (1934) intercorrelated four kinds of tests used in the Character Inquiry study, including tests of honesty, helpfulness, self-control, and persistence. He concluded that the intercorrelations, though small, indicated one common factor—a general disposition of good character. The presence of some zero correlations in his table suggest that there must have been more than one factor. We have seen in the listing of factors above that there are separate factors of honesty and persistence, and Brogden found one called self-control (although it did not arise from the kind of self-control tests of the Character Inquiry). We shall see later one or two factors that might qualify, benevolence, for example. It seems likely, then, that when a thorough coverage is made of these and other kinds of character tests, analysis will show additional character factors. We already find more than one.

From common experience, however, we should expect positive correlations among the primary character factors, for the social pressures that do or do not bring about their development tend to operate on an all-or-none basis. Good character is held up as a single goal, including all areas of conduct. The inculcation of *principles* of conduct is usually attempted in a general way. The pressures are by no means uniform, and they come from different directions, so that exceptions are also learned. We therefore have apparent bases for both a general character factor and for group factors of character. Cattell (1946a) has consistently insisted upon a general factor of "stable character," and he is probably right. But it is in the nature of a higher-order factor, or a syndrome, with lower-order factors needed to complete the picture of structure in the area of personality traits known popularly as "character."

Factors of Social Needs

Social needs require other human individuals more or less directly in their satisfaction or fulfillment. It cannot be said that they are the only needs in which other human beings are involved in some way, for this also applies to some of the other traits mentioned in this chapter. The motives in the social-need group call for doing something *with* others, *for* others, or *to* others.

> *Gregariousness:* Liking to be with others, to participate in group activities

One could hardly think of a class of social-need factors without expecting to find in it a primary trait of gregariousness. This factor is also commonly called "sociability." In view of the definition, the chosen term is more appropriate, since "sociability" has too many popular connotations. The choice of "gregariousness" has no implication that the trait is instinctive; it could be or it could not. The finding of a factor tells us nothing about its origin.

From a number of analyses involving inventory methods we gain the following rather clear picture of this factor:

Likes social affairs
Likes to be with people
Likes to have friends and acquaintances
Likes to work with others
Finds people more stimulating than anything else

From observations of young children the following behaviors indicate gregariousness: [48] engages in cooperative play, converses with others, participates in group work, and does not play alone.

From other observations of young children we have information con-

---

[43] Koch (1942); Williams (1935).

cerning development of gregariousness.[44] The trait appears to increase in strength during ages one to five, with correlations of .6 to .7 being reported between ratings of amount of social behavior and age. In spite of universal social development, large individual differences exist at any age, and individual children are rather consistent from one year to another. As the amount of social behavior increases with development, the social-behavior manifestations tend to go in two directions—one toward a differentiation into friendliness vs. quarrelsomeness [45] and the other toward a differentiation described as sympathy vs. aggressiveness.[46] In either case, boys tend to go more in the direction of quarrelsomeness or aggressiveness. These differentiations suggest very strongly that other factors have come into the picture, factors resembling one or two that will be mentioned next or one in the preceding chapter—friendliness vs. hostility.

The factor of gregariousness has some rather obvious logical relationships to vocational-adjustment problems. A person with a very high score on this trait would probably be unhappy if his work did not involve contacts with other people. A person with a very low score on the trait might be unhappy if he had many face-to-face contacts. A person with a moderate score could probably adjust himself in either direction, if necessary.

In the prediction of college grades correlations of $-.28$ and $-.34$ have been reported.[47] There is consistent indication that the more sociable student makes lower average grades, as might have been predicted. In connection with the prediction of criteria of leadership behavior, correlations all the way from .10 to .98 have been reported, with a median value of .45.[48] It should be expected that the trait would be of more importance in face-to-face situations and where skills in interacting with people are needed in the process of leading. The more gregarious person has developed social skills that are assets in leading.

Benevolence: A kindly, generous, sympathetic, and sensitive attitude toward others

Inventory scores for the following qualities are indicators of the benevolent person: [49]

---

[44] Arrington (1943).
[45] Green (1933a, 1933b).
[46] Murphy (1937).
[47] Goedinghaus (1954); Bass, Wurster, Doll, and Clair (1953).
[48] Stogdill (1948).
[49] Holley (1951). A similar factor has been reported by Harding (1941), who called it "idealism," by Gordon (1951), who called it "generosity," and by Adcock (1952), who called it "kindliness."

Is sympathetic (e.g., the fellow who is picked on arouses his sympathy)

Is generous (e.g., believes in being a "good Samaritan")

Is moral (e.g., believes people would be better off if they paid more attention to what is right and wrong)

Is sensitive (e.g., wants the other person to think well of him; would dislike hurting another person's feelings)

Need for discipline: Desire to have strict discipline enforced

Found in two analyses, this factor is related to a limited number of relevant inventory-score qualities.[50]

Is severe (e.g., favors maximum jail sentences for "hit-and-run" drivers)

Is punctual (e.g., believes most people would not be happier if they could throw away their timepieces)

Is strict (e.g., believes that a good leader is strict)

Aggressiveness: Need to coerce others, with inclination toward physical violence

The term "aggressiveness" has been used very ambiguously in descriptions of individuals. It is sometimes regarded as a favorable trait and sometimes as an unfavorable one. When applied in the favorable sense, aggressiveness has probably referred to the factor of ascendance vs. timidity. As applied to the factor in question, it takes on a quality that is generally frowned upon in modern culture. A factor of this kind is found in human subjects of widely varying ages and in lower animals. Let us begin with the attributes as indicated from inventory results: [51]

Overt aggression (e.g., believes that attack is the best defense)

Coercion (e.g., would like to make a witness talk)

Sadism (e.g., believes that husbands and wives should resort to "caveman" tactics now and then)

Biting (e.g. has had habit of chewing his pencil)

Defiant resentment (e.g., has often violated school regulations)

Indirect expression of hostility (e.g., likes to see the villain in a movie punished)

From observations of behavior problems of boys and girls we find the following cluster of attributes: [52] temper tantrums, assaultiveness, violence, fighting, quarrelsomeness, negativism, overaggressiveness, destructiveness, and incorrigibility.

From observed behavior of young children we are told that there is a pattern involving the following qualities: [53] pouting and sulking, in-

[50] Holley (1951); Guilford, Christensen, Frick, and Merrifield (1957).

[51] Brogden (1940); Cattell (1946a); Barnes (1952); Guilford, Christensen, Bond, and Sutton (1954). Brogden uses the term "hard-boiled aggression" and Cattell speaks of "hypomanic aggressiveness."

[52] Hart et al. (1943); Lorr and Jenkins (1953).

[53] Koch (1942).

dulgence in indirect attacks, much flitting about, indulgence in verbal attacks, and indulgence in physical attacks.

A fighting-pattern factor has been reported from observations of the behavior of dogs [54] and of rats,[55] with the following indicators in the latter case: biting, showing or gnashing the teeth, jumping at tormenter, hissing, laying back ears, fighting, erection of hair, etc.

The kind of aggression in question is obviously the type involved in consequence of frustration in the well-known frustration-aggression hypothesis. It is one of several common reactions to frustrating circumstances. From the picture of the factor found in human subjects we have the impression that the expression of the trait is not always overt. There are covert or indirect ways of showing the trait. It is probable that people more prone to the indirect expressions of aggressiveness are low on the dimension of ascendance or some other dimension.

One indicator of some interest in the first list of qualities given above is the tendency of biting. In one analysis in which the factor was found, an investigation was being made of certain Freudian hypotheses regarding personality development.[56] A collection of items was included on tendencies toward biting habits and satisfactions from biting and chewing, as hypothesized residuals from the oral-biting stage. The relationships between the biting score and other indicators of aggressiveness seem to support Freudian theory at this point. There was very little support on most other points.

DIMENSIONS OF AVOCATIONAL INTERESTS

As was pointed out in Chapter 9, the use of vocational categories has been, for practical purposes, the dominating practice in the measurement of interests. It was also pointed out that the vocational-interest traits fall far short of covering the whole range of human interests. We shall now give more substance to the latter assertion by surveying first the factors of interest that have no direct or obvious connection with vocations.

The avocational interests pertain to the things human beings like to do or find satisfaction in doing. The emphasis is on classes of activities, which are liked or not liked in fairly reasonable groupings under the different factors. We shall begin with dimensions of interest that have more to do with selected overt activities, followed by a group that emphasizes certain properties of activities, then a group having to do with aesthetic appreciation, and finally a group having to do with different kinds of thinking.

---

[54] Royce (1955).
[55] Hall (1941).

[56] Barnes (1952).

Factors of Interest in Overt Activities

> *Liking for adventure vs. security:* Deriving satisfaction from risk-taking vs. from security with tolerance of monotony

This bipolar dimension has been found in three analyses, with the following typical indicators: [57]

Likes to explore (e.g., to cross the Sahara desert)

Likes to take personal risks (e.g., to run river rapids in a small boat)

Likes to travel

Does not avoid harm (e.g., rough and dangerous games)

Dislikes monotony (e.g., would rather not settle down and spend rest of his life in one place)

It is not easy to say where the emphasis should be placed in interpreting this factor. It should probably not be placed too strongly on tolerance of monotony, for there is another factor, to be mentioned shortly, that involves liking for variety and has been found in the same analysis with this factor. We can also then say that the interests in travel and exploration exhibited in connection with this factor are not so much for the sake of change of scene as for the opportunities they afford for thrills arising from experiencing danger. The stay-at-home monotony at the opposite pole is disliked, not because of lack of variety, but because it offers no opportunity for risk taking.

From some information based upon analysis of animal behavior we may have further light on this factor in men. A factor that could be designated as boldness vs. timidity was indicated in results with rats.[58] The pattern of timid behavior was shown by reactions such as hiding, squealing, trembling, refusing to eat, jumping, freezing, and so on. This suggests a trait based upon what was formerly regarded as an instinct of fear, some individuals being "born" more fearful than others. By breeding two strains of rats, in fact, an investigator produced increasing separation into bold and timid strains.[59]

Although we do not have among these results positive descriptions of the bold rats, presumably they would show their boldness by tendencies to explore unfamiliar places without hesitation. This would be the counterpart to the adventure-loving attribute in humans. Whether rats experience thrills from escape from risks is something else again. Risk taking for thrills would seem to be something more than curiosity.

In men this adventure-loving disposition and risk-taking urge may be

[57] Guilford, Christensen, Bond, and Sutton (1954). Gernes (1940), in analysis of items from the Strong Vocational Interest Blank for Women, reported a factor that could be called "desire for security."

[58] Hall (1941).

[59] Hall (1938).

one of the most important traits for the business executive. As distinguished from those lower in an organization, the executive is the one who must make the decisions that are accompanied with the most risks. Similar inclinations to take rare chances may be a characteristic of the more original and trail-blazing scientists.[60] The adventure vs. security factor has not been found related to performance in tests of fluency, flexibility, or originality, however.[61] From Stogdill's (1948) review we learn that assessments of a trait of "adventuresomeness" have correlated from .57 to .78 with criteria of leadership behavior. Where risk taking is an important need in the situation, the successful leader seems to require a high position on this factor.

Liking for diversions: Deriving satisfaction from play, amusements, and other diversions

According to one analysis, the person who is high on this dimension: [62]

Likes to play (nonathletic)

Likes amusements (as a spectator)

Likes romanticism (idealized or fanciful events)

Likes athletics (participation in noncompetitive sports)

Likes to solve puzzles

A similar factor found among women is indicated by preferences for movie magazines, romantic stories, amusement parks, women's pages of a newspaper, formal affairs, and visits to the zoo.[63] The great variety of things for which there is common expression of liking indicates the generality of this interest, and the common element is clearly some form of diversion.

Factors of Interest in Activities with Certain Properties

Liking for variety: Satisfaction from change of task, activity, or scene

In two analyses the person high on this trait shows it by saying that he likes a position with varied tasks, he likes to deal with varied and unusual objects, and he enjoys travel and nature.[64] Not much more can be said about the trait, except to point out its possible relationships to creativity. There is some reason to expect that persons who are fluent thinkers, flexible thinkers, or original thinkers might also have a strong interest in variety. Results show that scores for liking for variety correlate zero with measures of fluency and originality factors, and correlate an insignificant .19 with scores for semantic spontaneous flexibility.[65] The

---

60 McClelland (1956).

61 Guilford, Christensen, Frick, and Merrifield (1957).

62 Guilford, Christensen, Bond, and Sutton (1954).

63 Gernes (1940).

64 Guilford and Guilford (1939*b*); Guilford, Christensen, Bond, and Sutton (1954).

65 Guilford, Christensen, Frick, and Merrifield (1957).

relation to figural spontaneous flexibility is unknown. It is interesting that, of all these aptitude factors, that of semantic spontaneous flexibility is the one whose definition stresses a *diversification* of responses. The lack of correlation of this interest factor with originality indicates that the latter factor is not a desire to be different for the sake of variety.

> *Liking for precision:* Preference for activity calling for exactness and attention to detail

As reported from one study using inventory scores, the following variables apply to this factor: [66]

Likes exactness (e.g., in comparing finger prints)

Likes laboratory work in science (e.g., work with a microscope)

Likes detailed operations (e.g., work with precision tools, as in engraving and etching)

Likes number computations

Appreciative Interests

The following factors are listed in order of decreasing generality. There seems to be a broad cultural interest; a less-general factor of aesthetic interest, which fairly covers the arts; and some special factors for appreciation of various visual-art forms and for appreciation of different brands of humor. Thus, within the area of appreciative interests alone, we find a good example of what seems to be a hierarchy of traits. More details concerning the nature of this hierarchy awaits empirical studies of intercorrelations among these traits.

> *General culture:* Liking for intellectual, artistic, and civic activities

The person who stands high on this dimension of general-culture interest indicates by inventory scores that he: [67]

Likes to take part in civic affairs (e.g., develop plan to get people to register for voting)

Likes writing persuasive material (e.g., send letter to the newspaper explaining his views)

Likes writing explanatory material (e.g., prepare booklet explaining the traffic laws)

Appreciates literature

Likes the social sciences

Appreciates drama, music, and the arts

Likes to write something of literary merit

---

[66] Guilford, Christensen, Bond, and Sutton (1954). See also Gernes (1940) who found a factor that emphasized liking for number computations.

[67] Guilford, Christensen, Bond, and Sutton (1954). Brogden (1952) reported a factor called "culture for its own sake," and Cattell and Miller (1952) reported a factor that seems similar but which for some reason they called "curiosity."

Aesthetic appreciation: Enjoyment of art in all forms as a spectator

The earliest analysis involving interests in various artistic matters demonstrated that liking art as an observer or consumer is one thing and liking to express one's self or to be a producer of art is something else.[68] Subsequent analyses have fully supported this distinction.[69] Furthermore, factor analysis does not show that there are further breakdowns of interest along the lines of the different arts—graphic arts, writing, music, and drama—but that interest in one form of art is likely to carry with it interest in the other forms. This is true to such an extent, at least in terms of responses to inventory items, that the results show one factor of aesthetic appreciation and one of aesthetic expression. The latter we shall find classified among the vocational-interest factors. It does have its avocational significance, too, but strong interest in artistic expression is likely to seek appropriate vocational outlets.

It would be natural to ask whether there is a substantial correlation between the two aesthetic-interest factors, and the answer is that probably there is. It is quite conceivable that there are people who have a high degree of appreciation for art and yet who have little urge to try to produce it. On the other hand, it is hardly conceivable that there are people who have a strong urge to express themselves artistically but have little or no appreciation to go with it. The relationship is thus likely to be rather one-sided. It may be that those with high appreciation but low desire to produce art have come to realize that they lack the necessary talents, or have never discovered that they have any latent talents. In general, it is found that the correlations between corresponding interests and aptitudes are not very strong. We shall return to this general problem later.

SOME SPECIAL AESTHETIC-APPRECIATION FACTORS

A factor of appreciation of a particular property of art has been found several times. It can be called *liking for simplicity vs. complexity.* It has been found in connection with preferences for silhouette figures,[70] for poems,[71] and for designs and pictures.[72] Relationships with other rated traits have been pointed out; one relationship of particular interest is that those who prefer complex designs are more likely to be original.[73]

A number of special, unverified factors have been found in a study of preferences for different silhouette figures.[74] Individuals could be typed

[68] Lurie (1937).
[69] Gernes (1940); Brogden (1952); Guilford, Christensen, Bond, and Sutton (1954).
[70] Harsh et al. (1939).
[71] Eysenck (1940).
[72] Guilford and Holley (1949); Eysenck (1941a, 1947).
[73] Barron (1952, 1953).
[74] Harsh et al. (1939).

in terms of the classes of forms that they tended to prefer. One group tended to favor figures with rounded contours, to prefer, for example, octagons to squares or triangles. A second group tended to prefer figures showing symmetry, either bilateral or rotational. A figure with rotational symmetry might be a circular one with repeated identical projections, such as a rimless wheel with spokes. A third group seemed partial to objects with sharp or upward-reaching points. These three factors, confined to silhouette figures so far as we know, suggest that there may be other factors that could be discovered in the area of aesthetic experience. This baffling phenomenon in behavior may turn out to be describable in terms of a number of dimensions of appreciation.

FACTORS OF HUMOR

Probably the best factor analysis that has been done of varieties of humor is that of Andrews (1943). The factors and their definitions are: [75]

a. *Derisive humor:* Laughter at weaknesses (particularly stupidity) in others, moral weaknesses excluded

b. *Immoral humor:* Laughter at debauchery and disgusting situations

c. *Insight humor:* Laughter at sudden insight into a puzzling situation

d. *Pun humor:* Laughter at a play on words or ideas

e. *Risque humor:* Laughter at sex jokes (probably those with some subtlety)

f. *Incongruity humor:* Laughter at ridiculous situations, the ludicrous, and "wisecracks"

Examples of these six types of jokes or laugh-provoking situations are easy to find. Factors *a, d,* and *f* have been indicated in some experimental work by Kambouropoulou (1926), and factor *e* in an analysis by Eysenck (1942). From the same sources there are some indications that we may have two higher-order humor factors. Kambouropoulou distinguishes between "personal" and "impersonal" humor. The former involves laughter at individuals and the latter, laughter at situations. Eysenck (1943, 1947) distinguishes between "orectic" humor and "cognitive" humor. Orectic humor is shown by preference for "funny," sex, and aggressive jokes, to use Eysenck's terminology, whereas cognitive humor is shown by preferences for complex and "clever" jokes. These two classes are not so far from those of Kambouropoulou.[76]

The popular conception, shared by some psychologists, is that there is

---

[75] It should not be assumed that these six factors exhaust the varieties of humor; there may be others.

[76] The factors found by Cattell and Luborsky (1947) do not agree with those of other investigators, with the possible exception of their factor of "resigned derision," and their factor of "urbane sophistication," which might be equivalent to Andrews' factor of insight humor.

one unitary "sense-of-humor" trait. A person has a sense of humor or he has not. When a holder of this view is pressed for a more precise definition of humor, he is likely to stress one or more of the factors listed above. Perhaps the one or ones stressed in his conception are those in which he himself is stronger. Perhaps when he admits that another person has a "sense of humor" he means that that person is strongest in those forms that he himself appreciates. Or he may regard anyone as having a sense of humor who laughs at least at one kind of joke; it may not matter which one. This would be an implicit recognition that there are varieties of humor and that a personal sense of humor involves a different pattern of humor appreciations in different individuals.

Down the ages different theories of humor and laughter have emphasized different types of humor, often setting one type up as the model for all humor. Each theory might have been correct as far as it went, but probably none went far enough. Of all the more prominent theories, that of Freud probably accounts for more of the types than any other. He proposed essentially the idea that we find things funny or laughable if they suddenly relieve us of some of our tensions, which are due to repressions, restrictions, or feelings of guilt. We make stupid mistakes, hence when we see others doing the same we laugh. We want to commit certain immoral acts but do not permit ourselves to do so, or we have committed the acts and feel guilty about them, hence we laugh at moral lapses of others. We like puns because they provide sudden escapes from the restrictions of conventional terminology and expression. We like risque humor for the vicarious reliefs that it provides. The other two varieties of humor, insight humor and incongruity humor, are not as easily accounted for in terms of Freudian theory.

There are some indications of relationships between certain humor factors and other traits of temperament as well as interests.[77] Individuals with a tendency toward rhathymia (of the restraint vs. rhathymia factor) showed preferences for risque humor and pun humor. Sex humor was also preferred by those who are more sociable and those who are low on the Theoretical scale of the Allport-Vernon Study of Values. Incongruity humor seemed to be preferred by those who are high on the Aesthetic scale of the same inventory. The correlations were high enough to be of some theoretical interest and they add a little information regarding the organization of personality structure. Additional information is needed for more meaningful interpretations.

Factors of Interest in Thinking

There has been a growing list of factors that emphasize interest in different kinds of thinking activity. Some kinds of thinking appeal more

[77] Cattell and Luborsky (1947); Grizwok and Scodel (1956).

to certain individuals and other kinds to other individuals. When we quiz individuals in a searching manner regarding their likes and dislikes for different specific acts of thinking, and when we intercorrelate their responses to groups of such questions, we find some interesting and apparently significant dimensions of interests, some better demonstrated than others.

Reflectiveness: Liking to indulge in meditative, ruminative, and philosophical types of thinking

This factor has sometimes been referred to as "thinking introversion," indicating a tendency to withdraw from the outer world into an inner world of thought. Since many other types of thinking also have the implication of introversion, it is better to accept the name given to the factor here. Indicative inventory scores are: [78]

Likes serious thinking (e.g., likes to discuss serious questions with friends)

Analyzes self and others (e.g., often speculates about why people behave as they do)

Frequently meditates (e.g., likes to have time to be alone with his thoughts)

Reflectiveness has shown small relationships to some aptitude factors. When scores for both are correlated, the correlations are approximately .20 with logical evaluation and expressional fluency, and .22 and .25, respectively, with semantic spontaneous flexibility and originality.[79] Scores for reflectiveness have correlated .34 with average grades in college.[80] Thus, the person who shows a liking for reflective thinking is likely to show some intellectual superiority in one or more ways.

Autistic thinking: Enjoyment of wishful, fanciful thinking that serves the end of enhancing self-esteem

Common inventory indicators show that the person high on the autistic-thinking scale: [81]

Appreciates humor (probably of the derisive type, e.g., likes to watch circus clowns)

Likes autistic thinking (e.g., dreams of heroic actions performed by himself)

Shows indirect expression of aggression (e.g., would like to see disliked person getting a traffic ticket)

[78] Guilford and Guilford (1939a); Brogden and Thomas (1943); Guilford and Zimmerman (1956).

[79] Guilford, Christensen, Frick, and Merrifield (1957).

[80] Goedinghaus (1954).

[81] Guilford, Christensen, Bond, and Sutton (1954). Other factors that may be much the same are reported by Mosier (1937) and by Harding (1941).

Likes amusements (e.g., likes to have fun)

Should it be demonstrated some time in the future that this dimension is bipolar, the opposite quality might be called "realistic thinking."

A syndrome of behavior symptoms of young children that have been identified with autistic thinking include ocular mannerisms, lack of compliance, daydreaming, playing alone, and playing with fingers.[82]

Rigorous thinking: Deriving satisfaction from thinking of a logical or mathematical character

When first found, this factor was called "liking for thinking," since it was the first of its kind.[83] The finding of a number of other factors of interest in thinking has called for a more differentiating name. The common indicators from inventories are: [84]

Likes mathematical thinking (e.g., to study algebra or geometry)

Likes logical thinking (e.g., to look for errors of reasoning in an argument)

Likes organizing and system (e.g., to design a new and efficient administrative system)

Likes solving problems (e.g., to plan strategy in a bridge game)

Likes to solve puzzles

It is not surprising to find that scores for the factor rigorous thinking correlate with scores for general reasoning and for logical evaluation to the extent of .15 and .22, respectively.[85] If we may accept the hypothesis that the Theoretical score from the Allport-Vernon Study of Values bears a substantial relationship to rigorous thinking, we have evidence that the factor has some relation to criteria of leadership, based upon correlations ranging .23 to .30.[86]

Recent unverified analysis of inventory scores from items pertaining to types of thinking hitherto unexplored by factorial methods indicates possible additional dimensions of thinking interest.[87] They happen to parallel some of the categories of thinking aptitudes mentioned in Chapter 15. Two of these factors will be mentioned here.

Convergent thinking is indicated by scores designed to measure goal-directed thinking (e.g., likes to choose one method of solution and follow it through), decisiveness in others (e.g., a strong person will be able to make up his mind even on the most difficult questions), and decisiveness

---

[82] Koch (1942).

[83] Guilford and Guilford (1939a). Whisler's (1934) factor, "criticalness and interest in truth," may be the same.

[84] Guilford, Christensen, Bond, and Sutton (1954); Guilford, Christensen, Frick, and Merrifield (1957).

[85] Guilford, Christensen, Frick, and Merrifield (1957).

[86] Carter and Nixon (1949b).

[87] Guilford, Christensen, Frick, and Merrifield (1957).

in one's self (e.g., have no difficulty in making up his mind). Scores for this factor correlated .23 with scores for the factor of general reasoning, which it will be remembered has to do with problem solving.

Divergent thinking is indicated by scores designed to measure adaptive, divergent thinking (e.g., likes to examine a new idea from all possible angles) and dilettantism (e.g., likes conversation that flits from one thing to another). Scores for this factor correlated .16 with scores for originality.

INTOLERANCE OF AMBIGUITY AS AN INTEREST DIMENSION

The University of California group that has devoted considerable effort to the study of what they call the "authoritarian personality" has made much of a hypothesized dimension called "intolerance of ambiguity." More will be said regarding the first of these two concepts later. We shall consider the second here because it apparently belongs with the general class of thinking-interest traits.

In theorizing about the trait intolerance of ambiguity, Frenkel-Brunswik (1949) has speculated about its origin in young children. It is said to depend largely upon how children are handled by their parents. Some children are able to see both the good and bad features of their parents, while other children cannot do this. The latter must repress one of the two views of their parents, for such children tend to see their parents as all good or all bad. The kind of parents who are likely to foster this outcome apply very strict, threatening, and unenlightening discipline which imposes external controls and the routine learning of rules of conduct. Children who develop under this regimen generalize their tendency to dichotomize. Other things, too, are regarded either as all good or all bad, including people in general. Thus do strong ethnic prejudices develop, according to this theory.

A factor analysis of inventory scores has lent some support to the concept.[88] It has shown a factor whose two definitive scores were Black-White Thinking (e.g., feels there are just two ways to attack any problem —the right way and the wrong way) and Need for Definiteness (e.g., does not like things to be indefinite and uncertain).

It may or may not be significant that the factor proved to be negatively correlated with a score for self-confidence (−.43) and positively with a score for depression (.33). The factor also correlated significantly with scores for thinking abilities, including associational fluency (−.15), originality (−.11), and the important verbal-intellectual factor of verbal comprehension (−.21). From this we obtain the impression that the person who strongly dislikes ambiguity is likely to be less intelligent and particularly less creative.

[88] Guilford, Christensen, Frick, and Merrifield (1957).

Interests of Young Children

Little attention has been given to dimensions of interest in children. One pioneer factor study is worth mentioning for its attempt in this direction.[89] Analyses were appropriately made in groups of boys and girls separately, both in the fourth grade. Unfortunately, the variables analyzed involved what children dislike rather than what they like, hence the factors appear to be aversions. They are represented by classes of activities or work that boys do not regard appropriate for boys and that girls do not regard appropriate for girls. Boys at that educational level characteristically reject things that girls like to do and girls reject things that boys like to do. A much more comprehensive analysis, stressing positive preferences, needs to be done.

Relations of Interests to Aptitudes

At several places in this section we have had occasion to consider some relations between interest dimensions and aptitude dimensions. This is an important general problem that has received considerable attention in the past because of the interest of vocational psychologists in it. Study of the problem has been on a very unsatisfactory basis until recent years because there were no well-defined variables of either interests or aptitudes. We have seen a growing tendency for factors in the one area to be paralleled by factors in the other. This situation makes more urgent and more inviting a reexamination of the whole problem.

Correlations between interest and aptitude variables have been typically quite small, even when there is logical correspondence between pairs of traits correlated.[90] Perhaps the best study to date, and the one showing higher-than-usual correlations, is that of Wesley, Corey, and Stewart (1950). They used scores from the Kuder Preference Record (Vocational) as measures of interests. Although the Kuder categories do not correspond very fully with interest factors, they are operational variables with recognized meanings. The investigators attempted to use parallel tests of abilities, including such tests as the Meier Art Judgment test, the Seashore tests of musical talent, and the Minnesota Test for Clerical Workers. Information tests were given in the areas of science, literature, and mechanics.

The correlations of corresponding pairs of variables averaged .30 when the Kuder raw scores were used. The reader may recall the discussion of the peculiarity of the Kuder scores mentioned in Chapter 9, to the effect that they evaluate each person's various interests around his own average rather than around the average of his group. To take this into

[89] Tyler (1955).
[90] For example, see Adkins and Kuder (1940).

account, these investigators applied two different procedures. They converted the aptitude scores also to the ipsative kind, with each student's aptitude scores distributed around his own mean. The correlations of corresponding pairs of scores then rose for the different traits to produce an average of .42. The second procedure was to compute a correlation for each and every student separately, each student having seven pairs of scores. These correlations ranged from −.57 to 1.00, with an average of .46. These results are more like what we should expect where correlations are between certain broad, well-recognized areas of interests and abilities. If there were not considerable agreement, we should have many more people who are frustrated because their interests and abilities are inconsistent. There is sufficient disagreement, even so, to require assessment of both aptitudes and interests.

Considering all kinds of studies of relationships between corresponding interests and aptitudes, we may extract a few more general conclusions. One is that such correlations within *persons* are higher than correlations within *populations*. The other is that correlations are higher between recognized *patterns* of interests and recognized *patterns* of aptitudes than between single, corresponding dimensions. This is seen in the comparison of the correlations mentioned earlier between certain thinking-interest factors and thinking-aptitude factors with the correlations involving the Kuder scores and corresponding measures of ability. Some of the latter were also measures of achievement, which should give higher correlations.

Gebhard (1949a) has suggested a plausible theoretical basis for expecting correlations between corresponding interest and aptitude factors. It is thought to be a matter of rewards and lack of rewards in learning to perform different kinds of tasks. Gebhard hypothesized that tasks should rise in attractiveness when the individual succeeds, whether or not he expects to succeed, and they should fall in attractiveness when he expects to succeed but fails. He may fail for lack of the necessary aptitude or aptitudes. We can also bring into the picture the phenomenon of generalization. When a task becomes more or less attractive, similar tasks, in other words, *classes* of tasks, share the change in attractiveness. Repetitions of such experiences serve to strengthen the interest thus developed, or rather to confirm the individual's trait position on the scale of that trait. Gebhard presented some experimental evidence in support of his hypothesis, finding the greatest changes in attractiveness of tasks when expectation and degree of success were in opposite directions.

DIMENSIONS OF VOCATIONAL INTEREST

The meanings of vocational-interest factors will be so clear from their very familiar names that they do not require definition. A brief mention of the chief areas of activity involved in each case will sharpen the boundaries of each trait. For convenience, these factors can be roughly grouped according to familiar socioeconomic categories.

Professional-level Interest Factors

The vocational-interest factors do not compose a numerous group. Only three appear at the professional level—interests in *science,* in *aesthetic expression,* and in *social welfare.*

Scientific interest

Interest in science is shown by high scores on inventory variables indicating liking for scientific theory, scientific investigation, laboratory work, mechanical designing, social science studies, and theory in general.[91] Relationship with the factor of rigorous thinking (logical and mathematical) is suggested by correlational information. There is also some indication of relationship with the factor of need for precision.

Aesthetic expression

In the preceding section we saw that there is a factor of aesthetic appreciation distinct from, but in some intimate way related to, this factor of aesthetic expression. The inventory indicators include liking for performing or composing music, writing things of literary merit, participating in drama, producing graphic-art effects, writing persuasive material, and producing humorous effects.[92]

A score for aesthetic expression has correlated significantly and reasonably with certain aptitude-factor scores, namely, .16 with expressional fluency, .26 with originality, and .25 with verbal comprehension.[93]

Social welfare

Let us begin by presenting the details of the composite picture. Those high on social-welfare interest are concerned about the welfare of others, particularly of the "underprivileged." They like to explain things to others; to perform personal services for others; to participate in civic affairs; to promote health and healing; to make business contacts, such as in public-relations activities; to coerce others (e.g., control crowds at a parade); and to direct others (e.g., tell people what to do in an emergency).[94]

The picture painted by the trait indicators listed above is very coherent and reasonable, except for the last two references to dominance and

---

[91] Thurstone (1931); Lurie (1937); Guilford, Christensen, Bond, and Sutton (1954).

[92] Gernes (1940); Guilford, Christensen, Bond, and Sutton (1954).

[93] Guilford, Christensen, Frick, and Merrifield (1957).

[94] Lurie (1937); Gernes (1940); Brogden (1952); Guilford, Christensen, Bond, and Sutton (1954). Cattell and Miller (1952) report a factor they call "parental protectiveness." See also, Morris and Jones (1955).

coercion. This aspect may come as a surprise and calls for comment. It must not be assumed from this that the desire to dominate others is the chief source of motivation behind those who give their time to the altruistic work of social welfare. An active interest in the underprivileged naturally calls for changing the underprivileged person and his environment. This person has somehow failed to cope with his problems as self-manager, and someone who has enough concern about his condition and who feels that he is able to do a better job of managing must take over, at least temporarily. Individuals engaged in welfare work no doubt differ among themselves in the weighting of this component. There may be some whose main satisfaction comes from managing people and others who minimize this aspect. Some of this difference may be attributed to the amount of aggressiveness involved.

Commercial-interest Factors

Two factors constitute this group, at two levels of socioeconomic status —those who manage and take responsibilities and those who do the office work.

Business interest

The person with strong business interest: [95]
Likes administrative duties (e.g., managing a department store)
Likes selling activities (e.g., selling advertising space)
Likes making business contacts (e.g., arranging for demonstrations)
Likes writing persuasive material (e.g., advertising copy)

Clerical interest

Several kinds of office work appeal to the person who is high on this trait, for he: [96]
Likes numerical computations (e.g., figure out a payroll)
Likes clerical work (e.g., look up letters in a file)
Likes mathematical thinking (e.g., understand the principles of an electronic computing machine)
Likes making business contacts (e.g., arrange for demonstrations)
The factor is also shown by women who say they would like to be a cashier, bookkeeper, stenographer, private secretary, commercial teacher, office manager, or public-health nurse.[97] All these things are mentioned

[95] Thurstone (1931); Gundlach and Gerum (1931); Gernes (1940); Guilford, Christensen, Bond, and Sutton (1954). Lurie's (1937) "philistine" factor is probably business interest in part.

[96] Guilford, Christensen, Bond, and Sutton (1954). See also, Gundlach and Gerum (1931).

[97] Gernes (1940).

here because it is so often apparently believed that clerical interest is much more restricted than these activities indicate. The correlation between numerical-computational work and other kinds of clerical work is so high that a separate interest in number work, as such, seems remotely possible.

A curious bit of validity information that is available probably concerns this factor. It was found that the Kuder Clerical score correlated to the extent of −.44 with criteria of leadership in a situation in which subjects were doing a clerical task.[98] This means that those with the higher Clerical scores were *less* inclined to take the lead in performing a joint task. This kind of result is not typical when other areas of interest and activity are considered. A reasonable hypothesis would be that those more interested in clerical work are by nature less interested in leading, even in the performance of clerical tasks.

Physical-activity Interest Factors

Three vocational-interest factors are grouped for no other reason than that relatively more handwork is involved, more brawn and relatively less brain than in the other cases.

Mechanical interest

It would be nothing short of miraculous if factor analysis did not bring out a variable of mechanical interest. What may be somewhat surprising is that there is not more than one such factor, for example, one having more to do with handwork (constructing, repairing, etc.) and another having more to do with brain work (inventing and designing). The following indicators are statistically quite coherent.[99] The person with strong mechanical interest likes mechanical manipulation; mechanical construction; manual activity, either in the form of just working with materials or of manual construction, such as carpentry; and mechanical designing. There is also liking for detailed work, such as working with precision instruments.

Unlike the finding in connection with the Kuder Clerical score, there is a positive correlation of .40 between the Kuder Mechanical score and leadership criteria in group performance of a mechanical task.[100] This kind of result is more typical and reasonable. In general, he who knows more technical information in a field is likely to find himself in the position of leadership, particularly if outcomes in those fields of operation are of critical importance.

[98] Carter and Nixon (1949*b*).
[99] Guilford, Christensen, Bond, and Sutton (1954).
[100] Carter and Nixon (1949*b*).

Outdoor interest

A scoring category for outdoor interest has been coming into the standard interest inventories in recent years. The recognition of this variable and its utilization is supported by factor-analysis results.[101] The person with strong outdoor interest likes agricultural tasks, such as planting and harvesting; outdoor work, such as lumbering; to construct things, as in carpentry; and manual work, such as working with materials.

Aviation interest

The indicators of this interest factor are in the form of behavior tests. It represents the only known instance in which information tests have been used successfully to measure interest traits. The information test is a technical-vocabulary test, scored for both pilot and navigator knowledge. Another test of the factor is a Biographical Data Blank scored for predicting success in pilot training.[102]

Some Possible Interest Factors Unique to Women

The interest factors mentioned thus far were found mainly in populations of men. In the instances in which reference was made to the work of Gernes (1940), the factors were also found for women. Gernes factor-analyzed several large groups of items from the Strong Vocational Interest Blank for Women. She found some other factors, as yet unverified, that pertain, so far as we know, only to women.

Career-woman interest

Women who respond in ways indicating this trait strongly are likely to say that they would like to be a judge, lawyer, chemist, biologist, musical director, college professor, farmer, or member of some other vocational group, mainly at the professional level. For men, fairly obviously, such a long and varied list would break up to indicate more than one factor. These results indicate a general principle to the effect that women's vocational interests are not as differentiated as men's.

Domestic interest

Women show high status in a factor of domestic interest by expressing a liking for cooking, sewing, doing own laundry work, teaching children, decorating, and raising flowers and vegetables. This factor and the one preceding are relatively independent, not strongly negatively correlated as some might expect. This means that there are some women who can be high on both interests and some who can be low on both.

---

[101] Guilford, Christensen, Bond, and Sutton (1954).
[102] Guilford and Lacey (1947).

Mathematics

In naming and defining this factor it is difficult to know whether to place the emphasis on interest in mathematics or on numbers. It may not be confined to the female population, but it has not been found in studies with male subjects. It is shown by expressions of liking for arithmetic, bookkeeping, algebra, geometry, ancient languages, and literature. The last two fields in this list will come as a surprise. Their presence might indicate something broader and more fundamental than mathematics. We can admit that mathematics is a branch of our language or a special language, which helps somewhat to bridge the gap. In the discussion of factors of intellect it was pointed out that operations with both numbers and other mathematical materials probably belong with language in the symbolic category of aptitudes. It is not an uncommon finding that a score for a test of number operations predicts grades in courses in language and literature.[103] An interest variable in common to mathematics and literature should not be absurd after all.

DIMENSIONS OF ATTITUDES

The known dimensions of attitude are quite small in number, but they have received a large amount of attention and they are of considerable social importance. They are of first importance to the understanding of social behavior, for they all have persistent and far-reaching social implications. Social organization and social processes both depend very much upon the attitudes of individuals and also have very much to do with the formation of those attitudes. The institutions of government, religion, and social welfare all owe their forms to human attitudes, and they in turn influence the attitudes of individuals who come in contact with them.

Known Factors of Attitude

Liberalism vs. conservatism

Although there may be much difference of opinion as to the qualities to be included in the factor of liberalism vs. conservatism, there is little question of its existence as a fairly comprehensive unity. It can be defined as a tendency to favor changes in social, economic, political, and aesthetic practices. Of the important areas of social life, religion is omitted from the definition for the reason that there is a relatively separate and more limited factor of *religionism,* to be discussed following this one.

From several analyses we gain the impression that a liberal person believes in evolution of the species, favors birth control, believes in easy

---

[103] Razor (1949).

divorce, is relatively in favor of communism, favors the new, and has relatively low regard for capitalism.[104]

Some investigators find the factor more related to one of these attributes and some find it more related to others. For example, Sanai (1951) found political attitudes more relevant, whereas Lorr (1951) found both political and economic attitudes more relevant. There are empirical indications that radicalism and reactionism belong on the same scale and are merely more extreme positions.[105] Arguments are sometimes presented against a unitary dimension of liberalism vs. conservatism, but the evidence for special areas of liberalism is weak.[106] Individuals tend to be fairly consistent in their positions with respect to all the relevant areas.[107]

Numerous studies have indicated that many personal and background conditions are related to the trait positions of individuals on this dimension. Persons over the age of forty tend to be more conservative, in keeping with popular opinion.[108] Some investigators find that males tend to be more liberal,[109] but others find no sex difference.[110] As might be expected, a negative correlation (one report of −.30) is found between liberalism and socioeconomic status of the individual.[111] Several correlations ranging from .05 to .45, all positive, have been reported between measures of liberalism and measures of intelligence.[112] Positive correlations have also been reported with amount of education of the individual[113] and of his parents.[114]

Sometimes it is found that liberals have better general information;[115] sometimes no over-all difference is found, but some differences in both directions are found when we consider different areas of knowledge. For example, liberals are better informed on new issues of the day, whereas conservatives are better informed on money and banking and on government policies. Liberals tend to travel more than conservatives.[116] In political affiliations in the United States, the expected order appears, from most liberal to most conservative: Communist, Socialist, Democrat, and Republican.[117] Both extremes on this attitude continuum tend to

104 Thurstone (1934); Ferguson (1939); Lorr (1951).
105 Vetter (1947).
106 Kerr (1952).
107 Lentz (1938).
108 Kerr (1944).
109 Lentz (1939).
110 Breemes et al. (1941).
111 Gundlach (1939); Fay and Middleton (1940c).
112 Whisler and Remmers (1938); Kerr (1944).
113 Lentz (1939); Kerr (1944).
114 Lentz (1939).
115 Kerr (1944).
116 Pace (1939); Smith (1948).
117 Lentz (1939); Kerr (1944).

become fascist in their outlook. It has been an interesting finding that extreme conservatives will endorse certain communistic ideas if those ideas are sufficiently disguised or if not labeled as communistic.[118] In religious affiliation, some of the more liberal groups are the Jews, Unitarians, and some Protestant groups; among the more conservative are the Catholics and fundamentalist Protestant groups.[119]

Some of the apparent consequences of the attitudes of this dimension are of interest. Liberals tend to admire scientists, inventors, authors, poets, and statesmen; conservatives tend to admire military leaders, athletes, financiers, industrialists, and entertainers.[120] More liberal students tend to choose specialization in journalism, social work, law, and agriculture; more conservative students tend to choose banking, dentistry, music, and government service.[121] Family influences are no doubt somewhat effective in these respects. Creative students in the arts and sciences tend to be more liberal than noncreative students, with a correlation of .38 reported.[122] This is in line with the popular opinion that creative people tend to be nonconformists.

Religionism

Probably the best conception of the attitude dimension of religionism is that it represents the strength of ties a person has to some organized religious group or religious doctrine. In Western culture this means Christian attitudes and beliefs. In early investigations religionism appears to have remained submerged in the general orbit of liberalism vs. conservatism.[123] In later work religionism was separated from the more general dimension, but remains related to it, obviously. The three defining indicators are belief in God, low belief in evolution, and rejection of birth control.[124] The last two of these also help to indicate liberalism vs. conservatism.

There seems to be agreement on the conclusion that women average higher on religionism than men. Religionism seems to have a negative correlation with socioeconomic status in the case of women but not in the case of men.[125] The smaller the population of the community in which the person lives, the greater the average degree of religionism.[126] The relation to membership in different religious groups is almost exactly the same as for liberalism vs. conservatism.[127] United States students with foreign-born parents tend to be higher on the religionism scale than students with native-born parents. The more religious students tend to choose specialization in the ministry, homemaking, medicine, music, and

[118] Kerr (1944).
[119] Lentz (1939); Kerr (1944).
[120] *Ibid.*
[121] Nelson and Nelson (1940).
[122] Drevdahl (1956).
[123] Thurstone (1934); Ferguson (1939).
[124] Ferguson (1941, 1944*a*).
[125] Ferguson (1944*b*).
[126] *Ibid.*
[127] Lawson and Stagner (1954).

teaching; the less religious students choose aviation, journalism, law, and commerce.[128]

Humanitarianism

The factor of humanitarianism is also sometimes referred to as "tender-mindedness vs. tough-mindedness," to use terms coming down to us from William James. The distinguishing qualities are: belief in capital punishment, tough treatment of criminals, and war.[129] Sanai (1951) called a somewhat similar factor "sentimental vs. efficient attitude." Keehn (1955) reports a factor such as humanitarianism in a population of Arabs, thus indicating that the trait transcends national and cultural lines. Eysenck (1953) supports the last conclusion in a more general fashion from his finding of similar factor results on attitudes in three different countries of Europe as well as the United States.

It is not surprising to learn that women tend to be more humanitarian than men. A possible basis may be in the maternal drive. A possible relation of tough-mindedness to the male sex drive may add to this difference. Although the religious groups that are more or less humanitarian differ somewhat for men and women, in general, the more humanitarian people are members of the Jewish and Congregational faiths and the less humanitarian belong to the Catholic faith and to certain Protestant groups.[130] United States students with native-born parents are more humanitarian than those with foreign-born parents. Little relationship has been found to political affiliation or to course of study selected in college.[131]

Nationalism

The person who is high on the attitude scale for nationalism believes in the importance of patriotism and in the value of war. He believes in applying measures of censorship, but he rejects communism.[132] In responding to particular items he expresses belief in keeping a large navy and in protecting foreign trade by force. He thinks that labor agitators are troublesome. He is against being liberal with regard to immigration and is against the practice of buying foreign goods.[133]

Gradualness vs. Revolution

Little is known about a suggested factor of belief in gradual change vs. sudden or revolutionary change. Cattell (1946a) mentions such a factor, and Sanai (1951) provides new support for the idea in a factor that he calls "social evolution vs. communism." The key to the difference between persons high and low on this continuum would seem to be in the degree

---

[128] Nelson and Nelson (1940).
[129] Ferguson (1939, 1941, 1944a).
[130] Ferguson (1944b).

[131] *Ibid.*
[132] Thurstone (1934); Ferguson (1942, 1944).
[133] Stagner and Katzoff (1942).

of patience they show in connection with social, economic, or political changes. There should be some degree of negative relationship between this primary attitude and liberalism vs. conservatism.

The General Place of Attitude Factors in Personality

In terms of complexity and generality, the primary attitudes would seem to be rather high in the hierarchy of personality structure. Almost no attention has been given, however, to relating them to other dimensions of temperament or motivation. It may be that each of the attitude dimensions can be largely accounted for in terms of combinations of those other variables to which something has been added.

A little speculation suggests some hypotheses concerning possible involvements of temperamental or hormetic traits in each primary attitude. Liberalism may rest in part upon the factors of liking for variety, liking for adventure vs. security, and aesthetic appreciation, whereas conservatism may rest more positively upon interest in business. The latter, of course, may also be based upon some of the more fundamental primary traits.

Humanitarianism may be based upon the primary traits of benevolence, with low aggressiveness and low need for discipline. More fully related may be the vocational interest of social welfare, but this, in turn, may be accounted for in terms of more basic variables. Nationalism, as described above, seems to rest upon high levels of aggressiveness, self-sufficiency, and cultural conformity. Gradualism is reminiscent of the restraint pole of the factor restraint vs. rhathymia, and perhaps of reflectiveness, friendliness, and tolerance. The side of revolution suggests general ambition, with its impatient aspect, and impulsiveness. Basic primary traits related to religionism are not so easy to see, unless depression is a possible contributor. It should be remembered that all of these suggested relationships are hypothetical and call for empirical examination.

OTHER POSSIBLE HORMETIC DIMENSIONS

Two aspects of personality that have received considerable attention from investigators remain to be treated here. One is a relative newcomer as a concept in personality study—the authoritarian personality. It is appropriately discussed at this place because it is primarily a motivational phenomenon and comes nearer to the class we have called attitudes than to any other. The other is a popular concept that has had a long history of study, particularly by the vocational psychologist. It is the phenomenon of leadership. As we shall see, leadership has relationships to many kinds of traits other than those in the hormetic category. We have previously seen references in many places to results indicating relationships of aptitudes, temperament dimensions, and motivational dimensions to leadership behavior. The topic of leadership could not be given adequate treatment without having at our disposal background information concerning all these kinds of traits.

The Authoritarian Personality

The title of this proposed trait suggests that it refers to a *type* of personality rather than to a single variable such as a primary trait. The history of the origin of the concept is somewhat revealing. Following the institution of the Third Reich, with its fascistic excesses under Hitler, there arose considerable interest concerning the nature and origin of anti-Semitic attitudes. Scales for the measurement of anti-Semitic attitudes were developed and studies were made with them. The conception of an anti-Semitic attitude was broadened to a conception of adverse attitude generalized to all minority groups. An ethnocentrism scale, or *E* scale, was developed for measuring this more general attitude.[134] Additional qualities were attributed to those high on the *E* scale, qualities that gave to the type the picture that justified the label of "fascist." A fascism scale, or *F* scale, was then developed. Largely from interview studies of very extreme individuals, the picture of the type was further developed and the label of authoritarian personality was applied.[135]

ATTRIBUTES OF THE AUTHORITARIAN PERSONALITY

The authoritarian type of person is regarded as having a general outlook or a set of attitudes toward his family and his fellow men, an outlook that involves his social and political philosophy. The following traits are commonly attributed to the authoritarian person: [136]

Is conventional, with rigid adherence to middle-class values

Is submissive to authority, with uncritical acceptance of an idealized moral authority

Is aggressive, condemning, rejecting, and punishing violators of the conventional code

Is superstitious, believing in fate

Has stereotyped thinking, in rigid, black-white categories

Stresses power, toughness, and domination

Projects, believing that others are indulging in "evil goings-on"

Is antiscientific, being inclined to autistic thinking and perhaps to animistic views of nature

The reader who has become acquainted with factors in the earlier part of this chapter will be able to guess what combinations of them probably

[134] Levinson (1949).
[135] Adorno et al. (1950).
[136] F. Sanford (1950); N. Sanford (1956).

go a long way to make up this picture. It should be said that there is not complete agreement among investigators concerning all the components. A question arises concerning the possible bipolar nature of the type as described. An opposite pattern has sometimes been called "equalitarian" and sometimes "democratic." There is much doubt whether the opposites of the components of the authoritarian type do cohere as well.

STATUS OF THE AUTHORITARIAN CONCEPT

Questions have been raised as to just how unitary the proposed type is. Sanford (1956), for example, recognizes several subtypes. Luchins (1950) has severely criticized the experimental operations of the research on which the major conclusions concerning the type were based. Rigorous correlational studies are needed to determine whether there is a more or less stable pattern of traits of this kind that some people have, what its most constant components are, whether there is an opposite type, and if the authoritarian type exists, how common and significant it is in the general population. The issue of the authoritarian personality belongs to the general problem of determining what higher-order syndrome types exist in personality. Correlational studies of the authoritarian syndrome type are appearing, but the picture has not yet become very clear.[137]

Leadership

Leadership was formerly studied as if it were a single human quality, and as if we could say, paraphrasing Gertrude Stein, "a leader is a leader is a leader." The statement "Bill is a born leader" is still typical in many circles. Empirical studies have given rather bewildering results. No one kind of score or rating or other assessment predicts it consistently in all situations, yet a very large variety of disparate qualities predict it in different studies. The latter statement has been evident earlier in this volume as we have noted one factor after another to be evidently related to leadership behavior.

PRESENT CONCEPTIONS OF LEADERSHIP

There is considerable agreement among those who have given the matter extended thought and examination that leadership is definitely not a unitary human commodity.[138] As a concept, leadership is a property of behavior more than it is of persons. We do better to speak of leadership behavior than of a leadership trait or even of leadership traits.

Leadership behavior is a function of many circumstances. First, it is a function of the kind of group in which it occurs. Groups vary in having different objectives and different operations or procedures to attain those

---

[137] See Hofstaetter (1952); O'Neil and Levinson (1954); Rokeach and Fruchter (1956).
[138] Stogdill and Shartle (1948); Hemphill (1949); Sanford (1950).

objectives. Groups are composed of individuals who differ in kind from one group to another. The followers have personalities and they have aspirations and expectations. Groups face different kinds of situations, situations that exert different demands upon a leader and upon the followers.[139] Sometimes the situation is a critical one demanding prompt action, sometimes not. Some groups may be face-to-face groups and others will rarely meet in one place.

It is true that, depending upon the needs of the situation and the members of the group, certain personal traits will be more pertinent and more in demand than others. Some persons have the qualities that match more nearly the pattern of desired attributes than others have. It is also true that over a considerable range of situations and groups there are, after all, certain attributes required in common. In this sense it is meaningful to speak of leadership qualities, qualities that have a greater probability of being needed and of ensuring success in situations that require leaders.

The shifting pattern of leadership qualities, however, makes it rather futile to talk about a leadership syndrome or a leader type. The number of leader types is very large. The interaction of leader, situation, and followers is the significant principle, and each combination of these involves its own type.[140] Superimposed upon the working of this principle, we have the fact that some persons seem more motivated than others to seek and to assume positions of leadership—the ascendant, the one lacking self-consciousness, and the active, for example. How well they succeed may depend more upon other traits.

Some of the implications of this view are interesting. It means that almost everyone has potentialities for leadership behavior under the right circumstances. It means that a leader may succeed with distinction under some circumstances but fail under other circumstances. It means that we should not select leaders, as such, but leaders for particular groups, each with its own purposes and methods and its own kind of followers. It means paying attention to the organization and composition of groups so as to achieve optimal group performance. From the standpoint of basic research, it means the study of situations and groups as well as leaders. Such studies have been made only fairly recently.[141]

TRAITS RELATED TO LEADERSHIP BEHAVIOR

What traits are more commonly related to successful leadership behavior? In addition to those mentioned from time to time in preceding surveys of factors, a few others may be mentioned. The total list is actually long if we include every trait that has any probability at all of contribut-

[139] Carter and Nixon (1949*a*).
[140] Stogdill and Shartle (1948).
[141] Hemphill (1949); Sanford (1950).

ing to success. One kind of quality that is perhaps most often found related to leadership behavior is information of some sort, particularly if the information is specialized and technical.[142] The person who knows more than others about the situation and its problems is looked to for guidance. He can lead at least as long as his superior knowledge is of use to the group.

Many studies have sought for some of the secrets of leaders in their physical characteristics. Height is usually found to be positively related. It has long been known that men in executive positions average taller than their followers.[143] This is also true among groups of boys.[144] An average correlation of .30 has been reported in connection with height and leadership.[145] Similar results have been found for weight, with slightly lower correlations. A good hypothesis would be that the taller and heavier group member can be accepted as fulfilling a "father image," which most individuals evidently continue to apply to their leaders.

Among other more incidental qualities, general appearance of the person has some importance in boys' groups but not in girls'.[146] Health and energy are sometimes important. Physical prowess and athletic ability are sometimes important, with correlations of .38 to .62 in boys' groups, and with some relationship in girls' athletic groups.[147] As to age, leaders are sometimes younger and sometimes older than their followers, with correlations ranging from $-.32$ to $+.71$. In student activities, for example, they are younger.[148] In terms of scores on the Bernreuter Personality Inventory, leaders among students were found to have higher average scores for adjustment, dominance, and self-sufficiency.[149] Contrary to popular belief, leaders need not show quick decisions, unless the situation is of a kind that calls for quick decisions.[150] There is some disagreement on whether a successful leader has superior empathy (ability to sense thoughts, feelings, and attitudes),[151] but it is a reasonable conclusion that leaders tend to be similar to their followers in interests and social background.[152] It is also noted that the kind of behavior shown by the leader is influenced by his followers, their traits, and what they do.[153]

[142] Jenkins (1947).
[143] Gowin (1915).
[144] Caldwell and Wellman (1926); Partridge (1934).
[145] Stogdill (1948).
[146] Dunkerley (1940); Stogdill (1948).
[147] Stogdill (1948).
[148] *Ibid.*
[149] Hanawalt and Richardson (1944).
[150] Hemphill (1949).
[151] Campbell (1955); Chowdhry and Newcomb (1952); Bell and Hall (1954).
[152] Jenkins (1947).
[153] Sanford (1950); Haythorn et al. (1956).

DEVELOPMENT OF LEADERSHIP BEHAVIOR

There are said to be few signs of leadership behavior before the ages of two or three, at which time it can be observed in nursery school children.[154] At that age level it takes the form of one child's dominating another, or trying to dominate him. Active leadership is observed at about the ages nine to ten.[155] As children grow into adolescence, dominating leaders are increasingly resented, except among those who have something of the authoritarian pattern of traits.[156] Incidentally, leaders who *emerge* in a group are more likely to be of the authoritarian type than are appointed or selected leaders.[157]

Among older adolescents and young adults, a certain amount of consistency has developed in leadership habits. The level of consistency is not very great, however, for the highest correlation found between different criteria was .39.[158] A factor analysis of leadership criteria suggested two broad classes, including intellectual leadership and leadership in work with the hands.[159] The more similar the groups, the more consistency an individual shows regarding leadership behavior, as, for example, in discussion groups.[160] Reliability of scores in the LGD test indicates this. There is some consistency even when tasks are varied somewhat.[161] In military groups, where the kinds of tasks are somewhat varied but regulations are fairly uniform, there is much predictability of leadership behavior. Correlations of .42 to .51 have been mentioned between ratings in officer-training schools and military performance some months later.[162]

SUMMARY

Hormetic dimensions are variables of the motivational aspects of personality. They include the general categories of needs, interests, and attitudes.

In spite of the transitory and fluctuating nature of organic needs, there are a few recognized personality traits based upon them. Other classes of needs pertain to kinds of environmental conditions desired; various needs for personal achievement; needs for self-determination, involving what are popularly known as character traits; and social needs, in which the needs prominently involve other individuals.

The largest number of hormetic dimensions is found in the group of avocational interests, which have to do with valued classes of activities

[154] Parten (1933); Stogdill (1948).
[155] Pigors (1933).
[156] Stogdill (1948); Hollander (1954).
[157] Carter et al. (1951).
[158] Carter et al. (1950).
[159] *Ibid.*
[160] Bell and French (1950).
[161] Gibb (1947).
[162] Baier (1947).

without any direct implications of vocations. These are grouped in several subclasses—interest in kinds of overt activity; interest in activities having certain properties, such as variety or precision; and various areas of appreciation, some broad and some narrow. The latter group contains some special factors of aesthetic interest and interests in different types of humor. Other avocational interests are concerned with liking for different types of thinking, some of which seem to be parallel with thinking aptitudes and to be correlated slightly with them. The general question of correlations between pairs of interest and aptitude dimensions deserves increased attention, as does the question of dimensions of interest among children.

A small group of vocational-interest factors can be classified in terms of well-known socioeconomic categories, some of them being in professional areas, some in commercial areas, and some in manual or physical areas. Women share many of men's interest categories, especially in the case of avocational interests, but present a few that are probably unique to their sex.

Five dimensions at present cover the variables in the domain of attitudes—liberalism vs. conservatism, religionism, humanitarianism, nationalism, and gradualism vs. revolution. Numerous studies have indicated relationships of these variables to demographic variables such as age, sex, socioeconomic level, and religious and political affiliations, as well as to vocational choices and to other traits of personality. It seems appropriate to regard attitudes as syndrome types that can eventually be largely accounted for in terms of combinations of primary traits of motivation and temperament.

In examining the hypothesized concept of the authoritarian personality, its significance, and its proposed composition as a complex syndrome type, it becomes evident that the boundaries of the authoritarian personality, its coherence, and its composition are yet to be determined. The associated hypothesis of a dimension of intolerance of ambiguity is reported to have some support from factor analysis.

In the light of considerable investigation and current thinking, the popular concept of leadership cannot be considered a unitary trait, nor is it a very stable composite of traits, since leadership behavior depends upon interactions of leaders, group functions, followers, and situations. The more common traits related to leadership have been mentioned in the preceding chapters and in this chapter, which also contains a thumbnail sketch of the development of leadership behavior.

Chapter 18

DIMENSIONS OF PATHOLOGY

IN THIS volume the view has been adopted that we should not attempt to describe normal individuals in terms of concepts born to describe pathological conditions. Instead, we should recognize the applicability of terms descriptive of normals to pathological individuals and find additional concepts with which to take care of varieties of pathology. We shall see how this policy works out in this chapter. Our primary interest will be to see what categories of pathology are needed; a secondary interest will be to note which traits of normal populations have significant relations to them, as indicated by intercorrelational studies of symptoms.

There will be no attempt to relate the dimensions of pathology systematically to any general theory of pathology, for the major interest here, as in preceding chapters, is descriptive. Much further work will have to be done in order to develop a thoroughgoing theory of pathology in terms of factors.

CONCERNING TRADITIONAL CATEGORIES OF PATHOLOGY

We shall begin by considering the past and present situations with regard to categories of pathology and the diagnosis of patients by the use of those categories. The varieties of pathology that are still in vogue today are very much as they were when handed down by Kraepelin, the founder of modern psychiatry. The persistence of their use attests strongly to the fact that there must be considerable soundness in them, but possibly, also, to the lack of procedures by which improvements could be introduced. There is considerable indication that improvements are needed, as we shall see.

Needs for More Rigorous Diagnostic Concepts

We do not have to go very far to find evidence that there is something wrong with current practices of psychiatric diagnosis where the traditional diagnostic concepts are used. There is also considerable uncertainty in distinguishing between the normal and the pathological. We are told that at 55 different induction stations in the United States Army during August, 1945, the percentages of rejections for psychiatric reasons varied from 0.5 per cent to 50.6 per cent.[1] There may have been some actual differences in populations from different regions, but it is unlikely that the differences were so great as these figures indicate. In the British Air Ministry, 541 men who were borderline or doubtful cases were interviewed by two psychiatrists. There was disagreement in 31 per cent of the cases.[2]

There is also considerable disagreement in the assignment of patients to diagnostic categories. This is shown indirectly by the fact that at induction stations in the United States Army, there was considerable variation in the proportions of the disqualified men who were diagnosed in the different nosological categories.[3] At civilian hospitals receiving mental patients, different psychiatrists also show marked differences in proportions that they assign to the categories.[4] Where more than one psychiatrist examines and diagnoses the same patients, there is considerable agreement on the assignment of patients to very broad classes, but rather poor agreement when patients are assigned to more limited categories. In one instance in which three psychiatrists were involved, there was complete agreement on 46 per cent of the diagnoses when very broad categories were used and agreement on 20 per cent when more specific diagnostic categories were used.[5] Between pairs of psychiatrists the agreement is higher. In another study, for example, for classification in three major categories—character defects, organic, and psychotic—there was 80 per cent agreement. When there was classification in minor categories the agreement dropped to 50 per cent.[6] Agreement is an index of interjudge consistency and has no necessary implication of validity. Agreement does not necessarily mean that the categories are sound or that the diagnosticians are using them properly.

Coherence of Present Diagnostic Categories

As implied in the last sentence, some of the difficulty in agreement may be due to faulty concepts of disease entities. We need to consider the extent to which disease entities exist and the stability of syndromes or trait patterns that indicate them.

A study by Page, Landis, and Katz (1934) reveals some of the difficulties in the search for consistent trait patterns. In this study 50 inventory items (which may be regarded as one way of listing potential symptoms) that were accepted by 12 psychiatrists as describing schizophrenics were first

[1] Stouffer et al. (1950, vol. 4).
[2] Eysenck (1952*b*).
[3] Stouffer et al. (1950, vol. 4).
[4] Mehlman (1952).
[5] Ash (1949).
[6] Schmidt and Fonda (1956).

selected. We may regard the 50 items as a representation of the psychiatrists' stereotype of the schizophrenic syndrome. The 50 items were then administered to three groups of individuals who were to answer them, describing themselves. There were two abnormal groups, schizophrenics and manic-depressives, and a third group of nonpathological individuals who matched the abnormal groups in other respects. The average number of symptoms that these groups applied to themselves were approximately 18, 14, and 18, for schizophrenics, manic-depressives, and normals, respectively. On 17 of the items, the three groups gave the schizophrenic responses about equally often. On 11 items normals gave more schizophrenic responses than the schizophrenics themselves.

The results are subject to differing interpretations, of course. The schizophrenic stereotype held in common by the 12 psychiatrists could have been incorrect. It could be that there is a considerable discrepancy between self-report and observer report of symptoms. Yet, presumably a psychiatrist uses information based upon answers to interview questions of a nature similar to those presented for self-description in this experiment to help in arriving at a diagnostic decision. Perhaps schizophrenics do not recognize their own symptoms. Perhaps abnormals and normals do not interpret items alike. Perhaps very few of the symptoms were actually very relevant for distinguishing schizophrenics from other groups. Within the category of schizophrenia there is still much room for variation in the kinds of qualities implied by the items, and perhaps none hit upon the distinguishing marks of pathology in this direction.

Correlational Study of Symptoms

For various reasons it is obvious that further, more rigorous study is needed of the nosological categories. We need to know where revisions are required and to know what the more dependable indicators are for each pathological concept. The obvious type of solution lies in making intercorrelational studies of symptoms, and to do this thoroughly means factor analysis.

Kraepelin and others who have contributed to the adoption of current categories of pathology have based their decisions largely on observations of concomitant variations of symptoms. Concomitant variation is most accurately determined by correlation methods. There can surely be no objection to substituting a rigorous procedure for studying the extent of the concomitant variations among symptoms for considerably less rigorous ones.

THE FACTOR-ANALYTICAL APPROACH TO PATHOLOGICAL CATEGORIES

As an example of what may be accomplished by means of the approach of factor analysis we may note a study of Wittenborn (1952). Intercorrelating approximately 50 symptoms as recorded for a large number of patients, Wittenborn had arrived at a set of factor categories that were somewhat different from the customary ones. The results also told him what symptoms should be used to indicate an individual's membership in each category, with appropriate weight for each symptom. Each patient could then be given a score for each category and a profile could be drawn for him. When patients were grouped in the new categories, the ones in each category had greater similarity of profiles than did patients who were grouped according to the traditional categories. Such a procedure provides a much more objective method of assigning patients to nosological categories than do ordinary diagnoses. If such a procedure still lacks full consistency and accuracy, there is always the possibility of improving it by incorporating new, pertinent information and perhaps new revisions of categories.

In the factor-analytical approach to pathology the variables of observation that are usually intercorrelated are symptoms. The symptoms may be recorded as merely being present or absent or as being present to different degrees, which means ratings for degree of manifestation. Other variables that have been observed and intercorrelated are in the form of overt behavior manifestations, such as pouting, crying, or fighting, and inferences drawn from overt signs of such symptoms as absentmindedness, daydreaming, or hallucinations. Behavior tests have been used very little for diagnosis except by Eysenck (1952).

In the domain of psychopathology the factors obtained by analysis should probably all be regarded as syndrome types. They are dimensions of variation higher in the structure of personality than the primary traits that we have been considering in the preceding chapters. Even within the domain of pathology we have factors representing different levels of complexity and generality. As we come to them we shall give some attention to their apparent level of complexity, and to possible relations to combinations of primary traits. We have some empirical basis for the latter in places. Pratt (1952) administered two personality inventories [7] to a large number of patients diagnosed in 10 nosological categories and determined some significant patterns of high and low scores for the different groups in certain inventory traits.

The factors of pathology can be grouped in the traditional major classes of neurotic and psychotic.

DIMENSIONS OF NEUROSIS

In the area of the neuroses we find that factor analysis supports the three traditional major categories of *neurasthenia, compulsion neurosis,*

[7] An Inventory of Factors STDCR and An Inventory of Factors GAMIN.

and *conversion hysteria* very well. It adds some more specialized disorders of *neurotic inadequacy, neurotic emotionality, neurotic anxiety, neurotic hostility,* and *sex conflict,* plus a couple of psychosomatic disorders.

The Traditional Neurotic Syndrome Types

Neurasthenia: Excessive fatigue, low energy level, low motivational level, and resistance to activity in any form

In addition to the qualities included in the definition of neurasthenia, three analyses provide similar ones—low achievement motivation, low confidence, and dislike for crowds.[8] The low motivational level suggests a consistently low status on the dimensions of need and interest mentioned in the preceding chapter, including the dimension of general drive for physical activity. The resistance to activity is not an active negativism, but rather a matter of inertia. The low motivational level all along the line seems to be the key to the pathological condition. Other symptoms, such as dependency, lack of confidence, and dislike for crowds, may be more incidental, as is true of the apparent negativism.

Compulsion neurosis: Beset by phobias, obsessions, and compulsions

On the three symptoms given in the definition of compulsion neurosis there is general agreement from four analyses. There are a number of accompanying symptoms, most of which are confined to one analysis each, so that it is difficult to tell whether they are consistent parts of the picture. These more incidental symptoms include distressful anxiety, guilt feelings, self-consciousness, marked distortions of reality, ideas of reference, preoccupation with self, skin eruptions, and respiratory symptoms.[9] It is unlikely that all of these are necessary components of the compulsion-neurosis picture.

Conversion hysteria: Using psychologically induced ailments to gain some advantage

Two analyses agree completely upon four symptoms—no organic basis for complaints, use of physical symptoms, no concern over physical handicaps, and physical disorders from emotional causes.[10] This is the traditional picture of conversion hysteria and of the person who finds that a physical disorder, such as a paralysis, is a way out of some difficulty or a gain to some personal end. Because the disorder enables the person to gain what he wants and because recovery would apparently be worse than continuation, he shows no concern about his handicap and little or no

8 Degan (1952); O'Connor (1953); Lorr and Rubenstein (1956).

9 Wittenborn and Holzberg (1951a); O'Connor (1953); Lorr et al. (1953); Lorr and Rubenstein (1955, 1956).

10 Wittenborn (1951); Wittenborn and Holzberg (1951a).

desire for recovery. The production of the disorder by his nervous system is of course beyond his voluntary control; it is not something he can turn on and off at will.

Some Neurotic Dimensions of Narrower Scope

Neurotic anxiety: Morbidly intense apprehension or dread

Since the days of Freud it would be surprising if a dimension of pathological anxiety did not come out of the analysis of symptoms. From two analyses we have the rather clear picture of a syndrome in which anxiety is the focal symptom.[11] Other descriptive symptoms are tenseness, tremors, weakness, difficulty in breathing and in sleeping, and possible depression and irritability.

It is necessary to distinguish between neurotic anxiety as a syndrome type and anxiety as a symptom. There are a number of other dimensions of pathology in which anxiety may be reported as a more or less constant aspect. In the preceding chapters we did not find anything that looked like a primary trait of anxiety, unless the dimension of nervousness vs. composure be regarded as the basic trait of anxiety. There is considerable lack of agreement upon just what anxiety as a psychological phenomenon is, although most theories link it in some way with fear. It is not an ordinary fear in connection with which there is a fear-provoking object. There is some agreement that anxiety, as such, is fear without a specific object to fear.

When it comes to the detection of anxiety or the assessment of its strength in individuals, we have a number of proposed ways of measuring it with inventories and behavior tests. Inventories have varied in the degree of success with which they separate cases with and without diagnosed anxiety.[12] They have correlated only moderately with one another [13] and not at all with such behavior tests as the galvanic skin response.[14] One reason for such results is probably that the inventories themselves are factorially complex, and differ in composition from one another and from the behavior tests. The anxiety cases they have been called upon to discriminate from other cases are also not simply anxiety-neurosis cases, but cases of varied diagnosis in categories in which anxiety is a symptom but not the only symptom.

Neurotic inadequacy: Morbid lack of self-confidence

In one analysis a limited syndrome appeared, focused around inferiority feelings. A person in this category is reported to feel inadequate, to have

[11] O'Connor (1953); Lorr and Rubenstein (1956).
[12] Freeman (1953); Taylor (1956).
[13] Kendall (1954).
[14] Gordon and Sarason (1955); Calvin et al. (1956).

little belief in himself, to give way to others, to crave approval, and to conceal his hostility.[15]

Neurotic emotionality: Emotionally reactive to a morbid extent

In the same analysis the following syndrome was segregated: [16] emotional overresponsiveness; unrestrained feelings; self-dramatization; overt expressions of hostility; frequent mood changes; and strong, active interests. The picture is that of the extreme of immaturity on the dimension emotional immaturity vs. maturity combined with a low degree of control, or a low position on the dimension of stability vs. cycloid disposition.

Neurotic hostility: A morbidly hostile attitude

Still another special neurotic syndrome of limited scope came from the same analysis.[17] Besides reporting the symptom of hostility for a person in this category, observers say that he is resentful of authority, is suspicious, is resistful of regulations, is defensive, sees the world as hostile, and blames others for his difficulties. There is first of all a strong picture of a person low on the scale of friendliness vs. hostility. This appears to be combined with a high position on need for freedom and with a somewhat low position on tolerance vs. criticalness.

Sex conflict: Preoccupation with guilt and fears with regard to sex behavior and sex desires

The most common symptoms involved (in male patients) are concern or guilt over masturbation or homosexual tendencies. Accompanying these symptoms there may also be phobias, compulsive acts, and cardiovascular symptoms, with some tendency to be effeminate in manner.[18]

Psychosomatic Disorders

Respiratory-cardiovascular disorder

The person suffering from this psychosomatic disorder has both respiratory and cardiovascular complaints, often very severe. The patient complains of lack of energy; he uses his physical symptoms to his advantage and is at the same time concerned about them.[19] He is thus in some respects like the hysteric and in other respects very different. Like the person in the next psychosomatic disorder to be mentioned, he shows a general overconcern with his body functions.

Gastrointestinal disorder

The focal symptoms pertain to functions of the stomach, intestines, and bowels. There may also be complaints of headache and of other bodily disorders.[20]

---

[15] Lorr and Rubenstein (1956).
[16] Lorr and Rubenstein (1956).
[17] *Ibid.*

[18] Lorr and Rubenstein (1955, 1956).
[19] *Ibid.*
[20] *Ibid.*

Is There a General Neuroticism Factor?

A factor of general neuroticism has been proposed by Eysenck (1944) and has been found repeatedly in his analyses. His method of analysis is such as to ensure a general factor even when some of the variables analyzed correlate zero with one another. Further analysis by other methods would undoubtedly show a number of group factors such as we have seen in the survey of neurotic dimensions above. To the extent that there are correlations among these group factors, there is an over-all syndrome that sets neurotics as a class off from normals on the one hand and from psychotics on the other.

Eysenck has a much better case for a higher-order syndrome of general neuroticism when he finds a collection of symptoms and of behavior tests that discriminate among these three classes of individuals.[21] The most discriminating symptoms are dependence, narrow range of interests, little energy, few social-group contacts or memberships, and poor muscle tone. It is possible that most of these qualities are the mark of a person who is not well mentally, but they have little to do essentially with the core of the disorder. Tests that have rather consistently discriminated neurotics from normals are Body Sway, Dark Vision, and Manual Dexterity. Again, these differences may not indicate essential properties of mental disease, but rather some of the psychological consequences. However, they can still be used as indicators for discriminating between normals and neurotics.

Eysenck (1944) has also consistently found a second factor, a bipolar dimension, which he interprets as a distinction between hysterics and dysthymics, or between hysteria and dysthymia. The more important symptoms of the hysterical pole are conversion hysteria, narrow interests, low energy, and sexual anomalies. The symptoms of the dysthymic pole are anxiety, depression, obsession, apathy, and irritability. Eysenck believes that the underlying dimension is an important one in personality—extraversion vs. introversion. Other methods of analysis than that used by Eysenck would either separate these two groups into two relatively independent, not directly opposite, factors or would break up each set of symptoms into smaller, more homogeneous clusters such as we have seen above. Of the dimensions listed in the survey above, those of conversion hysteria and compulsion neurosis come nearest to accounting for most of the symptoms, but some of the qualities Eysenck mentions for the two poles would go elsewhere in a complete analysis. It can be said again that Eysenck may have detected some genuine higher-order syndromes. Testing his hypotheses calls for study of interrelationships of the group factors.

[21] Eysenck (1956*b*).

DIMENSIONS OF PSYCHOSIS

There is no fully satisfactory distinction between neurosis and psychosis. One difference is that, as classes of disorders, neuroses are all psychogenic, whereas psychoses are sometimes clearly of organic origin and at other times are suspected of having some organic basis, even when the case is ordinarily regarded as psychogenic, as, for example, with schizophrenia. A psychological distinction that can be applied to some extent is that in psychoses we are more likely to find some degree of break with "reality" on the part of the patient. The distinction we live with is largely the operational one of diagnosis. If a patient is diagnosed in a neurotic category, it is a neurosis; if in a psychotic category, it is a psychosis. In some respects a psychosis appears to be a more serious neurosis, but in other respects the differences are qualitative rather than quantitative. As we review the psychotic dimensions we shall see certain parallels between some of them and certain neurotic dimensions, but in other cases we find pathological traits that are definitely new.

Psychotic Factors of Narrower Scope

We begin with some factors of psychosis in which the disorder seems to be more limited to one or another phase of mental functioning—*cognitive, emotional,* or *psychomotor.*

FACTORS PRIMARILY OF COGNITIVE DISORDER

The cognitive disorders pertain more obviously to perception or thinking or both. This classification is determined by their superficial appearance and is not intended to mean that there is no motivational or emotional involvement or determination. Three factors are recognized in this category.

Disorientation: Loss of awareness of place and time

The patient showing this particular disorder probably does not know where he is and the day, month, or year. He is confused with respect to where he is and when it is, to say the least. A symptom commonly reported to accompany the pattern is an affective state of euphoria (unusual and unwarranted cheerfulness). Degan (1952), who has reported the factor, suggests that the euphoria indicates that the patient's non-recognition of time and place is a happy solution to his conflict. Since this condition is frequently associated with a sudden and severe onset of a psychosis, Degan also suggests that the disorientation is a phase of a "traumatic shock." That it is a kind of crisis is indicated by common recovery from disorientation as the disease progresses.

Hyperprojection: Weakened distinction between what is real and what is not, to the extent that subjective products are taken for real

According to one analysis, there is a rather coherent picture of proneness to hallucinations and to delusions.[22] The hallucinations may be visual, auditory, tactual, or of other sense modalities. The delusions may be hypochondriacal or they may be rational or bizarre. Another analysis identifies a factor as "perceptual distortion," but it is probably the same, for delusions are also a part of the picture.[23] Also reported are the symptoms of feelings of unreality and obsessive hostile impulses.

The two pictures tend to agree that if there are hallucinations in one sense modality there are likely to be hallucinations in another, and that delusions and hallucinations tend to go together. This is not new information, but the relative absence of other symptoms from the picture suggests some underlying mechanism or condition that is unique in pathology. The choice of the term "hyperprojection" recognizes the Freudian interpretation of these phenomena.

Paranoid disposition: Suspicion coupled with grandiose ideas

The pattern of paranoid symptoms is well known, and the definition indicates the most consistent core components. Four analyses have contributed accessory aspects to the paranoid picture.[24] The lack of full agreement among them may be due in part to the fact that different investigators included different symptoms in their analyses and in part to possibly different populations of paranoids in different analyses; their numbers represented in any one analysis must have been small. The aspect of suspicion in a paranoid patient is indicated by symptoms such as ideas of reference and belief that people talk about him. The aspect of grandeur is indicated by such descriptions as boastfulness, stilted speech, and exaggerations of own abilities and condition of well-being. An aspect of hostility should also be recognized, although it seems not to be as essential as the others. This aspect is indicated by reports of obsessive hostile impulses and destructiveness. One or two investigations found the added symptom of the patient's feeling that he has changed or that things are unreal. The last symptoms are perhaps a result of some degree of self-insight into his own condition, particularly insight into gross inconsistencies in his cognition and thinking.

FACTORS PRIMARILY OF EMOTIONAL DISORDERS

In this category there is a factor representing a picture of generally increased emotionality and three more limited ones that represent in-

---

[22] Degan (1952).

[23] Lorr et al. (1955).

[24] Wittenborn and Holzberg (1951*a*); Lorr et al. (1953); Lorr and Rubenstein (1955); Lorr et al. (1955).

creased emotionality of three forms—anxiety, depression, and irritability.

Hyperexcitability: State of increased strength and speed of activity

Four analyses indicate a similar pattern with variations, the core of which is a greatly heightened activity level and readiness to respond.[25] The heightened activity shows itself in a variety of ways, none of which may be an essential part of the syndrome but many of which are common components. The fact that a person is hyperexcitable does not necessarily tell us what he will probably do. Since the persons involved in analytical studies are usually hospitalized cases, the picture obtained may be colored by these environmental conditions, either in the way of limitation or of special emphasis.

Symptoms most commonly reported as a part of the picture, in addition to the one of general excitement, include spontaneously and rapidly changing ideas, varied rate of speech, and faulty memory. The faulty memory is probably a consequence of poor observation by a person who is too busy to observe. There is some indication of assaultiveness and destructiveness, but these are said to be merely from excess activity rather than from any serious feelings of hostility. There may or may not be euphoria. This aspect, plus other considerations, indicate that the pattern is not sufficiently extensive to be called mania or even hypomania. It is not bipolar with depression, which comes out as a separate factor in most analyses.

Psychotic depression: A state of simple but severe dejection and pessimism

Clinical experience would lead us to expect a factor of relatively uncomplicated depression of a psychotic nature. Three reports of analyses can be cited in support of such a factor.[26] The usual picture is that of retardation, loss of interest in food, tendency to withdraw, feelings of unworthiness, and lack of self-confidence. There may be thoughts of committing suicide, but the patient appears to lack the energy to carry out such ideas.

Hyperirritability: Lowered threshold for reaction to frustration with anger, hostility, or aggression

This psychotic condition, which features anger and aggression, has been shown to involve the following symptoms: irritability, hostility, bitterness, tantrums, anxiety, tremors, and talking to voices.[27] The reaction is not always an overt aggressive one, as in tantrums. The talking to voices may be regarded as one indirect form of expression of hostility.

[25] Wittenborn (1951); Wittenborn and Holzberg (1951a); Wittenborn et al. (1951); Degan (1952).

[26] Degan (1952); O'Connor (1953); Lorr et al. (1953).

[27] Degan (1952); O'Connor (1953).

The mention of anxiety here as a symptom is another example of how that quality gets around, adding to the suspicion that there are different kinds of anxiety, or different functional significances of anxiety. This syndrome seems parallel to that of neurotic hostility, but has no indication, in the analysis, at least, of the same emphasis on resistance to authority. In terms of the primary traits that we may associate with the two syndromes, it appears that they have in common a low status on friendliness vs. hostility, but where the neurotic syndrome involves a high status on need for freedom, the psychotic one involves a strong component of aggressiveness.

A FACTOR OF PRIMARILY PSYCHOMOTOR DISORDER

Catatonia: A systematic avoidance of motor activity

The definition of this factor is in accordance with that suggested by Degan (1952), whose list of symptoms for this variable does suggest a minimum of motor activity. There is refusal to talk, refusal to eat, and a more general negativism. There are stereotyped postures and movements. Reactions such as grimacing, giggling, and loud talking occur spasmodically and are apparently unrelated to other actions.[28] There are periods of more active motor involvement, and some individuals show more of these exceptions than others. Degan reported a negative relation of the factor to the symptom of anxiety, which means that catatonics show relatively little anxiety compared with other patients. This might mean that the blocking of movement generally serves as an abnormal solution to a problem. On the other hand, it may mean that there is anxiety but it is not apparent for lack of overt signs.

SOME PARALLELS WITH NEUROTIC DIMENSIONS

It was suggested that one or two of the psychotic dimensions just described bear much resemblance to some of the neurotic factors of narrower scope. Further examination of other factors extends this impression. In order to point out the similarities, a matrix of factors is given in Table 18.1.

Five psychotic factors are listed parallel with five neurotic factors.[29] The first pair, neurotic inadequacy and psychotic depression, have in common the qualities of low confidence and depression, to describe these syndromes in terms of primary traits of temperament. Under each syndrome are listed other qualities that have not thus far been shown to be held in common by the two—low ascendance, high need for sympathetic

[28] Lorr et al. (1955).

[29] In order to include all parallels that there appear to be, it is necessary to include the factor of *psychotic anxiety*, which is discussed later among the more complex syndromes.

Table 18.1

Some parallel dimensions of neurosis and psychosis

Components in common	Neurosis	Psychosis
Low confidence with depression	*Neurotic inadequacy* Low ascendance High need for a sympathetic environment Low hostility	*Psychotic depression* Low general activity
Emotional immaturity	*Neurotic emotionality* Cycloid disposition High aggressiveness	*Hyperexcitability* High general activity High impulsiveness Low reflectiveness
Nervousness with depression	*Neurotic anxiety* Strong need for security	*Psychotic anxiety*
Hostility	*Neurotic hostility* High need for freedom Low tolerance	*Hyperirritability* Aggressiveness
High male sex drive with high cultural conformity	*Neurotic sexual conflict* Low masculinity (in males) Depression	*Paranoid disposition* Low objectivity Low friendliness High confidence

environment, and low hostility (high status on friendliness vs. hostility) for the neurotic syndrome and low general activity for the psychotic syndrome. We should not accept these differences too hastily. The reason none of them is mentioned as a common component of the two syndromes may be that analyses have not yet explored this possibility. There should be some differences, to be sure, to account for the differentiation of neurotic vs. psychotic. Perhaps the latter differentiation probably cannot always be stated in terms of primary traits. A general difference, stated earlier, is that psychosis involves some degree of loss of contact with reality. This may be shown in the form of delusions, hallucinations, and so on, symptoms that are foreign to neuroses.

Further inspection of Table 18.1 will provide summaries of some of the differences already pointed out in the discussion of some of the psychotic factors—hyperirritability, for example, in comparison with neurotic hostility. In three rows of the matrix there are two primary traits in common and in two rows only one, so far as results now indicate. As suggested above, we may find additional common components when more is known about the syndromes.

Perhaps the most uncertainty about appropriate pairing of syndromes pertains to the last pair. There is a clinical basis for linking the paranoid disposition with sexual conflict, and obviously the same linking applies to the corresponding neurotic syndrome. The naming of the "components in common" is the most questionable aspect of the last row. No analyses have shown that either group tends to be high in both sex drive and need for cultural conformity. The heading is therefore in the form of a hypothesis, on the logical ground that the most favorable conditions for sexual conflicts would be such a combination.

Psychotic Factors of Somewhat Broader Scope

The factors mentioned in the section above tend to be somewhat restricted to cognitive, emotional, and psychomotor areas of behavior. There are two factors, which are indicated by symptoms that are primarily associated with psychosis, that cut across those areas of behavior. They represent conditions that may not constitute disease entities in themselves but that are prominent features of psychoses.

Schizophrenic dissociation: Incongruity of perception, thoughts, feelings, and motor actions, with general apathy

The list of symptoms that have been found associated with this factor gives one immediately the impression that this is the picture of simple schizophrenia.[30] The patient lacks interests; has a "shut-in" personality; is low in energy; does stereotyped acts and says stereotyped things; talks to voices; lacks cheerfulness but is not depressed, just apathetic; speaks incoherently and irrelevantly; shows inconsistencies between thoughts, feelings, and actions; is preoccupied and may also be disoriented. The pattern may be observed to some extent in exceptional children, with such traits as queerness of behavior, ineffectiveness at work and at play, absentmindedness, daydreaming, and telling falsehoods.[31]

Deterioration: Egocentric indifference to the normal proprieties of behavior [32]

This factor presents a somewhat heterogeneous list of symptoms: [33] loss of finer sensibilities, anxiety, unawareness of feelings of others, opposi-

---

[30] Lorr et al. (1951); Degan (1952); Lorr et al. (1955).
[31] Lorr and Jenkins (1953).
[32] From a definition suggested by Degan (1952).
[33] Wittenborn (1951); Wittenborn et al. (1951); Degan (1952).

tional behavior, incontinence through negligence, assaultive actions, homicidal and suicidal tendencies, and destructiveness.

The picture is not that of a disease entity, by any means. It is often shown by patients who have been hospitalized for some length of time. They become slovenly in appearance and show disregard for life and property. The attitude is not so much a vicious one as a lack of feeling regarding conduct.

Psychotic Types of Still Broader Scope

From obtained intercorrelational information concerning the dimensions of psychosis at the levels already discussed, and from other factor-analytical information, we have evidence of some very broad psychotic syndromes, most of which come close to some of the Kraepelinian categories.

> *Paranoid schizophrenia:* Combines schizophrenic dissociation with paranoid disposition

The most probable symptoms, from most to least probable presence, are feeling of being systematically persecuted, belief that others are influencing him, delusional thinking, hallucinations, grandiose ideas regarding self, unjustified false beliefs about nature, and assaultive behavior.[34]

> *Hebephrenic schizophrenia:* Combines schizophrenic dissociation with disorientation and hyperprojection

The symptoms listed for the three narrower dimensions of psychosis mentioned in the definition would be probable aspects of the hebephrenic-schizophrenia picture. Clinical accounts of this type of schizophrenia are likely to stress the idea that there has been general regression of the patient to some lower level of development. This aspect seems not to have been brought into the picture in one factor analysis,[35] but it was prominent in the other.[36]

> *Catatonic schizophrenia:* Combines schizophrenic dissociation with catatonia

For particular distinguishing symptoms the reader is referred to the list under catatonia. Of the other, more narrow psychotic dimensions, the following may be involved at times: freedom from depression, disorientation, hyperirritability, and deterioration.[37] Hyperirritability is found in the state of catatonic excitement.

[34] Wittenborn (1951); Wittenborn and Holzberg (1951a); Wittenborn et al. (1951); Lorr and O'Connor (1955).

[35] Degan (1952).

[36] Geist (1952).

[37] Degan (1952).

Mania: Combines hyperexcitability and hyperirritability

We should probably add elation and confidence as important qualities in the picture of mania. Various analyses have agreed somewhat on other common symptoms, most of which were probably not mentioned in connection with hyperexcitability and hyperirritability. These include [38] sociability, shouting, singing, and loud talking; sudden and drastic changes in mood; lack of restraint; easy decisions; attention-demanding actions; exaggeration of own ability, health, and well-being; and poor compliance.

There is serious disagreement as to whether the factor that represents this syndrome is bipolar. Degan (1952) declares that it is not. Other writers insist that such a factor is a bipolar manic-depressive dimension, but their results provide little evidence that symptoms of depression have much negative relationship to it.[39] In only one study were much of the traditional manic and depressive syndromes found in direct opposition on a single bipolar dimension.[40] We should not expect complete opposition of all associated symptoms because there can be some apparently contradictory concomitances of qualities, as will be seen in connection with the next factor.

Psychotic anxiety: A state of depressed or melancholy agitation

In this factor we see that depressed states are not always negatively associated with excitability or hyperactivity. Four analyses have verified the common observation that there are many patients who are agitated with their depression, and the key to this state seems to be anxiety. In addition to anxiety, the most commonly mentioned psychotic symptoms are the patient's belief that he is evil, expectation of impending doom, fear that he will commit an abhorred act, and attempts to commit suicide.[41] While these seem to be the most constant symptoms, there are others more or less commonly associated, including phobias, obsessive thoughts, and retarded or blocked associative responses. Overtly, there may be tearfulness, if not crying spells, refusal of food, withdrawal from social contacts, and insomnia.

Introjection vs. projection: Combines neurasthenia and psychotic depression at one pole, with hyperprojection and hyperirritability at the other

This factor, as defined, was reported by Degan (1952). It seems to represent two opposed general ways in which individuals deal with their

[38] Wittenborn (1951); Wittenborn and Holzberg (1951a); Degan (1952); Lorr and Rubenstein (1955); Lorr et al. (1955).

[39] Wittenborn (1951); Wittenborn and Holzberg (1951a).

[40] Lorr et al. (1955).

[41] Wittenborn (1951); Wittenborn et al. (1951); Wittenborn and Holzberg (1951a); Lorr et al. (1955).

conflicts. One is a self-accusatory, defeatist approach and the other is an active, defensive approach. The same kind of opposition has been detected by other investigators. In the one case the opposition was described as overcontrol, overrestraint, and conformity vs. psychopathic personality.[42] In the other there was recognition of overcontrol vs. undercontrol, as exhibited most clearly by patients classified as anxiety cases on the one hand and as psychopathic-personality cases on the other.[43]

Is There a General Dimension of Psychoticism?

At various times Eysenck has proposed a comprehensive dimension that extends from normal to psychotic in addition to another dimension that extends from normal to neurotic. His best evidence is in the form of behavior tests that discriminate psychotics from normals and neurotics.[44] Psychotics were found to be inferior to normals, on the average, in tests of fluency, continuous addition, mirror drawing, memory, speed of reading, and tapping speed. Differences were also found in expressive-test results. Psychotics tended to be slower in making decisions regarding social attitudes, and they tended to make larger movements and to overestimate distances.[45] Such tests are not the same ones that discriminate neurotics from normals. Eysenck also points out that the same tests that discriminate psychotics from normals tend to be intercorrelated in the normal population.

It is still to be determined how much there is to be gained by describing in terms of a general psychoticism dimension and how much meaning such a dimension may have in a normal population. Where decisions as to normal vs. neurotic vs. psychotic are needed, it is desirable, of course, to have discriminating tests that will aid us in making such decisions. In discriminating between psychotics and normals by means of tests, however, we should find out what the differences in test performance mean. As it was pointed out in connection with the tests that help to discriminate neurotics from normals, many of the differences may be incidental or secondary effects. They may not reflect any general underlying variable along which normals differ, as Eysenck believes. In view of the very great heterogeneity of psychotic types, it is difficult to accept the idea of such a unitary variable.

SUMMARY

Experience in diagnosing patients in the traditional nosological categories shows a rather unsatisfactory state of affairs. Discriminations between normal individuals and pathological individuals reflect great

[42] Lorr and Rubenstein (1955).
[43] Geist (1952).

[44] Eysenck (1955*b*).
[45] Eysenck (1952).

variations in standards of normality and pathology. Classification of patients in different categories of pathology shows considerable disagreement among diagnosticians, except for the use of the grossest distinctions. Such a state of affairs calls for more rigorous methods of reexamining the traditional categories of pathology. The natural approach is through the study of concomitance of symptoms, which means intercorrelational studies of symptoms. Factor analysis has indicated many verified dimensions of both neurosis and psychosis, at different levels of complexity.

At higher levels of complexity the traditional neurotic disorders of neurasthenia, compulsion neurosis, and conversion hysteria have been supported. Other dimensions of neurosis have been indicated at lower levels of complexity, including neurotic inadequacy, neurotic emotionality, neurotic anxiety, neurotic hostility, and neurotic sexual conflict, plus a pair of psychosomatic disorders of cardiovascular reaction and gastrointestinal reaction. The usefulness and significance of a proposed over-all neurotic-tendency dimension are still to be determined.

Among the less complex psychotic variables we have three involving cognitive symptoms primarily—disorientation, hyperprojection, and paranoid disposition. We find four variables involving primarily emotional symptoms—hyperexcitability, psychotic depression, psychotic anxiety, and hyperirritability. A primarily psychomotor disorder is catatonia. Some of these dimensions exhibit pictures somewhat parallel to corresponding dimensions of neurosis.

Psychotic dimensions of somewhat broader scope include schizophrenic dissociation and deterioration. Still more complex syndromes correspond fairly well with traditional categories of pathology—paranoid schizophrenia, hebephrenic schizophrenia, and catatonic schizophrenia—all of which combine the syndrome of schizophrenic dissociation with other syndromes of like complexity. Also recognized at the higher level of complexity are mania and a bipolar variable called introjection vs. projection.

The hypothesis of an over-all psychotic disposition which extends into the normal population, like that for a general neuroticism, still needs to be examined. The point of view of this volume has been against the idea of extending pathological variables into the normal population. Instead, it proposes the extension of descriptive variables of the normal population into pathological groups, thus accounting to a large extent for their syndromes. Involvements of some of the patterns of primary traits in some of these syndromes of pathology have been pointed out.

APPENDIX

SOME BASIC STATISTICS

FROM TIME to time in this volume some basic statistics are mentioned, including the *arithmetic mean* (usually referred to as simply the "mean"), the *variance,* the *standard deviation,* the *coefficient of correlation,* and the *factor loading.* For the benefit of the readers whose acquaintance with statistics is very limited, the illustrations that follow should be helpful.

Table A.1

Formulas for the six hypothetical scores, each with different weights for the two factors

Score	Formula
1	l
2	w
3	$2l + w$
4	$2l + 2w$
5	$l + 2w$
6	$4l + w$

The "experimental data" that we shall use are included in Table A.2. Nine hypothetical individuals *A* through *I* have been assumed for the

Table A.2

Six scores for each of nine hypothetical persons

Person	1	2	3	4	5	6
A	7	1	15	16	9	29
B	5	3	13	16	11	23
C	4	4	12	16	12	20
D	3	5	11	16	13	17
E	1	7	9	16	15	11
F	5	5	15	20	15	25
G	3	3	9	12	9	15
H	1	1	3	4	3	5
I	7	7	21	28	21	35

purposes of illustration. Each person has six "scores," which we shall assume came from six different tests. Each score scale is considered to be a variable, a continuum along which individuals differ.

In Table A.3 we find illustrated the steps by which means, variances, standard deviations, and coefficients of correlation may be computed. Two sets of scores, for tests 2 and 3, have been selected for this purpose from Table A.2. For convenience during the computations, we let X stand for test 2 and Y for test 3.

THE ARITHMETIC MEAN

The mean is most directly computed by summing the scores in a set and then dividing by the number of cases N. This is demonstrated just below Table A.3 for variables X and Y, the means being 4.0 and 12.0, respectively.

VARIANCE

As it was pointed out in early chapters, the variance of a set of measurements indicates the amount of scatter or dispersion; when each measurement comes from a different individual, variance indicates the extent of the individual differences within the group. In computing the variance we first determine how far every score deviates from the mean. In the illustration the deviations are symbolized by x and y. The next step is to square all the deviations. The squares of x and y are seen in the later columns of Table A.3. For each set the mean of the squared deviations gives us the variance. This requires the division of the sum of the squared deviations by N, the number of cases. The variances of X and Y are 4.44 and 22.22, respectively. Individual differences in Y (score 3) are five times as great as in X (score 2).

THE STANDARD DEVIATION

A standard deviation of a distribution of scores is equal to the square root of the variance. Taking the square roots of V_x and V_y, we find the two standard deviations to be 2.11 and 4.71, respectively. The standard deviation is a measure of variability, another index of the extent of the individual differences of measurements. For some purposes it is more meaningful than the variance, for it is a distance on the score scale. If a distribution of scores is approximately normal, we may expect that two-thirds of the cases will fall within one standard deviation from the mean, that is, between a point one standard deviation below the mean and a point one standard deviation above the mean.

THE COEFFICIENT OF CORRELATION

A coefficient of correlation tells us how much agreement there is between two sets of scores, that is, whether they vary together and to

Table A.3

Illustration of some basic statistics, showing the computation of arithmetic means, variances, standard deviations, and the correlation between score 2 and score 3

(Score 2) X	(Score 3) Y	$(X - M_x)$ x	$(Y - M_y)$ y	x^2	xy	y^2
1	15	-3	$+3$	9	-9	9
3	13	-1	$+1$	1	-1	1
4	12	0	0	0	0	0
5	11	$+1$	-1	1	-1	1
7	9	$+3$	-3	9	-9	9
5	15	$+1$	$+3$	1	3	9
3	9	-1	-3	1	3	9
1	3	-3	-9	9	27	81
7	21	$+3$	$+9$	9	27	81
Σ 36	108	0	0	40	40	200
M 4.0	12.0	0	0	4.44	4.44	22.22

$$M_x = \frac{\Sigma X}{N} = \frac{36}{9} = 4.0$$

where M_x = mean of the X's,
ΣX = sum of the X's
N = number of X's

Similarly,

$$M_y = \frac{\Sigma Y}{N} = \frac{108}{9} = 12.0$$

$$V_x = \sigma_x{}^2 = \frac{\Sigma x^2}{N} = \frac{40}{9} = 4.44$$

where V_x = variance of the X's
Σx^2 = sum of squared deviations of X's

Similarly,

$$V_y = \frac{\Sigma y^2}{N} = \frac{200}{9} = 22.22$$

$$\sigma_x = \sqrt{V_x} = \sqrt{4.44} = 2.11$$

where σ_x = standard deviation of the X's

Similarly,

$$\sigma_y = \sqrt{V_y} = \sqrt{22.22} = 4.71$$

$$r_{xy} = \frac{\Sigma xy}{N\sigma_x\sigma_y} = \frac{40}{9(2.11)(4.71)} = \frac{40}{89.46} = .45$$

where r_{xy} = coefficient of correlation between X and Y

what extent. The coefficient can vary in different samples of data from
+1.0 when there is perfect, positive agreement, through 0.0 when there
is no relationship whatever, to −1.0 when there is perfect agreement in
the reverse direction. Examination of the two sets of scores in Table A.3
will show some slight tendency for high scores in the one set to go with
high scores in the other, but there are many exceptions. We should
expect some degree of positive correlation, but certainly not perfect
correlation. In Table A.2 we can find other pairs of columns of scores
in which the agreement is much closer—scores 1 and 6, for example, or
4 and 5. Inspection is a poor way of deciding upon the amount of agreement. A coefficient of correlation tells us exactly how much relationship
exists in a sample.

The coefficient of correlation for the relationship between scores 2 and 3
(X and Y) is computed in the last row beneath Table A.3. For this
purpose, one new value that we have not already computed is needed,
namely, the sum of the cross products. A cross product is the product of
the two deviations for each person. The xy products are given in the
next to the last column of Table A.3, with appropriate algebraic sign,
which must be observed in summing them. We divide this sum by the
product of the two standard deviations multiplied by N. The result is a
coefficient of correlation r_{xy}, equal to .45. This indicates what we would
usually call a *moderate* amount of correlation. Various uses and interpretations of correlation coefficients are mentioned in some of the chapters,
particularly Chapters 4 and 5.

SOME ELEMENTARY FACTOR THEORY

Some illustrations will be given here to lend additional meaning to the
discussions of factors in Chapters 4 and 5 and elsewhere. We shall start
with some ideas presented in Chapter 4, to the effect that each scalable
trait may be represented as a straight line and each person's characteristic
position on the trait may be represented as a point on that line. We shall,
in fact, make use of the general dimensional conception of personality
as illustrated in Figure 4.7.

A TWO-FACTOR CASE

Let us restrict our interest to two hypothetical independent (orthogonal,
uncorrelated) basic dimensions, representing two primary traits, which
can also be discovered as factors. Let us call these traits L and W. Let us
arbitrarily assume nine individuals who have trait positions on L and W
as indicated in Table A.2 as scores 1 and 2, respectively, and as shown
graphically in Figure A.1. We see the individuals represented in Figure
A.1 as they might appear if they were rectangles, with only two "traits,"

length (*L*) and width (*W*). We see the same individuals represented in a more abstract fashion in Figure A.2 as points in a two-dimensional space located with reference to two axes, *L* and *W*. This type of representation is like that in Figure 4.7.

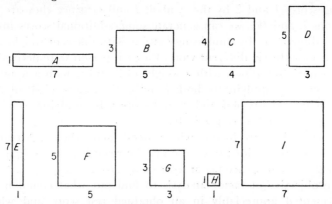

Fig. A.1 Representations of "individuals" *A* through *I*, each with two factor scores. Scores in factor *L* are represented by the horizontal dimensions of the rectangles and scores in factor *W* by the vertical dimensions.

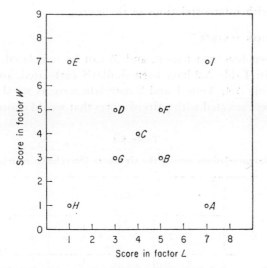

Fig. A.2 Diagram showing each "person," *A* through *I*, in terms of his two scores for factors *L* and *W*, where scores are represented as coordinates in a space in which factors *L* and *W* are orthogonal, or Cartesian axes.

TEST SCORES FROM FACTOR SCORES

We have two basic scores for each person (scores 1 and 2 in Table A.2). These happen to be along the dimensions *L* and *W*. Scores 1 and 2 are "pure" factor scores, which we should often like to know regarding individuals, although this is a goal we very rarely achieve. The kind of scores that we do obtain are likely to be determined by more than one primary trait. Let us assume some other scores of this type for our nine individuals. Denoting scores 1 and 2 by the symbols l and w (since they are on the dimensions L and W), we can generate some additional scores involving these two dimensions by combining l and w with different weights. Table A.1 shows how the six different scores for each person were derived. Score 3 comes from combining l with a weight of 2 and w with a weight of 1. Score 4 comes by applying to both l and w the same weight of 2; score 5 by applying weights of 1 and 2; and score 6 by applying weights of 4 and 1 to scores l and w, respectively.

These operations are in line with general factor theory. According to factor theory, an obtained test score may be regarded as a weighted composite of factor scores, each factor score being given an appropriate weight. It is one objective of factor analysis to find out what common factors are represented appreciably in an obtained test score and what the weights are. The weights, when the factors are orthogonal (independent), are the correlations of the obtained scores with the factors. They are called factor loadings. We learn this information from the factor analysis, which starts with intercorrelations of the scores.

THE CORRELATION MATRIX

We have seen how two tests (2 and 3) can be correlated. All possible pairs of tests in Table A.2 have been similarly correlated, and the results appear in Table A.4. Tests 1 and 2 correlate zero, as we should expect. Individuals were selected with pairs of scores that would ensure this. Other

Table A.4

Intercorrelations among the six scores (correlation matrix)

	Scores					
	1	2	3	4	5	6
1	1.00	.00	.89	.71	.45	.97
2	.00	1.00	.45	.71	.89	.24
3	.89	.45	1.00	.95	.80	.98
4	.71	.71	.95	1.00	.95	.86
5	.45	.89	.80	.95	1.00	.65
6	.97	.24	.98	.86	.65	1.00

correlations are large or small, depending upon how similar their compositions are in terms of the factors and their weights.

The intercorrelations can be represented geometrically as in Figure A.3. There each score variable is represented as a *vector* extending from the origin in a reference frame provided by the two coordinate axes, L and W, or as points at the ends of the vector. The nearer two vectors are to each other, the higher the correlation between the tests that they represent.

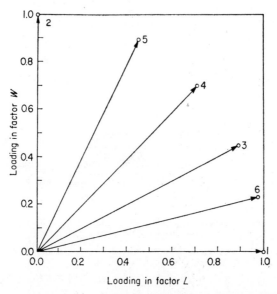

Fig. A.3 Showing six "tests" as vectors in a reference frame provided by the two factors *L* and *W*. In this particular case, two tests, 1 and 2, happen to coincide with factors *L* and *W*, respectively, since they are pure measures of those factors.

Vectors for tests 3 and 6 are closest together, and their correlation is .98. Vectors 1 and 2 are at a right angle since they are correlated zero. Vector 1 is also far from vector 5, consistent with a correlation of .45, and vector 2 is far from vector 6, with a correlation of only .24.

The locations of these six vectors with respect to one another in the plane are completely determined by the intercorrelations. The two axes, which happen to coincide with score variables 1 and 2, represent the two factors. The two factors give us all the information that the six tests would give us regarding the individuals. Test 4 measures both factors, L and W, to equal extents, and if one wanted a single score that indicated something about the combined effects of L and W in each individual, this score would be an impartial indicator. From the formula for score 4, we can see that it actually represents the perimeter of each rectangle in

Figure A.1. This would be one index of general size of each "person," but for two people of equal size, like *A* and *E*, we would not know whether the score of 16 means a person with 7 units on *L* and 1 unit on *W* or vice versa. For information regarding shape we need two un-ambiguous scores for each person. Many scores of psychological tests now in use are ambiguous, like scores 3 to 6 in our illustration.

THE FACTOR MATRIX

A factor analysis comes out with information like that in Table A.5, which we call a *factor matrix*. The values in the matrix are the correla-

Table A.5

Correlations of six tests with two factors (factor matrix)

Tests	Factors	
	L	*W*
1	1.00	.00
2	.00	1.00
3	.89	.45
4	.71	.71
5	.45	.89
6	.97	.24

tions of the tests with the factors. There are almost invariably fewer factors than tests. The factor matrix contains all the information that is contained in the correlation matrix. It is ordinarily derived from the correlation matrix, but when we know a factor matrix, we can, if we like, generate from it the intercorrelations among all pairs of tests.

The factor loadings are represented geometrically in Figure A.3. The two coordinates of each point for a test, that is, its projections on axes *L* and *W*, are the factor loadings. Test 4 has projections of .71 on both axes; test 5 has a projection of .45 on *L* and of .89 on *W*, and so on.

It was said earlier that the weights used in the equations for scores such as those for tests 3 to 6 are factor loadings. We shall have to explain one discrepancy that follows from that statement, for the weights actually given in Table A.1 are obviously not the factor loadings. For convenience, simple integers were adopted as weights. They are directly proportional to the factor loadings. As long as they are proportional, the other rela-tionships we have seen—correlations and factor loadings—will still be true. The loadings for test 3 are .89 and .45, not precisely in the ratio of 2 to 1, owing to rounding of values to the nearest second-decimal digit. The loadings for test 6 are .97 and .24, not quite in ratio of 4 to 1, but again, as close as rounding operations will allow.

PROPORTIONS OF TOTAL SCORE VARIANCES ACCOUNTED FOR

In several places in the text, the total variance of scores for a test are said to be accounted for by different proportions contributed by different sources. Sometimes the sources are factors, as in Table 5.2 and as represented graphically in Figure 5.2. For each factor component of each test, the proportion of the total test-score variance that can be accounted for by the factor is the square of the factor loading. This follows a more general principle. A coefficient of correlation indicates the degree of concomitant variation of two variables, such as two sets of scores. A square of that coefficient is known as the *coefficient of determination*. It indicates the extent to which the variance of the one thing correlated is accounted for by variance in the other. When factor loadings are coefficients of correlations, as they are with orthogonal factors, we may square them and treat them as coefficients of determination, determination of total test score by the factor component.

We could square all the loadings in Table A.5 and find that variance on test 1 is determined 100 per cent by variance in factor L, while variance in test 2 is determined similarly by factor W. The variance in test 3 is determined 80 per cent by L and 20 per cent by W, whereas in test 5 the reverse is true. The variance in test 4 is determined to the extent of 50 per cent by each factor, but test 6 has the most lopsided determination of all, as we should expect from the weights—94 per cent by factor L and only 6 per cent by factor W. It will be noted that in each case the two percentages add up to 100. This is because we are dealing with perfectly reliable "tests" and also "tests" in which only two common factors account for all variances. In Table 5.2 we see that more than two factors are commonly involved, and that even all the known factors fail to account for all of a test's variance in common practice, because no actual test is completely reliable nor are all its common-factor contributions known.

REFERENCES

Aaronson, B. S., and Welch, G. S. (1940). The MMPI as diagnostic differentiator: a reply to Rubin. *J. consult. Psychol.,* 14, 324–325.

Abelson, R. P. (1953). *Spectral analysis and the study of individual differences in the performance of routine, repetitive tasks.* Princeton, N.J.: Educational Testing Service.

Ackerson, L. (1943). Inferiority attitudes and their correlations among children examined in a behavior clinic. *J. genet. Psychol.,* 62, 85–96.

Adams, C. R. (1946). The prediction of adjustment in marriage. *Educ. psychol. Measmt,* 6, 185–193.

Adams, H. E. (1927). The good judge of personality. *J. abnorm. soc. Psychol.,* 22, 172–181.

Adamson, R. E. (1952). Functional fixedness as related to problem solving: a repetition of three experiments. *J. exp. Psychol.,* 44, 288–291.

Adcock, C. J. (1950). A note on the factorial analysis of Sheldon's personality traits. *Aust. J. Psychol. Phil.,* 2, 114–115.

Adcock, C. J. (1952). Temperament and personality. *Aust. J. Psychol. Phil.,* 4, 149–165.

Adkins, D. C., and Kuder, G. F. (1940). The relation of primary mental abilities to activity preferences. *Psychometrika,* 5, 251–262.

Adorno, T. W., Frenkel-Brunswik, E., Levinson, D. J., and Sanford, R. N. (1950). *The authoritarian personality.* New York: Harper.

Ahmavaara, Y. (1957). *On the unified factor theory of mind.* Helsinki: Akademiae Scientiarum Fennicae.

Allport, F. H., Walker, L., and Lathers, E. (1934). Written composition and characteristics of personality. *Arch. Psychol., N.Y.,* 26, No. 173.

Allport, G. W. (1937). *Personality: a psychological interpretation.* New York: Holt.

Allport, G. W. (1942). *The use of personal documents in psychological science.* New York: Social Science Research Council.

Allport, G. W., and Allport, F. H. (1928). *The A-S reaction study.* Boston: Houghton Mifflin.

Allport, G. W., and Odbert, H. S. (1936). Trait-names: a psycho-lexical study. *Psychol. Monogr.,* 47, Whole No. 211.

Allport, G. W., and Vernon, P. E. (1931). *A study of values.* Boston: Houghton Mifflin.

Allport, G. W., and Vernon, P. E. (1933). *Studies in expressive movement.* New York: Macmillan.

Amatora, M. (1956). Validity in self evaluation. *Educ. psychol. Measmt,* 16, 119–126.

Anastasi, A. (1948). A methodological note on the "controlled diary" technique. *J. genet. Psychol.*, 3, 237–241.

Anastasi, A., Fuller, J. L., Scott, J. P., and Schmitt, J. R. (1955). A factor analysis of the performance of dogs on certain learning tests. *Zoologika*, 40, 33–46.

Anderson, E. E. (1937). Interrelationships of drives in the male albino rat. I. Intercorrelations of measures of drives. *J. comp. Psychol.*, 24, 73–118.

Anderson, H. H. (1940). An examination of the concepts of domination and integration in relation to dominance and ascendance. *Psychol. Rev.*, 47, 21–37.

Anderson, J. E. (1939). An evaluation of certain indices of linguistic development. *Child Develpm.*, 8, 62–68.

Anderson, R. G. (1938). Technological aspects of counseling adult women. *J. appl. Psychol.*, 22, 455–469.

Andrews, T. G. (1943). A factorial analysis of responses to the comic as a study in personality. *J. gen. Psychol.*, 28, 209–224.

Ansbacher, H. L. (1951). The history of the leaderless discussion group technique. *Psychol. Bull.*, 48, 383–391.

Arnold, D. C. (1943). *The clinical validity of the Humm-Wadsworth temperament scale in psychiatric diagnosis.* Doctor's dissertation, Minneapolis: University of Minnesota.

Arrington, R. E. (1943). Time sampling in studies of social behavior. *Psychol. Bull.*, 40, 81–124.

Ash, P. (1949). The reliability of psychiatric diagnoses. *J. abnorm. soc. Psychol.*, 44, 272–276.

Atkinson, J. W., and McClelland, D. C. (1948). The projective expression of needs. II. The effect of different intensities of hunger drive on thematic apperception. *J. exp. Psychol.*, 38, 643–658.

Atwell, S. (1939). Color vision in relation to artistic ability. *J. Psychol.*, 8, 53–56.

Auld, F., Jr., and Mahl, G. F. (1956). A comparison of the DRQ with ratings of emotion. *J. abnorm. soc. Psychol.*, 53, 386–388.

Ausubel, D. F., and Schiff, H. M. (1955). A level of aspiration approach to the measure of goal tenacity. *J. gen. Psychol.*, 52, 97–110.

Ayad, J. M., and Farnsworth, P. R. (1953). Shifts in the values of opinion items: further data. *J. Psychol.*, 36, 295–298.

Baier, D. E. (1947). Note on "A review of leadership problems with particular reference to military problems." *Psychol. Bull.*, 44, 466–467.

Baldwin, A. L. (1946). The study of individual personality by means of the intraindividual correlation. *J. Pers.*, 14, 151–168.

Balinsky, B. (1941). An analysis of the mental factors of various age groups from nine to sixty. *Genet. Psychol. Monogr.*, 23, 191–234.

Balinsky, B. (1945). The multiple choice group Rorschach test as a means of screening applicants for jobs. *J. Psychol.*, 19, 203–208.

Barnes, C. A. (1952). A statistical study of the Freudian theory of levels of psychosexual development. *Genet. Psychol. Monogr.*, 45, 105–175.

Barnett, G. J., Stewart, L. H., and Super, D. E. (1953). Level of occupational interest: deadweight or dynamism. *Educ. psychol. Measmt*, 13, 193–208.

Barron, F. (1952). Personality style and perceptual choice. *J. Pers.*, 20, 385–401.

Barron, F. (1953a). Complexity-simplicity as a personality dimension. *J. abnorm. soc. Psychol.*, 48, 163–172.

Barron, F. (1953*b*). Some test correlates of responses to psychotherapy. *J. consult. Psychol.,* 17, 234–241.

Barron, F. (1955*a*). The disposition toward originality. *J. abnorm. soc. Psychol.,* 51, 478–485.

Barron, F. (1955*b*). Threshold for the perception of human movement in ink-blots. *J. consult. Psychol.,* 19, 33–38.

Bartlett, F. C. (1938). The cooperation of social groups: a preliminary report and suggestion. *Occup. Psychol.,* 12, 30–42.

Bartlett, F. C. (1939). *The study of society.* London: Routledge.

Bartlett, N. (1950). Review of research and development in examination for aptitude for submarine training, 1942–1945. *Medical Research Laboratory Reports,* 9, 11–53. No. 153, New London, Conn.: U.S. Naval Submarine Base.

Bass, B. M. (1951). Situational tests. I. Individual interviews compared with leaderless group discussions. *Educ. psychol. Measmt,* 11, 67–75.

Bass, B. M. (1954). The leaderless group discussion. *Psychol. Bull.,* 51, 465–492.

Bass, B. M., and Klubeck, S. (1952). Effects of seating arrangement on leaderless group discussion. *J. abnorm. soc. Psychol.,* 47, 724–727.

Bass, B. M., Klubeck, S., and Wurster, C. R. (1953). Factors influencing reliability and validity of leaderless group discussion assessment. *J. appl. Psychol.,* 37, 26–30.

Bass, B. M., McGehee, C. R., Hawkins, W. C., Young, P. C., and Gebel, A. S. (1953). Personality variables related to leaderless group discussion behavior. *J. abnorm. soc. Psychol.,* 48, 120–128.

Bass, B. M., and Norton, F. T. M. (1951). Group size and leaderless discussions. *J. appl. Psychol.,* 35, 397–400.

Bass, B. M., and White, O. L. (1951). Situational tests. III. Observers' ratings of leaderless group discussion participants as indicators of external leadership status. *Educ. psychol. Measmt,* 11, 355–361.

Bass, B. M., Wurster, C. R., Doll, E. A., and Clair, D. J. (1953). Situational and personality factors in leadership among sorority women. *Psychol. Monogr.,* 67, Whole No. 366.

Bass, R. I. (1939). An analysis of the components of tests of semicircular canal function and of static and dynamic balance. *Res. Quart. Amer. Ass. Hlth phys. Educ.,* 10, 33–52.

Beaver, A. P. (1955). Temperament and nursing. *Psychol. Rep.* 9, 339–344.

Beck, S. J. (1944). *Rorschach's test. I. Basic processes.* New York: Brune & Stratton.

Beck, S. J. (1951). The Rorschach test: a multi-dimensional test of personality. In H. H. Anderson and G. L. Anderson (Eds.), *Introduction to projective techniques.* Englewood Cliffs, N.J.: Prentice-Hall.

Beck, S. J. (1953). The science of personality: nomothetic or idiographic? *Psychol. Rev.,* 60, 353–359.

Bell, G. B., and French, R. L. (1950). Consistency of individual leadership position in small groups of varying membership. *J. abnorm. soc. Psychol.,* 45, 764–767.

Bell, G. B., and Hall, H. H., Jr. (1954). The relationship between leadership and empathy. *J. abnorm. soc. Psychol.,* 49, 156–157.

Bell, H. M. (1939). *The theory and practice of personal counseling.* Stanford, Calif.: Stanford University Press.

Bell, J. E. (1948). *Projective techniques: a dynamic approach to the study of personality.* New York: Longmans,

Bellak, L. (1944). The concept of projection. *Psychiat.*, 7, 353–370.

Bellak, L. (1950). Thematic apperception: failures and the defenses. *Trans. N.Y. Acad. Sci.*, 12, 122–126.

Bellak, L. (1956). Psychoanalytic theory of personality. In J. L. McCary (Ed.), *Psychology of Personality*. New York: Logos Press.

Bendig, A. W. (1955). Ability and personality characteristics of introductory psychology instructors rated competent and empathetic by their students. *J. educ. Res.*, 48, 705–709.

Bendig, A. W., and Sprague, J. L. (1954). The Guilford-Zimmerman Temperament Survey as a predictor of achievement level and achievement fluctuation in introductory psychology. *J. appl. Psychol.*, 38, 409–413.

Benton, A. L. (1945). The Minnesota Multiphasic Personality Inventory in clinical practice. *J. nerv. ment. Dis.*, 102, 406–420.

Benton, A. L., and Bandura, A. (1953). "Primary" and "secondary" suggestibility. *J. abnorm. soc. Psychol.*, 48, 336–340.

Benton, A. L., and Probst, K. A. (1946). A comparison of psychiatric ratings with Minnesota Multiphasic Personality Inventory. *J. abnorm. soc. Psychol.*, 41, 75–78.

Benton, A. L., and Stone, I. R. (1937). Consistency of response to personality inventory items as a function of length of interval between test and retest. *J. soc. Psychol.*, 8, 143–145.

Berger, R. M., Guilford, J. P., and Christensen, P. R. (1957). A factor-analytic study of planning. *Psychol. Monogr.*, 71, Whole No. 435.

Bernard, J. (1949a). The Rosenzweig Picture-Frustration Study. I. Norms, reliability, and statistical evaluation. *J. Psychol.*, 28, 325–332.

Bernard, J. (1949b). The Rosenzweig Picture-Frustration Study. II. Interpretation. *J. Psychol.*, 28, 333–343.

Bernreuter, R. G. (1933a). The theory and construction of the personality inventory. *J. soc. Psychol.*, 4, 387–405.

Bernreuter, R. G. (1933b). Validity of the personality inventory. *Personnel J.*, 11, 383–386.

Bijou, S. W. (Ed.) (1947). *The psychological program in AAF convalescent hospitals. Army Air Forces Aviation Psychology Research Program Reports*, No. 15. Washington: GPO.

Billingslea, F. Y. (1942). Intercorrelational analysis of certain behavior salients in the rat. *J. comp. Psychol.*, 34, 203–211.

Binet, A. (1906). *Les révélations de l'écriture d'après un controle scientifique.* Paris: Alcan.

Birch, H. G., and Rabinowitz, H. S. (1951). The negative effect of previous experience on productive thinking. *J. exp. Psychol.*, 41, 121–125.

Birge, W. R. (1954). An experimental inquiry into the measurable handwriting correlates of five personality traits. *J. Pers.*, 23, 215–223.

Blade, M. F., and Watson, W. S. (1955). Increase in spatial visualization test scores during engineering study. *Psychol. Monogr.*, 69, Whole No. 397.

Bloom, B. S. (1936). Further validation of the Bernreuter Personality Inventory. *Penn. State Coll. Stud. Educ.*, 6, No. 14.

Blum, G. S., and Hunt, H. F. (1952). The validity of the Blacky pictures. *Psychol. Bull.*, 49, 238–250.

Blumenfeld, W. (1946). The invariability of certain coefficients of correlation during human development. *J. genet. Psychol.*, 68, 189–204.

Bolanovich, D. J., and Goodman, C. H. (1944). A study of the Kuder Preference Record. *Educ. psychol. Measmt*, 4, 315–325.

Borg, W. R. (1950). The interests of art students. *Educ. psychol. Measmt*, 10, 100–106.

Borg, W. R., and Hamilton, E. R. (1956). Comparison between a performance test and criteria of instructor effectiveness. *Psychol. Rep.*, 2, 111–116.

Botzum, W. A. (1951). A factorial study of the reasoning and closure factors. *Psychometrika*, 16, 361–386.

Bouvier, E. A. (1954). *A study of scores designed to measure intra-trait variability on a test of temperament.* Master's thesis, Los Angeles: University of Southern California.

Brand, H. (Ed.) (1954). *The study of personality.* New York: Wiley.

Brayfield, A. H., and Crockett, W. H. (1955). Employee attitudes and employee performance. *Psychol. Bull.*, 52, 396–424.

Breemes, E. L., Remmers, H. H., and Morgan, C. L. (1941). Changes in liberalism-conservatism of college students since the depression. *J. soc. Psychol.*, 14, 99–107.

Brockway, A. L., Gleser, G. C., and Ulett, G. A. (1954). Rorschach concepts of normality. *J. consult. Psychol.*, 18, 259–265.

Brogden, H. E. (1940). A factor analysis of forty character tests. *Psychol. Monogr.*, 52, Whole No. 234.

Brogden, H. E. (1944). A multiple-factor analysis of the character trait inter-correlations published by Sister Mary McDonough. *J. educ. Psychol.*, 35, 397–410.

Brogden, H. E. (1952). The primary personal values measured by the Allport-Vernon test "A Study of Values." *Psychol. Monogr.*, 66, Whole No. 348.

Brogden, H. E., and Thomas, W. F. (1943). The primary traits in personality items purporting to measure sociability. *J. Psychol.*, 16, 85–97.

Brolyer, C. R., Thorndike, E. L., and Woodyard, E. (1927). A second study of mental discipline in high school subjects. *J. educ. Psychol.*, 18, 377–404.

Bryan, A. I. (1952). *The public librarian.* New York: Columbia University Press.

Burgess, E. W. (1928). Factors determining success or failure on parole. In A. A. Bruce (Ed.), *The workings of the indeterminate sentence law in the parole system in Illinois.* Springfield, Ill.

Burt, C. (1949a). Subdivided factors. *Brit. J. Psychol., Stat. Sec.*, 2, 41–63.

Burt, C. (1949b). The structure of mind: a review of the results of factor analysis. *Brit. J. Educ. Psychol.*, 19, 100–111, 176–199.

Busemann, A. (1925). *Die Sprache der Jugend als Ausdruck der Entwicklungs-rhythmic.* Jena, Germany: Gustav Fischer Verlagsbuchhandlung.

Busemann, A. (1926). Über typische und phasische Unterschiede der Kategoricalen Sprachform. *Z. pädag. Psychol.*, 27, 415–419.

Butler, J. M., and Fiske, D. (1955). Theory and techniques of assessment. In C. P. Stone and Q. McNemar (Eds.), *Annual Review of Psychology.* Palo Alto, Calif.: Annual Reviews.

Buzby, D. E. (1924). The interpretation of facial expression. *Amer. J. Psychol.*, 35, 602–604.

Cabot, P. S. de Q. (1938). The relationship between characteristics of personality and physique in adolescents. *Genet. Psychol. Monogr.*, 20, 3–120.

Caldwell, C. W., and Weilman, B. (1926). Characteristics of school leaders. *J. educ. Res.*, 14, 1–13.

Calvin, A. D., McGuigan, F. J., Tyrell, S., and Soyars, M. (1956). Manifest anxiety and the palmar perspiration index. *J. consult. Psychol.*, 20, 356.

Cameron, D. E. (1936). Studies in depression. *J. ment. Sci.*, 82, 148–161.

Campbell, A. A. (1932). Community of function in performance of rats on alley mazes and Maier reasoning apparatus. *J. comp. Psychol.*, 14, 225–235.

Campbell, D. T. (1950). The indirect assessment of social attitudes. *Psychol. Bull.*, 47, 15–38.

Campbell, D. T. (1955). An error in some demonstrations of the superior social perceptiveness of leaders. *J. abnorm. soc. Psychol.*, 51, 694–695.

Canning, W., Harlow, G., and Reglin, C. (1950). A study of two personality questionnaires. *J. consult. Psychol.*, 14, 414–415.

Carlson, H. B. (1937). Factor analysis of memory ability. *J. exp. Psychol.*, 21, 477–492.

Carlson, H. B., Fischer, R. P., and Young, P. T. (1945). Improvement in psychology related to intelligence. *Psychol. Bull.*, 42, 27–34.

Carmichael, D. M. (1938). The cooperation of social groups. *Brit. J. Psychol.*, 29, 209–231.

Carp, A. L., and Shavzin, A. R. (1950). The susceptibility to falsification of the Rorschach psychodiagnostic technique. *J. consult. Psychol.*, 14, 230–233.

Carpenter, A. (1941). An analysis of the relationships of the factors of velocity, strength, and dead weight to athletic performance. *Res. Quart. Amer. Ass. Hlth phys. Educ.*, 12, 34–40.

Carr, H. A., and Kindbury, F. A. (1938). The concept of traits. *Psychol. Rev.*, 45, 497–524.

Carroll, J. B. (1941). A factor analysis of verbal abilities. *Psychometrika*, 6, 279–307.

Carroll, J. B. (1943). The factorial representation of mental ability and academic achievement. *Educ. psychol. Measmt*, 3, 307–332.

Carroll, J. B. (1952). Ratings on traits measured by a factored personality inventory. *J. abnorm. soc. Psychol.*, 47, 626–632.

Carter, L., Haythorn, W., and Howell, M. (1950). A further study of the criteria of leadership. *J. abnorm. soc. Psychol.*, 45, 350–358.

Carter, L., Haythorn, W., Shriver, B., and Lanzetta, J. (1951). The behavior of leaders and other group members. *J. abnorm. soc. Psychol.*, 46, 589–595.

Carter, L., and Nixon, M. (1949a). An investigation of the relationship between four criteria of leadership ability for three different tasks. *J. Psychol.*, 27, 245–261.

Carter, L., and Nixon, M. (1949b). Ability, perceptual, personality, and interest factors associated with different criteria of leadership. *J. Psychol.*, 27, 377–389.

Castelnuovo-Tedesco, P. (1948). A study of the relationship between handwriting and personality variables. *Genet. Psychol. Monogr.*, 37, 167–220.

Cattell, R. B. (1943). Fluctuation of sentiments and attitudes as a measure of character integration and of temperament. *Amer. J. Psychol.*, 56, 195–216.

Cattell, R. B. (1944a). Psychological measurement: normative, ipsative, interactive. *Psychol. Rev.*, 51, 292–303.

Cattell, R. B. (1944b). Projection and the design of projective tests of personality. *Charact. & Pers.*, 12, 177–194.

Cattell, R. B. (1945). The description of personality: principles and findings in a factor analysis. *Amer. J. Psychol.*, 58, 69–90.

Cattell, R. B. (1946*a*). *The description and measurement of personality.* Yonkers, N.Y.: World.

Cattell, R. B. (1946*b*). The riddle of perseveration. I. "Creative effort" and disposition rigidity. *J. Pers.,* 14, 229–238.

Cattell, R. B. (1946*c*). The riddle of perseveration. II. Solution in terms of personality structure. *J. Pers.,* 14, 239–267.

Cattell, R. B. (1950). The main personality factors in questionnaire, self-estimate material. *J. soc. Psychol.,* 31, 3–38.

Cattell, R. B. (1955). The principal replicated factors discovered in objective personality tests. *J. abnorm. soc. Psychol.,* 50, 291–314.

Cattell, R. B. (1957). *The sixteen personality factor questionnaire.* (Rev. ed.) Champaign, Ill.: Institute for Personality and Ability Testing.

Cattell, R. B., and Beloff, H. (1958). *The high school personality questionnaire.* Champaign, Ill.: Institute for Personality and Ability Testing.

Cattell, R. B., Cattell, A. K. S., and Rhymer, R. M. (1947). P-technique demonstrated in determining psychophysiological source traits in a normal individual. *Psychometrika,* 12, 267–288.

Cattell, R. B., and Gruen, W. (1954). Primary personality factors in the questionnaire medium for children eleven to fourteen years old. *Educ. psychol. Measmt,* 14, 50–76.

Cattell, R. B., Heist, A. B., Heist, P. A., and Stewart, R. G. (1950). The objective measurement of dynamic traits. *Educ. psychol. Measmt,* 10, 224–248.

Cattell, R. B., and Luborsky, L. B. (1947). Personality factors in response to humor. *J. abnorm. soc. Psychol.,* 42, 402–421.

Cattell, R. B., and Miller, A. (1952). A confirmation of the ergic self-sentiment patterns among dynamic traits (attitude variables) by the R-technique. *Brit. J. Psychol.,* 43, 280–294.

Challman, R. C. (1945). The validity of the Harrower-Erickson multiple choice test as a screening device. *J. Psychol.,* 20, 41–48.

Chein, J. (1939). An experimental study of verbal, numerical, and spatial factors in mental organization. *Psychol. Rec.,* 3, 71–94.

Chen, Tso-Yu L., and Chow, H. H. (1948). A factor study of a test battery at different educational levels. *J. genet. Psychol.,* 73, 187–199.

Child, I. L. (1950). The relation of somatotype to self-ratings on Sheldon's temperamental traits. *J. Pers.,* 18, 440–453.

Child, I. L., Frank, K. F., and Storm, T. (1956). Self-ratings and TAT: their relations to each other and to the childhood background. *J. Pers.,* 25, 96–114.

Child, I. L., and Sheldon, W. H. (1941). The correlation between components of physique and scores on certain psychological tests. *Charact. & Pers.,* 10, 23–34.

Chowdhry, K., and Newcomb, T. M. (1952). The relative abilities of leaders and non-leaders to estimate opinions of their own groups. *J. abnorm. soc. Psychol.,* 47, 51–57.

Christal, R. E. (1958). Factor analytic study of visual memory. *Psychol. Monogr.,* in press.

Churchill, R. D., Curtis, J. M., Coombs, C. H., and Harrell, T. W. (1942). Effect of engineer school training on the Surface Development test. *Educ. psychol. Measmt,* 2, 279–280.

Clark, R. A. (1952). The projective measurement of experimentally induced levels of sexual motivation. *J. exp. Psychol.,* 44, 391–399.

Coffin, T. E. (1944). A three-component theory of leadership. *J. abnorm. soc. Psychol.,* 39, 63–83.

Cole, D. (1951). The reliability of a single Szondi profile. *J. clin. Psychol.,* 7, 383–384.

Comrey, A. L. (1949). A factorial study of achievement in West Point courses. *Educ. psychol. Measmt,* 9, 193–209.

Comrey, A. L., and High, W. S. (1955). Validity of some ability and interest scores. *J. appl. Psychol.,* 39, 247–248.

Conrad, H. S. (1933). The personal equation in ratings. II. A systematic evaluation. *J. educ. Psychol.,* 24, 39–46.

Coombs, C. H. (1941). A factorial study of number ability. *Psychometrika,* 1941, 6, 161–189.

Corey, S. M. (1937). Professed attitudes and actual behavior. *J. educ. Psychol.,* 28, 271–280.

Crockett, W. H., and Meidinger, T. (1956). Authoritarianism and interpersonal perception. *J. abnorm. soc. Psychol.,* 53, 378–380.

Cronbach, L. J. (1946). Response sets and test validity. *Educ. psychol. Measmt,* 6, 475–494.

Cronbach, L. J. (1955). Processes affecting scores on "understanding of others" and "assumed similarity." *Psychol. Bull.,* 52, 177–193.

Cronbach, L. J., and Gleser, G. (1953). Assessing similarity between profiles. *Psychol. Bull.,* 50, 456–473.

Crosby, R. C., and Winsor, A. L. (1941). The validity of students' estimates of their interests. *J. appl. Psychol.,* 25, 408–414.

Cross, O. H. (1950). A study of faking on the Kuder Preference Record. *Educ. psychol. Measmt,* 10, 271–277.

Cummings, J. D. (1939). The variability of judgment and "steadiness" of character. *Brit. J. Psychol.,* 29, 345–369.

Curtis, H. A. (1949). A study of the relative effects of age and of test difficulty upon factor patterns. *Genet. Psychol. Monogr.,* 40, 99–148.

Darrow, C. W. (1947). Psychological and psychophysiological significance of the electroencephalogram. *Psychol. Rev.,* 54, 157–168.

Davidson, W. M., and Carroll, J. B. (1945). Speed and level components in time-limit scores: a factor analysis. *Educ. psychol. Measmt,* 5, 411–427.

Davis, R. C. (1942). Methods of measuring muscular tension. *Psychol. Bull.,* 39, 329–346.

Davis, R. C., Buchwald, A. M., and Frankman, R. W. (1955). Autonomic and muscular responses, and their relation to simple stimuli. *Psychol. Monogr.,* 69, Whole No. 415.

de Cillis, O. E., and Orbison, W. D. (1950). A comparison of the Terman-Miles M-F Test and the Mf scale of the MMPI. *J. appl. Psychol.,* 34, 338–342.

Degan, J. W. (1952). Dimensions of functional psychosis. *Psychometr. Monogr.,* No. 6.

Deri, S., Dinnerstein, D., Harding, J., and Pepitone, A. D. (1948). Techniques for the diagnosis and measurement of intergroup attitudes and behavior. *Psychol. Bull.,* 45, 248–271.

Diamond, S. (1947). Three impossibilities: a verbal projective technique. *J. Psychol.,* 24, 281–292.

Doering, C. R. (1934). Reliability of observations of psychiatric and related characteristics. *Amer. J. Orthopsychiat.,* 4, 249–257.

Dollard, J., and Mowrer, O. H. (1947). A method of measuring tension in written documents. *J. abnorm. soc. Psychol.*, 42, 3–32.

Donceel, J. F., Alimena, B. S., and Birch, C. M. (1949). Influence of prestige suggestion on the answers of a personality inventory. *J. appl. Psychol.*, 33, 352–355.

Dorcus, R. M. (1944). A brief study of the Humm-Wadsworth Temperament Scale and the Guilford-Martin Personnel Inventory in an industrial situation *J. appl. Psychol.*, 28, 302–307.

Downey, J. E. (1922). *The will-temperament and its testing.* Yonkers, N.Y.: World.

Drevdahl, J. E. (1956). Factors of importance for creativity. *J. clin. Psychol.*, 12, 21–26.

Dubin, S. S. (1940). Verbal attitude scores predicted from responses in a projective technique. *Sociometry*, 3, 24–28.

Dubin, S. S., Burke, L. K., and Neel, R. G. (1954). Characteristics of hard and easy raters. *PRB Technical Research Note 36.* Washington: The Adjutant General's Office.

Dudek, F. J. (1948–49). The dependence of factorial composition of aptitude tests upon population differences among pilot trainees. I. The isolation of factors. II. The factorial composition of tests and criterion variables. *Educ. psychol. Measmt*, 8, 613–633; 9, 95–104.

Dudycha, G. J. (1938). A qualitative study of punctuality. *J. soc. Psychol.*, 9, 207–217.

Dudycha, G. J. (1939). The dependability of college students. *J. soc. Psychol.*, 10, 233–245.

Duffy, E. (1946). Level of muscular tension as an aspect of personality. *J. gen. Psychol.*, 35, 161–171.

duMas, F. M. (1949). The coefficient of profile similarity. *J. clin. Psychol.*, 5, 123–131.

duMas, F. M. (1955). Science and the single case. *Psychol. Rep.*, 1, 65–75.

Duncker, K. (1945). On problem solving. (Trans. by L. S. Lees.) *Psychol. Monogr.*, 58, Whole No. 270.

Dunkerley, M. D. (1940). A statistical study of leadership among college women. *Stud. Psychol. Psychiat. Cath. Univer. Amer.*, 4, 1–65.

Dunlap, J. W. (1933). The organization of learning and other traits in chickens. *Comp. Psychol. Monogr.*, 9, No. 4.

Dunlap, J. W., and Wantman, M. J. (1944). An investigation of the interview as a technique for selecting aircraft pilots. *CAA Airman Development Division Report*, No. 33. Washington: Civil Aeronautics Administration.

Dymond, R. F., Hughes, A. S., and Raabe, V. L. (1952). Measurable changes in empathy with age. *J. consult. Psychol.*, 16, 202–206.

Dysinger, Dale W. (1950). Factorial study of speed of responses in simple cancellation tasks. *Iowa Acad. Sci.*, 57, 373–378.

Dysinger, Don W. (1939). A critique of the Humm-Wadsworth Temperament Scale. *J. abnorm. soc. Psychol.*, 34, 73–83.

Edwards, A. L. (1953a). The relationship between the judged desirability of a trait and the probability that the trait will be endorsed. *J. appl. Psychol.*, 37, 90–93.

Edwards, A. L. (1953b). *Edwards personal preference schedule.* New York: Psychological Corp.

Edwards, A. L. (1957). *Techniques of attitude scale construction.* New York: Appleton-Century-Crofts.

Eisenberg, P. (1937). Expressive movements related to feeling of dominance. *Arch. Psychol., N.Y.,* No. 211.

Eisenberg, P. (1938). Judging expressive movement. I. Judgments of sex and dominance-feeling from handwriting samples of dominant and non-dominant men and women. *J. appl. Psychol.,* 22, 480–486.

Eisenberg, P., and Reichline, P. B. (1939). Judging expressive movement. II. Judgments of dominance-feeling from motion pictures of gait. *J. soc. Psychol.,* 10, 345–357.

Eisenberg, P., and Wesman, A. G. (1941). Consistency in response and logical interpretation of psychoneurotic inventory items. *J. educ. Psychol.,* 32, 321–338.

Eisenberg, P., and Zalowitz, E. (1939). Judging expressive movement. III. Judgments of dominance-feeling from phonograph records of voice. *J. appl. Psychol.,* 22, 620–631.

Ekman, G. (1951). On the number and definition of dimensions in Kretschmer's and Sheldon's constitutional systems. In *Essays in psychology dedicated to David Katz.* Uppsala, Sweden: Almquist & Wiksell.

Eliasberg, W. (1943). Political graphology. *J. Psychol.,* 16, 177–201.

Elkin, F. (1946). Specialists interpret the case of Harold Holzer. *J. abnorm. soc. Psychol.,* 42, 99–111.

El Koussy, A. A. H. (1935). An investigation into the factors in tests involving the visual perception of space. *Brit. J. Psychol.,* Monogr. Suppl., 20, 1–89.

Ellingson, R. J. (1956). Brain waves and problems of psychology. *Psychol. Bull.,* 53, 1–34.

Ellis, A. (1946). The validity of personality questionnaires. *Psychol. Bull.,* 43, 385–440.

Ellis, A., and Conrad, H. S. (1948). The validity of personality inventories in military practice. *Psychol. Bull.,* 45, 385–426.

Ellison, M. L., and Edgerton, H. A. (1941). The Thurstone Primary Mental Abilities tests and college marks. *Educ. psychol. Measmt,* 1, 399–406.

Ellson, D. G., and Ellson, E. C. (1953). Historical note on the rating scale. *Psychol. Bull.,* 50, 383–384.

Emmett, W. G. (1949). Evidence of a space factor at 11+ and earlier. *Brit. J. Psychol., Stat. Sec.,* 2, 3–16.

Eppinger, H. (1917). "Vagotonia." *Nerv. ment. Dis. Monogr.,* 20.

Escolona, S. K. (1940). The effect of success and failure upon the level of aspiration and behavior in manic-depressive psychoses. *Univer. Iowa Stud. Child Wel.,* 16, No. 3.

Eysenck, H. J. (1940). Some factors in the appreciation of poetry, and their relation to temperamental qualities. *Charact. & Pers.,* 9, 160–167.

Eysenck, H. J. (1941). "Type"-factors in aesthetic judgments. *Brit. J. Psychol.,* 31, 262–270.

Eysenck, H. J. (1942). The appreciation of humour: an experimental and theoretical study. *Brit. J. Psychol.,* 32, 295–309.

Eysenck, H. J. (1943). An experimental analysis of five tests of "appreciation of humor." *Educ. psychol. Measmt,* 13, 191–214.

Eysenck, H. J. (1944). Types of personality: a factorial study of seven hundred neurotics. *J. ment. Sci.,* 90, 851–861.

Eysenck, H. J. (1945). A comparative study of four screening tests for psychoneurotics. *Psychol. Bull.,* 42, 659–662.

Eysenck, H. J. (1947). *Dimensions of personality.* London: Routledge.

Eysenck, H. J. (1950). Cyclothymia and schizothymia as dimensions of personality. I. Historical review. *J. Pers.,* 19, 123–152.

Eysenck, H. J. (1951). The organization of personality. *J. Pers.,* 20, 101–117.

Eysenck, H. J. (1952a). Schizothyme-cyclothyme as a dimension of personality. *J. Pers.,* 20, 345–384.

Eysenck, H. J. (1952b). *The scientific study of personality.* New York: Macmillan.

Eysenck, H. J. (1953a). *The structure of personality.* New York: Wiley.

Eysenck, H. J. (1953b). Primary social attitudes: a comparison of attitude patterns in England, Germany, and Sweden. *J. abnorm. soc. Psychol.,* 48, 563–568.

Eysenck, H. J. (1954a). The science of personality: nomothetic! *Psychol. Rev.,* 61, 339–342.

Eysenck, H. J. (1954b). *The psychology of politics.* London: Routledge.

Eysenck, H. J. (1955a). Cortical inhibition, figural aftereffects, and theory of personality. *J. abnorm. soc. Psychol.,* 51, 94–106.

Eysenck, H. J. (1955b). Psychiatric diagnosis as a psychological and statistical problem. *Psychol. Rep.,* 1, 3–17.

Eysenck, H. J., and Furneaux, W. D. (1945). Primary and secondary suggestibility: an experimental and statistical study. *J. exp. Psychol.,* 35, 485–503.

Falk, J. L. (1956). Issues distinguishing idiographic from nomothetic approaches to personality theory. *Psychol. Rev.,* 63, 53–62.

Farnsworth, P. R. (1938a). The measure of emotional maturity. *J. soc. Psychol.,* 9, 235–237.

Farnsworth, P. R. (1938b). Auditory acuity and musical ability in the first four grades. *J. Psychol.,* 6, 95–98.

Farnsworth, P. R. (1938c). A genetic study of the Bernreuter Personality Inventory. *J. genet. Psychol.,* 52, 5–13.

Farnsworth, P. R. (1941). Further data on the Adlerian theory of artistry. *J. gen. Psychol.,* 24, 447–450.

Farnsworth, P. R. (1943). Shifts in the values of opinion items. *J. Psychol.,* 16, 125–128.

Faterson, H. F. (1931). Organic inferiority and the inferiority attitude. *J. soc. Psychol.,* 2, 87–101.

Faubian, R. W., Cleveland, E. A., and Harrell, T. W. (1942). The influence of training on mechanical aptitude test scores. *Educ. psychol. Measmt,* 2, 91–94.

Fay, P. J., and Middleton, W. C. (1939). Judgment of Spranger personality types from the voice as transmitted over a public-address system. *Charact. & Pers.,* 8, 144–155.

Fay, P. J., and Middleton, W. C. (1940a). Judgment of intelligence from the voice as transmitted over a public address system. *Sociometry,* 3, 186–191.

Fay, P. J., and Middleton, W. C. (1940b). Judgment of Kretschmerian body types from the voice as transmitted over public address system. *J. soc. Psychol.,* 12, 151–162.

Fay, P. J., and Middleton, W. C. (1940c). Certain factors related to liberal and conservative attitudes of college students. I. Father's occupation; size of home town. *J. soc. Psychol.,* 11, 91–105.

Fay, P. J., and Middleton, W. C. (1941a). Judgment of emotional balance from the transmitted voice. *Charact. & Pers.,* 10, 109–113.

Fay, P. J., and Middleton, W. C. (1941b). The ability to judge truth-telling or lying from the voice as transmitted over a public-address system. *J. gen. Psychol.*, 24, 211–215.

Fay, P. J., and Middleton, W. C. (1941c). The ability to judge sociability from the voice as transmitted over a public address system. *J. soc. Psychol.*, 13, 303–309.

Fay, P. J., and Middleton, W. C. (1942a). Judgment of introversion from the transmitted voice. *Quart J. Speech*, 28, 226–228.

Fay, P. J., and Middleton, W. C. (1942b). Measurement of the persuasiveness of the transcribed voice. *J. Psychol.*, 14, 259–267.

Fay, P. J., and Middleton, W. C., (1943). Judgment of leadership from the transmitted voice. *J. soc. Psychol.*, 17, 99–102.

Fay, P. J., and Middleton, W. C. (1944). Judgment of confidence from voice. *J. gen. Psychol.*, 30, 93–95.

Fearing, F. (1942). The appraisal interview. In Q. McNemar and M. A. Merrill (Eds.), *Studies in personality*. New York: McGraw-Hill.

Ferguson, G. A., (1954). On learning and human ability. *Canad. J. Psychol.*, 8, 95–112.

Ferguson, L. W. (1939). Primary social attitudes. *J. Psychol.*, 8, 217–223.

Ferguson, L. W. (1941). The stability of the primary social attitudes. I. Religionism and humanitarianism. *J. Psychol.*, 12, 283–288.

Ferguson, L. W. (1942). The isolation and measurement of nationalism. *J. soc. Psychol.*, 16, 215–228.

Ferguson, L. W. (1944a). A revision of the primary social attitude scales. *J. Psychol.*, 17, 229–241.

Ferguson, L. W. (1944b). Socio-psychological correlates of the primary attitude scales: I. Religionism; II. Humanitarianism. *J. soc. Psychol.*, 19, 81–98.

Ferguson, L. W. (1944c). An analysis of the generality of suggestibility to group opinion. *Charact. & Pers.*, 12, 237–243.

Ferguson, L. W. (1952). *Personality measurement*. New York: McGraw-Hill.

Fisher, S. (1950). Patterns of personality rigidity and some of their determinants. *Psychol. Monogr.*, 64, Whole No. 307.

Fiske, D. W. (1944). A study of the relationships to somatotypes. *J. appl. Psychol.*, 28, 504–519.

Fiske, D. W., and Rice, L. (1955). Intra-individual response variability. *Psychol. Bull.*, 52, 217–250.

Fleishman, E. A. (1954). Dimensional analysis of psychomotor abilities. *J. exp. Psychol.*, 48, 437–454.

Fleishman, E. A., and Hempel, W. E., Jr. (1954a). A factor analysis of dexterity tests. *Personnel Psychol.*, 7, 14–32.

Fleishman, E. A., and Hempel, W. E., Jr. (1954b). Changes in factor structure of a complex psychomotor test as a function of practice. *Psychometrika*, 19, 239–252.

Fleishman, E. A., and Hempel, W. E., Jr. (1955). The relation between abilities and improvement with practice in a visual discrimination reaction task. *J. exp. Psychol.*, 49, 301–312.

Fleishman, E. A., and Hempel, W. E., Jr. (1956). Factorial analysis of complex psychomotor performance and related skills. *J. appl. Psychol.*, 40, 96–104.

Ford, C. F., and Tyler, L. E. (1952). A factor analysis of Terman and Miles' M-F test. *J. appl. Psychol.*, 36, 251–253.

Forer, B. R. (1949). A fallacy of personal validation: a classroom demonstration of gullibility. *J. abnorm. soc. Psychol.*, 44, 118–123.

Franck, K., and Rosen, E. (1949). A projective test of masculinity-femininity. *J. consult. Psychol.*, 13, 247–256.

Frandsen, A. (1947). Interests and general educational development. *J. appl. Psychol.*, 31, 57–66.

Frandsen, A. N., and Sessions, A. D. (1953). Interests and school achievement. *Educ. psychol. Measmt*, 13, 94–101.

Frank, G. H. (1955). A test of the use of a figure drawing test as an indicator of sexual inversion. *Psychol. Rep.*, 1, 137–138.

Frank, G. H. (1956). The Wechsler-Bellevue and psychiatric diagnosis: a factor analytic approach. *J. consult. Psychol.*, 20, 67–69.

Frank, J. D. (1935). Individual differences in certain aspects of the level of aspiration. *Amer. J. Psychol.*, 47, 119–128.

Frank, J. D. (1941). Recent studies of the level of aspiration. *Psychol. Bull.*, 38, 218–226.

Franklin, G. H., Feldman, S., and Odbert, H. S. (1948). Relationship of total bodily movement to some emotional components of personality. *J. Psychol.*, 26, 499–506.

Franklin, J. C., and Brozek, J. (1949). The Rosenzweig test as a measure of frustration response in semi-starvation. *J. consult. Psychol.*, 13, 293–301.

Franklin, J. C., Schiele, B. C., and Brozek, J. (1948). Observations on human behavior in experimental semi-starvation and rehabilitation. *J. clin. Psychol.*, 4, 28–45.

Franks, C. M. (1956). Conditioning and personality: a study of normal and neurotic subjects. *J. abnorm. soc. Psychol.*, 52, 143–150.

Freeman, G. L. (1948). *The energetics of human behavior.* Ithaca, N.Y.: Cornell University Press.

Freeman, G. L., and Manson, G. E. (1942). The stress interview. *J. abnorm. soc. Psychol.*, 37, 427–447.

Freeman, M. J. (1953). The development of a test for the measurement of anxiety: a study of its reliability and validity. *Psychol. Monogr.*, 67, Whole No. 353.

French, J. W. (1948). The validity of a persistence test. *Psychometrika*, 13, 271–276.

French, J. W. (1951). Description of aptitude and achievement tests in terms of rotated factors. *Psychometr. Monogr.*, No. 5.

French, R. L. (1950). Changes in performance on the Rosenzweig Picture-Frustration Study following experimentally induced frustration. *J. consult. Psychol.*, 14, 111–115.

Frenkel-Brunswik, E. (1949). Intolerance of ambiguity as an emotional and perceptual variable. *J. Pers.*, 18, 108–143.

Frick, J. W. (1955). Improving the prediction of academic achievement by use of the *MMPI*. *J. appl. Psychol.*, 39, 49–52.

Frick, J. W., and Keener, H. E. (1956). A validation study of the prediction of college achievement. *J. appl. Psychol.*, 40, 251–252.

Fricke, B. G. (1956). A configurational-content-intensity item for personality measurement. *Educ. psychol. Measmt*, 16, 54–62.

Friedlander, J. W., and Sarbin, T. W. (1938). The depth of hypnosis. *J. abnorm. soc. Psychol.*, 33, 453–475.

Fruchter, B. (1948). The nature of verbal fluency. *Educ. psychol. Measmt*, 8, 33–47.

Fruchter, B. (1954). *Introduction to factor analysis*. Princeton, N.J.: Van Nostrand.

Furneaux, W. D. (1946). The prediction of susceptibility to hypnosis. *J. Pers.*, 14, 281–294.

Gage, N. L. (1952). Judging interests from expressive behavior. *Psychol. Monogr.*, 66, Whole No. 350.

Gage, N. L., and Cronbach, L. J. (1954). Conceptual and methodological problems in interpersonal perception. *Studies in the generality and behavioral correlates of social perception*, Report No. 4. Urbana, Ill.: Bureau of Educational Research.

Gage, N. L., and Exline, R. V. (1953). Social perception and effectiveness in discussion groups. *Hum. Relat.*, 6, 381–396.

Gage, N. L., Leavitt, G. S., and Stone, G. C. (1954). Social perception in the classroom. *Studies in the generality and behavioral correlates of social perception*, Report No. 5. Urbana, Ill.: Bureau of Educational Research.

Galton, F. (1908). *Memories of my life*. London: Methuen.

Gardner, J. W. (1939). Level of aspiration in response to a prearranged sequence of scores. *J. exp. Psychol.*, 25, 601–621.

Gardner, J. W. (1940). The relation of certain personality variables to level of aspiration. *J. Psychol.*, 9, 191–206.

Garrett, H. E. (1938). Differentiable mental traits. *Psychol. Rec.*, 2, 259–298.

Garrett, H. E. (1946). A developmental theory of intelligence. *Amer. Psychologist*, 1, 374–378.

Gates, G. S. (1923). An experimental study of the growth of social perception. *J. educ. Psychol.*, 14, 449–462.

Gebhard, M. E. (1949). Changes in the attractiveness of activities: the effect of expectation preceding performance. *J. exp. Psychol.*, 39, 404–413.

Geist, H. (1952). A comparison of personality test scores and medical psychiatric diagnosis by the inverted factor technique. *J. clin. Psychol.*, 8, 184–188.

Gelb, A., and Goldstein, K. (1920). *Psychologische Analysen hirnpathologischer Falle*. Leipzig: Barth.

Gernes, E. (1940). *A factorial analysis of selected items of the Strong Vocational Interest Blank for Women*. Doctoral dissertation, Lincoln, Nebr.: University of Nebraska.

Gesell, A. (1937). Early evidence of individuality in the human infant. *Sci. Mon.*, 45, 217–225.

Ghiselli, E. E., and Barthol, R. P. (1953). The validity of personality inventories in the selection of employees. *J. appl. Psychol.*, 37, 18–20.

Ghiselli, E. E., and Brown, C. W. (1948). The effectiveness of intelligence tests in the selection of workers. *J. appl. Psychol.*, 32, 575–580.

Ghiselli, E. E., and Brown, C. W. (1951). Validity of aptitude tests for predicting trainability of workers. *Personnel Psychol.*, 4, 243–260.

Gibb, C. A. (1942). Personality traits by factorial analysis. (II). *Austr. J. Psychol. Phil.*, 20, 86–110.

Gibb, C. A. (1947). The principles and traits of leadership. *J. abnorm. soc. Psychol.*, 42, 267–284.

Gibson, J. J. (1947). Motion picture testing and research. *AAF Aviation Psychology Research Program Reports*, No. 7. Washington: GPO.

Gilbert, C. (1950). The Guilford-Zimmerman Temperament Survey and certain related personality traits. *J. appl. Psychol.*, 34, 394–396.

Gilinsky, A. S. (1949). Relative self-estimate and the level of aspiration. *J. exp. Psychol.*, 39, 256–259.

Gilliland, A. R. (1951). The Humm-Wadsworth and the Minnesota Multiphasic. *J. consult. Psychol.*, 15, 457–459.

Gilliland, A. R., and Newman, S. E. (1953). The Humm-Wadsworth Temperament Scale as an indicator of the "problem" employee. *J. appl. Psychol.*, 37, 176–177.

Gilliland, A. R., Wittman, P., and Goldman, M. (1943). Patterns and scatter of mental abilities in various psychoses. *J. gen. Psychol.*, 29, 251–260.

Glad, D. D., and Shearn, C. R. (1956). An emotional projection test. *Percept. mot. Skills,* Monogr. Suppl. 1, 6, 1–12.

Gladstone, R. (1953). A group test of palmar sweat. *J. gen. Psychol.*, 48, 29–49.

Glaser, R. (1950). Multiple operation measurement. *Psychol. Rev.*, 57, 241–252.

Glaser, R. (1951). The application of the concepts of multiple operation measurement to the response patterns on psychological tests. *Educ. psychol. Measmt,* 11, 372–382.

Glaser, R. (1952). The reliability of inconsistency. *Educ. psychol. Measmt,* 12, 60–64.

Gobetz, W. (1953). A quantification, standardization, and validation of the Bender-Gestalt test on normals and neurotic adults. *Psychol. Monogr.*, 67, Whole No. 356.

Goedinghaus, C. H. (1954). *A study of the relationship between temperament and academic achievement.* Master's thesis, Los Angeles: University of Southern California.

Goodenough, F. L. (1942). The use of free association in the objective measurement of personality. In Q. McNemar and M. A. Merrill (Eds.), *Studies in personality.* New York: McGraw-Hill.

Goodenough, F. L. (1945). Sex differences in judging the sex of handwriting. *J. soc. Psychol.*, 22, 61–68.

Goodenough, F. L. (1949). *Mental testing.* New York: Rinehart.

Goodman, C. H. (1944). Prediction of college success by means of Thurstone's primary abilities tests. *Educ. psychol. Measmt,* 4, 125–140.

Goodman, C. H. (1947). The MacQuarrie test for measuring mechanical ability. II. Factor analysis. *J. appl. Psychol.*, 31, 150–154.

Goodstein, L. D. (1954). Interrelationships among several measures of anxiety and hostility. *J. consult. Psychol.*, 18, 33–39.

Gordon, E. M., and Sarason, S. B. (1955). The relationship between "test anxiety" and "other anxieties." *J. Pers.*, 23, 317–323.

Gordon, L. V. (1951). Validities of the forced-choice and questionnaire methods of personality measurement. *J. appl. Psychol.*, 35, 407–412.

Gordon, L. V. (1953). A factor analysis of the Szondi pictures. *J. Psychol.*, 36, 387–392.

Gordon, L. V., and Stapleton, E. S. (1956). Fakability of a forced-choice personality test under realistic high school employment conditions. *J. appl. Psychol.*, 40, 258–262.

Gordon, S. (1947). Exploration of social attitudes through humor. Master's thesis, Urbana, Ill.: University of Illinois.

Gottschaldt, K. (1926). Über den Einfluss der Erfährung auf die Wahrnehming von Figuren. *Psychol. Forsch.*, 8, 261–317.

Gough, H. G. (1946). An additional study of food aversions. *J. abnorm. soc. Psychol.*, 41, 86–88.

Gough, H. G. (1953a). What determines the academic achievement of high school students? *J. educ. Res.*, 46, 321–331.

Gough, H. G. (1953b). The construction of a personality scale to predict scholastic achievement. *J. appl. Psychol.*, 37, 361–366.

Gould, R. (1938). Factors underlying expressed "level of aspiration." *J. Psychol.*, 6, 265–279.

Gould, R., and Lewis, H. B. (1940). An experimental investigation of changes in the meaning of level of aspiration. *J. exp. Psychol.*, 27, 422–438.

Gowin, E. B. (1915). *The executive and his control of men.* New York: Macmillan.

Granick, S., and Smith, L. J. (1953). Sex sequence in the Draw-a-Person Test and its relation to the MMPI masculinity-femininity scale. *J. consult. Psychol.*, 17, 71–73.

Green, E. H. (1933a). Friendships and quarrels among preschool children. *Child Develpm.*, 4, 237–252.

Green, E. H. (1933b). Group play and quarreling among preschool children. *Child Develpm.*, 4, 302–307.

Green, R. F. (1951). Does a selection situation induce testees to bias their answers on interest and temperament tests? *Educ. psychol. Measmt*, 11, 503–515.

Green, R. F., Guilford, J. P., Christensen, P. R., and Comrey, A. L. (1953). A factor-analytic study of reasoning abilities. *Psychometrika*, 18, 135–160.

Greene, E. B. (1943). An analysis of random and systematic changes with practice. *Psychometrika*, 8, 37–52.

Greene, J. E., and Staton, T. F. (1939). Predictive value of various tests of emotionality and adjustment in guidance of prospective teachers. *J. educ. Res.*, 32, 653–659.

Gregory, W. S. (1946). *Gregory academic interest inventory.* Beverly Hills, Calif.: Sheridan Supply Co.

Grings, W. W. (1942). The verbal summator technique and abnormal mental states. *J. abnorm. soc. Psychol.*, 37, 529–545.

Grziwok, R., and Scodel, A. (1956). Some psychological correlates of humor preferences. *J. consult. Psychol.*, 20, 42.

Guertin, W. H. (1951). A factor analysis of some Szondi pictures. *J. clin. Psychol.*, 7, 232–235.

Guertin, W. H., and Schmidt, A. W. (1955). Constellations of religious attitudes of paranoid schizophrenics. *Psychol. Rep.*, 1, 319–322.

Guilford, J. P. (1934). Introversion-extroversion. *Psychol. Bull.*, 31, 331–354.

Guilford, J. P. (1940). *An inventory of factors STDCR.* Beverly Hills, Calif.: Sheridan Supply Co.

Guilford, J. P. (1946). New standards for test evaluation. *Educ. psychol. Measmt*, 6, 427–438.

Guilford, J. P. (1948). Factor analysis in a test-development program. *Psychol. Rev.*, 55, 79–94.

Guilford, J. P. (1952). When not to factor analyze. *Psychol. Bull.*, 49, 26–37.

Guilford, J. P. (1954). *Psychometric methods.* (2d ed.) New York: McGraw-Hill.

Guilford, J. P. (1956a). *Fundamental statistics in psychology and education.* (3d ed.) New York: McGraw-Hill.

Guilford, J. P. (1956b) The structure of intellect. *Psychol. Bull.*, 53, 267–293.

Guilford, J. P. (1957a). A revised structure of intellect. *Rep. psychol. Lab.*, No. 19. Los Angeles: University of Southern California.

Guilford, J. P. (1957*b*). Description de la morphologie humaine: types, composantes et facteurs. *Biotypologie,* 18, 88–105.

Guilford, J. P. (1957*c*). Creative abilities in the arts. *Psychol. Rev.,* 64, 110–118.

Guilford, J. P., and Christensen, P. R. (1956). A factor-analytic study of verbal fluency. *Rep. psychol. Lab.,* No. 17. Los Angeles: University of Southern California.

Guilford, J. P., Christensen, P. R., and Bond, N. A. (1954). *The DF opinion survey. Manual of instructions and interpretations.* Beverly Hills, Calif.: Sheridan Supply Co.

Guilford, J. P., Christensen, P. R., Bond, N. A., and Sutton, M. A. (1953). A factor analysis study of human interests. *Res. Bull.,* 53–11. San Antonio, Texas: Human Resources Research Center.

Guilford, J. P., Christensen, P. R., Bond, N. A., and Sutton, M. A. (1954). A factor analysis study of human interests. *Psychol. Monogr.,* 68, Whole No. 375.

Guilford, J. P., Christensen, P. R., Frick, J. W., and Merrifield, P. R. (1957). The relations of creative-thinking aptitudes to non-aptitude personality traits. *Rep. psychol. Lab.,* No. 20. Los Angeles: University of Southern California.

Guilford, J. P., and Comrey, A. L. (1948). Prediction of proficiency of administrative personnel from personal-history data. *Educ. psychol. Measmt,* 8, 281–296.

Guilford, J. P., Frick, J. W., Christensen, P. R., and Merrifield, P. R. (1957). A factor-analytic study of flexibility in thinking. *Rep. psychol. Lab.,* No. 18. Los Angeles: University of Southern California.

Guilford, J. P., Fruchter, B., and Zimmerman, W. S. (1952). Factor analysis of the Army Air Forces Sheppard Field battery of experimental aptitude tests. *Psychometrika,* 17, 45–68.

Guilford, J. P., Green, R. F., Christensen, P. R., Hertzka, A. F., and Kettner, N. W. (1954). A factor-analytic study of Navy reasoning tests with the Air Force Aircrew Classification Battery. *Educ. psychol. Measmt,* 14, 301–325.

Guilford, J. P., and Guilford, R. B. (1931). A prognostic test for students in design. *J. appl. Psychol.,* 15, 335–345.

Guilford, J. P., and Guilford, R. B. (1934). An analysis of the factors in a typical test of introversion-extroversion. *J. abnorm. soc. Psychol.,* 28, 377–399.

Guilford, J. P., and Guilford, R. B. (1936). Personality factors *S, E,* and *M* and their measurement. *J. Psychol.,* 2, 109–127.

Guilford, J. P., and Guilford, R. B. (1939*a*). Personality factors *D, R, T,* and *A. J. abnorm. soc. Psychol.,* 34, 21–36.

Guilford, J. P., and Guilford, R. B. (1939*b*). Personality factors *N* and *GD. J. abnorm. soc. Psychol.,* 34, 239–248.

Guilford, J. P., and Holley, J. W. (1949). A factorial approach to the analysis of variance of esthetic judgments. *J. exp. Psychol.,* 39, 208–218.

Guilford, J. P., and Hunt, J. McV. (1931). Some further experimental tests of McDougall's theory of introversion-extroversion. *J. abnorm. soc. Psychol.,* 26, 324–332.

Guilford, J. P., Kettner, N. W., and Christensen, P. R. (1955). The relation of certain factors to training criteria in the U.S. Coast Guard Academy. *Rep. psychol. Lab.,* No. 13. Los Angeles: University of Southern California.

Guilford, J. P., Kettner, N. W., and Christensen, P. R. (1956*a*). The nature of the general reasoning factor. *Psychol. Rev.,* 63, 169–172.

Guilford, J. P., Kettner, N. W., and Christensen, P. R. (1956*b*). A factor-analytic study across the domains of reasoning, creativity, and evaluation. II. Administration of tests and analysis of results. *Rep. psychol. Lab.*, No. 16. Los Angeles: University of Southern California.

Guilford, J. P., and Lacey, J. I. (Eds.) (1947). Printed classification tests. *AAF Aviation Psychology Research Program Reports* No. 5. Washington: GPO.

Guilford, J. P., and Martin, H. G. (1943*a*). *Personnel inventory: manual of directions and norms.* Beverly Hills, Calif.: Sheridan Supply Co.

Guilford, J. P., and Martin, H. G. (1943*b*). *The Guilford-Martin inventory of factors GAMIN: manual of directions and norms.* Beverly Hills, Calif.: Sheridan Supply Co.

Guilford, J. P., and Martin, H. G. (1944). Age differences and sex differences in some introvertive and emotional traits. *J. gen. Psychol.*, 31, 219–229.

Guilford, J. P., Shneidman, E., and Zimmerman, W. S. (1948). *The Guilford-Shneidman-Zimmerman interest survey.* Beverly Hills, Calif.: Sheridan Supply Co.

Guilford, J. P., and Zimmerman, W. S. (1947). *The Guilford-Zimmerman aptitude survey.* Beverly Hills, Calif.: Sheridan Supply Co.

Guilford, J. P., and Zimmerman, W. S. (1949). *The Guilford-Zimmerman temperament survey: manual of instructions and interpretations.* Beverly Hills, Calif.: Sheridan Supply Co.

Guilford, J. P., and Zimmerman, W. S. (1956*a*). Fourteen dimensions of temperament. *Psychol. Monogr.*, 70, Whole No. 417.

Guilford, J. P., and Zimmerman, W. S. (1956*b*). *The Guilford-Zimmerman aptitude survey: manual of instructions and interpretations.* (2d ed.) Beverly Hills, Calif.: Sheridan Supply Co.

Guilford, J. S. (1952). Temperament traits of executives and supervisors measured by the Guilford personality inventories. *J. appl. Psychol.*, 36, 228–233.

Gundlach, R. H. (1939). Emotional stability and political opinions as related to age and income. *J. soc. Psychol.*, 10, 577–590.

Gundlach, R. H., and Gerum, E. (1931). Vocational interests and types of ability. *J. educ. Psychol.*, 22, 505.

Guthrie, E. R. (1927). Measuring introversion and extroversion. *J. abnorm. soc. Psychol.*, 22, 82–88.

Guthrie, E. R. (1944). Personality in terms of associative learning. In J. McV. Hunt, *Personality and the behavior disorders.* New York: Ronald.

Guthrie, G. M. (1950). Six MMPI profile patterns. *J. Psychol.*, 30, 317–323.

Hake, D. T., and Ruedisili, C. H. (1949). Predicting subject grades of liberal arts freshmen with the Kuder Preference Record. *J. appl. Psychol.*, 33, 553–558.

Hall, C. S. (1937). Emotional behavior in the rat. IV. The relationship between emotionality and stereotyping of behavior. *J. comp. Psychol.*, 24, 367–375.

Hall, C. S. (1939). The inheritance of emotionality. *Sigma XI Quart.*, 26, 17–27.

Hall, C. S. (1941). Temperament: a survey of animal studies. *Psychol. Bull.*, 38, 909–943.

Hall, C. S., and Lindsley, D. B. (1938). The relation of the thyroid gland to the spontaneous activity of the rat. *Endocrinology*, 22, 179–186.

Hall, C. S., and Lindzey, G. (1957). *Theories of personality.* New York: Wiley.

Hall, D. M., and Wittenborn, J. R. (1942). Motor fitness tests for farm boys. *Res. Quart. Amer. Ass. Hlth phys. Educ.*, 13, 432–443.

Halpern, F. (1951). The Bender Visual Motor Gestalt Test. In H. H. Anderson and G. L. Anderson (Eds.), *Introduction to projective techniques*. Englewood Cliffs, N. J.: Prentice-Hall.

Hammond, K. R. (1948). Measuring attitudes by error-choice; an indirect method. *J. abnorm. soc. Psychol.*, 43, 38–48.

Hammond, W. H. (1942). An application of Burt's multiple general factor analysis to the delineation of physical types. *Man*, 42, 4–11.

Hanawalt, N. G., and Richardson, H. M. (1944). Leadership as related to the Bernreuter Personality Inventory measures. IV. An item analysis of responses of adult leaders and non-leaders. *J. appl. Psychol.*, 28, 397–411.

Hanks, L. M., Jr. (1936). Prediction from case material to personality data. *Arch. Psychol., N.Y.*, 29, No. 207.

Hanley, C. (1956). Social desirability and responses to items from three MMPI scales: D, Sc, and K. *J. appl. Psychol.*, 40, 324–328.

Hanna, J. V. (1950). Estimating intelligence by interview. *Educ. psychol. Measmt*, 10, 420–430.

Harding, J. (1941). A scale for measuring civilian morale. *J. Psychol.*, 12, 101–110.

Hargreaves, H. L. (1927). The "faculty" of imagination. *Brit. J. Psychol.*, Monogr. Suppl. 10, 74.

Harlow, R. G. (1951). Masculine inadequacy and compensatory development of physique. *J. Pers.*, 19, 312–323.

Harrell, W., and Faubian, R. (1941). Primary mental abilities and aviation maintenance courses. *Educ. psychol. Measmt*, 1, 59–66.

Harris, W. W. (1948). A bas relief projective technique. *J. Psychol.*, 26, 3–17.

Harrison, R. (1941). Personal tempo and the interrelationships of voluntary and maximal rates of movement. *J. gen. Psychol.*, 24, 343–379.

Harrison, R., and Dorcus, R. M. (1938). Is rate of voluntary bodily movement unitary? *J. gen. Psychol.*, 18, 31–39.

Harrower, M. R. (1950). The Most Unpleasant Concept Test: a graphic projective technique. *J. clin. Psychol.*, 6, 213–233.

Harrower-Erikson, M., and Steiner, E. (1945). *Large scale Rorschach technique*. Springfield, Ill.: Charles C Thomas.

Harsh, C. M., Beebe-Center, J. G., and Beebe-Center, R. (1939). Further evidence regarding preferential judgment of polygonal forms. *J. Psychol.*, 7, 345–350.

Hart, H., and Olander, E. (1924). Sex differences in character as indicated by teachers' ratings. *Sch. & Soc.*, 20, 381–382.

Hart, H. H., Jenkins, R. L., Axelrod, S., and Sperling, P. I. (1943). Multiple factor analysis of traits of delinquent boys. *J. soc. Psychol.*, 17, 191–201.

Hartshorne, H., and May, M. A. (1928). *Studies in the nature of character. I. Studies in deceit*. New York: Macmillan.

Hartshorne, H., May, M. A., and Maller, J. B. (1929). *Studies in the nature of character. II. Studies in service and self control*. New York: Macmillan.

Hartson, L. D. (1936). Does college training influence test intelligence? *J. educ. Psychol.*, 27, 481–491.

Hastorf, A. H., and Bender, I. E. (1952). A caution respecting the measurement of empathic ability. *J. abnorm. soc. Psychol.*, 47, 574–576.

Hathaway, S. R., and McKinley, J. C. (1940). A multiphasic personality schedule (Minnesota). I. Construction of the schedule. *J. Psychol.*, 10, 249–254.

Hathaway, S. R., and McKinley, J. C. (1942). A multiphasic personality schedule (Minnesota). III. The measurement of symptomatic depression. *J. Psychol.*, 14, 73–84.

Hathaway, S. R., and McKinley, J. C. (1943). *Manual for the Minnesota Multiphasic Personality Inventory.* New York: Psychological Corp.

Hathaway, S. R., and Meehl, P. E. (1951a). The Minnesota Multiphasic Personality Inventory. In *Military clinical psychology.* Washington: GPO.

Hathaway, S. R., and Meehl, P. E. (1951b). *Atlas of clinical interpretation of the MMPI.* Minneapolis: University of Minnesota Press.

Hawkes, G. R. (1952). A study of the personal values of elementary school children. *Educ. psychol. Measmt,* 12, 654–663.

Haythorn, W., Couch, A., Hoefner, D., Langham, P., and Carter, L. (1956). The effects of varying combinations of authoritarian and equalitarian leaders and followers. *J. abnorm. soc. Psychol.,* 53, 210–219.

Healy, I., and Borg, W. R. (1951). Personality characteristics of nursing school students and graduate nurses. *J. appl. Psychol.,* 35, 275–280.

Heath, H. (1952). A factor analysis of women's measurements taken for garment and pattern construction. *Psychometrika,* 17, 87–100.

Heathers, L. B. (1942). Factors producing generality in the level of aspiration. *J. exp. Psychol.,* 30, 393–406.

Heese, K. W. (1942). A general factor in improvement with practice. *Psychometrika,* 7, 213–223.

Heidbreder, E. (1930). Self ratings and preferences. *J. abnorm. soc. Psychol.,* 25, 62–74.

Helgerson, E. (1943). The relative significance of race, sex, and facial expression in choice of playmate by the pre-school child. *J. Negro Educ.,* 12, 617–622.

Helson, H. (1948). Adaptation-level as a basis for a quantitative theory of frames of reference. *Psychol. Rev.,* 55, 297–313.

Helson, H. (1953). Perception and personality—a critique of recent experimental literature. *USAF Air University School of Aviation Medicine Project Report.* Randolph Air Force Base, Tex.

Helson, H., Blake, R. R., Mouton, J. S., and Olmstead, J. A. (1956). Attitudes as adjustments to stimulus, background, and residual factors. *J. abnorm. soc. Psychol.,* 52, 314–322.

Hempel, W. E., Jr., and Fleishman, E. A. (1955). A factor analysis of physical proficiency and manipulative skill. *J. appl. Psychol.,* 39, 12–16.

Hemphill, J. K. (1949). *Situational factors in leadership. Ohio Studies in Personnel.* Columbus, Ohio: Ohio State University Press.

Henry, E. M., and Rotter, J. H. (1956). Situational influence on Rorschach responses. *J. consult. Psychol.,* 20, 457–462.

Henry, S. (1947). Children's audiograms in relation to reading attainment. II. Analysis and interpretation. *J. genet. Psychol.,* 71, 3–48.

Henshaw, L. S. (1937). Selection for paper sorters. *Hum. Factors, Lond.,* 11, 146–153.

Heron, A. (1956). The effects of real-life motivation on questionnaire response. *J. appl. Psychol.,* 40, 65–68.

Hersey, R. (1955). *Zest for work.* New York: Harper.

Hertzka, A. F., Guilford, J. P., Christensen, P. R., and Berger, R. M. (1954). A factor-analytic study of evaluative abilities. *Educ. psychol. Measmt,* 14, 581–597.

Herzberg, F. (1954). Temperament measures in industrial selection. *J. appl. Psychol.,* 38, 81–84.

Herzberg, F., and Bouton, A. (1954). A further study of the stability of the Kuder Preference Record. *Educ. psychol. Measmt,* 14, 326–331.

Herzberg, F., Bouton, A., and Steiner, B. J. (1954). Studies on the stability of the Kuder Preference Record. *Educ. psychol. Measmt*, 14, 90–100.

Heston, J. C. (1948). A comparison of four masculinity-femininity scales. *Educ. psychol. Measmt*, 8, 375–387.

Hewer, V. H. (1956). A comparison of successful and unsuccessful students in the medical school at the University of Minnesota. *J. appl. Psychol.*, 40, 164–168.

Highland, R. W., and Berkshire, J. R. (1951). A methodological study of forced-choice performance ratings. *Res. Bull.* 51–9. San Antonio, Texas: Human Resources Research Center.

Hildreth, G. (1949a). The development and training of hand dominance: I. Characteristics of handedness. *J. genet. Psychol.*, 75, 197–220.

Hildreth, G. (1949b). The development and training of hand dominance: II. Developmental tendencies in handedness. *J. genet. Psychol.*, 75, 221–254.

Hildreth, G. (1949c). The development and training of hand dominance: III. Origins of handedness and lateral dominance. *J. genet. Psychol.*, 75, 255–275.

Hills, J. R. (1955a). The measurement of levels of aspiration. *J. soc. Psychol.*, 41, 221–239.

Hills, J. R. (1955b). The relationship between certain factor-analyzed abilities and success in college mathematics. *Rep. psychol. Lab.*, No. 15. Los Angeles: University of Southern California.

Hilton, A. C., Bolin, S. F., Parker, J. W., Jr., Taylor, E. K., and Walker, W. B. (1955). The validity of personnel assessments by professional psychologists. *J. appl. Psychol.*, 39, 287–293.

Himmelweit, H. T. (1950). Student selection—an experimental investigation. I. *Brit. J. Sociol.*, 1, 328–346.

Himmelweit, H. T., and Summerfield, A. (1951). Student selection—an experimental investigation. II. *Brit. J. Sociol.*, 2, 59–75.

Hofstaetter, P. R. (1952). A factorial study of prejudice. *J. Pers.*, 21, 228–239.

Hollander, E. P. (1954). Authoritarianism and leadership choice in a military setting. *J. abnorm. soc. Psychol.*, 49, 365–370.

Hollander, E. P. (1956). Interpersonal exposure time as a determinant of the predictive utility of peer ratings. *Psychol. Rep.*, 4, 445–448.

Holley, J. W. (1951). *The isolation of traits in the domain of military leadership.* Doctoral dissertation, Los Angeles: University of Southern California.

Holsopple, J. Q., and Miale, F. R. (1954). *Sentence completion.* Springfield, Ill.: Charles C Thomas.

Holt, R. R., and Luborsky, L. (1952). Research in the selection of psychiatrists: a second interim report. *Bull. Menninger Clin.*, 16, 125–135.

Holtzman, W. H. (1952). Adjustment and leadership; a study of the Rorschach test. *J. soc. Psychol.*, 36, 179–189.

Holtzman, W. H., and Sells, S. B. (1954). Prediction of flying success by clinical analysis of test protocols. *J. abnorm. soc. Psychol.*, 49, 485–490.

Horowitz, E. L. (1936). The development of attitude toward the Negro. *Arch. Psychol., N.Y.*, No. 194.

Hovland, C. I., and Sherif, M. (1952). Judgmental phenomena and scales of attitude measurement: item displacement in Thurstone scales. *J. abnorm. soc. Psychol.*, 47, 822–832.

Howells, T. H. (1933). An experimental study of persistence. *J. abnorm. soc. Psychol.*, 28, 14–29.

Howells, W. W. (1951). Factors of human physique. *Amer. J. phys. Anthrop.,* 9, 159–192.

Howells, W. W. (1952). A factorial study of constitutional types. *Amer. J. phys. Anthrop.,* 10, 91–118.

Hull, C. L. (1933). *Hypnosis and suggestibility.* New York: Appleton-Century-Crofts.

Humm, D. G., and Humm, K. A. (1950). Humm-Wadsworth Scale appraisals. *J. Psychol.,* 30, 63–75.

Humm, D. G., and Wadsworth, G. W. (1935). The Humm-Wadsworth Temperament Scale. *Amer. J. Psychiat.,* 92, 163–200.

Hunt, J. McV., and Guilford, J. P. (1933). Fluctuation of an ambiguous figure in dementia praecox and in manic depressive patients. *J. abnorm. soc. Psychol.,* 27, 443–452.

Hunter, E. C., and Jordan, A. M. (1939). An analysis of qualities associated with leadership among college students. *J. educ. Psychol.,* 30, 497–509.

Husband, R. W. (1939). Intercorrelations among learning abilities. I. *J. genet. Psychol.,* 55, 353–364.

Ives, V., Grant, M. Q., and Ranzoni, J. H. (1953). The "neurotic" Rorschachs of normal adolescents. *J. genet. Psychol.,* 83, 31–61.

Jackson, J. (1946). The relative effectiveness of paper-pencil test, interview, and ratings as techniques for personality evaluation. *J. soc. Psychol.,* 23, 35–54.

Jackson, T. A. (1929). Errors of self-judgment. *J. appl. Psychol.,* 13, 372–377.

Jacobs, A., and Schlaff, A. (1955). *Falsification scales for the Guilford-Zimmerman Temperament Survey.* Beverly Hills, Calif.: Sheridan Supply Co.

James, W. (1890). *Principles of psychology.* New York: Holt.

James, W. T. (1949). Dominant and submissive behavior in puppies as indicated by food intake. *J. genet. Psychol.,* 75, 33–43.

James, W. T. (1955). Behaviors involved in expression of dominance among puppies. *Psychol. Rep.,* 1, 299–301.

Janoff, I. Z., Beck, L. H., and Child, I. L. (1950). The relation of somatotype to reaction time, resistance to pain, and expressive movement. *J. Pers.,* 18, 454–460.

Jastak, J. (1949). Problems of psychometric scatter analysis. *Psychol. Bull.,* 46, 177–196.

Jastak, J. (1953). Ranking Bellevue subtest scores for diagnostic purposes. *J. consult. Psychol.,* 17, 403–410.

Jenkins, W. O. (1947). A review of leadership studies with particular reference to military problems. *Psychol. Bull.,* 44, 54–79.

Jensen, M. B., and Rotter, J. B. (1945). The validity of the multiple choice Rorschach test in officer candidate selection. *Psychol. Bull.,* 42, 182–185.

Jersild, A. T. (1933). The constancy of certain behavior patterns in young children. *Amer. J. Psychol.,* 45, 125–129.

Johnson, D. M., and Vidulich, R. N. (1956). Experimental manipulation of the halo effect. *J. appl. Psychol.,* 40, 130–134.

Jones, D. S., Livson, N. H., and Sarbin, T. R. (1955). Perceptual completion behavior in juvenile delinquents. *Percept. mot. Skills,* 5, 141–146.

Jones, F. N. (1948). A factor analysis of visibility data. *Amer. J. Psychol.,* 61, 361–369.

Jones, F. N. (1950). A second factor analysis of visibility data. *Amer. J. Psychol.,* 63, 206–213.

Jones, H. E. (1950). The study of patterns of emotional expression. In M. L. Reymert, *Feelings and emotions.* New York: McGraw-Hill.

Jones, L. V. (1949). A factor analysis of the Stanford-Binet at four age levels. *Psychometrika,* 14, 299–331.

Jost, H., and Sontag, L. W. (1944). The genetic factor in autonomic nervous system function. *Psychosom. Med.,* 6, 308–310.

Jucknat, M. (1937). Leistung, Anspruchsniveau und Selbstbewustsein. *Psychol. Forsch.,* 22, 89–179.

Jung, C. G. (1923). *Psychological types.* New York: Harcourt, Brace.

Kambouropoulou, P. (1926). Individual differences in the sense of humor, and their relation to temperamental differences. *Amer. J. Psychol.,* 37, 268–277.

Karlin, J. E. (1942). A factorial study of auditory function. *Psychometrika,* 7, 251–279.

Katz, E. (1940). The relationship of IQ to height and weight from three to five years. *J. genet. Psychol.,* 57, 65–82.

Keehn, J. D. (1955). An examination of the two-factor theory of social attitude in a near eastern culture. *J. soc. Psychol.,* 42, 13–20.

Kelley, H. P. (1954). *A factor analysis of memory ability.* Princeton, N.J.: Educational Testing Service.

Kelley, T. L. (1935). *Crossroads in the mind of man.* Cambridge, Mass.: Harvard University Press.

Kelly, E. L. (1954). Theory and techniques of assessment. In C. P. Stone and Q. McNemar (Eds.), *Annual review of psychology.* Stanford, Calif.: Annual Reviews.

Kelly, E. L. (1955). Consistency of the adult personality. *Amer. Psychologist,* 10, 659–681.

Kelly, E. L., and Ewart, E. (1942). A preliminary study of success in civilian pilot training. *CAA Div. Res. Rep.,* No. 7. Washington: Civil Aeronautics Administration.

Kelly, E. L., and Fiske, D. W. (1951). *The prediction of performance in clinical psychology,.* Ann Arbor, Mich.: University of Michigan Press.

Kelly, E. L., Miles, C. C., and Terman, L. M. (1936). Ability to influence one's score on a pencil-and-paper test of personality. *Charact. & Pers.,* 4, 206–215.

Kelly, G. A. (1955). *The psychology of personal constructs.* New York: Norton.

Kendall, E. (1954). The validity of Taylor's Manifest Anxiety Scale. *J. consult. Psychol.,* 18, 429–432.

Kennard, M. A. (1956). The electroencephalogram and disorders of behavior. *J. nerv. ment. Dis.,* 124, 103–124.

Kerr, W. A. (1944). Correlates of politico-economic liberalism-conservatism. *J. soc. Psychol.,* 20, 61–77.

Kerr, W. A. (1952). Untangling the liberalism-conservatism continuum. *J. soc. Psychol.,* 35, 111–125.

Kerr, W. A., and Speroff, B. J. (1954). Validation and evaluation of the empathy test. *J. gen. Psychol.,* 50, 269–276.

Kettner, N. W., Guilford, J. P., and Christensen, P. R. (1956). A factor-analytic investigation of the factor called general reasoning. *Educ. psychol. Measmt,* 16, 438–453.

Keys, A., Brŏzek, J., Henschel, A., Mickelson, O., and Taylor, H. L. (1950). *The biology of human starvation.* Minneapolis: University of Minnesota Press.

Kimber, J. A. M. (1947). The insight of college students into the items of a personality test. *Educ. psychol. Measmt,* 7, 411–420.

King, G. F. (1954). Research with neuropsychiatric samples. *J. Psychol.,* 38, 383–387.

King, G. F., Erhmann, J. C., and Johnson, D. M. (1952). Experimental analysis of the reliability of observations of social behavior. *J. soc. Psychol.,* 35, 151–160.

Kinsey, A. C., Pomeroy, W. B., and Martin, C. E. (1948). *Sexual behavior in the human male.* Philadelphia: Saunders.

Kinsey, A. C., Pomeroy, W. B., Martin, C. E., and Gebhard, P. H. (1953). *Sexual behavior in the human female.* Philadelphia: Saunders.

Kirkpatrick, J. J. (1956). Validation of a test battery for the selection and placement of engineers. *Personnel Psychol.,* 9, 211–227.

Kleemeier, R. W., and Dudek, F. J. (1950). A factorial investigation of flexibility. *Educ. psychol. Measmt,* 10, 107–118.

Klein, G. S. (1956). Perception, motives, and personality. In J. L. McCary (Ed.), *Psychology of Personality.* New York: Logos Press.

Klopfer, B., and Kelley, D. McG. (1946). The Rorschach technique. Yonkers, N.Y.: World.

Klubeck, S., and Bass, B. M. (1954). Differential effects of training on persons of different leadership status. *Hum. Relat.,* 7, 59–72.

Knopf, I. J. (1956). Rorschach summary scores in differential diagnosis. *J. consult. Psychol.,* 20, 99–104.

Knott, J. R., Friedman, H., and Bardsley, R. (1942). Some electroencephalographic correlates of intelligence in eight-year- and twelve-year-old children. *J. exp. Psychol.,* 30, 380–391.

Koch, H. L. (1934). A multiple-factor analysis of certain measures of activeness in nursery school children. *J. gen. Psychol.,* 45, 482–487.

Koch, H. L. (1942). A factor analysis of some measures of the behavior of preschool children. *J. gen. Psychol.,* 27, 257–287.

Kounin, J. S. (1943). Intellectual development and rigidity. In R. G. Barker, J. S. Kounin, and H. F. Wright (Eds.), *Child behavior and development.* New York: McGraw-Hill.

Kreezer, G. (1940). The relation of intelligence level and the electroencephalogram. *Yearb. Nat. Soc. Stud., Educ.* 39, 130–133.

Kretschmer, E. (1926). *Physique and character.* New York: Harcourt, Brace.

Kretschmer, E. (1948). *Körperbau und Charact.* Berlin: Springer.

Krüger, H., and Zietz, K. (1933). Das Verifikationsproblem. *Z. angew. Psychol.,* 45, 140–171.

Krumboltz, J. D., and Farquar, W. W. (1957). Reliability and validity of the n-achievement test. *J. consult. Psychol.,* 21, 226–227.

Kuder, G. F. (1946). *Revised manual for the Kuder Preference Record.* Chicago: Science Research Associates.

Lacey, J. I. (1950). Individual differences in somatic response patterns. *J. comp. physiol. Psychol.,* 43, 338–350.

Lacey, J. I., Bateman, D. E., and Van Lehn, R. (1953). Autonomic response specificity. An experimental study. *Psychosom. Med.,* 15, 8–21.

Lacey, J. I., and Lacey, B. C. (1958). The relationship of resting autonomic activity to motor impulsivity, in The brain and human behavior. *Proc. Ass. Res. nerv. ment. Dis.* Baltimore: Williams and Wilkins.

Lacey, J. I., and Van Lehn, R. (1952). Differential emphasis in somatic response to stress. *Psychosom. Med.,* 14, 71–81.

Laird, D. A. (1925). Detecting abnormal behavior. *J. abnorm. soc. Psychol.,* 20, 128–141.

Landis, C. (1936). Questionnaires and the study of personality. *J. nerv. ment. Dis.,* 83, 125–134.

Landis, C., and Katz, S. E. (1934). The validity of certain questions which purport to measure neurotic tendencies. *J. appl. Psychol.,* 18, 343–356.

Landis, C., Zubin, J., and Katz, S. E. (1935). Empirical evaluation of three personality adjustment inventories. *J. educ. Psychol.,* 26, 321–330.

Landreth, C. (1940). Consistency of four methods of measuring one type of sporadic emotional behavior (crying) in nursery school children. *J. genet. Psychol.,* 57, 101–118.

LaPiere, R. T. (1934). Attitudes vs. actions. *Soc. Forces,* 13, 230–237.

Lawson, E. D., and Stagner, R. (1954). The Ferguson religionism scale: a study in validation. *J. soc. Psychol.,* 39, 245–256.

Layman, E. M. (1940). An item analysis of the adjustment questionnaire. *J. Psychol.,* 10, 87–106.

Leeds, C. H. (1956). Teacher attitudes and temperament as a measure of teacher-pupil rapport. *J. appl. Psychol.,* 40, 333–337.

Lehman, R. T. (1944). Interpretation of the Kuder Preference Record for college students of home economics. *Educ. psychol. Measmt,* 4, 217–223.

Lentz, T. F. (1934). Reliability of opinionaire technique studied intensively by the retest method. *J. soc. Psychol.,* 5, 338–364.

Lentz, T. F. (1938). Generality and specificity of conservatism-radicalism. *J. educ. Psychol.,* 29, 540–546.

Lentz, T. F. (1939). Personage admiration and other correlates of conservatism-radicalism. *J. soc. Psychol.,* 10, 81–93.

Levine, A. S., and Zachert, V. (1951). Use of biographical inventory in the Air Force classification program. *J. appl. Psychol.,* 35, 241–244.

Levine, P. R., and Wallen, R. (1954). Adolescent vocational interests and later occupations. *J. appl. Psychol.,* 38, 428–431.

Levinson, D. J. (1949). An approach to the theory and measurement of ethnocentric ideology. *J. Psychol.,* 28, 19–39.

Lewinson, T. S., and Zubin, J. (1942). *Handwriting analysis.* New York: King's Crown.

Lewis, W. D. (1947). Some characteristics of children designated as mentally retarded, as problems, and as geniuses by teachers. *J. genet. Psychol.,* 70, 29–51.

Licht, M. (1947). The measurement of one aspect of personality. *J. Psychol.,* 24, 83–87.

Likert, R. (1932). A technique for the measurement of attitudes. *Arch. Psychol., N.Y.,* 22, No. 140.

Lindberg, B. J. (1940). Suggestibility in different personality types. *Amer. J. Psychol.,* 55, 99–108.

Lindsley, D. B. (1951). In S. S. Stevens (Ed.), *Handbook of experimental psychology.* New York: Wiley.

Lindzey, G., and Goldwyn, R. M. (1954). Validity of the Rosenzweig Picture-Frustration Study. *J. Pers.,* 22, 519–547.

Lindzey, G., Prince, R., and Wright, H. K. (1952). A study of facial asymmetry. *J. Pers.,* 21, 68–84.

Lipsett, L., and Wilson, J. W. (1954). Do "suitable" interests and mental ability lead to job satisfaction? *Educ. psychol. Measmt,* 14, 373–380.

Littell, S. (1946). The role of suggestibility in susceptibility to the size-weight illusion and the phenomenon of autokinetic streaming. *Denison Univer. Bull., J. sci. Lab.,* 39, 156–170.

Little, K. B., and Shneidman, E. S. (1955). The validity of thematic projective technique interpretation. *J. Pers.*, 23, 285–294.

Long, L., and Perry, J. D. (1953). Academic achievement in engineering related to selection procedures and interests. *J. appl. Psychol.*, 37, 468–471.

Long, W. F., and Lawshe, C. H., Jr. (1947). The effective use of manipulative tests in industry. *Psychol. Bull.*, 44, 130–148.

Longstaff, H. P. (1948). Fakability of the Strong Interest Blank and the Kuder Preference Record. *J. appl. Psychol.*, 32, 360–369.

Longstaff, H. P., and Jurgensen, C. E. (1953). Fakability of the Jurgensen Classification Inventory. *J. appl. Psychol.*, 37, 86–89.

Lord, E. E. (1950). Experimentally induced variations in Rorschach performance. *Psychol. Monogr.*, 64, Whole No. 316.

Lord, F. M. (1956). A study of speed factors in tests and academic grades. *Psychometrika*, 21, 31–50.

Lorge, I. (1935). Personality traits by fiat. *J. educ. Psychol.*, 26, 273–278.

Lorr, M. (1951). A factorial isolation of two social attitudes. *J. soc. Psychol.*, 34, 139–142.

Lorr, M., and Fields, V. (1954). A factorial study of body types. *J. clin. Psychol.*, 10, 182–185.

Lorr, M., and Jenkins, R. L. (1953). Patterns of maladjustment in children. *J. clin. Psychol.*, 9, 16–19.

Lorr, M., Jenkins, R. L., and O'Connor, J. P. (1955). Factors descriptive of psychopathology and behavior of hospitalized psychotics. *J. abnorm. soc. Psychol.*, 50, 76–86.

Lorr, M., Lepine, L. T., and Golder, J. V. (1954). A factor analysis of some handwriting characteristics. *J. Pers.*, 22, 348–353.

Lorr, M., and Meister, R. K. (1941). The concept of scatter in the light of mental test theory. *Educ. psychol. Measmt*, 1, 303–310.

Lorr, M., and Rubenstein, E. A. (1955). Factors descriptive of psychiatric outpatients. *J. abnorm. soc. Psychol.*, 51, 514–522.

Lorr, M., and Rubenstein, E. A. (1956). Personality patterns of neurotic adults in psychotherapy. *J. consult. Psychol.*, 20, 257–263.

Lorr, M., Rubenstein, E. A., and Jenkins, R. L. (1953). A factor analysis of personality ratings of outpatients in psychotherapy. *J. abnorm. soc. Psychol.*, 48, 511–514.

Lorr, M., Wittman, P., and Schanberger, W. (1951). An analysis of the Elgin prognostic scale. *J. clin. Psychol.*, 7, 260–263.

Lovell, G. D., and Haner, C. F. (1955). Forced-choice applied to college faculty rating. *Educ. psychol. Measmt*, 15, 291–304.

Lubin, A. (1950). A note on Sheldon's table of correlations between temperamental traits. *Brit. J. Psychol., Stat. Sec.*, 3, 186–189.

Luchins, A. S. (1950). Personality and prejudice: a critique. *J. soc. Psychol.*, 32, 79–94.

Luchins, A. S., and Luchins, E. H. (1953). Effects of varying the administration of the digit-symbol subtest of the Wechsler-Bellevue Intelligence Scale. *J. gen. Psychol.*, 49, 125–142.

Luft, J. (1950). Implicit hypotheses and clinical predictions. *J. abnorm. soc. Psychol.*, 45, 756–760.

Lundholm, H. (1921). The affective tone of lines. *Psychol. Rev.*, 28, 43–60.

Lundin, W. H. (1949). Projective Movement Sequences: motion pictures. *J. consult. Psychol.*, 13, 407–411.

Luria, A. R. (1932). *The nature of human conflicts.* New York: Liveright.

Lurie, W. A. (1937). A study of Spranger's value-types by the method of factor analysis. *J. soc. Psychol.,* 8, 17–37.

Lykken, D. T. (1956). A method of actuarial pattern analysis. *Psychol. Bull.,* 53, 102–107.

Lynn, J. G., and Lynn, D. R. (1938). Face-hand laterality in relation to personality. *J. abnorm. soc. Psychol.,* 33, 291–322.

Lynn, J. G., and Lynn, D. R. (1943). Smile and hand dominance in relation to the basic modes of adaptation. *J. abnorm. soc. Psychol.,* 38, 250–276.

Machover, K. (1951). Drawing the human figure: a method of personality investigation. In H. H. Anderson and G. L. Anderson (Eds.), *Introduction to projective techniques.* Englewood Cliffs, N.J.: Prentice-Hall.

Mackie, R. R. (1948). *Norms and validity of sixteen test variables for predicting success of foremen.* Master's thesis, Los Angeles: University of Southern California.

Madigan, M. E. (1938). A study of oscillation as a unitary trait. *J. exp. Educ.,* 6, 332–339.

Magaret, A., and Wright, C. (1943). Limitations in the use of intelligence test performance to detect mental disturbances. *J. appl. Psychol.,* 27, 387–398.

Magill, J. W. (1955). Interest profiles of college activity groups. Kuder Preference Record validation. *J. appl. Psychol.,* 39, 53–56.

Maier, N. R. F. (1931). Reasoning in humans. II. The solution of a problem and its appearance in consciousness. *J. comp. Psychol.,* 12, 181–194.

Maller, J. B. (1934). General and specific factors in character. *J. soc. Psychol.,* 5, 97–102.

Malmo, R. B., Shagass, C., and Davis, F. H. (1950). Specificity of bodily reactions under stress. *Res. Publ. Ass. nerv. ment. Dis.,* 29, 231–261.

Malmo, R. B., and Smith, A. A. (1955). Forehead tension and motor irregularities in psychoneurotic patients under stress. *J. Pers.,* 23, 391–406.

Mandell, M. (1950). Validation of group oral performance test. *Personnel Psychol.,* 3, 179–185.

Martin, H. G. (1944). Locating the troublemaker with the Guilford-Martin Personnel Inventory. *J. appl. Psychol.,* 28, 461–467.

Mayman, M., and Kutner, B. (1947). Reliability in analyzing Thematic Apperception Test stories. *J. abnorm. soc. Psychol.,* 42, 365–368.

Mayman, M., Schafer, R., and Rapaport, D. (1951). Interpretation of the Wechsler-Bellevue Intelligence Scale in personality appraisal. In H. H. Anderson and G. L. Anderson (Eds.), *Introduction to projective techniques.* Englewood Cliffs, N.J.: Prentice-Hall.

McCandless, B. R. (1949). The Rorschach as a predictor of academic success. *J. appl. Psychol.,* 33, 43–50.

McCleary, R. A. (1953). Palmar sweat as an index of anxiety: a field method suitable for large groups. *USAF Air University School of Aviation Medicine Project Report* No. 1, iii, Project No. 21-1207-0004. Randolph Air Force Base, Tex.

McClelland, D. C. (1956). The calculated risk: an aspect of scientific performance. In C. W. Taylor (Ed.), *The 1955 University of Utah research conference on the identification of creative scientific talent.* Salt Lake City, Utah: University of Utah Press.

McClelland, D. C., Atkinson, J. W., Clark, R. A., and Lowell, E. L. (1953). *The achievement motive.* New York: Appleton-Century-Crofts.

McClelland, D. C., Clark, R. A., Roby, T. B., and Atkinson, J. W. (1949). The projective expression of needs. IV. The effect of needs for achievement on thematic apperception. *J. exp. Psychol.,* 39, 242–255.

McCloy, C. H. (1940a). An analysis for multiple factors of physical growth at different age levels. *Child Develpm.,* 11, 249–277.

McCloy, C. H. (1940b). The measurement of speed in motor performance. *Psychometrika,* 5, 173–182.

McCloy, C. H., and Young, N. D. (1954). *Tests and measurements in health and physical education.* (3d ed.) New York: Appleton-Century-Crofts.

McCulloch, T. L. (1935). A study of the cognitive abilities of the white rat with special reference to Spearman's theory of two factors. *Duke Univer. Contrib. Psychol. Theor.,* 1, No. 2.

McKeachie, W. J. (1952). Lipstick as a determiner of first impressions of personality: an experiment for the general psychology course. *J. soc. Psychol.,* 36, 241–244.

McKinley, J. C., and Hathaway, S. R. (1940). A multiphasic personality schedule (Minnesota). II. A differential study of hypochondriasis. *J. Psychol.,* 10, 255–268.

McKinley, J. C., and Hathaway, S. R. (1942). A multiphasic personality schedule (Minnesota). IV. Psychasthenia. *J. appl. Psychol.,* 26, 614–624.

McKinley, J. C., and Hathaway, S. R. (1944). The Minnesota Multiphasic Personality Inventory. V. Hysteria, hypomania, and psychopathic deviate. *J. appl. Psychol.,* 28, 153–174.

McMurray, R. N. (1947). Validating the patterned interview. *Personnel J.,* 23, 263–272.

McMurray, R. N. (1952). Efficiency, work-satisfaction, and neurotic tendency. A study of bank employees. *Personnel J.,* 11, 201–210.

McMurray, R. N., and Johnson, D. L. (1945). Development of instruments for selecting and placing factory employees. *Advanced Mgmt.,* 10, 113–120.

McNemar, Q. (1957). On WAIS difference scores. *J. consult. Psychol.,* 21, 239–240.

McQuitty, L. L. (1941). An approach to the nature and measurement of personality integration. *J. soc. Psychol.,* 13, 3–14.

McReynolds, P. (1951). Perception of Rorschach concepts as related to personality deviations. *J. abnorm. soc. Psychol.,* 36, 131–141.

Mead, M. (1956). The cross-cultural approach to the study of personality. In J. L. McCary (Ed.), *Psychology of personality.* New York: Logos Press.

Meehl, P. E. (1945). The dynamics of structured personality tests. *J. clin. Psychol.,* 1, 296–303.

Meehl, P. E. (1946). Profile analysis of the Minnesota Multiphasic Personality Inventory in differential diagnosis. *J. appl. Psychol.,* 30, 517–524.

Meehl, P. E. (1954). *Clinical versus statistical prediction.* Minneapolis: University of Minnesota Press.

Meehl, P. E., and Hathaway, S. R. (1946). The K factor as a suppressor variable in the Minnesota Multiphasic Personality Inventory. *J. appl. Psychol.,* 30, 525–564.

Mehlman, B. (1952). The reliability of psychiatric diagnoses. *J. abnorm. soc. Psychol.,* 47, 577–578.

Meier, N. C. (1939). Factors in artistic aptitude: final summary of a ten-year study of a special ability. *Psychol. Monogr.,* 51, Whole No. 231, 140–158.

Meili, R. (1949). Sur la nature des facteurs d'intelligence. *Acta Psychol.,* 6, 40–58.

Melton, A. W. (1947). Apparatus tests. *AAF Aviation Psychology Research Program Reports,* No. 4. Washington: GPO.

Melville, S. D., and Frederiksen, N. (1951). Achievement of freshmen engineering students and the Strong Vocational Interest Blank. *J. appl. Psychol.*, 36, 169–173.

Michael, W. B. (1949). Factor analyses of tests and criteria: a comparative study of two AAF pilot populations. *Psychol. Monogr.*, 63, Whole No. 298.

Michael, W. B., Guilford, J. P., Fruchter, B., and Zimmerman, W. S. (1957). The description of spatial-visualization abilities. *Educ. psychol. Measmt*, 17, 185–199.

Michael, W. B., Zimmerman, W. S., and Guilford, J. P. (1950). An investigation of two hypotheses regarding the nature of the spatial-relations and visualization factors. *Educ. psychol. Measmt*, 10, 187–213.

Michael, W. B., Zimmerman, W. S., and Guilford, J. P. (1951). An investigation of the nature of the spatial-relations and visualization factors in two high-school samples. *Educ. psychol. Measmt*, 11, 561–577.

Middleton, W. C. (1941). The ability of untrained subjects to judge neuroticism, self-confidence, and sociability from hand-writing samples. *Charact. & Pers.*, 9, 227–234.

Miles, D. W., Wilkins, W. L., Lester, D. W., and Hutchins, W. H. (1946). The efficiency of a high speed screening procedure in detecting the neuropsychiatrically unfit at a U.S. Marine Corps Recruit Training Depot. *J. Psychol.*, 21, 243–268.

Misiak, M., and Franghiadi, G. J. (1953). The thumb and personality. *J. gen. Psychol.*, 48, 241–244.

Mohr, G. J., and Gundlach, R. H. (1927). The relation between physique and performance. *J. exp. Psychol.*, 10, 117–157.

Mohr, G. J., and Gundlach, R. H. (1929). A further study of the relation between physique and performance in criminals. *J. abnorm. soc. Psychol.*, 14, 91–103.

Montalto, F. D. (1946). An application of the group Rorschach technique to the problem of achievement in college. *J. clin. Psychol.*, 2, 254–260.

Mooney, C. M. (1954). A factorial study of closure. *Canad. J. Psychol.*, 8, 51–60.

Mooney, C. M., and Ferguson, G. A. (1951). A new closure test. *Canad. J. Psychol.*, 6, 129–133.

Moore, T. V. (1938). The psychotic and prepsychotic character. *Charact. & Pers.*, 7, 14–18.

Moore, T. V. (1941). The prepsychotic personality and the concept of mental disease. *Charact. & Pers.*, 9, 169–187.

Moore, T. V., and Hsü, E. H. (1946). Factorial analysis of anthropological measurements in psychotic patients. *Human Biol.*, 18, 133–157.

Morgan, J. J. B. (1943). Distorted reasoning as an index of public opinion. *Sch. & Soc.*, 57, 333–335.

Morgan, J. J. B. (1945). Attitudes of students toward the Japanese. *J. soc. Psychol.*, 21, 219–246.

Morgan, J. J. B., and Morton, J. T. (1944). The distortion of syllogistic reasoning produced by personal convictions. *J. soc. Psychol.*, 20, 39–59.

Morris, C., and Jones, L. V. (1955). Value scales and dimensions. *J. abnorm. soc. Psychol.*, 51, 523–535.

Morris, W. W. (1951). Other projective methods. In H. H. Anderson and G. L. Anderson (Eds.), *Introduction to projective techniques*. Englewood Cliffs, N.J.: Prentice-Hall.

Mosier, C. I. (1937). A factor analysis of certain neurotic tendencies. *Psychometrika*, 2, 263–287.

Moursy, E. M. (1952). The hierarchical organization of cognitive levels. *Brit. J. Psychol., Stat. Sec.,* 5, 151–180.

Mullen, F. A. (1940). Factors in the growth of girls. *Child Develpm.,* 11, 27–42.

Munroe, R. L. (1942). An experiment in large-scale testing by a modification of the Rorschach method. *J. Psychol.,* 13, 229–263.

Murdock, K., and Sullivan, L. R. (1923). A contribution to the study of mental and physical measurements in normal children. *Amer. phys. Educ. Rev.,* 28.

Murphy, L. B. (1937). *Social behavior and child personality: an exploratory study of some roots of sympathy.* New York: Columbia University Press.

Murray, H. A. (1938). *Explorations in personality: a clinical and experimental study of fifty men of college age.* New York: Oxford University Press.

Murray, H. A. (1943). *Thematic Apperception Test.* Cambridge, Mass.: Harvard University Press.

Murray, H. A. (1951). Thematic Apperception Test. In *Military clinical psychology.* Washington: GPO.

Myers, C. T. (1952). The factorial composition and validity of differently speeded tests. *Psychometrika,* 17, 347–352.

Naccarati, S. (1921). The morphological aspect of intelligence. *Arch. Psychol., N.Y.,* No. 45.

Nance, R. D. (1949). Masculinity-femininity in prospective teachers. *J. educ. Res.,* 42, 658–666.

Napoli, P. J. (1951). Finger painting. In H. H. Anderson and G. L. Anderson (Eds.), *Introduction to projective techniques.* Englewood Cliffs, N.J.: Prentice-Hall.

Neel, M. O., and Mathews, C. O. (1935). Need for superior students. *J. higher Educ.,* 6, 29–34.

Neilon, P. (1948). Shirley's babies after fifteen years: a personality study. *J. genet. Psychol.,* 73, 175–186.

Nelson, E., and Nelson, N. (1940). Student attitudes and vocational choices. *J. abnorm. soc. Psychol.,* 35, 279–282.

Noll, V. H. (1951). Simulation by college students of a prescribed pattern on a personality scale. *Educ. psychol. Measmt,* 11, 478–488.

O'Connor, J. P. (1953). A statistical test of psychoneurotic syndromes. *J. abnorm. soc. Psychol.,* 48, 581–584.

O'Connor, N. (1952). The prediction of psychological stability and anxiety-aggressiveness from a battery of tests administered to a group of high grade male mental defectives. *J. gen. Psychol.,* 46, 3–17.

Odbert, H. S. (1934). *The consistency of the individual in his imaginal processes.* Cambridge, Mass.: Harvard College Library.

Older, H. J. (1944). An objective test of vocational interests. *J. appl. Psychol.,* 28, 99–108.

Oléron, P. (1957). *Les composantes de l'intelligence.* Paris: Presses Universitaires de France.

Oliver, J. A., and Ferguson, G. A. (1951). A factorial study of tests of rigidity. *Canad. J. Psychol.,* 5, 49–59.

O'Neil, W. M., and Levinson, D. J. (1954). A factorial exploration of authoritarianism and some of its ideological concomitants. *J. Pers.,* 22, 449–463.

Osborne, H. T., and Sanders, W. B. (1949). Multiple-choice Rorschach responses of college achievers and non-achievers. *Educ. psychol. Measmt,* 9, 685–691.

Osburn, H. G., Lubin, A., Loeffler, J. C., and Tye, V. M. (1954). The relative validity of forced choice and single stimulus self description items. *Educ. psychol. Measmt,* 14, 407–417.

OSS Assessment Staff (1948). *Assessment of men.* New York: Rinehart.

Owens, W. A., Jr. (1954). The retest consistency of Army Alpha after thirty years. *J. appl. Psychol.,* 38, 154.

Pace, C. R. (1939a). A situations test to measure social-political-economic attitudes. *J. soc. Psychol.,* 10, 331–344.

Pace, C. R. (1939b). The relationship between liberalism and knowledge of current affairs. *J. soc. Psychol.,* 10, 247–258.

Pace, C. R. (1950). Opinion and action: a study in validity of attitude measurement. *Educ. psychol. Measmt,* 10, 411–419.

Page, H. E. (1945). Detecting psychoneurotic tendencies in Army personnel. *Psychol. Bull.,* 42, 645–658.

Page, J., Landis, C., and Katz, S. E. (1934). Schizophrenic traits in functional psychoses and in the normal individual. *Amer. J. Psychiat.,* 13, 1213–1225.

Parrish, J., and Rethlingshafer, D. (1954). A study of the need to achieve in college achievers and non-achievers. *J. gen. Psychol.,* 50, 209–226.

Parten, M. B. (1933). Leadership among pre-school children. *J. abnorm. soc. Psychol.,* 27, 430–440.

Partridge, E. D. (1934). Leadership among adolescent boys. *Teach. Coll. Contr. Educ.,* No. 608.

Pascal, G. R. (1943a). The analysis of handwriting: a test of significance. *Charact. & Pers.,* 12, 123–144.

Pascal, G. R. (1943b). Handwriting pressure: its measurement and significance. *Charact. & Pers.,* 11, 235–254.

Pascal, G. R., and Suttell, B. (1947). Testing the claims of a graphologist. *J. Pers.,* 16, 192–197.

Pastore, N. (1949). Need as a determinant of perception. *J. Psychol.,* 28, 457–475.

Paterson, D. G. (1930). *Physique and intellect.* New York: Appleton-Century-Crofts.

Paterson, D. G., and Ludgate, K. E. (1922). Blond and brunette traits: a quantitative study. *J. Personnel Res.,* 1, 122–128.

Pederson, R. A. (1940). Validity of the Bell Adjustment Inventory when applied to college women. *J. Psychol.,* 9, 227–236.

Pemberton, C. L. (1952a). The closure factors related to other cognitive processes. *Psychometrika,* 17, 267–288.

Pemberton, C. L. (1952b). The closure factor related to temperament. *J. Pers.,* 21, 159–175.

Penfield, W. (1958). Some mechanisms of consciousness discovered during electrical stimulation of the brain. *Proc. Nat. Acad. Sci.,* 44, 51–66.

Pepinsky, H. B., Siegel, L., and Vanatta A. (1952). The criterion in counseling: a group participation scale. *J. abnorm. soc. Psychol.,* 47, 415–419.

Phillips, W. S., and Osborne, R. T. (1949). A note on the relationship of the Kuder Preference Record scales to college marks, scholastic aptitude and other variables. *Educ. psychol. Measmt,* 9, 331–337.

Pickford, R. W. (1956). Colour-blindness and its inheritance. *Biol. & hum. Affairs,* 1–8.

Pierce-Jones, J., and Carter, H. D. (1954). Vocational interest measurement using a photographic inventory. *Educ. psychol. Measmt,* 14, 671–679.

Pigors, P. (1933). Leadership and domination among children. *Sociologus,* 9, 140–157.

Pillsbury, W. B. (1936). Body form and success in studies. *J. soc. Psychol.,* 7, 129–139.

Plutchik, R. (1954). The role of muscular tension in maladjustment. *J. gen. Psychol.,* 50, 45–62.

Poffenberger, A. T., and Barrows, B. E. (1924). The feeling value of lines. *J. appl. Psychol.,* 8, 187–205.

Polansky, N. A. (1941). How shall a life history be written? *Charact. & Pers.,* 9, 188–207.

Porter, E. L. H. (1938). Factors in the fluctuation of fifteen ambiguous figures. *Psychol. Rec.,* 2, 231–253.

Powell, M. G. (1948). Comparisons of self-ratings, peer-ratings, and expert's-ratings of personality adjustment. *Educ. psychol. Measmt,* 8, 225–234.

Powers, M. K. (1956). Permanence of measured vocational interests of adult males. *J. appl. Psychol.,* 40, 69–72.

Pratt, S. H. (1952). *The study of differential personality dynamics within and between various nosological groups and subgroups using objective type self-report inventories.* Doctoral dissertation, Purdue University.

Proshansky, H. M. (1943). A projective method for the study of attitudes. *J. abnorm. soc. Psychol.,* 38, 383–395.

Prothero, E. T. (1955). The effect of strong negative attitude on the placement of items in a Thurstone scale. *J. soc. Psychol.,* 41, 11–17.

Rabin, A. I., and Guertin, W. H. (1951). Research with the Wechsler-Bellevue test. *Psychol. Bull.,* 48, 211–248.

Rapkin, M. (1953). The projective motor test: a validation study. *J. proj. Tech.,* 17, 127–143.

Razor, B. A. L. (1949). *The relation of the Guilford-Zimmerman Aptitude Survey to success in various college courses.* Master's thesis, Los Angeles: University of Southern California.

Redlener, J. (1949). *A comparative study of the efficiency of the Kuder Preference Record and the Strong Vocational Interest Blank in the prediction of job satisfaction.* Master's thesis, Los Angeles: University of Southern California.

Reed, P. H., and Wittman, P. (1942). "Blind" diagnoses of several personality questionnaires checked with each other and the psychiatric diagnoses. *Psychol. Bull.,* 39, 592.

Rees, W. L., and Eysenck, H. J. (1945). A factorial study of some morphological and psychological aspects of human constitution. *J. ment. Sci.,* 91, 8–21.

Remmers, H. H., Cutler, M., and Jones, P. (1940). Waking suggestibility in children: general or specific? *J. genet. Psychol.,* 56, 87–93.

Remmers, H. H., and Silance, E. B. (1934). Generalized attitude scales. *J. soc. Psychol.,* 5, 298–312.

Rethlingshafer, D. (1942). The relation of tests of persistence to other measures of continuance of action. *J. abnorm. soc. Psychol.,* 37, 71–82.

Ricciuti, H. N. (1955). *The prediction of academic grades with a projective test of achievement motivation. II. Cross-validation at the high school level.* Princeton, N.J.: Educational Testing Service.

Rich, G. H. (1928). Biochemical approach to the study of personality. *J. abnorm. soc. Psychol.,* 23, 158–175.

Richards, T. W. (1940). Factors in the personality of nursery school children. *J. exp. Educ.,* 9, 152–153.

Richards, T. W. (1941). Genetic emergence of factor specificity. *Psychometrika,* 6, 37–42.

Richards, T. W., and Ellington, E. (1942). Objectivity in the evaluation of personality. *J. exp. Educ.,* 11, 228–237.

Richards, T. W., and Nelson, V. L. (1939). Abilities of infants during the first eighteen months. *J. genet. Psychol.,* 55, 299–318.

Rim, Y. (1955). Perseveration and fluency as measures of introversion-extraversion in abnormal subjects. *J. Pers.,* 23, 324–334.

Rimoldi, H. J. A. (1951). Personal tempo. *J. abnorm. soc. Psychol.,* 46, 283–303.

Roback, A. A. (1955). *Present-day psychology.* New York: Philosophical Library.

Roberts, K. E., and Fleming, V. V. (1943). Persistence and change in personality patterns. *Monogr. Soc. Res. Child Develpm.,* 8, No. 1.

Roe, A. (1946). The personality of artists. *Educ. psychol. Measmt,* 6, 401–408.

Roe, A. (1953). A psychological study of eminent psychologists and anthropologists, and a comparison with biological and physical scientists. *Psychol. Monogr.,* 67, Whole No. 352.

Roff, M. (1952). A factorial study of tests in the perceptual area. *Psychometric Monogr.,* No. 8.

Rogers, C. A. (1953). The structure of verbal fluency. *Brit. J. Psychol.,* 44, 368–380.

Rohde, A. R. (1946). Explorations in personality by the sentence completion method. *J. appl. Psychol.,* 30, 169–181.

Rohde, A. R. (1957). *The sentence completion method.* New York: Ronald.

Rokeach, M., and Fruchter, B. (1956). A factorial study of dogmatism and related concepts. *J. abnorm. soc. Psychol.,* 53, 356–360.

Rorschach, H. (1942). *Psychodiagnostistics, a diagnostic test based on perception* (Trans. by P. Lemkau and B. Kronenburg). Bern: Huber.

Rosanoff, A. (1920). *Manual of psychiatry.* (4th ed.) New York: Wiley.

Rosenbaum, M. E. (1956). The effect of stimulus and background factors on the volunteering response. *J. abnorm. soc. Psychol.,* 53, 118–121.

Rosenberg, N. (1953). Stability and maturation of Kuder interest patterns during high school. *Educ. psychol. Measmt,* 13, 449–458.

Rotter, J. B. (1942). Level of aspiration as a method of studying personality. *Psychol. Rev.,* 49, 463–474.

Rotter, J. B. (1951). Word association and sentence completion methods. In H. H. Anderson and G. L. Anderson (Eds.), *Introduction to projective techniques.* Englewood Cliffs, N.J.: Prentice-Hall.

Rotter, J. B., Rafferty, J. E., and Schachtitz, E. (1949). Validation of the Rotter Incomplete Sentences Blank for college screening. *J. consult. Psychol.,* 13, 348–356.

Rotter, J. B., and Willerman, B. (1947). The incomplete sentence test as a method of studying personality. *J. consult. Psychol.,* 11, 43–48.

Royce, J. R. (1955). A factorial study of emotionality in the dog. *Psychol. Monogr.,* 69, Whole No. 407.

Rubin, H. (1948). The Minnesota Multiphasic Personality Inventory as a diagnostic aid in a Veterans hospital. *J. consult Psychol.,* 12, 251–254.

Ruch, F. L. (1942). A technique for detecting attempts to fake performance on the self-report type of personality tests. In Q. McNemar and M. A. Merrill (Eds.), *Studies in personality.* New York: McGraw-Hill.

Rundquist, E. A. (1933). Inheritance of spontaneous activity in rats. *J. comp. Psychol.,* 16, 415–438.

Rusmore, J. T. (1956). Fakability of the Gordon Personal Profile. *J. appl. Psychol.,* 40, 175–177.

Rust, R. M., and Ryan, F. J. (1953). The relationship of some Rorschach variables to academic behavior. *J. Pers.,* 21, 441–456.

Ryans, D. G. (1938). A study of the observed relationship between persistence test results, intelligence indices, and academic success. *J. educ. Psychol.,* 29, 573–580.

Sacks, J. M., and Lewin, H. S. (1950). Limitations of the Rorschach as sole diagnostic instrument. *J. consult. Psychol.,* 14, 479–481.

Samuelson, C. O., and Pearson, D. T., Sr. (1956). Interest scores in identifying the potential trade school dropout. *J. appl. Psychol.,* 40, 386–388.

Sanai, M. (1951). An experimental study of social attitudes. *J. soc. Psychol.,* 34, 235–264.

Sanford, F. H. (1942). Speech and personality. *Psychol. Bull.,* 39, 811–845.

Sanford, F. H. (1950). *Authoritarianism and leadership.* Philadelphia: Stephenson Bros.

Sanford, N. (1956). The approach of the authoritarian personality. In J. L. McCary (Ed.), *Psychology of personality.* New York: Logos Press.

Sanford, R. N. (1936). The effects of abstinence from food upon imaginal processes: a preliminary experiment. *J. Psychol.,* 2, 129–136.

Sanford, R. N. (1937). The effects of abstinence from food upon imaginal processes. *J. Psychol.* 3, 145–159.

Sanford, R. N., Adkins, M., Miller, R. B., and Cobb, E. A., et al. (1943). Physique, personality, and scholarship: a cooperative study of school children. *Monogr. Soc. Res. Child Develpm.,* 8, No. 1.

Sarbin, T. R. (1942). A contribution to the study of actuarial and individual methods of prediction. *Amer. J. Sociol.,* 48, 593–603.

Saudek, R. (1928). *Experiments in handwriting.* New York: Morrow.

Schaie, K. W. (1955). A test of behavioral rigidity. *J. abnorm. soc. Psychol.,* 51, 604–610.

Schanck, R. L. (1932). A study of a community and its groups and institutions conceived of as behaviors of individuals. *Psychol. Monogr.,* 43, No. 2.

Scheier, I. N., and Ferguson, G. A. (1952). Further factorial studies of tests of rigidity. *Canad. J. Psychol.,* 6, 18–30.

Schmid, J., and Leiman, J. M. (1957). The development of hierarchical factor solutions. *Psychometrika,* 22, 53–62.

Schmidt, H. O. (1945). Test profiles as a diagnostic aid: the Minnesota Multiphasic Inventory. *J. appl. Psychol.,* 29, 115–131.

Schmidt, H. O. (1948). Notes on the Minnesota Multiphasic Personality Inventory: the *K* factor. *J. consult. Psychol.,* 12, 337–342.

Schmidt, H. O., and Fonda, C. P. (1956). The reliability of psychiatric diagnoses: a new look. *J. abnorm. soc. Psychol.,* 52, 262–267.

Schofield, W. (1953). A study of medical students with the MMPI. III. Personality and academic success. *J. appl. Psychol.,* 37, 47–52.

Schroder, H. M., and Rotter, J. B. (1952). Rigidity as learned behavior. *J. exp. Psychol.,* 44, 141–150.

Schultz, D. G., and Ricciuti, H. N. (1954). Level of aspiration measures and college achievement. *J. gen. Psychol.,* 51, 267–275.

Schwegler, E. A. (1929). A study of introvert-extravert responses to certain test situations. *Teach. Coll. Contr. Educ.,* No. 361.

Seashore, R. H., Buxton, C. E., and McCollum, I. N. (1940). Multiple factor analysis of fine motor skills. *Amer. J. Psychol.*, 53, 251–259.

Seashore, R. H., Starmann, R., Kendall, W. E., and Helmick, J. S. (1941). Group factors in simple and discrimination reaction time. *J. exp. Psychol.*, 29, 346–349.

Seashore, S. H., and Seashore, R. H. (1941). Individual differences in simple auditory reaction times of hands, feet, and jaws. *J. exp. Psychol.*, 29, 342–345.

Secord, P. F. (1949). Studies of the relationship of handwriting to personality. *J. Pers.*, 17, 430–448.

Secord, P. F. (1952). A note on the problem of homogeneity-heterogeneity in the use of the matching method in personality studies. *Psychol. Bull.*, 49, 41–42.

Secord, P. F. (1953). An analysis of perceptual and related processes occurring in projective testing. *J. gen. Psychol.*, 49, 65–85.

Secord, P. F. (1955). "Personality integration" in responses to self-inventories. *J. Pers.*, 23, 308–316.

Secord, P. F., and Muthard, J. E. (1955). Personalities in faces. IV. A descriptive analysis of the perception of women's faces and the identification of some physiognomic determinants. *J. Psychol.*, 39, 269–278.

Seeleman, V. (1940–41). The influence of attitude upon the remembering of pictorial material. *Arch. Psychol., N.Y.*, 36, No. 258.

Segel, D., and Brintle, S. L. (1934). The relation of occupational interest scores to achievement test results and college marks. *J. educ. Res.*, 27, 442–445.

Semeonoff, B. (1952). On the reliability of the leaderless group discussion technique. *Psychol. Bull.*, 49, 540–541.

Shagass, C. (1946). An attempt to correlate the occipital alpha frequency of the electroencephalogram with performance on a mental ability test. *J. exp. Psychol.*, 36, 88–92.

Shakow, D., and Rosenzweig, S. (1940). The use of the tautophone ("verbal summator") as an auditory apperceptive test for the study of personality. *Charact. & Pers.*, 8, 216–226.

Shapiro, J. J. (1947). *A factor analysis of twenty tests for pilots given by the Army Air Forces to West Point Cadets.* Master's thesis, University of Southern California.

Shaw, D. C. (1949). A study of the relationships between Thurstone primary mental abilities and high school achievement. *J. educ. Psychol.*, 40, 239–249.

Sheldon, W. H. (1940). *The varieties of human physique.* New York: Harper.

Sheldon, W. H. (1942). *The varieties of temperament.* New York: Harper.

Shen, E. (1925). The validity of self-estimates. *J. educ. Psychol.*, 16, 104–107.

Shepler, B. F. (1951). A comparison of masculinity-femininity measures. *J. consult. Psychol.*, 15, 484–486.

Sherman, M., and Jost, H. (1945). Quantification of psychophysiological measures. *Psychosom. Med.*, 7, 215–219.

Shevach, B. J. (1938). A note on racial differences in perseveration. *J. Psychol.*, 5, 271–279.

Shipley, W. C. (1940). A self-administering scale for measuring intellectual impairment and deterioration. *J. Psychol.*, 9, 371–377.

Shipley, W. C., Gray, F. E., and Newbert, N. (1946). The Personal Inventory—its derivation and validation. *J. clin. Psychol.*, 2, 318–322.

Shirley, M. M. (1932). The first two years. A study of twenty-five babies. Vol. II. Intellectual development. *Univer. Minn. Inst. Child Welfare Monogr. Ser.*, No. 7. Minneapolis: University of Minnesota Press,

Shneidman, E. S. (1943). A note on the experimental study of the appraisal interview. *J. appl. Psychol.*, 27, 196–205.

Shneidman, E. S. (1948). Schizophrenia and the MAPS test: a study of certain formal psycho-social aspects of fantasy production in schizophrenia as revealed by performance on the Make a Picture Story (MAPS) Test. *Genet. Psychol. Monogr.*, 38, 145–224.

Shuey, H. (1937). The fundamental principles of typology. *Psychol. Rev.*, 44, 170–182.

Simrall, D. (1947). Intelligence and the ability to learn. *J. Psychol.*, 23, 27–43.

Slater, E. (1943). The neurotic constitution. A statistical study of two thousand neurotic soldiers. *J. Neurol. Neurosurg. Psychiat.*, 6, 1–16.

Slater, E. (1944). A heuristic theory of neuroses. *J. Neurol. Neurosurg. Psychiat.*, 7, 49–55.

Smith, F. V., and Madan, S. K. (1953). A projective technique based upon kinaesthetic and tactile modalities. *Brit. J. Psychol.*, 44, 156–163.

Smith, G. H. (1948). The relation of "enlightenment" to liberal-conservative opinions. *J. soc. Psychol.*, 28, 3–17.

Smith, H. C. (1949). Psychometric checks on hypotheses derived from Sheldon's work on physique and temperament. *J. Pers.*, 17, 310–320.

Smith, M. B., Bruner, J. S., and White, R. W. (1956). *Opinions and personality.* New York: Wiley.

Soar, R. S. (1956). Personal history data as a predictor of success in service station management. *J. appl. Psychol.*, 40, 383–385.

Spearman, C. (1927). *The abilities of man.* New York: Macmillan.

Spranger, E. (1928). *Lebensform.* (3d ed.) (Trans. by P. J. W. Pigors.) New York: Stechert.

Stagner, R. (1933). The relation of personality to academic aptitude and achievement. *J. educ. Res.*, 26, 648–660.

Stagner, R., and Katzoff, E. T. (1942). Fascist attitudes: Factor analysis of item correlations. *J. soc. Psychol.* 16, 3–9.

Stanley, J. C., and Waldrop, R. S. (1952). Intercorrelations of Study of Values and Kuder Preference Record scores. *Educ. psychol. Measmt,* 12, 707–719.

Stein, M. I., and Meer, B. (1954). Perceptual organization in a study of creativity. *J. Psychol.*, 37, 39–43.

Steinberg, D. L., and Wittman, M. P. (1943). Etiologic factors in the adjustment of men in the armed forces. *War Med.*, 4, 129–139.

Steinmetz, H. C. (1932). Measuring ability to fake occupational interest. *J. appl. Psychol.*, 16, 123–130.

Steinmetz, H. C. (1945). Directive psychotherapy: measuring psychological understanding. *J. clin. Psychol.*, 1, 331–335.

Steinmetz, H. C. (1948). Obfuscating personality. *Sci. Mon.*, 66, 87.

Stewart, B. M. (1950). *A study of the relationship between clinical manifestations of neurotic anxiety and Rorschach test performance.* Doctoral dissertation, University of Southern California.

Stogdill, R. M. (1948). Personal factors associated with leadership: a survey of the literature. *J. Psychol.*, 25, 35–71.

Stogdill, R. M., and Shartle, C. L. (1948). Methods for determining patterns of leadership behavior in relation to organization structure and objectives. *J. appl. Psychol.*, 32, 286–291.

Stone, D. R. (1950). A recorded auditory apperception test as a new projective technique. *J. Psychol.*, 29, 349–353.

Stone, G. C., Leavitt, G. S., and Gage, N. L. (1954). Generality of accuracy in perceiving standard persons. *Studies in the generality and behavioral correlates of social perception.* Report No. 1. Urbana, Ill.: Bureau of Educational Research.

Stott, L. H. (1938). An analytical study of self-reliance. *J. Psychol.,* 5, 107–118.

Stouffer, S. A., Guttman, L., Suchman, E. A., Lazersfeld, P. F., Star, S. A., and Clausen J. A. (1950). *Measurement and prediction. Studies in, social psychology in World War II,* Vol. IV. Princeton, N.J.: Princeton University Press.

Street, R. F. (1931). *A Gestalt Completion test.* New York: Teachers College, Columbia University.

Strong, E. K., Jr. (1931). *Change in interests with age.* Stanford, Calif.: Stanford University Press.

Strong, E. K., Jr. (1943). *Vocational interests of men and women.* Stanford, Calif.: Stanford University Press.

Strong, E. K., Jr. (1945). *Manual for Vocational Interest Blank for Men.* Stanford, Calif.: Stanford University Press.

Strong, E. K., Jr. (1951). Interest scores while in college of occupations engaged in 20 years later. *Educ. psychol. Measmt,* 11, 335–348.

Sulzman, J. H., Cook, E. H., and Bartlett, N. R. (1947). The reliability of visual scores yielded by three commercial devices. *J. appl. Psychol.,* 31, 236–240.

Sundberg, N. D. (1955). The acceptability of "fake" versus "bona fide" personality test interpretations. *J. abnorm. soc. Psychol.,* 50, 145–147.

Super, D. E. (1941). Avocations and vocational adjustment. *Charact. & Pers.,* 9, 51–61.

Super, D. E. (1942). The Bernreuter Personality Inventory. *Psychol. Bull.,* 39, 94–125.

Sweet, L. (1929). *The measurement of personal attitudes in younger boys.* New York: Association Press.

Symonds, P. M. (1949). *Adolescent fantasy: an investigation of the picture-story method of personality study.* New York: Columbia University Press.

Taft, R. (1950). *Some correlates of the ability to make accurate social judgments.* Doctor's dissertation, Berkeley, Calif.: University of California.

Taft, R. (1955). The ability to judge people. *Psychol. Bull.,* 52, 1–23.

Tate, M. W. (1948). Individual differences in speed of response in mental test materials of varying degrees of difficulty. *Educ. psychol. Measmt,* 8, 353–374.

Taylor, C. W. (1947). A factorial study of fluency in writing. *Psychometrika,* 12, 239–262.

Taylor, J. A. (1956). Drive theory and manifest anxiety. *Psychol. Bull.,* 53, 303–320.

Terman, L. M., and Merrill, M. (1937). *Measuring intelligence.* Boston: Houghton Mifflin.

Terman, L. M., and Miles, C. C. (1936). *Sex and personality. Studies in masculinity and femininity.* New York: McGraw-Hill.

Thomas, W. F., and Young, P. T. (1938). Liking and disliking persons. *J. soc. Psychol.,* 9, 169–188.

Thompson, G. G., and Witryol, S. L. (1946). The relationship between intelligence and motor learning ability, as measured by a high relief finger maze. *J. Psychol.,* 22, 237–246.

Thorndike, E. L., Bregman, E. O., Cobb, M. V., Woodyard, E., et al. (1926). *The measurement of intelligence.* New York: Teachers College, Columbia University.

Thornton, G. R. (1939). A factor analysis of tests designed to measure persistence. *Psychol. Monogr.*, 51, Whole No. 229.

Thornton, G. R. (1943). The effect upon judgments of personality traits of varying a single factor in a photograph. *J. soc. Psychol.*, 18, 127–148.

Thornton, G. R. (1944). The effect of wearing glasses upon judgments of personality traits of persons seen briefly. *J. appl. Psychol.*, 28, 203–207.

Thorpe, L. P., Clark, W. W., and Tiegs, E. W. (1939). *California Test of Personality*. Los Angeles: California Test Bureau.

Thune, J. B. (1949). Personality of weight lifters. *Res. Quart. Amer. Ass. Hlth phys. Educ.*, 20, No. 3.

Thurstone, L. L. (1928). Attitudes can be measured. *Amer. J. Sociol.*, 33, 529–554.

Thurstone, L. L. (1931). A multiple factor study of vocational interests. *Personnel J.*, 10, 198–205.

Thurstone, L. L. (1934). Vectors of mind. *Psychol. Rev.*, 41, 1–32.

Thurstone, L. L. (1937). Ability, motivation, and speed. *Psychometrika*, 2, 249–254.

Thurstone, L. L. (1938). Primary mental abilities. *Psychometric Monogr.* No. 1.

Thurstone, L. L. (1944). A factorial study of perception. *Psychometric Monogr.*, No. 4.

Thurstone, L. L. (1946). Factor analysis and body types. *Psychometrika*, 11, 15–21.

Thurstone, L. L. (1947). Factorial analysis of body measurements. *Amer. J. phys. Anthrop.*, 5, 15–28.

Thurstone, L. L., and Thurstone, T. G. (1930). A neurotic inventory. *J. soc. Psychol.*, 1, 3–30.

Thurstone L. L., and Thurstone, T. G. (1942). Factorial studies of intelligence. *Psychometric Monogr.*, No. 2.

Thurstone, L. L., and Thurstone, T. G. (1947). *SRA Primary Mental Abilities*. Chicago: Science Research Associates.

Tiffin, J., and Greenly, R. J. (1939). Employee selection tests for electrical fixture assemblers. *J. appl. Psychol.*, 23, 450–460.

Tilton, J. W. (1949). Intelligence test scores as indicative of ability to learn. *Educ. psychol. Measmt*, 9, 291–296.

Tindall, R. H. (1955). Relationships among indices of adjustment status. *Educ. psychol. Measmt*, 15, 152–162.

Tolman, E. C. (1948). Cognitive maps in rats and men. *Psychol. Rev.*, 55, 189–208.

Tomkins, S. S. (1947). *The Thematic Apperception Test*. New York: Grune & Stratton.

Travers, R. M. W. (1941). A study in judging the opinions of groups. *Arch. Psychol., N.Y.*, No. 266.

Tresselt, M. E. (1948). The effect of experience of contrasted groups upon the formation of a new scale of judgment. *J. soc. Psychol.*, 27, 209–216.

Tryon, C. McC. (1939). Evaluation of adolescent personality by adolescents. *Monogr. Soc. Res. Child Develpm.*, 4, No. 4.

Tupes, E. C. (1950). An evaluation of personality-trait ratings obtained by unstructured assessment interviews. *Psychol. Monogr.*, 64, Whole No. 317.

Tyler, F. T., and DiMichaelis, J. U. (1953). K scores applied to MMPI scales for college women. *Educ. psychol. Measmt*, 13, 459–466.

Tyler, L. E. (1955). The development of "vocational interests." I. The organization of likes and dislikes in ten-year-old children. *J. genet. Psychol.*, 86, 33–44.

Uhrbrock, R. S. (1948). The personal interview. *Personnel Psychol.*, 1, 273–302.

U.S. War Manpower Commission, Division of Occupational Analysis (1945).

Factor analysis of occupational aptitude tests. *Educ. psychol. Measmt,* 5, 147–155.

Van Steenberg, N. J. (1939). Factors in the learning behavior of the albino rat. *Psychometrika,* 4, 179–200.

Van Zelst, R. H. (1953). Validation evidence on the empathy test. *Educ. psychol. Measmt,* 13, 474–477.

Vaughn, C. L. (1937). Factors in the rat. *Comp. Psychol. Monogr.,* 14, No. 3.

Vernon P. E. (1933). Some characteristics of the good judge of personality. *J. soc. Psychol.,* 4, 42–57.

Vernon, P. E. (1936a). The matching method applied to investigations of personality. *Psychol. Bull.,* 33, 149–177.

Vernon, P. E. (1936b). The evaluation of the matching method. *J. educ. Psychol.,* 27, 1–17.

Vernon, P. E. (1938). *The assessment of psychological qualities by verbal methods.* London: H. M. Stationery Office.

Vernon, P. E. (1950a). *The structure of abilities.* New York: Wiley.

Vernon, P. E. (1950b). The validation of Civil Service Selection Board Procedures. *Occup. Psychol. Lond.,* 25, 75–95.

Vetter, G. B. (1947). What makes attitudes and opinions "liberal" and "conservative"? *J. abnorm. soc. Psychol.,* 42, 125–130.

Viteles, M. W. (1945). The aircraft pilot: five years of research, a summary of outcomes. *Psychol. Bull.,* 42, 489–526.

Wallen, R. (1943). Individuals' estimates of group opinion. *J. soc. Psychol.,* 17, 269–274.

Wallen, R. (1945). Food aversions of normal and neurotic males. *J. abnorm. soc. Psychol.,* 40, 77–81.

Wallon, E. J., and Webb, W. B. (1956). *The effect of varying degrees of projection on test scores.* Research Project No. NM 011 108 100, Report No. 12. Pensacola, Fla.: U.S. Naval School of Aviation Medicine.

Walter, W. G. (1953). *The living brain.* New York: Norton.

Walton, R. D. (1936). Relations between amplitude of oscillation in short period efficiency and steadiness of character. *Brit. J. Psychol.,* 27, 181–188.

Walton, R. D. (1939). Individual differences in amplitudes of oscillation and their connection with steadiness of character. *Brit. J. Psychol.,* 30, 36–46.

Walton, W. E. (1936). Empathic responses in children. *Psychol. Monogr.,* 48, Whole No. 213, 40–67.

Warren, H. C. (1934). *Dictionary of psychology.* Boston: Houghton Mifflin.

Wauck, L. A. (1950). Schizophrenia and the MMPI. *J. clin. Psychol.,* 6, 279–282.

Webb, E. (1915). Character and intelligence. *Brit. J. Psychol.,* Monogr. Suppl., 1, No. 3.

Webb, S. C. (1955). Scaling of attitudes by the method of equal-appearing intervals: a review. *J. soc. Psychol.,* 42, 215–239.

Wechsler, D. (1944). *The measurement of adult intelligence.* (3d ed.) Baltimore: Williams & Wilkins.

Wedeck, J. (1947). The relationship between personality and "psychological ability." *Brit. J. Psychol.,* 37, 133–151.

Weingarten, E. M. (1949). Selective perception in clinical judgment. *J. Pers.,* 17, 369–406.

Weinland, J. D. (1930). An objective method for the measurement of attitudes. *J. appl. Psychol.,* 14, 427–436.

Weinland, J. D. (1947). A five month strength curve. *J. appl. Psychol.,* 31, 498–501.

Weisgerber, C. A. (1955). Factor analysis of a questionnaire test of perseveration. *J. gen. Psychol.,* 53, 341–345.

Weisskopf, E. A., and Kieppa, J. J. (1951). Experimentally induced faking of TAT responses. *J. consult. Psychol.,* 15, 469–474.

Welch, L., and Kubis, J. (1947). The effect of anxiety on the conditioning rate and stability of the PGR. *J. Psychol.,* 23, 83–91.

Wendler, A. J. (1938). A critical analysis of test elements used in physical education. *Res. Quart. Amer. Ass. Hlth phys. Educ.,* 9, 64–76.

Wenger, M. A. (1941–42). A further note on the measurement of autonomic balance. *Psychosom. Med.,* 3, 427–434; 4, 94.

Wenger, M. A. (1942). A study of physiological factors: the autonomic nervous system and the skeletal musculature. *Hum. Biol.,* 14, 69–84.

Wenger, M. A. (1943a). A further note on the measurement of autonomic balance. *Psychosom. Med.,* 5, 148–151.

Wenger, M. A. (1943b). An attempt to appraise individual differences in level of muscular tension. *J. exp. Psychol.,* 32, 213–225.

Wenger, M. A. (1948). Studies of autonomic balance in Army Air Forces Personnel. *Comp. Psychol. Monogr.,* 19, No. 101.

Weschler, I. R. (1950). An investigation of attitudes toward labor and management by means of the error-choice method. I. *J. soc. Psychol.,* 32, 51–62.

Wesley, S. M., Corey, D. Q., and Stewart, B. M. (1950). The intra-individual relationship between interest and ability. *J. appl. Psychol.,* 34, 193–197.

Wherry, R. J. (1939). Factorial analysis of learning dynamics. *J. comp. Psychol.,* 28, 263–272.

Wherry, R. J. (1940). A test by factorial analysis of Honzik's exteroceptive data. *J. comp. Psychol.,* 29, 75–95.

Wherry, R. J. (1941). Determination of the specific components of maze learning for Tryon's bright and dull rats by means of factor analysis. *J. comp. Psychol.,* 32, 237–252.

Whisler, L. D. (1934). Multiple-factor analysis of generalized attitudes. *J. soc. Psychol.,* 5, 283–297.

Whisler, L. D., and Remmers, H. H. (1938). Liberalism, optimism, and group morals: a study of student attitudes. *J. soc. Psychol.,* 9, 451–467.

Whyte, W. H., Jr. (1954). The fallacies of "personality" testing. *Fortune,* 50, 117–121.

Williams, H. L., and Lawrence, J. F. (1953). Further investigations of Rorschach determinants subjected to factor analysis. *J. consult. Psychol.,* 17, 261–264.

Williams, H. W. (1935). A factor analysis of Berne's "Social Behavior Patterns in Young Children." *J. exp. Educ.,* 4, 142–146.

Williams, R. J. (1953). *Free and unequal: the biological basis of individual liberty.* Austin, Tex.: University of Texas Press.

Williams, R. J. (1955). Implications of humanics for law and science. Law and medicine, a symposium. *J. public Law,* 3, 328–344.

Willoughby, R. R., and Morse, M. E. (1936). Spontaneous reactions to a personality inventory. *Amer. J. Orthopsychiat.,* 6, 562–575.

Wilmer, H. A., and Husni, M. (1953). The use of sounds in a projective test. *J. consult. Psychol.,* 17, 377–383.

Wilson, I. (1949). The use of the sentence completion test in differentiating between well-adjusted and maladjusted secondary school pupils. *J. consult. Psychol.*, 13, 400–402.

Wilson, R. C., Guilford, J. P., and Christensen, P. R. (1953). The measurement of individual differences in originality. *Psychol. Bull.*, 50, 362–370.

Wilson, R. C., Guilford, J. P., Christensen P. R., and Lewis, D. J. (1954). A factor-analytic study of creative-thinking abilities. *Psychometrika*, 19, 297–311.

Winfield, M. C. (1946). The use of the Harrower-Erickson multiple choice Rorschach test with a selected group of women in military service. *J. appl. Psychol.*, 30, 481–487.

Witkin, H. A., Lewis, H. B., Hertzman, M., Machover, K., Meissner, P. B., and Wapner, S. (1954). *Personality through perception.* New York: Harper.

Wittenborn J. R. (1943). Factorial equations for tests of attention. *Psychometrika*, 8, 19–35.

Wittenborn, J. R. (1945a). Mechanical ability, its nature and measurement. I. An analysis of the variables employed in the preliminary Minnesota experiment. *Educ. psychol. Measmt*, 5, 241–260.

Wittenborn, J. R. (1945b). Mechanical ability, its nature and measurement. II. Manual dexterity. *Educ. psychol. Measmt*, 5, 395–409.

Wittenborn, J. R. (1949). A factor analysis of discrete responses to the Rorschach ink blots. *J. consult. Psychol.*, 13, 335–340.

Wittenborn, J. R. (1950a). A factor analysis of Rorschach scoring categories. *J. consult. Psychol.*, 14, 261–267.

Wittenborn, J. R. (1950b). Level of mental health as a factor in the implications of Rorschach scores. *J. consult. Psychol.*, 14, 469–472.

Wittenborn, J. R. (1951). Symptom patterns in a group of mental hospital patients. *J. consult. Psychol.*, 15, 290–310.

Wittenborn, J. R. (1952). The behavioral symptoms for certain organic psychoses. *J. consult. Psychol.*, 16, 104–106.

Wittenborn, J. R., Bell, E. G., and Lesser, G. S. (1951). Symptom patterns among organic patients of advanced age. *J. clin. Psychol.*, 7, 328–331.

Wittenborn, J. R., and Holzberg, J. D. (1951a). The generality of psychiatric syndromes. *J. consult. Psychol.*, 15, 372–380.

Wittenborn, J. R., and Holzberg, J. D. (1951b). The Rorschach and descriptive diagnosis. *J. consult Psychol.*, 15, 460–463.

Wittenborn, J. R., and Larsen, R. P. (1944). A factorial study of achievement in college German. *J. educ. Psychol.*, 35, 39–48.

Wittenborn, J. R., and Sarason, S. B. (1949). Exceptions to certain Rorschach criteria of pathology. *J. consult. Psychol.*, 13, 21–27.

Wittman, M. P. (1941). A scale for measuring prognosis in schizophrenic patients. *Elgin Papers*, 4, 20–33.

Wittman, M. P., and Huffman, A. V. (1945). A comparative study of development, adjustment, and personality characteristics of psychotics, psychoneurotics, delinquents, and normally adjusted teen aged youths. *J. genet. Psychol.*, 66, 167–182.

Wittman, M. P., and Steinberg, L. (1944). Follow-up of an objective evaluation of prognosis in dementia praecox and manic-depressive psychoses. *Elgin Papers*, 5, 216–227.

Wittson, C. L., Hunt, W. A., and Older, H. J. (1944). The use of the multiple choice group Rorschach test in military screening. *J. Psychol.*, 17, 91–94.

Wolf, W. (1943). *The expression of personality.* New York: Harper.

Wolfson, R. (1951). Graphology. In H. H. Anderson and G. L. Anderson (Eds.), *Introduction to projective techniques.* Englewood Cliffs, N.J.: Prentice-Hall.

Wolpert, E. A. (1955). A new view of rigidity. *J. abnorm. soc. Psychol.,* 51, 589–594.

Woodrow, H. (1938). The relation between abilities and improvement with practice. *J. educ. Psychol.,* 29, 215–230.

Woodrow, H. (1939a). The relation of verbal ability to improvement with practice in verbal tests. *J. educ. Psychol.,* 30, 179–186.

Woodrow, H. (1939b). The common factors in fifty-two mental tests. *Psychometrika,* 4, 99–108.

Woodrow, H. (1939c). The application of factor-analysis to problems of practice. *J. gen. Psychol.,* 21, 457–460.

Woodrow, H. (1939d). Factors in improvement with practice. *J. Psychol.,* 7, 55–70.

Woodworth, R. S. (1920). In S. I. Franz, *Handbook of mental examination method.* New York: Macmillan.

Wrenn, C. G., Ferguson, L. W., and Kennedy, J. L. (1936). Intelligence level and personality. *J. soc. Psychol.,* 7, 301–308.

Young, P. C. (1941). Experimental hypnotism: a review. *Psychol. Rev.,* 38, 92–104.

Young, P. T. (1941). The experimental analysis of appetite. *Psychol. Bull.,* 38, 129–164.

Young, P. T. (1948). Appetite, palatability and feeding habits: a critical review. *Psychol. Bull.,* 45, 289–320.

Zimmerman, W. S. (1953). A revised orthogonal rotational solution for Thurstone's original mental abilities test battery. *Psychometrika,* 18, 77–93.

Zubin, J. (1937). The determination of response patterns in personality adjustment inventories. *J. educ. Psychol.,* 28, 401–413.

Zubin, J. (1948). Recent advances in screening the emotionally maladjusted. *J. clin. Psychol.,* 4, 56–63.

NAME INDEX

Aaronson, B. S., 181, 503
Abelson, R. P., 68, 503
Ackerson, L., 411, 419, 503
Adams, C. R., 422, 503
Adams, H. E., 152, 503
Adamson, R. E., 380, 503
Adcock, C. J., 122, 434, 436, 445, 503
Adkins, D. C., 267, 457, 503
Adkins, M., 300, 301, 536
Adler, A., 125, 126
Adorno, T. W., 468, 503
Ahmavaara, Y., 103, 503
Alimena, B. S., 116, 511
Allport, F. L., 39, 115, 172, 284, 503
Allport, G. W., 2, 22, 38, 39, 77, 92, 115, 122, 151, 152, 172, 222, 271, 284, 285, 453, 455, 503
Amatora, M., 57, 151, 503
Anastasi, A., 158, 421, 434, 504
Anderson, E. E., 434, 435, 504
Anderson, G. L., 529, 531
Anderson, H. H., 418, 504, 529, 531
Anderson, J. E., 284, 504
Anderson, R. G., 175, 504
Andrews, T. G., 452, 504
Ansbacher, H. L., 260, 504
Arnold, D. C., 176, 177, 504
Arrington, R. E., 157, 445, 504
Ash, P., 181, 475, 504
Atkinson, J. W., 300, 303, 504, 529
Atwell, S., 126, 504
Auld, F., 325, 504
Ausubel, D. F., 253, 504
Axelrod, S., 437, 446, 521
Ayad, J. M., 226, 504

Baier, D. E., 472, 504
Baldi, C., 274
Baldwin, A. L., 326, 504
Balinsky, B., 296, 405, 504
Bandura, A., 429, 506
Bardsley, R., 129, 526
Barker, R. G., 526
Barnes, C. A., 433, 434, 436, 437, 440, 441, 447, 504
Barnett, G. J., 209, 504
Barron, F., 312, 320, 389, 451, 504, 505
Barrows, B. E., 279, 534
Bartlett, F. C., 233, 505
Bartlett, N., 163, 505
Bartlett, N. R., 138, 539

Bartol, R. P., 202, 516
Bass, B. M., 163, 186, 260–262, 413, 419, 420, 422, 424, 435, 445, 505, 526
Bass, R. I., 346, 353, 505
Bateman, D. E., 136, 340, 526
Beaver, A. P., 186, 505
Beck, L. H., 122, 524
Beck, S. J., 24, 290, 291, 505
Beebe-Center, J. G., 451, 521
Beebe-Center, R., 451, 521
Bell, E. G., 484, 487–489, 543
Bell, G. B., 261, 471, 472, 505
Bell, H. M., 172, 503
Bell, J. E., 291, 505
Bellak, L., 90, 300, 301, 506
Beloff, H., 188, 509
Bender, I. E., 150, 521
Bender, L., 307
Bendig, A. W., 186, 506
Benton, A. L., 181, 193, 200, 429, 506
Berger, R. M., 347, 371, 375, 378, 386, 388, 389, 506, 522
Berkshire, J. R., 145, 523
Bernard, J., 305, 306, 506
Bernreuter, R. G., 173–175, 195, 196, 420, 506
Bijou, S. W., 278, 294, 506
Billingslea, F. Y., 417, 506
Binet, A., 91, 240, 242, 245, 258, 274, 506
Birch, C. M., 116, 511
Birch, H. G., 380, 506
Birge, W. R., 278, 506
Blade, M. F., 402, 506
Blake, R. R., 38, 40–42, 522
Blakey, R. I., 373, 380
Bloom, B. S., 175, 506
Blum, G. S., 308, 506
Blumenfeld, W., 334, 506
Bolanovich, D. J., 219, 507
Bolin, S. G., 187, 523
Bond, N. A., 66, 198, 216, 223, 420, 434–438, 440, 442, 446, 448–451, 454, 455, 459–461, 519
Borg, W. R., 58, 186, 219, 263, 507, 522
Botzum, W. A., 386, 507
Bouton, A., 217, 522, 523
Bouvier, E. A., 68, 507
Brand, H., 10, 507
Brayfield, A. H., 231, 507
Breemes, E. L., 464, 507
Bregman, E. O., 395, 539
Brintle, S. L., 211, 537

Brockway, A. L., 295, 507
Brogden, H. E., 19, 415, 427, 439, 441–443, 446, 450, 451, 454, 459, 507
Brolyer, C. R., 401, 507
Brown, C. W., 373, 516
Brozek, J., 37, 72, 185, 306, 515, 525
Bruner, J. S., 310, 538
Bryan, A. I., 186, 507
Buchwald, A. M., 136, 510
Burgess, E. W., 319, 507
Burke, L. K., 145, 146, 511
Burt, C., 99, 118, 331, 332, 336, 362, 507
Buxton, C. E., 351, 537
Buzby, D. E., 151, 507

Cabot, P. S. de Q., 118, 507
Caldwell, C. W., 471, 507
Calvin, A. D., 479, 508
Cameron, D. E., 384, 508
Campbell, A. A., 400, 508
Campbell, D. T., 233, 471, 508
Canning, W., 181, 508
Carlson, H. B., 362, 363, 508
Carmichael, D. M., 233, 508
Carp, A. L., 298, 508
Carpenter, A., 351, 508
Carr, H. A., 52, 508
Carroll, J. B., 185, 352, 377, 385, 398, 399, 508, 510
Carter, H. D., 222, 533
Carter, L., 373, 381, 382, 392, 419, 461, 470–472, 508, 522
Castelnuovo-Tedesco, P., 278, 508
Cattell, A. K. S., 326, 509
Cattell, J. McK., 241
Cattell, R. B., 91, 92, 102, 187, 188, 191, 214, 250, 309, 326, 410, 415, 417, 419, 426, 427, 433, 434, 438, 440, 446, 450, 452, 453, 459, 466, 508, 509
Challman, R. C., 294, 509
Chein, J., 373, 509
Chen, T. L., 405, 509
Child, I. L., 122, 300, 301, 509, 524
Chow, H., 405, 509
Chowdhry, K., 471, 509
Christal, R. E., 362, 509
Christensen, P. R., 66, 86, 198, 216, 221, 223, 347, 353, 366, 368–371, 373, 374, 377, 380, 382, 383, 385–389, 393, 394, 410, 412, 420, 426, 434–438, 440, 442, 446, 448, 451, 454, 455, 459, 461, 506, 518, 519, 522, 525, 543
Churchill, R. D., 402, 509
Cicero, 2
Clair, D. J., 424, 435, 445, 505
Clark, R. A., 300, 303, 509, 529
Clark, W. W., 187, 540
Clausen, J. A., 475

Cleveland, E. A., 402, 513
Cobb, E. A., 300, 301, 536
Cobb, M. V., 395, 539
Coffin, T. E., 122, 510
Cole, D., 306, 510
Comrey, A. L., 190, 220, 371, 373, 380, 399, 510, 518, 519
Conrad, H. S., 152, 200, 510, 512
Cook, E. H., 138, 539
Coombs, C. H., 392, 402, 510
Corey, D. Q., 457, 542
Corey, S. M., 230, 510
Couch, A., 471, 522
Crockett, W. H., 148, 231, 507, 510
Cronbach, L. J., 199, 250, 510, 516
Crosby, R. C., 217, 510
Cross, O. H., 220, 510
Cross, R. B., 99, 510
Cummings, J. D., 427, 510
Curtis, H. A., 405, 510
Curtis, J. M., 402
Cutler, M., 258, 534

Darrow, C. W., 129, 510
Darwin, C., 241
Davidson, W. M., 398, 510
Davis, F. H., 340, 529
Davis, R. C., 136, 510
de Cillis, O. E., 423, 510
Degan, J. W., 478, 482–485, 487–489, 510
Deri, S., 233, 510
Diamond, S., 308, 510
Dieppa, J. J., 302, 542
DiMichaelis, J. U., 180, 540
Dinnerstein, D., 233, 510
Doering, C. R., 181, 510
Doll, E. A., 424, 435, 445, 505
Dollard, J., 324, 511
Donceel, J. F., 116, 511
Dorcus, R. M., 177, 425, 511, 521
Downey, J. E., 284, 285, 511
Drevdahl, J. E., 381, 389, 420, 465, 511
Dubin, S. S., 145, 146, 233, 511
Dudek, F. J., 387, 401, 511, 526
Dudycha, G. J., 20, 76, 230, 511
Duffy, E., 338, 511
duMas, F. M., 24, 322, 511
Duncker, K., 380, 511
Dunkerley, M. D., 471, 511
Dunlap, J. W., 165, 400, 511
Dymond, R. F., 151, 511
Dysinger, Dale W., 392, 511
Dysinger, Don W., 177, 183, 511

Edgerton, H. A., 248, 512
Edwards, A. L., 197, 223, 229, 511, 512
Eisenberg, P., 193, 278, 282, 283, 512

Ekman, G., 120, 121, 336, 512
Eliasberg, W., 274, 512
Elkin, F., 181, 512
El Koussy, A. A. H., 372, 512
Ellingson, R. J., 129, 512
Ellington, E., 154, 434, 535
Ellis, A., 170, 200, 512
Ellison, M. L., 248, 512
Ellson, D. G., 142, 512
Ellson, E. C., 142, 512
Emmett, W. G., 372, 512
Eppinger, H., 133, 512
Erhmann, J. C., 148, 152, 526
Escalona, S. K., 254, 512
Ewart, E., 165, 525
Exline, R. V., 250, 516
Eysenck, H. J., 24, 91, 99, 102, 118, 129,
    138, 200, 253, 265, 266, 274, 275, 293,
    294, 331, 413, 428, 430, 451, 452, 466,
    475, 477, 481, 490, 512, 513, 534

Falk, J. L., 24, 513
Farnsworth, P. R., 88, 125, 126, 193, 226,
    411, 504, 513
Farquar, W. W., 303, 526
Faterson, H. F., 125, 513
Faubian, R. W., 248, 402, 513, 521
Fay, P. J., 281, 464, 513, 514
Fearing, F., 163, 514
Feldman, S., 283, 515
Ferguson, G. A., 312, 387, 401, 402, 426,
    514, 531, 532, 536
Ferguson, L. W., 211, 228, 229, 411, 429,
    465, 514, 544
Fields, V., 336, 528
Fischer, R. P., 400, 508
Fisher, S., 387, 514
Fiske, D. W., 68, 166, 263, 320, 429, 514,
    525
Fleishman, E. A., 346, 350–356, 402, 403,
    514, 522
Fleming, V. V., 72, 535
Fonda, C. P., 475, 536
Ford, C. F., 423, 514
Forer, B. R., 116, 515
Franck, K., 309, 515
Frandsen, A., 219, 515
Frandsen, A. N., 217, 219, 515
Franghiadi, G. J., 116, 531
Frank, G. H., 268, 307, 515
Frank, J. D., 254, 515
Frank, K. F., 300, 301, 509
Franklin, F. C., 306, 515
Franklin, G. H., 283, 515
Franklin, J. C., 72, 515
Frankman, R. W., 136, 510
Franks, C. M., 185, 413, 515
Frederiksen, N., 211, 531

Freeman, G. L., 161, 163, 164, 339, 340, 515
Freeman, M. J., 198, 479, 515
French, J. W., 395, 439, 515
French, R. L., 261, 306, 472, 505, 515
Frenkel-Brunswik, E., 468, 503, 515
Freud, S., 90, 103, 147, 308, 434, 453
Frick, J. W., 182, 379, 383, 386, 387, 412,
    426, 437, 442, 446, 449, 454, 455, 459,
    515, 519
Fricke, B. G., 190, 515
Friedlander, J. W., 430, 515
Friedman, H., 129, 526
Fruchter, B., 93, 372, 373, 384, 469, 515,
    516, 519, 531, 535
Fuller, J. L., 421, 434, 504
Furneaux, W. D., 429, 430, 513, 516

Gage, N. L., 150, 250, 516, 539
Galen, 90
Galton, F., 142, 240, 241, 362, 516
Gardner, J. W., 253, 254, 516
Garrett, H. E., 404, 405, 516
Gates, G. S., 151, 516
Gebel, A. S., 186, 413, 419, 420, 422, 505
Gebhard, M. E., 458, 516
Gebhard, P. H., 433, 526
Geist, H., 488, 490, 516
Gelb, A., 426, 516
Gernes, E., 421, 435–437, 440, 448–451, 459,
    460, 462, 516
Gerum, E., 460, 520
Gesell, A., 71, 516
Ghiselli, E. E., 202, 373, 516
Gibb, C. A., 415, 472, 516
Gibson, J. J., 238, 516
Gilbert, C., 185, 516
Gilinsky, A. S., 254, 517
Gilliland, A. R., 177, 182, 267, 517
Glad, D. D., 308, 517
Gladstone, R., 135, 517
Glaser, R., 68, 517
Gleser, G. C., 295, 507, 510
Gobetz, W., 517
Goedinghaus, C. H., 186, 413, 420, 424,
    445, 454, 517
Golder, J. V., 278, 528
Goldman, M., 267, 517
Goldstein, K., 426, 516
Goldwyn, R. M., 306, 527
Goodenough, F. L., 259, 278, 309, 517
Goodman, C. H., 219, 248, 355, 507, 517
Goodstein, L. D., 416, 517
Gordon, E. M., 479, 517
Gordon, L. V., 189, 306, 414, 441, 445, 517
Gordon, S., 232, 517
Gottschaldt, K., 386, 517
Gough, H. G., 201, 266, 517, 518
Gould, R., 253, 254, 518

Gowin, E. B., 123, 471, 518
Granick, S., 307, 518
Grant, M. Q., 295, 524
Gray, F. E., 188, 537
Green, E. H., 445, 518
Green, R. F., 195, 220, 370, 371, 373, 380, 393, 518, 519
Greene, E. B., 402, 518
Greene, J. E., 201, 518
Greenly, R. J., 355, 540
Gregory, W. S., 212, 214, 234, 518
Grings, W. W., 298, 518
Grizwok, R., 453, 518
Gruen, W., 410, 416, 509
Guertin, W. H., 28, 268, 306, 518
Guilford, J. P., 44, 63, 66, 86, 89, 92, 95, 96, 99, 102, 111, 113, 127, 142, 154, 159, 165, 166, 178, 183–185, 190, 196, 198, 202, 216, 220, 221, 223, 234, 246, 248, 251, 263, 268, 279, 296, 297, 302, 317, 328, 347, 353, 354, 359, 362, 363, 366, 368–375, 377–380, 382–389, 391, 393–395, 399, 408, 410, 412–416, 418, 420–423, 426, 434–438, 440, 442, 446, 448–451, 454, 455, 459–461, 506, 518, 519, 520, 522, 525, 531, 543
Guilford, J. S., 187, 520
Guilford, R. B., 183, 279, 412, 413, 415, 416, 434, 454, 455, 519
Gundlach, R. H., 118, 460, 464, 520, 531
Guthrie, E. R., 16, 89, 520
Guthrie, G. M., 200, 520
Guttman, L., 475, 538

Hake, D. T., 219, 520
Hall, C. S., 10, 27, 427, 434, 435, 447, 448, 520
Hall, D. M., 350, 520
Hall, H. H., 471, 505
Halpern, F., 307, 520
Hamilton, E. R., 58, 263, 507
Hammond, K. R., 232, 521
Hammond, W. H., 331, 521
Hanawalt, N. G., 471, 521
Haner, C. F., 145, 528
Hanks, L. M., 151, 521
Hanley, C., 197, 521
Hanna, J. V., 163, 521
Harding, J., 233, 422, 445, 454, 510, 521
Hargreaves, H. L., 384, 388, 521
Harlow, G., 181, 508
Harlow, R. G., 127, 521
Harrell, T. W., 402, 513
Harrell, W., 248, 521
Harris, W. W., 298, 521
Harrison, R., 352, 425, 521
Harrower, M. R., 308, 521
Harrower-Erikson, M., 292, 294, 296, 521

Harsh, C. M., 451, 521
Hart, H., 146, 521
Hart, H. H., 437, 446, 521
Hartshorne, H., 18, 19, 143, 151, 252, 255–257, 443, 521
Hartson, L. D., 401, 521
Hastorf, A. H., 150, 521   [530
Hathaway, S. R., 176, 178–180, 521, 522,
Hawkes, G. R., 222, 522
Hawkins, W. C., 186, 413, 419, 420, 422, 505
Haythorn, W., 471, 472, 508, 522
Healy, I., 186, 522
Heath, H., 331–333, 522
Heathers, L. B., 254, 522
Heese, K. W., 400, 522
Heidbreder, E., 125, 196, 522
Heist, A. B., 250, 509
Heist, P. A., 250, 509
Helgerson, E., 233, 522
Helmick, J. S., 351, 537
Helson, H., 38–45, 264, 522
Hempel, W. E., 350, 351, 353–356, 402, 403, 514, 522
Hemphill, J. K., 469, 470, 522
Henchel, A., 37, 525
Henry, E. M., 298, 522
Henry, S., 344, 345, 522
Henschel, A., 185, 525
Henshaw, L. S., 355, 522
Heron, A., 196, 522
Hersey, R., 340, 522
Hertz, M., 290   [522
Hertzka, A. F., 347, 370, 371, 379, 393, 519,
Hertzman, M., 264, 543
Herzberg, F., 187, 217, 522, 523
Heston, J. C., 423, 523
Hewer, V. H., 182, 523
High, W. S., 220
Highland, R. W., 145, 523
Hildreth, G., 130, 523
Hills, J. R., 254, 374, 378, 523
Hilton, A. C., 187, 523
Himmelweit, H. T., 164, 254, 523
Hippocrates, 90, 117
Hitler, A., 274, 468
Hoefner, D., 471, 522
Hofstaetter, P. R., 469, 523
Hollander, E. P., 149, 472, 522
Holley, J. W., 154, 421, 422, 436, 438, 441, 445, 446, 451, 519, 522
Holsopple, J. Q., 304, 523
Holt, R. R., 166, 523
Holtzman, W. H., 296, 328, 523
Holzberg, J. D., 28, 268, 294, 478, 483, 484, 488, 489, 543
Horowitz, E. L., 233, 523
Hovland, C. I., 227, 523
Howell, M., 472, 508

Howells, T. H., 252, 522
Howells, W. W., 331, 332, 336, 524
Hsü, E. H., 119, 331–333, 531
Huffman, A. V., 185, 543
Hughes, A. S., 151, 511
Hull, C. L., 258, 259, 523
Humm, D. G., 175–177, 181–183, 524
Humm, K. A., 177, 524
Hunt, H. F., 308, 506
Hunt, J. McV., 89, 384, 519, 524
Hunt, W. A., 293, 294, 543
Hunter, E. C., 175, 524
Husband, R. W., 400, 524
Husni, M., 298, 542
Hutchins, W. H., 200, 531

Ives, V., 295, 524

Jackson, J., 188, 201, 524
Jackson, T. A., 152, 524
Jacobs, A., 184, 524
James, W., 91, 466, 524
James, W. T., 419, 524
Janoff, I. Z., 122, 524
Jastak, J., 268, 524
Jenkins, R. L., 28, 410, 416, 421, 437, 446,
    478, 483–485, 487, 489, 521, 528
Jenkins, W. O., 123, 471, 524
Jensen, M. B., 297, 524
Jersild, A. T., 159, 524
Johnson, D. L., 392, 530
Johnson, D. M., 148, 152, 524, 526
Jones, D. S., 367, 524
Jones, F. N., 343, 524
Jones, H. E., 134, 135, 415, 525
Jones, L. V., 405, 413, 420, 434, 459, 525,
    531
Jones, P., 258, 534
Jordan, A. M., 175, 524
Jost, H., 338, 340, 525, 537
Jucknat, M., 254, 524
Jung, C. G., 16, 90, 91, 412, 524
Jurgensen, C. E., 189, 528

Kambouropoulou, P., 452, 525
Karlin, J. E., 345, 346, 363, 367, 525
Katz, E., 123, 525
Katz, S. E., 193, 200, 475, 527
Katzoff, E. T., 466, 538
Keehn, J. D., 466, 525
Kelley, D. McG., 291, 526
Kelley, H. P., 362–364, 525
Kelley, T. L., 372, 525
Kelly, E. L., 72, 165, 166, 190, 195, 263,
    296, 320, 525
Kelly, G. A., 325, 525

Kendall, E., 479, 525
Kendall, W. E., 351, 537
Kennard, M. A., 130, 525
Kennedy, J. L., 411, 420, 544
Kerr, W. A., 249, 464, 465, 525
Kettner, N. W., 368–371, 373, 374, 377,
    378, 380, 393, 394, 519, 520, 525
Keys, A., 37, 185, 525
Kieppa, J. J., 302, 542
Kimber, J. A. M., 195, 196, 525
King, G. F., 148, 152, 181, 526
Kingsbury, F. A., 52, 508
Kinsey, A. C., 433, 526
Kirkpatrick, J. J., 186, 526
Kleemeier, R. W., 387, 526
Klein, G. S., 264, 526
Klopfer, B., 290, 291, 526
Klubeck, S., 260, 262, 505, 526
Knopf, I. J., 294, 526
Knott, J. R., 129, 526
Koch, H. L., 74, 159, 414, 416, 417, 434,
    441, 444, 446, 455, 526
Kounin, J. S., 426, 526
Kraepelin, E., 28, 178, 474, 476
Kreezer, G., 129, 526
Kretschmer, E., 90, 117, 124, 335, 336, 526
Krüger, H., 116, 526
Krumboltz, J. D., 303, 526
Kubis, J., 266, 542
Kuder, G. F., 206, 213–220, 234, 267, 321,
    457, 461, 503, 526
Kutner, B., 300, 529

Lacey, B. C., 137, 526
Lacey, J. I., 136–138, 159, 165, 166, 178,
    183, 190, 196, 202, 216, 220, 234, 246,
    248, 251, 263, 296, 297, 302, 328, 340,
    347, 353, 354, 362, 363, 372, 373, 375,
    391, 393, 399, 520, 526
Laird, D. A., 172, 173, 526
Landis, C., 147, 193, 196, 200, 475, 527
Landreth, C., 157, 158, 527
Langham, P., 471, 522
Lanzetta, J., 472, 508
LaPiere, R. T., 223, 527
Larsen, R. P., 363, 543
Lathers, E., 284, 503
Lawrence, J. F., 297, 542
Lawshe, C. H., 355, 528
Lawson, E. D., 465, 527
Layman, E. M., 183, 412, 416–418, 420, 527
Lazersfeld, P. F., 475, 539
Leavitt, G. S., 250, 516, 539
Leeds, C. H., 186, 527
Lehman, R. T., 321, 527
Leiman, J. M., 103, 536
Lentz, T. F., 193, 464, 465, 527
Lepine, L. T., 278, 528

Lesser, G. S., 484, 487–489, 543
Lester, D. W., 200, 531
Levine, A. S., 190, 527
Levine, P. R., 219, 527
Levinson, D. J., 468, 469, 503, 527, 532
Lewin, H. S., 295, 536
Lewinson, T. S., 275, 527
Lewis, D. J., 86, 366, 375, 379, 382, 383, 386, 388, 394, 543
Lewis, H. B., 254, 264, 518
Lewis, W. D., 146, 527
Licht, M., 388, 527
Likert, R., 229, 527
Lindberg, B. J., 258, 527
Lindsley, D. B., 134, 434, 435, 520, 527
Lindzey, G., 10, 27, 132, 306, 520, 527
Lipsett, L., 218, 527
Littell, S., 259, 428, 429, 527
Little, K. B., 301, 528
Livson, N. H., 367, 524
Loeffler, J. C., 189, 533
Long, L., 219, 528
Long, W. F., 355, 528
Longstaff, H. P., 189, 220, 528
Lord, E. E., 297, 528
Lord, F. M., 398, 528
Lorge, I., 88, 528
Lorr, M., 28, 268, 278, 336, 340, 410, 416, 421, 436, 440, 441, 446, 464, 478–480, 483–485, 487–490, 528
Lovell, G. D., 145, 528
Lowell, E. L., 303, 529
Lubin, A., 189, 528, 533
Luborsky, L., 166, 509, 523
Luborsky, L. B., 452, 453, 509
Luchins, A. S., 167, 239, 528
Luchins, E. H., 239, 528
Ludgate, K. E., 115, 533
Luft, J., 151, 528
Lundholm, H., 279, 528
Lundin, W. H., 309, 528
Luria, A. R., 266, 529
Lurie, W. A., 220, 451, 459, 460, 529
Lykken, D. T., 322, 323, 529
Lynn, D. R., 130, 131, 529
Lynn, J. G., 130, 131, 529

McCandless, B. R., 296, 529
McCary, J. L., 536
McCleary, R. A., 135, 529
McClelland, D. C., 300, 303, 449, 504, 529
McCloy, C. H., 331, 333, 334, 346, 347, 350, 351, 358, 530
McCollum, I. N., 351, 537
McCulloch, T. L., 400, 530
McGehee, C. R., 186, 413, 419, 420, 422, 505
McGuigan, F. J., 479, 508

Machover, K., 264, 307, 529
McKeachie, W. J., 155, 530
Mackie, R. R., 422, 529
McKinley, J. C., 179, 521, 522, 530
McMichaelis, J. U., 180, 183, 540
McMurray, R. N., 165, 392, 530
McNemar, Q., 268, 525, 530
McQuitty, L. L., 190, 530
McReynolds, P., 68, 530
Madan, S. K., 298, 538
Madigan, M. E., 427, 529
Magaret, A., 268, 529
Magill, J. W., 218, 529
Mahl, G. F., 325, 504
Maier, N. R. F., 380, 529
Maller, J. B., 19, 443, 529
Malmo, R. B., 136, 338, 340, 529
Mandell, M., 262, 529
Manson, G. E., 161, 163, 164, 515
Martin, C. E., 433, 526
Martin, H. G., 183, 185, 187, 520, 529
Mathews, C. O., 201, 532
May, M. A., 18, 19, 143, 151, 252, 255–257, 443, 521
Mayman, M., 267, 300, 309, 529
Mead, M., 11, 530   [530
Meehl, P. E., 176, 178–180, 198, 320, 522,
Meer, B., 367, 538
Mehlman, B., 475, 530
Meidinger, T., 148, 510
Meier, N. C., 356, 363, 457, 530
Meili, R., 530
Meissner, P. B., 264, 543
Meister, R. K., 268, 528
Melton, A. W., 238, 530
Melville, S. D., 211, 531
Merrifield, P. R., 379, 383, 386, 387, 412, 426, 437, 442, 446, 449, 454, 455, 459, 519, 530
Merrill, M., 242, 539
Miale, F. R., 304, 523
Michael, W. B., 372, 373, 401, 531
Mickelson, O., 37, 185, 525
Middleton, W. C., 278, 464, 513, 514, 531
Miles, C. C., 195, 259, 311, 525, 539
Miles, D. W., 200, 531
Miller, A., 433, 438, 440, 441, 450, 459, 509
Miller, R. B., 300, 301, 536
Mira, L. E., 284–286
Misiak, M., 116, 531
Mohr, G. J., 118, 531
Montalto, F. D., 296, 531
Mooney, C. M., 312, 366, 531
Moore, T. V., 29, 119, 331–333, 531
Morgan, C. L., 464, 507
Morgan, J. J. B., 232, 531
Morris, C., 413, 420, 434, 459, 531
Morris, W. W., 285, 298, 302, 307, 308, 531
Morse, M. E., 194, 542

Morton, J. T., 232, 531
Mosier, C. I., 183, 410, 414, 415, 417, 418, 454, 531
Moursy, E. M., 99, 532
Mouton, J. S., 38, 40–42, 522
Mowrer, O. H., 324, 511
Mullen, F. A., 331, 532
Munroe, R. L., 295, 296, 532
Murdock, K., 123, 532
Murphy, L. B., 74, 532
Murray, H. A., 21, 147, 223, 299, 532
Muthard, J. E., 155, 537
Myers, C. T., 398, 532

Naccarati, S., 117, 118, 532
Nance, R. D., 423, 532
Napoli, P. J., 307, 532
Neel, M. O., 201, 532
Neel, R. G., 145, 146, 511, 532
Neilon, P., 71, 72, 532
Nelson, E., 465, 466, 532
Nelson, N., 465, 466, 532
Nelson, V. L., 404, 535
Newbert, N., 188, 537
Newcomb, T. M., 471, 509
Newman, S. E., 177, 517
Nixon, M., 373, 381, 382, 392, 419, 461, 470, 508
Noll, V. H., 195, 532
Norton, F. T. M., 260, 261, 505

O'Connor, J. P., 28, 410, 478, 479, 483, 485, 488, 489, 528, 532
O'Connor, N., 265, 532
Odbert, H. S., 92, 163, 283, 503, 515, 532
Olander, E., 146, 521
Older, H. J., 222, 293, 294, 532, 543
Oléron, P., 395, 532
Oliver, J. A., 387, 420, 532
Olmstead, J. A., 38, 40–42, 522
O'Neill, W. M., 469, 532
Orbison, W. D., 423, 510
Osborne, H. T., 296, 532
Osborne, R. T., 219, 533
Osburn, H. G., 189, 533
Otis, A. S., 242
Owens, W. A., 244, 533

Pace, C. R., 230, 232, 464, 533
Page, H. E., 200, 533
Page, J., 475, 533
Parker, J. W., 187, 523
Parrish, J., 303, 533
Parten, M. B., 472, 533
Partridge, E. D., 471, 533
Pascal, G. R., 274, 278, 285, 533

Pastore, N., 300, 533
Paterson, D. G., 115, 123, 533
Pearson, D. T., 219, 536
Pederson, R. A., 172, 533
Pemberton, C. L., 366, 367, 386, 533
Penfield, W., 365, 533
Pepinsky, H. B., 262, 533
Pepitone, A. D., 233, 510
Perry, J. D., 219, 528
Phillips, W. S., 219, 533
Pickford, R. W., 344, 533
Pierce-Jones, J., 222, 533
Pigors, P., 472, 534
Pillsbury, W. B., 123, 534
Plutchik, R., 339, 534
Poffenberger, A. T., 171, 279, 534
Polansky, N. A., 151, 534
Pomeroy, W. B., 433, 526
Porter, E. L. H., 383, 534
Powell, M. G., 147, 534
Powers, M. K., 210, 534
Pratt, S. H., 186, 477, 534
Prince, R., 132, 527
Probst, K. A., 181, 506
Proshansky, H. M., 233, 534
Prothero, E. T., 225, 534

Raabe, V. L., 151, 511
Rabin, A. I., 268, 534
Rabinowitz, H. S., 380, 506
Rafferty, J. E., 304, 535
Ranzoni, J. H., 295, 524
Rapaport, D., 267, 309, 529
Rapkin, M., 307, 534
Razor, B. A. L., 463, 534
Redlener, J., 210, 218, 534
Reed, P. H., 177, 534
Rees, W. L., 331, 534
Reglin, C., 181, 508
Reichline, P. B., 282, 512
Remmers, H. H., 228, 258, 464, 507, 534, 542
Rethlingshafer, D., 303, 459, 533, 534
Rhymer, R. M., 426, 509
Ricciuti, H. N., 254, 534, 536
Rice, L., 68, 427, 514
Rich, G. H., 128, 534
Richards, T. W., 154, 404, 405, 419, 434, 442, 534, 535
Richardson, H. M., 471, 521
Rim, Y., 426, 535
Rimoldi, H. J. A., 351–353, 425, 535
Roback, A. A., 14, 31, 535
Roberts, K. E., 72, 535
Roby, T. B., 300, 529
Roe, A., 278, 297, 302, 535
Roff, M., 347, 373, 386, 535
Rogers, C. A., 385, 535

Rohde, A. R., 303, 535
Rokeach, M., 469, 535
Rorschach, H., 288–290, 292–298, 309, 311, 312, 535
Rosanoff, A. J., 175, 176, 535
Rosen, E., 309, 515
Rosenbaum, M. E., 34–36, 535
Rosenberg, N., 217, 535
Rosenzweig, S., 298, 305, 537
Rostan, L., 117
Rotter, J. B., 233, 254, 279, 298, 303–305, 388, 522, 535, 536
Royce, J. R., 434, 447, 535
Rubenstein, E. A., 340, 410, 416, 421, 436, 440, 441, 478–480, 483, 484, 490, 528
Rubin, H., 181, 535
Ruch, F. L., 195, 535
Ruedisili, C. H., 219, 520
Rundquist, E. A., 434, 435, 535
Rusmore, J. T., 189, 536
Rust, R. M., 296, 535
Ryan, F. J., 296, 536
Ryans, D. G., 252, 536

Sacks, J. M., 295, 536
Samuelson, C. O., 219, 535
Sanai, M., 464, 466, 536
Sanders, W. B., 296, 532
Sanford, F. H., 468–471, 536
Sanford, N., 468, 536
Sanford, R. N., 300, 301, 503, 536
Sarason, S. B., 294, 479, 517, 543
Sarbin, T. R., 164, 319, 367, 524, 536
Sarbin, T. W., 430, 515
Saudek, R., 274, 536
Schachtitz, E., 304, 535
Schafer, R., 267, 309, 529
Schaie, K. W., 387, 536
Schanberger, W., 487, 528
Schanck, R. L., 223, 536
Scheier, I. N., 387, 536
Schiele, B. C., 72, 515
Schiff, H. M., 253, 504
Schlaff, A., 184, 524
Schmid, J., 103, 536
Schmidt, A. W., 28, 518
Schmidt, H. O., 180, 475, 536
Schmitt, J. R., 421, 434, 504
Schofield, W., 182, 536
Schroder, H. M., 388, 536
Schultz, D. G., 254, 536
Schwegler, R. A., 89, 536
Scodel, A., 453, 518
Scott, J. P., 421, 434, 504
Seashore, R. H., 351, 536, 537
Seashore, S. H., 351, 537
Secord, P. F., 155, 199, 278, 310, 327, 537
Seeleman, V., 232, 537

Segel, D., 211, 537
Sells, S. B., 296, 328, 523
Semeonoff, B., 261, 537
Sessions, A. D., 217, 219, 515
Shagass, C., 129, 340, 529, 537
Shakow, D., 298, 537
Shapiro, J. J., 350, 537
Shartle, C. L., 469, 470, 538
Shavzin, A. R., 298, 508
Shaw, D. C., 248, 537
Shearn, C. R., 308, 517
Sheldon, W. H., 118–122, 124, 167, 335, 336, 509, 537
Shen, E., 146, 537
Shepler, B. F., 423, 537
Sherif, M., 227, 523
Sherman, M., 340, 537
Shevach, B. J., 426, 537
Shipley, W. C., 188, 267, 537
Shirley, M. M., 71, 72, 537
Shneidman, E. S., 163, 220, 221, 301, 308, 520, 528, 538
Shriver, B., 472, 508
Shuey, H., 89, 538
Siegel, L., 262, 533
Silance, E. B., 228, 534
Simon, T., 241, 242
Simrall, D., 400, 538
Slater, E., 129, 138, 538
Smith, A. A., 136, 338, 529
Smith, F. V., 298, 538
Smith, G. H., 464, 537
Smith, H. C., 122, 538
Smith, L. J., 307, 518
Smith, M. B., 310, 538
Soar, R. S., 190, 538
Sontag, L. W., 338, 525
Soyars, M., 479, 508
Spearman, C., 68, 245, 369, 371, 425, 427, 538
Sperling, P. I., 437, 446, 521
Speroff, B. J., 249, 525
Sprague, J. L., 186, 506
Spranger, E., 281, 538
Stagner, R., 201, 465, 466, 538
Stanley, J. C., 218, 538
Stapleton, E. S., 189, 517
Star, S. A., 475, 538
Starmann, R., 351, 537
Staton, T. F., 201, 518
Stein, G., 469
Stein, M. I., 367, 538
Steinberg, D. L., 185, 538
Steinberg, L., 319, 543
Steiner, B. J., 217, 523
Steiner, E., 292, 521
Steinmetz, H. C., 249, 309, 538
Stern, W., 91
Stevens, S. S., 527

Stewart, B. M., 278, 294, 457, 538, 542
Stewart, L. H., 209, 504
Stewart, R. G., 250, 509
Stogdill, R. M., 385, 411, 422, 435, 445, 449, 469, 471, 472, 538
Stone, C. P., 525
Stone, D. R., 302, 538
Stone, G. C., 250, 516, 539
Stone, I. R., 193, 506
Storm, T., 300, 301, 509
Stott, L. H., 420, 421, 440, 539
Stouffer, S. A., 475, 539
Street, R. F., 312, 366, 539
Strong, E. K., 206–212, 214, 216, 219, 234, 539
Suchman, E. A., 475, 538
Sullivan, L. R., 123, 532
Sulzman, J. H., 138, 539
Summerfield, A., 164, 254, 523
Sundberg, N. D., 182, 539
Super, D. E., 174, 175, 201, 209, 221, 504, 539
Suttell, B., 275, 533
Sutton, M. A., 66, 198, 216, 221, 420, 434–438, 440, 442, 446, 448–451, 454, 455, 459–461, 519
Sweet, L., 151, 539
Symonds, P. M., 301, 539
Szondi, L., 306

Taft, R., 150–152, 539
Tate, M. W., 398, 539
Taylor, C. W., 382, 384, 385, 539
Taylor, E. K., 187, 523
Taylor, H. L., 37, 185, 525
Taylor, J. A., 479, 539
Terman, L. M., 123, 195, 242, 259, 311, 525, 539
Theophrastus, 89
Thomas, W. F., 56, 454, 507, 539
Thompson, G. G., 400, 539
Thorndike, E. L., 395, 401, 507, 539
Thornton, G. R., 155, 252, 439, 540
Thorpe, L. P., 187, 540
Thune, J. B., 126, 540
Thurstone, L. L., 38, 172, 173, 224, 228–230, 246–248, 331–333, 351, 366, 371, 372, 381, 384, 386, 391, 392, 398, 404, 459, 460, 466, 540
Thurstone, T. G., 172, 173, 248, 404, 540
Tiegs, E. W., 187, 540
Tiffin, J., 355, 540
Tilton, J. W., 400, 540
Tindall, R. H., 295
Tolman, E. C., 372, 540
Tomkins, S. S., 300, 540
Travers, R. M. W., 233, 540
Tresselt, M. E., 44, 540

Tryon, C. McC., 419, 540
Tupes, E. C., 165, 540
Tye, V. M., 189, 533
Tyler, F. T., 180, 540
Tyler, L. E., 73, 180, 183, 423, 457, 514, 540
Tyrell, S., 479, 508

Uhrbrock, R. S., 163, 167, 540
Ulett, G. A., 295, 507

Vanatta, A., 262, 533
Van Lehn, R., 136, 137, 240, 526
Van Steenberg, N. J., 372, 421, 425, 541
Van Zelst, R. H., 249, 541
Vaughn, C. L., 372, 421, 425, 541
Vernon, P. E., 122, 150, 152, 191, 222, 262, 271, 284, 285, 327, 453, 455, 503, 541
Vetter, G. B., 464, 541
Vidulich, R. N., 148, 524
Viola, G., 117, 118
Viteles, M. W., 165, 310, 541

Wadsworth, G. W., 175–177, 181–183, 524
Waldrop, R. S., 218, 538
Walker, W. L., 187, 284, 503, 523
Wallen, R., 219, 233, 266, 527, 541
Wallon, E. J., 198, 541
Walter, W. G., 129, 130, 541
Walton, R. D., 427, 541
Walton, W. E., 151, 541
Wantman, M. J., 165, 511
Wapner, S., 264, 543
Warren, H. C., 4, 541
Watson, W. S., 402, 506
Wauck, L. A., 181, 541
Webb, E., 443, 541
Webb, S. C., 227, 541
Webb, W. B., 198, 541
Wechsler, D., 239, 243, 541
Wedeck, J., 150, 541
Weingarten, E. M., 147, 541
Weinland, J. D., 259, 340, 541, 542
Weisgerber, C. A., 426, 542
Weisskopf, E. A., 302, 542
Welch, G. S., 181, 503
Welch, L., 266, 542
Wellman, B., 471, 507
Wendler, A. J., 351, 542
Wenger, M. A., 133, 134, 136, 139, 337–339, 542
Weschler, I. R., 232, 542
Wesley, S. M., 457, 542
Wesman, A. G., 193, 512
Wherry, R. J., 372, 542
Whisler, L. D., 440, 441, 455, 464, 542
White, O. L., 262, 505

White, R. W., 310, 538
Whyte, W. H., 170, 542
Wilkins, W. L., 200, 531
Willerman, B., 233, 535
Williams, H. L., 297, 542
Williams, H. W., 444, 542
Williams, R. J., 11, 279, 542
Willoughby, R. R., 194, 542
Wilmer, H. A., 298, 542
Wilson, I., 305, 542
Wilson, J. W., 218, 527
Wilson, R. C., 86, 366, 375, 379, 382, 386,
    388, 394, 543
Winfield, M. C., 295, 543
Winsor, A. L., 217, 510
Witkin, H. A., 264, 543
Witryol, S. L., 400, 539
Wittenborn, J. R., 28, 268, 294, 297, 347,
    350, 352, 355, 363, 392, 476, 478, 483,
    484, 487–489, 520, 543
Wittman, M. P., 185, 319, 538, 543
Wittman, P., 177, 185, 267, 487, 517, 528,
    534, 543
Wittson, C. L., 293, 294, 543
Wolf, W., 132, 544
Wolfson, R., 273, 544

Wolpert, E. A., 387, 544
Woodrow, H., 347, 398, 400–402, 544
Woodworth, R. S., 171, 544
Woodyard, E., 401, 507, 539
Wrenn, C. L., 411, 420, 544
Wright, C., 268, 529
Wright, H. F., 526
Wright, H. K., 132, 527
Wurster, C. R., 262, 424, 435, 445, 505

Yerkes, R. M., 242
Young, N. D., 346, 347, 351, 358, 530
Young, P. C., 186, 413, 419–421, 428, 505,
    544
Young, P. T., 56, 400, 433, 508, 539, 544

Zachert, V., 190, 527
Zalowitz, E., 282, 512
Zietz, K., 116, 526
Zimmerman, W. S., 95, 96, 184, 185, 248,
    317, 363, 373, 374, 378, 408, 410, 412–
    418, 421–423, 434, 454, 519, 520, 531,
    544
Zubin, J., 171, 190, 200, 274, 527, 544

SUBJECT INDEX

Ability, analyzing, 86–87
    definition, 342
    primary mental, 247–248
    synthesizing, 86–87
Abnormal personality, 28–30
Abnormal syndrome, 29–30
Academic achievement, and ascendance,
    420
    and friendliness, 422
    and gregariousness, 445
    and the GZTS, 186
    prediction of, 164, 201, 219
    and the Rorschach, 296
Achievement factors, 398–399
Achievement need, factors of, 437–439
Adaptation-level theory, 43–45
Adjectives and lines, 279–280
Adjustment, personality as, 5
    problems of, 11–12
Adler hypothesis, 125–127, 411
Adventure, factor of interest in, 448–449
    and leadership, 449
    in rats, 448
    in scientists, 449
Aesthetic-appreciation factor, 451

Aesthetic-expression factor and aptitudes,
    459
Age, differences in, 333
    and liberalism, 464
    and rating ability, 151
Aggressiveness, 418
    factor of, 446–447
    in lower animals, 447
Agility, 358
Alertness factor, 412
Allport A-S Reaction Study, 39, 172, 173
Allport-Vernon Study of Values, 122, 453,
    455
Anthropology and personality, 11
Anxiety factor, inventories for, 479
Aptitude, definition, 342
Aptitude factors, 343–395
    learning and, 401–403
Aptitude tests, 238–239, 246–248
Aptitudes, clerical, 247
    differential, tests of, 247
    and impulsiveness, 412
    intellectual, 348–395
    and interests, 457–458
    mechanical, 246

Aptitudes, perceptual, 343–348
  psychomotor, 348–358
  vocational, 246–247
Army Alpha Examination, 242, 244, 368
Arm, aiming factor, 354
  speed factor, 352
  steadiness factor, 353
Art aptitude, 363, 390
Articulation-speed factor, 352
Artistic sensitivity and rating ability, 52
Artistic talent, 356, 363
Ascendance, development of, 419
  in puppies, 419
Ascendance factor, 96, 418
  and leadership, 419
Aspiration level, 252–254
  tests of, 253–254
Associational-fluency factor, 384–385
Associative-memory factors, 363–364
Attention factor, 347
Attitude, toward Chinese, 223–224
  definition, 223
  factors of, 463–467
  toward football, 226
  toward Jews, 225
  toward labor, 232
  toward Negroes, 227, 232
Attitude-scale construction, 224–225
Attitude scales, reliability of, 228
  Remmers, 228
  Thurstone, 226, 234
  validity of, 228, 230–231
Attitudes, objective tests of, 232
  primary, 229, 463–467
  in relation to other factors, 467
Auditory-cognition factor, 366
Auditory-integral factor, 345
Auditory-memory factor, 363
Auditory-sensitivity factors, 344–346
Authoritarian personality, 468–469
Autistic-thinking factor, 454–455
Autokinetic phenomenon, 429
Autonomic balance, 133
  factor of, 337–338
Autonomic patterns, 136–137, 340
Aviation-interest factor, 462

Behavior, consistency in, 158–159
  determination of, 45–47
  expressive (*see* Expressive behavior)
  and inferiority feelings, 411
  leadership (*see* Leadership behavior)
  parolee, prediction of, 320
  traits as determiners of, 37
Behavior problems, 12
Behavioral content, 395–396
Bender-Gestalt test, 307
Benevolence factor, 445

Bernreuter Personality Inventory, 173–175,
  185, 201, 203, 276, 281
Binet-Simon scale, 242
Biochemistry, 127
Biographical data, 189
Biology and personality, 11
Blacky pictures, 308
Blood-sugar factor, 339
Body-sway test, 430
BPI (*see* Bernreuter Personality Inventory)
Business-interest factor, 460

California Personality Inventory, 201
California Test of Personality, 187
Case-history method, 323–324
Catatonia, 485
Catatonic schizophrenia, 488
Cattell inventories, 187
Character factors, 439–444
  general, 443
  oscillation and, 427
Cheerfulness factor, 415
Chevreul pendulum, 258, 428, 429
Clerical-aptitude tests, 392
Clerical-interest factor, 460–461
  and leadership behavior, 461
Clinical vs. actuarial predictions, 318–321
Clinical methods, validity of, 326–328
Clinical psychologists, 11, 106, 151, 165–
  166
  selection of, 320
Cognition, of classes, 368–369
  of implications, 374–376
  of relations, 369–371
  of systems, 371–374
  of units, 366–368
Cognitive factors, 365–376
  matrix of, 365
Cognitive map, 372
Colgate Mental Hygiene Test, 172, 173
Color blindess, 64, 343–344
Color sensitivity, 64
  factors of, 343–344
Community size and religionism, 465
Complex Coordination test, 402–403
Complexity, preference for, 389
Composure factor, 416
Compulsion-neurosis factor, 478
Concept-naming factor, 377
Concepts, empirical, 27
  operational, 27
Conceptual-foresight factor, 375
Confidence, 410–411
  and leadership behavior, 411
Configural scoring, 190–191
Consistency in behavior, 158–159
Controlled-diary method, 157–158

Convergent thinking, factor of interest in, 455
  factors of, 376–381
    matrix of, 378
Conversion-hysteria factor, 478
Coordination factors, 354–355
  gross body, 354
Correlates, production of, 377–378
Correlation coefficient, computation of, 494–496
  matrix of, 498
Creativity, in chemists, 366–367
  and intellect, 389–390
  and liberalism, 465
Criticalness factor, 422
Cultural-conformity factor, 441
  and verbal comprehension, 441
Cycloid disposition, 417

Deduction factor, 392
Deliberateness, 412
Delinquents, test scores of, 367
Dependence factor, 440
Depression factor, 413
Deterioration factor, 487–488
Determination, of behavior, 45–47
  coefficient of, 501
Development, problems of, 13
  of traits, 30–31
Dextrality (handedness), 130
DF Opinion Survey, 223
Differential psychology, 14–15
Direct-observation methods, 156–159
Discomfort-relief ratio (DRQ), 324
Disorientation factor, 482
Divergent thinking, factor of interest in, 456
  factors of, 381–390
    matrix of, 382
Diversion, factor of interest in, 449
Docility, 421
Dominance, 418
  cortical, 130
  and leadership behavior, 471
Downey Will-Temperament Test, 284–285
Draw-a-Person test, 288, 307
Dynamic-balance factor, 354
Dynamic traits, 205
Dysplasia, definition, 127

E scale, 468
Edwards Personal Preference Schedule, 223
Ego concept, 27
Elaboration factor, 389
Electroencephalogram (EEG), 129, 136

Emotional factors, 414–418
  immaturity vs. maturity, 415
  poise, 417–418
  stability, 417
Empathy, 249, 395
  tests of, 150
Endocrinology, 128
Endurance, factor of, 439
  psychomotor, 358
Environmental-need factors, 436–437
Epileptic sign, 130
Equal-appearing-intervals method, 225
Equalitarian personality, 469
Equations, summative, 315–316
Evaluation factors, 390–394
  matrix of, 390
Exhibitionism, 437
Experiential-evaluation factor, 393
Expressional-fluency factor, 385
  and leadership behavior, 385
Expressions, as indicators, 273
Expressive behavior, 271–273
  in dancing, 283
  ratings of, 280–284
  in speaking, 281–282
  in walking, 283
  in written speech, 284

F scale, 468
Faces, composite, 132
Factor analysis, 95
Factor composition and learning, 402–403
Factor loading, 95
Factor matrix, 500
Factor theory, 94, 496–498
Factors, genesis of, 404
  nature of, 97–98
  and transfer of learning, 401
  (*See also* specific factors)
Ferguson theory, 401
Figural adaptive flexibility, 386
Figural-classification factor, 368
Figural content, 360
Figural-identification factor, 391–392
  and leadership behavior, 392
  validity of, 392
Figural-relations factor, 370
Figural spontaneous-flexibility factors, 383
Finger, dexterity factor, 355
  tests of, validity of, 355–356
  speed factor, 353
Flexibility, factors of, 356, 383–384, 386–388
  learning of, 387–388
  and transfer of learning, 387
Fluency factors, 381–382, 384–385
Freudian types, 90
Friendliness factor, 421

Friendliness factor, in lower animals, 421
  validity of, 422
Frustration-aggression hypothesis, 447
Functional fixedness, 380
Functional fluctuation, 110
  definition, 66

Galton types, 362
Galvanic skin response (GSR), 133–134,
  251, 413
  and anxiety, 479
  in children, 134–135
Garrett theory, 404
Gastrointestinal-disorder factor, 480
General activity, 434–435
  heredity and, 435
    and leadership behavior, 435
    in lower animals, 434
General-ambition factor, 438
General-culture factor, 450
General neuroticism, 481
General psychoticism, 490
General-reaction-time factor, 351
General-reasoning factor, 374
General-strength factor, 350
Geometry aptitude, 393
Goal-discrepancy score, 253
Goal-satisfaction factor, 394
Gradualness-vs.-revolution factor, 466
Graphology, 273–280
  acceptability of, 279
  and anatomy, 279
  validity of, 275–277
Gregariousness factor, 444–445
  and academic achievement, 445
  development of, 445
  and leadership behavior, 445
Group factors, 245
GSR (*see* Galvanic skin response)
Guilford inventories, 183–187
Guilford-Shneidman-Zimmerman Interest
  Survey, 220–221, 234
Guilford-Zimmerman Aptitude Survey,
  248, 371–372, 374, 378, 380, 391
Guilford-Zimmerman Temperament Sur-
  vey (GZTS), 184–185, 187, 198, 201,
  204, 262, 317, 323

Hand, aiming factor, 354
  dexterity factor, 355
  speed factor, 353
Handedness, 130
Head-size factor, 331
Hebephrenic schizophrenia, 488
Heredity of traits, 30–31
Hexis, definition, 99
Hierarchy of traits, 99–103

High School Personality Questionnaire,
  188
Hippocrates types, 117
Honesty factor, 442
Hormetic dimensions, 432
Hormetic traits, 205, 250
Hostility factor, 421
House-Tree-Person test, 307–308
Humanitarianism factor, 466
Humm-Wadsworth Temperament Scale,
  175–178, 198, 201, 203
Humor factors, 452–453
Hunger for substances, 432–433
Hyperexcitability factor, 484
Hyperirritability factor, 484
Hyperprojection factor, 483
Hypersensitivity factor, 413
Hypnosis and suggestibility, 428–430
Hypnotizability, 430
Hypomania, 415
Hysterics, conditioning in, 413
  vs. dysthymics, 481

Ideational-fluency factor, 382
Ideomotor-action tests, 258
Idiographic approach, 23–24
Implications, factors for production of,
  380–381, 389
Impulsion factors, 351–352
Impulsiveness factor, 412
  and aptitudes, 412
Incident-sampling method, 157
Inferiority-feelings factor, 96, 410–411
Integration of information, 315, 323
Intellect, classification of, 360
  dimensions of, 359–398
  general problems of, 395–405
  general theory of, 396–397
  model for, 397
  speed factors of, 398
Intelligence, and EEG, 129
  and inferiority feelings, 411
  and learning ability, 399–401
  and liberalism, 464
  and physique, 123
  and rating ability, 151–152
  as unitary trait, 245–246
  and voice, 281
Intelligence tests, 240–244
  evaluation of, 244–245
Interest, definition, 205
Interest Maturity scale (Strong), 208
Interests, appreciative, 450–453
  and aptitudes, 267, 457–458
  avocational, 221, 447–458
  of children, 457
  in overt activities, 448–449
  vocational, 206, 458–462

Interests, of women, 462–463
Interview, and aviation, 165–166
  in industry, 165, 167
  reliability of, 162–163
  types of, 160, 162
  validity of, 163–165
Intolerance-of-ambiguity factor and aptitudes, 456
Intraindividual differences, 23, 83, 267
Introjection-vs.-projection factor, 489–490
Introversion-extraversion, 16, 89, 91, 412,
  413
Intuition, clinical, 25
  need for, 318
  scientific, 26
Inventories, attitude, 229–230
  biographical, 189–190
  change of responses in, 192–193
  for children, 187–188
  criticisms of, 191–199
  evaluation of, 191–203
  falsification in, 194–198
  forced-choice, 188, 214–215
  general nature of, 170
  history of, 171
  interest, for children, 222
    empirical, 206
    general, 213
    pictorial, 222
  of needs, 222–223
  self-knowledge and, 191–192
  validity of, 200–203
  vocational use, 202–203
Inventory of Factors, GAMIN, 183, 337,
  477
  STDCR, 183, 283, 337, 477
Ipsative scores, 214
IQ, 242
Item analysis, with external criterion, 176,
  207
  with internal criterion, 173

Judgment, commonsense, 394
  factor of, 393
  of identity, 391–392
  and leadership behavior, 394
  of relations, factors of, 392–393
  of systems, factors of, 393–394

Kerr Empathy Test, 249
Kinesthetic memory, 362
Kinesthetic-sensitivity factor, 346
Kretschmer types, 90, 117–119, 281, 335,
  336
Kuder Preference Record (Vocational),
  213–220, 234, 457
  biased scores on, 220

Leaderless-group-discussion (LGD) test,
  260–263
Leadership behavior, determiners of, 469–
  470
  related traits, 470–471
  development of, 472
  military, 472
Learning, and intelligence, 399–401
  and memory factors, 364
  rate of, measurement of, 399–401
Leg-flexibility factor, 356
Length-of-body factor, 332
Length-estimation factor, 347
Level of aspiration, 437
LGD test, 260–263
Liberalism-vs.-conservatism factor, 463–
  465
Limb-strength factor, 350
Limb-thrust factor, 351
Logical-evaluation factor, 392
Loudness-discrimination factor, 345
Luria test, 266

Male-sex-drive factor, 433–434
Mania factor, 489
Masculinity-femininity, 423–424
  and academic achievement, 424
  and leadership behavior, 424
Masculinity-Femininity scale (Strong), 209
Mathematics-interest factor, 463
Maudsley Medical Questionnaire, 185
Mean, arithmetic, computation of, 484
Mechanical-interest factor, 461
  and leadership behavior, 461
Meier Art Judgment Test, 457
Memory, associative, meaningful, 364
  rote, 363
  factors of, 361–365
  matrix of, 362
  physiology of, 365
  substance, auditory, 363
    visual, 362
Memory systems, spatial order, 364
  temporal order, 364
Meticulousness factor, 436–437
  and aptitudes, 437
Minnesota Multiphasic Personality Inventory (MMPI), 178–183, 201, 203, 295,
  423
  correlations with Humm-Wadsworth,
    181–182
  validation keys, 179
Minnesota Test for Clerical Workers, 457
Mira myokinetic tests, 285, 286
MMPI (*see* Minnesota Multiphasic Personality Inventory)
Modalities, 6–8
Model of personality, 78–81, 99–104

Morale, measurement of, 231
Morphological factors, 330–336
  and behavior traits, 335
  hypotheses for, 334
Morphological methods, appeal of, 116–117
Motivation, 37
  in testing, 238–240
Motive, definition, 205
Motor-speed factors, 352–353
Multiple-regression equation, 316
Munroe check-list method, 295
Muscular-thickness factor, 333

Naming factors, 377
Nationalism factor, 466
Need-for-attention factor, 437
Needs, definition, 205
  factors of, 432–447
    discipline, 446
    freedom, 440
    soft environment, 436
  organic, 432–435
Nervous system, autonomic, 132–133
  central, 128–132
Nervousness factor, 96, 416
Neurasthenia factor, 478
Neurosis, dimensions of, 477–481
Neurotic-anxiety factor, 479
Neurotic-emotionality factor, 480
Neurotic-hostility factor, 480
Neurotic-inadequacy factor, 479–480
Neurotic vs. normal personality, tests for, 481
Neurotic and psychotic factors, matrix, 486
Neuroticism, 265–266
  and autonomic condition, 338
  and facial symmetry, 132
  general, 481
  and hypnotizability, 430
    and suggestibility, 430
  and sensory functions, 129
Nomothetic approach, 23–24
Normative scores, 215
Numerical-facility factor, 380
  and leadership behavior, 381

Object-naming factor, 377
Objectivity factor, 414
Occupational Level scale (Strong), 209
Ordering factor, 378
Organic conditions, 37
Organic need, dimensions of, 432–435
Originality factor, 388
  as flexibility, 389
Originality tests, validity of, 389

Oscillation, 427
Outdoor-interest factor, 462

Paranoid disposition, 483
Paranoid schizophrenia, 488
Parolee behavior, prediction of, 320
Pathology, and figural flexibility, 384
  and graphology, 275
  and inventories, 200
  perseveration in, 426
  traditional categories, 8, 474
  traits and, 28–30
Pattern (configural) scoring, 190–191
Penetration factor, 375
Perceptual-foresight factor, 375
Perceptual-speed factor, 391
Perseveration, 383, 425–426
  factors of, 426
  in pathology, 426
  sensory, 425
Persistence in thinking, 387
Persistent-effort factor, 439
Personal constructs, 325
Personal documents, 324
Personality, definitions, 2–5
  descriptions of, 26–27, 85–89
  sphere of, 80–82
  as stimulus, 3
  structure of, model for, 99–103
  views of, 56–57
Personnel Inventory, 184, 337
Phallic level, 434
Phrenology, 114–115
Physical-fitness interest, 435
Physiognomy, 115
Physiological factors, 336–341
  variability of, 340
Physique and leadership, 471
Pitch-discrimination factor, 345
Polarity of traits, 65–66
Posture, 272
Precision, interest in, 450
  psychomotor factors of, 353–354
Prediction, information used in, 33–34
  value of, 33
Primary traits, 100
  definition, 82
Productive-thinking factors, 376–390
Profiles, 316–318
  ideal, 321
  interpretation of, 321–323
  similarity of, 322
Projection, nature of, 289
Projective principle, use of, 311
Projective techniques, in attitude measurement, 233
  construction tasks, 308
  evaluation of, 309–313

Projective techniques, motor tasks, 306–308
  as unstructured tests, 288
  validity of, 310
Psychiatric diagnosis, reliability of, 475
Psychiatrists, 11, 151
  selection of, 166
Psychology, points of view in, 13
Psychomotor factors, 348–359
  matrix of, 357
Psychopathology, factor approach to, 476–477
Psychosis, dimensions of, 482–490
  and neurosis, 482
Psychosomatic disorders, 480
Psychotic anxiety, 489
Psychotic depression, 484
Psychotic factors, cognitive, 482–483
  emotional, 483–485
  motor, 485

Raters, qualities of, 149–152
Ratings, accuracy of, 47
  check-list, 143
  by children, 57
  errors in, 145–149
  of expressive behavior, 280–284
  factor analysis of, 154
  forced-choice, 144
  graphic, 142
  halo effect, 146
  and irrelevant cues, 155
  numerical, 142
  reliability of, 153–154
  sociometric, 145
  validity of, 154–156
Reaction time, general, 351
Reading retardation, 367
Redefinition factors, 379
Reflectiveness factor, 454
  and aptitudes, 454
Reliability, and change of responses, 193
  coefficient of, 110
  of measurements, 109–111
  of physiological measures, 138
Religion, and humanitarianism, 466
  and liberalism, 465
Religionism factor, 465–466
Respiratory-cardiovascular-disorder factor, 480
Response generalization, 18
Restraint factor, 413
Rhathymia factor, 413
  and humor, 453
  validity of, 413
Rigidity, 387
  disposition, 426
  factors of, 426

Rigorous thinking, factor of interest in, and aptitudes, 455
Role Construct Reperatory (Rep) Test, 325
Rorschach ink blots, 276, 366
Rorschach scores, 293–297
Rorschach technique, 288–298
  and academic achievement, 296
  administration, 290
  biased scores in, 298
  criticisms, 309
  and diagnosis, 294
  history, 289–290
  and maladjustment, 295
  multiple-choice form, 292
  and pathology, 293–295
  scoring, 291
  and vocational predictions, 296
Rosanoff theory, 175–176
Rosenzweig Picture-Frustration Test, 303, 305–306
Rostan types, 117
Rote-memory factor, 363

Sargent Paper-and-Pencil test, 302
Scalability of traits, 62–63
Scatter principle, 267–268
Schizophrenic-dissociation factor, 487
Scientific-interest factor, 459
Security factor, 448
Self, concept of, 27
Self-assertion factor, 418
Self-consciousness, 417–418
Self-determination, factors of, 439–444
Self-reliance factor, 440
Self-sufficiency factor, and creativity, 420
  and intelligence, 420
Semantic-classification factor, 368
Semantic content, 360
Semantic-correlates factor, 378
Semantic-redefinition factor, 379
Semantic-relations factor, 371
Semantic-spontaneous-flexibility factor, 383
Semicircular canals, factors of, 346
Sensitivity, dimensions of, 343–347
  to problems, factor of, 394
Sensory tests, 129
Sentence-completion test, 303–305
Sex, and humanitarianism, 466
  and religionism, 465
Sex-conflict factor, 480
Sex differences, 333
Sheldon components, 119–121, 335, 336
Shneidman Make-a-Picture-Story technique, 308
Simplicity, factor of liking for, 451
Skinner's verbal summator, 298

Smiling, dominance in, 130–131
Sociability (*see* Gregariousness factor)
Social-disposition factors, 418–422
Social-initiative factor, 420–421
Social intelligence, 396
Social-needs factors, 444–449
Social timidity, 418
Social traits, intercorrelations of, 95
Social-welfare-interest factor, 459–460
Socialization factor, 420
Socioeconomic status, and liberalism, 464
    and religionism, 465
Sociology and personality, 11
Somatic traits and psychomotor factors, 359
Spatial-orientation factors, 371–373
Spatial-orientation tests, validity of, 373
Spearman's g, 245, 246
Speed, intellectual, 398
    psychomotor, 352–353
Stability of measurements, 110
Standard deviation, computation of, 494–495
Static-balance factor, 353
Stereotypes, 280, 282
Stimulus generalization, 17
Street Gestalt Completion test, 311–312, 366–367
Strength factors, 350
Stress, interview, 161–162
    reactions to, 136–137
Strong Vocational Interest Blank, 206–212, 234, 320, 423, 448
    group scales, 209–210
    for women, 212, 234
Structure of intellect, general plan, 359
    theory, 395–398
Suggestibility, 257–259
    factors of, 427–429
    and neuroticism, 430
    prestige, 429
    primary, 428
    secondary, 429
    tests of, 257–259, 430
Superego, 103
Symbol-manipulation factor, 393
Symbol-substitution factor, 380
Symbolic adaptive-flexibility factor, 386
Symbolic-cognition factor, 367
Symbolic content, 360
Symbolic-correlates factor, 377
Symbolic-identification factor, 392
Symbolic-pattern factor, 373–374
Symbolic-redefinition factor, 379
Symbolic-relations factor, 370
Sympathetic vs. parasympathetic dominance, 337–338
Syndrome, neurotic, 478

Syndrome, types of, 92
System-production factor, 378
Szondi test, 303, 306

Tameness, 421
Tapping factor, 352
TAT (*see* Thematic Apperception Test)
Tautophone, 298
Temperament, factors, 409–410
    matrix of, 409
    in industry, 186
    and physiology, 139
    problems of, 407–408
    Sheldon components, 121
    tests of, 257–263
Tempo, personal, 424–425
Tendermindedness vs. toughmindedness, 466
Tension, factor of, 338
    muscular, 135–136
Terman-Miles M-F test, 259, 423
Test, leaderless-group-discussion, 260–263
Test materials, 238
Tests, character, 255–257
    empathy, 249–250
    experimental control in, 48–49
    expressive-behavior, 283–286
    factors in, 94–97
    history of, 240–242
    honesty, 255
    of hormetic traits, 250–257
    of interests, 250–252
    of level of aspiration, 252–254
    masculinity-femininity, 259
    nonaptitude, 238–240
    of pathology, 265–268
    perceptual, 262–265
    persistence, 252
    of primary mental abilities, 248
    principles of, 236–240
    situational, 259–263
    of suggestibility, 257–259
    temperament, 257–263
    of unselfishness, 256
    (*See also* specific tests)
Thematic Apperception Test (TAT), 233, 276, 288, 299–302
    adaptations of, 303
    biased scores in, 302
    evaluation of, 300–302
    vocational use of, 302
Therapy, prediction in, 319, 320
Thinking, factors of interest in, 453–456
Thurstone attitude scales, 224–228
Thurstone Identical Forms test, 392
Thurstone Personality Schedule, 172–173
Thurstone Primary Mental Ability tests, 248

Thyroid-function factor, 339
Time-sampling method, 157
Timidity, social, 418
Tolerance factor, 422
  in industry, 422
  in marriage, 422
Trait, concepts of, requirements for, 86–89
  definition, 5–6
  generalization, 19–20
Trait indicators, behavior as, 236–237
  definition, 53
  kinds of, 54–55
Trait position, consistency of, 66–67
  inference of, 62–63
Traits, common, 22–23
  as determiners of behavior, 37
  development of, 30–31
  durability of, 70–71
  dynamic, 205
  flexibility of, 70–71
  generality of, 74–75, 99
  heredity of, 30–31
  hexitic, 100
  hierarchy of, 99–103
  hormetic, 205, 250
  independence of, 78–83
  levels of, 99–102
  organization of, 75–77
  origin of, 52–53
  and pathology, 28–30
  polarity of, 65–66
  primary, 82, 100
  scalability of, 62–63
  social, 95
  somatic and psychomotor, 359
  specific vs. general, 16–18
  universality of, 73–74
  variability of, 67
Transformation-production factors, 378–379
Traumatic-shock factor, 482
Trunk factors, depth, 332
  flexibility, 356
  length, 331
  strength, 350
  width, 332
Types, 89–92
  continuous, 92

Types, emotional, 135
  morphological, 117–120, **335**
  species, 91
  syndrome, 92, 101–102

Unit-production factors, 381–382

Validation keys, of GZTS, 184
  of Humm-Wadsworth Temperament Scale, 176
  of MMPI, 179, 198
Validity, face, 238
  of measurements, 111–112
Variance, accounted for, 501
  components of, 97
  computation of, 494–495
  definition, 46
  sources of, 46–47
Variety, factor of interest in, 449–450
Vectors, 499
Verbal-comprehension factor, 368
  learning and, 402
View, differential, 14–15
  functionalistic, 15–15
  general-trait, 19–20
  impersonal, 21–22
  personal, 21
  specific-trait, 16–18
Viola index, 118
Viola types, 117
Visual-cognition factor, 366
Visual-memory factor, 362
Visual-movement factor, 348
Visualization factor, 378
  learning and, 402
Vocational psychologist, 12, 106

Wechsler-Bellevue Intelligence Scale, 239, 243, 268
Wechsler Intelligence Scale for Children, 243
Witkin perceptual tests, 264
Word-fluency factor, 381
  and creativity, 381
  and leadership behavior, 382
Woodworth Personal Data Sheet, 171